The Cambridge Companion to
ALEXANDER THE GREAT

Has any ancient figure captivated the imagination of people over the centuries so much as Alexander the Great? In less than a decade he created an empire stretching across much of the Near East as far as India, which led to Greek culture becoming dominant in much of this region for a millennium. Here, an international team of experts clearly explains the life and career of one of the most significant figures in world history. They introduce key themes of his campaign as well as describing aspects of his court and government and exploring the very different natures of his engagements with the various peoples he encountered and their responses to him. The reader is also introduced to the key sources, including the more important fragmentary historians, especially Ptolemy, Aristobulus and Clitarchus, with their different perspectives. The book closes by considering how Alexander's image was manipulated in antiquity itself.

Daniel Ogden is Professor of Ancient History at the University of Exeter. His previous publications include: *Polygamy, Prostitutes and Death: The Hellenistic Dynasties* (1999; 2nd ed., 2023); (ed.) *The Hellenistic World: New Perspectives* (2002); (co-ed. with Elizabeth Carney) *Philip and Alexander: Father and Son, Lives and Afterlives* (2010); *Alexander the Great: Myth, Genesis and Sexuality* (2011); and *The Legend of Seleucus* (Cambridge, 2017).

CAMBRIDGE COMPANIONS TO THE ANCIENT WORLD

The Cambridge Companion to
ALEXANDER THE GREAT

Edited by

Daniel Ogden
University of Exeter

CAMBRIDGE UNIVERSITY PRESS

CAMBRIDGE UNIVERSITY PRESS

Shaftesbury Road, Cambridge CB2 8EA, United Kingdom

One Liberty Plaza, 20th Floor, New York, NY 10006, USA

477 Williamstown Road, Port Melbourne, VIC 3207, Australia

314–321, 3rd Floor, Plot 3, Splendor Forum, Jasola District Centre,
New Delhi – 110025, India

103 Penang Road, #05–06/07, Visioncrest Commercial, Singapore 238467

Cambridge University Press is part of Cambridge University Press & Assessment, a department of the University of Cambridge.

We share the University's mission to contribute to society through the pursuit of education, learning and research at the highest international levels of excellence.

www.cambridge.org
Information on this title: www.cambridge.org/9781108840996
DOI: 10.1017/9781108888349

© Cambridge University Press & Assessment 2024

This publication is in copyright. Subject to statutory exception and to the provisions of relevant collective licensing agreements, no reproduction of any part may take place without the written permission of Cambridge University Press & Assessment.

First published 2024

A catalogue record for this publication is available from the British Library.

A Cataloging-in-Publication data record for this book is available from the Library of Congress

ISBN 978-1-108-84099-6 Hardback
ISBN 978-1-108-74467-6 Paperback

Cambridge University Press & Assessment has no responsibility for the persistence or accuracy of URLs for external or third-party internet websites referred to in this publication and does not guarantee that any content on such websites is, or will remain, accurate or appropriate.

In memoriam

Eugene N. Borza

1935–2021

Contents

List of Figures	page x
List of Tables	xiii
List of Maps	xiv
List of Abbreviations	xv
Notes on Contributors	xvi
Acknowledgements	xxiv
Introduction DANIEL OGDEN	1

I Alexander's Life and Career — 27

1. Alexander's Birth and Childhood — 29
   DANIEL OGDEN

2. The Crises Leading up to Alexander's Accession — 42
   DANIEL OGDEN

3. Alexander and the Greeks — 55
   BORJA ANTELA BERNÁRDEZ

4. To the Ends of the World: What the Campaign Was All About — 67
   EDWARD M. ANSON

5. Alexander and Egypt — 82
   TIMOTHY HOWE

6. Alexander and the Persian Empire — 97
   SABINE MÜLLER

7. Alexander and India — 111
   RICHARD STONEMAN

8 Alexander's Death, Last Plans and Burial 129
JOSEPH ROISMAN

II Contexts 145

9 Macedonia 147
CAROL J. KING

10 Kingship 165
WILLIAM S. GREENWALT

11 Court and Companions 179
JEANNE REAMES

12 Changes and Challenges at Alexander's Court 192
JEANNE REAMES

13 The Women of Alexander's Court 213
ELIZABETH D. CARNEY

14 Religion 226
HUGH BOWDEN

15 Army and Warfare 243
CAROLYN WILLEKES

16 Alexander's Modern Military Reputation 256
F. S. NAIDEN

17 Finance and Coinage 273
KYLE ERICKSON

18 The Administration of Alexander's Empire 290
MAXIM M. KHOLOD

19 Geography, Science and Knowledge of the World 317
ANTONIO IGNACIO MOLINA MARÍN

III The Historical and Biographical Tradition 331

20 Arrian's Alexander 333
DANIEL W. LEON

21 Plutarch's Alexander 348
PHILIP BOSMAN

22	Curtius' Alexander ELIZABETH BAYNHAM	364
23	Ptolemy and Aristobulus FRANCES POWNALL	379
24	Clitarchus' Alexander LUISA PRANDI	392
25	Callisthenes, Chares, Nearchus, Onesicritus and the Mystery of the *Royal Journals* CHRISTIAN THRUE DJURSLEV	406
IV	THE ANCIENT WORLD'S MEMORY OF ALEXANDER	423
26	The Successors and the Image of Alexander DANIEL OGDEN	425
27	Alexander and the Roman Emperors SULOCHANA ASIRVATHAM	438
28	The *Alexander Romance* CHRISTIAN THRUE DJURSLEV	452
29	Alexander in Jewish and Early Christian Literature ALEKSANDRA KLĘCZAR	471
30	Alexander in Ancient Art AGNIESZKA FULIŃSKA	488
	Alexander's Timeline 356–321 BC DANIEL OGDEN	518
	References	523
	Index	576

Figures

1.1 Olympias gives birth to Alexander; the siring serpent hovers above. Master of the Jardin de vertueuse consolation (*c.* 1470–1475). Getty Museum: Ms. Ludwig xv 8 (83.MR.178), fol. 15 (*Livre des fais d'Alexandre le grant*). — page 31

2.1 Donato Creti, *Alexander the Great Threatened by His Father* (*c.* 1700–1705). National Gallery of Art, Washington, DC, Samuel H. Kress Collection: 1961.9.6. — 44

6.1 Alexander at the tomb of Cyrus the Great. Pierre-Henri de Valenciennes (1796). Art Institute, Chicago, 1983.35. — 108

7.1 Pillar at Besnagar in Central India, *c.* 110 BC, with Prakrit inscription of Heliodorus. Photo: Richard Stoneman. — 127

8.1 Alexander the Great on his death bed with his generals. Master of Jean de Mandeville. Getty Museum, Ms. 1, v2 (84.MA.40.2), fol. 138. — 134

9.1 Upper Macedonia, from Elimeia, with the middle Haliacmon to the left and a view towards Eordaea and western Pieria. Photo: Carol J. King. — 150

9.2 The Strymon at Amphipolis. Photo: Carol J. King. — 161

12.1 Master of the Jardin de vertueuse, *The Execution of Philotas*. (*c.* 1470–1475). Getty Museum: Ms. Ludwig XV 8 (83.MR.178), fol. 149. — 204

15.1 The Battle of the Granicus: initial battle order; reprinted with modifications from Heckel 2008: 47. — 249

15.2 The Battle of Issus: initial battle order; reprinted with modifications from Heckel 2008: 62. — 251

15.3 The Battle of Gaugamela: initial battle order; reprinted with modifications from Heckel 2008: 76. — 253

17.1 Percentage of Alexander's coinage by metal. — 283

17.2 Percentage of Alexander's silver coinage by denomination. 283
17.3 Gold stater, 8.57 g. Obv.: helmeted Athena. Rev.: Nike standing, facing left, holding a wreath in her right hand and a stylis in her left hand; legend, ALEXANDROU. Magnesia Mint. Yale Numismatic Collection, 2001.87.9969. 284
17.4 Gold quarter stater, 2.15 g. Obv.: helmeted Athena. Rev.: lightning bolt; legend, DROU; bow and club; legend, ALEXAN. Pella Mint. Yale Numismatic Collection, 2001.87.9971. 285
17.5 Silver tetradrachm, 17.15 g. Obv.: beardless head of Heracles, facing right. Rev.: Zeus seated on a stool, facing left, holding an eagle on his outstretched right hand and a sceptre in his left; legend, ALEXANDROU. Damascus Mint. Yale Numismatic Collection, 2007.182.343. 286
26.1 Gold pentadrachm of Ptolemy Soter. Obv.: Ptolemy. Rev.: Zeus-eagle carrying thunderbolt. Harvard Art Museums: 1.1965.2740. 430
26.2 Silver tetradrachm of Seleucus I. Obv.: Alexander. Rev.: Zeus with eagle and the Seleucid anchor mark. Harvard Art Museums: 1.1965.2557. 432
28.1 Alexander is lowered into the sea. Folio from a Khamsa (Quintet) of Amir Khusrau Dihlavi, illustrated by Mukunda (attributed), 1597–1198. Metropolitan Museum of Art, 13.228.27. 454
29.1 Italian, active first half sixteenth century, *Alexander and the High Priest of Jerusalem*. National Gallery of Art, Washington, DC: 1968.18.20. 475
30.1 The *Azara Herm*. Paris, Louvre, Ma 436. 492
30.2 Euphranor. *The Alexander Rondanini*. Munich, Staatliche Antikensammlung, 9007172307. 494
30.3 Bronze figurine after Lysippus, Paris, Louvre, Br 370. 498
30.4 Equestrian Alexander: bronze figurine. Naples, National Archaeological Museum, inv. 4996. 499
30.5 The *Schwarzenberg Alexander*. Munich, Staatliche Antikensammlungen, inv. GL 559. 499
30.6 The Alexander Mosaic. Naples, National Archaeological Museum, inv. 10020. 502
30.7 Alexander with ram's horns. Tetradrachm of Lysimachus. Paris, Louvre, FG 128. 505

30.8   Sarcophagus of Abdalonymus. Istanbul, Archaeological   506
       Museum.
30.9   Lion Hunt mosaic. Pella, Archaeological Museum.   508
30.10 Lion Hunt relief, Messene. Paris, Louvre, Ma 858.   508
30.11 Contorniate with Olympias and the serpent. London,   509
       British Museum, R.4803.
30.12 Gold medallion with frontal portrait of Alexander. Berlin, 510
       Münzkabinett, Staatliche Museen zu Berlin, 18200016
       (1907/230).
30.13 Bronze statuette of Alexander. London, British Museum   512
       1868,0520.65.
30.14 Alexander Aegiochus. Bronze statuette. London, British   514
       Museum, 1922,0711.1.

Tables

18.1 Alexander's satrapies *page* 294
18.2 Alexander's satraps 301
24.1 Narrative material attributed to Clitarchus 397

Maps

5.1 Alexander in Africa: places of interest. Drawn by David Hollander. *page* 83
7.1 Alexander in India: places of interest. Reproduced from Stoneman 2019: 43, fig. 2.1, with kind permission of Princeton University Press. 112
9.1 Alexander's Macedonia. Drawn by Gabe Moss and the Ancient World Mapping Center. Previously reproduced at King 2018: xix. 148
18.1 Satrapies of Alexander's empire. 293

Abbreviations

AR or *AR* (A)	The Greek *Alexander Romance*, MS A.
AR (Arm.)	The Armenian *Alexander Romance*.
AR (L)	The Greek *Alexander Romance*, MS L.
BNJ	Worthington 2007–.
CIG	Boeckh et al. 1828–1877.
FGrH	Jacoby et al. 1923–.
FHG	Müller 1841–1870.
GEMF	Faraone and Torallas Tovar 2022.
GHI	Rhodes and Osborne 2003.
IG	*Inscriptiones Graecae* 1873–.
IGR	Cagnat et al. 1906–1927.
IK Priene	Blümel and Merkelbach 2014.
LIMC	Kahil et al. 1981–1999.
OCRE	Online Coins of the Roman Empire: http://numismatics.org/ocre/
P.Oxy.	Grenfell et al. 1898–.
PGM	Preisendanz and Henrichs 1973–1974.
PIR^2	Groag et al. 1933–2015.
RE	Pauly, Wissowa, and Kroll 1893–.
RIC	Mattingly et al. 1923–1994.
SEG	*Supplementum Epigraphicum Graecum* 1923–.
SHA	Scriptores Historiae Augustae.
SIG or *Syll.*^{3}	Dittenberger 1915–1924.

Notes on Contributors

EDWARD M. ANSON is Distinguished Professor of History at the University of Arkansas, Little Rock, USA. His research interests range over the period of Macedonian history from the early Argead Dynasty through the Hellenistic Period. He has authored *Philip II, the Father of Alexander the Great: Themes and Issues* (Bloomsbury Academic, 2020); *Eumenes of Cardia: A Greek among Macedonians* (Brill, 2004; 2nd rev. ed., 2015); *Alexander's Heirs: The Age of the Successors* (Wiley-Blackwell, 2014); *Alexander the Great: Themes and Issues* (Bloomsbury, 2013). He has co-edited *After Alexander: The Time of the Diadochi (323–281 BC)* (Oxbow, 2013) with Victor Alonso Troncoso; and *Affective relations and personal bonds in Hellenistic Antiquity: A Festschrift Honouring the Career of Elizabeth D. Carney* (Oxbow, 2020), with Monica D'Agostini and Frances Pownall.

BORJA ANTELA-BERNÁRDEZ is Lecturer in the Departamento de Ciencias de la Antigüedad y la Edad Media, at the Autonomous University of Barcelona. He has published widely on Alexander the Great and is the editor of *Karanos: Bulletin of Ancient Macedonian Studies*.

SULOCHANA ASIRVATHAM is Professor of Classics and General Humanities at Montclair State University, USA. Her main research interests include the reception of Alexander the Great, imperial Greek literature, ancient ethnic identity and ancient historiography. She is co-editor of *Between Magic and Religion: Interdisciplinary Studies in Ancient Mediterranean Religion and Society* (Rowman and Littlefield, 2001), with Corinne Pache and John Watrous; and *The Courts of Philip II and Alexander the Great: Monarchy and Power in Ancient Macedonia* (De Gruyter, 2022), with Frances Pownall and Sabine Müller.

ELIZABETH BAYNHAM is Adjunct Research Fellow at Victoria University of Wellington, New Zealand. She was formerly Senior Lecturer in the School of Humanities and Social Science, University of Newcastle, New South Wales. She is the author of *Alexander the Great: The Unique History of Quintus Curtius* (Michigan University Press, 1998). She has co-edited *Alexander the Great in Fact and Fiction* (Oxford University Press, 2000) with Brian Bosworth; *East and West in the World Empire of Alexander* (Oxford University Press, 2015), with Pat Wheatley; and *Alexander the Great and Propaganda* (Routledge, 2021), with John Walsh.

PHILIP BOSMAN is Professor of Ancient Greek at Stellenbosch University. His main research interest lies in the intellectual history of ancient Greece and he has edited a number of theme-based volumes in this broad area, among them *Intellectual and Empire in Greco-Roman Antiquity* (Routledge, 2019). More specifically, he has published on the early Cynics and their legacy in the Roman period. Alexander the Great is a side-interest entered via Plutarch's biography. He was the editor of a collection of articles on *Alexander in Africa* (UNISA, 2014), and recently wrote book chapters on 'Two conceptions of court at Persepolis' and 'Philosophers Naked and Other', the latter for the catalogue of the British Library exhibition entitled *Alexander the Great: Legend of a Life* (British Museum, 2022).

HUGH BOWDEN is Professor of Ancient History at King's College London. His main areas of research are ancient religious experience and Alexander the Great. He has written extensively about the interaction between gods and mortals, in particular in the area of mystery cults and oracles and divination. His books include *Classical Athens and the Delphic Oracle: Divination and Democracy* (Cambridge University Press, 2005); *Mystery Cults in the Ancient World* (Thames and Hudson/Princeton University Press, 2010); and *Alexander the Great: A Very Short Introduction* (Oxford University Press, 2014). He is co-editor of the *Oxford Handbook of Ancient Mystery Cults* (Oxford University Press, 2025).

ELIZABETH D. CARNEY is Professor of History, Emerita, at Clemson University. Her focus has been on Macedonian monarchy and the role of royal women in ancient monarchy. She has written *Women and Monarchy in Ancient Macedonia* (Oklahoma University Press, 2000); *Olympias, Mother of Alexander the Great* (Routledge, 2006); *Arsinoë of Egypt and Macedon: A Royal Life* (Oxford University Press, 2013); and

Eurydice and the Birth of Macedonian Power (Oxford University Press, 2019). Some of her articles dealing with monarchy are collected in *King and Court in Ancient Macedonia: Rivalry, Treason and Conspiracy* (Classical Press of Wales, 2015). She has co-edited *Philip II and Alexander the Great* (Oxford University Press, 2010) with Daniel Ogden; *Royal Women and Dynastic Loyalty* (Springer, 2018) with Caroline Dunn; and *The Routledge Companion to Women and Monarchy in the Ancient Mediterranean World* (Routledge, 2021) with Sabine Müller.

CHRISTIAN THRUE DJURSLEV is Associate Professor of Classics in the Department of History and Classical Studies at Aarhus University, Denmark. He has published widely on the reception of Alexander from antiquity to modernity, including his first book, entitled *Alexander the Great in the Early Christian Tradition: Classical Reception and Patristic Literature* (Bloomsbury, 2020).

KYLE ERICKSON is Professor of Ancient History at the University of Wales Trinity Saint David, where is also Director of Academic Experience. His primary research interest is the political and cultural interactions between the Greek world and the Near East. He is the author of *The Early Seleukids, their Gods and Their Coins* (Routledge, 2018); editor of *The Seleukid Empire, 281–222 BC: War within the Family* (Classical Press of Wales, 2018); and co-editor of *The Alexander Romance in Persia and the East* (Barkhuis, 2012); and *Seleucid Dissolution: The Sinking of the Anchor* (Harrassowitz, 2011).

AGNIESZKA FULIŃSKA is affiliated to the Institute of History at the Jagiellonian University, Kraków. Her research focuses on the reception of Alexander the Great in art and allied topics.

WILLIAM S. GREENWALT is Emeritus Professor of Classical History, Santa Clara University. He has published over thirty papers on Argead Macedon and related topics. He is actively pursuing scholarship and is currently preparing a manuscript on the evolution of Macedonian kingship through the Argead Period.

TIMOTHY HOWE is Professor of History at St Olaf College, Minnesota. He is the author of *Pastoral Politics: Animals, Agriculture and Society in Ancient Greece* (Regina Books, 2008). He is editor of *Traders in the Ancient Mediterranean* (Association of Ancient Historians, 2016). He is co-editor, with Jeanne Reames, of *Macedonian Legacies: Studies in Ancient Macedonian History and Culture in Honour of Eugene N. Borza* (Regina Books, 2008); with E. Edward Garvin and Graham

Wrightson, of *Greece, Macedon and Persia* (Oxbow, 2015); with Lee L. Brice, of *Brill's Companion to Insurgency and Terrorism in the Ancient Mediterranean* (Brill, 2015); with Sabine Müller, of *Folly and Violence in the Court of Alexander the Great and His Successors* (Projekt Verlag, 2016); and, with Sabine Müller and Richard Stoneman, of *Ancient Historiography on War and Empire* (Oxbow, 2016).

MAXIM M. KHOLOD is Associate Professor of Classics in the Department of the History of Ancient Greece and Rome at St Petersburg State University. He is author of more than eighty publications on Ancient History in Russian (mainly) and in English. His research interests focus on Philip II of Macedon and Alexander the Great, in particular on the relationships between them and the Greek cities, primarily those of Asia Minor. He has also studied a number of aspects of the political history of the late Achaemenids. His most recent projects deal with the local administration of Alexander's Empire.

CAROL J. KING is Associate Professor of Classics at Grenfell Campus Memorial University in Newfoundland, Canada. Her primary areas of research are Alexander the Great, Argead Macedonia and the early Hellenistic period of the Successors. She is the author of *Ancient Macedonia* (Routledge, 2017). She holds a PhD from Brown and is an alumna of the American School of Classical Studies at Athens, Regular Member and James Rignall Wheeler Fellow 2000–2002.

ALEKSANDRA KLĘCZAR works at the Institute of Classical Philology, Jagiellonian University, Kraków. Her research concentrates on the legends of Alexander the Great, especially in ancient Jewish Literature, as well as on Classical Reception in popular culture. She is the author of *Ha-Makdoni: Images of Alexander the Great in Ancient and Medieval Jewish Literature* (Archeobooks, 2019).

DANIEL W. LEON works in the Department of the Classics at the University of Illinois at Urbana-Champaign. His research focuses on Greek and Roman historical narrative, particularly as it reflects intercultural relations and the political uses of the past. He is the author of *Arrian the Historian: Writing the Greek Past in the Roman Empire* (University of Texas, 2021).

ANTONIO IGNACIO MOLINA MARÍN is Research Fellow at the University of Alcalá de Henares, Madrid. He earned his doctorate in Ancient History at the University of Murcia and has been a visiting researcher at the Universities of Exeter (2014) and Santa Clara (2017). He specializes in ancient Macedonia, Alexander the Great, and ancient geography. His main publications are *Geographica: Ciencia del espacio y tradición narrativa de Homero a Cosmas Indicopleustes* (Universidad de Murcia, 2011); *Alejandro Magno (1916–2015): Un siglo de estudios sobre Macedonia Antigua* (Libros Pórtico, 2018); and *El orden y el caos: El monstruo y el héroe* (Editorial Dilema, 2021). He is a member of the editorial board of *Karanos: Bulletin of Ancient Macedonian Studies*.

SABINE MÜLLER is Professor of Ancient History at the History Department of Marburg University, Germany. She has studied Medieval and Modern History, Art History and Ancient History. Her research focuses on the Persian Empire, Argead Macedonia, the Hellenistic Empires, Macedonian royal women, Lucian of Samosata, and Reception Studies. Her publications include monographs on Alexander the Great, Ptolemy II and Arsinoë II, and Perdiccas II. She is co-editor of the *Lexicon of Argead Makedonia* (Franke and Timme, 2020) and *The Routledge Companion to Women and Monarchy in the Ancient Mediterranean World* (Routledge, 2021).

F. S. NAIDEN, Professor of History at the University of North Carolina at Chapel Hill, studies ancient Greek law, religion and warfare, including Near-Eastern parallels, especially among the Western Semites. Chief periods of interest are the Classical and Hellenistic. Recently completed is *Soldier, Priest, and God* (Oxford University Press, 2020), a study of Alexander the Great, his officers, and the role of religion in Macedonian conquests, which combines his interests in warfare, religion and the Near East.

DANIEL OGDEN is Professor of Ancient History at the University of Exeter. Publications relevant to this volume include *Polygamy, Prostitutes and Death: The Hellenistic Dynasties* (Duckworth and Classical Press of Wales, 1999); (ed.) *The Hellenistic World: New Perspectives* (Duckworth and Classical Press of Wales, 2002); (co-ed. with Elizabeth Carney) *Philip and Alexander: Father and Son, Lives and Afterlives* (Oxford University Press, 2010); *Alexander the Great: Myth, Genesis and Sexuality* (University of Exeter Press, 2011); and *The Legend of Seleucus* (Cambridge University Press, 2017). Other recent publications include *Drakōn: Dragon Myth and Serpent Cult in the Greek and Roman Worlds* (Oxford University Press, 2013); *The Werewolf in the Ancient World* (Oxford University Press, 2021); *The Dragon in the*

West (Oxford University Press, 2021); (ed.) *The Oxford Handbook of Heracles* (Oxford University Press, USA, 2021); and *The Strix-Witch* (Cambridge University Press, 2021).

FRANCES POWNALL is Professor of Classics at the University of Alberta. She has published widely on Greek historiography, and has contributed extensively to the online resource, *Brill's New Jacoby*. Recent publications include *Ancient Macedonians in the Greek and Roman Sources* (co-edited with Timothy Howe, Classical Press of Wales, 2018); *Lexicon of Argead Macedonia* (co-edited with Waldemar Heckel, Johannes Heinrichs and Sabine Müller, Franke and Timme, 2020); *Affective Relations & Personal Bonds in Hellenistic Antiquity* (co-edited with Edward M. Anson and Monica D'Agostini, Oxbow, 2020); and *The Courts of Philip II and Alexander the Great: Monarchy and Power in Ancient Macedonia* (co-edited with Sulochana Asirvatham and Sabine Müller, De Gruyter, 2022).

LUISA PRANDI is Full Professor of Greek History at Verona University, Italy. Her research interests focus on the history of Athens and Boeotia, Greek culture in Roman age and, mainly, historiography. She has published extensively on the sources for Alexander the Great. Recently she has focused on the Greek city of Byzantium (principally the open-access book, *Bisanzio prima di Bisanzio*, L' 'Erma' di Bretschneider 2020), and has been interested in the relationships between the ancient Near East and the Greek world: she is the editor of the proceedings of the conference *EstOvest: Confini e conflitti fra Vicino Oriente e mondo Greco-Romano* (L' 'Erma' di Bretschneider, 2019); and co-editor, with S. Ponchia, of the proceedings of the conference *Shaping Boundaries in the Eastern Mediterranean Area in the First Millennium* BC (Verona, January 2022), forthcoming from Zaphon as a Melammu Workshop.

JEANNE REAMES is Associate Professor and Director of the Ancient Mediterranean Studies Program at the University of Nebraska, Omaha. She has published widely on Alexander, including articles on 'The mourning of Alexander' (*Syllecta Classica*, 2001); 'The cult of Hephaistion' (in Paul Cartledge et al. eds. *Responses to Oliver Stone's Alexander*, Wisconsin University Press, 2010); and 'Becoming Macedonian' (*Karanos*, 2020). She has co-edited, with Timothy Howe, *Macedonian Legacies: Studies on Ancient Macedonian History and Culture in Honor of Eugene N. Borza* (Regina Books, 2008). Currently, she is at work on a monograph examining Hephaestion and Craterus as both cooperating and clashing figures at the court. In addition, she dabbles occasionally in Reception Studies works to further knowledge about Macedonia (not just Alexander) in social media spaces, and has even written a pair of novels, *Dancing with the Lion: Becoming* and *Dancing with the Lion: Rise* (Riptide, 2019), about the young Alexander before he became 'the Great'.

JOSEPH ROISMAN is Professor of Classics, Emeritus, at Colby College. His primary research areas are Alexander the Great, ancient Macedonia, Greek military history and Attic oratory. His publications include *Lycurgus Against Leocrates* (with Michael Edwards, trans., Oxford University Press, 2019); *The Classical Art of Command: Eight Greek Generals Who Changed the History of Warfare* (Oxford University Press, 2017); *Lives of the Attic Orators: Texts from Pseudo-Plutarch, Photius and the Suda* (co-authored with Ian Worthington, and with Robin Waterfield, trans., Oxford University Press, 2015); *Alexander's Veterans and the Early Wars of the Successors* (University of Texas, 2012); *Ancient Greece from Homer to Alexander: The Ancient Evidence* (with John Yardley, trans., Wiley-Blackwell, 2011); *A Companion to Ancient Macedonia* (co-edited with Ian Worthington, Wiley-Blackwell, 2010); *The Rhetoric of Conspiracy in Ancient Athens* (University of California, 2006); *The Rhetoric of Masculinity: Manhood According to the Attic Orators* (University of California, 2005); and, *Brill's Companion to Alexander the Great* (edited, Brill, 2003).

RICHARD STONEMAN is an Honorary Visiting Professor at the University of Exeter. His research has focused on the legends of Alexander the Great, and more recently on Greek interactions with India following Alexander's expedition. His publications include *Alexander the Great: A Life in Legend* (Yale University Press, 2008); *Xerxes: A Persian. Life* (Yale University Press, 2011); *The Greek Experience of India* (Princeton University Press, 2019); and *Megasthenes, Indica: A New Translation of the Fragments with Commentary* (Routledge, 2021). He is editor of the catalogue for the 2022–2023 British Library exhibition, 'Alexander the Great: The Making of a Myth'.

CAROLYN WILLEKES is Assistant Professor at Mount Royal University, Canada. Her research focuses on horses and horsemanship in the ancient world, with a particular interest in the role of the cavalry and the training of the military horse. She is the author of *The Horse in the Ancient World: From Bucephalus to the Hippodrome* (Bloomsbury, 2016). She has also contributed chapters to *A Companion to Greek Warfare*

(Wiley, 2021); *Greece, Macedon and Persia: Studies in Social, Political and Military History* (Oxbow, 2015); *The Oxford Handbook of Animals in Classical Thought and Life* (Oxford University Press, 2014); *Philip II and Alexander the Great: Father and Son, Lives and Afterlives* (Oxford University Press, 2010); and *The Herodotus Encyclopedia* (Wiley, 2021).

Acknowledgements

The editor thanks above all Frances Pownall for indulgently allowing him to exploit her splendid 2018 Alexander conference in Edmonton to recruit the bulk of the contributors to this book, which may, accordingly, be considered a second fruit of that happy and productive week, alongside its own conference volume *The Courts of Philip II and Alexander the Great: Monarchy and Power in Ancient Macedonia* (Pownall, Asirvatham and Müller, 2022). He expresses special gratitude to Fiona Carroll (Exeter) for realizing the handsome map of Alexander's satrapies (Map 17.1) with patience and painstaking care. He thanks Waldemar Heckel for kindly allowing him to reprint modified versions of three of the battle plans from his *Conquests of Alexander the Great* (Figures 14.1–14.3; Heckel, 2008). And he thanks Michael Sharp of the Press for shepherding the project through from proposal to publication.

Introduction

Daniel Ogden

This volume presents the latest wisdom on Alexander the Great and his contexts as fostered principally in 'the Alexander équipe', by which I mean the loose association of leading Alexander scholars that has spoken and conferred at an informal chain of conferences first inspired by a meeting organized in Newcastle (New South Wales) by Brian Bosworth and Elizabeth Baynham in 1997. The chain was then given the head of steam to continue by a pair of meetings organized by Waldemar Heckel in Calgary in 2002 and 2005. Since then, there have been meetings in Otago (2007, organized by Pat Wheatley), Clemson (2008, organized by Elizabeth Carney), La Coruña (2010, organized by Victor Alonso Troncoso), Grahamstown (2011, organized by Philip Bosman), Sydney (2013, organized by John Walsh and Elizabeth Baynham), Salt Lake City (2014, organized by Lindsay Adams), Milan (2015, organized by Franca Landucci-Gattinoni) and Edmonton (2018, organized by Frances Pownall). The links between these extraordinarily constructive meetings have, as I say, not been formal: they consist principally in collective memory and self-consciousness. The only individual scholar to have attended all of them is the distinguished professor Pownall; the respective groups of speakers are connected otherwise by what Wittgenstein would have called a 'family resemblance' – a strong but, of course, a gradually evolving one.[1] The views expressed here represent, accordingly, the latest state of understanding on the part of an experienced community of scholars.

---

[1] The Salt Lake City conference has not been published. The others have been published as, respectively: Bosworth and Baynham 2000; Heckel and Tritle 2003; Heckel, Tritle and Wheatley 2007; Wheatley and Hannah 2009; Carney and Ogden 2010; Alonso Troncoso and Anson 2013; Bosman 2014; Walsh and Baynham 2021; Bearzot and Landucci Gattinoni 2016; Pownall, Asirvatham and Müller 2022.

Some Visions of Alexander

> Everyone uses him as a projection of their own private truth, their own dreams and aspirations, fears and power-fantasies. Each country, each generation, sees him in a different light. Every individual biographer, myself included, inevitably puts as much of himself, his own background and convictions, into that Protean figure as he does of whatever historical truth he can extract from the evidence.
>
> Green 1974: 480

Perhaps there is something in this, but a related phenomenon that certainly can be identified is the tendency for critics to interpret and explain the visions of Alexander espoused by his modern biographers in the light of what they think they know about the biographers' personal background and context.

The first modern – in the sense of critical – history of Alexander's campaign is that of Gustav Droysen's *Geschichte Alexanders des Grossen*, published in 1833. This strongly Arrian-centred account (there are large tracts of paraphrase) was written with great drive and at great pace, with the result that errors of haste are sometimes apparent. The remarkable Droysen – who, inter alia, served as tutor to the young Felix Mendelsohn – was influenced by Luther and the Hegelian notion of synthesis, and so understood Alexander as God's instrument in the merging of the Greeks and the peoples of the Near East, together with that of their respective religions, a fusion from which Christianity and the salvation of the human race were destined to emerge. It was Droysen, indeed, in his sequel-history *Geschichte des Hellenismus* (1836–1843) that established the now standard use of the terms 'Hellenism' and 'Hellenistic' to describe the expanded Greek world created by Alexander. These terms derived from ancient Greek words (*hellēnismos*, *hellēnistēs*) originally developed in antiquity to express the access of the Jews to Greek language and culture – the more immediate fusion from which Christianity was indeed to be born.[2] For Droysen,

---

[2] The publication history of Droysen's works can confuse: the *Geschichte Alexanders des Grossen* was initially published as a stand-alone history in Berlin in 1833. He followed this up with a two-volume history on the early Hellenistic period, published in Hamburg in 1836 and 1843 respectively, *Geschichte des Hellenismus*; of these the first volume was devoted to the Diadochi or Successors, the second to the Epigoni. Half a century later Droysen published much revised editions of both works in a consolidated form in Gotha (1877–1878), with the Alexander history now brought under the *Geschichte des Hellenismus* aegis and presented as its first volume, and the volumes on the Diadochi and the Epigoni now being rebranded as vols ii and iii respectively. This new edition, both in its revisions and indeed in its very repackaging strengthened Droysen's claim about the relationship between Alexander and 'Hellenism'. The revised version of *Geschichte Alexanders* incorporated into the new *Hellenismus* has recently been translated into

accordingly, 'the Hellenistic period ended not with Augustus but with Jesus'.³ As to the king himself, Droysen saw Alexander as a superman on the Aristotelian model, a man who is himself the embodiment of law.⁴ Critics of Droysen's work have found in his grand narrative trajectory a projection of his own historical circumstances, and his work towards the unification of Germany under the Prussian monarchy and in the promotion of German culture. Thus, Badian tells us how Droysen 'saw God's purpose in history, and Alexander's semi-barbarian kingdom on the fringes of the fragmented Greek world was a model for the role that he hoped the semi-Livonian kingdom [of Prussia] on the eastern marches of the fragmented German world was destined to play in uniting the nation and spreading its superior Kultur'.⁵

In 1926 Helmut Berve published his two-volume *Das Alexanderreich auf prosopographischer Grundlage*. This marked a new stage in Alexander scholarship less because Berve enunciated a distinctive conceptualization of Alexander in himself (his focus was rather the organization of Alexander's army and the administration of his empire), than because the introduction of the prosopographical method of itself entailed a shift away from a vision of the king as an untrammelled actor to a vision of him rather as enmeshed, as the node of an expansive network of competing interests and agendas. The work also marked a step-change in the level of philology brought to the study of Alexander. The second volume constitutes a vast prosopographical register of all those individuals that came into contact with the king, 883 individuals in numbered entries. This register at once became an indispensable tool for further study. Its fundamental role is recognized in a quartet of English-language publications by the great Alexander-prosopographer of our own age, Waldemar Heckel, which have updated it and advanced it in its various aspects. In his *Marshals of Alexander's Empire* (1992), Heckel developed more detailed and discursive entries for the most prominent members of Alexander's army. In 2016 he revised and republished the text as *Alexander's Marshals: A Study of the Makedonian Aristocracy and the Politics of Military Leadership*, narrowing further the range of individuals treated, but giving updated, enhanced and more relaxed treatments to those that remained. This pair of volumes was complemented by his *Who's Who in the Age of Alexander the Great: Prosopography of Alexander's Empire* (2006), which

English: Droysen 2012. Droysen was a persistent source of fascination for Bosworth, who frequently returned to his work and his legacy: see Bosworth 2003: 186–193, 2006, 2009, 2012.
³ Bosworth 2012: xix.   ⁴ Aristotle *Politics* 1284a; cf. Bosworth 2009: 3, 2012: xvi.
⁵ Badian 1974; cf. Green 1974: 482–483.

more directly represented an updated version of Berve's broader register, albeit with slightly fewer entries, c. 820, these unnumbered.[6] In 2021, Heckel published a further expanded version of this book in turn to incorporate all individuals coming into contact with Alexander's Successors also, down to the end of the fourth century, *Who's Who in the Age of Alexander and His Successors: From Chaironeia to Ipsos (338–301 BC)*: this volume now contains 1,279 entries, once again numbered, as Berve's had been.[7] The reputation of Berve's study survives on the basis of its profound philology, and by virtue of the fact that (in contrast to the case of Schachermeyr) its publication preceded its author's engagement with Nazism.[8]

After a distinguished academic career (he was a pioneer in papyrology) Ulrich Wilcken published his *Alexander der Grosse* in 1931 at the age of sixty-nine; it was an immediate success and translated into English the following year.[9] Wilcken's image of Alexander shows the continuing influence of Droysen, but is more nuanced. He has Alexander set on the conquest of a universal empire, driven by a fervid mysticism and self-confidence, but pragmatic nonetheless. In his own summary, he describes Alexander as 'a personality of quite unique genius, a marvellous mixture of demonic passion and sober clearness of judgement' and as an 'iron-willed man of action' with a 'firm belief in his mission', but he also credits him with 'a non-rational element . . . his "longing" for the undiscovered and the mysterious' and a 'simple piety', whilst balancing all this with the assertion that he was 'a realist in policy if anyone ever was'.[10]

In his two-volume *Alexander the Great* of 1948 (after beginnings in 1927) the independent British scholar William Tarn took it as his mission to excise the negative aspects of Alexander's portrayal in the ancient tradition, which he ascribed to the hostility of the Peripatetics, and to restore to history an Alexander that was all-but faultless: a gentleman, a military

---

[6] *Pace* Heckel himself, who denies (2006: viii) that his work is an English equivalent of 'the master's', or even a 'Son of Berve'. Unlike its predecessor, this volume also contains helpful (if necessarily skeletal) entries for Alexander himself and his father Philip.

[7] Heckel's frustration at not being able to take his biographies all the way down to Ipsos in the first *Who's Who* was apparent: Heckel 2006: vii.

[8] Another important technical advance in Alexander Studies was made in 1927–1930, shortly after Berve's first publication, with the appearance of volumes ii.B and ii.D of Felix Jacoby's monumental *Die Fragmente der griechischen Historiker (FGrH)*. However, since the collection of these fragments does not in itself entail a vision of Alexander as such, we shall say no more of it here.

[9] For Wilcken's career see Borza 1967: xix–xxi, who explains that personal information is hard to come by. In contrast to Berve and Schachermeyr, there is no suggestion of Nazi sympathies on Wilcken's part (he lived until 1944).

[10] The quotations are derived from Wilcken 1932: 239; cf. Ferguson 1932; Larsen 1932; Robinson 1932; Borza 1967: xxi.

genius, albeit one uninterested in conquest for its own sake, an enlightened monarch, a philosopher-king, a paragon of self-restraint and sexual continence, a messianic promoter of the 'Brotherhood of Man' or 'Unity of Mankind' (this being the greater purpose of his empire), and a Jesus avant-la-lettre: the teleology latent in Droysen's project moves centre-stage.[11] The tales of his drunkenness, cruelty, mistresses and homosexuality are accordingly pushed aside.[12] In Tarn's case too critics have found an Alexander scholar to be projecting himself, or the ideals of the environment to which he belonged, into his portrait of the king. Welles refers to Tarn's 'gentlemanly and sporting Alexander ... with the extreme views toward life and death and honor, and temperance in love and wine which are associated with the English gentry'.[13] Badian implicitly interprets Tarn's approach to Alexander as determined by the English-public-school culture of his day, characterizing Tarn's king as follows: 'moderate and scholarly in his habits and interests, he sought conquest, strictly according to the code of Arnold of Rugby, only to bring nations together in harmony and brotherhood'.[14] Green, on the other hand, more charitably and more persuasively, sees Tarn's conception of Alexander as forged in the light of enthusiasm for the League of Nations, which was in its heyday in the early 1920s.[15]

Fritz Schachermeyr's large-scale biography of Alexander, first published in 1949 (and then again in a more heavily annotated edition in 1973), was admired for its strong geographical foundations and its detailed treatment of individual episodes in the king's life, to which it brought many new observations. The armature over which

---

[11] Tarn 1927, 1948. Bosworth 2019: 78 [1983]: '... conceived in isolation without exposure to serious academic criticism, and most of the traits of his characterisation of Alexander, for all their strong delineation, are in flat contradiction of the consensus of the ancient sources. All too often its basis is emotional intuition, and the source material becomes an embarrassment, to be explained away or selectively expurgated.' (Bosworth's review of Tarn's *Alexander* – first printed on the occasion of the book's belated republication in Australia, and now accessibly reprinted in the journal *Karanos* – is essential reading for an insight into the man's character and context.) Borza 1967: xiv–xv: 'Tarn took the basic Droysen conception of Alexander as world-mover and added to it the dimension of a new social philosophy.' For a more sympathetic assessment of Tarn's work in the round see Todd 1964.

[12] As I have noted elsewhere (Ogden 2011a: 3–4), while Tarn's determination to eliminate all traces of Alexander's homosexual behaviour from the tradition may in some ways seem old-fashioned and suitably Victorian (Tarn was born in 1869), his fixation on his sexuality as in some way a vital determinant of the man – hence the importance of 'straighten[ing] the matter out' (1948: ii, 319) – also marks Tarn out as curiously modern.

[13] Welles 1951: 433, cited with approval by Borza 1967: xv. Whilst Tarn was born in London and spent his earlier career as a lawyer there, he almost certainly identified as Scottish: he married a Scottish wife (Flora MacDonald), retired to a highland estate near Inverness to pursue his academic writing, and wrote a Skye-set fairytale (*The Treasure of the Isle of Mist*, 1919) for his sick daughter, who went on, as Otta Swire, to become an expert on the island's folklore (publishing *Skye: The Island and its Legends*, 1952).

[14] Badian 1974.   [15] Green 1974: 483–486.

Schachermeyr pastes these treatments is a distinctive one. He confers upon Alexander, to whom he characteristically refers as 'the Titan', a striking arc of character development: a genius with unlimited military ability, he was driven mad by his own success to the extent that he came to believe himself possessed of magical abilities and capable of the impossible.[16] The portrait is all the more compelling for being delivered in a prose style at once lapidary and emotive, with Bosworth remarking that Schachermeyr's king is 'the most galvanic and evocative Alexander of all time'.[17] Not all have been swept along to the same degree. In a review published shortly after the book's appearance, Brown observes that the hypothesis of a 'mad' Alexander conveniently allows for the endorsement of just about every story preserved of him in the source tradition, however contradictory, without discrimination.[18] Once again, the critics have found in Schachermeyr's Alexander a projection of his own circumstances, the scholar having aligned himself with the Nazis until the end of the war. Welles characterizes Schachermeyr's conception of Alexander as 'impossible before Hitler and World War II'.[19] Burn, writing in 1951, characterizes his Alexander as 'a ruthless, mystical-minded Führer', who 'behaves like a young Nazi let loose in the Alps'. He finds Schachermeyr's disavowals of dictatorship, at the top and tail of his work, cosmetic, and considers that the intervening contents could have been published ten years previously.[20] Bosworth describes Schachermeyr's Alexander as 'an emanation of frightening power, conceived during the dark days of the Third Reich ... He was capable of impulsive acts of generosity or of savage blood lust ... Above all the wish to dominate was paramount ... Alexander had a burning desire for world empire ....'[21]

In an extensive series of articles beginning in 1958,[22] Ernst Badian brought a renewed and philological attention to the detail of the Alexander sources and their *Quellenforschung*, in explicit opposition to Tarn's project and methods. Badian's Alexander was the polar opposite of Tarn's idealized figure. He had no interest in culture, philosophy, brotherhood or the promotion of these; he was a pragmatist, an ultra-realist; his motivations were above all military success in itself and, in the

---

[16] Cf. in particular Schachermeyr 1949: 477. [17] Bosworth 2019: 86–88 [1983], 1988a: xii.
[18] Brown 1951: 75.
[19] Welles 1951: 434; cf. Borza 1967: xvii. Schachermeyr had retained his chair in Graz under the Nazis, producing observations on race of sort acceptable to the regime in his *Indogermanen und Orient* of 1944. He was accordingly ejected from it at the end of the war.
[20] Burn 1951: 101–102. [21] Bosworth 2019: 86–88 [1983].
[22] Badian 1958a, 1958c; Badian's principal works on Alexander (27 of them) are collected in the posthumous Badian 2012.

first instance, financial profit (he had inherited an empty treasury from his father); the individual choices he made (and Badian admired Alexander for his ruthless decisiveness at least) served these ends, and to a cynical degree. Beyond this, Badian's own conception of Alexander and his development did retain a slight reminiscence of Schachermeyr's arc: he was initially an inventive and energetic military and political leader, but he ended up distancing himself from the Macedonian nobility upon which he depended as he evolved into an oriental despot and withdrew 'into a tragic isolation, plagued by insecurity and loneliness'.[23]

Still a popular starting-point for those interested in Alexander today, Robin Lane Fox's 1973 biography *Alexander the Great* is written with pace and verve. It is to be regretted that the evidence and telegraphic argumentation supporting its many striking and independent insights is submerged in the most rebarbative and intractable variety of annotation known to Alexander scholarship. The book is noteworthy for combining a post-Badian rejection of Tarn's work ('persistently mistaken both in method and in evidence'), with a distinctively Tarnian romanticism in its approach to the king, for all that Lane Fox sees Alexander as a more sinister figure.[24] In Lane Fox's case too, the critics have turned to projectionism, and suggested that his image of Alexander as an effortlessly self-confident, dashing leader of men is influenced by the paradigms the author assimilated in the cloisters of Eton and Oxford, institutions admittedly advertised prominently on his fly-leaf. Badian: 'The only real interest in this book is in the light it casts on the author's personality and (like so many books on ancient history)

---

[23] The quotation is Bosworth's encapsulation (2019: 89 [1983]) of Badian's 1962 piece, 'Alexander the Great and the loneliness of power.' Corey Brennan is currently working on (the refugee) Badian's unexpectedly charitable attitude towards Schachermeyr and his work. Badian always rejected the idea of writing a biography of the king himself, and he offered synoptic views on Alexander only in this 1962 article and in a 1958 summary of the king's career drafted for a popular audience and published in *History Today* (1958b). Unfortunately, he chose to withhold the latter piece from his 2012 retrospective. See Borza at Badian 2012: xvi–xviii on both pieces and, for a characterization of Borza's conceptualization of Alexander, 1967: xvii–xviii.

I take this opportunity to add a note on the notorious riot at the heart of which Professor Badian, Dr Kate Mortensen and I found ourselves in Thessaloniki in 2002. I supplied an account of this at Ogden 2011a: 2–3, but withheld a detail it seemed unfair and possibly unsafe to print whilst the professor remained alive. When we had finally been extracted from the baying crowd of self-proclaimed 'nationalists', shaken myself, I asked the frail 77-year-old, with concern, whether he was in any distress: 'Not at all', he replied with a twinkle in his eye, 'I've been persecuted by far better fascists than these.' I have since learned (from Borza at Badian 2012: xvii) that he subsequently professed that the episode reminded him of his experience of Kristallnacht – the same underlying comparison, but disturbingly less disjunctive. Perhaps the joke and the twinkle were for my sake.

[24] Cf. Bosworth 2019: 92 [1983].

on the values of the environment and the society in which it was written.'[25]

The most profound and philological Alexander scholar of the modern age has been Brian Bosworth, whom Badian took under his wing.[26] Bosworth published the first volume of his commentary on Arrian (covering Books i–iii) in 1980[27] and then in 1988 published both a detailed monograph of the king and a technical work on the historiographical principles that must underpin work on the Alexander tradition.[28] He insisted that his monograph was not a biography of Alexander: such a thing would be 'impossible to achieve ... Alexander the man will always elude us, thanks to the distorting filter of ancient (and modern) judgements and our grossly inefficient documentation'.[29] But, despite himself, synoptic views of Alexander and his character peeped out here and there. In Milns' encapsulation, Bosworth sees the character of Alexander as 'vainglorious; imperious; self-willed and autocratic; resentful and unforgiving when thwarted ... ; and utterly ruthless in his treatment of real or imagined enemies ... an altogether unlikeable and distasteful personality'.[30]

Having completed our brief review, let us return to the point at which we began this Introduction.[31] A notorious review by James Davidson of Bosworth's and Baynham's proceedings from the pivotal and inspirational 1997 conference opens with the following paragraphs:

---

[25] Badian 1974; cf. Briscoe 1976: 234. Whatever value one accords this as a hermeneutic approach to Lane Fox's Alexander (I do not myself find it convincing), I cannot forebear to note that it is leadership qualities acquired at Eton and Oxford that have, over the last decade, brought catastrophe upon my country.

[26] Professor Bosworth once sympathized with me for the dismal trajectory of my academic career: it was a pity that I had never had a Badian, he observed. It must be conceded, however, that while Badian did indeed aid some, he also attempted to destroy the careers of others – including some of those recognized as the Alexander scholars of the first rank today.

[27] Bosworth 1980b. The second volume (covering Books iv–v) appeared in 1995. Bosworth died before he could complete the third and final volume. The work is now being completed by the capable hands of Professors Elizabeth Baynham and Pat Wheatley.

[28] Bosworth 1988a, 1988b.   [29] Bosworth 1988a: 5.

[30] Milns 1992. In 1987 an Oxford Ancient History don declared to me that one could encompass all one needed to know about Alexander by reading the work only of scholars whose names began with B, namely Berve, Badian, Brunt and Bosworth. Brunt – translator of the Arrian Loeb, with its admittedly useful appendices – was doubtless added to the list primarily for reasons of that university's narcissism. He was, however, Bosworth's tutor and held in a degree of respect by him, receiving conspicuous acknowledgement in his major books.

[31] Among the lesser accounts of Alexander over the course of the era reviewed, we may single out above all O'Brien's 1992 book, *Alexander the Great: The Invisible Enemy*. This, at least, has a distinctive take on the king, viewing his career consistently as it does through the lens of his alcoholism. Other keys to Alexander's personality have been found in an Oedipus complex (Thomas 1995) and in paranoia (Worthington 1999). For a most helpful and all-but exhaustive review of Alexander scholarship between the years 1916 and 2015, see Molina Marín 2018.

> For those suffering from millennial panic about the current state of history – all those Postmodernists on the non-fiction bestseller lists, all those fact-deniers occupying important professorial chairs, all those poor students who know what Marie Antoinette had for breakfast but not how she died – Classics departments all over the country are offering courses of therapy: Alexander the Great.
>
> In Alexanderland scholarship remains largely untouched by the influences which have transformed history and classics since 1945. Some great beasts, having wandered in, can still be found here decades later, well beyond reach of the forces of evolution. Secluded behind the high, impassable peaks of prosopography, military history and, above all, Quellenforschung, Alexander historians do what Alexander historians have done for more than a hundred years: try to discover the facts about Alexander the Great between his accession to the throne of Macedon in October 336 and his death in Babylon on the evening of 10 June 323 BC; what really happened on the expedition, what really happened during the three big battles against the Persians, what really happened during the march into India and back again, what happened to Alexander, what happened at Court.
>
> (Davidson 2001: 7)

Since this review, a number of scholars have appropriated, rehearsed and indeed misused the term 'Alexanderland' for a glib dismissal of the work of the équipe. They are wrong to do so.

The effect of Alexander's campaign on the history of the world, not merely the western world, cannot be overstated. If we lay aside the teleology, Droysen was right. Were it not for the Hellenistic world that Alexander created – despite himself, no doubt! – by integrating the indigenous cultures of the Middle East with that of Greece (and Macedon), there would have been no Roman Empire as we know it (the emperors – to whom in turn we owe the popes – effectively constituting the last and greatest of the Hellenistic dynasties); there would have been no Christianity (a synthesis of, inter alia, Jesus' apocalyptic Judaism and Paul's Hellenism) – with all that that entails (including no Islam); accordingly, there would have been no Byzantium; and, accordingly again, there would have been no Italian Renaissance – with, yet again, all that that entails. In the light of this, it is the critical first duty of the ancient historian to pin down, as closely as possible, every fact (if I may be permitted the reach for such a tastelessly old-fashioned concept) about Alexander, his campaign and its context. And it is his critical second duty to understand the relationships between these facts, in other words, how and why it all happened. This is not to underestimate the pesky slipperiness of facts, nor to deny that as often as not 'as closely as possible' may not be very close at all. Yes, indeed, there are many other kinds of history one can pursue on the theme of Alexander the Great, including those with more modern flavours, but these must ever remain of no better than tertiary and derivative import (I write, guiltily, as being myself primarily a practitioner of matters of tertiary and derivative import).

But it is as true today as it was a hundred years ago that there is no better – indeed no alternative – way to approach *the facts*, the *truth*, that chill wind, of Alexander, than by the philological methods of, precisely, 'prosopography, military history and, above all, Quellenforschung'. *There is nothing else to put in their place.* It is implied in the remainder of Davidson's review that the exercise of these philological techniques, after more than a century of vigorous application, now moves in ever narrower and more footling circles of *s'entendre parler*; that the équipe is doing nothing more than idly rearranging the bibelots on the mantlepieces of Alexander's palace, back and forth; that we stand on the soldiers of the nineteenth-century giants of philology in cheerleader-pyramids of ever more diminutive homunculi. Well, so what if all that were true? The exercise would remain primary and essential, nonetheless. Knowledge survives only in its exercise and manipulation: it asphyxiates in closed books. But in every generation, whatever else they want to do with the information, people will always want and deserve to know what Alexander actually did, to return to the source, and will need scholars able to teach them how to do this.

Davidson does not really offer a positive articulation of what he sees as the alternative to Alexanderland, the non-Alexanderland approach to Alexander. He does, however, express regret that love and sex in particular are absent from the utopia, and he laments a failure to accommodate new finds within it. It was hardly true that love and sex had been ignored, even at the time he wrote. Indeed, they had formed the focus of one of the pair of 1958 articles by Badian considered the starting-point of the new rigour in Alexander Studies, 'The eunuch Bagoas' (admittedly, Badian's approach to such matters is hardly Davidson's). Of the 'earth-shattering new finds' he begs to have imported to Alexanderland, these are inevitably going to be few and far between. Indeed, the one find he specifies in this regard is the Alexander sarcophagus made for Abdalonymus of Sidon, discovered as recently as . . . 1887. A better example of an 'earth-shattering new find' – one that came to light in 2007, after Davidson wrote, is the Oxyrhynchus papyrus (*P.Oxy.* 4808) that, on one interpretation, specifies that Clitarchus was the tutor to Ptolemy IV, with the implication that this crucial lost Alexander historian's *floruit* and the writing of his history fell during the reign of Ptolemy III, as opposed to early in the reign of Ptolemy I. Alexander scholars seem equally divided, as one group now rides away on the tectonic plate of Ptolemy III, whilst the other clings still to the Ptolemy I plate, and a chasm yawns open between them (see the discussion by Luisa Prandi in Chapter 24 of this volume). There is no better indication than this that Alexander Studies of a traditional cast do not, after all, move in ever decreasing circles.

One might speculate that the alternative vision of Alexander Studies Davidson hints at turns the focus away from the facts of the campaign, supposedly unknowable or at any rate unknowable to any further degree than they are known already, and towards the knowable ones that we can derive from the relevant evidence, from the surviving Alexander histories as secure artefacts in their own right, which can be contextualized within their own spheres of production, and that too in infinite ways. This is indeed a project of critical importance, but it had always, necessarily, formed an ancillary part of the *Quellenforschung* exercise: as soon as one asks how an imperial author may have represented or even mispresented the words of any given prior source, one is asking questions about his own agenda and his context. Such questions had in fact been brought into more concentrated focus already before Davidson wrote, for example in Diana Spencer's 2002 book, *The Roman Alexander: Reading a Cultural Myth*. These questions rightly continue to be prioritized in this volume too (Chapters 20–30).

But it is absurd to pursue such questions about the imperial texts *at the expense of* – as opposed to *in addition to* – trying to come to terms with and engage with the historical events that inspired them and lie behind them. We are reminded, indirectly, of the position adopted by Tom Townsend in Whit Stillman's marvellous 1990 film comedy *Metropolitan*. We are privileged to witness a shy conversation between a couple of intellectualist teenagers that find themselves alone at a party:

AUDREY ROUGET: What Jane Austen novels have you read?
TOM TOWNSEND: None. I don't read novels. I prefer good literary criticism. That way you get both the novelists' ideas as well as the critics' thinking. With fiction I can never forget that none of it really happened, that it's all just made up by the author.

We appreciate the purity and rigour of Tom's stance, of course: novels have no (tangible) referent, no object, they are not about anything that exists or can be pinned down. By contrast, the literary criticism devoted to them does indeed have a tangible, existent referent or object: the novels themselves. But poor Tom . . . .

The Volume's Shape and Contents

The book is structured as follows. The eight chapters of Part I offer, if not a biography of Alexander, then a broadly chronological survey of his life and his career. This is topped and tailed by chapters on his childhood, accession and death. The five intervening chapters take as their primary focus the major regions of Europe and Asia with which Alexander was primarily engaged at the successive stages of his reign and campaign. We look, accordingly, at the nature of Alexander's interactions with the Greek cities, with Egypt, with the Persian Empire and with India. How did Alexander interact with these various regions? What was his impact upon them? What was his legacy in them? We include here also an overview of the Asian campaign as a whole, asking what Alexander's objectives were in initiating it, and how these objectives mutated in the face of brilliant successes.

Chapter 1, 'Alexander's Birth and Childhood' (Daniel Ogden), collects what can be known of Alexander's life prior to his accession in 336 BC, for which the source of primary importance is Plutarch's biography. It attempts to sift what may plausibly be regarded as historical from embellishments of various kinds, contemporary and subsequent, propagandist, folkloric or mythologizing. Particular attention is given to: Alexander's three birth myths; his education at the hands of Aristotle and others; Aeschines' vignette of him as nine-year-old boy; the intriguing traditions bearing upon his taming of his horse Bucephalas; his regency during the Byzantine campaign; his foundation of Alexandropolis; his dealings with Persian ambassadors; his role in the battle at Chaeronea; and the tradition of Philip and Olympias' concerns about his sexuality. Chapter 2, 'The Crises Leading up to Alexander's Accession' (Daniel Ogden), follows directly on, reviewing the two major crises Alexander faced (or brought upon himself) before shortly succeeding his father Philip II on the throne of Macedon: his dispute with Attalus at Philip's wedding to Cleopatra and the Pixodarus affair. It also gives consideration to Alexander's whereabouts at the point of his father's assassination, and the stages by which Alexander did indeed secure the throne for himself and his recognition as king.

Chapter 3, 'Alexander and the Greeks' (Borja Antela Bernárdez), the first of the regional studies, focuses on Alexander's relationship with the city-states, with which he was engaged in a direct way during the brief period between his accession in 336 BC and the first phase of his Asian campaign in 334 BC, and thereafter in a more remote though nonetheless impactful fashion, as exemplified by the Exiles Decree. After a relatively smooth start with his seemingly easy succession to his father in his role as leader of the League of Corinth, Alexander dealt the Greek world a devastating lesson with his complete extirpation of Thebes after its 335 BC rebellion. It could be considered effective: the only further rebellion amongst the Greek states during Alexander's lifetime was that of Sparta under Agis III, which Antipater, the regent he left in control of Macedon, was able to quell. The manner of his engagement with the Greek states of Asia Minor appears to have been determined principally by the degree of loyalty they displayed to him.

We then interrupt our series of chronological-regional studies to try to get a sense of what Alexander's campaign, in the course of which he was to engage with the non-Greek peoples, was all about. Chapter 4, 'To the Ends of the World: What the Campaign Was All About' (Edward M. Anson), makes the forceful case that Alexander's prime motivation was the pursuit of endless, remorseless conquest for its own sake, an ambition most clearly written in the evolving composition and organization of his army. His personal martial glory was all. Other stated aims, such as the taking of revenge for the Persians' 480–479 BC invasion of Greece (and, we might ask, why revenge for the unsuccessful invasion of Greece as opposed to revenge for the successful subjection of Macedon during the years 510–479 BC, or some part thereof?) or, subsequently, the acquisition of booty, were mere diplomatic or persuasive conveniences.

Our second regional study, Chapter 5, 'Alexander and Egypt' (Timothy Howe), focuses on Alexander's engagement with that land, in which he spent eight months at the most between 332 BC and 331 BC. The visit has, nonetheless, given rise to some of the most distinctive controversies of his career in its entirety. Amongst these: What did Alexander do in Memphis? How did Alexander speak to his Egyptian subjects? To what extent can Alexander be said to have founded the city of Alexandria, and what, in any case, might we mean by 'foundation' in this context? What were the purpose and subsequent significance of his visit to Siwah? A fresh look is taken at these questions on the basis of an integrated approach to all available sources, with archaeological findings and (striking) Egyptian-language inscriptions pitted against the familiar web of texts offered by the Graeco-Roman literary tradition. The third regional study, Chapter 6, 'Alexander and the Persian Empire' (Sabine Müller), turns to the major focus of Alexander's campaign (331–323 BC). Compatibly with Edward M. Anson's understanding of Alexander's motivations, Müller stresses that the war in the Persian territories did not serve the aims of 'liberation' or 'reprisal', but those of the acquisition of territory, influence and wealth. The attempt to view Alexander's campaign from the perspective of the Persians themselves is doomed by the want of suitable sources, but we can at least partly redress the balance between the two enemies by realizing that the Graeco-Roman sources' projection of the Persian Empire as weak, decadent and riven by strife, an apple ready to be picked, is conditioned by the long-ingrained stereotypes our ancient authors had assimilated. Indeed, the general robustness of the Achaemenid administrative system is demonstrated by the fact that, for the most part, Alexander merely took it over, lock, stock and barrel. Paradoxically, the Achaemenid structures served to support his conquest. The fourth regional study, Chapter 7, 'Alexander and India' (Richard Stoneman), looks at the last of the great regions into which Alexander ventured (327–325 BC). Compatibly with Sabine Müller and Edward M. Anson again, Stoneman sees Alexander's motivation for carrying the campaign forwards into India as ambition in itself. Particular attention is given to the long-term impact of the difficult Indian adventure, including the Indo-Greek dynasties that thrived in its wake for a further two centuries. But Alexander's engagement with India also had an impact on Greek culture more widely: formerly a soldier in Alexander's army, Megasthenes wrote up an account of the land for the Successor Seleucus; this was to be a widely influential document, with many substantial fragments of it surviving. In a different way, a line can be drawn from the thinking of the 'naked philosopher' that Alexander acquired in Taxila, Calanus, and that of Pyrrho, the founder of the philosophical school of Scepticism, who also travelled with Alexander.

Finally in this section, Chapter 8, 'Alexander's Death, Last Plans and Burial' (Joseph Roisman), brings Alexander's story to an end with a look at his death in Babylon and a consideration of what Alexander might have gone on to do had he lived: were the 'last plans' attributed to him authentic and, either way, why were they rejected? The cultural significance of the omens retrospectively developed to foreshadow Alexander's death is investigated as are the conspiracy theories, ancient and modern, that surround the circumstances of it. The chapter closes with a review of the tussle between the Successors, in which Ptolemy was to prevail, for control of Alexander's totemic corpse.

Part II offers treatments of eleven contexts and important themes in Alexander's life and campaign. First, Chapter 9, 'Macedonia' (Carol J. King) looks at Alexander's Macedonian background. The Macedonia that Alexander grew up in, after its resurgence and recovery under his father Philip, resembled in its extent the Macedonian state that Alexander I had previously established after the retreat of Xerxes' army in 479 BC. After his Anschluss of Upper Macedonia, Philip had in fact doubled in size the kingdom he had inherited, and he was able, further, to dominate the neighbouring regions of Epirus and Thessaly by means direct and indirect. The stability that Philip had brought to the kingdom (assassination plots aside) and its broader region was an indispensable foundation, a *sine qua non*, for his son's Asian adventure. Inter alia, the region was now able to provide him with the resources of manpower upon which his campaign would initially depend.

The following four chapters focus on Alexander as a king in his court: we look at his kingship in itself, his relations with his aristocratic entourage, the trouble that ensued when these relations broke down, and the women of the court, in their contrasting capacities. Chapter 10, 'Kingship' (William S. Greenwalt) looks at the conservative and personal nature of Macedonian kingship that Alexander came to occupy. The Argead (Temenid) family was differentiated from the rest of the Macedonian population by a collective charisma. The king was maintained in power by his relationship with the members of the Companion class, alongside whom, on horseback, he faced battle, and with whom he drank. His relationship with them was performed, endorsed and legitimated in stagey and ideologically rich contexts – not only that of the symposium but also, and especially, that of the royal hunt. Next, a linked pair of chapters focuses on Alexander's court. Chapter 11, 'Court and Companions' (Jeanne Reames), investigates the nature of the Macedonian royal court from the perspectives of its historical development and its structure and composition under Alexander. Consideration is given to the elite institutions of the Companions, the Royal Pages, the Bodyguards and the Royal Hypaspists. Attention is again turned to the symposium and the royal hunt, but now from a different angle, as it is shown how the king exploited these contexts also to engage with his Companions and to attempt to read their mood. Chapter 12, 'Changes and Challenges at Alexander's Court' (Jeanne Reames), takes the story of the court further forward, looking at the Persianising innovations

Alexander began to bring to it and to the broader army from 330 BC, and the modes by which opposition to these was articulated both by the existing elite and by the common troops. Further light is shed on Alexander's actions in this regard and the resistance to them by consideration of the innovations introduced by the previous Argead kings, a topic for which, surprisingly, archaeological evidence is of some value. And this in turn allows us to recover an original Macedonian perspective on Alexander's innovations, a perspective that tends to be occluded by the agendas of the literary sources upon which we have traditionally depended. Chapter 13, 'The Women of Alexander's Court' (Elizabeth D. Carney), investigates the role of the royal women in Alexander's mobile court. His mother Olympias, with whom he maintained communication throughout the campaign, and his sister Cleopatra continued to exercise influence remotely, even whilst remaining behind in the Macedonian–Greek peninsula. The women Alexander brought into his court in the course of his campaign were able to exercise influence in a more immediate way, often by virtue of the expansive networks in which they were embedded and, inevitably, in alliance with males. There is no greater testament to the influence they could wield – and the threats they could constitute – than the fact that, amongst others of the royal women, Olympias and at least two of Alexander's three wives, Roxane and Barsine-Stateira, met with violent ends in just the same way that Macedonian princes jostling for power at the court could expect to do.

Chapter 14, 'Religion' (Hugh Bowden), looks at Alexander's religious role as king and as military commander, both in relation to the Greek world and to that of the Achaemenid Empire. It gives particular attention to Alexander's exploitation of the Greek sanctuaries as media for communication with the cities, and to his engagement with the religious practices and expectations of the territories he conquered, especially Egypt and Babylon. The well-known tale of his visit to the Oracle of Amun at Siwah testifies to his acceptance of divine filiation, at least at the level of titulature, within an Egyptian context, but to no more than this.

The next two chapters return to the single most fundamental aspect of Alexander's campaign, the military one, building on the discussions of the campaign as a whole in Part I (especially Chapter 4). No apology is offered for devoting a total of three chapters directly to military matters (indeed it pricks my conscience that there are not more): without the army, there could have been no Alexander, in any sense. We can be sure that Alexander himself would have been appalled to find that, with his life being captured in thirty chapters, only three of them should take warfare as their focus. Chapter 15, 'Army and Warfare' (Carolyn Willekes), devoted to Alexander's organization of his army and his deployment of it in the field, focuses on the success of his adaptable use of combined-arms tactics, especially in his deployment of the cavalry as both his primary offensive and primary defensive arm, in both cases in conjunction with different forms of infantry. At the heart of these innovations lay Alexander's profound understanding of Macedonia's long equestrian tradition. Brief treatments are offered of his three great battles against the Persians, those of the Granicus, Issus and Gaugamela. Chapter 16, 'Alexander's Modern Military Reputation' (F. S. Naiden), explores the peculiar impact that this modern reputation, in its various guises, can exercise upon the scholarly interpretation and evaluation of his military activity in its historical context. So far-reaching is this impact that it requires that we make an exception to the volume's general principle of not pursuing questions of reception beyond the frame of antiquity itself (of which more anon). Even so, the debate about Alexander's military reputation has hallowed and ancient roots, and is found already in Julian's *Caesares*. It is contended that the reason that Alexander's military reputation remains a continuing source of debate and fascination in Europe and America is his carelessness about his own life and the lives of his troops. Both were repeatedly risked for trifling reasons, with the result that 'This paradigmatic soldier was very much at odds with familiar rationales for combat.'

The following pair of chapters address the finance and administration of Alexander's empire. Chapter 17, 'Finance and Coinage' (Kyle Erickson), shows that the process of conquest, as pursued by Alexander, did not show a net profit. His vast minting operation – which consumed in Persian bullion the weight of the gold in Fort Knox – was wholly absorbed by the financing, principally the pay, of his army. It was for others, his Successors, to reap the financial benefits of his conquests, with the cities he founded generating new source of income. Chapter 18, 'The Administration of Alexander's Empire' (Maxim M. Kholod), examines the satrapal system through which Alexander managed his empire. He took over the Achaemenid system (cf. Chapter 6) but adapted it as needed to the new circumstances of his conquest. Such alterations and innovations as he did make, whether they involved Macedonian or new Persian administrators, were ad hoc, and were not made in the service of any grand administrative vision or principle – beyond, that is, the goal of ensuring the efficient control and exploitation of the subject peoples. Alexander's tutelage of and tinkering with the satrapal system may be considered broadly successful, insofar as his empire was generally stable at the point of his death.

Finally in this section, we consider the impact that Alexander's campaign, which all at once brought his men direct experience of vast new swathes of territory and countless new cultures, had on the Greeks' general understanding of the world, and upon their science and geography in particular. Without Alexander it is difficult to imagine the work of Megasthenes, Agatharchides of Cnidus or indeed Eratosthenes. Chapter 19, 'Geography, Science and Knowledge of the World' (Antonio Ignacio Molina Marín), maintains that, while exploration and the expansion of knowledge were undoubtedly positive goals for Alexander, we should not think of him as carrying out some rarified or abstract Aristotelian commission in pursuit of knowledge for knowledge's sake. Rather, exploration and the acquisition of knowledge of foreign parts and peoples were indissociable from the Argead king's traditional role as a conqueror: 'Alexander wanted to know the *kosmos* in order to make it easier to conquer. Alexander the explorer was another facet of the Argead king that wished to surpass his mythical models ... by the spear.'

With Part III we turn, in six chapters, to the basis of our knowledge of Alexander and his deeds, the texts of the historical and biographical tradition for him. Students of Alexander are often presented with the facts of his career in the form of a judicious concoction arrived at after the application of a series of additive, subtractive, qualifying and revisionary processes to the material in the extant sources, with the identities, the individualities, the agendas and the voices of those sources being stripped out along the way. Here we attempt let some of the major sources for Alexander speak for themselves and to understand the different ways in which they viewed and conceived of the king, and what was important to them in the way they chose to project him. Establishing this helps us, at the historical level, to manipulate our evidence-base for Alexander with greater subtlety and sophistication, and at the literary level to understand the reception of Alexander and his work hundreds of years after the fact, in the high days of the Roman Empire.

The most important of these source texts fall into two broad groups. First, and more tractably, we have a series of five (almost) complete, full-scale narratives of the campaign, composed in the Roman Imperial period or (in the case of Diodorus) on the eve of it. Second, and more challengingly, we have a protracted series of fragments from earlier historians, some of whom participated in the campaign and were personally close to Alexander, on whose work the imperial historians depended; of these much can be said, whilst much remains disputed or unknown.

Of the five full-scale narratives that remain to us, a chapter is devoted to each of the three most important and interesting, Arrian, Curtius and Plutarch. In these the authors are situated in their own immediate context, and their particular perspectives, moral, philosophical and other, and agendas in writing about Alexander are laid out. Arrian, writing his *Anabasis* probably during the reign of Hadrian (r. AD 117–138) is by far the most important of these, covering the campaign in serious, sober and coherent detail, and basing his work primarily on the histories of two eyewitnesses to it, Ptolemy and Aristobulus. The work occupies c. 375 pages of Greek in the Loeb edition. Chapter 20, 'Arrian's Alexander' (Daniel W. Leon), shows how Arrian perceives an alteration in Alexander's behaviour occasioned by the increasing complexity of his political and personal circumstances, and represents this change for us by aligning his portrait of Alexander with Herodotus' portraits of despotic Persian kings. Plutarch's *Life of Alexander*, written c. AD 100, occupies 107 pages of Greek in the Loeb edition. It is unique amongst this group of five for offering us not a history of Alexander's campaign but a very personal biography of the man himself, and it is from this that its advantages and disadvantages as a source flow. On the plus side, Plutarch offers us much material of a particularly interesting sort, and much material that his unique to him; as the only one the five authors not in effect confining himself to an account of Alexander's campaign or earlier military activities, he is of incomparable value for Alexander's life prior to them, his childhood and youth. On the minus side, because he is not giving us a systematic account of the campaign (or purporting to do so), many of his intriguing anecdotes are, frustratingly, chronologically unhitched. Plutarch also gives us a further series of anecdotes about and sayings of Alexander – in a fashion more chronologically unhitched still – in the course of some of his moral essays. Chapter 21, 'Plutarch's Alexander' (Philip Bosman), shows how, in his epideictic speeches, Plutarch projects Alexander's successes as due to his own efforts rather than bestowed upon him by fortune, but has no particular axe to grind: the demands of the genre require only bravura rhetorical display in the manipulation of evidence drawn from ready knowledge. His portrait of Alexander in the *Life* explores the extent to which the great-souled king's ambition is directed by his education and by philosophy. It is a lesson in the way that governance is determined by personal morality. Quintus Curtius Rufus, writing his Latin history of Alexander's campaign probably, as it is now thought, in the AD 30s, has bequeathed us the most substantial of the extended accounts to survive, even despite the fact that large chunks of it are missing (the first two of his ten books; an expanse covering the end of Book 5 and the beginning of Book 6; and parts of Book 10). What remains occupies *c.* 460 pages of Latin in the Loeb edition; complete, the work would perhaps have occupied *c.* 600 pages – almost twice the length of Arrian, therefore. The extra length – compared with Arrian – is achieved, however, less by the incorporation of further substantive detail than by rhetorical inflation. Chapter 22, 'Curtius' Alexander' (Elizabeth Baynham), investigates the sources and the structure of Curtius' work, his use of intertextuality, and his characterization of Alexander. Of particular interest are the excursuses in which the historian seems to speak about the king's personality in his own voice, and his handling of the theme of his relationships with and interactions with women (cf. Chapter 13), notably the courtesan Thais, the Amazon queen Thalestris and Sisygambis, the Persian Queen Mother.

The two full-scale narratives to which we have not considered it a priority to assign dedicated chapters are those of Diodorus of Sicily and Justin. Diodorus, writing *c.* 30 BC, devotes Book 17 of his universal history, his *Library of History*, to the campaign. This is a detailed book by Diodorus' standards, but unfortunately his narrative of events between the second half of 330 BC and early 326 BC has been lost to a lacuna. What remains occupies *c.* 175 pages of Greek in the Loeb edition; on a proportionate basis, we can expect the complete narrative to have extended to *c.* 225 pages. For an introduction to Diodorus' Alexander, one may turn to Luisa Prandi's commentary on the relevant book (in Italian).[32] The Gallo-Roman Trogus, from Vaison-la-Romaine, completed his substantial forty-four-book *Philippic Histories* in *c.* AD 9.[33] This text constituted a world history that focused on the Hellenistic age and took relatively little interest in Rome herself. The *Histories* survive principally in an epitome made by Justin, who wrote at some point between the second and the fourth centuries AD, possibly in Africa (the prime centre of Latin literary production during those centuries). As Justin tells us, he selected Pompeius' material particularly for what he considered enjoyable or morally improving – the usual Roman obsession with the 'exemplary'; he may have seen his primary readership as rhetoricians. Books 11–12 of Trogus' *Histories* were devoted to Alexander's campaign, and these are refracted in the corresponding

---

[32] Prandi 2013. [33] See Yardley and Heckel 1997: 4–6.

books of Justin's *Epitome*. These two books are equivalent to *c.* 40 Loeb pages of Latin (the work – bafflingly – not yet featuring in the Loeb series itself). For an introduction to Trogus-Justin's Alexander, one may turn to John Yardley and Waldemar Heckel's translation of and commentary upon the relevant pair of books.[34] A useful 'Eusebian canons' aligning the common places of these five principal texts is provided in the first part of the first volume of Robinson's *The History of Alexander the Great* (Robinson described his project as an 'Alexander harmony').[35]

The fragmentary historians of Alexander are collected in Jacoby's *Die Fragmente der griechischen Historiker* (vol. ii.B: *FGrH / BNJ* nos 117–153), with commentaries, often vestigial, in German (in vol. ii.D).[36] For translations of these one long had to depend, once again, on the first volume of Robinson's *History*, which could be frustratingly difficult to get hold of.[37] However, up-to-date translations are now more easily accessible in an online resource that conveniently adopts Jacoby's numeration for the fragments, *Brill's New Jacoby* (*BNJ* nos 117–153); this resource also carries much fuller commentaries, in English.[38] Of the fragmentary historians of the first rank of importance we have already mentioned Ptolemy and Aristobulus, upon whom Arrian bases his work. Also of the first rank of importance is Clitarchus. It is upon his lost Alexander history (in fifteen books?) that Diodorus, Trogus-Justin, Curtius and Plutarch – the authors of the so-called 'vulgate' tradition – are held to have based their Alexander material.[39] Indeed, significant correspondence between the texts of Curtius and Diodorus in particular is generally taken to indicate that Clitarchus lies beneath. These three historians are accordingly given focal treatments, with Ptolemy and Aristobulus being taken together, given their concatenation in Arrian. Chapter 23, 'Ptolemy and Aristobulus' (Frances Pownall), shows that their remaining fragments are sufficient to give an insight into how Alexander himself presented some of the more controversial aspects of

---

[34] Yardley and Heckel 1997; note in particular the authoritative Introduction to this volume, by both authors, at pp. 1–41.
[35] Robinson 1953–1963: i.1–29. A similar function is also served by the citations of parallel sources in the notes to Ziegler's Teubner edition of Plutarch's *Alexander* (1968).
[36] Jacoby 1923–. The volumes in question were published in 1927 and 1930. Jacoby's fragment collection builds on Müller's *Fragmenta historicorum graecorum* (*FHG*, published 1841–1870).
[37] Robinson 1953–1963: i, 30–276.   [38] For general discussion of these see Pearson 1960.
[39] The concept of the Clitarchan vulgate was first properly developed at Jacoby 1921: 626–628; see Hamilton 1977 (for a strong affirmation of it) and Bosworth 2019: 83 [1983]. When it used to be believed that it was Diodorus' technique to follow a single source slavishly for large slabs of his work, his Alexander material was assumed to be all the more purely Clitarchan. Justin's chief sources for his material on Alexander and his Successors were (ultimately) Clitarchus, Duris and Hieronymus of Cardia: Yardley and Heckel 1997: 30, 34–41.

his campaign to his contemporaries. His general Ptolemy's account had an appropriately military focus and inflated his own role in and importance to the expedition to an egregious and narcissistic degree, all in the service, no doubt, of establishing and legitimating his own rule in Egypt during its early years. Since we know little of Aristobulus beyond the remains of his history itself, we cannot be sure of the immediate context in which he wrote, or, accordingly, of his personal agenda in writing, but his account seems to have been generally eulogistic of Alexander, though not exclusively so, and to have foregrounded the king's clemency. If we have been unable to give Diodorus and Justin chapters of their own, we have at least been able to accord that privilege to the Clitarchus that underpins them. Chapter 24, 'Clitarchus' Alexander' (Luisa Prandi), investigates the contexts in which the extant authors that depend upon Clitarchus make mention of him, and gives attention to his reputation as a fine writer. The pesky issue of Clitarchus' own chronological setting – the court of Ptolemy I or that of Ptolemy III? – continues to haunt us still. Chapter 25, 'Callisthenes, Chares, Nearchus, Onesicritus and the Mystery of the *Royal Journal*' (Christian Thrue Djurslev), is then devoted to surveys of a further five fragmentary Alexander histories, those of Callisthenes, Chares, Nearchus, Onesicritus and the *Royal Journal* or *Ephemerides*, the last perhaps compiled by Eumenes of Cardia (*FGrH / BNJ* nos 117, 124–125, 133–134). The importance of these texts lies in the fact that they were the earliest-produced histories of Alexander of which we know and represent the first generation of information about him. Given that these authors were, in their different ways, at the heart of Alexander's campaign and had good access to the king himself, it is dispiriting to realize (as we are still able to do, despite the fragmentary nature of their works) that they often preferred the demands of literary convention to those of direct reporting, and imbued their writings with the elaborations and inventions of a venerable tradition of history-writing that had its roots in Herodotus and even in Homer. But then what else could we have expected them to do? For discussions of the remaining fragmentary Alexander historians, the reader is referred in the first instance to the corresponding entries in *BNJ*.[40]

---

[40] Namely: Strattis of Olynthus (118), Baeton (119), Diognetus of Erythrae (120), Philonides of Crete (121), Amyntas (122), Archelaus of Cappadocia (123), Ephippus of Olynthus (126), Nicobule (127), Polyclitus of Larissa (128), Medius of Larissa (129), Cyrsilus of Pharsalus (130), Menaechmus of Sicyon (131), Leon of Byzantium (132), Marsyas of Pella (135), Marsyas of Philippi (136), Anticlides of Athens (140), Antigenes (141), Hegesias of Magnesia (142), Aristus of Salamis (143), Asclepiades (144), Dorotheus of Athens (145), Nicanor (146),

Each of the authors discussed in Part III can be said to have remembered Alexander in their own way. We carry this theme further forward in Part IV, in which we look more broadly at the way Alexander was remembered within the confines of the ancient world. With the partial exception of Chapter 16 on Alexander's military reputation, this volume does not attempt to address the reception of Alexander *after* antiquity: the reception of Alexander within antiquity is a rich and important enough subject in itself, whilst that of Alexander after it is vast and, in any case, the focus of our contributor Richard Stoneman's fine new edited volume, *A History of Alexander the Great in World Culture*, also published by Cambridge University Press.[41] Furthermore, consideration of the reception of Alexander within antiquity can have a critical bearing on how we interpret the raw data upon which we depend for an understanding of the historical Alexander; this is only exceptionally true of Alexander's reception after antiquity (Chapter 16 is again a case in point). One notable consequence of our general policy of pursuing only traditions of reception that are already rooted in antiquity is that we give attention here to Alexander's reception in Jewish and Christian literature, but not to his (rich) reception in Muslim literature: this lack is made good by Professor Stoneman's book, which devotes two chapters to Alexander's reception in Persian writings and a third to his reception in Arabic ones.

The Part accordingly begins by investigating the manipulation of the image of Alexander in association with the figures of his immediate Successors, the first generation of the magnificent Hellenistic kings, and then its manipulation in association with the figures of the Hellenistic kings' effective successors in turn, the emperors of Rome. Chapter 26, 'The Successors and the Image of Alexander' (Daniel Ogden), looks at the appropriation of Alexander's image in the broader sense – and principally through the medium of texts – in connection with the legends constructed for the founders of the greater two of the Successor dynasties, those of the Ptolemies and the Seleucids. In the case of the figure of Seleucus I, the Alexander-imagery tended to be focused on the person of Seleucus himself. Some of the relevant tales celebrate Seleucus' personal interaction with Alexander, whilst others serve to establish a typological parallel between his actions and those of Alexander. In the case of Ptolemy I, the legend-generation tends to focus less upon developing a relationship between

---

Potamon of Mytilene (147), *P.Oxy* 1798 (148), Varro (149), Amyntianus (150), *Fragmentum Sabbaiticum* (151), Antidamas of Heracleopolis (152), varia (153).

[41] Stoneman 2022a; cf. also Moore 2018.

Alexander and the person of Ptolemy (though there is some of that) and rather more upon developing Alexander's relationship with – Ptolemy's own – city of Alexandria. Chapter 27, 'Alexander and the Roman Emperors' (Sulochana Asirvatham), looks at the fundamental subject of the way in which Alexander was represented in the Roman empire – fundamental because, as we have noted, all the extant, substantial and coherent narrative sources for his life were produced under it (Diodorus' account possibly preceded the formal commencement of the Imperial period by a few years). It is, accordingly, the Roman Empire's Alexander that we know first and best. To what extent did the Romans of this age consciously imitate Alexander, and to what extent did they emulate him? It seems that imitation of Alexander to an unsubtle degree could incur mockery in the city itself, but it could be received more indulgently in the east, where Alexander could be looked upon as a city-founder or the progenitor of a local people.

Two varieties in particular of literature produced within the ancient world were to be responsible for carrying knowledge of and thought about Alexander forward beyond the confines of that world. The first is the *Alexander Romance* tradition, which had roots in the early Ptolemaic period, and achieved the earliest form in which we have access to it (the 'alpha recension') in the early third century AD, but kept Alexander's story alive in many of the languages of Europe and the Middle East throughout the medieval period, and indeed continued to thrive in the Early Modern period and even into the present in the form of the Greek *Phyllada*.[42] Chapter 28, 'The *Alexander Romance*' (Christian Thrue Djurslev), offers of an overview of the central issues bearing upon the alpha recension, some potential solutions to them and some possible directions for future study. Attention is given to the constitution of the text, its problematic dating, its contents and structure, its sources, its characterization of Alexander, its (particularly problematic) genre and the possible contexts of its original composition.

The second impactful variety of literature produced within the ancient world was the selection of Alexander episodes and commonplaces filtered into Jewish and Christian traditions through biblical and apocryphal texts, and on occasion invented by them, which were accordingly manipulated in the works of early Jewish scholars, the Church Fathers and the Christian Chroniclers. Chapter 29, 'Alexander in Jewish and Early Christian Literature' (Aleksandra Kłeczar), shows that there was no single, uniform Jewish or Christian

---

[42] For the *Phyllada* see Stoneman 2012.

vision of Alexander. In Jewish and Christian sources alike the figure constructed for Alexander exhibited some continuities with his representation in Classical sources, but there were striking innovations too. This Judaeo-Christian projection was a composite one: complex, centrifugal and fragmentary, and ever subject to creation and recreation, as suited the immediate agenda of the given text in which the king was to feature.

All the preceding chapters in this volume have perforce had to concentrate on the literary sources for Alexander's life, career and context. In the final chapter we turn to his representation in visual media. Chapter 30, 'Alexander in Ancient Art' (Agnieszka Fulińska), explains how images of Alexander deriving from his own lifetime can be classified into two broad categories: on the one hand, representations without attributes, which are more or less what we would now term 'portraits'; and, on the other hand, representations with attributes, which have an allegorical function, their purpose being to tell a story about him, rather than merely to convey his likeness. The distinction tended to coincide with the medium. Images of Alexander in sculpture tended towards 'realism', whilst images of him in paintings and glyptics tended towards allegorization. The attributes given to Alexander in art during his own lifetime are restricted in their epistemological content, being predominantly of a military sort, such as a spear or armour. But a much richer repertoire of attributes emerges for him in the posthumous representations of the king generated by and for his successors in the Hellenistic age. Above all, these new attributes allowed for his direct association with the divine: the aegis associated him with Zeus and Athena; ram's horns with Zeus-Ammon; goat's horns with Pan; bull's horns with Dionysus; the lion-scalp with Heracles; the elephant-scalp with Dionysus; and the radiate crown with Apollo-Helios.

Part I

Alexander's Life and Career

1: ALEXANDER'S BIRTH AND CHILDHOOD

Daniel Ogden

THE FONS ET ORIGO: PLUTARCH

Plutarch's *Alexander* (c. AD 110–115) occupies a predominant position in the extant sources for Alexander's life prior to his accession, this by virtue of the fact that it offers us a biography of the king, as opposed to an account of his campaigns. Accordingly, much of this essay is perforce a footnote to the first ten chapters of Plutarch's work. His attention to the king's childhood derives not from a desire to narrate his life in full (rather, he apologizes for his inability to be exhaustive), nor from a belief that the child is the father of the man, but from the conviction that a man's character is better conveyed by his smaller deeds, the ones often overlooked, than it is by his greater ones (indeed it is in the Preface to the *Alexander* that he supplies his programme for the *Parallel Lives* as a whole).[1]

BIRTH AND BIRTH MYTH (356 BC)

Alexander is rather unique amongst ancient figures in that we actually know – thanks to Plutarch – not only the year of his birth, 356 BC, but its actual date: 20 July (or so we may translate the 6th day of the Macedonian month of Lous, equivalent to the Athenian Hecatombeion).[2] He tells us too that it coincided with the day of his father's chariot victory at Olympia: a nice omen, though it may be that the birth-date was massaged to make it;

---

[1] Plutarch *Alexander* 1–10 (§1 for the programmatic material). Hamilton's outstanding 1969 commentary, with its full and lucid introduction, should be consulted on all passages; for the dating of the *Alexander*, see xl–xliii; for Plutarch's aims and methods in composing the *Parallel Lives*, see xliii–lv; note also Tarn 1948: ii.296–309 and Chapter 21 in this volume. For surveys of Alexander's childhood see Wilcken 1932 [1931]: 53–60; Hamilton 1965, 1969: 1–28, 1973: 29–43; Lane Fox 1973: 43–67; Green 1974: 35–110; Bosworth 1988a: 19–28; O'Brien 1992: 8–42; Hammond 1997b especially 1–7, 21–24, 27–31 (effectively unreferenced, alas); Worthington 2003: 89–94; Adams 2005: 21–46 (largely pedagogical); Müller 2016b: 278–282; Landucci 2018. For the full range of scholarship on these matters published up until 2015, see Molina Marín 2018: 76–82. Did Curtius cover Alexander's childhood in the lost first book of his *Histories*? See Chapter 22.

[2] Plutarch *Alexander* 3.

it may also be that the name of Alexander's Epirote-princess mother was changed from Myrtale (?) to Olympias to salute it.[3]

Plutarch and others preserve a suite of three extravagant birth myths for the king: first, before her marriage, Olympias dreamed that her womb was struck by a thunderbolt (the imagery of Zeus); secondly, after the marriage Philip dreamed that he was sealing Olympias' womb with a lion-device signet ring (the imagery of Heracles); thirdly, Philip espied Olympias in sexual congress with a gigantic serpent (the imagery perhaps of Asclepius, or of an ostentatiously unidentifiable power; Figure 1.1). Of these, the signet-ring myth at least must have been developed in Alexander's own lifetime, since it was referred to by Ephorus, who is thought to have died c. 330 BC.[4] The claim that Alexander was the son of Ammon presumably did not antedate the king's visit to the god's oracle, though it seems to have flourished immediately after it; the tradition often misleadingly conflates Alexander's siring by Ammon with that of his siring by the serpent.[5]

EDUCATION: LANICE, LYSIMACHUS OF ACARNANIA, LEONIDAS OF EPIRUS AND ARISTOTLE

No doubt Alexander received his first education on the lap of his nurse Hellanice, whose name was affectionately abbreviated to Lanice (she is also referred to as Alcrinis). The tradition remembers her because she was sister to Clitus the Black. When Alexander subsequently murdered him at Samarkand in a fit of drunken range, he was remorseful not least for the sake of the man's sister: 'What a fine repayment for rearing (*tropheia*) this was!'[6]

Two tutors (*paidagōgoi*) are named for Alexander's early years; they were remembered because the king maintained relationships with them during his campaign. The more important was Leonidas of Epirus,

---

[3] So Bosworth 1988a: 19; Hammond 1992c: 356–361; Heckel 2006: 10, 2021: 18; note also Ferrando 1998, arguing for a birth-date in January 355. For Olympias' names see Heckel 1981b and Carney 2006: 15–16, 93–95.

[4] Plutarch *Alexander* 2–3. Ephorus *FGrH* / *BNJ* 70 F217 = Tertullian *De anima* 46. For my latest views on the birth myths, their datings and their various significances, see Ogden 2022a, building on my previous studies at, *inter alia*, 2009a, 2009c, 2011a: 7–78 (and cf. 2017b: 23–67); note also Sales 2005; Collins 2012b. For the elaboration of these myths in the *Alexander Romance* tradition, see Feis 1918–1919; Aufrère 1999; Stoneman 2008: 6–26; Ogden 2015 and the commentaries of Stoneman 2007– and Nawotka 2017 on *AR* (A) 1.1–14. For Olympias see, *in primis*, Carney 1987, 2006.

[5] See Ogden 2014b: 9–14, 2022a. Note the inscribed pedestal from the temple of Ammon at Bahariya, near Siwah, supposedly dedicated by Alexander in 332–331 BC: 'King Alex<a>nder to Ammon, his father'; see Bosch-Puche 2008.

[6] Justin 12.6, Curtius 8.1.21, 8.2.8 (with the full version of the name), Arrian *Anabasis* 4.9 (from whom the quote), Aelian *Varia historia* 12.26, Athenaeus 129a, *AR* (A) 1.13 ≃ Julius Valerius 1.13

1.1 Olympias gives birth to Alexander; the siring serpent hovers above. Master of the Jardin de vertueuse consolation (*c.* 1470–1475). Getty Museum: Ms. Ludwig xv 8 (83.MR.178), fol. 15 (*Livre des fais d'Alexandre le grant*).

a relative of Olympias and an advocate of austerity. Plutarch tells, first, that he gave Alexander the best of cooks, namely a night-march (i.e. to add savour to his breakfast) and a tiny breakfast (i.e. to add savour to his dinner); second, that he would examine Alexander's linen chests, to make sure that his mother was not hiding treats for him in them; and, third, that he reproved Alexander for being wasteful with incense at the altar, telling him that he could only afford to be so lavish once he had conquered the lands of the spices (accordingly, after he had taken Gaza, Alexander sent back to Leonidas 500 talents of frankincense and a 100 of myrrh).[7] The second was Lysimachus of Acarnania, who, Plutarch explains,

---

≃ *AR* (Arm.) §29 Wolohojian. For Lanice, see above all Alonso Troncoso 2007 and Asirvatham 2018; for the killing of Clitus see Carney 1981 and Tritle 2003.

[7] Plutarch *Alexander* 5, 22, 25; cf. Plutarch *Moralia* 179e–179f, Pliny *Natural History* 12.62, *AR* 1.13 ≃ Julius Valerius 1.13 (where the name is given as Leuconides) ≃ *AR* (Arm.) §29 Wolohojian,

was rough, but admired for his conceit that he was Phoenix to Alexander's Achilles (was it he, then, that was responsible for ensuring that Alexander had Homer's *Iliad* off by heart, if Dio may be believed?). Lysimachus was with Alexander during the siege of Tyre, when, during a side-expedition against the Arabs of Mt Libanus, the king risked his life in order to look after his ailing tutor, who struggled when the party had to proceed on foot. He was with him still for the downfall of Callisthenes, in which he played a part, resenting as he did the latter's airs and graces.[8]

For the years 343 to 340, Philip hired Aristotle to teach Alexander; these years preceded the philosopher's fame, though Plutarch suggests that he was already able to command a considerable fee. Aristotle had an existing family connection to the court: his father Nicomachus had been doctor to Philip's father Amyntas III. He had another family connection of interest too: his father-in-law was Hermias, the dynast of Atarneus on the Troad, which had the potential to offer a bridgehead for a sally into Asia Minor. For a school Philip assigned Aristotle the shady precinct of the Nymphs at Mieza at the foot of Mt Bermion. It was here he supposedly taught Alexander a full curriculum, with medicine the prince's favourite subject. He is also said to have taught him some secret doctrines, with Alexander subsequently being disappointed to learn, in the course of his expedition, that Aristotle had now published them: he feared that he had now lost an advantage over other men. Plutarch further tells (after Onesicritus) that the philosopher made a special edition of the *Iliad* for him. When Alexander subsequently seized Darius' baggage after the battle of Issus, the most precious item among the Persian king's possessions was held to be a casket, and it was in this that Alexander decided to keep the edition, thereby indicating that it was his most treasured possession.[9] Scholars have speculated that Aristotle wrote his lost works *On Kingship* and *Alexander, or, On behalf of the Colonies* for the boy-prince.[10] The relationship with Aristotle presumably deteriorated when Alexander murdered his nephew Callisthenes, his expedition historian, in 327 BC. It may be, as Plutarch

---

Quintilian 1.1.9 (after Diogenes of Babylon); see Berve 1926 no. 469; Heckel 2006: 146–147, 2021: 273.

[8] Plutarch *Alexander* 5, 24 (incorporating Chares *FGrH* / *BNJ* 125 F7), 55; Dio Chrysostom *Orations* 4.39; see Berve 1926 no. 481; Heckel 2006: 153, 2021: 284.

[9] Plutarch *Alexander* 7–8 (incorporating Onesicritus *FGrH* / *BNJ* 134 F38), 26, *Moralia* 327e–327f, Justin 12.16, Pliny *Natural History* 8.44, Diogenes Laertius 5.4–5.5, Athenaeus 398e, Aelian *Varia historia* 4.19, Quintilian 1.1.23–1.1.24, Dio Chrysostom 49.4. Discussion at Hamilton 1965: 118–119, 1969 on §7; O'Brien 1992: 19–21 and, more generally, Carney 2003a.

[10] Hamilton 1969 on §7, p.18; the precarious notion is that the latter text was penned in association with Alexander's foundation of Alexandropolis, for which see below.

claims, that Alexander subsequently threatened, in a letter to Antipater, to punish Aristotle for having introduced his nephew to him,[11] though the notion that Aristotle had himself been involved in a plot to poison Alexander is presumably an elaboration of the tradition.[12]

Aeschines on the Boy of Nine (346 bc)

A unique near-contemporary view of the almost ten-year old Alexander in 346 BC is provided by a difficult passage of Aeschines' speech *Against Timarchus*, composed the following year. This tells how the boy had performed on the *kithara* and held a quick-fire debate with another boy for the entertainment of Athenian and other Greek ambassadors at a banquet Philip had laid on for them. Aeschines further tells that his opponent Demosthenes had previously made sexual innuendos against the boy and implies that he is now accusing him himself, Aeschines, of having tried to seduce him.[13]

Alexander Becomes a Man (1): Bucephalas

The tale of Alexander's acquisition of the horse Bucephalas ('Ox-head') and the tale considered next, that of Alexander as a *gynnis*, constitute the only significant episodes in the tradition of direct interaction between Alexander and his father, other than in the context of dynastic disputes (the latter will be discussed in the following chapter).[14] The original hook for this tale appears to have been Alexander's subsequent foundation of the city of Bucephala on the banks of the Hydaspes (Jhelum) in honour of (and around the tomb of) the animal, after the horse died in the aftermath of the battle against Porus in 326 BC. Fragments of two of the historians that were personally close to Alexander, Chares of Mytilene, Alexander's chamberlain, and Onesicritus, Alexander's chief helmsman in India, both speak of this.[15]

---

[11] Plutarch *Alexander* 55, Diogenes Laertius 5.10; for the introduction, see Valerius Maximus 7.2. ext. 11 and *Suda* s.v. Καλλισθένης.

[12] Plutarch *Alexander* 77, Arrian *Anabasis* 7.27; cf. Heckel 2006: 51, 2021: 98. For a detailed and sensitive examination of the literary tradition of Alexander's education, see now Djurslev 2022; see also Müller 2019: 54–56.

[13] Aeschines 1.166–1.169, with Fisher 2001: 311–315 (*ad loc.*); cf. Lane Fox 1973: 46 (Lane Fox is a rarity amongst Alexander's biographers for noting this text) and Koulakiotis 2006: 34–38.

[14] For the Bucephalas tradition in general, see Anderson 1930; Baynham 1995b; Ogden 2021b.

[15] Chares *FGrH* / *BNJ* 125 F18 *apud* Gellius 5.2.1–5.2.5; Onesicritus *FGrH* / *BNJ* 134 F20 *apud* Plutarch *Alexander* 61. Bucephalas' tomb: Pliny *Natural History* 8.154; cf. Greenwalt 2016. Bucephalas may have entered the iconographic tradition at an even earlier point, if we accept

Once again, we have to wait until Plutarch for the key tale of the boy Alexander's taming of Bucephalas. According to this account, Philonicus of Thessaly offers to sell Bucephalus to Philip for 13 talents, but the king declines the offer on the ground of the animal's intractability. Alexander appreciates his latent quality and protests, whereupon Philip offers him a deal: if Alexander can master him, he will buy the horse for him; otherwise, Alexander himself will forfeit the price of the horse. Alexander has noticed that the horse is frightened of his own shadow, and so calms him down by turning him towards the sun and successfully mounts and rides him. Philip, the proud father, congratulates the boy and tells him to seek out a kingdom equal to himself, Macedonia being too small for him.[16] The early-third-century AD *Alexander Romance* offers a gloriously elaborated version of this tale in which Bucephalas is presented actually as a man-eater, no less.[17]

There is a good chance, however, that Plutarch's tale may already have appeared in Chares. His fragment's claim that Bucephalas was bought for 13 talents and then given to Philip – the donor is unspecified in Gellius' account of the fragment – is a reasonably close match for Plutarch's claim that Philonicus sold Bucephalas to Philip for 13 talents, and in the context of Plutarch's narrative this claim is, as we see, the starting point for his story of the boy Alexander's taming of the horse.[18] Chares did, it again appears from Gellius, also have the claim that Bucephalas would allow no other person to mount him when caparisoned, a detail which is broadly compatible with the taming story.[19]

Whatever the historical roots of this taming-of-Bucephalas tale – and Chares might be thought to inspire confidence – its broader

with Stewart 1993: 130–150 (with colour figs. 4–5a) that (a) the horse Alexander rides in the Alexander Mosaic identifies itself as Bucephalas with an ear contrived to salute an ox-horn: and (b) that the mosaic reproduces a painting (by Philoxenus?) completed immediately after the 333 BC Battle of Issus. The origin of the name must – despite the tradition's other claims – have lain in the horse's brand-type: see Pliny *Natural History* 8.154, Arrian *Anabasis* 5.19.4–5.19.6, Solinus 45.5–45.5.8, *AR* (A) 1.15, with the discussions of Anderson 1930: 3–7; Bosworth 1995: 314; and Chandezon 2010: 178–179.

[16] Plutarch *Alexander* 6; this material is recycled at Zonaras 4.8 (xii AD). For general commentary on the Plutarch narrative see Hamilton 1969: 14–16.

[17] *AR* (A) 1.13, 15, 17: see Stöcker 1976; Stoneman 2007– : i, 500–508, Ogden 2015; Nawotka 2017: 73–77.

[18] The later tradition partly supplements and partly varies Chares' details. Diodorus 17.76 has Demaratus of Corinth give the horse directly to Alexander. Pliny *Natural History* 8.154 agrees with Plutarch in having Philip buy the horse for 13 talents from Philonicus of Pharsalus. The *AR* (A) 1.13 has him given to Philip by the rulers of Cappadocia. Discussion at Anderson 1930: 8–10; Lane Fox 1973: 47–48; Stoneman 2007– : i, 500.

[19] A suspicion shared by Jacoby and Müller on Chares (*FGrH* and *BNJ ad loc.* respectively) and also by Hamilton 1965: 118, 1969: 15, 1973: 32; Bosworth 1995: 313–314; and Baynham 1995b: 5–6 n.27.

function in the tradition is to align Alexander with a series of great mythical tamers of (super-)wild horses. Bellerophon, for example, with the help of Athena, had been able to bridle the flying horse Pegasus before embarking upon the three great Labours with which he is credited in the *Iliad*.[20] In this case the feat of taming seems to serve as a rite of passage from boyhood to manhood; in Alexander's case we have a transition not merely to manhood but, as we see, actually to kingliness. And Alexander's own Heracles, too, famously tamed some very wild horses in the course of his eighth Labour, that of the Mares of the wicked Thracian Diomede. Diodorus, for example, tells how they had bronze mangers because of their wildness, and that they had to be bound with iron chains because of their strength. For their food they hacked apart the limbs of the unfortunate strangers fed to them by their master. In order to render them manageable, Heracles fed Diomede himself to them. By sating the creatures' hunger with the flesh of the man that had taught them to violate their natures he was able to render them docile. He then took the mares back to Eurystheus, and Eurystheus in turn dedicated them to Hera. Diodorus concludes by noting that the horses' descendants endured until the reign of Alexander.[21] With this final point he telegraphically conveys the belief that Bucephalas himself was the ultimate descendant of Diomede's horses – and this further entails that Diodorus already (in *c*. 30 BC) understood him to be a man-eater. It may be, accordingly, that the seemingly extravagant *Alexander Romance* is not magnifying the more sober tale found in Plutarch, but that Plutarch is partly rationalizing an already extravagant tradition.

Alexander Becomes a Man (II): Alexander as *Gynnis*, and His Sexuality

A chronologically unhitched anecdote, which must nonetheless relate to the time when Alexander was on the cusp of adulthood, unites both Philip and Olympias with their son in cosy domestic trio:

> Hieronymus in his *Letters* tells that Theophrastus said that Alexander was not well predisposed towards sex.

---

[20] Bridling of Pegasus: Pindar *Olympians* 13.63–13.66 and 84–90; cf. *Isthmians* 7.44–7.47. Bellerophon's Labours: Homer *Iliad* 6.152–195. For the horse-taming imagery associated with Perseus' transition to manhood (a somewhat complex case), see Ogden 2008: 26–28 and 2021a: 120–121.
[21] Diodorus 4.15.3–4.15.4. For further sources for this Labour, and discussions of it, see Robert 1921: i.458–462; Brommer 1986, 34–36; Boardman 1990; Gantz 1993, 395–397; Bader 1998, 151–156; and Ogden 2021a. Bader sees the Labour as reflecting an Indo-European rite of male initiation by horse-taming; however, she makes the case more by assertion than argument.

> Accordingly, Olympias actually sent the outstandingly beautiful Thessalian courtesan Callixeina to bed with him, and Philip abetted her in this, for they were taking precautions lest he should be a eunuch [*gynnis*]. Olympias frequently begged her to have sex with Alexander.
>
> Athenaeus 435a, incorporating Hieronymus of Rhodes F38 Wehrli = F10 Hiller (iii BC) and Theophrastus F578 Fortenbaugh (late iv BC – early iii BC)

For all that this engaging tale must have been composed soon after Alexander's death, the chain beginning with Theophrastus, it can hardly be historical.[22] Rather, Theophrastus has seized upon the rare term *gynnis* for its capacity to encapsulate retrospectively some distinctive aspects of the adult Alexander and his activities during the campaign: the effeminacy of his projected image, beardless, limpid-eyed and with a coy tilt to the neck;[23] his engagement with the Persian royal family and its harem, and indeed with the actual eunuch Bagoas;[24] and his growing identification (according to early, but possibly posthumous, tradition) with the god Dionysus.[25] The tale shares a function with that of Bucephalas, in that it articulates for us Alexander's transition from boyhood to manhood, albeit a manhood of an unusual kind in this instance.[26] Had the tale been historical, then Alexander's parents need not have worried: for all that Alexander today tends to have the reputation of poor fertility (and perhaps the same was true already for Theophrastus), his attested rate of child-production was actually slightly superior to that of his father Philip, who is regarded as rather fecund.[27]

I take this opportunity to make just some brief points about Alexander's sexuality, or rather its representation in the ancient tradition, the subject now being mined out in current scholarship.[28] Cumulatively, our sources indicate that Alexander participated in the

---

[22] See Ogden 2011a: 174–184. [23] Plutarch *Alexander* 4, *Pyrrhus* 8, *Moralia* 335ab.
[24] Plutarch *Alexander* 67, Curtius 6.5.22–6.5.23. For Bagoas see Badian 1958c; Ogden 2011a: 167–171.
[25] For Dionysus as a eunuch see, for example, Aeschylus frr. 62, 78a *TrGF*, Aristophanes *Thesmophoriazusae* 136–137. Whatever we think of the tradition's claims that Alexander Dionysus-ized during the campaign, as, for example, in the context of the revel in Carmania (Curtius 9.10.24–9.10.29, Diodorus 17.106.1, Plutarch *Alexander* 67), in *c.* 305–301 BC Seleucus minted a series of tetradrachms depicting Alexander wearing a panther-skin helmet and cloak in evocation of the god; Mørkholm 1991 no. 139, Stewart 1993: 7–80 and 234–238, with fig. 116.
[26] An observation I owe, with gratitude, to Ignacio Molina Marín.
[27] Ogden 2011a: 121–123: Philip has an attested impregnation rate (after the age of 24) of one pregnancy every 3.1 years; Alexander one every 2.7 years.
[28] For the traditions of Alexander's homosexual relationships, see Ogden 2011a: 155–184 (building on 2007b, 2009b).

martially-driven bisexual culture of the Macedonian court into which he was born and into which he was socialized, just as his father did before him, as we learn vividly from the circumstances of the latter's assassination (see the following chapter).[29] Had this not been the case, one way or the other, it might have been easier to establish more particular claims about his personal sexuality. Any attempt to go further is stymied not only by the general impossibility of knowing the secrets of the boudoir, let alone an individual's 'reel thorts' on matters of love and sex (did Alexander even know his own?), but also by the fact that all pronouncements on the subject of his sexuality in the extant sources, mostly composed hundreds of years after his lifetime, are demonstrably enmeshed in a literary game or contest of one sort or another. So it is, for example, with the only text in our source tradition *seeming* to assert directly that Alexander had a sexual relationship with Hephaestion:

> (Note) that Alexander garlanded the tomb of Achilles and Hephaestion that of Patroclus, the latter riddling [*ainittomenos*] that he too was a beloved [*erōmenos*] of Alexander, just as Patroclus was of Achilles.
> (Aelian *Varia historia* 12.7)

In fact, there is no direct assertion here. Rather, Aelian is having fun with an ancient conundrum. Hephaestion is made to suggest, teasingly, that he is the *erōmenos* of Alexander in just the same way that Patroclus was the *erōmenos* of Achilles. All and well and good – except that the nature of the relationship between Homer's Patroclus and Achilles was already in his day an ancient and notorious mystery: it had ever been disputed whether their relationship was sexual or homosocial, and, in the former eventuality, whether Patroclus, Achilles' elder but lower in status, had been the active lover (*erastēs*) or the passive *erōmenos*.[30]

'The only text in our source tradition *seeming* to assert directly that Alexander had a sexual relationship with Hephaestion': however, it may be inferred that an anonymous *erōmenos* of Alexander mentioned by Epictetus was intended to be Hephaestion on the basis of Arrian's *Discourses of Epictetus*, where he is reported to have spoken, in an illustrative rhetorical flourish, of Alexander 'order[ing] the temples of

---

[29] For the homosexual culture that provided the context to Philip's assassination, see Mortensen 2007; Antela-Bernárdez 2010, 2012; Skinner 2010. For the typically martial context of attested homosexual relationships in Macedon (as in Greece, with the possible exception of Athens), see Ogden 1996 especially 119–123 (47–49 in the 2020 reprint).
[30] For discussion and further sources, see Ogden 2011a: 155–167. For Hephaestion, see also Reames-Zimmermann 1999; Müller 2019: 231–236.

Asclepius to be burned when his *erōmenos* died'. The reason for supposing that the *erōmenos* in question is intended to be Hephaestion is that Arrian, in his own voice, *denies* the tradition that Alexander ordered the temple of Asclepius (evidently the *interpretatio Graeca* of an indigenous deity) at Ecbatana to be razed in his grief at his death. In this respect too, Hephaestion was evidently at the heart of an established literary debate (in this case we see it actually being fought out between teacher Epictetus and pupil Arrian), and we can easily hariolate the issues it concatenated: How many temples, if any at all, did Alexander destroy? How great was his grief? How much – and in what way – did he love Hephaestion?[31]

Regency, Thrace, Alexandropolis and the Persian Ambassadors (340 BC)

Plutarch tells that, when Alexander was 16, Philip felt able to appoint him regent whilst he besieged Byzantium at the far end of Thrace, leaving him 'in charge of [*kyrios*] affairs and the seal'.[32] He further tells that during this time he took responsibility for dealing with the rebellious Maedi of the Upper Strymon and the Mt Rhodope massif in central Thrace. He succeeded in expelling them from their mountain city and refounded it as his own mixed-race and military-colony city of Alexandropolis (evidently there was some sort of coordination with Philip's own Thracian foundation, some two years previously, of Philippopolis, the modern Plovdiv).[33] It is not clear how substantial or how well-ensconced Alexander's new city was, but it appears to have disappeared almost immediately.[34]

Plutarch twice tells an anecdote of a Persian embassy visiting the Macedonian court in Philip's absence and interacting with the prince. The ambassadors are impressed with the lad's precocity, as he asks them not the predictable questions about the Great King's wealth (his golden vine, etc.), but about the size of his army, his battle formations and the lengths of his roads. The ambassadors conclude that here indeed is

---

[31] Arrian *Discourses of Epictetus* 2.22.17, *Anabasis* 7.14.5. See Reames-Zimmermann 1999: 90; Ogden 2011a: 159.
[32] Plutarch *Alexander* 9. Heckel 2006: 11: 'though under the watchful eye of Antipater'; cf. Hamilton 1973: 35 for the same claim.
[33] This city acquired the name of Poneropolis ('Wicked-town'). Pliny *Natural History* 4.41 implausibly implies that Poneropolis was the city's original name, this being converted to Philippopolis when (re-)founded by Philip. Cf. also Strabo C320 and Theopompus FGrH / BNJ 115 F110.
[34] Hammond and Griffith 1979: 558; Cohen 1995: 82.

a 'Great King', whereas their own king is merely rich. The conversation is no doubt apocryphal, and crafted with a heavy dose of retrospect, but some nonetheless regard the tale as founded upon a historical Persian embassy to the Macedonian court that must have taken place at some point during Philip's Thracian expedition, and some have speculated too that the subject of the embassy was Philip's siege of Byzantium. But one has to wonder why Persian ambassadors would travel to a Philip-less Macedon for such a purpose, when Philip himself was so much more accessible to them than ever, tarrying as he was on their very doorstep.[35]

However, the tale displays a certain parallelism with a famous one in Herodotus: in both cases an Alexander, a boy-prince and the king-to-be, is seen dealing in striking fashion with a group of Persian ambassadors at the Macedonian court in the absence of his father the king. In Herodotus' tale the young Alexander I (to be) sends his father Amyntas I away before ambushing the ambassadors and killing them with the help of his peers, a band of smooth-chinned youths disguised as women.[36] One wonders, accordingly, whether the tale has been constructed in dialogue with Herodotus' — to show the later boy Alexander (III to be) pursuing the long-game war against the Persians with rather greater subtlety and effectiveness than his namesake predecessor?[37]

Scythia and Chaeronea (339–338 BC)

In 339 Philip abandoned his siege of Byzantium, which was compromised by the efforts of the Athenians and the Persians alike. In order to recoup some of his losses, he took his army north to subdue and plunder the Scythians under Atheas at the Danube mouth. According to Justin, he summoned Alexander from Pella to join him in the expedition and to gain experience in warfare. Unfortunately, most of the ample booty seized — vast numbers of slaves and cattle — was lost as Philip had to fight his way back to Macedon through hostile Triballian territory.[38]

---

[35] Plutarch *Moralia* 342b–342c (*Fortune of Alexander*), *Alex.* 5, 9 (the last for Alexander's regency in Macedon whilst Philip was in Thrace). The fundamental historicity of the embassy is championed by Hammond and Griffith 1979: 579.
[36] Herodotus 5.18–5.22.
[37] At Ogden 2011a: 131–132, I argued that the tale of Alexander the Great's first meeting with Roxane and his marriage to her — as narrated in various conflicting versions at Strabo C517, Curtius 8.4.21–8.4.30, Plutarch *Alexander* 47, Arrian *Anabasis* 4.18.4, 4.19.4–4.19.6, 4.20.4 and *Metz Epitome* 28–31 — also operates in response with Herodotus' tale of Alexander I: in both cases the subject dynasts, with some humiliation, bring out their own womenfolk for the entertainment of their conquerors, albeit the tables are reversed between Macedonians and Persians.
[38] Justin 9.1–9.3.

In the pivotal pitched battle against the Athenians and the Thebans at Chaeronea in 338 BC, Diodorus tells that Philip put Alexander in charge of one of the wings, and stationed his most experienced generals adjacently to him, taking charge of the other himself, where he stationed his picked men. On the other side, the Athenians took one wing, the Boeotians the other. It was Alexander that first succeeded in breaking the line of the enemy phalanx before him and in putting them to flight as the corpses piled up. Then Philip similarly broke the line opposite him. In total, 1,000 Athenians were killed and 2,000 were captured, and so too 'many' of the Boeotians were killed and captured.[39]

Plutarch mentions the battle only briefly in his *Life of Alexander*, for all that it was evidently a momentous one in the rise of the young prince, and for all that he himself was (valuably) a native of Chaeronea, but he supplies us with some important clues about the battle order and the topography of the clash. He tells us that in his own day an ancient oak beside the Cephisus river was known as 'Alexander's oak' and held to indicate the spot at which he had pitched his tent. This entails that Alexander must have commanded the Macedonian left wing, and therefore that Philip commanded the Macedonian right. The enemy troops he broke through into were none other than the Thebans' Sacred Band, the three-hundred-strong elite infantry force, hitherto undefeated and the foundation upon which the Theban miracle of the last three decades had been built. This in turn tells us that they occupied the allies' right wing, and that the Athenians, accordingly, occupied the left, opposite Philip.[40]

Justin tells that it was Alexander himself that negotiated peace terms with Athens after the victory, with Antipater as his aide.[41] This mission was to be Alexander's one and only visit to the city.[42] (It is a remarkable fact indeed that, so far as our sources indicate, Philip himself never set foot in Athens.)[43] It was presumably at this point that the Athenians erected their statues of Philip and Alexander in their *agora*.[44]

In the afterglow of Chaeronea, most observers must have considered Alexander's succession to Philip assured, but also long in the future still. They would have been wrong on the second count, and perhaps too on the first – at least in Alexander's own eyes, as we shall see in the following chapter.

[39] Diodorus 16.85–16.86.   [40] Plutarch *Alexander* 9.2.   [41] Justin 9.4; cf. Polybius 5.10.
[42] As Cawkwell 1978: 167 observes.
[43] As Hammond and Griffith 1979: 606 and 620–621 note, whilst debating whether his staying away was a token of diplomatic caution or cultural philistinism. It remains conceivable that Philip had visited the city in his childhood years.
[44] Pausanias 1.9.4.

Guide to Further Reading

The matters discussed here are covered in the standard biographies of both Philip and Alexander. For the historical events, Hammond and Griffith 1979 continue to provide the most substantial framework. Useful prosopographical biographies of the minor players may be found in Heckel 2021. For Plutarch's Alexander, see Chapter 21 in this volume, with further bibliography. For Olympias, see Heckel 1981b; Carney 1987, 2006. For the myths of Alexander's birth, see Ogden 2011a: 7–110, with Ogden 2022a now superseding the former on the particular issue of the serpent sire; compare also Aufrère 1999; Stoneman 2008: 6–26; Collins 2012b. For Lanice, see Alonso Troncoso 2007 and Asirvatham 2021. For Alexander's education, see Carney 2003a, 2003b and especially Djurslev 2022. For the tradition of Bucephalas, see Anderson 1930; Baynham 1995b; Chandezon 2010; Green 2016; Ogden 2021b. For Alexander's sexuality and partners, see Badian 1958c; Reames-Zimmermann 1999; Mortensen 2007; Antela-Bernárdez 2010, 2012; Skinner 2010; Ogden 2011a: 124–184 and Chapter 13 in this volume.

2: The Crises Leading up to Alexander's Accession

Daniel Ogden

As we have seen in the previous chapter, in the 338 BC Battle of Chaeronea against the Thebans and the Athenians the young Alexander had commanded the left wing, balancing Philip on the right, and played the decisive role with his successful strike against the most elite unit amongst the opposing forces, the Thebans' Sacred Band. He then went on, titularly at any rate, to take the lead role in negotiating peace terms with Athens. In the eyes of most Macedonians he must have seemed at this point to be in pole position to succeed his father. That succession would come a mere two years later, but not before Alexander had had to negotiate a pair of crises that threatened to undermine his suit. The tradition – for what it is worth – leaves us with the impression that these crises were largely of his own making, and that the prince's impetuousness and hot-headedness had much to answer for.

Philip's Wedding to Cleopatra, Niece of Attalus, and Its Aftermath (337 BC)

Two major dynastic disputes between Alexander and Philip are recorded for the period shortly prior to the latter's assassination, namely the Attalus affair and the Pixodarus affair. Both are founded in the competitive free-for-all of the Macedonian court's polygamous culture.[1]

As to the first, Plutarch tells of a rift between Philip and Alexander shortly after the Battle of Chaeronea, in which the lad had so

---

[1] For the culture of polygamy at the Argead and earlier Hellenistic courts (Alexander's own court included), its rationale (such as it was), its structuring and its effects, see Greenwalt 1989; Carney 1992, 2000 especially 23–27, 2006 especially 21–26; Ogden 1999, 2011b especially 93–96. For a once typical but now distinctly old-fashioned approach to Philip's marriages see, for example, Hammond and Griffith 1979: 676–678 (Olympias was Philip's 'official queen'), 681 ('Cleopatra had been queen') and Hatzopoulos 2020: 138–142.

distinguished himself, this being fuelled by the jealousy and difficulty of Alexander's mother Olympias.² The rift occurred during the feasting after Philip's marriage to what was to be his final wife, the Macedonian noblewoman Cleopatra, niece of the increasingly powerful Attalus, probably in early 337 BC.³ Attalus, in an advanced state of drunkenness, bade the Macedonians ask the gods to produce a legitimate successor to the kingdom from Philip and Cleopatra. An infuriated Alexander challenged Attalus with the defiant question, 'Do you consider us to be bastards [*nothoi*], evil head?'⁴ and threw a cup at him. Philip in turn now lunged at Alexander with his sword, but fell over owing to a combination of fury and drunkenness. Alexander mocked him with the observation that the man that was preparing to cross from Europe to Asia could not even cross from one couch to another (Figure 2.1). As a result of this Alexander took Olympias off to stay with her birth family in Epirus, whilst he occupied himself in Illyria. (The Alexandrists dispute whether or not Alexander was formally exiled as a result of this fight – whatever 'formally' might mean in such a context.)⁵ Philip was in due course persuaded to summon Alexander home by a sharp observation of Demaratus of Corinth. When Philip had asked him how well the Greeks were getting on with each other (inevitably in the context of the League of Corinth), Demaratus chided him for taking an interest in such an issue, when he had filled his own house with dissent.

The same story is briefly recounted in an important fragment of Satyrus. After a careful exposition of Philip's total of seven wives and his system of polygamy with them, he tells that Philip threw his household into turmoil by bringing Attalus' niece Cleopatra in on top of Olympias. According to him, Attalus' quip ran, 'So now legitimate kings instead of bastard ones will be produced.' Alexander then threw his cup at Attalus and Attalus threw his cup in turn. There is no mention of Philip, but again Olympias is said to have fled to the Molossians and Alexander to the Illyrians.⁶

---

² Plutarch *Alexander* 9. Justin's briefer account of this episode (9.7) offers no variant details. For the date of the marriage, see Hammond and Griffith 1979: 681 n.1: the very end of 338 BC at the earliest.
³ Attalus was to be one of the three leaders of Philip's upcoming Asian campaign: Diodorus 16.91, 93, 17.2, Justin 9.5. At some indeterminate point he acquired the daughter of Parmenion, and sister of Philotas, as his wife. According to Curtius 6.9.17, Alexander was subsequently to cite the fact that Philotas had given his sister in marriage to Attalus, his most dangerous enemy, as proof of the former's disloyalty to him. An at least partly tendentious claim, surely: since Attalus predeceased Parmenion, it must have been he, rather than his son Philotas, that had given the woman. Discussion of the Attalus affair: Ellis 1976: 211–217; Hammond and Griffith 1979: 676–679; Heckel 1992: 4–5; Hammond 1994: 170–176; Ogden 1999: 17–27; Carney 2000: 70–76, 2006: 31–35; Heckel, Howe and Müller 2017: 94–96.
⁴ Why plural? The 'royal we', or does Alexander include his full sister, (another) Cleopatra?
⁵ Badian 1963(yes); Hammond and Griffith 1979: 678 (no).
⁶ Satyrus F21 Kumaniecki, *apud* Athenaeus 557b–557e.

2.1 Donato Creti, *Alexander the Great Threatened by His Father* (*c.* 1700–5). National Gallery of Art, Washington, DC, Samuel H. Kress Collection: 1961.9.6.

Attalus' agenda is self-evident. In order to enhance his niece's – that is to say his own – influence at court, he was tendentiously attempting to assert a principle of legitimacy and succession that had evidently never held any purchase with the Argeads previously: namely that, just as, notoriously, in Classical Athens, a condition of legitimacy should be that both of one's parents were citizens of the state (whatever 'citizen' might mean in a Macedonian context at this point). Had Alexander bothered to articulate a reply, he could of course have made appeal: (a) to the fact that he was of higher birth, being born not merely of a noblewoman but of an Epirote princess; (b) to the fact that he had already served as regent (we cannot know whether any formal role of 'crown prince' existed, nor, if so, whether it had been conferred upon him); (c) to the fact that he had served with distinction as Philip's deputy at Chaeronea; and (d) to the fact that in the light of his (elder?) half-brother Arrhidaeus' incapacity (for which see below), he was the only child of Philip capable of taking on the kingship until, at least, any male child of Cleopatra's should approach an age of majority.[7]

It is too easy, from the cosy vantage-point of hindsight, to view, as Satyrus did, Philip's marriage to Cleopatra as reckless and irresponsible. Given his own – and now also Alexander's – intense and unremitting involvement in warfare, it was imperative for him to produce more sons to secure his line and indeed, from one perspective, the stability of Macedon. Had, for instance, Chaeronea gone the other way, both he and Alexander would have been wiped out. It remains unclear whether Philip got as far as producing from Cleopatra the male child for which Attalus hoped. The Satyrus fragment tells that she gave birth to daughter, Europe, whilst Justin has Alexander have an (unnamed) little daughter killed on her lap upon his accession.[8] However, Justin also mentions Alexander butchering a son from this marriage, one Caranus.[9]

ARRHIDAEUS AND THE PIXODARUS AFFAIR (336 BC)

A distinctive effect of the polygamous system was to render a king's wives not merely rivals but actually enemies of each other, as they fought to secure the succession for one of their own sons: at stake, typically, was not just the prize of kingship, but also that of survival, given that the elimination of his half-brothers and their mothers was often, quite understandably, the privilege and courtesy of a newly

---

[7] Cf. Ogden 1999: 21.   [8] Satyrus F21 Kumaniecki, *apud* Athenaeus 557b–557e; Justin 9.7.
[9] Justin 11.2. Discussion: Berve 1926 no. 411; Tarn 1948: ii. 260–262; Lane Fox 1973: 18; Hammond and Griffith 1979: 681n. 1; Heckel 1979, 2006: 78 ('non-existent'), 2021: 237 ('fictitious'); O'Brien 1992: 40–41.

established king. Macedonian princes appear to have enjoyed much tighter bonds of loyalty with their mothers, upon whom they could always depend, than they did actually with their fathers, upon whom they could not. We note that, when Alexander fled from Macedon in the aftermath of the Attalus affair, his mother did too.[10]

According to the final words of Plutarch's *Alexander*, the competition between, on the one side, Alexander and his mother Olympias and, on the other side, Arrhidaeus and his Thessalian-noblewoman mother Philinna became established at an early point. As a child Arrhidaeus had displayed an accomplished, charming and noble nature, and so Olympias had deployed 'drugs', 'poisons' or 'spells' (the term *pharmaka* can mean all three of these) to destroy his mind.[11] The supposed result of this was that when, in 323 BC, the Macedonians were compelled, in default of able candidates, to elevate him to the throne after Alexander's death (together with his newborn nephew Alexander IV), they could only do so by placing him in the care of a guardian (*prostatēs*), Craterus, and under the power of a regent, Perdiccas.[12] Olympias' antipathy towards Arrhidaeus was only to be sated when she acquired control of him herself in 317 BC and put him to death.[13] The tale of Olympias corrupting the boy Arrhidaeus' mind with drugs is too extravagant to be trustworthy. I have argued previously that it should be combined with a tradition found in the Greek Magical Papyri of a charm credited to a Thessalian Philinna for the cure of headaches (the papyrus in question is dateable to the first century BC). Thereby we are able to reconstruct an even more extravagant tale of a 'war of witches' at Philip's court, as Olympias strove to deploy witchcraft against Arrhidaeus, whilst his mother Philinna strove to deploy it in protection of him.[14]

A more tangibly historical demonstration of the rivalry between Alexander and Arrhidaeus and indeed their respective mothers is provided by the Pixodarus affair, for which once again Plutarch is our sole source. He locates the episode just after the point at which Philip had

---

[10] See Ogden 1999 especially ix–xxxiii. [11] Plutarch *Alexander* 77.
[12] The sources for Arrhidaeus' condition, including Diodorus 18.2 and Plutarch *Alexander* 10, 77, are reviewed and discussed at Carney 2001 and Ogden 2007a: 267–269; Carney argues that the evidence points to what would today be classified as 'mental retardation'. Craterus' guardianship and Perdiccas' regency: Curtius 10.7, 10.10, Diodorus 18.2–18.3, Justin 13.2–13.4, Arrian *Successors* 1.1–1.7, Pausanias 1.6.2, Appian *Syriace* 52.261, Dexippus *FGrH* / *BNJ* 100 F8.4, Porphyry *FGrH* / *BNJ* 260 F2.
[13] Diodorus 19.11 (cf. 19.52), Justin 14.5, Pausanias 1.11, 8.7.
[14] *PGM* XX = *GEMF* 3 (with disappointing commentary); see Ogden 2007a ≈ Ogden 2011a: 115–121.

persuaded Alexander home from Illyria.[15] Pixodarus, the satrap of Caria, wanted to construct a military alliance with Philip and sent one Aristocritus to Macedonia with the proposal that Philip's son Arrhidaeus should marry his eldest daughter, Ada. Olympias and Alexander's friends persuaded Alexander that Philip was trying to line Arrhidaeus up to succeed himself by arranging this brilliant match for him. So Alexander sent the tragic actor Thessalus in turn to Pixodarus, to tell him to ignore Arrhidaeus, who, he said, was a bastard and an idiot (*nothos, ou phrenērēs*), and to choose himself instead. Pixodarus was delighted by the prospect of such an upgrade. But when Philip got wind of what was afoot, he took Alexander's friend Philotas along with him to Alexander's chamber and told him off: he was ignoble and unworthy of his rank, he said, if he wanted to become son-in-law to a mere Carian and a slave of a barbarian king. Philip had the Corinthians return Thessalus to him in chains (why was he in Corinth?), though seemingly without further consequence, and banished some of Alexander's companions, evidently regarding them as a poor influence. These included Harpalus, Nearchus, Erigyius and Ptolemy. After his accession Alexander would recall them all and bestow upon them the highest offices in his regime.[16] Arrian too speaks of Philip's banishment and Alexander's retrieval of these same men, together with Erigyius' brother Laomedon, but he makes no mention of Pixodarus. Rather, he tightly aligns the banishment with the former dispute, asserting that Philip banished the men for being adherents of Alexander when the prince fell under suspicion with the king after he humiliated Olympias with his marriage to Eurydice (i.e. Cleopatra).[17]

Why was a satrap of the Persian empire trying to make a military alliance with Philip? According to Heckel, his messenger Aristocritus arrived in Macedon shortly after Philip's advance forces under Parmenion, Attalus and Amyntas had crossed over into Asia in the

[15] But Bosworth 1988a: 22 holds that the episode is narrated out of sequence (as so often with Plutarch) and that the Pixodarus affair preceded the Attalus affair, in part because he believes that the story entails Olympias' presence in Macedon (possibly so) at a time when she ought to have remained confined to Epirus.

[16] Plutarch *Alexander* 10; cf. Justin 13.2 ('the son of a Larissaean whore'); for Ada see Strabo C656–C657. Justin 9.7 speaks more allusively of Alexander's fear of his step-mother-born brother as a rival for the throne. Discussion of the Pixodarus affair: Badian 1963, 2007: 397–400; Ellis 1976: 217–219; Hammond and Griffith 1979: 679–680; Hatzopoulos 1982, 2005; French and Dixon 1986a, 1986b; O'Brien 1992: 31–33; Heckel 2006: 4 and 265, 2021: 6, 488 (for Ada and Thessalus); Ruzicka 2010; Heckel, Howe and Müller 2017: 100–105; Müller 2019: 59–61. Hammond and Griffith make the point that the Pixodarus affair at least serves to show that Philip was not planning to make his nephew Amyntas his heir, despite his estrangement from Alexander.

[17] Arrian *Anabasis* 3.6.

spring of 336 with the explicit mission to liberate the Greek cities there.[18] If so, the move looks like a protective insurance policy. Philip's anger is to be explained, concomitantly, by the fact that the fiasco cost him a potential ally in his Asian campaign, since Pixodarus then chose to consolidate his loyalty to the Persian king Darius by giving Ada rather to the distinguished Persian Orontopates.[19] Ruzicka holds that the initiative for the marriage-alliance came rather from a Philip eager to gain a strategic ally for his Persian campaign and that Alexander – supposedly in exile still at the relevant point – intervened in order to beat a path back into the Macedonian court for himself.[20]

The Assassination of Philip (336 BC): Pausanias of Orestis

There was much speculation in antiquity about the ultimate culprit behind Philip's assassination, and indeed people continue to speculate about it today. However, the truth of the matter is clear, being adumbrated for us by the best of all possible contemporary sources, Aristotle, tutor to Alexander, and then being laid out by Diodorus in uncharacteristically rich, compelling and persuasive detail (albeit not without error or detectable accretion), with Justin's briefer account supplying some extra details but probably inventing at least some of them.[21] The interest of alternative ancient accounts of the assassination therefore lies in the determination of the reasons for their concoction, whilst alternative modern accounts of the assassination are merely idle.[22]

---

[18] Diodorus 16.91; cf. 17.24. See Heckel 1981a: 55, 2006: 4, 2021: 6.
[19] Strabo C656–C657; cf. Arrian *Anabasis* 1.23. Cf. Badian 1963; Hamilton 1969 on §10; and Hammond and Griffith 1979: 680.
[20] Ruzicka 2010.
[21] Aristotle *Politics* 1311ab, Diodorus 16.93–16.5, Justin 9.6–9.7. A sober reading of the undatable and frustratingly fragmentary *P.Oxy.* 1798 = *FGrH* / *BNJ* ('Anonymous on Alexander') 148 F1 + F17 offers nothing to contradict or supplement these accounts. The letters απετυπα may derive from the verb ἀποτυμπανίζω and refer to the crucifixion of Pausanias' dead body, as mentioned at Justin 9.7. See Parsons 1979 and now Prandi 2012a *ad loc.*, superseding some speculative reconstructions. As an example of a clear error on Diodorus' part, he makes Attalus the nephew instead of the uncle of the Cleopatra that was Philip's bride; as an example of a detectable accretion, we may point to the role given to the orator Hermocrates.
[22] One such modern theory implicates Philip's nephew Amyntas in the murder of the boy whose throne he had somehow appropriated in 360/359 BC: he is connected with the Attalus–Cleopatra axis by Badian 1963: 245 and Bosworth 1971a: 103–105; contra, Hammond and Griffith 1979: 686. For discussion of the assassination see Badian, 1963, 2007; Bosworth 1971b; Ellis 1971, 1976: 222–234; Fears 1975; Hammond and Griffith 1979: 675–698; Develin 1981; O'Brien 1992: 34–42; Hammond 1994: 170–176; Kapetanopoulos 1996; Carney 2006: 31–41; Antela-Bernárdez 2012; Anson 2013: 74–81; Müller 2016b: 268–276; Heckel, Howe and Müller 2017 especially 105–113; Müller 2019: 64–67; Hatzopoulos 2020: 142–147.

As Diodorus and Justin tell, Philip was assassinated by his former lover, Pausanias of Orestis, who considered that the king had insufficiently avenged and compensated him for a gang rape organized by the ever-baleful Attalus with the help of his muleteers. He planned his attack for the magnificent wedding Philip held at Aegae for his daughter Cleopatra, Alexander's full sister, and her uncle and Olympias' brother, Alexander of Epirus: a timely match, since Justin tells us that the disaffected and fugitive Olympias had been egging her brother on to declare war on Philip. On the second day of the festivities, Philip, clad in a striking white cloak, sent his entourage ahead and asked his bodyguards to stand back, seemingly so that he could give his adoring audience a clear and uninterrupted view of his entrance as he emerged, through a narrow passageway, into the theatre, where competitions were to be held. Pausanias seized his moment, rushed at Philip in the passageway and stabbed him in the ribs with a dagger of the sort later termed 'Celtic'. The bodyguards ran the assassin through with their javelins before he could make it to the horses he had stationed for his escape.

Justin tells that, as he walked, Philip was flanked by the two Alexanders, his son and the bridegroom. But this does not fit at all with Diodorus' more detailed account, and the claim would appear to be a rhetorical embellishment. However, the embellishment does indeed prompt us to ask where our Alexander actually was at the time of the deed. We can only infer that he was somewhere in the offing. If we discount Justin, it is Arrian that gives us our first glimpse of Alexander in the immediate aftermath of the assassination. He tells that the suspect Alexander of Lyncestis was amongst the first of the prince's friends to come to him after the assassination, and that he helped him put his breastplate on and escorted him to the palace. The donning of the breastplate was presumably for safety – who knew what other conspirators might lurk? But why to the palace? Was the palace regarded as a place of safety? The place at which Alexander could be calmly united with the recovered body of his father? Or did he rather make a dash to the physical centre of royal power in order, a greater priority, to establish his claim to the succession?[23]

Over-determination gives the lie to Justin's striking and wonderfully elaborate claim that Pausanias was encouraged in his work by

---

[23] Arrian *Anabasis* 1.25; cf. Bosworth 1980b *ad loc*. And what of Olympias' whereabouts at the time of the assassination? Justin 9.7 implies that she was still based in Epirus and had to rush back to Aegae for the funeral, though it is curious that she should not have returned to Macedon if only for the sake of the wedding of both her brother and her daughter.

Olympias with the complicity of Alexander. She it was, he tells, that provided the horses for Pausanias' getaway. After the killing she hastened back to Aegae, and on the night of her arrival put a golden crown on the head of the body of the dead Pausanias, which had been crucified. She subsequently had Pausanias' remains burned on Philip's own funeral pyre and made a tomb for him in the same place as Philip's. Her revenge upon Attalus' niece Cleopatra was savage: she had her little daughter killed in her lap before having the woman forced into a noose, before her own eyes. Finally, she dedicated the sword with which Pausanias had killed Philip to Apollo, under her childhood name of Myrtale. All, these things, Justin asserts, Olympias did not merely publicly but openly, as if she feared that it might not be clear to all that she had been the sponsor of the deed.[24] Our own Plutarch accepts that Pausanias acted alone, but nonetheless reports some entertaining rumours associated with the climate of suspicion that had looked to Alexander and Olympias, such as the rumour that Alexander had encouraged Pausanias to the deed by quoting a line of Euripides' *Medea* that referred darkly to the planned murder of the giver of the bride (i.e. Creon/Attalus), the bridegroom (i.e. Jason/Philip) and the bride herself (i.e. Glauce/Cleopatra).[25]

Arrian offers another theory. For him, three Lyncestian brothers, Heromenes, Arrhabaeus and Alexander, the sons of Aeropus, had been involved in the murder. Upon becoming king Alexander had executed the former two, but he spared the third, despite accusations against him, because he was amongst the first of his friends to come to him after the assassination (as just noted).[26] It is hard to see how these brothers can have been involved in the assassination if the protestations of Aristotle and Diodorus about the motives of the assassin Pausanias are accepted.[27] On the other hand, it is easy to see how one might have put Pausanias of Orestis together with the three Lyncestian brothers to construct the

---

[24] For the view that Olympias was the instigator of the assassination, see Beloch 1912–1927: iii.1, 606–607; contra, Badian 1963: 249 n. 25 and Hammond and Griffith 1979: 678, 682, 685–686, with the latter in particular holding that Olympias did not return to Macedon between her departure after the Attalus episode and the murder of Philip, and accordingly 'exonerating' her of all involvement in Philip's death.

[25] Plutarch *Alexander* 10; Euripides *Medea* 289.

[26] Arrian *Anabasis* 1.25, who goes on to tell that Alexander of Lyncestis was eventually executed, after allegations of further involvement in conspiracy against Alexander, in 330 BC; cf. also Diodorus 17.2, 17.32, 17.80, Justin 11.2, 11.7, 12.14, Curtius 3.7.1–3.7.15, 7.1.5–7.1.7. He may have owed his initial preservation also to the fact (as these sources tell) that he was the son-in-law of Antipater; cf. Hammond and Griffith 1979: 690; Bosworth 1980b *ad loc.*, 1988a: 26; Carney 1980; Badian 2000: 56–60; Heckel 2006: 19, 2021: 29.

[27] Nonetheless, Bosworth 1971b accepts the possibility; contra, Hammond and Griffith 1979: 688–689.

notion of a grand Upper Macedonian conspiracy against Philip, fuelled by resentment at the emasculation of the principalities under him. And so too perhaps Amyntas the son of Perdiccas, also executed by Alexander soon after his accession, the former baby king whose throne Philip had usurped, and who might have been imagined to consider that it should now revert to him.[28] Hammond and Griffith see the creation of the notion of the involvement of the Lyncestian brothers not merely as an opportunist move on Alexander's part to unburden himself of rivals, but also as an act of rationalization of the killing on the part of the Macedonian establishment as a whole, which could not come to terms with the actual circumstances: the great man deserved better assassins with more dignified motivations. One suspects this says more of the values and perspectives of Cambridge in the AD 1970s than it does of those of Macedon in the 330s BC. They further protest that the brothers cannot themselves have been candidates for the throne – but that is to view the Macedonian succession from a quaintly constitutionalist perspective.[29]

The Stages by Which Alexander Secured the Succession

What were the stages by which Alexander secured the throne, given that all was up for grabs on the death of an Argead king, and that we must not be misled by hindsight into assuming that Alexander's succession was inevitable?

Step 1: Arrian, as we have seen, tells that Alexander spared one of Pausanias' supposed conspirators, Alexander of Lyncestis, because he had been one of the first to come to Alexander after the killing. Justin more pointedly declares that Alexander of Lyncestis had been the very first after the killing to hail Alexander as king. Whether specifically true or not, this perhaps gives us a hint that the first step on the journey to recognition lay precisely in receiving hails from the Companions.[30]

---

[28] Curtius 6.9.17, 6.10.24, Justin 12.6. Alexander also took an early opportunity to unburden himself of another proven rival, Attalus, dispatching Hecataeus to the forward forces in Asia to engineer his death there, with the help of Parmenion: Diodorus 17.2, 17.5, Curtius 7.1.3. It was left to Olympias, as we have seen, to finish off his niece Cleopatra and her baby daughter: Justin 11.5. For Amyntas the son of Perdiccas, see Ellis 1971; Heckel 2006: 23, 2021: 41.
[29] Hammond and Griffith 1979: 685–686.   [30] Arrian *Anabasis* 1.25; Justin 11.1–11.2.

Step 2: Arrian further tells us that Alexander made a bee-line for the royal palace; if occupancy of the palace was a token of kingship, clearly no rival claimant could be permitted to get there first.

Step 3: Diodorus, Justin and the *Alexander Romance* tell that the twenty-year-old Alexander held an immediate public assembly in which he reassured and encouraged the Macedonians. Diodorus and Justin agree that Alexander made a stabilizing claim to the effect that the king had changed in name only. For Diodorus, Alexander proclaimed that he would run the state in the same way as his father had done; for Justin, he proclaimed relief from all taxes and impositions for the Macedonians, beyond that of service in the army. Diodorus adds that Alexander also addressed himself to the embassies of the Greeks present in Macedon – presumably the ones that had come for the wedding and stayed on for the funeral – and bade them to transfer their loyalty to him.[31] It should be made clear that the notion, which has found acceptance in the most respectable scholarship, that Alexander was presented to the assembly for its endorsement by Antipater – a winning vignette – is effectively a myth. The only authority for it is the fifteenth-century Leiden MS (L) of the *Alexander Romance*, which preserves a version of the (fifth-century AD?) β recension, modified at some point prior to the eighth century; it does not appear in the remainder of the β recension, which, we may assume, was the only basis for L's treatment of this episode.[32]

Step 4: Justin also tells of Alexander's conducting of his father's funeral. This was a critical point. The conducting of the funeral was an important, graphic means of declaring oneself the dead man's successor. Justin further specifies that Alexander killed all those that had been complicit in the murder and that they were put to death at Philip's place of burial, again with the exception of Alexander of Lyncestis (whom Justin mistakenly identifies as the brother of Pausanias).[33]

---

[31] Diodorus 17.2, *AR* (A) 1.25–1.26.

[32] *AR* (L) 1.26; accepted by, inter alios, Badian 1963: 248; Hammond and Walbank 1988: 4 (tentatively); Heckel 1992: 40; and Hatzopoulos 2020: 147. For the MS L in the context of the *Romance* tradition see Stoneman 2008: 231; Jouanno 2002: 271–280; it is edited by Van Thiel 1974, and forms the principal basis for the translations of Dowden 1989 and Stoneman 1991.

[33] Cf. Diodorus 17.2 again, Plutarch *Alexander* 10 and the possible reference to crucifixion in P.Oxy. 1798 = FGrH / BNJ ('Anonymous on Alexander') 148 F1 + F17, discussed above.

Step 5: Justin next tells of Alexander's disposal of his potential rival for the throne, Caranus, the little son of Cleopatra (as noted above). This looks like a doublet of Justin's own account of Olympias having Cleopatra's little daughter killed on her knee, but perhaps there could have been two children already, with Alexander killing the male and Olympias the female. Plutarch tells that Olympias killed Cleopatra herself during Alexander's absence, and that he was angry with her for this. Perhaps, specifically, he had wanted to marry her for quasi-levirate purposes, given that it seems to have been a practice among the polygamous Argead kings to legitimate their rule by marrying one of their father's later and younger widows (and thereby also mitigate the potential for conflict between the rival lines).[34]

Step 6: The final stage was to secure the acceptance of the wider Greek community, building on his work with the ambassadors in Step 3. Justin again tells how Alexander summoned the Greeks to Corinth and had them appoint him their leader in the League of Corinth in Philip's place. Also for the consumption of the wider Greek community was Alexander's reorganization of the Philippeum monument that his father had started to construct at Olympia in the wake of Chaeronea. Whatever his father had planned for it, the circular building was now to enshrine and virtually divinize five figures: in the centre stood that of Philip himself; on the right side he was flanked by those of his parents, Amyntas and Eurydice; on the left he was flanked by those of his son Alexander and Alexander's mother Olympias. Here the exotic polygamy and associated successional chaos of the Macedonian court was discreetly occluded, to be replaced by a cosy tableau of three loving generations of a respectable nuclear family, and of a crown passing seamlessly, unproblematically, uncontestedly and *inevitably* from grandfather to father to son.[35]

---

[34] Plutarch *Alexander* 10. Levirate considerations: see Ogden 2011b: 102–104. For detailed discussion of the murder of Cleopatra and its context at Heckel, Howe and Müller 2017: 114–120; note also Baynham 1998c.

[35] For the Philippeum see Pausanias 5.17.4, 5.20.10 and Arrian *Anabasis* 3.6.5. Discussion (including quite radically different interpretations of the monument and its development): Schultz 2007, 2009; Carney 2007 (reprinted with a valuable afterword at 2015, 61–90); Palagia 2010; Müller 2019: 58–59; Ogden 2023: 286.

Guide to Further Reading

The material discussed in this chapter is chewed over in every modern biography of Philip and Alexander alike, for example Lane Fox 1973: 17–27; Hammond and Griffith 1979: 675–698; O'Brien 1992: 28–42; Hammond 1997b: 21–31; Squillace 2022: 197–203. Useful prosopographical biographies of all minor players can be found in Heckel 2021. For Attalus and the fiasco at Cleopatra's wedding, see Heckel 1979, 1981a. For the Pixodarus affair, see Hatzopoulos 1982; French and Dixon 1986a; 1986b; Ruzicka 2010; for Arrhidaeus more specifically, see Carney 2001; Ogden 2007a. For the polygamous context of both of these disputes, see Greenwalt 1989; Carney 1992, 2000: 51–81, 2006: 19–41, Ogden 1999 *passim* especially 3–40. For the assassination of Philip and its sundry controversies, the item of first resort is now Heckel, Howe and Müller 2017; see also Badian 1963, 2000, 2007; Ellis 1971, 1981; Fears 1975; Carney 1980; Develin 1981; Kapetanopoulos 1996; Hatzopoulos 2005; Antela-Bernárdez 2012. For the Philippeum, see Carney 2007; Schultz 2007, 2009; Palagia 2010.

3: ALEXANDER AND THE GREEKS

Borja Antela-Bernárdez

THE LEAGUE OF CORINTH

In the late hours of 9 August 338, the arrival of the news of the city's defeat in the battle of Chaeronea must have had a tremendous impact in Athens. The distinguished orator Lycurgus of Boutadai recalls, in around 330, how on that night the old men had left the warmth of their beds to take up positions on the fortifications, equipped with arms collected from the temples and chosen from among those that had been dedicated to the gods, while the women stood in the doorways of their homes asking passers-by for news of their sons, husbands, brothers or fathers (*Against Leocrates* 1.2). This terrifying vignette, a reminder of the collective trauma that resulted from the Chaeronea disaster and also a reflection of different ways in which the genders responded in such circumstances,[1] is fashioned for us by Lycurgus in his blunt epitaph to the Classical era: the freedom of the Greeks lay buried in Chaeronea (*Against Leocrates* 1.49–1.50).

However, the immediate reaction to the Macedonian victory could not have been one of mere despair: Demosthenes' Funeral Oration for those slain in the battle expresses great pride, depicting the defeat in a very different light. Despite Philip's success, Demosthenes clearly insists in describing the Athenians as undefeated, and he even claims that the Macedonian king's careful handling of relations with Athens after the battle was a sure sign that he feared the prospect of facing an Athenian army on the field of battle again.[2] The citizens that fell at Chaeronea were therefore nothing less than heroes of all Greece, and they deserved a place beside Zeus's throne. Philip had simply been favoured by good fortune (*tyche*), which had bestowed victory upon him (*Funeral Speech* 19–22).

---

[1] Antela-Bernárdez 2007a.
[2] Justin 9.4.1–9.4.3; Plutarch *Moralia* 177e–177f records Philip's magnificent treatment of Athens, with no punishment. The funeral embassy to Athens for the men that had fallen at Chaeronea was led by Alexander and Antipater: this demonstrates a clear intention to honour Athens and to retain her loyalty with a view to constructing a diplomatic settlement for Greece under Macedonian rule.

Nevertheless, the orator cannot avoid mention of the mourning of the fate of the dead, and herein lies the point of contact between both narratives – Demosthenes' and Lycurgus' – since, for all the honour paid to their glorious past, after Chaeronea the Athenians had been placed at the mercy of Philip's diplomatic designs.[3] The collective trauma seems evident in the Athenian laws against tyranny, voted for after Chaeronea, which are indicative of contemporary anxiety about an immediate political threat to the democracy.[4] Memories arose of Athens' final defeat in the Peloponnesian War at the Battle of Aegospotami, and it was feared that the city might experience a similar destiny now: that it might be destroyed, or subjected to tyranny by Philip, as it had been by Lysander. The perception that Chaeronea represented a historiographical boundary, the closure of an era, has been disseminated by almost every work of modern scholarship,[5] but in fact the changes that took place after Chaeronea did not entail a radical break with preceding Greek diplomatic tradition, nor even a rupture in Athens' democratic history.[6]

Philip's indisputable victory allowed him to forge a series of bilateral peace accords with each member of his enemies' coalition (Aelian *Varia historia* 6.1). Macedonian garrisons were established in Thebes, Corinth and Ambracia (Polybius *Histories* 18.11.5). The remaining cities kept their internal autonomy. Athens was forced to dismantle her Second Naval Confederacy definitively but, in exchange, she received control of Oropus, to the detriment of Thebes. All the other Greek leagues and confederations remained active. Thus, after just a few weeks of negotiations, the post-Chaeronea settlement was resolved.[7] Only Sparta challenged the new Macedonian rule over Greece, openly rejecting any alliance. Philip eventually dealt with the city through a brief campaign in the Peloponnese, this as a token of his support for his local allies in their border disputes with Sparta.[8] Philip's next move was meant to unite all the Greeks in a project of Common Peace: the League of Corinth.[9]

---

[3] The brilliant account by Habicht (1997: 6–35) of life in Athens between Chaeronea and the Lamian War includes both a comprensive portrait of the political voices in the city and a valuable consideration of Philip's peace from the Athenian perspective.

[4] Rhodes and Osborne 2003 no. 79.   [5] Antela-Bernárdez 2018: 43–100.   [6] Faraguna 2011.

[7] The presence at the Pythian Festival, in the autumn of 338, of most of the Greek states that had opposed Philip proves that peace had probably been restored by that point: Hammond and Griffith 1979: 615; cf. Cloché 1916: 119–128.

[8] Polybius *Histories* 9.28.26; Plutarch *Moralia* 218f, 219f, 233e, 235b; Pausanias *Description of Greece* 3.24.6, 5.4.9. McQueen 1995: 168. On Philip and the Peloponnese after Chaeronea, cf. Magnetto 1994.

[9] The ancient sources call it 'the Hellenic League'. The first use of the modern name of which I am aware occurs, in the form '*Korinthische Bund*', at Wieland 1796:106. This was probably the model for Droysen's use of the term in his *Geschichte Alexanders des Grossen* of 1833 (*passim*). Oskar Jäger and the brilliant German scholar Ernst Curtius subsequently deployed '*Korinthische Bündniss*'

Ever since the Peloponnesian War and throughout the fourth century BC, many voices had been raised in favour of a Panhellenic campaign that could unite the Greeks against the barbarians, this as a solution to the endless strife among the Greek cities that was bleeding them dry. The influence of Gorgias' and Lysias' calls for Panhellenism was later reflected in Isocrates' exhortations to Philip and in Aristotle's deliberations on the capacity of the Greeks for governing barbarians.[10] Thucydides had already used the word *hēgemonia* ('leadership') to refer to the Athens' leadership of Greece after the Persian Wars (*History of the Peloponnesian War* 1.96.1).[11] Throughout the fourth century there were constant recourses to the establishment of different forms of Common Peace (*Koine Eirene*) and, from the Great King's Peace (or Peace of Antalcidas) onwards, these treaties had enshrined the presence of a guarantor of peace and of the Greeks' freedom:[12] a *hēgemōn*. The structure of Philip's League of Corinth followed both the precedents of the Greek ideal of *Koine Eirene* and the advice of the Panhellenic authors.[13] Diodorus records how Philip invited the Greeks to a general congress (*koinon synedrion*) in Corinth, where he was elected *stratēgos autokratōr* (plenipotentiary general)[14] to lead the war against Persia.[15] Each member-state sent a number of delegates (*synedrioi*) to the

(Jäger 1866: 547; Curtius 1867–1869: iii.740: 'Der neue Hellenenbund gegen Persien wurde auf dem Isthmos vereinbart zur Erinnerung an das Korinthische Bündniss zur Zeit des Themistokles, und der ganze Perserkrieg, als nationale Pflicht aufgefasst, war ja eine Idee der Kimonischen Zeit' – note that the terms '*Hellenenbund*' and '*Korinthische Bündniss*' stand side-by-side here). Grote did not pick up on the term in his own distinguished work (Grote 1853: 287, 1857: 20) preferring 'general league of Greeks' and 'Grecian League'. The term seems to have been introduced to English-language scholarship by Ward's translation of Curtius (Curtius 1873: 467): 'The new Hellenic League against Persia was concluded on the Isthmus in remembrance of the League of Corinth in the times of Themistocles.' (I thank Hayden Ausland for kindly drawing many of these references to my attention.) For discussion of the Common Peace, see Worthington 2008a.

[10] Cf. Perlman 1957, 1967, 1969; Antela-Bernárdez 2007b: 70–74, 77–83. For Aristotle, see *Politics* 7.7.3 = 1327b 29–33; cf. 4.11.19 = 1296a37-b2; cf. Lord 1978: 350–352. On Alexander and Panhellenism, cf. Flower 2000.

[11] Even Demosthenes was a supporter of Panhellenism, but again, as with many Greek politicians, Panhellenism was for him a way to justify imperialism. Cf. Luccioni 1961; Perlman 1976; Low 2018.

[12] Seager and Tuplin 1980; Seager 1981.

[13] Our sources for the League of Corinth are problematic. The best evidence is epigraphical: Patsavos 1973: 1–37; Harding 1985: 123–124; Rhodes and Osborne 2003 no. 76, with a detailed description of the sources and a full bibliography. Cf. Diodorus 16.89.2; Polybius *Histories* 3.6.13. See also Ryder 1965: 102–105, 150–162; Hammond and Griffith 1979: 604–623; Bosworth 1988a: 187–197; Faraguna 2003: 100–1003; Poddighe 2012.

[14] Diodorus 17.4.9; Arrian *Anabasis* 1.1.1–1.1.3; Plutarch *Alexander* 14.1; Justin 11.2.5. Cf. Poddighe 2012: 131. Although Diodorus uses the form *stratēgos autokratōr* (16.60.5; 16.89.3; 17.4.9), other sources refer to Philip as *hēgemōn*: Rhodes and Osborne 2003 no. 76, l. 2; Arrian *Anabasis* 2.14.4; 1.2.2 (*hēgemonia*); 7.9.5 (*hēgemōn autokratōr*). Cf. McQueen 1995: 169.

[15] Diodorus 16.89.3. At 16.89.1–16.89.2, Diodorus refers to the impact of Chaeronea ('he had dashed the confidence of the leading Greek cities'), to the control of public opinion ('He spread the word that he wanted to make war on the Persians') and, above all, to the friendly attitude

synedrion, where they were joined by the leader of the League, the *hēgemōn*, in the role of peace keeper. All the Greeks, except Sparta, were bound into this structure.

In any case, the new Hellenic League clearly agreed, probably in the course of various meetings at Corinth, to establish an offensive-defensive alliance:[16] first, it set up a body to deal with any conflicts between the cities, and at the same time it guaranteed the independence, freedom and internal autonomy of each community ([Demosthenes] *On the Treaty with Alexander* 8); second, it conceded Greece's military power to Philip, as *hēgemōn* and *stratēgos autokratōr*, giving him full authority to lead the Greek armies in the conquest of Asia, to conduct war against the common enemy, the Persians, with the aim (a clear *casus belli*) of avenging the Persians' acts of sacrilege during Xerxes' invasion. It is hard to determine whether Philip's aim was really, at least at the outset, to conquer the Achaemenid Empire, or whether he was simply seeking, as had been the case in Agesilaus' earlier campaign, merely to gain control of Asia Minor and 'liberate' the Greeks across the Aegean from the authority of the Great King ([Demosthenes] *On the Treaty with Alexander* 9). Philip's premature death at the hands of the assassin Pausanias prevents us from knowing towards which of these goals the initial steps taken in the campaign, with Parmenion and Attalus disembarking in Asia, were directed.

Nor can we know whether Alexander fully shared in his father's plans, or whether he intended from the first to take Philip's idea further and contemplated the total conquest of Persia. After all, Alexander's unstoppable advance through Asia and his constant victories may have gradually modified an initial plan that was much less ambitious. In any case, we can observe a number of differences between Alexander and Philip in terms of their governing styles and personal aims, and perhaps even in how they envisaged the relationship between themselves as kings of Macedonia and the cities of the League. One good example can be seen at the very beginning of Alexander's reign, if we are to believe the contents of the oration *On the Treaty with Alexander*, included in the Demosthenic corpus.[17] In this speech, the author draws the attention of the Athenian Council

---

Philip displayed ('He showed a kindly face to all in private and in public'), as key stages in the build-up to the meeting of the *synedrion*. Translations are taken from Welles 1963.

[16] Against the use of the concept *symmachia*, see Faraguna 2003: 102.

[17] The doubts about the authorship of this speech arose even in antiquity: Libanius, in his *hypotheses* to the speeches of Demosthenes already argued against an attribution to Demosthenes on the basis of style. See Bosworth 1988a: 190; MacDowell 2009: 377–381. Culasso Gastaldi 1984 offers a detailed commentary on the text, with a very different interpretation of the speech and its date (especially 149–183).

to a series of irregularities, accusing Alexander of breaching the terms of the accords sworn to in the founding of the Hellenic League. The transgressions described include the restoration of tyrants in Messene (4) and the transformation of Pellene's democracy into a tyranny at the hands of Chaeron (10), both in the Peloponnese. The orator also points out that it is the duty of the Council of the League to guarantee that there will be no executions or banishments contrary to the laws of each city, and notes that the confiscation of property, the cancellation of debts and even the emancipation of slaves with a view to promoting revolution are also forbidden by the oaths and regulations of the Council (15). These measures seem to be related to the aim of guaranteeing the autonomy of each city, and the speech stresses that if any constituent state supports exiles in revoking the constitution in place when the oaths for the Council were taken, then it shall be excluded from the peace, and the orator argues that Macedon, that is Alexander and the states under his control, did this in some cases, such as that of Sicyon (16). The author turns to the issue of security on the seas, also under the protection of the alliance sworn to in Corinth, and he accuses the Macedonians of forcing the Athenian ships coming from the Black Sea to moor in Tenedos, a situation that was not resolved until the Athenians threatened, through a decree, to dispatch a hundred-strong fleet under Menestheus to rescue their ships. In short, the text returns to several themes that were already present in Demosthenes' *Funeral Oration* and the author urges the Athenians, yet again, to stand up to Macedonian power, as though the latter has been showing signs of waning or the Macedonians have been showing signs of fearing Athens. He concludes by openly calling Alexander a tyrant, a new Agamemnon in his dealings with those included in the peace. However, the author's real concern seems to be the prospect of the Athenians' constitution being overthrown, or of some other compromise of their prized political freedom.[18] At all points his words point to the conclusion that Macedonia has breached the terms of the treaty and therefore deserves to be expelled from the coalition, to be regarded as a common enemy and to be attacked by the member-states (30).

---

[18] Demosthenes *On the Crown* 295 lists the names of supposed tyrants in Greece in Philip's early days. The accusation seems, therefore, to be levelled not only at the Macedonians, but above all at the citizens who fostered governments of this type, no doubt as a warning to the Athenians about the orators who were favourable towards Macedon. The orations of the Lycurgan age are, in fact, full of prosecutions against those in collaboration with Macedonia. Cf. Faraguna 2011: 71–77.

Rebellions

The fact that the oration *On the Treaty with Alexander* does not mention Thebes permits us to date it before 335 BC. Certainly, the destruction of Thebes was a turning-point in the relations between Alexander and the Greek cities. The Macedonians had destroyed other cities in the past, as in the case of Olynthus, but Thebes was one of the main cities of Greece, and its destruction by Alexander must have had a huge impact. Athens itself, which had intended to support the Theban rebels in their uprising against the Macedonian garrison on the Cadmea, opted to wait and see after being surprised by the appearance of Alexander before the walls of Thebes with his army, following a meteoric advance that caught the Greeks unawares. After the siege and capture of the city, the Thebans were sold as slaves and the city laid waste (Arrian *Anabasis* 1.7–1.9; Diodorus 17.8.3–17.13.6; Plutarch *Alexander* 11.6–11.12; Justin 11.3.4–11.3.11). The Theban lands were shared out among the neighbouring allies of Macedonia. Moreover, the aim of the sources is to exonerate Alexander of responsibility for the final decision against the Thebans, which is laid rather on his allies (Diodorus 17.14.1; Arrian *Anabasis* 1.9.9; Justin 11.3.8).[19] However, Alexander's message to the Greeks was clear and simple: any sedition against Macedonian hegemony would be put down severely and without hesitation by the tremendous force of Macedonian arms. The instantaneous repression of Thebes also stressed not just the force of Alexander's authority and his army's skilfulness, but also the strength of the bonds between Macedonia and her Greek allies. Not only the Thessalians, who adhered to Alexander as closely as they had previously done Philip, but many other small states too were now able to deal with the traditional great Greek cities face to face. This was the threat the rise of Macedonian power constituted for the great cities. In the case of Athens, reprisals were feared, and Alexander asked the Athenian Assembly to hand over the politicians that had shown hostility to him, but Demades' diplomatic efforts were fruitful and secured Alexander's pardon for them (Arrian *Anabasis* 1.10.3; Demades *On the Twelve Years* 17). But the Athenians learned well the lesson that Macedonian arms had taught at Thebes: they did not contemplate any new move against Macedonia until the flight of Harpalus to Athens (in 324 BC) even though, internally, the policy of Lycurgus and his followers was to take reprisals against any citizen who might have been on the side of the enemy (as in the cases of the trials against Leocrates and Euxenippus, etc.).

---

[19] Bosworth 1980a: 87–91.

Alexander's benevolence towards Athens has usually been attributed to strategic motives: Macedonia needed the Athenian fleet for the Asian campaign. But the Athenian contingent in the allied fleet was, in fact, rather small, making up only 20 of Alexander's total of 160 ships.[20] It seems more likely that the respect shown to Athens was rooted in matters of ideology. Alexander had deployed historical arguments against Thebes, such as the accusation that the city had collaborated with the invader during the Persian invasion. However, Macedonia had also been an ally of Persia at that time,[21] and it was Athens that had been the figurehead of the struggle against the Persians, the struggle that Alexander now intended to revive. With Sparta outside the Hellenic League and against it, and Thebes destroyed for its *philomedism*, Alexander could not attack Athens without undermining his war propaganda that called for revenge upon the Great King.[22] On the other hand, though, there are signs that Alexander intended to display understanding towards Athens, such as the dedication to Athena Polias of the enemy arms Alexander sent to the city after the battle at the Granicus (Arrian *Anabasis* 1.16.7; Plutarch *Alexander* 16.8).[23] We also know that the king was putting pressure on her, for example, by means of the Athenian mercenaries captured among the Persian ranks, who were held hostage and condemned to forced labour in Macedonia.[24] Their liberation surely had a lot to do with Athens' fidelity to the Macedonian peace during Agis' revolt.

If Athens must have been the cultural reference point for resistance to Macedonia, for all its inevitable submission after Chaeronea, and Thebes was the scapegoat used by Alexander to show Greece the risks that any kind of defection entailed, Sparta stood for rejection of the League of Corinth, and then, armed resistance to domination. In 331, with some financial support from Persia (Arrian *Anabasis* 2.13.5–2.13.6), King Agis III recruited disaffected Greek mercenaries, former soldiers of the Persian king defeated by Alexander (Diodorus 17.48.1; Curtius 4.1.39), to forge an alliance with Elis, Achaea and much of Arcadia

---

[20] Hammond and Walbank 1988: 253. Frequent reference has also been made to Diothymus' campaign against piracy as an example of the deployment of Athenian sea power under the aegis of the League of Corinth and in line with its accords. However, the campaign (which actually consisted of only three ships) probably pre-dated the League's accords and is therefore irrelevant. Cf. Verdejo Manchado and Antela-Bernárdez 2021.
[21] Brosius 2003b.
[22] Regarding the propaganda of vengeance, see Squillace 2010; Antela-Bernárdez 2016a.
[23] The sources tell that the dedication was inscribed with the text 'Alexander, son of Philip, and the Greeks, except for the Lacedaemonians, set up these spoils from the barbarians dwelling in Asia' – a clear reference to the League of Corinth.
[24] Arrian *Anabasis* 1.29.5; 3.6.2; Curtius 4.8.12–4.8.13.

and form a front against Macedonia. This revolt began more as a reaction against the territorial encroachment of Macedonia's allies in the Peloponnese (Arrian *Anabasis* 1.11.3; Diodorus 17.17.5) than a major Greek insurrection against Macedonian rule. Meanwhile, Agis' initial successes proved to be just a misleading illusion, and the reality of Macedonia's formidable military power eventually prevailed when Antipater succeeded in marching his army to Megalopolis, then under siege by Agis, and defeating the rebels (Aeschines *Against Ctesiphon* 165, 167; Dinarchus *Against Demosthenes* 34; Diodorus 17.62.6–17.63.4; Curtius 6.1.1–6.1.20; Justin 12.1.4–12.1.11). Agis died in battle, bringing an end to any hopes of liberation on the part of the Greeks.[25]

In fact, Alexander established many forms of domination over the Greek cities. The long tradition of Panhellenic Leagues and the use of taxes as systems of control and punishment were well-known among the Greeks. The rigours of the war against Persia and the difficulties in transporting consumer products due to the conflict in the Aegean, which raised the price of basic foodstuffs and led to famine and other hardships, were mitigated by Alexander by means of grain handouts. But there were also political motives behind these handouts, with loyal allies being rewarded with larger amounts and potential dissidents punished with smaller rations.[26] Measures of this sort served to maintain the Greeks' loyalty without the need for armed interventions or for meddling in their internal politics. Nevertheless, although the League of Corinth guaranteed the internal autonomy of its members, its purpose was the war against Persia. Alexander's victory over Darius and his proclamation as King of Asia[27] put an end to this strategy and, for all we know, to the League itself. Whatever the case, at the Olympic Games of 324 BC Aristotle's son-in-law Nicanor of Stagira proclaimed the Exiles Decree on Alexander's orders (Diodorus 18.8.3–18.8.4; Diogenes Laertius 5.12; Hyperides *In Defence of Lycophron* 14; 18.9–18.10; Dinarchus *On the Twelve Years* 169; 175; Diodorus 17.109.1; Curtius 10.2; Justin 13.5.3–13.5.4). This allowed political exiles to return to their homelands. We know few details of this return, nor do we know whether it related also to exiles that were enemies of Philip or Alexander, but it was an early indication that the King of Macedonia was challenging the limits to his power in relation to the internal politics of

---

[25] For Agis III, see Heckel 2006: 7–8. For his revolt, see Badian 1994; Bosworth 1988a: 198–204.
[26] Cf. Antela-Bernárdez 2022. For Alexander's impact on Greek economies, see also Adams 1996.
[27] Fredricksmeyer 2000; Badian 1996. On Alexander as the 'Last of the Achaemenids', see Briant 1979: 1414 and the response of Lane Fox 2007.

his Hellenic League allies.[28] Much about the Decree remains an enigma: its actual impact; the exact nature of the shift it potentially signifies in Alexander's policy towards the Greek cities, which it seems, in its implications, to fashion as subjects more than as allies; and the role that Harpalus' money could play in this scenario. Alexander's death in Babylon in June 323 BC rendered the riddle forever insoluble.

THE GREEKS IN ASIA

Looking beyond the relationship between Alexander and the cities of mainland Greece, the Greek cities of Asia Minor received a very different treatment. Although the liberation of the Greeks of Asia was one of the arguments used to justify the campaign against Persia (Diodorus 16.91.1, 17.24.1), these cities' reaction towards Alexander's advance would determine their status and the conditions of their submission to the Macedonians. Resistance, or any kind of support for the Persians, could entail a punishment as severe as that given to Thebes, as seen in the case of Gryneum, which was subdued by Parmenion in 335 and whose entire population was enslaved (Diodorus 17.7.9). Some cities were pardoned *in extremis*, such as Miletus (Arrian *Anabasis* 1.19.6; Diodorus 17.22.4–17.22.5), despite having given resistance to the Macedonian invaders. This can be explained by their potential strategic or military value to the campaign. But most cities that put up a fight lost part of their autonomy or had to pay various kinds of tribute once they had been taken by force. As a result, there was great deal of variation in the conditions imposed by Alexander on the different Greek communities of Asia.

The cities of Asia Minor were not brought into the League of Corinth. There has been much debate on this topic,[29] but clues like the inscribed treaty between Alexander and Priene make it clear that what the former established with the Asian cities was a series of individual accords, together with the substitution, on occasion, of the *phoros* ('tribute') that they paid to the Persian king with a new kind of impost, known as *syntaxis* ('contribution'),[30] this in line with the tradition of the Second Athenian League.[31] The cities, moreover, were incorporated

---

[28] Faraguna 2003: 126–130; Dmitriev 2004; Worthington 2015.
[29] Badian 1966; Bosworth 1988a: 250–258.
[30] Rhodes and Osborne 2003 no. 86 (at p. 434); Kholod 2013; Faraguna 2020: 277–278.
[31] As maintained by Bosworth 1988a: 254, the Athenian *syntaxis* was a special, irregular tax; perhaps, accordingly, Alexander's *syntaxis* was of a similar nature: possibly it was sporadic and associated with the specific needs that arose in the different phases of the campaign to conquer Persia.

into the royal territory (the *chōra basilikē* of the later Hellenistic kingdoms),[32] and the king could grant them in their accords the use and exploitation of territories and resources, as was the case, for example, with Iasus, to which Alexander restored permission to exploit the so-called 'Little Sea'.[33] Though it is difficult to establish the point with certainty, such cases seem to have been the norm in relations between the Argeads and the cities within their kingdoms.[34] Depending upon how their surrender had taken place, cities offering resistance could end up with Macedonian garrisons stationed in them.[35]

Furthermore, Alexander tried to impose widespread constitutional reforms in the cities 'liberated' from the Persians. This should serve as definitive proof that they were not incorporated into the League of Corinth, the regulations of which prohibited this type of interference, as pointed out by the author of *On the Treaty with Alexander*. The spread of democracies among the Greek cities of Asia, which we can document clearly from the increase in the numbers of epigraphic decrees surviving,[36] resulted in part from the discourse of the legitimacy of the war on Persia and of the liberty of the Greeks.[37] Local oligarchies and tyrannies had been associated with the Persians since the Persian Wars and so, by overturning them, Alexander could be seen to fulfil his alleged mission of liberation. In fact, Arrian (*Anabasis* 1.18.2) mentions that Alexander restored each city's own particular laws, imposing democracies as the system he considered inherent to the Greeks of Asia, as if the period of Persian domination had constituted a *parenthesis* during which they had to obey foreign laws.[38] As a result of these complex dealings between Alexander and the Greeks of Asia, many local cults to Alexander sprang up in the cities, these with the aim of establishing a relationship of goodwill with the king and of showing him gratitude.[39]

Alexander also founded many new cities in Asia, using them for the settlement of Greek mercenaries, Macedonian soldiers and sometimes local populations. Although the cities were probably designed as a mechanism for keeping watch over the lands and retaining control of the conquered territories, Alexander granted the Greek and Macedonian inhabitants many kinds of privilege. Even so, Alexander probably expected

---

[32] Antela-Bernárdez 2016b. [33] Kholod 2013; Faraguna 2020: 259.
[34] Hatzopoulos 1996: i.219–230. [35] Kholod 2010.
[36] The importance of epigraphy in the scholarship of Alexander consists in the fact that it furnishes us with our only significant evidence for the king from his own age (one might otherwise point to some problematic oratory, of which the chief example is the speech *On the Treaty with Alexander*, classified as Demosthenes 17, but spurious). Invaluable on the epigraphy of Alexander are Heisserer 1980; Schwenk 1985; and Rhodes and Osborne 2003.
[37] Nawotka 2003. [38] Bosworth 1988a: 252. [39] Kholod 2016.

to extract resources and taxes from them, and towards the end of his life the royal treasury was in sore need of these. Many rebellions arose in these later years, and many more again when the news of Alexander's death spread to every corner of his kingdom.

Beyond Politics: Alexander and Greek Culture

Although Alexander's life, as reflected in our sources, was characterized by conquest and war, in fact the king was also a formidable champion of Greek culture, arts and sciences. Moreover, this was a common feature of the Argead kings, who regularly invited and welcomed artists, physicians, philosophers and inventors to their courts.[40] Alexander's education by Aristotle at Mieza and his subsequent well-known interest in reading seem to have led him, for example, to seek out the company of intellectuals of all kinds.[41] Throughout the campaign, the sources depict Alexander as being surrounded by Olympic champions like Dioxippus, historians and sophists like Callisthenes of Olynthus and Anaxarchus of Abdera, and philosophers and artists like Pyrrho, who would go on to found the school of Scepticism, together with actors and artists of all kinds.[42] Alexander's close links with visual artists related to his attempt to control his own image: Pliny says that Alexander forbade the free representation of himself, granting permission to represent him only to Apelles, Lysippus and Pyrgoteles, each within his own discipline.[43] Likewise, the corpus of anecdotes and *exempla* bearing upon Alexander includes a large number of episodes in which he encounters characters like Diogenes 'the Dog' or the gymnosophists, which further illustrates the king's strong engagement with Greek (and other) thought.

By virtue of his conquests and foundations, Alexander was the main vehicle of the dissemination of Greek culture in Asia and, accordingly, in the new Hellenistic world that was to emerge upon his death.[44]

---

[40] Tomlinson 1970: 308–315; Faure 1982: 65–66, 207–208. For the importance of intellectuals in the Hellenistic courts, see Smith 1993.
[41] For Alexander's reading, see Brown 1967; Molina Marín 2022. For Alexander's particular interest in Euripides, see Bosworth 1996a.
[42] See Heckel 2006 for all these names. On Alexander and the philosophers at his court, see Sirinelli 1993: 55–67.
[43] Pliny *Natural History* 7.38. Antela-Bernárdez 2005: 184–192.
[44] The famous sentence from the opening of Droysen's *Geschichte Alexanders des Grossen* (1833; at p. 4 in the 1998 Darmstadt reprint), 'Der Name Alexander bezeichnet das Ende einer Weltepoche und den Anfang einer neuen', so often quoted, is in fact questionable: cf. Bosworth 2009; Almagor 2023.

Some scholars have cast doubt on the degree of Alexander's success, contrasting his conquests and victories with the rapid dismemberment of his empire, but what remains unquestionable is that the impact of his conquests led to the emergence of a culture that amalgamated the traditions of the conquered territories under the ascendancy of Greek language and culture, and that in this amalgam were the seeds of much of the culture of imperial Rome and indeed modern-day Europe. Alexander's real triumph lies, essentially, in transforming Greek culture into a universal and ecumenical heritage for mankind.

Guide to Further Reading

For sources contemporary to the age of Alexander, the work of first resort still is Heisserer 1980, supplemented by Rhodes and Osborne 2003. The latter review the main arguments about the League of Corinth, and provide a detailed bibliography for it, but see also Poddighe 2012; for the league working as a court, see Antela-Bernárdez 2011a. On the impact of Alexander's campaign in Asia upon Greece, see Adams 1996 and Domínguez Monedero 2022, together with Antela-Bernárdez 2022 on the specific case of Athens. For rebellions against Macedon and resistance towards it, Agis in particular, see Badian 1994. Faraguna 2003 provides a brief and clear overview of the Greek states' relations with Alexander, including those outside the mainland. Alexander's treatment of the Hellenic communities of Asia Minor and his treaties with them have been brilliantly revisited recently by Kholod 2010, 2013 and 2016. There is a large bibliography on Alexander's relationship with and impact upon Greek culture more generally, but the reader may find Sirinelli 1993 to be of particular interest. On the discourses and ideas on Panhellenism in this period, Perlman 1969 and 1976 still deserve attention; to these items should be added also Flower 2000, mostly focusing on Alexander himself, and Antela-Bernárdez 2007b.

4: To the Ends of the World: What the Campaign Was All About

Edward M. Anson

Why did Alexander wish to pursue a career of conquest? What was his ultimate goal? It had been suggested certainly in the propaganda surrounding the beginning of the campaign itself that this was to be a war of revenge. The Persians had invaded Greece in 480/479, committing destruction and sacrilege, and while this campaign failed in its purpose to conquer the Greek peninsula, the Persians were later to involve themselves repeatedly in Greek affairs. This created animosity towards the Persians which was amplified by the Greek view that all other peoples were barbarians and natural enemies of the Greek people (Plato *Republic* 470c). The Athenian rhetorician and orator Isocrates writes of the eternal hatred between Asians and Greeks (4.157; 12.163) and advocated 'compelling the barbarians ... [to] be serfs of the Greeks' (*Letter* 3.5). For Isocrates, such a campaign would also serve as a cause for Greek unity (5.16). The actual campaign was not initially the brainchild of Alexander, but rather that of his father Philip, who at least for propaganda purposes adopted the concept of a crusade against the old enemy of Persia (Lane Fox 1973: 93). This was, of course, a bit paradoxical since Macedonia and Persia had a long history, going back at least to a time when Macedonia was a dependency of the Persian Empire in the late sixth century prior to and during the Persian invasion of Greece (Borza 1990: 102–105; Olbrycht 2010: 342–345). The Macedonians had fought alongside the Persians during the great invasion (Herodotus 8.34; 8.136.1–8.136.2; 8.140a), but tradition said such service was forced and not freely given (Herodotus 7.173.3; 175.1; 8.140b; 9.45). Philip, as a result of his victory at Chaeronea, stood in a position to dominate the Greek world. His Peace and League of Corinth were his mechanisms to achieve this domination. For Philip II, this war was to give his new world order a purpose.[1] In fact, he had already sent an advance

---

[1] Anson 2020a: 166–178.

force to secure a beachhead in Asia for the full-scale invasion when he was assassinated, leaving the task of fulfilling the expedition to his son Alexander. Given Philip's assassination before he could do more than begin the preliminaries for his invasion, it is unknown what Philip's ultimate plans may have been.[2] Previously, Philip had portrayed himself as the avenger of Apollo in the Third Sacred War against the Phocians, even supposedly having his soldiers wear wreaths of laurel, the plant sacred to Apollo (Justin 8.2.3). His campaign in Asia was also to carry religious overtones.

The proposed campaign energized the Greek world, but the fact that Alexander, once having conquered the Persian heartland, gave up his war of revenge most readily and began a rapprochement with his former enemies suggests that whatever Philip's purpose, for Alexander the proclamation of a war of revenge was simply a means to some other end. Indeed, Alexander's adoption of his father's 'war of revenge' was, like so much of Alexander's campaign, his army, his general staff, simply an inheritance from his father.[3] While it is uncertain what Philip's ultimate goal was, since he died before his invasion was much under way with his advance force, it is likely he also used the revenge theme as a ploy to unite the Greeks behind his 'crusade'.[4] If not as proclaimed in the early propaganda, what then was the goal?

To discover the real Alexander and the reason for his life and work is made most difficult by the virtual absence of contemporary sources and the development of a body of literature today referred to as the '*Alexander Romance*'. The latter presents Alexander as someone worthy of a cape and a new superhero movie. In the *Romance*, one finds Alexander the Dragon Slayer, Alexander at Gog and Magog, Alexander and the Amazons, the Mermaids and the 'Wilting Maidens'. Alexander today is a national hero claimed by two states, Greece and North Macedonia (formerly the Former Yugoslav Republic of Macedonia), and a figure in the music of several heavy metal bands. In the 1986 Iron Maiden song 'Alexander the Great', 'His name struck fear into hearts of men. Alexander the Great became a legend 'mongst mortal men.' Yet, our sources, both historical and fantastical, present a picture that owes much to its subject. Alexander cultivated his own

---

[2] For an examination of what may have been Philip's intent, see Anson 2020a: 151–161.
[3] On the use of this particular theme by both Philip II and Alexander III, see Squillace 2010: 76–80, 2004: 60–71, 130–138.
[4] Rather cynically many Greeks may have been enthusiastic about the coming invasion simply because it would remove Philip and the bulk of his forces from the Greek mainland, not to mention that the Persians might succeed in defeating and, perhaps, even killing the Macedonian king.

self-image. This was an evolving and complex image that he wished to project in life to demonstrate that he was anything but an ordinary man. The image was complex in that it was a combination of a number of base beliefs that changed little over time and his desire to project himself in ways that would be receptive to whoever was his current audience. This image evolved as his view of his exceptionality grew, enhanced by his every success. He was an individual who brought with him on his invasion of Asia his own historian, Callisthenes (Arrian *Anabasis* 4.10.1–4.10.2), a personal sculptor, Lysippus (Plutarch *Alexander* 4.1–4.2), a painter, Apelles (Cicero *Ad familiares* 5.12.7), and an engraver, Pyrgoteles (Pliny *Natural History* 7.125, 37.8). He wanted to control every aspect of his image. Alexander founded numbers of Alexandrias across his empire, not to mention two Nicaeas to emphasize his victories, a Bucephala to honour his horse,[5] and, perhaps, even a Peritas after his dog (Plutarch *Alexander* 61.1). Even as a sixteen-year-old he founded Alexandropolis in Thrace (Plutarch *Alexander* 9.1). All of these foundations were to trumpet his name down through the ages. Alexander is supposed to have lamented that unlike his ancestor Achilles he did not have a Homer to extol his achievements and virtues (Arrian *Anabasis* 1.12.1). His inferior Homer, Callisthenes, is reported to have proclaimed that Alexander's fame depended on him, including 'his share in divinity' (Arrian *Anabasis* 4.10.1–4.10.2).

Everything Alexander did was about Alexander. After his father's death, he stayed in Europe just long enough to secure his back before leaving for Asia; he was not interested in supplying his homeland with an heir prior to his departure as suggested by his principal advisors (Diodorus 17.16.2); after his successes in Asia, he planned on centering his empire in Asia with its capital in Babylon (Strabo C731; cf. Diodorus 17.108. 4). 'Alexander was not just a legend in his own time but also a legend in his own mind.'[6] For Alexander, conquest was the goal, an ongoing, ever continuing and expanding, objective. Alexander wished to conquer the entire world (Arrian *Anabasis* 7.1.4; Diodorus 17.94.3; Curtius 9.2.11, 6.18). This puts the Macedonian in a very rarified company. Cyrus the Great is reported by Herodotus to have attacked the Massagetae 'for there were many weighty reasons that impelled and encouraged him to do so: first, his birth, because of which he seemed to be something more than mortal; and next, his victories in his wars: for no nation that Cyrus undertook to attack could escape from him'

---

[5] Arrian *Anabasis* 4.22.6; 5.194; Diodorus 17.955; Curtius 9.3.23. [6] Anson 2021a: 15.

(1.204). While this is Herodotus' assessment, it is to be remembered that Cyrus died in the midst of his last expedition of conquest (Herodotus 1.214; cf. 178, 201; [Ctesias] *FGrH / BNJ* 688 F9).[7] A similar statement would also suit Genghis Khan and his conquests[8] 'You have pacified all our people, you have unified all other peoples, and the Khan's throne has been assigned to you' (de Rachewiltz 2015: 201). Genghis Khan died in August 1227, during an invasion of Western Xia (de Rachewiltz 2015: 268–269). According to Babus Rashidzad, a translator of *I Am Timour, World Conqueror: Autobiography of a 14th Century Central Asian Ruler*, 'Amur Timour's passion in life was conquest' (2009: ix). Alexander's desire for glory through conquest then is certainly not unknown through history.

While Aristotle (*Politics* 1252a35–1252b5) associates imperialism and conquest with racism and Thucydides (5.89) has an Athenian ambassador proclaim that it is a natural law that 'the strong do what they can and the weak suffer what they must', Alexander's desire for conquest was not racist, nor part of some natural law, it was entirely personal. Much debate concerning Alexander's ultimate goals in recent literature has come to centre on his supposed failure to conquer India. In this regard, the sources all state that Alexander wished to conquer India (Arrian *Anabasis* 4.16.6; 5.26.1–5.26.2; Curtius 9.2.2–9.2.12; Justin 12.7.4; Plutarch *Alexander* 62.2, 5; Diodorus 17.93.4–94.5),[9] and that this goal was only stopped when on the Hyphasis river his troops silently protested continuing this conquest. Despite Alexander's attempt to entice them to follow his lead, the campaign to the east was over and Alexander returned to the Indus and sailed and battled down the river to the Indian Ocean (Arrian *Anabasis* 528.3–528.4; Curtius 9.3.19–9.3.20; Justin 12.7.16–12.8.1; Plutarch *Alexander* 62.6–62.7; Strabo C697–C698). The sources are uniform in describing the role of the army in this end to the eastward campaign. Alexander wished to continue, but the army showed its reluctance and Alexander retraced his steps to the Indus. His 'insatiable' ambitions were thwarted by his troops.

In 1999, Philip Spann, however, brought forth the argument that, after Alexander's defeat of Porus, the Conqueror 'once apprised

---

[7] Xenophon (*Cyropaedia* 8.7) has Cyrus dying at home surrounded by his family, but this is a highly suspect biography. In the words of Cicero, *Cyrus ille a Xenophonte non ad historiae fidem scriptus sed ad effigiem justi imperi* (*Ad Quintum fratrem* 1. 1. 23).

[8] De Rachewiltz 2015: 186–187, 189, 193, 214, 239, 247–257, 259, 265–266, 270, 272.

[9] Diodorus (2.37.3; 18.6.1) does state that, on reaching the Ganges, Alexander turned around fearing what lay ahead. Bosworth (1995: 337) suggests that these comments may come originally from Hieronymus, but the reference to the Ganges puts the source and the statement in question.

of what lay ahead ... did not wish to proceed, that he in fact encouraged what history might record as a "mutiny" in his army in order to preserve his public image and his own mythopoetic vision of himself' (1999: 62). Alexander's ambitions were, then, satiable. Spann's argument is that Alexander had earlier in his expedition stated his intention to conquer all the way to the eastern ocean, but in light of more precise knowledge of what lay ahead he had now decided that this goal was too difficult. Waldemar Heckel likewise argues that Alexander staged the entire Hyphasis episode, but not because of any doubt in his ability to conquer India. For Heckel, Alexander's goal was the conquest of the Persian Empire, nothing more and certainly nothing less (Heckel 2003a: 147–174). Alexander had proclaimed that he was going to conquer the civilized world. It was only in the Punjab, continues Heckel, that Alexander discovered that the end of this world was not the same as the end of the Persian Empire: 'How can he continue to style himself *Kosmokrator* and ignore these new regions?' (Heckel 2003a: 172). To both Spann and Heckel, Alexander pushed his troops to stage the so-called mutiny on the Hyphasis. The decision to stop was then ostensibly the army's. Alexander would then be seen as wanting to conquer India, but his troops 'refused' to proceed. The troops then brought Alexander's march to the east to an end, but an end which was, in fact, desired by their commander. There was then no mutiny on the Hyphasis; in point of fact, no order was given to proceed further into India and none was refused, because for Spann and Heckel none was ever intended. The entire incident was staged by Alexander to save face, leaving his image for invincibility intact. The failure to conquer all of civilized Asia was due to his army not to himself. Claims that Alexander wished to conquer India and then proceed to the Straits of Gibraltar and even to Britain were just part of the *Romance* tradition that has tainted our surviving sources. Along these lines of mistrust of our sources regarding this incident, Timothy Howe and Sabine Müller proclaim the entire Hyphasis incident was invented tradition and that Alexander saw the Hyphasis as his stopping point from the very beginning (2012: 24, 37–38). While it is true that our surviving historical sources come to us from the Roman period and it is further true that every generation interprets the past through the filter of its present, still this usually involves interpretation and not outright invention of events. Moreover, Aristobulus (*FGrH / BNJ* 139 F56 = Strabo C741), Alexander's companion and historian, proclaims that the Conqueror 'wanted to be lord of all'. There is, also, evidence that the ultimate source of the Hyphasis episode at least in Arrian's account was Alexander's close companion and the future king of Egypt, Ptolemy, the son of Lagus.[10] Howe and Müller note that Ptolemy was likely one of the sources used, but believe that he gave a very abbreviated account with a purpose of downplaying any appearance that Alexander was in any sense the successor of the Achaemenid tradition (2012: 31–32): 'Ptolemy had good reason to cover up anything that made Alexander look too Persian' (Howe and Müller 2012: 32). However, this argument for a limited account in Ptolemy's history is pure speculation. Ptolemy's history may, indeed, be the mainstay of Arrian's entire account of this incident (Hammond 1993: 259–260; cf. Bosworth 1995: 337). Arrian does proclaim that he has based his history primarily on the histories written by Aristobulus and Ptolemy, and of these two primarily Ptolemy (*Anabasis* Pref.1; 5.7.1; 6.2.4; 7.15.6). At the beginning of his description of the crossing of the Indus and the beginnings of the Indian campaign, Arrian (*Anabasis* 5.7.1) states 'as for the method by which Alexander bridged the Indus, neither Aristobulus nor Ptolemy, the authors whom I chiefly follow, describe it'. The implication is that here with the Indian campaign as elsewhere, Arrian's primary authorities are Ptolemy and Aristobulus, but here he is noting that for this particular episode, he has turned to a different source. Certainly, Ptolemy was an individual in a position to know Alexander's most intimate thoughts and who was present during this incident, and is, therefore, likely Arrian's source for this episode.[11] Arrian does not say otherwise. He had cited Ptolemy earlier in his description of the Acesines river (*Anabasis* 5.20.8) and notes in his discussion of the incident on the Hyphasis: 'But when there continued dead silence through the camp, and it was clear that the men were ... in no mood to change their minds ... then, Ptolemy son of Lagus tells us he nonetheless offered sacrifices with a view to crossing the river' (*Anabasis* 5.28.4). So, when Arrian states that the reports of what lay beyond the Hyphasis in India 'only stirred Alexander to a desire for still further advance' (*Anabasis* 5.25.2), it is reasonable to assume that he is getting this information from a contemporary source. This passage itself certainly suggests that Alexander was not hesitant to proceed nor preparing to cease his advance. While Ptolemy in his surviving fragments never specifically speaks of Alexander's insatiable desire for conquest, Arrian's other

---

[10] See the analysis in Holt 1982: 42–43. However, Brunt (1976–1983: ii.532) believes that for the bulk of this episode Arrian relied on Aristobulus, not Ptolemy.

[11] See Hammond 1993: 251; Bosworth 1995: 344; 1980a: 16–17; Holt 1982: 41–47. Brunt (1976–1983: ii.532–533), however, believes that Aristobulus was Arrian's source for these speeches.

major source, Aristobulus, however, as noted earlier, did. The notice that Alexander's eastward conquest was ended by the reluctance of his army to proceed is found in all our major surviving sources. This overall acceptance of Alexander's desire to continue to the east suggests that the situation took place as described; the army was majorly responsible for the end of Alexander's eastward campaign despite his wish to proceed. Arrian (*Anabasis* 5.23.1–5.29.1) proclaims that it was Alexander's knowledge of morale problems that led him to address his commanders in order to reinstill their enthusiasm to proceed. According to Curtius (9.2.27), Arrian (*Anabasis* 5.26.8), and Diodorus (17.94.3–17.94.4), Alexander attempted to bribe his soldiers with material rewards so that they would agree to the advance. The incident found in all our surviving sources in accordance with which the army by its silence forced Alexander to forego his conquest of India represents the truth of the situation. Might Ptolemy or Aristobulus have invented the entire incident? Possibly, but unlikely. While the expedition in the East ended at the Hyphasis, this was not to be the end of Alexander's search for new lands to conquer. Alexander did not simply turn around and retrace his steps back to Babylon; he sailed and fought his way down the Indus. When he had returned to Babylon, he planned new conquests in Arabia and in the West (Diodorus 18.4.2–18.4.4; Arrian *Anabasis* 7.20.1–7.20.2). The contemporary source Aristobulus also notes Alexander's desire to conquer Arabia (Strabo C741).

Heckel's claim that Alexander only wished to conquer what had been the Persian Empire is challenged not only as recorded in our sources by his stated desire for further conquests, but also by his progress beyond the Indus, the border of that same empire (Strabo C688–C689; cf. Herodotus 4.44.1–4.44.3; Arrian *Anabasis* 3.8.6; Pseudo-Aristotle *De Mundo* 398a25).[12] In the words of A. K. Narain, 'Doubtless therefore

---

[12] While the Achaemenid direct administrative apparatus did not extend to the Indian regions entered by Alexander, it has been suggested (Vogelsang 1990: 108) that Persian influence in these areas may have operated under some 'flexible and varied' system. The actual areas under clear Achaemenid administrative control, however, are to the west of the Indus. Heckel also points out that there was a fleet all ready for Alexander on the Hydaspes for sailing down the Indus and concludes that this proves Alexander had planned on sailing down the Indus from the beginning. However, Arrian (*Anabasis* 5.7.1–5.7.2) is likely correct that Alexander crossed the Indus on a bridge of boats and it was these ships that were broken down and carried forward for the fording of the Hydaspes (Arrian *Anabasis* 5.8.4–5.8.5; 6.1.1). Strabo (C689), following the contemporary Aristobulus (*FGrH / BNJ* 139 F56), notes that many ships built at Alexander's direction were constructed with bolts and could be taken apart and transported over land. It was likely ships of this type that Alexander found when he returned to the Hydaspes after turning back from the Hyphasis. It would be these that then had to be made ready for sailing down the Indus (Arrian *Anabasis* 6.1.6).

Alexander did nourish an ambition to conquer India, ... Otherwise the crossing of the Indus was meaningless.'[13] Heckel emphasizes that the Hyphasis was part of the Indus river system, and implies that this was simply a slight deviation from the Persian eastern border. Howe and Müller see the Hyphasis as the limit of Darius' conquest, but present no such evidence (2012: 31). But, why the deviation? Hephaestion had in advance of Alexander's arrival already bridged the Indus (Arrian *Anabasis* 5.3.5; Diodorus 1786. 3; Curtius 8.12.4). Perhaps he meant this advance beyond the Indus as a demonstration of his power. He had crossed the Danube but did not acquire the submission of this area and he crossed the Jaxartes against the Scythians, but did not subjugate that land. However, once he crossed the Indus he did acquire the territories that existed between the Indus and the Hydaspes. He founded a Nicaea and a Bucephala in the summer of 326 on the eastern side of the Indus in the plain of the Hydaspes (Arrian *Anabasis* 5.19.4), and an Alexandria on the Acesines (5.29.3). All three were settled east of the Hyphasis. The Hydaspes was past the boundary of the Persian Empire proper and the Hyphasis well beyond that.

Moreover, with respect to Heckel's and Spann's scenarios, anyone who has ever been in a leadership position knows that, while asking advice from immediate subordinates is never wrong, letting others make decisions for you is an easy way to lose that leadership. Alexander was too good a commander to encourage his own loss of authority simply to save face about changing a decision. As Beth Carney (1996b: 35) states,

> This minimal description of the scene on the Hyphasis is enough in itself to make untenable the view that Alexander intentionally staged this event to avoid going further east. Voluntarily risking his prestige – yielding, that thing no Greek hero wants to do – would have been unimaginable because it made it appear that the army rather than the king was in charge.

What makes this even less likely is that he simply had to claim that the sacrifices were not favourable, which is what he actually did before then sailing down the Indus (Arrian *Anabasis* 5.28.4).

At the start of his expedition, Alexander, as had his father, presented his objective as punishment of the Persian Empire, a 'war of

---

[13] Narain 1965: 156; cf. Briant 2002: 754–757; Magee et al. 2005: 711–741, Kuhrt 2007: 873–875. Strabo (C688–C689; cf. Herodotus 4.44.1–4.44.3, Pseudo-Aristotle *De Mundo* 398a25) states that the eastern border was the Indus.

revenge'. However, Alexander, once having conquered the Persian heartland, gave up this war of revenge most readily and began a rapprochement with his former enemies, which suggests that for him the war of revenge was always simply a means to an end. As propaganda, the proclaimed campaign of revenge against the Persians, with references to the Trojan War and to Achilles, had played well with his allies and his Greek and Macedonian troops. Agesilaus had likewise attempted to associate his invasion of Asia Minor with the expedition to Troy by attempting to offer sacrifice at Aulis, emulating the departure of the Trojan expedition, but was thwarted by the Boeotians (Xenophon *Hellenica* 3.4.3–3.4.4). With the defeat of the Persians at Gaugamela and the subsequent deaths of Darius and the usurper Bessus, Alexander wished to continue his march to the East and was in need of a new incentive to keep up the enthusiasm of his Macedonians. It was clear with the death of Darius that most of the troops assumed the expedition was over, and on the strength of a rumour that Alexander planned now to return to Macedonia, the Macedonians enthusiastically prepared to leave Asia (Curtius 6.2.15–6.2.16). To secure these soldiers' support, Alexander addressed the troops, explaining that these Asian lands were not yet secure and Bessus was rallying support against them, and convinced them to continue on the campaign (Curtius 6.3.6–6.4.1; Diodorus 17.74.3–17.74.4; Plutarch *Alexander* 47.1–47.4; Justin 12.3.2–12.3.4).

Even with the pacification of the Persian heartland and the death of the pretender Bessus, Alexander had no intention of stopping. He did, however, change the stated purpose of his campaign. The war would cease to be one of revenge and become one of ongoing conquest. Whereas in 329 Alexander convinced his troops to continue the campaign based on patriotic objectives, now he emphasized the riches and booty to be won (Curtius 9.2.27; Arrian *Anabasis* 5.26.8; Diodorus 17.94.3–17.94.5, 104.5–104.7). But, more importantly, if Alexander were to continue his advance deeper into Asia, he would need additional troops beyond what could be raised in Macedonia or Greece. He would need the services of many of these conquered Asians.

To mark the change, he needed some act to demonstrate the end of the war of revenge and the beginning of a shared war of conquest. In the late spring of 330, despite what appears to have been the peaceful surrender of the Persian capital Persepolis, Alexander permitted his troops to sack the city, with the exception of the royal palace, much of which he later burned (Curtius 5.6.1–5.6.8; Diodorus 17.70). The men of the city were killed, the city plundered and the women carried off into slavery. According to Curtius (5.6.1), Alexander had earlier proclaimed that Persepolis was 'the city from which troops without number had poured forth, from which first Darius and then Xerxes had waged an unholy war on Europe. To appease the spirits of their forefathers they should wipe it out'. Certainly, the theme of revenge is offered by our sources as an explanation for both the initial plundering of the city and the later destruction of the palace (Arrian *Anabasis* 3.18.12; Diodorus 17.70.2, 72.6; Curtius 5.6.1; Strabo C729–C730).[14] This was to be an act of catharsis. The revenge was now ended, at least as seen by Alexander, and a new partnership could be begun.[15] However, Alexander had to be very careful in this process of assimilation. Alexander had already in 331, shortly after his victory at Gaugamela, and perhaps even earlier in his letter to Darius in 334 (Arrian *Anabasis* 2.14.8), begun to call himself the 'King of Asia' (Plutarch *Alexander* 34.1). He did not and could not become king of Persia in the same fashion he had become Pharaoh of Egypt or King of Babylonia (Fredricksmeyer 2000: 136–137). To proclaim himself the successor of the Achaemenids would be too offensive to his Macedonian troops. King of Asia was a title that transcended Persia and the Achaemenid dynasty and, also, pointed to his desire for conquests beyond the limits of the Persian Empire.

Alexander accelerated his inclusion of Persians in his personal entourage; he began to adopt Persian dress and court procedure, to secure Persian advisors and increasingly to incorporate Asian units into his ever-growing army (Arrian *Anabasis* 7.11.1–7.11.3; Diodorus 17.110.1). Alexander's increasing embrace of Persian practices and his incorporation of Asian troops in his army led W. W. Tarn in the mid-twentieth century to proclaim that Alexander was attempting to create a 'brotherhood of man' (1933, 1948: ii.399–449). While the thesis has over the years been seriously challenged,[16] its basic premise still has its supporters (Hammond 1989c: 226). Alexander ultimately did marry three eastern princesses, two of whom were Persian (Plutarch *Alexander* 47.7–47.8; Diodorus 17.107.6; Arrian *Anabasis* 7.4.4), and he did oversee the mixed marriages of a wide assortment of officers and soldiers to Asian women performed according to Persian ceremony (Arrian *Anabasis* 7.4.4–7.4.8). Even though Plutarch proclaims that

---

[14] An indication of the symbolic nature of this destruction was that it was limited. The city soon after is not only found to be inhabited but serving as a satrapal capital (Diodorus 19.21.2, 22.1, 46.6). Indeed, the archaeological evidence suggests that even the destruction of the palace was limited to the three main buildings closely associated with King Xerxes (Sancisi-Weerdenberg 1993: 181–182).

[15] See Anson 2013: 157–172. [16] Badian 1958a: 425–444; Bosworth 1980a.

Alexander 'came as the heaven-sent governor of all, and as a mediator for the whole world, ... bringing together into one body all men everywhere, uniting and mixing in one great crater' (*Moralia* 329c), the truth is clearly otherwise. The Macedonian king's desire that 'the Macedonians and Persians should enjoy harmony as partners in the government' (Arrian *Anabasis* 7.11.9) was not based on some philosophical principle, but rather on Alexander's own self-interest. He was, after his conquest of Egypt, proclaimed the son of Zeus, and by the end of his reign desirous of receiving the honours typically bestowed on a god;[17] all others were hence inferior and his subjects. It is within this context that Alexander's incorporation of the conquered in his administration and increasingly in his army must be understood. Clearly, Alexander was not motivated by racist claims of Greek superiority, but he was no idealist proponent of racial equality either. His needs were personal and immediate.

The 'unpleasantness' on the Hyphasis caused Alexander, while never abandoning his claim to be the king of Macedonia, as King of Asia to begin the process of altering dramatically his relationship with the Macedonians in his army, to ensure that in the future his desires would be carried out without even silent opposition.[18] To guarantee this outcome he began to build what would be his army, not a national force, but one loyal to him personally. This was to be an army far less reliant on Macedonia. To accomplish his goal of a personal army he wanted to retain at least for the immediate future a core of Macedonian veterans, but where possible to replace these with those not imbued with the traditions of Macedonia, or indeed with those of any other nations either. One way to ensure this loyalty was to begin the indoctrination of his new troops at an early age and primarily those with Asian origins. The traditions of true autocracy were embedded in Asia, but not found in Alexander's homeland. The traditions of Macedonia ran counter to Alexander's ambitions. When he had returned from India, Alexander began seriously to create this new army. In Susa in 324 came the arrival of the *Epigoni* (Arrian *Anabasis* 7.6.1–7.6.2).[19]

---

[17] Anson 2013: 114–119.
[18] Diodorus 17.108.3 states that the incidents on the Hyphasis and the later one at Opis were not isolated occurrences.
[19] Hammond argues that Alexander was recruiting and training regular corps of young men throughout his empire in the pattern of the Macedonian Pages (1990: 276, 278, 286–287, 1996b: 101). These troops initially were for satrapal defence, but later would also be used to replace frontline troops (Hammond 1990: 285–286). Hammond based this argument on a passage in the *Suda* (*s.v.* Βασίλειοι), which states, 'Six thousand royal boys by order of Alexander the Macedonian were doing military drill in Egypt.' The passage, however, is likely

Perhaps, as early as 330,[20] or as late as 327,[21] Alexander had ordered his satraps and city commanders to recruit 30,000 Asian young men of roughly the same age to be taught Greek and trained in the techniques of Macedonian warfare (Curtius 8.5.1; Diodorus 17.108.1–17.108.3; Plutarch *Alexander* 71.1). This unit was to remain separate from the Macedonian phalanx, and Diodorus (17.108.3) calls it an *antitagma*, an 'anti-phalanx', certainly suggesting that Alexander had more in mind than simply beefing up his numbers. Despite Plutarch's (*Alexander* 47.6) claim that their creation was to produce harmony between the two ethnic groups, Alexander wished to use this unit as a counterpoise to his increasingly unruly Macedonians. His father Philip had used the *Pezhetairoi*, his newly created heavy infantry, in part as just such a counter to the Hetairoi,[22] the long-standing aristocratic king's companions. Even more significant with these mostly Iranian recruits was their very name, *Epigoni*, seriously implying that they were to be the new phalanx, replacing their Macedonian counterpart. Brian Bosworth describes this unit as 'a corps of troops without roots in Europe or permanent home in Asia, the janissaries of the new Empire, whose loyalty would be to Alexander alone' (1980a: 18).

Alexander's dream of a new army was accelerated at Opis in northern Babylonia. Here, he called a meeting of his Macedonians to announce the discharge of many of his Macedonian veterans,[23] an action seemingly long sought by the veterans themselves. Many of the soldiers, however, now interpreted this discharge as an insult; they believed that they were to be replaced by Asians,[24] a conclusion obviously not without merit. At Opis, unlike on the Hyphasis, where silence was the reaction to Alexander's proposal to march further east, the commander had to endure insults and calls for him to carry on alone with his father Ammon.[25] To these insults Alexander reacted quickly, arresting thirteen of the most vocal protesters and executing them that same day.[26] Alexander now

a confused version of Alexander's creation of the *Epigoni*. Without the *Suda* passage there is no evidence for these empire-wide academies.

[20] Hammond 1996 b:101; cf. Plutarch *Alexander* 47.1–47.3.
[21] Curtius 6.5.1; Bosworth 1988a: 272.
[22] On the traditional relationship of these aristocratic companions and the king and the revolutionary changes brought to this relationship by Philip II, see Anson 2020a: 90–91.
[23] Curtius 10.2.8, 19; Arrian *Anabasis* 7.8.1; Diodorus 17.109.1–17.109.3; Justin 12.11.4–12.11.8.
[24] Arrian *Anabasis* 7.8.2; Curtius 10.2.12; Plutarch *Alexander* 71.3; Justin 12.11.6; Diodorus 17.109.2.
[25] Curtius 10.2.12–10.4.3; Arrian *Anabasis* 7.8.1–7.11.9; Diodorus 17.109.2–17.109.3; Justin 12.11.1–12.12; Plutarch *Alexander* 71.2–71.9. On Alexander's claims to be the son of Zeus/Ammon and his pretensions to be a living god, see Anson 2013: 83–120.
[26] Curtius 10.2.30, 3.4; Arrian *Anabasis* 7.8.3; Diodorus 17.109.2–17.109.3; Justin 12.11.8.

accelerated his transformation of his army. In the next two days he began to create Iranian military units with traditional Macedonian names from his Asian troops (Arrian *Anabasis* 7.11.1–7.11.3; Diodorus 17.110.1). There would now be even a Persian Hypaspist guard (Arrian *Anabasis* 7.11.3).[27] The insolence ended with the Macedonians begging forgiveness. However, even with the disturbance quelled, Alexander proceeded with his plans and demobilized many of these veterans.[28] The Iranian parallel units were retained. Those veterans who were initially to be dismissed and sent back to Macedonia were still sent. Alexander was determined on future campaigning and the need for a more dependable force. Macedonians in the future would make up only a minority of his forces, a veteran corps, essential until his new recruits had achieved a similar status.

Alexander was looking to create a core in his army whose loyalty would be to him personally and only to him (Bosworth 1980a: 18). The core of this new force was to be Alexander's *Epigoni*. Highly praised by Alexander for their skill in weaponry and drill, they were to provide the future core phalanx (Diodorus 17.108.1–17.108.3). Even though for a time the dominant numbers in his army were Iranian, Alexander's purpose was to create an army without national identity. As Bosworth (1988a: 273) states, '[the army] would become deracinated, the only constant being their employer, Alexander'. Alexander was preparing an Arabian campaign and was content to use his current army without waiting for any promised Macedonian reinforcements (Arrian *Anabasis* 7.19.3–7.22.5). With his new army anchored on the *Epigoni*, Alexander would proceed to the conquest of Arabia.

It was also in Susa that Alexander established a future source of recruits that would be separated from any homeland. This new area of recruitment was to be the children born in the camp. At Opis, when he sent so many of his veterans home, he ordered that they leave their children born in the camp with him.[29] These children numbered roughly 10,000 (Diodorus 17.110.3). Alexander promised to educate his soldiers' children in Greek culture and arms (Arrian *Anabasis* 7. 12.1–7.12.2).[30] Now, none of these youths would be old enough to serve

---

[27] Plutarch *Alexander* 71.4–71.6; Curtius 10.3.5–10.3.14; Diodorus 17.108.3.
[28] Bosworth 1986: 4–6, 1988a: 267 estimates that at Opis there were 18,000 Macedonian veterans of which Alexander eventually dismissed 10,000 (Arrian *Anabasis* 7.12.1). Hammond 1980a: 245 estimates that at Alexander's death the grand army contained around 10,000 Macedonians.
[29] Arrian *Anabasis* 7.12.1–7.12.2; Diodorus 17.110.3; Justin 12.4.6; cf. Plutarch *Alexander* 71.5.
[30] The obvious implication of the martial training suggests Alexander was really only interested in the male offspring.

immediately. Alexander's campaign was barely a decade old. They would be the future recruits to fill the ranks of the fallen and those retired from service. This was a further extension of Alexander's plan to create an army not tied to the traditions of any specific ethnic group, but rather tied to the camp and to him personally. As Justin (12.4.6) comments, 'They would be all the more steadfast for having spent not just their training but even their infancy right in the camp', and he also refers to them as '*Epigoni*' (12.4.11).[31] Over time, with the camp as home, more soldiers' children would follow their fathers into the army. The new army would be in a sense Alexander's children. He would become the chief of a tribe of warriors ever pursuing their commander's dreams of conquest.[32]

To proclaim Alexander's major reason for his invasion of Asia as the pursuit of glory is not to declare that his expedition was not rooted in reality. His campaign was well-planned and methodically carried out. Arrian's assessment, 'Alexander had no small or mean conceptions, nor would ever have remained contented with any of his possessions so far, ... being always the rival if of no other, yet of himself' (*Anabasis* 7.1.4), is a correct assessment, which in no way conflicts with Alexander's singular ability to carry out his ambitions brilliantly. What must not be forgotten is that Alexander at the time of his death in 323 was still a young man of not quite thirty-three years. His father had prepared to lead his expedition to Asia in his mid-forties. Maybe after another decade of further conquest, Alexander would have ceased his pursuit of personal glory and begun to give his empire administrative stability with a unified administrative system, if it had lasted that long, and a regularized succession process with a clear heir, but at the time of his death these goals were not his immediate ones, glorious conquest was.

Guide to Further Reading

Tarn in 1933 presented a talk on 'Alexander the Great and the unity of mankind' (Tarn 1933; cf. 1948: ii.399–449). Following the opinion of Plutarch, he proclaimed Alexander a philosopher king who dreamed of uniting the world's peoples. This view was attacked by Badian 1958a, but has since received renewed attention in a more modified form, so far

---

[31] Hammond 1990: 276 believes that Justin is here confusing these youths with those officially called the *Epigoni*, but in the context it would appear that Justin is using the term in a general sense.

[32] See Anson 2020b: 239.

as pertains to the fusion of Greeks and Persians only (Thomas 1968). By contrast, Bosworth 1980a contends that in reality the Persians were used by Alexander as a counterweight to the increasingly mutinous behaviour of the Macedonians. On the proclaimed 'war of revenge', see Squillace 2004 and 2010. With respect to Alexander's limited ambition, see Spann 1999; Heckel 2003a; and Howe and Müller 2012. Additionally, on Alexander's pursuit of glory, see Joseph Roisman 2003b and Anson 2021a.

5: ALEXANDER AND EGYPT

Timothy Howe

Alexander spent at most eight months in Egypt (mid/late October of 332[1] to late June of 331[2]), but his brief time there has sparked more scholarly debate than any other similar period in his eleven-year campaign,[3] in part because the founding of his most famous city – Egyptian Alexandria – and his most famous side-trip – the visit to the oracular sanctuary of Ammon in the Siwah Oasis – date from this period (Map 5.1). This attention derives from the fact that these events figured prominently in the propaganda of Alexander, as seen in the surviving fragments from the history of his court historian Callisthenes,[4] and in the legitimation efforts of his Successors, especially the Ptolemaic dynasty, which took over Egypt after Alexander's death.[5] Throughout the Hellenistic and Roman periods, Alexander continued to interest the peoples of the Mediterranean, with the result that each generation reframed events for their own audiences as they found new meaning in his story and actions.[6] In part, contemporary Egyptian-language sources, such as Alexander's royal titulature, temple

---

[1] A graffito from the Luxor temple allows us to date the Egyptian reception of Alexander's official power precisely: *Topographical Bibliography of Ancient Egyptian Hieroglyphic Texts, Reliefs and Paintings*[2] ii: 335, no. 219. A priest named Ankhpakhered writes that building began under his direction 'on the first day of the first month of Alexander's year one' (*rnpt-zp 1, 1. 3ḫt, sw 1 ḥr ḥm (n) nswt-byt 3rksndrys*), which corresponded to 15 November 332; Ladynin 2016: 261–262. Cf. Bosch-Puche 2013: 153–154, especially n.139, who argues that this date is a later invention. Not in dispute, but not as precise, *Oriental Institute Hawara Papyri* 2, a Demotic annuity contract, dates Alexander's official control over Egypt to November of 332; Hughes and Jasnow 1997, 16–19, pls. 8–13.

[2] Egyptian New Year (late June in 331 BCE) provides a *terminus post quem*: Bowden 2014a: 41–42; cf. Łukaszewicz 2012: 207. Egyptian kings were formally crowned on New Year's Day; so Morris 2010: 206.

[3] Bloedow 2004 offers insightful historical context for nineteenth- and twentieth-century scholarship.

[4] E.g. Pownall 2014; 2021; O'Sullivan 2015.   [5] Ogden 2009c; Howe 2018b, 2018a.

[6] For the fragmentary sources, see the commentaries in *Brill's New Jacoby* – Aristobulus: Pownall 2013; Callisthenes: Rzepka 2016; Clitarchus: Prandi 2016; Ptolemy: Howe 2018b. For specific focus on the Hellenistic and Roman overlays, see Papadoulou 2017 and Howe 2013, 2014, with references to earlier studies. For the methods of the Roman historians and the expectations of their audiences, see Bosworth 2003.

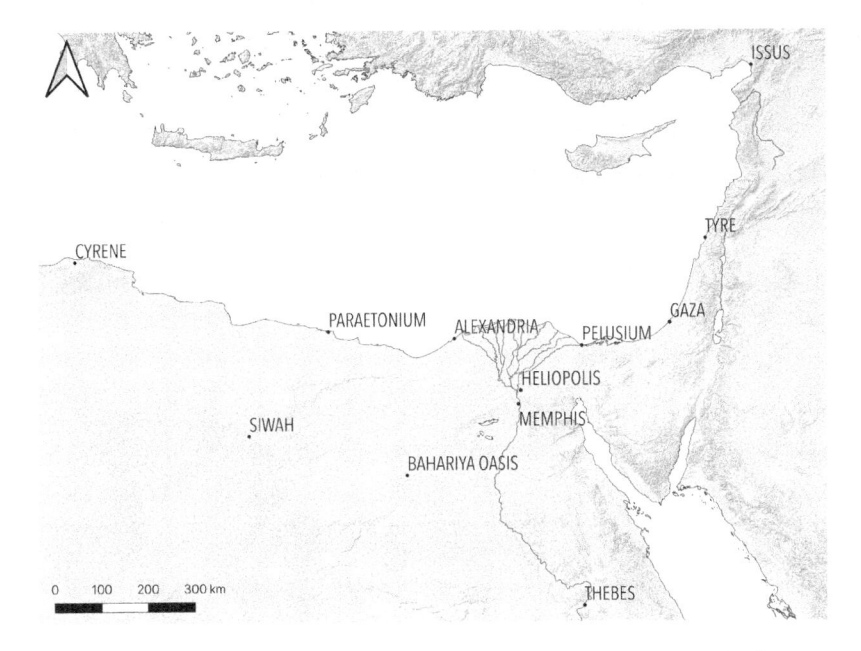

MAP 5.1 Alexander in Africa: places of interest. Drawn by David Hollander.

dedications, Demotic ostraca and papyri, and archaeological remains, such as the temples and sanctuaries Alexander visited and commissioned, offer some ways to provide context to the Greco-Roman literature, but, even then, these sources often do not tell us what we most want to know – the reasons why Alexander did what he did, in the way that he did. Consequently, the modern scholar has a complicated pastiche of ancient opinion and contemporary Egyptian evidence to draw on, which has, in turn facilitated a wide diversity of opinion.[7] This chapter surveys these diverse bodies of evidence and opinion through four main events: Alexander's arrival in Memphis, his founding of Alexandria, his visit to Siwah, and his return to Memphis and departure from Egypt.

Arrival

After the two-month siege of Gaza ended in success, Alexander crossed into Egypt at the great border fortress of Pelusium, likely travelling along the 'Ways of Horus', an ancient Egyptian military highway

[7] Borza 1995.

begun in the New Kingdom to link the Eastern Delta to the Levant and facilitate (or contain) traffic to and from Egypt. Recent excavations have uncovered a network of fortresses, rest stations and water reservoirs that were in use throughout Antiquity.[8] Alexander's smooth passage from Gaza to Pelusium (six days to move 200 km) suggests that such logistical support was at his disposal and that not even token resistance was offered. The literary sources report that Pelusium willingly surrendered to the Macedonians and that the Egyptians warmly welcomed them.[9] Before moving on, Alexander stationed a garrison at Pelusium to guard his flank. He then proceeded to Heliopolis, one of the oldest and most important religious centres of Egypt, where he likely visited the famous temple of the sun god Re, the chief deity of the Egyptians and personal patron of the Egyptian kings.[10] The fleet and the rest of his army he sent up the Nile to rendezvous at Memphis.[11] Once at Memphis (the main administrative capital of Egypt since at least the beginning of Persian rule in the sixth century BCE) Alexander was welcomed by Darius III's recently-appointed satrap Mazaces, who surrendered the city and the royal treasuries, which according to Curtius, totalled 800 talents (*c.* 28,800 kg of gold).[12] Thus, with apparently little effort, Alexander gained control over the smooth-running administrative and financial systems of the Persians.[13]

After the handover of power, Alexander sacrificed to the Apis bull, a living deity connected to the cult of Ptah, the chief god of Memphis. At the same time, Alexander held Greek-style athletic and musical contests to commemorate the event for both the army and his new subjects.[14] Alexander's choice to engage Apis likely derived from Herodotus' famous account of Cambyses' murder of the bull in 523 BCE and (if they are not the product of later invention) the rumours that Artaxerxes III Ochus had killed and eaten the Apis bull eleven years previously (343 BCE).[15] By Alexander's time, Persian impiety towards the Apis bull had been entrenched in Greek historical tradition and, as

---

[8] Hussein 2019.   [9] Curtius 4.7.2; Arrian *Anabasis* 3.1.1.
[10] Pfeiffer 2014: 92 sees this visit to Heliopolis as an important step in Alexander's 'official' process to become a recognized king of Egypt.
[11] Arrian *Anabasis* 3.1.2; cf. Curtius 4.7.3, who reports that Alexander *sailed* to Memphis with only a small force of elite troops.
[12] Curtius 4.7.4; Heckel 2021: 294.
[13] Burstein 2008; Schütze 2017; Agut-Labordère 2021: 177–178, 183.
[14] Arrian *Anabasis* 3.1.4. Bosch-Puche 2012 contends that Alexander took a genuine interest the cults of sacred animals.
[15] Cambyses: Herodotus 2.42; Depuydt 1995. Artaxerxes III: Plutarch *On Isis and Osiris* 11, 31; Aelian *On the Nature of Animals* 10.28; *Varia historia* 4.8; 6.8; Pfeiffer 2014: 94–96; Colburn 2015: 184; cf. Lloyd 2011: 85, who argues that the Artaxerxes story is post-Alexander.

with so many other local traditions in the course of his campaign, Alexander took the opportunity to cast himself as 'righting the past wrongs' inflicted by the Persians.[16] That Greeks *and* Egyptians were the target audience of these events is underscored by the contemporary Greek-language dedication to Apis, now housed in the Ashmolean Museum, as well as the Greek-style athletic games Alexander held for the god.[17] The Apis sacrifice was, first and foremost, a political event that Alexander wanted both Greeks and Egyptians to comprehend and witness. The Persian injustices done to Apis offered a poignant backdrop against which Alexander could not only contextualize his recent triumphs over Darius III at Issus, but also proclaim his agenda to both the Egyptians and his Greco-Macedonian army, to the effect that he would protect the traditional Egyptian order and harmony of things – the pivotal native concept of *ma'at* ($m3^c.t$).[18] In this one public act, Alexander could portray himself as an advocate for two of the most distinctive features of Egyptian religiosity – the king's duty to protect and maintain *ma'at and* the worship of native divinities through their earthly manifestations in the form of animals.[19] Whether this was spontaneous opportunism or a long-planned and choreographed event is impossible to discern, but the fact that the festivities included famous musicians and athletes who travelled from Greece implies that some advance planning was required. As for the comments in the sources about spontaneity, the many other games and festivals that Alexander sponsored throughout his campaign were also portrayed by the literary sources as 'spontaneous' but in reality were carefully ritualized events, designed not only to keep the army devoted to Alexander and informed about his next policy aims, but also to engage the new peoples he encountered in their local idiom.[20] The events in Memphis, then, fit a general pattern often seen during Alexander's campaign – the style of the celebration was Greek but the venue and themes were carefully chosen to teach about, and honour, local traditions and institutions.

After Memphis, Curtius observes that Alexander sailed up the Nile 'to ensure that there were no changes in the customs of the Egyptians'.[21]

---

[16] Lloyd 2011; Llewellyn-Jones 2012. For Alexander making use of the tradition: Schäfer 2014: 164; Ogden 2014b: 3–4; Colburn 2015: 171–172. For Alexander's engagement with Persian *topoi*, see Flower 2000.

[17] '[A]lexander to Ap[is]' [– Ἀ|λέξανδρος ΑΠ|–]: Ashmolean Accession no. G 1205; Bowman, Crowther and Savvopoulos 2016: 101.

[18] Menu 1999 argues that Alexander understood well that the primary role of the Egyptian kings was to preserve *ma'at*. Cf. Ladynin 2016.

[19] Bosch-Puche 2012; Agut-Labordère 2024. [20] Lunt 2014; Mann 2020.

[21] Curtius 4.7.5: *compositisque rebus ita ut nihil ex patrio Aegyptiorum more mutaret*.

This is certainly in keeping with the duties of a prospective Egyptian king: in order to be crowned, the royal candidate must travel on his royal barge, in view of the people, and visit the important cult centres of the kingdom.[22] Most importantly, Curtius' phrasing suggests a direct engagement with *ma'at*. For their part, the other literary sources move on after observing Alexander's arrival in Memphis, intent on discussing what they consider the more significant events of the Egyptian sojourn – the founding of Alexandria and the visit to Siwah Oasis. Nonetheless, we should see the proclamation to preserve tradition as in keeping with Alexander's other actions in Memphis and not be quick to dismiss Curtius' evidence out of hand, simply because it lacks corroboration.

ALEXANDRIA

Up to this point, the literary gaze has centred round Alexander's actions and policies, but after Memphis, there is a shift in tone in all of the narratives, as the authors pivot to explore Alexander's perception of himself.[23] Arrian is the most dramatic, portraying the founding of Alexandria and the journey to Siwah as the product of Alexander's deep-seated desires (*pothos*). As a result, Alexander's personal emotions and the evolution (or devolution) of his character have played a large role in the scholarship.[24]

As one might expect with such a close focus on the persona of Alexander, the accounts of the founding of Alexandria abound with intertextual allusions and heroic and mythical elements.[25] The most fabulous include a dream sequence in which Homer guides Alexander to the site[26] and a dramatic tale of birds swooping down to eat the grain used to mark out the city's new boundaries.[27] The more mundane, but still heroic, have the king himself, much like Herodotus' King Amasis

---

[22] Discussion and references at Bowden 2014a: 41.
[23] Arrian *Anabasis* 3.1.5, 3.2.3; Curtius 4.7.8; Plutarch *Alexander* 26. Scholars have largely followed the sources in this regard: references at Grieb 2014 n. 1 (Alexandria) and Ogden 2014b n. 37 (Siwah).
[24] E.g. Worthington 2004: 84–92; Zahrnt 2016; Naiden 2019a: 103–108; cf. Bosworth 1988a: 71–74; Ogden 2014b: 4–14.
[25] These accounts contain many layers, added over time as the Ptolemies and Alexandrians constructed the city's mythology: Howe 2014 and Papadoulou 2017.
[26] Plutarch *Alexander* 26.2–26.7.
[27] The sources, in approximate chronological order, are: Strabo C792 (= 17.1.6), Valerius Maximus 1.4 ext. 1; Curtius 4.8.6; Plutarch *Alexander* 26.5–26.6; Arrian *Anabasis* 3.2.1–3.2.2; Stephanus of Byzantium s.v. Ἀλεξάνδρειαι (incorporating Jason of Argos); Amyntianus, *Fragmentum Sabbaiticum*, *FGrH* / *BNJ* 151 §11; *Alexander Romance* 1.32.4; *Itinerarium Alexandri* 49; Ammianus Marcellinus 22.16.7; Eustathius *Commentary on Dionysius Periegetes* 254. Arrian *Anabasis* 3.2.1–3.2.2, while noting that grain was used, does not include the rapacious birds.

when he set up Naucratis, personally planning Alexandria's religious and commercial spaces.[28] Indeed, all of the stories recorded in the ancient sources reference the special nature of Alexandria and the fact that the gods had willed Alexander to create such a famous place of wealth and prosperity.[29]

Two main issues make it difficult to discern the historicity of these foundation accounts: (1) the sources themselves do not agree on *when* the foundation occurred relative to the visit to Siwah;[30] and (2) the sources all originate from a time when Alexandria had already developed as a major economic and political centre and tend to view Alexander's acts from the perspective of hindsight. Issue number one has typically been solved by reference to geography: Alexander *could* have passed through the site of Alexandria on his way to the Oasis of Siwah and then come back through it again on his return to Memphis.[31] But this is not without its problems, foremost of which is the fact that Ptolemy, our earliest surviving source, has Alexander cross the desert from Siwah to Memphis and therefore not pass through Alexandria on his return.[32] There have been various responses to Ptolemy's evidence, ranging from 'Arrian must be in error regarding what Ptolemy actually wrote',[33] to 'Ptolemy altered the route for propaganda reasons of his own'.[34] At this point, the *Alexander Romance*, a dubious source for historicity at best, is brought into the conversation because it offers a hard date (25 Tybi = 7 April, 331 BCE) for the official foundation of Alexandria, which supports the 'return via Alexandria' argument's timeline.[35] Issue number two is more troublesome: the archaeological work in the region so far has offered no evidence for Alexander's presence – in fact, the physical evidence unambiguously has Alexandria's construction taking place many years after Alexander's death, under Ptolemies I and II.[36] The contemporary written sources also support a later date for Alexandria's construction: the only

---

[28] Arrian *Anabasis* 3.1.5. Amasis: Herodotus 2.178. Cf. Homer *Odyssey* 6.1–6.12; Plato *Laws* 745b–745e.
[29] Plutarch *Alexander* 26.10; Curtius 4.8.6; Arrian *Anabasis* 3.2.2.
[30] Alexandria first, then Siwah: Plutarch *Alexander* 26.3–26.10; Arrian *Anabasis* 3.1–3.2. Siwah first, then Alexandria: Diodorus 17.52; Curtius 4.8.1–4.8.6; Justin 11.11.13; *Alexander Romance* 1.30–1.31; Amyntianus, *Fragmentum Sabbaiticum*, FGrH / BNJ 151 §§10–11; *Itinerarium Alexandri* 49–50; Orosius 3.16.14
[31] For example, Welles 1962; Bosworth 1976b: 137–138, 1988a: 71–74; Bagnall 1979. Further discussion at Ogden 2014b: 4–5.
[32] Arrian *Anabasis* 3.4.5 = Ptolemy FGrH / BNJ 138 F9.   [33] Bosworth 1976b.
[34] Howe 2014; Pownall 2021.
[35] *Alexander Romance* 1.32; discussion and references at Grieb 2014 et al.: 206–210; Wojciechowska and Nawotka 2014: 49–51.
[36] Empereur 2018. Excavation reports and syntheses reviewed at Howe 2014.

contemporary Greek source, the Aristotelian *Oeconomica,* places Alexandria's foundation in the future, after Alexander has departed Egypt,[37] and the Egyptian-language *Stele of the Satrap,* written in 9 November, 311, refers to the area as a 'construction site' (*rᶜqd(y)t*) and a 'fort/stronghold' (*nḫtw*).[38] All of this suggests a less prominent role for Alexander in the creation of Egyptian Alexandria, a role that corresponds well to the otherwise rather low urbanistic ambitions of the Macedonian king, who did not appear as an ambitious city founder either before or after his stay in Egypt.[39]

Thus, scholars in recent years have focused on the regional economic and military nature of Alexandria's origins rather than Alexander's construction of (or desire to construct) a great city.[40] Here, the island of Pharos is of particular interest, for all of the sources mention it as playing a primary role in Alexander's plans, and, as an offshore island, Pharos would provide a safe haven for both an occasional emporium (as mentioned in the Aristotelian *Oeconomica*) and a military garrison (as noted in the *Stele of the Satrap*). A garrison on the Canopic branch of the Nile in the Western Delta also makes good military sense: it would balance that of Pelusium to the east, thus blocking land access to the rich agricultural resources of Egypt from both directions. In addition, the garrison at Alexandria could be a staging post for future conquests to the west, if we take the sources at their word that Alexander was planning an expedition to Carthage just before his unexpected death in 323.[41] The military focus would certainly fit the context of Alexander's immediate actions after the visit to Alexandria, when he moved to secure the coast as far as Paraetonium, some 300 km to the west. In any event, Alexander's presence in the region seems to have sent a clear message, for envoys from Cyrene met Alexander along the route to Paraetonium and offered an alliance.[42]

---

[37] Pseudo-Aristotle *Oeconomica* 1352a29–1352b30: 'When King Alexander commanded him [Cleomenes of Naucratis] to found a city near Pharos and to establish there a trading centre which was formerly held at Canopus', Ἀλεξάνδρου <τε> τοῦ βασιλέως ἐντειλαμένου αὐτῷ οἰκίσαι πόλιν πρὸς τῇ Φάρῳ καὶ τὸ ἐμπόριον τὸ πρότερον ὂν ἐπὶ τοῦ Κανώβου ἐνταῦθα ποιῆσαι. Grieb 2014: 210–212.

[38] Egyptian Museum no. 22182; discussion and references at Howe 2018b, 2018a: 161–164. For the Greek place name Rhacotis, derived from *rᶜqd(y)t*, see Ogden 2014b n. 25.

[39] Fraser 1996; Cohen 2006, 2013; Anson 2021b: 5–11 surveys the primarily military and strategic nature of Alexander's many settlements.

[40] Military: Howe 2014; Anson 2021b. Economic: Łukaszewics 2012; Grieb et al. 2014.

[41] Diodorus 18.4; Arrian *Anabasis* 7.1.2; Ogden 2014b: 17–19.

[42] Diodorus 17.49.2–17.49.3. Cf. Curtius 4.7.9, who reports that Alexander had met the envoys at Lake Mareotis.

Siwah

From Paraetonium, with Cyrene now nominally under his control, Alexander headed inland to visit the oracle of Zeus-Ammon at the Siwah Oasis. The Siwah expedition – a 1,300 km journey, including more than 1,000 km in an hyper-arid environment – is unique to Alexander's Egyptian sojourn and has generated the most attention. Whether the trip to Siwah was the original intent of the coastal expedition, or a result of the surrender of Cyrene, is difficult to discern: the literary accounts understood the journey to Siwah as a destination in and of itself and used it as an opportunity to explore Alexander's character and personal religiosity.[43] As with Alexander's actions at Alexandria, the surviving narratives abound with intertextual allusion, personal disclosure and the miraculous: Alexander suffers from thirst, but a providential rain renews his water supply; his army becomes lost in the dunes, but two ravens – or as Ptolemy has it, talking snakes[44] – appear to guide them through the sands to the Siwah Oasis, which is fed by a miraculous spring that alternately boils or chills. This wondrous journey only serves to set the tone for the revelations made to the Macedonian king by the oracle. Here, through a combination of direct (private) communication,[45] signs and nods,[46] or a 'lost in translation' greeting,[47] the will of the god was revealed: Alexander was, in fact, the unconquerable son of Zeus-Ammon. Given the prominence of the oracular consultation in the ancient accounts, the main scholarly debates have centred round the method by which responses were delivered to the king in order to discern whether or not (and in what manner) Alexander was hailed as 'son of Ammon' and how being proclaimed the son of a god might affect Alexander's relationships with both his army and his Egyptian subjects.[48] While a cautious approach to the ancient evidence has largely prevailed,[49] some have prioritized the more dramatic and detailed Clitarchan

---

[43] Sources in approximate chronological order: Strabo, C813–C814 (17.1.43) = Callisthenes *FGrH / BNJ* 124 F14a; Diodorus 17.49–17.51; Curtius 4.7.5–4.7.32; Plutarch *Alexander* 26–28; Arrian *Anabasis* 3.3–3.4; Justin 11.11; *Itinerarium Alexandri* 49–50.

[44] Arrian *Anabasis* 3.3.5 = Ptolemy *FGrH / BNJ* 138 F8; Ogden 2009c.

[45] Strabo, C813–C814 (17.1.43) = Callisthenes *FGrH / BNJ* 124 F14a; Plutarch *Alexander* 27.5–27.7; Curtius 6.7.25–6.7.28; Diodorus 17.51.1–17.51.3; Collins 2014b, Collins 2014a.

[46] Callisthenes *FGrH / BNJ* 124 F14a; Bowden 2014a: 45 links this with other Egyptian oracular traditions.

[47] Plutarch *Alexander* 27.8–27.11 notes that the priest's poor knowledge of Greek allowed for Alexander to 'misunderstand' that he was the son of the god; Ogden 2014b: 12.

[48] References at Collins 2014a n.1. On the linkage between the oracle of Siwah and Alexander's 'divine' status as king of Egypt, see Burstein 1991; Menu 1999; Bosch-Puche 2008; Collins 2014b; Bowden 2014a; Pfeiffer 2014; Schäfer 2014; Caneva 2016: 19–22; Agut-Labordère 2024.

[49] Bosworth 1988a: 73–74; Ogden 2014b: 9–14.

tradition, best reported by Curtius, and thus have seen the visit to Siwah as an important stop in Alexander's personal journey to godhood.[50]

Unlike with the founding of Alexandria, however, we are fortunate to have Alexander's official motive from Callisthenes' history, as paraphrased by the Roman geographer Strabo.[51] According to Strabo-Callisthenes, Alexander travelled to Siwah so that he could follow the path of his ancestors, Heracles and Perseus. Of the other sources, only Arrian confirms this motive, though he adds that Alexander wished to consult the oracle both 'because it was said to be infallible' and 'because he traced his birth in part to Ammon'.[52] This need of Alexander to follow his heroic forebears stands in stark contrast to the Clitarchan sources, which frame the visit round questions of Alexander's divine parentage.[53] As with the founding of Alexandria, the source traditions are heavily influenced by hindsight: centuries later, when they are writing, Alexander's identity as the son of Zeus-Ammon has become well established as a result of Alexander's and his Successors' propaganda. And yet, in Callisthenes we can capture this tradition in formation: according to Callisthenes, Alexander did not reveal at the time what the priest told him, but rather kept it to himself until he returned to Memphis.[54] Only at that later time and place, when Alexander had a wide audience and supporting evidence in the form of the prophecies brought by the Milesian envoys from Greek oracles in Asia Minor that proclaimed his birth from Zeus and foretold of future military victories, did the king proclaim his divine sonship in public.[55] From the order of events in Callisthenes' account, we might conclude that the notion of divine sonship appealed to Alexander but that he delayed announcing it until he found the proper venue in which it would best serve his interests.

It is significant that Callisthenes links the Siwah expedition with the demi-gods Heracles and Perseus and a desire to visit the wilds of the

---

[50] Worthington 2004: 83–92, 199–204; Zarhnt 2016; Naiden 2019a: 103–108. See Howe 2013 for analysis of the different source traditions.
[51] Howe 2013; Collins 2014a; Agut-Labordère 2024.
[52] ὅτι ἀτρεκὲς ἐλέγετο εἶναι τὸ μαντεῖον τοῦ Ἄμμωνος ... καί τι καὶ αὐτὸς τῆς γενέσεως τῆς ἑαυτοῦ ἐς Ἄμμωνα ἀνέφερε. Arrian *Anabasis* 3.3.1–3.3.2.
[53] Curtius 4.7.8; Justin 11.11.2.
[54] Arrian confirms that Alexander kept the consulation secret for a time but that 'he said he heard the answer his heart desired' (καὶ ἀκούσας ὅσα αὐτῷ πρὸς θυμοῦ ἦν, ὡς ἔλεγεν). Arrian *Anabasis* 3.4.5
[55] Sekunda 2014b; Zarhnt 2016: 302–307; Caneva 2016: 12–13 argues that Alexander only learned of his divine parentage at Siwah. Sekunda goes further and suggests that Callisthenes invented the other oracles after the fact to underscore Alexander's message. Cf. Bosworth 1977 and Collins 2014a, who contend that Alexander already knew of his divine birth well before he entered Egypt. For the 'unconquerable Alexander' as a literary theme in Callisthenes' history, see O'Sullivan 2015.

Western Desert, as they had done. At the time, the army and the audience back in Greece would have certainly recalled the passage in book two of Herodotus, where Heracles sees the god Ammon wearing a ram's head.[56] Indeed, this might have special resonance with the Macedonian Companions, for the Macedonian-controlled Chalcidicean city of Aphytis had long put Ammon's ram's-headed image on its coins, and the sanctuary there to Zeus-Ammon saw considerable building activity in the decades before Alexander's journey to Egypt.[57] What the Greek and Macedonian audience might have done with Perseus in this context is not as clear, though Arrian's comments about Perseus consulting the oracle for information, before he set off on his quest for the gorgon, offer an important clue. The Perseus connection may even be an outright invention by Callisthenes, to serve as a reference to Persians in general, so that the audience might recall Herodotus' account of Cambyses' offenses against Siwah.[58] In a way, this oblique approach to Cambyses fits well with Alexander's earlier engagement with the Apis bull when he first arrived at Memphis. And by his actions at Siwah Alexander was certainly an anti-Cambyses: the Macedonian king's respectful consultation of the oracle and successful trip across the treacherous desert to the distant oasis are counter-images of Cambyses' hubris and failure, as told by Herodotus.[59] Furthermore, the choice to frame the expedition in terms of competition with demi-gods is a significant and recurring motif in Alexander's campaign. In India, for example, when Alexander wished to push beyond the limits of known space, the sources have Alexander rationalize such a going forward to the 'ends of the earth' as following in the steps of the demi-gods Heracles and Dionysus.[60] With this in mind, the Egyptian name of Siwah, 'the end of the farthest point' ($\underline{t}$3y-n-$\underline{d}$r.w/$\underline{d}$rw.w) takes on great significance. In any event, because of Callisthenes' evidence and its stress on competition and exploration, scholars have begun to shift the conversation away from Alexander's personal religiosity to his economic and political motives.[61]

---

[56] Herodotus 2.42; Ogden 2014b: 13. That this happened at Thebes and not Siwah may not have mattered, so Bowden 2014a: 45. For Herodotus' influence on Callisthenes, see Prandi 1985: 82–93.
[57] Archaeological excavations of the Ammon sanctuary: Leventopoulo-Giouri 1971: 667; Tsigarida 2011. Coins: Leclant and Clerc 1981.
[58] Herodotus 3.17.1, 3.26.2; Bowden 2014a: 51–52; Müller 2016c.
[59] Cambyses sent 50,000 men to take Siwah and all were lost in a sandstorm. Herodotus 3.25.3–3.26.2; Müller 2016c.
[60] For example, Arrian *Anabasis* 4.28.2; Bowden 2014a: 44–45.
[61] Bowden 2014a: 51–53; Müller 2016c; Agut-Labordère 2024.

This shift has been facilitated by the archaeological and epigraphic evidence. While the archaeology of Siwah has failed to resolve the details of Alexander's oracular consultation,[62] and what he may or may not have heard there, it does document the site's regional importance to the inhabitants of the Western Desert and Cyrene during the sixth and fourth centuries BCE. The main temple on the top of Aghurmi Hill was constructed by the usurper Amasis in the sixth century, the same Amasis whose foundation of Naucratis, as told by Herodotus, may have led Alexander to the site of Alexandria.[63] Herodotus gives some context for Amasis' rationale, which is similar to that provided by Arrian for Alexander: Amasis patronized only those oracles he considered infallible.[64] But Amasis did not sponsor the temple alone, he was joined by the 'Prince of the Two Deserts, Sethirtaios, son of Leloutek' (*wr ḫȝs.ty Sth-ir-di-s sȝ Rrwtk*), whose title suggests he ruled the deserts that surrounded Siwah to the east towards the Nile and the west towards Cyrene.[65] As a usurper, Amasis needed as many allies as he could get. That both Sethirtaios and Amasis collaborate in sponsoring the temple speaks to the regional significance of Siwah as a political nexus for forging alliances between the peoples of the Nile and the Western Desert.

The construction of the second temple at Siwah lends further context for the role of the shrine in regional politics in the decade before Alexander's visit. The second temple was dedicated by one Wenamun, 'Prince of the Desert' (*wr [ꜥȝ] ḫȝs.t*), a contemporary of Nectanebo II (360–342 BC), little more than a decade before Alexander made his journey.[66] In a temple dedication in the nearby oasis of Bahrain, Wenamun refers to himself with Egyptian royal titulature, suggesting he had aspirations on Nectanebo's throne. For Alexander's predecessors, then, the oasis of Siwah and, through it, the territory of the 'Two Deserts', were political and military objectives in themselves.[67] Seen from this context, Alexander's trip across the desert was not optional – he needed to secure his western flank before he continued his campaign against Darius III.[68] And Alexander, by his anti-Cambyses-style approach, won a victory at Siwah without a blow – as at Pelusium and Memphis, the Siwah elite welcomed him with open arms. They also

---

[62] Fakhry 1973; Kuhlmann and Brashear 1988; Bruhn 2010. The excavations carried out in Siwah raised many hopes but, in the end, failed to deliver decisive answers: Bowden 2014a: 46–47; Agut-Labordère 2024; cf. Collins 2014a.
[63] Kuhlmann 1988, 42–43. [64] Herodotus 2.174.2.
[65] Colin 1998: 339–341; Agut-Labordère 2024. [66] Fakhry 1973: 168; Gallo 2006.
[67] Kuhlmann 2013. [68] So Agut-Labordère 2024.

gave him a propaganda gift: divine birth. A familial connection to the god Zeus-Ammon, who was venerated by the Libyans and by the Greeks of the Western Desert, would legitimize Alexander's control over the region.[69]

The epithets attached to Ammon in the Western Desert illuminate how a personal connection to the god could so readily legitimate Alexander to both Libyans and Greeks. A group of inscriptions from Darb Ain Amur, dated to the second part of the second millennium BCE,[70] show the evolution of the unique cult of Ammon. Originally called 'Amun-Re, lord of the sky' (*'Imn-R^c nb p.t*), an epithet largely unknown in the Nile valley,[71] this deity developed an identity distinct from its Nilotic roots – 'Ammon Lord of the sky' (*'Imn nb p.t*), whose main temple Amasis built at Siwah in the sixth century.[72] Despite the patronage of Amasis, however, this oracle and its god Ammon, 'Lord of the sky', received no mention in the contemporary sources from the Nile valley. Egyptologists have taken this to mean that Ammon of Siwah held little direct importance to the inhabitants of the Nile.[73] In this light, it seems unlikely that the trip to its oasis would play an *initial* role in facilitating Alexander's formal recognition as King of Egypt.[74] And yet, according to Callisthenes, the announcement that Alexander was the son of Zeus-Ammon *later* played a pivotal role in Alexander's own propaganda to Egyptians, Macedonians and Greeks at Memphis. The unique epithet 'Beloved of Ammon' (*mr(y) 'Imn*), which is attested in the formal titulature of Alexander that was developed by the Egyptian priests later in Alexander's reign, implies that Siwah played some role in the construction of Alexander's royal identity.[75] We might see the Greek dedication by Alexander to his father Ammon at the Barhiya Oasis,[76] an important stop on the road between Memphis and Siwah, in this context as well.[77] In the end, because of the sources' focus on Alexander's character, the true purpose of the Siwah visit will likely never be resolved with certainty.

---

[69] See Collins 2014b, 2014a on the connections between Siwah and Cyrene, with references to earlier literature.
[70] Lazaridis 2012: 123–126; Lazaridis 2015.   [71] Lazaridis 2015: 50.   [72] Guermeur 2005: 563.
[73] Osing 1984 col. 965; Agut-Labordère 2024.
[74] So Burstein 1991: 139–140; Pfeiffer 2014; Agut-Labordère 2024, contra Bosworth 1988a: 73; Anson 2003: 127–129; Bowden 2014a: 47–48.
[75] Bosch-Puche 2013: 151–152; Ladynin 2016: 267. Cf. Pfeiffer 2014: 102–104; Schäfer 2014: 159.
[76] 'King Alexander to Ammon the father' Βασιλεὺς | Ἀλέξ<α>νδρος | Ἄμμωνι | τ[ῷ]ι πατρί; the inscription is published at Bosch-Puche 2008.
[77] Although Bosch-Puche 2008 sees this as a contemporary dedication by Alexander as he took the desert road back to Memphis, others have seen it as a later product. Analysis and references at Agut-Labordère 2024.

Return to Memphis and Departure

As noted earlier, Alexander's return from Siwah has become entangled with the date and details of the foundation of Alexandria. There are only two possibilities: to return the way he came, or to go through the desert directly to Memphis. The former is safer, and is preferred by most scholars,[78] the latter is more dangerous and has the benefit of successfully traversing the route that bested Cambyses.[79] In any event, Alexander made his way back to Memphis, where he sacrificed to Zeus the King and held athletic competitions to commemorate his recent military successes, welcomed envoys and ambassadors, publicized his status as Son of Zeus-Ammon, and set about putting his new province in order and preparing for the next round of his war with Darius III.[80]

The political organization of Egypt went according to the pattern already established in Asia Minor: Alexander divided the governance of Egypt into civilian and military roles and distributed them accordingly among Macedonians, Greeks and native Egyptians.[81] The civil administration (and tax collection) for the two central kingdoms of Upper and Lower Egypt was handed over to native Egyptians, Doloaspis and Petisis.[82] For reasons unknown, Petisis soon gave up the office and Doloaspis took over both Egypts. The important garrison at Memphis was commanded by Alexander's Companion, Pantaleon of Pydna.[83] The Macedonian troops who remained behind were under the overall command of Peucestas, son of Maracatus and Balacrus, son of Amyntas.[84] The fleet was overseen by Polemon, son of Theramenes,[85] the garrison of Pelusium by Polemon, son of Megacles from Pella.[86] Lycidas the Aetolian was put in charge of the mercenaries whom Alexander left, and Eugnostus, son of Xenophantes, was to assist him as secretary, while Aeschylus and Ephippus, son of Chalcideus, were to serve as overseers.[87] The outer territories to the west and the east were given over to Egypt-based Greeks, with Apollonius son of Charinus overseeing the Libyan desert and Cleomenes of Naucratis the Arabian one.[88] Cleomenes ultimately took over the entire kingdom and was confirmed as governing satrap by Alexander.[89]

---

[78] References and discussion at Pownall 2021. [79] Preferred by Müller 2016c.
[80] Arrian *Anabasis* 3.5; Strabo C813–C814 (17.1.43) = Callisthenes *FGrH* / *BNJ* 124 F14a.
[81] Arrian *Anabasis* 3.5; Curtius 4.8.4–4.8.5; Burstein 2008.
[82] Heckel 2021: 177 and 372, respectively.   [83] Heckel 2021: 351.
[84] Heckel 2021: 372 and 126, respectively.   [85] Heckel 2021: 410.   [86] Heckel 2021: 409.
[87] Heckel 2021: 280, 184–185, 16–17, and 180, respectively.
[88] Heckel 2021: 80 and 249, respectively.
[89] Pausanias 1.6.3 and Dexippus *FGrH* / *BNJ* 100 F8.2.

One of the large questions that hangs over Alexander's time in Memphis for modern scholars is whether or not he was formally crowned King of Egypt with Egyptian rituals.[90] Unfortunately, as with all other instances of non-Greek royal rituals, such as the substitute-king ceremony in Babylon and the taking of the throne in Susa, the Greco-Roman sources are silent or hostile.[91] But the fact remains that across the genres of Egyptian literature, from private notes and contracts in Demotic to the complete royal titulature of all five names, the Egyptians refer to Alexander as the ruler of Egypt.[92] Significantly, unlike other recent foreign rulers, such as Artaxerxes II Ochus and Darius III, Alexander was given all five royal titles and, as noted above, his titles include the unique phrases 'Son of Ammon' (*sꜣ-'Imn*) and 'Beloved of Ammon' (*mr(y) 'Imn*) alongside and in addition to the formulaic and ancient 'Son of Re' (*sꜣ Rꜥ*). Clearly, the priests were not simply 'cutting and pasting' when it came to acknowledging Alexander's royal authority over Egypt. In any event, whether he was formally crowned or not, the Egyptians integrated Alexander into their daily lives as their new ruler, and the fact that Alexander did not face any revolts during his lifetime, as had his Persian predecessors, implies that his efforts to insert himself into Egyptian tradition were well received.

Another question that has attracted attention is the date of Alexander's departure from Egypt. As with so much we might wish to know, the Greco-Roman sources do not give a precise time of departure, and only Arrian gives any details, noting that Alexander had bridges built so he could cross the canals and channels of the Eastern Delta before he left for Asia.[93] Because no precise date is forthcoming, scholars have tended to work backwards from the 25 Tybi (7 April 331), the date given by *Alexander Romance* for the founding of Alexandria.[94] Consequently, a timeframe anywhere from late April to late June/early July is possible, depending on whether one chooses to have Alexander remain in Egypt until New Year's Day (end of June/early July) for the formal coronation ceremony or depart soon after the founding of Alexandria.[95]

---

[90] The main analyses are Burstein 1991; Bowden 2014a: 40–43; Pfeiffer 2014; Schäfer 2014.
[91] Bowden 2014a: 42–43.
[92] For the official titulature, see Bosch-Puche 2013, 2014. For the demotic sources, see Moje 2014 and Bosch-Puche and Moje 2015. In the formal hieroglyphic titulature, Alexander was referred to as '[he] of sedge [and] bee' (*nswt-bjt(y)*), which is often translated for convenience as 'King of Upper and of Lower Egypt', or simply 'King'. The metaphorical title pharaoh (*pr ꜥꜣ*) – literally 'great house' – was used only in demotic documents as a form of shorthand reference to royal authority, Leprohon 2013.
[93] Arrian *Anabasis* 3.6.1.   [94] References and analysis at Bowden 2014a: 40–41.
[95] See above, n. 2.

Guide to Further Reading

Alexander's time in Egypt has produced such a wide array of specialist studies that some guidance is required. The studies of Bosworth 1988a and Heckel 2020b provide an important introduction to the wider historical context (and implications) of Alexander's time in Egypt in terms of his military campaign and political goals. Heckel's 2021 prosopographic study offers insight into all of the figures involved both during and after Alexander's lifetime, including the relevant ancient and modern sources. For the specific events of the Egyptian sojourn and their reception, there is much to be gained from the many conference volumes and edited collections dedicated to the subject, such as Hinge and Krasilnikoff 2009; Bosman 2014; Grieb, Nawotka and Wojciechowska 2014; and Zerefos and Voardinoyannis 2018. For an introduction and analysis of the royal titulature and naming conventions of the Egyptians in general see Leprohon 2013 and for Alexander in particular see Bosch-Puche 2013 and 2014 and Bosch-Puche and Moje 2015. To access these and other royal texts from the period, see the Trismegistos database[96] and the *Digital Topographical Bibliography of Ancient Egyptian Hieroglyphic Texts, Statues, Reliefs, and Paintings*.[97] For the archaeology of Alexandria and its surroundings, see Goddio and Fabre 2008; Robinson and Wilson 2010; and Blue and Khalil 2010. For the archaeology of the Siwah Oasis and its surroundings see Fakhry 1973; Kuhlmann and Brashear 1988; and Bruhn 2010. For commentary on, and translations of, the fragmentary Alexander sources see the entries in *BNJ*.

---

[96] www.trismegistos.org/tm/   [97] http://topbib.griffith.ox.ac.uk//pdf.html/

6: Alexander and the Persian Empire

Sabine Müller

Introduction: Macedonia and the Persian Empire before Alexander's Campaign

Macedonia and Achaemenid Persia had a shared history prior to Alexander's conquests. In about 513–512/11,[1] when Darius I established Persian rule over the Greek Hellespontine, Thracian and Paeonian districts, the Argead ruler Amyntas I became one of Darius' subordinate governors (Herodotus 5.17–5.18). Familial Macedonian–Persian connections followed, certainly distinguishing the Argead *primus inter pares* from his elite: Amyntas' daughter Gygaea was married to the high-ranking Persian Bubares, their son became the governor of a city in Asia Minor, and Amyntas I's successor Alexander I was chosen to be the ambassador the Persians sent to the Athenians during Xerxes' invasion.[2] In terms of courtly representation and the visualization of monarchy, the Achaemenids were an inevitable model for the Argeads.[3] Hence, the earliest Argead coins, minted by Alexander I (late 480s), show a Macedonian rider holding a Persian short sword (*akinakes*). Macedonian troops fought loyally on the Persian side during Xerxes' invasion. Only in the post-war era, when Alexander I had to save his country from the punishment meted out to 'friends of the Persians' by the Hellenic League, did he transform himself into a 'friend of the Greeks'.[4]

There is a gap in our knowledge about Persian–Macedonian relations between the Persian withdrawal from Thrace and Macedonia after the battle of Plataea in 479/8 and the reign of Philip II (360/59–336).

I am grateful to Daniel Ogden for inviting me to contribute to this *Companion*.

[1] All dates are BC if not stated otherwise.
[2] Marriage: Herodotus 5.21.2, 8.136.1; Justin 7.3.9. Cf. Carney 2000: 15–16; Olbrycht 2010: 343; Vasilev 2015: 109–12; Carney 2017: 140, 143; Heinrichs 2020b: 55–56. Alexander I as envoy: Herodotus 7.25.2, 143.3, 185.2; 8.34, 126.2; 9.31.5, 89.4. Cf. Vasilev 2015: 188–190; Heinrichs 2020b: 58.
[3] Spawforth 2007b: 92; Müller 2021a: 109–110.   [4] Heinrichs 2020b: 59–60.

There was probably no cessation in diplomatic contacts. Although anecdotally embroidered, Plutarch's reference to the presence of Persian envoys at Pella during Alexander's childhood seems to be reliable (*Alexander* 15.1; *Moralia* 342b). Persia and Macedonia were not worlds apart. There are no traces of any tension before Philip extended the borders of his realm to the shores of eastern Thrace in 341. Some scholars believe that Arrian's information about an alliance between Artaxerxes III and Philip (in the middle of the 340s) is authentic.[5] The fact that in 353/2 Philip granted refuge to the satrap of Hellespontic Phrygia, Artabazus, expelled by Artaxerxes III (Diodorus 16.22.1, 52.3), did not seem to have harmed Macedonian relations with Persia. The watershed was Philip's advance to the Hellespont in 340. By besieging the crucial strongpoints of Perinthus and Byzantium, he revealed his ambition to control the straits. This challenged the balance of power in the area, and led to a collision with the established powers involved. The Persian king, represented by his satraps of Asia Minor, Athens and the major Hellespontine cities brought Philip to a halt – for the time being.[6] But from that point on Macedonia was on a collision course with Persia: any further advance eastward by the Macedonians meant war.

After the establishment of Macedonia's hegemony over Greece (338), Philip integrated the Greek *poleis* (without reluctant Sparta) into the new order of the Corinthian League, a tool of Macedonian rule. Via the League, war was declared against Persia in 337 (Diodorus 16.77.2, 89.2–89.3). Most scholars think that Philip pursued the limited aim of the subjection of Asia Minor with its rich cities in order to secure a permanent income.[7] After his assassination in 336, Philip's successor Alexander was elected *hegemon* (leader) of the Corinthian League. He inherited the Persian war that had already begun: an advance force under Parmenion and Attalus had tried to secure footholds in Asia Minor for the safe landing of the main troops.[8] Alexander had grown up in a quickly expanding, militarized Macedonia in times of permanent war. For him, war would have been the 'normal' situation. He followed Philip's example and devoted his entire reign to the waging of it. At the start of the Persian campaign, his opponent was the militarily experienced Darius III, who had succeeded the short-lived king Artaxerxes IV, son of Artaxerxes III, in 338.

---

[5] Arrian *Anabasis* 2.14.1–2.14.2. Cf. Olbrycht 2010: 350; Wirth 2020: 418. Briant 1996: 708 believes that there were at least diplomatic negotiations.

[6] Diodorus 16.74.2–16.76.4, 77.2–77.3; Pausanias 1.29.10; Justin 9.1.2–9.1.6. Cf. Sealey 1993: 184; Worthington 2008b: 131–135; Müller 2020a: 14–15.

[7] Worthington 2008b: 170; Müller 2019: 46; Wirth 2020: 416.

[8] Diodorus 17.24.1; Polyaenus 5.44.4. Cf. Kholod 2018: 407–440; Rop 2019: 182–185.

The Evidence

The evidence is a problem. All the contemporary historiography bearing on Philip II and Alexander III is lost and we miss the Macedonian point of view. Only fragments are preserved by later Greek and Roman authors, who filtered them through their own cultural norms and values.

The primary historiographers of Alexander's campaign blended panhellenic motifs with stereotypes of Persian 'barbarians' that comprised all the negative qualities they held to be antithetical to their own culture: decadence, excessive luxury, unmanliness, cruelty, lack of *logos* (reason) and tyranny. The authors even retained their panhellenic colouring when they went on to record the later stages of the Macedonian war, by which point Alexander himself had already abandoned his panhellenic propaganda.[9]

Even the writers that participated in Alexander's campaign seem to have viewed Persia from a culturally prejudiced perspective, dominated by a series of pre-existing Greek images familiar from authors such as Herodotus, Xenophon, Ctesias and Dinon. For example, while Chares of Mytilene, Alexander's Master of Ceremonies (*eisangeleus*) from 330, certainly had some knowledge of Persian courtly architecture, he chose to project stereotypes at the expense of his own first-hand experience, recycling traditional Greek images of the Persian king's *tryphe* (*FGrH* / *BNJ* 125 F 2). In general, the primary Alexander historiographers showed little interest in Persian culture, except perhaps for Onesicritus. Apparently keen on Persian sepulchral culture in particular, Onesicritus mentions a reliable variant of Cyrus II's epitaph and gives us a Greek summary of the Old Persian text of Darius I's epitaph at Naqš-i Rustam: 'I was a friend to my friends, I was the first of horsemen and archers, I excelled as a hunter, I could do everything.'[10]

The secondary historiographers of Alexander's campaign, Trogus-Justin, Curtius, Plutarch and Arrian, associated the fourth-century BC Persians with the Parthians, Rome's eastern opponents in their own times. This parallelism entailed the application to the Parthians of traditional clichés about the shortcomings of 'orientals', the counter-images of western protagonists. This is particularly visible in Arrian's biased portrait of Darius as a soft, decadent weakling and an incapable

---

[9] Cf. Böhme 2009; Pownall 2020a. On the Greek stereotypes regarding the Persians: Madreiter 2012: 33–191.
[10] *FGrH* / *BNJ* 134 F 35. Cf. *Darius Naqš-i Rustam b* § 8h (Kent). Cf. Heinrichs 1987: 540; Müller 2021a: 107–108.

coward.[11] While Curtius treats Darius much more favourably, what he gives us is not a genuine appraisal but a literary image and a stylistic device. Curtius wanted to project Darius' character development as the mirror image of that of his Alexander figure, who becomes ever more depraved. Chastened by his setbacks, Curtius' Darius transforms himself from a corrupt, cowardly oriental tyrant back into his formerly mild, just self.

Often unjustly underestimated as an Alexander historiographer, Diodorus is very well-informed about Achaemenid Persia. His description of Persepolis' palace area with its citadel, terrace, adjacent royal graves, royal residences and courtiers' quarters (17.17.3–17.17.8) is reliable. He is also the only source to mention Alexander's introduction of Achaemenid ushers into court ceremonial in 330 (17.77.4). Recording the Tyrians' resistance to Alexander (332), Diodorus plausibly states that they wanted to help Darius by drawing the Macedonians into a difficult siege (17.40.3). This information meshes with the fact that at that time Tyre's ruler Azemilcus participated in the Persian Aegean counter-attack (Arrian *Anabasis* 2.15.7). Diodorus depicts Darius as an energetic, brave and deserving king (17.6.1, 7.2, 61.1) and provides a full picture of the resistance he carefully organized together with his crucial supporters (e.g. the house of Artabazus, aided by individual Athenian *strategoi* such as Chares and Ephialtes). Therefore, just as in the case of Curtius, who also provides unique information about Persia (e.g. about the royal road system and postal service), scholars debate whether Diodorus' knowledge originates in the reports of an anonymous professional Greek soldier (*misthophoros*) in Persian service.[12]

Persian evidence is particularly scarce. Since the dominant tradition of record-keeping in Persia was oral, they produced no historiography of their own. Extant contemporary Persian sources – coins, administrative documents and archaeology – cannot compensate for this lack or provide a counterweight to the Greek and Roman perspectives. Unfortunately, in contrast to the case with most of his predecessors, no royal inscriptions or archaeological monuments commissioned by Darius III are known. One of the four monumental rock-cut tombs at Persepolis has a cross-shaped façade, in imitation of Darius I's grave, but it was left incomplete and remained empty. Perhaps it was meant for him.

[11] Arrian *Anabasis* 2.10.1, 2.11.4–2.11.5, 3.14.3, 3.22.2–3.22.5. Cf. Nylander 1997: 145; Müller 2019: 104–105.
[12] For example, Curtius 5.6.13–5.6.15, 5.8.8, 7.2.36–7.2.37, 8.2.35. Cf. Baynham 1998a: 7; Lenfant 2011: 358–359.

As for coins, the silver *sigloi* and golden darics (*dareikoi*) minted by Darius III show the traditional Achaemenid iconography established by Darius I: the warrior king with his weapons, ready to protect his realm against the forces of evil.[13] After Darius III's death, Alexander carried on minting his issues for some time. This step served to stress his claim to political continuity, appease the conquered Persians and confirm that their money was still valuable.

As to archaeological evidence, the excavation report from the treasury of the Persepolis palace provides valuable information about the Macedonian treatment of what had been the ideological core of the Persian Empire.[14] It shows that the literary tradition, according to which the conflagration was a drunken act committed on impulse (Plutarch *Alexander* 38.1–38.4; Curtius 5.7.10–5.7.12; Diodorus 17.72.1–17.72.6), is a fiction. After the removal of the valuable objects, Xerxes' buildings were deliberately burnt by separate, controlled fires. The Macedonians destroyed or broke items that were too heavy or bulky to transport, such as sculptures (even those of Greek provenance such as the 'Penelope from Persepolis').

A collection of letters, lists of supplies, and tallies from a Bactrian satrapal archive (353–324) written on leather and wood in Aramaic (the official language of administration in Achaemenid Persia) gives us information about daily administrative matters. It contains information on the Bactrian satrap Bessus, who instigated Darius' assassination and who was acclaimed as Artaxerxes V. His throne name and preparations for departing from Bactra are mentioned.[15]

The Neo-Babylonian Chronicle Series, cuneiform tablets composed by Babylonian scholars, provide a database of astronomical observations and chronological references to events and to the lives and deaths of kings. They contain some information about Alexander's campaign. The Babylonian astronomical diaries record a lunar eclipse for 20 September 331 (considered a negative omen for the Persian king), a few days before the battle of Gaugamela. Other cuneiform texts mention the battle itself, Alexander's entry into Babylon, his benefactions to the temple of the main local deity

---

[13] Carradice 1987; Briant 1996: 226–227. On the ideology: Rollinger 2014: 157.
[14] Schmidt 1939: 16–17, 55, 65–82. Cf. Cahill 1985: 383; Sancisi-Weerdenburg 1993: 181–185.
[15] Naveh and Shaked 2012: 19–21, 177–80, C1 (Khalili I A 21). Cf. Shayegan 2007: 106; Briant 2009a: 148–151.

Marduk (restoration activity in the sanctuary area, donations of money for the rituals, gifts to the people) and Alexander's death in June 323: we learn that it occurred on a cloudy day in a clouded week.[16]

Events

In 334, reactivating the Royal Road once used by Xerxes along the coast of Aegean Thrace, the Macedonian army and its allies, comprising about 32,000 infantry, 5,100 cavalry and 160 ships, crossed the Hellespont (Diodorus 17.17.3–17.17.4; Arrian *Anabasis* 1.11.6). Prior to their crossing, Darius III had ordered Philip's former guest-friend, Memnon of Rhodes, to expel the Macedonian advance force from the coast of Asia Minor. However, the Macedonian control of Sestus on the European side and Abydus on the Asian side of the straits sufficed to ensure the army's safe crossing.

The Macedonians were the superior land force with the more effective strategy, drill and equipment. Their weak point was their small and inexperienced fleet, founded only in the 350s by Philip. While it was no match for the superior Persian fleet, with its long naval tradition, Persian ships nonetheless failed to prevent the Macedonian army from making the crossing, perhaps because they were preoccupied with trouble in Egypt. Darius sent his Asia Minor satraps and generals to intercept the invaders after their landing. The Persians were defeated at the battle of Granicus (334). The Macedonians conquered the rich satrapies of the Aegean coast.

Following in the footsteps of Philip, who had styled the war as a panhellenic campaign, Alexander claimed to be avenging the injuries inflicted on the Greeks by the Persians, particularly Xerxes, and to be 'liberating' the Ionians. This was nothing but a piece of propaganda. In fact, the war was about the expansion of territory, power, wealth and revenues. Thus, the tax exemption for the Ionian cities (Arrian *Anabasis* 1.18.2) was probably only temporary.

As for military strategy, in the early stage of the war, which was essentially orchestrated by Parmenion and Philotas,[17] the Macedonians avoided involvement in naval battles and tried to neutralize the Persian fleet by capturing its ports from the shore. The Persians tried to exploit Macedonian maritime weakness by launching a fierce naval counter-attack

---

[16] On the chronicles, see van der Spek 2003. According to the diary, Alexander died on the 11th of June: Depuydt 1997: 117–135.
[17] Heckel 2016: 44–59.

in the Aegean, led by Memnon and then, after his early death in 333, by his nephew Pharnabazus and his colleague Autophradates.[18] Both recaptured crucial bases and challenged the newly established Macedonian superiority in the Aegean. For example, owing to vigorous defence on the Persian part, the Macedonian conquest of the important port Halicarnassus in 334 was only partial. Alexander's alliance with and adoption by Ada of Caria, an aged member of the former Hecatomnid satrapal dynasty, did not succeed in getting him Halicarnassus, only the Carian hinterland.

At Halicarnassus too the impact of the rapprochement between Athens and Persia in the late 340s (owing to the Macedonian threat) became manifest. The Athenian *strategoi* Thrasybulus and Ephialtes fought as individuals (but in their *polis*' interest) for the Persian cause in hopes of a Macedonian defeat, these being fuelled by Demosthenes' faction in Athens. Demosthenes seems to have been in contact with Darius until just before Issus.[19] Officially, as a member of the Corinthian League, Athens was obliged to send troops and 20 triremes to support the Macedonians.

While the Macedonians concentrated on the strength of their land forces, Darius continued to organize his defence by land and sea. He gathered a large army in northern Mesopotamia and led it personally in the battle of Issus (333) in Cilicia, in an attempt to cut Alexander's lines of communication. The Persians were defeated, but Darius managed to escape. Contrary to the biased portrayal of the Alexander historiographers, this was no act of cowardice but an attempt to reorganize the defence and keep the spirit of resistance alive. Since Darius was the symbol and incarnation of Achaemenid rule, the continuation of the fight against the invaders, the motivation of the troops and the hopes of the population depended on his welfare.[20]

Darius' family, the royal treasure and the relatives of his elite were captured by the Macedonians. Alexander treated Darius' family honourably but refused to ransom the valuable hostages. Reportedly, Darius even offered the territory west of the Euphrates to Alexander (Diodorus 17.54.2; *Fragmentum Sabbaiticum, FGrH / BNJ* 151 F 1.5). However, if this claim is authentic, Alexander may have been offered merely the role of a subordinate petty king – an offer that was unacceptable to him.

---

[18] Ruzicka 1988; Briant 2010: 44–48; Heckel 2020b: 41–81.
[19] Aeschines 3.164. Other individuals were Chares and Charidemus. Cf. Landucci Gattinoni 1994: 39–40, 55, 57, 59–60; Rop 2019: 185–226; Müller 2020a: 16–18.
[20] Nylander 1997: 150–152; Heckel 2008: 80; Briant 2010: 42–52.

The defeat at Issus was a severe blow to the Persian cause but not decisive: Darius summoned levies from the eastern satrapies and the Persian fleet still dominated the Aegean. To neutralize Persian naval superiority, Alexander and his generals secured the Levantine coast before pursuing Darius. In 332, when the large Phoenician and Cyprian fleets defected from the Persians and the crucial port of Tyre was conquered, the Macedonians finally got the upper hand in the Aegean.

In 332/1 Mazaces, the Persian governor of Egypt, surrendered. Alexander took Egypt without any bloodshed, conquered the last naval bases of the Persians, and gained control of Cyrenaica (important for grain supplies) and the Libyan caravan routes (important for luxury goods from Nubia). Like the Persian kings before, Alexander played the role of the traditional pharaoh (including the acceptance of the pharaonic title 'Son of Amun'), as attested at two of the hubs for the routes through the desert, Siwah and Bahariya.[21]

In 331, after his return, Alexander entered Mesopotamia and defeated Darius at Gaugamela, but again failed to capture him. Darius sacrificed his rich capitals of Babylon, Persepolis, Susa and Pasargadae to the enemy and headed east to reorganize resistance. In 330, to mark the official end of the supposedly panhellenic campaign, the allied troops were dismissed. The deliberate conflagration of parts of the Persepolis palace built by Xerxes was probably another marker of the end of the 'panhellenic' war.

Darius fell victim not to the Macedonians but to his own officials. A circle of dissatisfied Bactrian-Sogdian potentates around Bessus, the satrap of Bactria (reputed for its manpower and cavalry), murdered him in 330.

War went on: Bessus, probably an Achaemenid himself, was acclaimed king under the throne name Artaxerxes V ('Having a kingdom of justice') that linked him with the successful reign of Artaxerxes III. While Bessus could only claim to control the eastern satrapies, he probably intended to reconquer the western parts in accordance with the Achaemenid tradition of rule. However, his responsibility for Darius' assassination proved to be a heavy burden. It cost Bessus much support amongst western Persians. The competition with Bessus transformed the ideology of Alexander's campaign: posing

---

[21] Bowden 2014c: 56–67; Müller 2019: 126–128. On the myths about Alexander and Ammon, see Ogden 2011a: 14–28, 2022a.

now as Darius' legitimate successor (Arrian *Anabasis* 3.22.1, 30.1–30.5), he claimed to be avenging him by hunting down his murderer.

From the start of the war Alexander had, out of political necessity, cooperated with willing parts of the Persian elite, adopted the Achaemenid administrative structures, made good use of the infrastructure (such as the Royal Road system), and showed respect for local customs and cults. During the pursuit of Bessus and after the latter's execution (329), in order to stress his legitimacy as Darius' successor, Alexander intensified this policy of appeasement. He adopted elements of Achaemenid court protocol (such as *proskynesis*) and representation (e.g. elements of the royal costume) and integrated Persians into his court, administration and army. However, since this new interpretation of Argead rulership, with its autocratic overtones, contradicted the traditional ideal of the Argead *primus inter pares*, parts of the Macedonian and Greek elite were offended and felt slighted. Opposition became particularly manifest by the conspiracies of Dimnus (330) and Hermolaus (327), the elimination of Clitus (328) and Callisthenes (327) and the Opis mutiny, in which Macedonian veterans protested against their replacement by Persian soldiers as recipients of booty (324).[22]

The death of Bessus failed to pacify Bactria and Sogdiana. Apparently disgruntled by the rigid Macedonian policy of conquest, the local dynasts continued resistance. Only the assassination of the focal leader Spitamenes by his own allies and Alexander's political marriage to Roxane, the daughter of a Sogdian-Bactrian leader, gave the Macedonians the upper hand.[23] But the area remained unruly.

The Indian campaign (327–325) led Alexander to the easternmost parts of the Achaemenid Empire in the Indus valley. Its regional dynasts, loosely bound to central Achaemenid power, had responded to Darius' call for help against Alexander (Diodorus 17.59.4; Arrian *Anabasis* 3.8.3, 11.5–11.6). The Hyphasis River marked the Persian Empire's easternmost limits and the end of the exhausting and challenging campaign that caused a lot of bloodshed on either side. Soon after Alexander had left India, Macedonian control faded away: the regions were difficult to rule directly.

On his return to Susa (324), in order to integrate himself and his elite into Persian family networks, Alexander married the captured daughters of Darius III and Artaxerxes III, Stateira and Parysatis, gave

---

[22] Carney 2015: 42–47, 141–154, 212–216; Roisman 2012a: 50.
[23] Ogden 2009b: 206; Heckel 2008: 87–88; Briant 2010: 55–58.

his generals Persian wives and registered the liaisons of his soldiers with Asian women (Arrian *Anabasis* 7.4.4–7.4.8; Diodorus 17.107.6).[24] Alexander spent his last months eliminating unrest in the area connecting Babylon and Susa to Ecbatana and planning an Arabian campaign. When he died in the summer of 323, his all-too-swiftly conquered empire was left susceptible to unrest.

The two daughters of Darius (and probably also Artaxerxes III's daughter, who vanishes from the records) were eliminated by Perdiccas in 323 to secure the throne rights of Roxane's unborn child with Alexander. Amastris, the niece of Darius III, made a career under the Successors as the wife of Lysimachus and regent of Heraclea Pontica. Apart from this and the career of Seleucus' wife, Apama, it is difficult to trace the lasting impact of the Persian families on Macedonian ones; the historiographers are not much interested in the matter.

During the Wars of the Successors, Achaemenid administrative structures and hierarchies in the western parts of the former Achaemenid Empire, particularly in Asia Minor, disintegrated.[25]

Participation in the conquest of Persia under Alexander became a symbol of Macedonian military glory and the prime factor of legitimization for the Successors. As for the Hellenistic legacy, for example, items of Macedonian booty are treated by epigrams of the Milan Papyrus attributed to Posidippus of Pella, a poet who worked at the Ptolemaic court in the third century. Persian gem stones are mentioned in a group of poems devoted to marvellous and precious stones (*Lithika*): former possessions of the Persians that had come to be owned by Macedonians.[26]

Trends in Scholarship

In the current scholarly debate, the traditional image of the Persian Empire as a giant with feet of clay is rejected.[27] Under Artaxerxes III, Persia had risen to a new strength. This was consolidated under Darius III, who was widely accepted and supported by the Persian elite. It was only after the third Persian defeat at Gaugamela that dissatisfaction emerged, particularly in the circles of Darius' easternmost officials.

---

[24] Arrian *Anabasis* 7.4.4–8; Justin 12.10.9. Cf. Ogden 1999: 44–45; Carney 2003b: 246–247; Heckel 2008: 137–141; Ogden 2009b: 206–207.
[25] Jacobs 2020: 465.
[26] Posidippus *ep.* 3, 4 and 5 Austin-Bastianini. Cf. Müller 2016e: 184–185.
[27] Briant 2009a: 141; Briant 2009b: 171–188; Rollinger 2014: 166–168.

However, even they may have tried to save Darius: perhaps, without understanding its proper implications, Curtius (5.9.3–5.9.9) preserves a tradition that Nabarzanes and Bessus proposed a substitute-king ritual to Darius to save the empire.[28] He was asked to hand over the rule to Bessus as a substitute king until the Macedonian danger was neutralized and he could be restored. However, Darius took the plan for treason (since the substitute-king ritual required the substitute king's death, which Bessus seemed unlikely to accept).

Contrary to the Alexander historiography's biased image of Darius as a cowardly king, scholars now characterize him as an energetic defender of his realm who threw himself into the diplomatic and military response and even initiated a military reform in which he took Macedonian weapons as his model.[29] Greek and Roman records of Persian warfare have been criticized as strongly biased, not least the reports of the uselessness of scythed chariots.[30] Contrary to the Macedonian propaganda regarding a war of 'liberation' and of 'reprisal', scholars now characterize the campaign as an expansionist war.[31]

A focal matter in recent scholarship has been Alexander's policy of consolidation and appeasement alongside the conquest.[32] In order to gain acceptance by the subjected Persians, he paid respect to their traditions, honoured the Teispid founder Cyrus II by visiting his tomb at Pasargadae (Figure 6.1), sat on the Achaemenid throne in Susa (in Greek eyes *the* Persian capital) and adopted elements of Achaemenid courtly etiquette. In this context, Alexander's attempted introduction of *proskynesis*, the ceremonial greeting-rite for a Persian king (which took various forms dependent on the status of the person performing it), is interpreted as an attempt to unify the greeting ceremonial at his multicultural court.[33] Contrary to Greek and Roman misunderstanding, the rite was not an act of worship but a ritualized way of acknowledging the king's superior political rank and status as Ahuramazda's chosen one on Earth. The Macedonian elite would have been informed about this. However, in view of the

---

[28] Nylander 1997: 152; Jamzadeh 2012: 75–76.
[29] Wirth 1993a: 33–172; Nylander 1997; Briant 2010: 42–52; Heckel 2017a; Heckel 2020: 82–97, 130–170.
[30] Manning 2020: 269–278.
[31] Worthington 2008b: 160–163; Briant 2010: 33–36; Müller 2019: 88–92; Heinrichs 2020c.
[32] Wiesehöfer 1993: 149–150; Briant 2010: 116–133; Olbrycht 2011a; Olbrycht 2016; Heckel 2020b: 265–278; Müller 2021a: 112–114.
[33] Heckel 2008: 107–108; Briant 2010: 123–126; Bowden 2013; Strootman 2014: 193–194; Pownall 2014: 64–65; Bowden 2014c: 76; Müller 2020c.

6.1 Alexander at the tomb of Cyrus the Great. Pierre-Henri de Valenciennes (1796). Art Institute, Chicago, 1983.35.

hierarchical downgrading it implied for Alexander's leading circles, this attempted unification of the greeting ceremonial met with so much disapproval that he dropped the plan.

An exception to Alexander's policy of appeasement was the burning of parts of the palace of Persepolis (330). The event is controversial in scholarship. Since the archaeological reports testify to a carefully arranged conflagration that affected only the parts of the palace identifiable (by inscriptions) as Xerxes' constructions, it is mostly interpreted as a propagandistic marker of the accomplishment of the alleged panhellenic mission of revenge.[34] The suggestion that it also had the aim of luring sympathizers away from the revolt of Agis III of Sparta is speculative, as the chronology of the revolt and synchronism with the burning is uncertain. Alternatively, the burning is thought to have addressed the Persians, and to have been an attempt to court their elite by signalling a return to the Teispid tradition of Cyrus II; or an attempt to intimidate Darius and his followers by destroying a visible symbol of Achaemenid rule; or an attempt to rid any rival of the opportunity of enthroning himself in Persepolis.[35]

Recent studies point out that Alexander adopted Achaemenid Persia's administrative structure, left its satrapal system almost untouched and was able to conquer the large empire in such a short space of time precisely because he appropriated the existing system of

---

[34] Bosworth 1988a: 93; Wirth 1993a: 226; Wiesehöfer 1993: 150; Heckel 2008: 84; Anson 2013: 7, 134, 153–157; Bowden 2014c: 73–74.
[35] Return to the Teispids: Wiesehöfer 1993: 150; Nawotka 2003: 150; Briant 2010: 110–111. Neutralizing rivals: Balcer 1978: 131–132.

administration that facilitated the exercise of power. In addition, its roads and supply systems supported the necessary troop movements.[36]

A formerly controversial matter, Alexander's march through the Gedrosian desert on his return from India (325), is now predominantly interpreted as a strategic necessity. Alexander took the route along the coastline of the desert in order to supply and protect the Indus fleet (Arrian *Anabasis* 6.21.3, 23.1). The bulk of the infantry and the invalids took the less rigorous route through Arachosia. Though precautions were taken, the march through the desert was gruelling, in particular because the neighbouring satraps ignored the demands for provisions. However, images of a horrible disaster seem to be exaggerated: it was probably not the army but the camp followers who suffered most. Casualties were mainly due to the attacks of the hostile local population.[37]

In sum, during the last decades, many traditional ideas about Alexander and Persia have been reassessed; the (re)search goes on. Artificial images of Alexander as the adventurer, the tyrant and butcher, the destroyer of Persia, the victim of 'eastern vices', the lover of Persian culture and suchlike, which formerly predominated, have now been rejected. Nowadays, so far as his attitude to Persia is concerned, Alexander is mainly seen as a military strategist and a political pragmatist.

Guide to Further Reading

On the ancient history of the Persian Empire before Alexander and during the Macedonian conquest, Briant 1996 and Kuhrt 2007 remain unreplaceable 'must reads', but the work of first resort is now Brosius 2021. As for Achaemenid administration before Alexander and during the Macedonian conquest and its traces in the Alexander historiographers, see Jacobs et al. 2017. On Alexander and Cyrus II, particularly the visit to Cyrus' tomb at Pasargadae and Alexander's propagandistic use of the memory of Cyrus, see Heinrichs 2020d. On the Achaemenid capitals, Pasargadae, Susa, Persepolis etc., from an archaeological point of view, see Jacobs 2021. On Alexander and the Persian conquest in the epigrams of the Milan Papyrus, ascribed to Posidippus, the works of first resort are now Barbantani 2016: 5–9, 15–17, 2017: 55–57, 90–101;

---

[36] Jacobs 1994; Briant 2010: 69–95; Jacobs 2020; Brosius 2021: 217–219.
[37] Engels 1978: 110–118; Heckel 2008: 131–134.

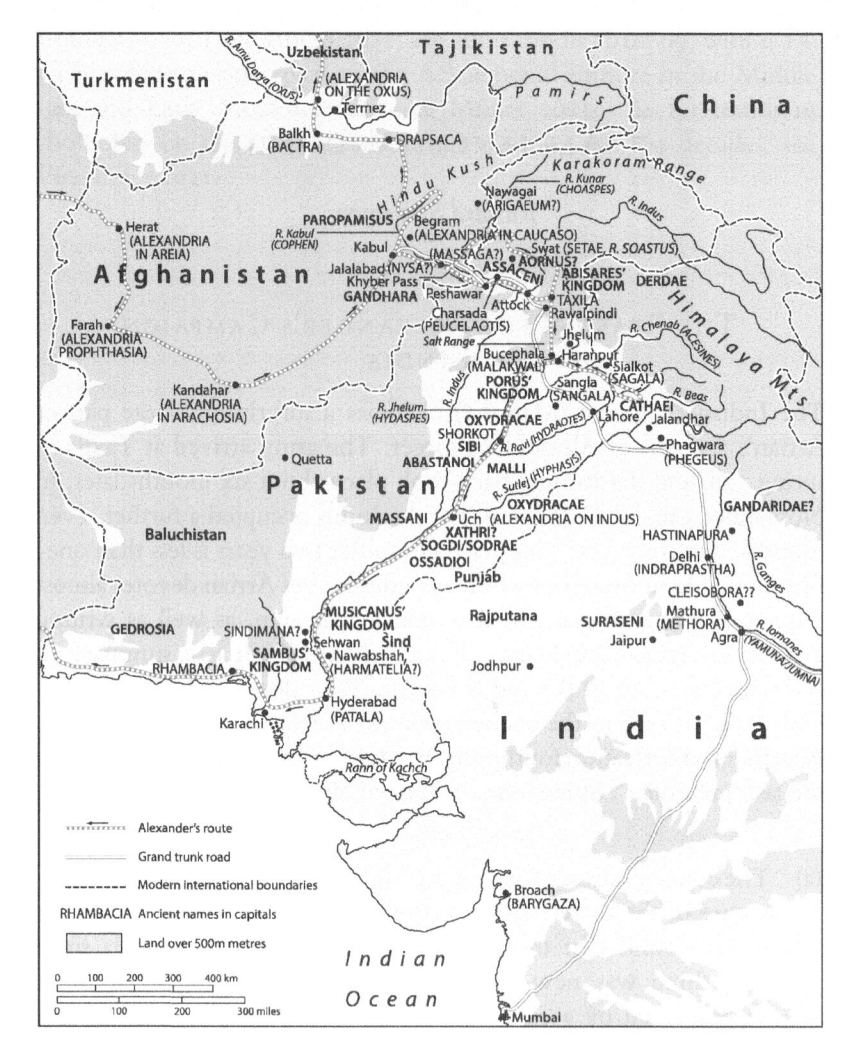

MAP 7.1 Alexander in India: places of interest. Reproduced from Stoneman 2019: 43, fig. 2.1, with kind permission of Princeton University Press.

story of Alexander's scientific patronage is a myth and that there is very little in Aristotle's works about India other than his information on the elephant[3] (Theophrastus has a little more).

(b) If Alexander did not enter India with a scientific mission, did he have a clear strategic aim? Punjab and Sind had been part of the

---

[3] Romm 1989; Bigwood 1993; Stoneman 2019: 41–42.

Achaemenid empire at its greatest extent, under Darius I, though in his successor Xerxes' time there is no evidence for Achaemenid rule beyond Bactria.[4] Darius' Foundation Charter from Susa states that his empire included Sattagydia (Upper Indus), Gandhara and Sind,[5] and Herodotus (3.89–3.95) specifies that tribute was paid to Persia from India. So Alexander may have believed that his conquest of the Achaemenid empire was not complete until he had secured the Indus region. But that would not explain his desire to march to eastern India.

(c) A third reason for the expedition – and for the sources' fascination with it – may lie in Alexander's famous *pothos*, his desire to go ever further. The idea is expressed several times by Arrian. Aristotle had suggested (*Meteorology* 1.13.15) that once one crossed the Hindu Kush the River of Ocean would be in sight. The end of the world would be in his grasp, and he could begin to style himself not just 'King of Asia' but 'King of the World'. In the speech that Arrian attributes to Alexander before the crossing of the Hyphasis, the king sets out a plan to circumnavigate and subdue the whole world (*Anabasis* 5.26.1–5.26.2).[6] If Alexander did not enter India with the scheme of becoming king of the world, it may have grown on him as he continued eastward.

The Course of the Campaign

The course of events in the campaign has been fully summarized by Bosworth (1988a: 104–139, cf. 1996b), and by the present author (Stoneman 2019: 42–79). Rather than repeat that narrative here, I draw attention to the main difficulty of constructing the narrative, which is, as usual, the problem of the sources.[7] In many cases these are contradictory or self-contradictory, because of the remoteness of the region. Problems begin with Alexander's descent into the plain of the Indus.[8] Hephaestion led the main army down the Kabul (Cophen) river and through the Khyber Pass.[9] Alexander, however, led the remainder of the troops northward along the River Kunar (Choaspes) into Bajaur and Swat. After several brutal campaigns the army reached a city named Nysa. Its ruler, Acuphis, approached him and persuaded him that their

---

[4] Badian 1998. [5] The inscription is D(arius) S(usa) e in the Kent 1950 series.
[6] Cf. Curtius 9.2.28, 'the limits of the inhabited world'. [7] Stoneman 2019: 64.
[8] Arrian *Anabasis* 4.22.8: 'the end of spring'. Bosworth 1988a: 119–125.
[9] Arrian *Anabasis* 4.22.7.

city was sacred because of the birth of a god there, whom the Macedonians, impressed by the coincidence of names, immediately identified as Dionysus. The troops held a Bacchic revel, perhaps joining in a local wine-festival and cult.[10] The city benefited and was granted its freedom under an aristocratic government. The location is unidentifiable but it may be Jalalabad.[11]

At the Rock of Aornus, Alexander was again able to deploy mythology, as well as engineering skills, to assist his conquest of the apparently inaccessible stronghold.[12] (The site was identified nearly a century ago by Sir Aurel Stein as Pir-Sar, in a bend of the Indus 5,000 feet above the river, but the identification has been challenged in favour of Mt Ilam by Giuseppe Tucci: debate will continue.) From here, Alexander began to return, probably down the Choaspes and via the city of Puśkalavati (Peuceolotis, modern Charsadda), to the main road into India. But Arrian contradicts himself about the capture of Peuceolotis, which he says (at 4.2.8) was subdued by Hephaestion, while (at 4.28.6) he says that Alexander himself received its surrender on his way to Aornus.[13]

The crossing of the Indus also involves a conflict in the sources. Curtius (8.10.3) writes simply of transportable boats. Arrian (*Anabasis* 5.7.1–8.2) notes that neither of his main sources states exactly how Alexander crossed the Indus, but surmises that a bridge of boats was used, as was traditional in the region.[14]

Indian states at this period of the 'second urbanization' were divided into oligarchies, *gana-sanghas*, and monarchies, *mahājanapadas*, the former more prevalent in the more Brahmanical north-west (while Buddhism was gaining sway in the Middle Ganges region).[15] The next two states Alexander encountered were monarchies, Taxila and the kingdom of Porus. The 'Taxiles' that presided over the former was also known as Omphis (*Ambhi), whilst 'Porus' is a dynastic name: the Puru tribe had been settled in the region since the middle of the second

---

[10] Carter 1992 and 2015: 355–376.
[11] Curtius 8.10.11–8.10.18 places Nysa high in the mountains in a wooded region, west of the Choaspes, and describes Alexander's arrival there before his conquest of Massaga. Arrian, however, locates Nysa 'between the Cophen and the Indus', therefore perhaps in the region of Peshawar. For further references see Stoneman 2004: 78–79.
[12] Arrian *Anabasis* 4.28.1.
[13] Bosworth 1988a: 125 n. 307 thinks that there must be two cities with the same name; but in his *Indica* (1.8) Arrian makes clear that they are the same. It looks as if Arrian has imperfectly combined the narratives in two different sources.
[14] So Rollinger 2013: 83; further, Stoneman 2019: 48–52.   [15] Stoneman 2019: 45–48.

millennium.[16] Alexander received a warm welcome at Taxila and stayed there for three months.

Taxila, close to modern Rawalpindi, was an ancient settlement at a position where three trade routes crossed. It may have had a notably Achaemenid character still when Alexander arrived: the absence of burials may imply exposure of the dead in the Zoroastrian style. It was also famous as a university centre (especially in Buddhist sources), and the future king Candragupta was a student here. Alexander was intrigued by the 'philosophers' of Taxila (see below). The description of the city in Philostratus' *Life of Apollonius of Tyana* may be largely fiction, though there are some intriguing correspondences to the archaeological remains.[17]

THE BATTLE ON THE HYDASPES

While Alexander was at Taxila a mission came from Abisares, offering token submission (Arrian *Anabasis* 5.8.3; but 5.20.5 puts his surrender after the defeat of Porus). Porus, the neighbouring king, whose lands lay between the Hydaspes (Jhelum) and Acesines (Chenab), was more recalcitrant. In May, Alexander advanced to meet Porus in the last major battle of his campaign, that on the River Hydaspes. Arrian's account (*Anabasis* 5.9–5.17) is fuller than any other and looks reliable. The conditions taxed Alexander's strategic genius. The armies met in June, when the monsoon rains had already begun (Strabo C691–C692), and it was the first time Alexander's army had faced elephants in battle. Alexander concentrated on confusing the enemy. Drawn up on the west bank of the Hydaspes, he lit fires at different points to give the impression of several camps, while he brought a large body of troops across the river some seventeen miles upstream, under cover of darkness. Once these troops had attacked, Craterus brought the main army across opposite the Indian troops. Porus' chariots proved useless in the muddy terrain, and conditions were made worse by a violent thunderstorm. Once the chariots were disposed of, the Indians were caught in a pincer movement, and Porus beat a retreat. Alexander presently restored Porus to power in exchange for promises of loyalty, and even extended his rule (5.20.4).

Alexander now set off in pursuit of another hyparch, also called Porus, who, according to Diodorus (17.9.11), retreated to the land of

---
[16] Habib and Jha 2004: 8.
[17] Dani 1986; Bäbler and Nesselrath 2016; Stoneman 2019: 463–469.

the Gandaridae. These lived on the Middle Ganges and Diodorus is probably thinking of Gandhara, in which case Porus may have withdrawn to the Mathura region.[18] Arrian compounds the topographical confusion by stating that Alexander's pursuit brought him as far as the Hydraotes (Ravi), from whence he continued his advance against the Cathaei of Sangala. Whichever this was of the two places called Sangala, neither is to be reached by a traveller crossing the Ravi. Presumably Arrian means the Acesines (Chenab), which is where the Cathaei are placed by Onesicritus. Arrian has misunderstood his source, or misread his map.[19]

The engagement at Sangala concluded in a massacre, and several neighbouring peoples submitted. Arrian places the advance to the Hyphasis immediately after the destruction of Sangala, but Strabo and Diodorus have him reach the kingdom of Sopeithes (*S(a)ubhuti?) next, in the region of the Salt Range.[20] But by Arrian's narrative the Salt Range should now be behind Alexander. The confusion is probably insoluble.[21]

The Retreat and the Voyage down the Indus

The River Hyphasis was to be the turning point of the expedition. A spirit of mutiny began to infiltrate the troops. 'There had been many losses among the soldiers, and no relief from fighting was in sight. The hooves of the horses had been worn thin by steady marching. The arms and armour were wearing out, and Greek clothing was quite gone.'[22] In addition to this, the monsoon had brought heavy rain and thunderstorms for the past seventy days.

Alexander himself was excited by the prospect of taking on the army of the Ganges peoples.[23] Some Indian historians, however, have seen the great power of the Prasii, the easterners of Magadha, as the main reason for Alexander's retreat, deriving support from Diodorus' comment that Alexander did not campaign against the Gandaridae because of the number of their elephants.[24]

Arrian gives Alexander a great set-piece speech to the brigade commanders (*Anabasis* 5.25.3–5.26.8) in which he attempts to revive

---

[18] Stoneman 2019: 64.   [19] Stoneman 2019: 65.
[20] Strabo C699–C700, Diodorus 17.91.4, Stoneman 2019: 66. Bosworth 1988a omits Sopeithes from his narrative altogether.
[21] Brunt 1976–1983, app. 17.20.   [22] Diodorus 17.94.1, cf. Arrian *Anabasis* 5.25.2.
[23] *Anabasis* 5.25.1.   [24] Diodorus 18.6.1; Majumdar 1960: 52.

the flagging spirits of his men.[25] As Curtius expresses it, '[H]e and his soldiers saw things differently: while his thought encompassed worldwide empire and his programme was still in its initial stages, the men were exhausted by the hardships of the campaign and wished only to enjoy what profits from it lay closest to hand, now that the danger was finally past.'[26] Alexander began by insisting that it was not far from here to the River Ganges. Craterus in a letter to his mother even told her that they had reached it.[27] But probably none of them knew quite how long the Ganges was.

After the Ganges, Alexander announced, they would reach the eastern sea, so the fleet would sail thence round Libya to The Pillars of Hercules and bring all of Europe and the west under Macedonian control.

The men and, more importantly, the officers were unmoved. Coenus responded to Alexander's speech point by point.[28] Alexander attempted to change their minds, but after three days, when the sacrifices offered prior to crossing the Hyphasis turned out unfavourable, he proclaimed to the army that they would be turning back. He erected twelve altars on the west bank of Hyphasis 'as thank-offerings to the gods who had brought him so far as a conqueror, and as memorials of his own exertions'.[29] These altars, which few from the west can ever have seen in subsequent centuries, became a fixed datum of Asian geography for two millennia: the *Tabula Peutingeriana* (XI 3A; but cf. XI 5 B) shows them to the east of the Caspian Sea, north of the Caucasus/Himalayas. The altars are described in different ways in the other ancient sources: Diodorus (17.95), Plutarch (*Alexander* 62), Justin (12.10.6) and Strabo (C171). Philostratus states that his hero Apollonius visited them and saw that they were dedicated to Ammon, Heracles, Athena Pronoia, Zeus, the Cabiri of Samothrace, the Indus, Helios and Apollo. This strange collection – which does not add up to twelve – is a little difficult to explain, though the inclusion of the rare cult of Athena Pronoia may

---

[25] *Anabasis* 5.25.3–5.26.8.
[26] Curtius 9.2.11. Cf. Diodorus 17.94, who refers to a 'carefully prepared speech', which cut no ice with the troops.
[27] FGrH / BNJ 153 F2 = Strabo C702. Bosworth 1996b: 186–200, is puzzled by Arrian's 'strange silence' about the Ganges, except in 5.25.1; but why should he say more? He apparently knew of the Nanda country, but while the Vulgate calls this a kingdom (which it was), for Arrian it is an oligarchy (194, 198). But there was more than one people beyond the Hyphasis, and the two traditions may be making different selections.
[28] Arrian *Anabasis* 5.27.1–5.27.9.
[29] Arrian *Anabasis* 5.29.1. Curtius 9.3.19 also has twelve altars. Pliny *Natural History* 6.62 implausibly places the altars on the east bank. See Brunt 1976–83, app. 16.5.

echo the importance of Pronoia as a goddess in the *Alexander Romance*, with which Philostratus seems to have been familiar.

Alexander now embarked on the Hydaspes on the boats that were waiting there from the previous crossing, while Craterus led a division down the right bank and Hephaestion advanced down the left bank to the kingdom of Sopeithes. Alexander had once believed that the Indus was the source of the Nile, since there were crocodiles and lotuses in both. He even wrote to his mother about it but cancelled that part of the letter when the local Indians gave him more accurate information about the course of the rivers in the Punjab; by this time he knew that he could expect to sail, not into the Nile, but into the encircling Ocean.[30]

Nearchus was admiral of the fleet, while Onesicritus was the skipper (κυβερνήτης) of Alexander's ship.[31] Though many of the 2,000 ships in the fleet were built for the purpose, the army must have commandeered a good many local vessels as well.

The rain had finally ceased by this time. Aristobulus' astronomical indications[32] mean that the voyage lasted from approximately November 326 to July 325 BC. Strabo calls this ten months, but it is somewhat less than that even by inclusive reckoning. Plutarch (*Alexander* 66.1) says it took seven months.[33]

It took five days to reach the junction of the Hydaspes and the Acesines. Diodorus (17.96.1–17.96.2) places a visit to the Sibi at this point;[34] Alexander got a good reception and gained the impression that these people were descendants of the army of Heracles that had attempted to besiege Aornus. But the next people, the Agalasseis, had drawn up 40,000 infantry and 3,000 cavalry against them. Alexander massacred most of them, enslaved the remainder, and pursued a rearguard into a large city which he set on fire, burning most of the occupants alive.

This hostile reception from the Agalasseis (who, like the Sibi, are not mentioned by Arrian), and the savagery it inspired in Alexander, begins the descent of what should have been a steady voyage home into a reign of terror. The reason for this is hard to determine: the need to raid the countryside for food must be relevant, and they had to go further from the river as the countryside along the Indus became more arid and mountainous.[35] But this hardly explains the ferocity. Brian Bosworth, in a chapter entitled 'The Justification of Terror',[36] pointed

---

[30] Arrian *Anabasis* 6.1.4–6.1.6. [31] Arrian *Anabasis* 6.2.3. [32] Strabo C687.
[33] See Hamilton 1969 *ad loc*. [34] The Śiva of Śivapura, near Shorkot (Patañjali 4.2.2).
[35] Engels 1978: 107–108. [36] Bosworth 1996b: 133–165.

out that Alexander went hundreds of miles out of his way to attack the Malli (see below). He concludes that their crime was not to have greeted him with signs of 'submission'. The policy of terror is perhaps a sign of increasing megalomania in the king, and increasing frustration and desperation among the troops. By this time, there was no sense in which this was a voyage of discovery or research. However, Onesicritus wrote interestingly about it, and Nearchus' account of the voyage through the Arabian Sea that followed the Indus voyage (= Arrian *Indica* 18–43) is invaluable.

The next target was the Malli, who, according to Diodorus, were waiting with a huge army of 80,000 infantry, 10,000 cavalry and 7,000 chariots. Alexander sent Nearchus ahead to the borders of their territory to prevent their neighbours coming to assist them, while he himself led the army eastwards through the desert. In a day and a night the army covered 500 stades, or an astonishing 56 miles, to reach a city where the Malli had taken refuge. The slaughter here was followed by a further night's march to cross the Hydraotes, and reach the Malli town.[37] Actually the total distance as the crow flies from the junction of the two rivers to the Ravi is about 60 miles, so Arrian may have included both nights' marches in the distance. In a brutal siege, the king himself scaled the walls with a ladder and found himself surrounded by angry defenders. He was left alone with a few companions in the midst of the enemy. He received a dangerous wound in the chest, from which, according to Ptolemy, both blood and breath spurted out. Peucestas protected him until he could be got away. Clitarchus attributed this feat to Ptolemy, but Ptolemy himself denied it.[38] The wound sounds like a punctured lung if Ptolemy's report is to be credited: it was without doubt severe and dangerous, and Alexander lay in a critical condition for many days, a condition which perhaps permanently weakened his constitution and contributed to his early death.

Both Diodorus (17.98.1) and Curtius (9.4.26–9.4.33) placed this crisis among a different people, the Oxydracae (Kśudrakas): Mālavas and Kśudrakas are mentioned in the same breath in the *Mahābhārata,* and seem to have been closely associated.[39] The Kśudrakas' 'nomarchs' diplomatically announced that their freedom dated back to the arrival of Dionysus in India, but that 'since the story prevailed that Alexander

---

[37] Arrian *Anabasis* 6.8.4. Sircar 1945: 33 indicates that the Mālavas later relocated from their fourth-century home on the Ravi to Malwa in Central India, a region centred on Indore.
[38] Arrian *Anabasis* 6.11.8; at 11.2 Arrian complains of the contradictions of the sources.
[39] The Kśudrakas had supplied troops to Cyrus: Strabo C687 ('Hydracae'), Prakash 1964: 145; so Alexander could still claim to be reclaiming Achaemenid territory.

too was born to a god, they would accept a satrap whom Alexander might appoint'.⁴⁰

During Alexander's convalescence many new ships were constructed. He was now able to sail on to the confluence with the Indus, where he was rejoined by Perdiccas and the land army. Here he built an Alexandria (probably Uch), which may be the city referred to as 'Alexandria of the Yonas [Greeks]' in the *Mahāvaṁsa*. Peithon was appointed satrap of the region from here to the sea.⁴¹

The next stage of the voyage passed smoothly and quickly, and by the time it reached the kingdom of Musicanus the king had only just learned that it was coming.⁴² Having no time to prepare an army, he received Alexander with gifts and submission, but later revolted in conjunction with the Brahmanes (see below, p. 123); he was crushed by Peithon, his cities razed and he himself was hanged. Despite the obvious hostility between the invaders and the people of Musicanus, Onesicritus wrote an admiring account of their society, which is one of the earliest documents of the utopian idealization of India.

The next ruler, called Oxicanus by Arrian and Porticanus by Diodorus, was ordered to surrender. Alexander took away his elephants, and the neighbouring cities also surrendered. Next came Sindimana, city of Sambus, the self-appointed satrap of the hill men. Arrian implies a peaceable surrender, but Diodorus says that he destroyed their city and killed 80,000 of the inhabitants.

The next target was the city of a people called the Brahmanes, named Harmatelia. The Brahmanes had been the movers behind the revolts of Sambus (Diodorus) and Musicanus (Arrian). Arrian tantalizingly writes that he will explain 'the wisdom of these men, if such it is, in my Indian treatise'. There is no such discussion in the *Indica*, raising the suspicion that the work meant may be the part of the treatise *On the Life of the Brahmans* that is attributed by its author Palladius to Arrian.⁴³ The puzzling name of the people is preserved in the older name of the ancient city of Harmatelia, which was Brahmanabad but is now the ruined site of Mansura, north-east of Hyderabad. Arrian also refers to a city of the Brahmanes much further north, in the region of the Malli town (*Anabasis* 6.7.4), but this looks like another confusion in his geography.

---

⁴⁰ Arrian *Anabasis* 6.14.2.   ⁴¹ Arrian *Anabasis* 6.15.4.
⁴² The name may reflect either the Mūshikas, on the west coast of South India (Lassen) or the Moghasis (Nilakanta Sastri 1957: 121).
⁴³ Stoneman 2012: xxvi, 2008: 98 and 2022b.

By the time the fleet reached Patala (Hyderabad) the people had fled the city. Alexander persuaded the fugitives to return, and they did so without molestation. Hephaestion fortified the city, and dockyards were constructed for the ocean voyage back to Persia. So Alexander left India, in high summer 325.

The ready submission of so many of these peoples may be explained not only by the ferocity meted out to those who resisted, but also to the sense they must have had that Alexander would not be staying long. A lightning visit to install a garrison was not going to be a long-term problem for the natives; and so it proved. Within months of Alexander's departure all the conquered peoples had revolted and regained their freedom. Jawaharlal Nehru dismissed Alexander's expedition as 'a minor and unsuccessful raid across the border';[44] Brian Bosworth concluded that the reason for the impermanence of Alexander's conquest was that he 'rode roughshod over the deepest sensitivities of his new subjects'.[45] A profounder reason is Indian self-sufficiency. What did Alexander have to offer? Nothing that India wanted.

THE NAKED PHILOSOPHERS

Alexander's stay in Taxila was the occasion for a memorable encounter which proved to be the most resonant episode of all the legends associated with him. On arrival in Taxila, Alexander was intrigued by a group of naked ascetics he observed in a grove outside the city, practising various yoga postures, and sent Onesicritus to find out something about them.[46] What is reported by Arrian and Strabo of what Onesicritus learned from the 'leader' of the philosophers, Dandamis (Arrian) or Mandanis (Strabo), consists mainly of commitment to vegetarianism, and the teaching that one should eliminate pleasure and pain from the soul. They are also described as experts in natural phenomena, and are said (all) to approve of suicide by fire in case of illness.

The descriptions in Arrian and Strabo offer a vivid portrait of a recognizable type of Indian *sādhu*, intent on spiritual enlightenment by ascetic means. Vegetarianism is characteristic of all renouncers, whether Hindu or Buddhist, though living on fruit alone is a step further. The *Sāmaññaphala Sutta* offers the reason: '[the true ascetic]

---

[44] Nehru 2004: 115.   [45] Bosworth 1996b: 97.
[46] Strabo C715–C716 = Onesicritus *FGrH / BNJ* 134 F17. Cf. Arrian *Anabasis* 7.2.2–7.2.4.

abstains from damaging seed and plant life'.[47] The vegetarianism of the naked philosophers is a fundamental feature of all later Greek descriptions, and is adduced by several later writers including Plutarch and Porphyry.[48]

In Arrian, Dandamis is regarded as the master of the philosophers, while the others are his disciples. Dandamis responds to Alexander with haughty arrogance (as he does later in the *Alexander Romance*), while Calanus (who rebuffed Onesicritus) was won over by the king.

The naked philosophers are all renunciants, but they need not be regarded as a 'school'.[49] Each of them probably thought the other fourteen were on the wrong path. However, we are told that, according to Megasthenes, 'the sophists themselves spoke opprobriously of Calanus, because, having left the happiness among them, he went to serve another master than God'.[50] Nearchus[51] says that Calanus is one of the seers, but Onesicritus places him in a different group from the advisers-and-seers. There is an echo of a controversy here: according to *Sāmaññaphala Sutta* 56,[52] renouncers are supposed to abstain from prophecy and fortune-telling, which are 'a wrong means of livelihood'. Thus Calanus looks like an example of a 'bad' renouncer.

There seems no doubt that Calanus changed his way of life when he met Alexander; but at the first encounter he presents as a fairly typical Indian *sādhu*, using mortification as a way to enlightenment. Such ascetics can be from any caste or sect. But Calanus' later suicide by fire may help to define him. There is only one sect in ancient India that systematically favours suicide by fire as an ascetic practice, and that is the Ajīvikas.

What we know of the Ajīvikas we mainly know from hostile sources, both Buddhist and Jain.[53] The Jain accounts list forty-eight different forms of death that Ajīvikas might seek. Death by self-torture was admired, since pain was pursued for its own sake. This sits rather oddly with the pursuit of luxury and (sexual) self-indulgence of which the Jains also accused the Ajīvikas, but this may indicate a devotion to Tantrik practices. Voluntary death is also acceptable for those who are very old, or incurably sick.

---

[47] *Sāmaññaphala Sutta* I. 46: Bodhi 1989: 31.   [48] Stoneman 1994b.
[49] Though they may constitute a 'society': Hausner 2007: 52.
[50] Arrian *Anabasis* 7.2.9 (= Megasthenes; cf. Megasthenes *FGrH / BNJ* 715 F 34b).
[51] Strabo C717–C718 = Nearchus *FGrH / BNJ* 133 F 23.
[52] Bodhi 1989: 35. They should not predict eclipses either: *ibid*. 37. On the diversity of the philosophical schools, see Singh 2009: 301–302.
[53] The standard work remains Basham 1951.

The criticisms levelled at Calanus by the other 'philosophers' resemble those directed at the Ajīvikas by the Jains, and his final suicide by fire, though allowable because of his illness, is also one of the methods that were habitual with Ajīvikas. If he abandoned his austerities to join the court of Alexander, he returned to them in his last act.

The other major source on the naked philosophers, the *Alexander Romance* (3.5–3.6) supplements Onesicritus' account. The date of composition of this much-rewritten work is a controversial question, but the essentials of this passage surely go back to a first-hand account of the visit to the philosophers, perhaps that of Onesicritus himself.[54] Here the naked philosophers are explicitly identified with 'the Brahmans or Oxydorkai'. The Oxydracae and the Brahmans are the objects of two campaigns by Alexander in Sind, and neither of them has anything to do with the naked philosophers of Taxila. The confusion seems to be due to Plutarch, who calls the rebellious Brahmans of Harmatelia 'gymnosophists'. Suspicion has arisen that Onesicritus, as a pupil of Diogenes, eagerly attributed Cynic ideas to the men he encountered under the trees of Taxila.[55]

In the *Alexander Romance* the philosophers invite Alexander to come and learn about their way of life. But the series of questions Alexander asks the philosophers appears in a different form on a papyrus dating from about 100 BCE.[56] It was known to Plutarch who incorporated it in his *Life* of Alexander. This version takes the form of a *Halsrätsel*, a riddle on the answer to which one's life depends. The papyrus begins in mid-sentence: '[whoever] I command to judge, he shall be your moderator; if I decide that he has judged well, he alone shall be let off alive'. At the end of the excerpt, Alexander asks the tenth philosopher to state which had given the worst answer; but 'the Indian did not want anyone to perish as a result of his answer, so he replied that each had answered worse than the other'. Alexander then says he will put them all to death, but the philosopher points out the logical fallacy and Alexander lets them all off.

The head-wager is not alien to Indian tradition. Indian sages who entered into debate with Tripitaka, the fictional version of the monk Xuan Zang in the famous Chinese novel, *Journey to the West*, showed themselves willing to forfeit their heads if they lost the argument.

---

[54] Stoneman 1994b, 1995.
[55] I looked favourably on this view in Stoneman 1995, but have since come to believe that he made an honest attempt to report Indian material. See further Stoneman 2008: 94–95. Woodcock 1966: 33 is a clear statement of the Cynic interpretation.
[56] Berlin Papyrus (*P. Berol.*) 13044; translation in Stoneman 2012: 77–78.

The get-out clause in this story is that Tripitaka, as a Buddhist, will not take life, and thus the sages do not die.[57]

The questions and answers themselves contain genuine information about the philosophers' way of life, while the riddles that follow can be paralleled in Indian sources.[58] The dialogue has sometimes been thought to be a thoroughly Greek confection, and Tarn was of the opinion that it influenced the Pali *Questions of King Milinda* (*Milindapañha*), a Greek version of which then further influenced the *Letter of Aristeas*.[59] In 1995 and 2008 (94–97) I assembled a good many examples to suggest that the dialogue takes a largely Indian form.

Dandamis now delivers a short sermon putting forward the same ascetic ideals as the other sources. The philosophers then ask Alexander for immortality, to which Alexander replies that that is not his to give. Immortality does not seem to be a typically Indian aspiration, but at *Buddhacarita* VII.18 the ascetics tell Prince Gautama that they are seeking Paradise. The mention of immortality enables the philosophers to point out the impermanence of Alexander's worldly conquests.[60] Alexander's response to Dandamis' quietism is an assertion that his own life of action and violence is also ordained by Providence. This contrast of temperaments is the basis for the later works, the *Correspondence of Alexander and Dindimus* and Palladius' *Life of the Brahmans*.[61]

Calanus remained with Alexander until his death. Also on the expedition was a young man, Pyrrho of Elis, who studied with Anaxarchus and 'travelled everywhere' with him (Diogenes Laertius 9. 61). He 'foregathered with the Indian Gymnosophists and with the Magi. This led him to adopt a most noble philosophy ... of agnosticism and suspension of judgment'.[62] He asserted 'about each single thing that it no more is than is not, or it both is and it is not, or it neither is nor is not'.[63]

This teaching resembles a crucial part of Buddhist philosophy, the tetralemma.[64] Buddha used the recognition that things are beyond the firm judgement of humans (Pyrrho calls them *anepikrita*; Buddha's term is *avyākrta*, 'insoluble or inexpressible')[65] to reject all forms of dogmatism.[66] The form of argument occurs close to the time of the Buddha, for

---

[57] Waley 1952: 54–55 and n. 271.
[58] Cf. *Śatapatha Brāhmaṇa* 13.5.2.17, 'What was the first conception? The sky'; also *Bṛhadāraṇyaka Upaniṣad* 1.1.2.
[59] See Stoneman 1995: 111 with further details. Kubica 2016: 146 also emphasizes the Indian quality of the *Questions of King Milinda*.
[60] The topos of the sage reproving the king appears in *Bṛhadāraṇyaka Upaniṣad* 4.1.
[61] Translations and earlier scholarship in Stoneman 2012. [62] Diogenes Laertius 9.61.
[63] Eusebius *Praeparatio evangelica* 14.18.1–14.18.5, quoting Timon. [64] Flintoff 1980.
[65] Flintoff 1980: 91. [66] Cf. Strabo C712–C713, Kuzminski 2008: 46–47.

example in *Sāmaññaphala Sutta* I. 31:⁶⁷ 'I do not say "it is this way", nor "it is that way", nor "it is otherwise." I do not say "it is not so", nor do I say "it is not not so".' It was soon well known: at *The Questions of King Milinda* I. 206 Nāgasena rejects the tetralemma as pointless. In the hands of the Greek Sceptics this developed into the radical suspension of judgement outlined by Sextus Empiricus.⁶⁸ If Pyrrho's ideas of metaphysical instability were acquired from conversation with Calanus (not himself a Buddhist), Alexander's legacy to philosophy was a long one.

MEGASTHENES' *INDICA*

Nehru's view that Alexander's campaign was no more than a temporary local skirmish ignored the longer-term effect of the campaign, namely that many of the veterans stayed on in the region and formed the nucleus of a Greek community that persisted for two centuries. Among these was Megasthenes (*c.* 350–290 BCE), the author of the most extensive description of India written by a Greek author. He had presumably travelled to India with Alexander's army, and was associated with Sibyrtius, the satrap of Arachosia and Gedrosia. His importance is due to the fact that, according to his own testimony, he travelled to India as ambassador for King Seleucus, residing at Pataliputra, the capital of the Maurya kingdom, perhaps for a long time. His account became a classic.

The rule of Taxiles and Porus, whom Alexander had re-established in their kingdoms in the north-west, collapsed soon after Alexander's departure when both were successively murdered by Eudamus, the military commander. In the meantime the Nanda kingdom of Magadha had been overthrown by Candragupta, who is probably the Meroes (i.e. Maurya) who had acted as a go-between for Alexander and Porus after the Hydaspes battle;⁶⁹ at that time Candragupta was, according to Indian sources, a student in Taxila. Candragupta was able to extend his power into the region where Taxiles and Porus had ruled and thus to establish the Maurya empire.⁷⁰

Seleucus, as Alexander's successor, continued to claim these regions and soon brought an army to the Indus and confronted Candragupta. The meeting ended with a treaty by which Seleucus

---

⁶⁷ Bodhi 1989: 24.
⁶⁸ See Garfield 1990 for a detailed exploration of eastern and western 'scepticism'.
⁶⁹ Arrian *Anabasis* 5.18.7–5.19.1.
⁷⁰ On the rise of Candragupta, Stoneman 2019: 156–163 and Mookerji 1966; the best study is Jansari 2023.

ceded territory to Candragupta, perhaps as far west as Arachosia, and in exchange received five hundred elephants. This 'Treaty of the Indus' also included an agreement on *epigamia*, probably not a presentation of one ruler's daughter to the other as has often been supposed, but an enablement of marriage between Greeks settled in the region, who were outside the Indian caste system, and local women. The treaty thus cemented the continuance of Greek settlement in north-west India, but also ensured the eventual assimilation of Greeks to Indians, in the manner of Anglo-Indians after 1947. It is a plausible hypothesis that Megasthenes was one of the negotiators of this treaty.[71]

Megasthenes' book became the classic account of India for the classical world.[72] Though Strabo's complaints about the tall stories he includes (from Indian informants) have led to the frequent denigration of Megasthenes in modern scholarship, it is apparent that he provided a largely sober account of Maurya India, where customs prevailed that were quite different from the north-west described by Alexander's companions. For example, Nearchus mentions the use of writing in the north-west, whereas Megasthenes makes clear that writing was unknown in Magadha. Strabo (and many later writers) were unable to recognize that India was a culturally diverse place.[73]

THE INDO-GREEKS

The Greeks settled in India in veteran colonies and garrison cities. Inevitably they intermarried with Indians, and various pieces of evidence inform us of assimilated Greeks and perhaps mixed-race descendants. The rise of the Indo-Greek kingdoms has been thoroughly traced in earlier scholarship and takes us beyond the subject of Alexander's India,[74] but it is worth pointing to three signal pieces of evidence of assimilation (besides the Hellenistic city of Ai Khanum in Afghanistan, not in India proper). First is the inscription of Sophytos from Kandahar, probably before 100 BCE, which in learned Greek recounts the career of

---

[71] Stoneman 2019: 377–378, drawing on Kosmin 2014: 33 for the involvement of Megasthenes, and Mairs 2014: 111–112 for the intermarriage idea.
[72] Dihle 1964.
[73] On Megasthenes see Stoneman 2019: 129–237, reviewing previous scholarship, and, for a translation and commentary, Stoneman 2021b.
[74] Tarn 1951, Woodcock 1966, Narain 2003; see also Mairs 2014. Stoneman 2019: 375–404 discusses some aspects.

7.1 Pillar at Besnagar in Central India, *c.*110 BC, with Prakrit inscription of Heliodorus. Photo: Richard Stoneman.

an Indian who rebuilt his family fortunes.[75] The name may be the same as the that of the ruler Sopeithes whom Alexander encountered: perhaps this is a descendant. The second is the inscription of Heliodorus in Prakrit on a pillar at Besnagar in Central India, erected about 110 BCE (Figure 7.1). It is a dedication to the Indian god Vasudeva by a man who came as ambassador from King Antalcidas to an otherwise unknown Indian king. This Greek has 'gone native' and is able to use his dual identity in a professional way as an ambassador. The third is the previously mentioned Pali work, *The Questions of King Milinda*, in which the Indo-Greek king Menander puts a series of questions to the Buddhist sage Nāgāsena and enables the latter to provide a full exposition of Buddhist doctrine. While not a historical document, it probably signifies a genuine interest in Buddhism on the part of this Greek king, who seems briefly to have extended Greek rule as far as Pataliputra.[76]

[75] Mairs 2014: 102–117, with earlier scholarship.   [76] Stoneman 2019: 391–396.

These three examples of different kinds of assimilation between Greeks and Indians provide a clue to the eventual end of the Greeks in India. While barbarian invasions in the late second century BCE obliterated the kingdoms, the people did not vanish; they gradually turned into Indians. As Narain wrote, 'they came, they saw, but India conquered'.[77] Nehru quotes Tarn, 'in matters of spirit Asia was quite confident that she could outstay the Greeks, and she did'.[78] Alexander's memory lasted long in the west, but in India he was virtually forgotten.

Guide to Further Reading

On the course of the Indian campaign, Bosworth 1988a remains the most comprehensive account. Some problems are addressed in the narrative in Stoneman 2019: 36–79. Bosworth 1996b: 133–165 discusses the voyage down the Indus. On the political structure of India at the time of Alexander's arrival, see Thapar 2002: 138–164; Singh 2009: 257–287; Prakash 1964; and the summary in Stoneman 2019: 45–48. The fragments of the Alexander historians are collected by Robinson 1953–1963 vol. i, and the authoritative discussion is Pearson 1960; see further Chapter 25 in this volume. On Onesicritus, see Brown 1949; the utopian aspects of Onesicritus' work are treated by Winiarczyk 2011. Megasthenes' *Indica* is the subject of a study and new translation by Stoneman 2021b. Discussion of the naked philosophers was opened by Stoneman 1994b and 1995; on Calanus, see Bosworth 1998. The philosophers' influence on Pyrrho is treated at length by Beckwith 2015 and Kuzminski 2008. The 'Treaty of the Indus' and relations between Greeks and Mauryas are discussed by Kosmin 2014: 31–58. The classic study of the Indo-Greeks by Tarn 1951 has been succeeded, but not replaced, by Narain 2003.

---

[77] Narain 2003: 18. [78] Nehru 2004: 160.

8: ALEXANDER'S DEATH, LAST PLANS AND BURIAL

Joseph Roisman

DEATH FORETOLD

In 324 Alexander lost two good friends, first the Indian philosopher Calanus and then his dearest companion and right-hand man, Hephaestion. Death was getting closer to Alexander, even though his death in Babylon on June 10/11, 323, came as a surprise for most people.[1] There were warning signs in the usual bad omens and prophecies that preceded the death of great men (cf. Arrian *Anabasis* 7.30.2). Omens also served the sources' narrative by paving the way for Alexander's fate, as well as illuminating others' reaction to his impending death. Roughly in chronological order, the major omens were as follows:

1. Apollodorus, the general of Babylonia, consulted his brother, the diviner Peithagoras, about his own and Alexander's fates. Peithagoras sacrificed and divined danger to the king (Arrian *Anabasis* 7.18.1–7.18.5; Plutarch *Alexander* 73; Appian *Civil War* 2.152).
2. Before Calanus died, he told Alexander that he would meet him in Babylon (Arrian *Anabasis* 7.18.6).
3. Alexander ordered the peoples of Asia to mourn Hephaestion and temporarily extinguish the sacred fire, as was customary when a Persian king died. This act was taken as a bad omen for Alexander himself (Diodorus 17.114.4).
4. Alexander dreamt sometime before the visit to his court of Cassander, Antipater's son, that he would die by Cassander's hand, but he dismissed the dream (Valerius Maximus 1.7. ext. 2).
5. Chaldaean diviners told Alexander about an oracle, or an astrological observation, that warned him against entering Babylon, at

---

[1] Deaths of Calanus and Hephaestion: Heckel 2021: 231, 218–219. Date of Alexander's death: Depuydt 1997; and as a surprise: Diodorus 17.116.1. Unless noted otherwise, all dates are BCE.

least by its western side. Alexander dismissed the prediction, either after reconsideration or because the difficult terrain forced him to enter Babylon from the west (Diodorus 17.112.1–17.112.5; Arrian *Anabasis* 7.16.5–7.17.6, 22.1; Plutarch *Alexander* 73; Justin 12.13.3–12.13.6).

6. On approaching the walls of Babylon, Alexander saw many crows flying and fighting, some of which dropped dead next to him (Plutarch *Alexander* 73).
7. A domestic ass kicked to death the biggest and best-looking lion in Alexander's park (Plutarch *Alexander* 73).
8. When Alexander sailed through the marshlands east of Babylon, his diadem fell into the water. A sailor, some say a Phoenician, retrieved it and swam back to Alexander's ship with the diadem on his head. Alexander rewarded him generously before flogging him, or, in another version, before having him beheaded him on the seers' advice. In another account again, he was distracted and failed to punish the man, and in a happier tradition the diadem's rescuer was the future Successor Seleucus, whose wearing of it portended his own future royalty (Arrian *Anabasis* 7.22.2–7.22.5; Diodorus 17.116.5–17.117.1).
9. A local woman gave birth to a monster resembling Scylla and brought it to Alexander's palace. The most honest of Alexander's seers told him that it heralded his death (*Liber de morte* 90–95; *Alexander Romance* 3.30).
10. An anonymous man, though named Dionysius of Messene in one version, sat himself on Alexander's vacant throne and put on the royal dress and diadem that happened to be there. He is also described as a prisoner who did it after he was miraculously freed from his chains. Depending on the source, the man claimed that he acted spontaneously, or said that the god Serapis had freed and instructed him. Alexander tortured him on suspicion of a plot, or, in another version, regarded it as an evil omen and executed the man on the seers' advice so that the trouble would pass over to him (Arrian *Anabasis* 17.24.1–17.24.3; Diodorus 17.116.2–17.116.4; Plutarch *Alexander* 73).
11. Shortly before the gravely ill Alexander died, several of his Companions asked the god Serapis at his temple if they should move Alexander under his care. The god responded that it was better for Alexander to stay where he was (Arrian *Anabasis* 7.26.2–7.26.4; Plutarch *Alexander* 76).[2]

---

[2] For the omens, see McKechnie 2009; Bowden 2016: 158, 161–162.

Ancient and modern scepticism about the omens' authenticity should not lead us to treat them all as inventions *ex eventu*. The story about Apollodorus and his brother Peithagoras (no. 1 above) can be traced back to the self-promoting Peithagoras himself, but it suggests nothing unlikely or unhistorical. Similarly, the Chaldaeans' warnings (no. 5) might be reconciled or even corroborated by contemporary Babylonian texts.[3] Serapis' cult likely postdated Alexander, but is locating omen no. 11 in its temple in Babylon enough to invalidate the entire story?[4] Other omens are valuable for their cultural and historical contexts. Alexander was intimately associated with lions, as witnessed by his Heraclid ancestry, his depictions on coins, his participation in lion hunts, and his displays of courage, masculinity and kingliness. It was easy to identify him with the mighty lion in omen no. 6, while the domestic donkey might refer to internal danger.[5] If a prevalent scholarly interpretation is correct, the stories of the men who paid with their lives for donning Alexander's regalia and sitting on his throne (nos 8, 10) reflect the sources' misconstruing of the Mesopotamian ritual of the substitute king. (To protect the reigning king from prophecies of danger, the Mesopotamians replaced him with another man for a short time. They then executed the substitute king to fulfil the bad omen, and the reigning king resumed his duties.) It appears, then, that the Babylonians were actually trying to protect Alexander when they warned him not to enter the city and, supposedly, replaced him with another man.[6]

Foul Play?

Ultimately, the omens proved right. The sources offer in essence two versions of how he died: one chronicles Alexander's activities and deteriorating condition in his last days up to his death with no explicit indication of foul play. The other claims that he was poisoned. The most detailed account of the first version is found in authors who relied on the so-called *Diaries* or *Ephemerides*. The *Diaries* were presumably based on royal chronicles put together by Alexander's former secretary and commander, Eumenes of Cardia, and the unknown Diodotus of Erythrae.[7]

---

[3] Van der Spek 2003: 332–340, though see also Lane Fox 2016: 105.
[4] See further Bosworth 1988b: 167–170.
[5] Alexander and lions: Palagia 2000; Ogden 2011a: 8–11.
[6] Van der Spek 2003: 91–92, 339; Collins 2013: 142; Bowden 2016: 161–162. Lane Fox 2016, however, rejects the ritualistic interpretation as misapplied to the Greek sources, and claims that the sources' reconstructions and embellishments of the story of the man on the throne go back to an historical incident.
[7] Anson 1996; Bearzot 2017. See also Curtius 10.5.1–10.5.6; Diodorus 17.117.1–17.117.5; Justin 12.14.1–12.16.1. Ephippus of Olynthus *FGrH* / *BNJ* 116 F3 ascribes Alexander's death to a drinking competition and Dionysius' revenge for Thebes' destruction.

Later authors, who used the *Diaries* directly or indirectly, describe with some variations Alexander's daily routine of consultations with commanders, sacrifices, baths, sleep and heavy drinking. He developed a high fever after attending a banquet hosted by his friend Medius, but he continued to function for few days before becoming incapacitated and losing his speech. He was still able to bid goodbye to his soldiers, who insisted on seeing him. A group of Companions hoping for divine intervention were told by the god Serapis to let things take their course (no. 11 above). He died shortly thereafter.

Scholars have challenged the authenticity of the *Diaries* as either a late fictional composition or a contemporary piece of propaganda designed to refute allegations that Alexander was poisoned (see below, p. 133). Yet there is little in the *Diaries* that indicates a work of fiction or anachronistic touches. Moreover, if the goal of the work was to fight charges of poisoning by merely ignoring them, it was too subtle or indirect to be effective. The royal *Diaries* can be largely trusted for their account of Alexander's last days.

I regard the claim that Alexander was poisoned as less reliable. Its best-known version tells that Aristotle supplied the poison, whose unique makeup and potency meant that it could be transported only in the hoof an ass, a mule or a horse (!). The chief plotter was Antipater, the regent of Macedonia, who (like Aristotle) feared for his life. Alexander told Antipater to hand over his regency to Craterus and present himself at his court, and the sources give Antipater additional reasons to feel threatened, including Alexander's arrogance, cruelty, envy and distrust of his loyalty. Several years earlier, Alexander had executed Antipater's friends and son-in-law, and he had punished errant governors with death in 324. Finally, Antipater had feuded with Alexander's mother, Olympias, who kept complaining about him to the king. Antipater then sent his son Cassander with the poison to Alexander's court, where his other son, Iolaus (Iollas), served as a royal butler or taster and could slip it into Alexander's drink and medication. Other versions add to the conspiracy several prominent commanders and friends, including Medius, who hosted Alexander's last banquet and was said to be Iolaus' lover. In one account, that of the *Liber de morte*, the generals and courtiers Eumenes, Perdiccas, Ptolemy, Asander and Holcias are exonerated as ignorant of the plot.[8]

---

[8] Diodorus 17.118.1–17.118.2; Arrian *Anabasis* 7.27.1–7.27.3; Curtius 10.14–10.20; Plutarch *Alexander* 77; Pliny *Natural History* 30.53; Justin 12.13.10–12.14.8; *Alexander Romance* 3.31; *Liber de morte* 87–89, 96; cf. [Plutarch] *Moralia* 849f., reproduced at Photius *Bibliotheca* cod. 266, p. 496a.

The tale of Alexander's poisoning was already rejected or qualified as rumour in antiquity (Arrian *Anabasis* 7.27.1–7.27.3; Plutarch *Alexander* 77; Curtius 10.10.14–10.10.19). Although there are historians who detect a conspiracy of prominent Macedonians against Alexander, many more scholars share the ancient scepticism, not because the story was improbable but because of its likely origins and prejudice.[9] First, it is not uncommon for the sudden death of a prominent figure to encourage conspiratorial speculations, in which those who happened to benefit from the death are the first suspects. Second, in the struggles over power and territories that followed Alexander's death, the major players sought to legitimize their claims and position through kinship, friendship and service to Alexander, and to delegitimize their opponents by belittling their connection to him or worse. If Plutarch is correct, Olympias' charge that Antipater poisoned her son through Iolaus (Iollas) did not predate 317, when she was at war with Cassander among other opponents (Plutarch *Alexander* 77; cf. Diodorus 19.11.7–19.11.9, 35.1). There were surely other possible culprits and earlier opportunities for poisoning charges, but their partisanship robs them of credibility. The composition we possess only in Latin known as 'The Book on the Death and Testament of Alexander the Great' (*Liber de morte testamentumque Alexandri Magni*), if based on an independent contemporary pamphlet and not merely translated from the fictional *Alexander Romance*, played a part in the propaganda war. It tells the poisoning story and distinguishes the alleged conspirators from those who were not involved. The work also purports to include the contents of Alexander's last will, even though no other Macedonian king, before or after Alexander, is known to have left such a document. In the will, Alexander distributed offices and lands to members of his elite staff, including appointments that we know postdate his death. The will's partiality to certain individuals and cities can be best explained as deriving from fictive claims to Alexander's bequests and goodwill. Its author may have been the little-known Holcias, and although there is no agreement on the composition's exact date and whose cause it best served, it clearly weaponized Alexander's death for and against his Successors and other rivals.[10]

The death of Alexander has also attracted the interest of scientists and historians, who, in the absence of forensic evidence, have tried to uncover its cause on the basis of ancient testimonies. There is no consensus among the sources on how Alexander spent his last days or the length and characteristics of his ailment (Figure 8.1). After a bout of

---

[9] Bosworth 1971b: 115–116, 134–16 credits a conspiratorial coup, but see n.12 below.
[10] Heckel 1988 (dates it to 317); Bosworth 2000 (dates to 309, with more followers).

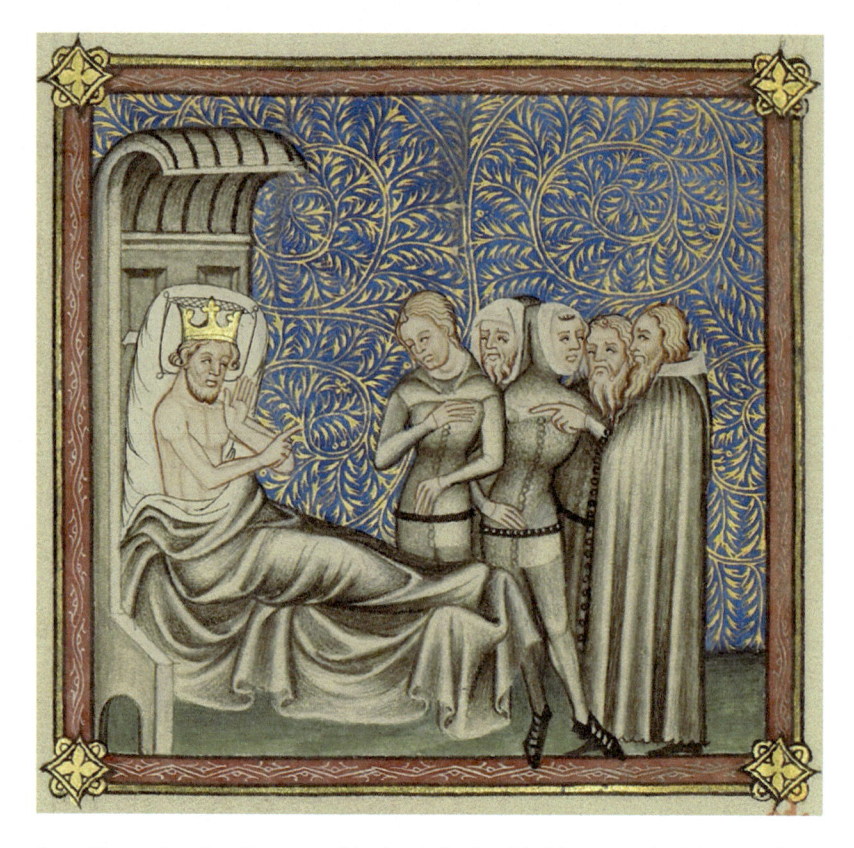

8.1 Alexander the Great on his death bed with his generals. Master of Jean de Mandeville. Getty Museum, Ms. 1, v2 (84.MA.40.2), fol. 138.

heavy drinking, his symptoms progressed from a rising fever that lasted about eleven days, through inability to move around independently, sharp back pain, difficulty sleeping, loss of speech, inability to conduct business in the last four days, a swollen tongue, movement limited to raising his head or hand, delirium and, in death, no signs of decay for at least six days, despite the June heat.[11] These symptoms have suggested different kinds of poison to different experts. Some scholars have detected long-term causes such as previous injuries, alcohol abuse and extended grief over Hephaestion, while others cite diseases commonly associated with the Babylonian environment or with poor hygiene, such

---

[11] Plutarch 75–77; Arrian *Anabasis* 7.25.1–7.26.1 (both deny the pain seizure); Diodorus 17.117.1–17.117.3; Justin 12.13.7–12.13.9, 15.1–16.1; Curtius 10.5.3–10.5.5 (allowing Alexander to speak moments before he died), 10.9–10.13; *Liber de morte* 99, 104–106.

as malaria, typhoid, and West Nile virus. Clearly, the multitude of proposals reflect their speculative nature. All are admittedly based on a choice of some symptoms to the exclusion of others, and on the presumption of unchanging diseases and environments since Alexander's time. Given the present state of the evidence, their main contribution is in demonstrating the limitations of rival theories.[12]

Alexander's Unsettled Succession

Whatever its cause, Alexander's death created a power vacuum. The king left no functioning or designated heir, probably because he believed he would overcome his medical condition, as in the past. As to possible royal successors, his wife Roxane was still pregnant, his brother Arrhidaeus was weak-minded, and his young son Heracles from the Persian Barsine was largely forgotten and far from Babylon. The failure to appoint an heir is illustrated by stories of Alexander's prophetic last words, which all look like *ex eventu* fabrications. The best known tells that when Alexander's friends asked to whom he left his kingdom, he answered 'to the best' or 'the strongest'. He also predicted that there would be mighty funeral games after his death, referring metaphorically to the coming conflicts over power and land.[13] Even the unlikely story about his suicide attempt shortly before he died suggests his failure to appoint an heir. It reports that the gravely ill Alexander tried to disappear into the River Euphrates so that people would think he had joined the gods. Roxane, however, prevailed upon the reluctant king to go back to his sickbed. This fictional tale is premised on Alexander's real disregard for his succession, and it may explain why, in the *Liber de morte*, he summons his friends to witness his will right after this incident.[14]

Less dubious (though not above suspicion) are traditions that Alexander gave his ring to his deputy (*chiliarch*), Perdiccas, and that he asked to be buried in Siwah, Egypt. The meaning of the handing over of the ring, with which Alexander authenticated his communications, was disputed even by those attending the scene and by other commanders. It certainly did not make Perdiccas an heir, but at best a caretaking regent.

---

[12] See the surveys of Atkinson, Truter and Truter 2009; Gamble and Bloedow 2017.
[13] Diodorus 17.117.4, 18.1.4–18.1.5; Curtius 10.5.5; Arrian *Anabasis* 7.26.3; Justin 12.15.5–12.15.8; *Alexander Romance* 3.33; Antela-Bernárdez 2011b.
[14] Arrian *Anabasis* 7.27.3 (dismissing the tale); *Liber de morte* 101–102. Lack of heir: Heckel 2008: 151.

In any case, when Perdiccas was eventually recognized as the (temporary) regent of the realm, it was not because of Alexander's directive or ring, but because Perdiccas himself eliminated those who challenged his leadership and made deals with other former generals and governors.[15]

In addition to failing to appoint an heir, Alexander left other unfinished business. The rest of the chapter deals with two items of it: his so-called last plans and his burial.

Alexander's Last Plans

Alexander's draft plans for his campaign and other projects came into the foreground in the context of the succession struggle that followed his death. On one side was the regent Perdiccas, who acted in the name of Alexander's unborn child and was supported by other members of the elite and the cavalry. On the other side was the infantry, led by the populist commander Meleager and united around Alexander's brother Arrhidaeus, who was crowned as king Philip (III). The conflict became violent, with intermittent agreements that were often broken, but the elimination of Meleager was followed by a more stable arrangement. There would be a joint kingship of Philip and Roxane's future child (if male) under the guardianship of Perdiccas, now the most powerful general. Many other commanders and officeholders were confirmed in their positions. Ptolemy was given the satrapy of Egypt, and Craterus also got a new assignment. His original mission was to lead an army of veterans back to Europe, where he was to replace Antipater as the governor of Macedonia, part of Thrace and Greece. But Craterus waited with his army in Asia Minor and was now instructed to share Antipater's rule.[16]

The historian Diodorus provides the sole account of what happened next. In the royal *hypomnemata* (notes or memoranda), Perdiccas found instructions to complete the pyre and burial site of Hephaestion as well as other projects. The most ambitious and noteworthy included a great military expedition to Libya, Carthage, Sicily and Spain that required the building of a military road along the north African coast all the way to the Straits of Gibraltar. The campaign also involved the construction of 1,000 large battleships in Phoenicia, Syria and Cilicia, in

---

[15] Ring: Diodorus 17.117.3; Curtius 10.5.5; Justin 12.15.12; Nepos *Eumenes* 2; *Liber de morte* 112; *Heidelberg Epitome FGrH / BNJ* 155 F1; cf. Plutarch *Alexander* 9. Atkinson 2009: 145–146 (doubtful of the story); Roisman 2012a: 64 (with n. 8), 92.

[16] Meeus 2008; Roisman 2012a: 61–81; and below pp. 136–7.

addition to the construction of ports and shipyards where necessary. More peaceful was the building of cities and mutual transplanting of population from Asia to Europe in order to create harmony and marital kinship between the continents. Fifteen hundred talents were allocated to the building of six temples in Greece and Macedonia, and another magnificent temple was planned for Troy. Finally, the plans included the building of a tomb for Alexander's father, Philip, that would resemble the biggest pyramid in Egypt. Diodorus adds that there were also (unspecified) written orders to Craterus, and that Perdiccas thought the plans were too costly and impractical. Not wishing to be held personally responsible for diminishing Alexander's reputation, however, he brought the plans to the Macedonian Assembly. The Macedonians paid due respect to Alexander, but they shared Perdiccas' view of the plans and voted them down (Diodorus 18.4.1–18.4.6).[17]

Modern discussions of Alexander's last plans focus largely on two questions: their authenticity and the motives for Perdiccas' and the Macedonians' actions. Although some historians regard the plans as an invention, the more dominant view, to which I subscribe, is that they were largely authentic. Indeed, some are corroborated independently by other sources. While differing from Diodorus regarding the amount Alexander intended to spend on the construction of temples in Greece – 10,000 vs 1,500 talents, respectively – Plutarch confirms the project (*Moralia* 343d). Similarly, Strabo cites Alexander's letter to the Trojans promising them a grand temple, among other things (C593). Variants of the planned western expedition can be found in other works that do not appear to share a common source or suggest their use of the *hypomnemata*. Before he died, Alexander was planning a campaign to Arabia, unmentioned in the 'last plans' but linked by the sources to the African and Mediterranean expedition. The plans' half-baked but grandiose nature is characteristic of Alexander.[18]

Perdiccas' and the Macedonians' treatment of the plans deserves an explanation.[19] Although Perdiccas disapproved of the plans, cancelling them on his own would have provided ammunition to his rivals, who already suspected or blamed him for his soloist style and ambitions for kingship. He could hardly hide or ignore the plans, because Craterus and others knew about them. There are problems, however, with the

---

[17] See recently Finn 2022: 84–122, who claims that the last plans are a construct of Diodorus that links Alexander to Heracles on the one hand and to Antony and Octavian on the other.
[18] Arrian *Anabasis* 7.1.1–7.11.4; Curtius 10.1.17–10.1.19; Plutarch *Alexander* 68; cf. Arrian *Anabasis* 4.7.5, 5.26.2; and see Badian 2012: 174–192.
[19] For the following, see Roisman, 2012a: 82–83.

claim that Perdiccas misrepresented the plans so that they would be rejected, fearing that Craterus would challenge his primacy by arguing in their favour. There is no evidence that Craterus supported any version of the plans, and there was already a consensus for their rejection. Diodorus approvingly reports that Perdiccas and the troops believed that the plans were too expensive and impractical. Furthermore, the power struggle in Babylon and the distribution of offices and territories left the leaders wishing not to expand the empire but either to preserve it, as in the case of Perdiccas and his supporters, or to establish their individual rule at the expense of the empire as a whole and of neighbours, as in the case of many satraps. There was no appetite for pet projects of Alexander's, such as developing religious centres in Macedonia and Asia Minor or glorifying the memory of his best friend and father. Perdiccas brought the decision about the last plans to the Assembly with just a slight degree of risk to himself, thus demonstrating his control over the army that had hitherto opposed him. Finally, while there is much to say in favour of the cancellation of Alexander's over-ambitious plans, Diodorus also strongly suggests that it looked like an insult to his name and vision. The treatment of Alexander's body suggests a similar disregard for his wishes.

ALEXANDER'S BODY

The best representations of Alexander's presence after his death were his regalia, personal weapons and body. They were all used by his former generals to create the fiction that his authority survived his death and supported their agendas. Alexander's body in particular became an object of contention, because it offered the strongest reminder of, and substitute for, the living king. It took time, however, for its value to be recognized. Plutarch claims that during the strife after Alexander's death his corpse remained unembalmed for some time, despite the heat and humidity of Babylon in June.[20]

Alexander's body made its first appearance when the division in the Macedonian camp solidified into two opposing groups, one led by Perdiccas and the other by Meleager and King Philip (see above, p. 136). According to Curtius (10.7.11–10.7.21), Philip went about in the chaotic infantry assembly wearing Alexander's robe and accompanied by Meleager in arms. Their appearance put the infantry in a belligerent

---

[20] Plutarch *Alexander* 77; Curtius 10.10.13; cf. Diodorus 18.26.3; Aelian *Varia historia* 12.63 (it is unlikely that it was unattended for thirty days); see p. 140 below.

mood, which frightened Perdiccas. He locked himself up where Alexander's body lay, together with Ptolemy and several hundred warriors.

There was more than panic to Perdiccas' and his supporters' reaction. King Philip gave the infantry a legitimacy that reinforced their superiority in numbers. But Philip was a new king and not universally acknowledged, while Perdiccas laid claim to Alexander, whose body (far more than his cloak) stood for the old regime and uncontested authority. By locking it up and guarding it, Perdiccas suggested that it needed protection from his opponents. Not surprisingly, his action triggered a struggle. When Philip, Meleager and the infantry burst into the death chamber, Perdiccas tried to play his big card by calling aside those who wished to protect Alexander's body. He was ignored because the issue was not loyalty to the dead king but who would win the contest. In the ensuing conflict, many were wounded, and after veteran infantrymen urged their opponents to yield peacefully, Perdiccas and his followers laid down their arms. At this point Meleager and Philip 'owned' the body, now a symbol of unity. Meleager appealed to Perdiccas' supporters, many of them cavalry, not to abandon the corpse. Since staying in Babylon meant accepting Meleager's power, they opted to leave the city and harass it from the plains. As the episode illustrates, the varied uses of Alexander's body turned it into the proverbial political football.

On both sides of the conflict there were those who fuelled it and others who favoured reconciliation. Eventually the latter gained the upper hand, and a compromise was reached that resembled the one discussed earlier (see p. 136). In essence, it recognized Philip as king of all Macedonians, with Alexander's unborn child, if a son, as his co-king. Perdiccas got command of the army, which he shared to a degree with Meleager and possibly also the absent Craterus.[21] Alexander's body played a part in the process. According to Curtius Rufus, when King Philip tried to persuade the infantry to accept reconciliation, he depicted the prospective funeral and burial of the body as a unifying event (10.8.18). Justin adds that the settlement was made over Alexander's body, which served as witness (13.4.4). It appears that Philip and Meleager brought Alexander's body along in the possibly naïve belief that it would deter violation of the agreement. The body also

---

[21] Arrian *Successors* 1–3; Curtius 10.8.22–10.8.23; Justin 12.4.2–12.4.5; Dexippus *FGrH / BNJ* 100 F8.4; Meeus 2008: 53–59. According to Justin 13.4.7–13.4.8, Alexander's death led to a purification ritual for the army, but Curtius' explanation that the ritual was due to later bloodshed is preferable: 10.9.11–10.9.21.

represented the lack of discord that (allegedly) characterized the army under Alexander.

It didn't take long for Perdiccas to get rid of Meleager and regain control of the entire camp, including Alexander's body, whose recent history as a shifting political asset was among the incentives for bringing it to its final rest. In Perdiccas' later distribution of satrapies and responsibilities, the hitherto-unknown Arrhidaeus (not the king) was tasked with burying Alexander. The dead king had reportedly wished to be buried in Siwah, where the temple of his divine father Ammon would support his own claim to divinity. It seems that the leadership in Babylon was willing at first to respect Alexander's wish. Even before the events described here, they sanctioned the embalming of his body, which followed Egyptian and Near Eastern (not Macedonian) practice.[22] Later, Perdiccas had second thoughts as his relationship with Ptolemy, the ruler of Egypt, deteriorated. Wishing to deprive Ptolemy of the patronage of Alexander's tomb and its accompanying cult, Perdiccas planned to bury Alexander rather in Aegae, Macedonia, with his ancestors. The act would have gained Perdiccas the Macedonians' goodwill, and there was not much that his rival Antipater could say against it. Moreover, royal burial was the responsibility of the royal heir or kinsman and legitimized a claim to the throne. Perdiccas, who was possibly related to the royal house and who asked for the hand of Alexander's sister, Cleopatra, seemed to entertain such ambitions. Ptolemy frustrated Perdiccas' plan by getting possession of Alexander's body and burying it first in Memphis and then in Alexandria. The sources for the story are prejudiced, some justifying Ptolemy's action and others suggesting criticism. Nevertheless, a reconstruction of the events is possible.[23]

It took almost two years for Arrhidaeus to prepare Alexander's last journey (321). Diodorus' detailed description of the hearse suggests a showiness designed to impress spectators with sights, sounds and size. The main components included Alexander's body in a golden coffin, a temple- or tomb-like structure above it, four large paintings

---

[22] Meeus 2008: 67; cf. Faust 2018: 88–89.
[23] Burial in Siwah: Diodorus 18.3.5; Curtius 10.5.4; Justin 12.15.7, 13.4.6. Perdiccas and Alexander's body: Pausanias 1.6.3; Diodorus 18.23.1–18.23.3; Justin 13.6.4–13.6.6; Worthington 2016b: 94. Ptolemy and the body: Diodorus 18.28.2–18.28.3; Pausanias 1.6.3; Arrian *Successors* 25 and *FGrH / BNJ* 156 F10.1; Strabo C794; *Alexander Romance* 3.34; Aelian *Varia historia* 12.64 (the last two are hopelessly pro-Ptolemy, telling respectively that he took the body from Babylon to Egypt by permission and that he deceived Perdiccas with a fake corpse); cf. *Parian Marble FGrH / BNJ* 239 B11. For additional reconstructions of the affair, see Errington 1970: 64–66; Erskine 2002: 170–173; Badian 2012: 175–177.

and an appropriately massive chariot that artfully absorbed the shocks of the road, all decorated with an abundance of gold, precious stones and purple fabric, and pulled by sixty-four large mules. There were images of lions and wreaths and Victories for the benefit of Greco-Macedonian viewers. The paintings depicted Alexander and his imperial army, including Macedonian and Persian infantry bodyguards, elephants with Indian soldiers, cavalry and even ships, most of them as if ready for battle. Bells of various size announced aloud the approach of the spectacle. There was also an entourage of troops and repair personnel. In short, the hearse invited people to celebrate and admire Alexander's fame as well as the grandeur, size, diversity, wealth, power and advanced technology of his empire.[24]

The sources (and, consequently, modern scholars) fail to agree on what happened after the chariot and body left Babylon. I follow the view that Arrhidaeus, for unknown reasons, disobeyed Perdiccas and let Ptolemy take the body to Egypt. Perdiccas, who was then in Asia Minor, sent two commanders, Polemon and Attalus, to stop Arrhidaeus on the way. They failed, either because of Arrhidaeus' successful resistance or because Ptolemy, taking no chances, anticipated them by bringing an army to Syria and taking the body for burial in Memphis.[25] Thus Ptolemy and Perdiccas, two of Alexander's closest friends, had no compunctions about violating his wish. The body's political and ideological value, as well as the belief that it would bless and protect the land of its burial (Aelian *Varia historia* 12.64), played a part in their competition over the body, but there were additional considerations. We have already discussed Perdiccas' motivation, but what was Ptolemy's?

Ptolemy appropriated the body with one eye to Egypt and the other looking beyond it. The act suggested that he was independent from Perdiccas and ruled Egypt by the grace of Alexander. If for Perdiccas the body represented Alexander's Macedonian identity and the integrity of his empire, Ptolemy's Alexander was an Egyptian ruler whom the Egyptian priesthood (and probably subjects) identified as their Pharaoh and god.[26] Alexander was also the founder of Alexandria in Egypt. But Ptolemy's perspective and ambitions were not narrowly local. Universally associated with conquest and empire,

---

[24] Diodorus 18.26.1–18.28.2, likely based on Hieronymus of Cardia: Athenaeus 206d–e. Stewart 1993: 214–225; Faust 2018: 87–91 (mistaking general Arrhidaeus for the king).
[25] See n. 23 above.
[26] Alexander and Ptolemy as Pharaohs: Schäfer 2011: 74–83; Worthington 2016b: 162–198; but see also Collins 2009.

the dead king linked him to Macedonians and Greeks both in Egypt and the old country. Yet grander ambitions could (and did) await. Ptolemy buried Alexander initially in Memphis using Macedonian rites, organized games in his honour and probably established a cult for him.[27]

In 320 Perdiccas led an invasion of Egypt. His primary goal was to bring the country under his rule by deposing its too-independent satrap. An additional goal, probably used to justify the campaign, was to retrieve Alexander's body for burial in Macedonia. Perdiccas also brought along the joint kings, Philip and Alexander's son, Alexander IV, thereby making Ptolemy an enemy of the royal house and of Alexander's heirs. We don't know how Ptolemy countered Perdiccas' propaganda, but he may have presented himself as the protector of Alexander's body from the invaders. The invasion failed largely because of Perdiccas' poor generalship, which resulted in his assassination. He was the first and last man to challenge Ptolemy's patronage of the body. When Antigonus I invaded Egypt in 306, the issue of Alexander's burial did not even come up. By then Ptolemy had already moved the body from Memphis to Alexandria, his preferred city and royal centre, where he instituted a new cult for Alexander. He may also have built his own tomb next to Alexander's at a site that was known as the *sema* (tomb) or *soma* (body). In the late third century, Ptolemy IV Philopator further identified Alexander with the Ptolemies by moving his Ptolemaic ancestors and Alexander to new quarters in the palace complex in Alexandria. According to the geographer Strabo (C794), the first-century Ptolemy (X?) surnamed Son of Cocce and Pareisaktos (usurper) looted Alexander's golden coffin and replaced it with one of glass or alabaster. Strabo thought the act deplorable, but in a way this Ptolemy too was continuing his ancestors' proprietary and exploitative use of Alexander's body.[28]

Evidence for the later history of Alexander's body is episodic. The Roman poet Lucan described Julius Caesar's visit to Alexander's tomb in 48. Of all Egypt's attractions, it was supposedly the only place the Roman conqueror wanted to see. Lucan makes the visit a compliment

---

[27] Pausanias 1.6.3; Diodorus 18.28.3–18.28.4; Fraser 1972 i.215–i.219; Worthington 2016b: 94–95, 129–133; see n. 23 above.

[28] Perdiccas' invasion: Arrian *Successors* 1.24; Roisman 2012a: 92–96. The body's transfer to Alexandria: Curtius 10.10.20; Pausanias 1.6.3; Diodorus 18.28.3–18.28.4; cf. *Alexander Romance* 3.34; Fraser 1972:i.215–i.219. Pausanias' claim (1.7.1; cf. Zenobius *Proverbs* 3.94) that Ptolemy's son, Argaeus, brought the corpse to Alexandria is contested by Worthington 2016b: 131; see also Caneva 2016: 39–42. Philopator's project: Zenobius 3.94; Erskine 2002: 166–167. Changing coffins: Strabo C794; Fraser 1972: i.15, ii.32. History and legends of Alexander and Alexandria: Thompson 2022.

to neither man, describing Alexander as a monstrous despot and bloodthirsty marauder whose remains should have been scattered (*Pharsalia* 1.1–1.52). Caesar's adopted son, the future Augustus, also asked to see Alexander's body when he came to Alexandria in 30. When it was brought to him, he placed a golden crown and flowers over the body – a gesture both honouring the Macedonian world ruler and laying claim to his legacy. It was also an act of reconciliation with and goodwill towards the Alexandrians by way of their founder. The rest of the story is less cheerful. It is told that when Octavian touched Alexander's face, he accidently broke his nose, and when Octavian was asked if he would be interested in seeing the remains of the Ptolemies, he responded with characteristic rudeness that he wanted to see a king, not corpses. The new Roman Alexander, who put an end to the Ptolemaic dynasty, thus closed the gap between himself and the legendary conqueror.[29] In 199/200 CE, the Emperor Septimius Severus toured Egypt and prohibited visits to Alexander's tomb and body. It appears that the site had become a centre for divination and prophesying, and Severus banned the practice elsewhere, too, to prevent its political misuse (Cassius Dio 76.13.1–76.13.2.). Severus' son and heir Caracalla, who was a hardcore Alexander admirer and imitator, visited Alexandria and the tomb in c. 215 CE. He paid respect to the dead king and left him his robe, rings, belts and other valuables carried on his body. Of all the honours given to Alexander by Roman leaders, Caracalla's was the most personal. But his respect for Alexander did not keep him from pillaging and slaughtering the Alexandrians, for uncertain reasons (Herodian 4.8.6–4.9.8; Cassius Dio 76.13.2). In the late fourth century CE, the orator Libanius identified Alexandria as the place where Alexander could be seen (*Oration* 49.12). However, around 500 CE John Chrysostom celebrated the victory of Christ over Alexander by boasting that not even the Alexandrians knew the site of Alexander's tomb or the day of his death, unlike those of Christ's apostles and servants. Alexander's tomb has never been found, though not for lack of trying. Perhaps this is for the best, since his remains were extensively used and misused when available.[30]

---

[29] Suetonius *Augustus* 18; Cassius Dio 51.16.3–51.16.5. Octavian also changed the sphinx on his seal to Alexander: Suetonius *Augustus* 50; Pliny *Natural History* 37.10. The Emperor Caligula claimed to own Alexander's breastplate, but the authenticity and the origin of the armour are uncertain: Suetonius *Caligula* 52; Cassius Dio 59.17.3.

[30] John Chrysostom *26th Homily On 2 Corinthians* 5. The search for Alexander's tomb: Chugg 2004.

Guide to Further Reading

McKechnie 2009 provides a detailed discussion of the omens that preceded Alexander's death and their historiography. Bosworth 1971b is still a relevant analysis of the political circumstances surrounding Alexander's death, though his conclusion in favour of a death by conspiracy is controversial. The various poisons or diseases suggested as the cause of death are described by Atkinson, Truter and Truter 2009 and Gamble and Bloedow 2017. Waterfield 2011 and Anson 2014 deal with the conflicts attending Alexander's death and their development into wars among his Successors. Erskine 2002 offers the most exhaustive treatment of the changing fortunes of Alexander's corpse.

Part II

Contexts

9: MACEDONIA

Carol J. King

Alexander left Macedonia in spring 334 BCE at the age of 21 and never returned.[1] The Macedonia he left was to a great extent the making of his father, Philip II, though Philip's 'Macedonia proper' had been largely a recovery of the Argead realm of Alexander I more than a century earlier. In addition to recovering and securing the old kingdom, through conquest and diplomacy Philip expanded the territory under Macedonian control well beyond what may be regarded as Macedonia's geographical boundaries. Philip's apocryphal remark, 'Son, ... Macedonia does not have enough room for you' (Plutarch *Alexander* 6.5), hardly reflects the size of his kingdom. It is, rather, a comment on Alexander's boundless ambition. At the time of Philip's death and Alexander's accession, Macedonia was at its greatest extent to date, both geographically and politically (Map 9.1).

EARLY ARGEAD EXPANSION AND THE GEOGRAPHICAL KINGDOM

In its geographical extent in Alexander's time Macedonia proper comprised three contiguous regions.[2] Lower Macedonia, the central region, included the core of the old Argead kingdom first established by the ancestors of Alexander and Philip, this being mainly the alluvial plain between the lower Haliacmon and Axios rivers, as formed by the silting of these two rivers together with the Loudias, and the foothills of the enclosing mountains, the Pierian range and Olympus to the south, Bermion and Barnous to the west and northwest.[3] The earliest Argead

---

[1] All ancient dates are BCE.
[2] Hatzopoulos 2020: 11–48 offers the most recent detailed description of Macedonia proper and the allied (subject) cities, regions and peoples. See also Thomas 2010; Borza 1992: 23–57. (Citations herein are limited mainly to the most recent scholarship, where the reader will be directed to other discussions.)
[3] Spelling of geographical features (rivers, lakes and mountains) follows that of Borza 1992.

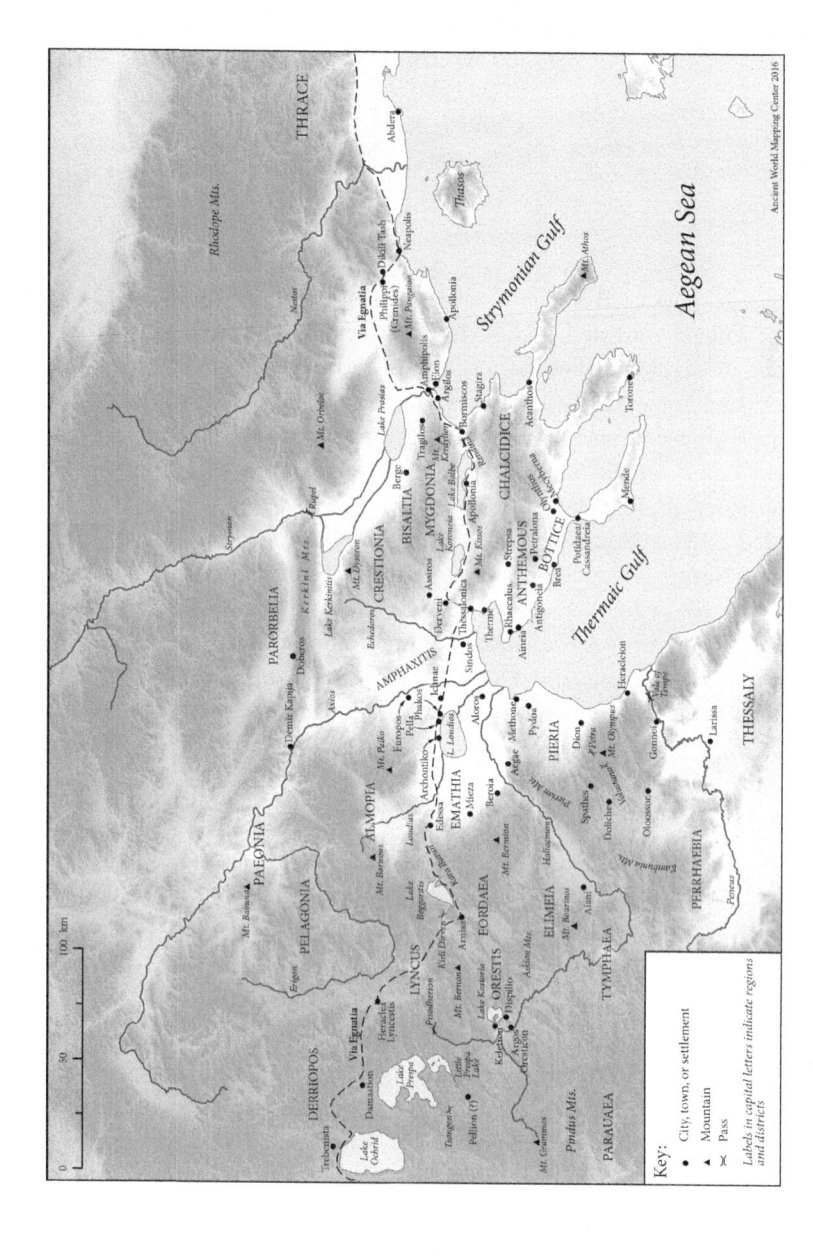

MAP 9.1 Alexander's Macedonia. Drawn by Gabe Moss and the Ancient World Mapping Center. Previously reproduced at King 2018: xix.

king, according to legend, was a descendant of Heracles originally from Argos in the Peloponnese (Herodotus 8.137–8.138).[4] Perdiccas I and his two brothers crossed to Orestis in Upper Macedonia from Illyria, and having set out from the highlands they established a stronghold at a settlement Perdiccas named or renamed Aegae, 'goat place', after consulting the Delphic oracle.[5] Aegae is identified as modern Vergina situated in the Pierian foothills just south of the Haliacmon as it enters the plain from the west, where it has a commanding view of the plain. All Argead kings evidently were buried at Aegae with the exception of Alexander III (Justin 7.2.1–7.2.4, Diodorus 22.12), who was buried in Egypt (see Chapters 5 and 8). The two unplundered tombs discovered at Vergina by Manolis Andronicos in 1977–1978, famously known as Tomb II and Tomb III (Tomb I was plundered), are believed to have belonged to Argeads.[6]

From either Aegae or a place near the Gardens of Midas under Mt Bermion (Herodotus 8.138), the early Argeads proceeded to expand their territory. Advancing into the Pierian plain south of the Haliacmon, they drove out the Thracian Pieres who were forced to resettle east of the Strymon River. In the central plain they took control of Bottiaea and Almopia, displacing the inhabitants there as well, and seized Paeonian territory along the lower Axios. The order of these early and other Argead conquests (discussed below) is uncertain. Some scholars read Thucydides' description at 2.99, the main evidence, as chronological and others take it as a geographical description,[7] but most agree that the Pierian and Emathian (Bottiaean) plains were conquered before the end of the archaic period. Also by the late archaic period, the Argeads had established a religious centre at Dion on the northeast foot of Olympus (Thucydides 4.78.6). However, in coastal Pieria, the port city Pydna was long a bone of contention between Argead kings and Greek traders until Philip II seized it for good (until the Roman conquest) in 357, and in 354 he secured the Greek port of Methone, famously losing an eye during the siege (Demosthenes 18.67; Diodorus 16.34.5).[8] Ports were vital for trade, particularly for the export of

---

[4] On Herodotus' account of the legend, see Vasilev 2012.
[5] Diodorus 7.15–7.16; Synkellos p. 288 Adler and Tuffin. The archaeological record suggests the take-over of an older settlement with occupation in the Iron and Bronze Ages.
[6] Andronicos 1984 remains essential for the excavations.
[7] For example, Hatzopoulos 2020: 11–33: (mainly) chronological; Vasilev 2011: geographical. See also Mari 2011a: 82–87; Sprawski 2010: 131–134.
[8] Hatzopoulos and Paschidis (2004: 806) claim that Pydna was a Macedonian city. Lane Fox 2011d: 267 suggests that Pseudo-Skylax 66 (Pydna is *polis hellēnis*) is specific to summer 360, when both Pydna and Methone were in Athenian hands.

agricultural goods and forest products. When the capital was shifted to Pella in the central plain perhaps near the end of the fourth century (at that time Pella was coastal and not yet silted), the move likely was in consideration of commerce, mainly timber and shipping.[9] By Alexander III's day, Lower Macedonia included the entire Pierian coastline extending as far south as the Peneios River.

Upper Macedonia, the western region (Figure 9.1), comprised the uplands stretching from the mountains bordering the southern and western edges of the central plain as far as the Pindus range and the Prespa lakes, later to Lake Ohrid (Lychnitis). It was dominated by the upper and middle courses of the Haliacmon and had several major thoroughfares passing through its wide valleys. In these highlands, several distinct principalities were essentially independent, each with its own ruling house, until Philip II's consolidation of Upper and Lower Macedonia. Thucydides (2.99.2) refers to the upper groups of people (*ethnē*) 'the Lyncestians and Elimiotes and others' as 'Macedonians' who

9.1 Upper Macedonia, from Elimeia, with the middle Haliacmon to the left and a view towards Eordaea and western Pieria. Photo: Carol J. King.

---

[9] Greenwalt 1999.

were 'allies and subordinates' of the Argeads.[10] A fragmentary inscription (*IG* I³ 89) of a treaty between Perdiccas II (r. c. 454–413) and Athens confirms the alliance at that point (the date is disputed) between the Argead king and Derdas of Elimeia and Antiochus of Orestis, as well as a reconciliation between Perdiccas and Arrhabaeus of Lyncus.[11] But alliances were not consistent. Both Perdiccas and his successor Archelaus (r. 413–399) came into military conflict with the Lyncestian Macedonians and Perdiccas also faced conflict with Elimeia (see below, p. 156). Eordaea, which bordered Lyncus, Elimeia and Orestis, is an exception, as it was taken over by the Argeads probably before the reign of Alexander I (r. c. 498–c. 454) and the inhabitants were either killed or resettled (Thucydides 2.99.5). Pelagonia, to the north, does not appear in the historical record until the fourth century. It had its own ruling house as late as c. 364 (*IG* II² 190; cf. *SEG* 41.42) and, along with Derriopus, was either part of or contiguous with Paeonia. Paeonia was subjugated (Diodorus 16.4.2) and with it probably Pelagonia, while Derriopus evidently was incorporated into Argead Macedonia with Philip's unification about 358.[12] To the south, Perrhaebia came under Archelaus' control late in the fourth century, while Tymphaea may have been incorporated later during Philip's reign, certainly by 336.[13]

By Alexander III's time, it is difficult to define the geographical extent of Upper Macedonia, that is, what had been annexed and what subjugated. While Strabo (C326) says some called all the territory west as far as Corcyra 'Macedonia', it be may be closer to a proper delineation to limit 'Upper' to the recruiting regions for the heavy infantry in Alexander's army. As Waldemar Heckel points out, five of the six phalanx commanders at Gaugamela are identified as coming from Upper Macedonia districts: Perdiccas and Craterus from Orestis, Coenus from Elimeia, Polyperchon and Amyntas (son of Andromenes) from Tymphaea.[14] Parmenion and his sons Philotas and Nicanor, the highest-ranking generals, also probably came from Upper

---

[10] See also Thucydides 2.100.5. On Strabo's identification at C434 of the Orestae, Pelagonians and Elimiotes as Epirote tribes, see Xydopoulos 2012b. For the meaning of *ethnē*, see Archibald 2002: 213–214. The rulers of Lyncus claimed Bacchiad Corinthian origin (Strabo C326).
[11] 423/2 is the favoured date. The district names Elimeia, Orestis and Lyncus, not present on the stele, are presumed from literary references.
[12] Xydopoulos (2012b: 521) includes Pelagonia, Derriopus and Eordaea among the Macedonian principalities. Hatzopoulos (2020: 41) argues that Paeonia may have become subject but 'was clearly a distinct entity'.
[13] Perrhaebia: Borza 1992: 164–165; see also Hatzopoulos 2020: 41–42. Tymphaea: Hatzopoulos 2020: 43–45.
[14] Heckel 2017b: 69–70; he suggests Meleager, the sixth taxiarch, is also from Upper Macedonia.

Macedonia, though their district is nowhere specified.[15] Of the seven elite bodyguards identified for the year 326/5 (Arrian *Anabasis* 6.28.4), four are Upper Macedonian: Leonnatus from Lyncus, Perdiccas from Orestis and Ptolemy and Aristonus from Eordaea. Peithon from Derriopus (or Eordaea) should be included as well.[16] So, in Alexander's highest offices six (at least) upper districts are represented, if Derriopus is included. The importance of Upper Macedonia to Alexander's military success cannot be overemphasized. As Heckel states: 'those with the greatest power and influence at Alexander's court were primarily Upper Macedonians'.[17]

The Thraceward region extended from the Axios River on the eastern fringe of Lower Macedonia to the Strymon River basin. Eastward expansion began probably during the reign of Amyntas I (*c.* 540–*c.* 498). Thucydides says (2.99.4) that after Alexander I 'and his ancestors' conquered Bottiaea and part of Paeonia along the lower Axios, across the Axios they drove the Thracian Edones out of Mygdonia, a narrow corridor stretching along lakes Koroneia and Volvi (Bolbe) between the mountains of the Chalcidice peninsula and Mt Kerdylion as far as the Strymon. Thucydides does not mention Amphaxitis (evidently the name did not come into use until later), the territory along the Axios and east to the so-called 'gold-bearing' Echedorus (Gallikos) River, but this must have been the first territorial gain east of the Axios, with Mygdonia farther south and east being conquered later.[18] It remains a best guess that Amphaxitis became part of Macedonia proper shortly after 512, when a Persian force left behind after Darius I's failed Scythian expedition entered the Strymon basin for the purpose of subduing the local Thracian and Paeonian tribes.[19] The Thracians submitted, but the Paeonians resisted and several tribes of Paeonians were deported to Asia Minor by Darius' general Megabazus, though according to Herodotus (5.14.1–5.16.1) not those around Mt Pangaion and Lake Prasias. The mining of silver and gold in Mt Pangaion, already commenced by locals in the seventh century, by the late sixth century had attracted the interest of the Persians as well as Greek tyrants as far away as Athens and Miletus, and it was later to

---

[15] Heckel 2017b: 72 with n. 32.
[16] Peithon, son of Crateuas, is from Eordaea at *Anabasis* 6.28.4 but at *Indica* 18.6 from Alcomenae (in Derriopus: see Hatzopoulos and Paschidis 2004: 796); Justin (13.4.13, 8.10) calls him Illyrian.
[17] Heckel 2017b: 70.
[18] See Hammond 1989c: 42–43, 45; Borza 1992: 87–88; Vasilev 2011: 101–102.
[19] Herodotus 4.143.3, 5.22. The earliest extant reference to Amphaxitis is Polybius 5.97. Annexation suggested by Hammond and Griffith 1979: 58; Errington 1990: 9, Borza 1992: 100. For Persian activity in the Strymon basin, see Vasilev 2015: 86–109.

become, together with the Dysoron mines, a major source of economic prosperity for Macedonia.[20]

The later reign of Amyntas I marks the beginning of Macedonian–Persian relations. About 510, following the subjugation of coastal Thrace and the deportation of the Paeonians, Megabazus sent a Persian embassy 'into Macedonia' to demand earth and water from Amyntas I as tokens of subjugation (Herodotus 5.17.1, 18.1; Justin 7.3.1–7.3.2: hostages). Herodotus' vague description of 'Macedonia' has led to confusion about topography and there continues to be dispute about the location of Lake Prasias and Mt Dysoron, over which Herodotus says lay the short route into Macedonia. If the embassy had to cross Mt Dysoron to enter Macedonia c. 510 (Herodotus 5.17.2 may suggest this), then we cannot equate Dysoron with modern Menoikion, as does Militades Hatzopoulos, but we may equate it with modern Dysoro, the more common identification.[21] Nicholas Hammond believes the Persian embassy met with Amyntas I in Amphaxitis, which he suggests Amyntas was able to annex to Macedonia in the wake of the collapse of Paeonian power.[22] Others suggest the embassy met with Amyntas in Aegae, where the royal residence was located. Herodotus' embellished tale of the Persian embassy culminating in the murder of all seven envoys at a *symposion* (5.17–5.22) is almost universally rejected, yet there is general agreement that Amyntas I did become a vassal of Persia c. 510. What has never been definitively settled is the debate about the nature of Macedonian subjugation. On one end of the spectrum, Hammond's view is that Macedonia was fully subject to Persia as the most westerly part of the Persian Empire for about thirty years, c. 510–479, while on the other end, Malcolm Errington maintains 'Amyntas did not yield to the Persians.'[23] Between extremes, Eugene Borza believes that Macedonia remained outside the Persian satrapal organization of the Balkans until 492 or later, this view being favoured more recently by Ioannis Xydopoulos, who argues that Macedonia was a client kingdom, not a satrapy, from Amyntas' reign, and by Miroslav Vasilev, who believes that Amyntas became a vassal c. 510 but that there was no Persian

---

[20] Macedonian wealth: Alexander I, see Herodotus 5.17.2, 8.121.2, Demosthenes 12.21; Perdiccas II, see Plato *Republic* 1. 336a; Philip II, see Diodorus 16.8.6–16.8.7.
[21] See Vasilev 2015: 93–103, 113; contra Hatzopoulos 2020: 33–34, who argues that Herodotus is referring to 'Macedonia' as it was when he was writing, not c. 510.
[22] Hammond 1989c: 42. Borza (1992: 101) and Vasilev (2015: 114) suggest Aegae.
[23] Hammond and Griffith 1979: 58–59; 1989c: 42–43; Errington 1990: 9.

garrison in the territory under Amyntas' control.[24] Slawomir Sprawski reiterates the suggestion that Alexander possibly broke free of Persian control after the Ionians revolted in 499 and for this reason was forced to pay tribute, a suggestion seemingly supported by Herodotus 3.96.1 and 7.108.1.[25] However, Johannes Heinrichs and Sabine Müller point out that there is no clear evidence for a Macedonian revolt, though they do regard the period 499–492 as a hiatus in a thirty-year period of subjugation.[26] The view taken here is that Amyntas I was a subordinate ally of Persia in the role of *hyparchos* of the Macedonians (Herodotus 5.20.4) and that relations were positive through the marriage tie of Amyntas' daughter Gygaea to the Persian noble Bubares (Herodotus 5.21, 8.136; Justin 7.3.7–7.4.1). Alexander I probably succeeded near the beginning of the Ionian Revolt, during which time Macedonian–Persian relations were probably interrupted. So Mardonius' arrival in 492 might have been the first dealing between the Persian court and Alexander I as the reigning Macedonian king. When Xerxes came in 480, he is said to have given Alexander control from Mt Olympus to Mt Haemus (Justin 7.4.1).

If Thucydides' account (2.99.6) is chronological, the annexation of Anthemus southeast of Mygdonia and, to the north, Crestonia and Bisaltia, came later than Mygdonia and in that order. Amyntas I offered Anthemus to Hippias for refuge a few years after the tyrant fled Athens (Herodotus 5.94), which seems to suppose that Anthemus was under Macedonian suzerainty about 505,[27] and it has been suggested that the westernmost part of Mygdonia was conquered early, during the reign of Amyntas I.[28] The conquest of eastern Mygdonia as far as the Strymon more likely came after the Persian retreat of 479–476, this being when Alexander I drove out the Thracian Edones, as Thucydides says.[29] The prevalent view is that Alexander I took full advantage of the power void

---

[24] Borza 1992: 104–105, Xydopoulos 2012a: 27, Vasilev 2015: 115–116 with n.360. Arguments hinge on Herodotus (at 6.44 Macedonians became subservient to Persia in 492, but at 7.108.1 Megabazus and Mardonius subjugated the lands as far as Thessaly and made them tributary) and Synkellos p. 359 Adler and Tuffin (Alexander gave earth and water). For the date, see Xydopoulos 2012a: 22 n.6, himself favouring 513–512.

[25] Sprawski 2010: 136–137. For similar views, see Xydopoulos 2012a: 29–30, n.47, though he says no revolt (30) but perhaps tribute (24). Vasilev 2015: 228: paying of tribute is debatable.

[26] Heinrichs and Müller 2008: 289–290. Borza 1992: 102–103 rejects the suggestion of a revolt.

[27] This is disputed. See Xydopoulos 2012a: 26, 33 and the summary of scholarly views at 24–26. See also Vasilev 2015: 116. Contra Hatzopoulos 2020: 17.

[28] Zahrnt 1984: 360, Vasilev 2015: 109. Contra Hammond 1989c: 43, Sprawski 2010: 133, n. 14.

[29] So Hammond and Griffith 1979: 61–62, 1989c: 45. Hatzopoulos 2020: 16: Archaic Macedonia did not extend as far as the Strymon basin. Herodotus 8.116: a local Thracian king refused to cooperate with Xerxes, so these districts were not part of Macedonia in 480. Vasilev (2015: 96) suggests *c.* 460 for the annexation of Bisaltia.

following the retreat of Xerxes' army to expand into the eastern region. After conquering eastern Mygdonia, Alexander succeeded in annexing Crestonia and Bisaltia between the Echedorus and the Strymon valley, with their rich supplies of mineral deposits and timber in the Dysoron–Kerdylion mountain range. The peoples were not displaced, resulting in a more mixed population in eastern Macedonian than in the central and western regions. By 450, however, a few years after the death of Alexander I, '[t]he whole lower Strymon valley was lost for Macedonia',[30] and it was not fully recovered until Philip II reconquered it. The boundary of Macedonia proper did not extend beyond the Strymon/Pangaion area until after Alexander III's time, though Macedonian interests and activity certainly did begin to extend farther early in Philip's reign.[31]

Philip II's Conquest, Consolidation and the Political Kingdom

In 336, when Alexander III succeeded Philip II (r. 360–336), the geographical extent of Macedonia proper was not much greater than during the later reign of Alexander I. It is estimated, however, that Philip II's subjugations more than doubled the politically controlled territory of Macedonia.[32]

Philip's subjugations began with Paeonia on the northern border. This was both necessary and practical, for the Paeonian campaign not only secured against incursions from the north, but it also tested the success of Philip's recent major military innovations. These were initiated in the wake of the battle against the Illyrians in 360 that left his brother Perdiccas III and more than 4,000 Macedonians dead on the field (Diodorus 16.2.4–16.2.5, 3.1; Justin 7.6.3–7.6.5). The Paeonians, who had been driven up the Axios and Strymon rivers in the late archaic period, took advantage of Macedonian weakness – a succession struggle on top of a demoralized and depleted military force – to raid into the north of Lower Macedonia (Diodorus 16.2.6). Philip sent an embassy and bought a brief period of peace with bribes, but when their king died shortly after, he quickly turned the tables and in 358 he invaded Paeonia and defeated the Paeonians in battle (Diodorus 16.1.5, 3.4, 4.2). The people were subjugated rather than driven out and the region retained

---

[30] Hatzopoulos 2020: 34; see his discussion at 34–35 for Athenian activity around this time.
[31] Hatzopoulos 2020: 38.   [32] Thomas 2010: 76, Hatzopoulos 2011: 49.

its own status as a subordinate ally under Philip's political control.[33] It was not fully annexed to Macedonia until the Antigonid period. A Paeonian unit of cavalry scouts crossed to Asia with Alexander in 334 and fought in the key battles at Granicus (Arrian *Anabasis* 1.14.1, 6), Issus (2.7.5, 2.9.2) and Gaugamela (3.12.3).

If anecdotes are any indication (Polyaenus 4.1; Justin 7.2.6–7.2.12), relations between Argead Macedonia and her Illyrian neighbours – Illyria was never a united kingdom but rather a group of independent tribes inhabiting the region mainly northwest of Upper Macedonia, among which the Dardanians and Taulantians were notable – were troubled from the earliest times. Illyrians did raid for stock (Arrian *Anabasis* 7.9.2), but it might have been a mutual concern over Argead expansionism that forged military cooperation between certain Illyrians and Lyncestians and perhaps between Orestians and certain Epirotes (Thucydides 2.80.5–2.80.6). During the first phase of the Peloponnesian War, when the Spartans were working against Athenian interests in the north, Perdiccas II, wanting to subjugate Arrhabaeus of Lyncus, seized the opportunity to form an alliance of convenience with Brasidas (Thucydides 4.79, 82–83). The first attempt in 424 failed when Brasidas came to an agreement with Arrhabaeus and withdrew. But, on the second attempt, Arrhabaeus was defeated in battle and Perdiccas was on the point of overrunning the Lyncestian villages with the aid of some Illyrian mercenaries, when Arrhabaeus bribed or convinced the Illyrians to switch sides, prompting Perdiccas' Macedonians to run away and Brasidas to make a forced retreat under fire (Thucydides 4.124–4.128). During the reign of Perdiccas' successor Archelaus, another conflict arose between the Argead king and Arrhabaeus and a certain Sirras (Aristotle *Politics* 5.1311b). Though Sirras is nowhere identified as such, it is certainly possible that he was an Illyrian ally of Arrhabaeus.[34] During this conflict, Archelaus formed a marriage alliance with the Elimiote royal house (giving his daughter to the Elimiote king), built forts and roads, and strengthened his military (Thucydides 2.100.2).

Despite Archelaus' measures, the Illyrian frontier was particularly problematic for the Argeads in the first half of the fourth century.[35]

---

[33] Excepting an occasional brief rebellion: Diodorus 16.22.3, *GHI* no. 53 (356); Demosthenes 1.13 (*c.* 352?). See n. 12 above.

[34] On the identity of Sirras, see Ogden 1999: 12–13 and Carney 2019: 24 with n. 48. I am inclined to think Sirras was Illyrian.

[35] Greenwalt 2010b: 282: Macedonians and Illyrians 'do not appear to have been mortal enemies until the fourth century'.

Following the assassination of Archelaus and the subsequent six-year period of succession turmoil, Amyntas III seized the throne in 393, only to be defeated in battle soon after by the Illyrians (Dardanians under Bardylis, it is supposed) and expelled from Lower Macedonia altogether, at which point he ceded his eastern territory to the Chalcidic League and thus effectively lost his entire kingdom (Diodorus 14.92.3–14.92.4; Isocrates 6.46), including the capital Pella (Xenophon *Hell.* 5.2.11–5.2.13). Amyntas' recovery might have been dependent on his marrying of Eurydice, daughter of Sirras and granddaughter of Arrhabaeus (Strabo C326), thereby allying himself with an Illyrian group (possibly) as well as the Lyncestian royal house.[36] Whether Amyntas was expelled a second time by the Illyrians c. 383 is debatable, but he was forced to pay tribute (Diodorus 16.2.2).[37] His successor Alexander II (r. 369–368) also paid tribute during his short reign (Justin 7.5.1). Perdiccas III (r. 365–360) was possibly trying to extricate himself from the burden of paying tribute when he was killed in 360 (Diodorus 16.2.4). Anyway, the fact that Antipater wrote a (lost) history of Perdiccas' Illyrian deeds is a good indication that the fatal battle was not a singular event.[38]

Riding the wave of his military success in Paeonia, Philip almost immediately invaded Illyrian-held territory. This time, the revitalized, retrained and well-equipped Macedonian army defeated Bardylis' Illyrians, leaving 7,000 enemy dead on the field and driving the remainder out of Lyncus in Upper Macedonia (Diodorus 16.4.3–16.4.7).[39] Philip was now able to extend the northwestern border of Macedonia proper to Lake Ohrid (Lychnitis) (Diodorus 16.8.1). For the first time (perhaps) an Argead king had control over Lyncus.[40] His marriage to Audata, possibly Bardylis' granddaughter, but in any case of the Illyrian royal line – mother of Philip's daughter Cynnane and grandmother of Adea, who married Arrhidaeus Philip III – was evidently part of the political settlement. Despite this, two years later Philip's general Parmenion won a campaign against the Illyrian Grabus and more than a decade after that Philip fought against Pleuratus and then in 337 against

---

[36] On the timing of the marriage, see Carney 2019: 27–28.
[37] Diodorus 15.19.2 (and 16.2.2) may be a doublet: see King 2018: 56–57 with n.58. Diodorus 16.2.2 and Justin 7.5.1 claim he had to hand over Philip as a hostage, but this is much disputed. See Anson 2020a: 46–47.
[38] *Suda* s.v. Ἀντίπατρος (*FGrH* / *BNJ* 114 T1) and see Polyaenus 4.10.1.
[39] See also Justin 7.6.7, Polyaenus 4.2.17, Frontinus 2.3.2; cf. Anson 2020a: 61–62.
[40] Hatzopoulos (2020: 35) claims that Arnisa in Eordaea was the westernmost point of Temenid (Argead) control in Upper Macedonia, prior to Philip II. Contra, Billows (2018: 27–28) suggests Alexander I controlled all the upper districts.

Pleurias.⁴¹ These wars of Philip, though, were quite likely offensive rather than defensive. When Alexander III went into self-exile after his falling out with Philip over the latter's seventh marriage (Argead kings were polygamous),⁴² he found refuge among some Illyrians, though no details are known about his time there (Plutarch *Alexander* 9.4–9.5). As soon as Philip was dead, Alexander faced a rebellion in Illyria (Diodorus 17.8.1; Justin 11.6) and fought a hard campaign near Pelion in 335 against the Dardanians led by Clitus and the Taulantians under Glaucias (Arrian *Anabasis* 1.5.1–6.11). This campaign was Alexander's testing ground as a general, his warm-up for the war against Persia that his father planned but did not live to carry out. Illyrian forces were incorporated into Alexander's army and crossed to Asia in 334 (Diodorus 17.17.4) and 3,000 Illyrian reinforcements reached him in 327 (Curtius 6.6.35).

The Illyrian threat, especially, by occasioning such innovative reforms to the military as the use of the *sarissa* and the strengthened phalanx, changed Macedonia permanently, as William Greenwalt points out.⁴³ But Philip was never one to rely on military might alone. His best defence against Illyria was both a united Upper Macedonia under his political control and a border secured by reliable allies to the west and south. In addition to Audata, Philip's marriage to Phila, sister of Machatas and Derdas of the Elimiote royal house, whatever the circumstance – it was said he 'always married according to war' (Athenaeus 13.557C) – was effectual diplomacy.⁴⁴ Also, Philip could offer individual land grants to loyal nobles as well as to pastoralists and serfs in exchange for military service (*Syll.*³ 332, Diodorus 16.34.5). Philip's heavy infantry, the formidable Macedonian phalanx, was built largely on a landed peasantry and served to deflate the independent power of the Upper Macedonian nobles. Some scholars suggest that tension between Upper and Lower Macedonia continued even after Philip's consolidation and that it is not coincidental that his assassin Pausanias was from Orestis, while two brothers executed for complicity hailed from Lyncus.⁴⁵ However, the Upper Macedonians had been amply compensated for their submission to Argead rule. Many held positions of high command in the military, others were chosen as hetairoi

---

⁴¹ Grabus: Plutarch *Alexander* 3.5, Diodorus 16.22.3, Justin 12.16.6; Pleuratus: Diodorus 16.69.7, Justin 8.6.3; Pleurias: Diodorus 16.93.6.
⁴² On Macedonian polygamy before Alexander, see Ogden 1999: 3–40.
⁴³ Greenwalt 2010b: 290.   ⁴⁴ For Argead marriage policy, see Carney 2017.
⁴⁵ E.g. Bosworth 1971a; contra Heckel 2017b and see Anson 2020a: 73–77. Assassins: Diodorus 16.94, Arrian *Anabasis* 1.25.1, Justin 9.6.3–9.6.4, 11.2.2.

(Companions) of the Argead king, sharing in the social practices of the *symposion* and hunting as well as in the king's *synedrion* (council), while sons of leading nobles were reared at court in royal servitude as *paides basilikoi* (royal pages), a few enjoying royal privilege as *syntrophoi* of the king's offspring (see Chapters 11 and 12).

Philip secured the southwestern border of Macedonia by marriage in 357 to a princess of the royal house of Epirus – Olympias, mother of Alexander III. The alliance, meant to be a mutual defence against raiding Illyrians, was evidently shaky at times (Demosthenes 1.13), until Philip placed Olympias' brother Alexander on the Epirote throne (Diodorus 16.72.1; Justin 8.6.3–8.6.8) and finally arranged the marriage of his own daughter Cleopatra to her uncle Alexander (Diodorus 16.91.4). Following Philip's assassination at that same wedding, Epirus remained a close political ally of Macedonia throughout Alexander III's reign and for a time came under the direct control of Cleopatra and Olympias (see Chapter 13).

Thessaly, south of Macedonia, gradually came to be absorbed into Philip's political sphere over the course of two decades. The two regions were always from the earliest times closely associated by the major travel and land-trade routes connecting mainland Greece with the rest of Europe and with Asia along the north Aegean coast: one over the Kamvouni Mts from Perrhaebia to Elimeia, another through the Vale of Tempe into southern Pieria. Early legend makes the eponymous founder of Macedonia, Macedon son of Zeus, a brother of Magnes, founder of the Magnetes in Thessaly, both 'delighting in horses' and both 'living around Pieria and Olympus'.[46] Horsemanship was a valuable skill shared by their respective elite societies and cavalry the most important unit in their military organizations. Relations between Argead kings and leading aristocrats in northern Thessaly, mainly the Aleuads at Larissa, were ongoing at least from the reign of Perdiccas II (Thucydides 4.78.2, 132.2). Archelaus' assassination involved a man of Larissa (Aristotle *Politics* 1311b). Thessalians helped Amyntas III recover Macedonia after the Illyrians drove him out (Diodorus 14.92.3–14.92.4), but at one point he was allied with the Aleuads' enemy Jason of Pherae (Diodorus 15.60.2). When Alexander II succeeded in 369, he marched an army into Thessaly to restore some of the exiled Aleuads, but when he installed a garrison at Larissa, the Theban Pelopidas removed it (Diodorus 15.61.3–15.61.5, 67.4). Soon after this, when

---

[46] *Eoiae* F 7, Hesiodic *Catalogue of Women*. See Billows 2018: 40–41 for some comparisons between Macedonia and Thessaly.

Pelopidas arbitrated in the dispute between Alexander II and his political rival Ptolemy of Alorus, a young Philip was taken to Thebes as a hostage, where he was greatly influenced by the military strategies of Epaminondas (Plutarch *Pelopidas* 26.3–26.4; Justin 7.5.2–7.5.3).

Philip's first foothold in Thessaly came *c.*358 at the invitation of the Aleuads against the tyrants of Pherae (Diodorus 16.14.1–16.14.2). At this time he married Philinna of Larissa, mother of Arrhidaeus (Philip III), though in his own political interest he did not favour the Aleuads at the expense of the Pheraeans (Polyaenus 4.2.19). In fact, at some point he married Jason's niece Nicesipolis, who bore him Thessalonice. The Aleuads invited him to intervene again *c.* 355 and this time he became embroiled in the Third Scared War against the Pheraeans, who were allied with Phocis (Diodorus 16.35). Ian Worthington sees this war as triggering Philip's shift of focus from the kingdom of Macedonia to the Macedonian Empire.[47] Philip's success in defeating the tyrants of Pherae won him widespread popularity in Thessaly and the honour of being elected the overall commander of the Thessalian military forces, most significantly the Thessalian cavalry (Justin 7.6.8–7.6.9). Eighteen hundred Thessalian cavalry crossed to Asia with Alexander III in 334 and played an exceptional role in his victories over Darius.[48]

The final outcome of the Third Sacred War gave Philip two votes in the Amphictyonic Council (Diodorus 16.60.1). This was the door to his political control in central and southern Greece, solidified with his victory at Chaeronea in 338. But, notably, Philip's hegemony over the Corinthian League (his creation) was personal, the oaths being sworn to Philip as king of the Macedonians and to his successors, not to Macedonia as a state (Diodorus 16.89.1). Nevertheless, the long ongoing debate about 'constitutionalism' vs 'autocracy' has not yet been put to rest.[49] Control of the Greek *poleis* in the Chalcidice peninsula near Lower Macedonia had already been secured by the dissolution of the Chalcidic League after Philip razed Olynthus in 348 (Diodorus 16.52.9, 54–55). That territory became royal land, which the king could then parcel out to his Companions (Demosthenes 7.28).[50]

---

[47] Worthington 2014: 50; but see Anson 2020a: 124–125. Further on Argeads and Aleuads, see Graninger 2010: 309–318.

[48] See especially Diodorus 17.17.4; Arrian *Anabasis* 1.14.3 (Granicus), 2.11.2–2.11.3 (Issus), 3.11.10 (Gaugamela); Plutarch *Alexander* 24.1 (Issus); Curtius 6.6.35 (dismissal).

[49] See King 2010: 374–375, also 2018: 165–167 and Billows 2018: 30–31, arguing for no formal constitution. Contra, Hatzopoulos 2020: 103–116.

[50] Hatzopoulos (2020: 239) includes Chalcidice in Macedonia proper; contra Borza 1992: 49 with n. 55.

Philip's Thraceward advance, initially a swift reclamation of the conquests of Alexander I, prompted the alliance in 356 of Athens with Thracian, Paeonian and Illyrian kings in a 'war' against Philip.[51] Like Illyria, Thrace was never united, though again a few groups dominated politically and militarily. The Odrysians after the Persian campaign in 512–511 were dominant in the eastern Strymon area. When Philip seized control of the new Thasian settlement east of Pangaion at Crenides, the future Philippi (Diodorus 16.3.7), he was carving out new territory for Macedonian control, at Odrysian expense. The abundance of natural resources, control over which was the king's prerogative, not only minerals (silver and gold, iron and copper) for currency and luxury items but also timber for shipbuilding (Herodotus 5.23), meant that rivalry was inevitable. This is exemplified by the long-standing dispute between the Argead kings and Athens over the control of Amphipolis (Figure 9.2), a city the Athenians, after a failed settlement in 465, successfully founded in 437 near the crossing of the Strymon southwest of Mt Pangaion.[52] The 'both-ways' city was strategically

9.2 The Strymon at Amphipolis. Photo: Carol J. King.

[51] See *GHI* no. 53; cf. n. 33 above.
[52] Herodotus 5.11, 124, 7.112, Thucydides 1.100.2–1.100.3, 5.102, Diodorus 16.3.3, 4.1, 8.2–8.3, 6–7.

situated astride the main east-west coastal route and the land route up the Strymon valley into the interior of the central Balkans. Control of the city, with access to the area's timber supplies and the nearby port at Eion (Thucydides 4.108.1), might have been imperative for Athens, especially if Perdiccas II had a monopoly on the supply of silver fir (*Abies alba*), the best timber for shipbuilding and oars, and found only (apparently) in the forests of Mt Paiko, a monopoly which Athenian policy perhaps was aimed at breaking.[53] The Athenians briefly supported a challenge to the Macedonian throne in 432 by Perdiccas' brother Philip, whom Perdiccas expelled from the *archē* ('rule') he held east of the Axios towards the Strymon (Thucydides 1.57.3, 59.2).[54] Again in 429 the Athenians promised to back the Odrysian king Sitalces when he invaded Lower Macedonia and attempted to depose Perdiccas. Perdiccas managed to hold onto the kingdom by giving his sister in marriage to Sitalces' nephew (Thucydides 2.95.2–2.95.101; Diodorus 12.50), and by instigating the alliance of Chalcidic *poleis* (the Chalcidic League – see above, p.157) against Athenian imperialism in the north Aegean.[55] But in 424 the Athenians lost Amphipolis to Brasidas, whom Perdiccas had invited into the mix and to whom he gave military support (Thucydides 4.102–4.107). Although successive Argead kings agreed to help restore Amphipolis to Athens (e.g. Aeschines 2.32–2.33), that never happened, and Perdiccas III evidently placed a Macedonian garrison there in the 360s, for Philip II is said to have made it autonomous and withdrawn a force in 359/8 (Diodorus 16.3.3). By summer 356, Philip had recaptured it (Diodorus 16.8.2–16.8.3; Polyaenus 4.2.17) and Amphipolis became a permanent 'Macedonian' city. A unit from Amphipolis fought in Alexander's Companion Cavalry as early as 335 (Arrian *Anabasis* 1.2.5, 3.11.8).

In addition, Philip established what was to be permanent (until the Roman conquest) political control of the Plain of Philippi, a garrisoned, colonized base for exploiting local resources and for further expansion (Diodorus 8.6–8.7). Successive campaigns in 352, 346 and 342–340 brought all of Odrysian Thrace into Macedonian vassalage and the coastal Greek cities all the way to the Hellespont into alliance or under Philip's control (Diodorus 16.71; Justin 8.3.6, 14–15). Thereby, even before he gained hegemony in southern Greece, Philip had established a secure route to the Hellespont, a secure communications and

---

[53] Karathanasis 2019.
[54] Hatzopoulos 1996: i.174–i.175, Psoma 2011: 118–119. See also Plato *Gorgias* 471a–b.
[55] Psoma 2011: 113–115.

supply line for future expansion into Asia. In 339 he imposed Macedonian control through inland Thrace as far as the Danube River and the Black Sea. Philip saw the potential of harnessing both natural and human resources, utilizing colonists, garrison towns such as Philippopolis and a *stratēgos* of Thrace (Arrian *Anabasis* 1.25.2) to manage the vast area.[56] The Triballians, whom Philip subjugated on the return from the Danube (Justin 9.3.1–9.3.3), revolted at the news of his assassination. Alexander, who would take from Philip's settlement of Thrace a model for his own conquests, marched out and defeated them and other independent Thracians in 335 (Arrian *Anabasis* 1.1.4–1.4.6). Both Odrysian Thracians and Triballians crossed the Hellespont with Alexander in 334, as did some Agrianians, a Paeonian tribe formerly subject to the Odrysian king (Diodorus 17.17.4).

The oft-quoted speech of Alexander at Opis in 324 (Arrian *Anabasis* 7.9–7.11), prompted by the soldiers' longing for home, purports to summarize Philip's transformation of Macedonia. Much of it is true: his subjugation of the Illyrians, Triballians and Thracians, his opening up of trade and securing of mining, his domination of Thessaly and bringing together of the Greek *poleis* under his own hegemony. However, that he transformed Macedonians from wandering herders in the uplands into lowland city-dwellers 'is not completely true'.[57] In the western uplands, transhumant pasturing was the principal way of life and the archaeological record shows that the predominant type of settlement in Upper Macedonia was the unfortified village (*kōmē*), though larger centres did exist, as at Aiane in Elimeia, whereas in Lower Macedonia urban development is evident from the end of the sixth century.[58] While some Macedonians were or became city-dwellers, many put down the shepherd's crook for the *sarissa* and thereafter saw little if any of Macedonia. Those who did return returned to Antipater's Macedonia, bringing great wealth and new influences that would transform Macedonia once again.

Guide to Further Reading

For the general Macedonian background of Alexander's career, Borza 1990/1992 is a good place to begin. His discussions of the reigns of Argead kings prior to Alexander are thorough and his detailed

---

[56] Loukopoulou 2011: 467–471.
[57] Thomas 2010: 74. See Hammond's discussion, 2000: 349–351.
[58] Hammond 2000: 348, Xydopoulos 2012b: 523, Hatzopoulos 2020: 95–103.

descriptions of geography are well illustrated with excellent maps. Unfortunately, his work is sometimes stigmatized in response to his view of the 'Macedonian Question', which is mainly a modern political one. Nevertheless, his treatment of early Macedonia is exceptionally lucid. Much of the same material, albeit with different views expressed, is also found in Hammond's older, magisterial *A History of Macedonia* (vol. II, 1979), co-authored with Griffith. This remains essential reading despite being now largely outdated for archaeology and taking a somewhat imaginative approach to origins and institutions (so also Hammond 1989c). Errington 1990 (the first two chapters), though less detailed, is also informative. More recently, Billows 2018 and Anson 2020a both offer particularly valuable insights into Macedonian society as well as in-depth discussions of Philip II. Hatzopoulos 2020 offers an informative, though subjective, discussion of the main scholarly debates, and his negative reception of Borza is best balanced by reading Borza 1999. For Macedonian relations with Persia in the late archaic and early classical periods, Vasilev 2015 is highly recommended. For shorter topical discussions of various aspects of Macedonian history, society and culture, see Müller et al. 2017 and Heckel et al. 2020.

10: Kingship

William S. Greenwalt

Background

By the time Alexander III ascended the throne (336), the Argead kingdom had been in existence for about 300 years.[1] Nevertheless, for most of its history, that realm knew only very primitive political institutions.[2] Despite the arguments of N. G. L. Hammond, M. Hatzopoulos (both rightly heralded as first-rate Macedonian scholars) and others who have argued along these lines, there were no established and regularly-meeting assemblies (civil or military), no political procedures overseen by any recognized body of citizens, there were no written laws, and no defined court procedures beyond an appeal to the King or one of his designated Hetairoi. The king had no title and was merely addressed or noted by his given name, with a patronymic if called for. There was no bureaucracy or elections giving power to anyone for any length of time.[3] There were the Hetairoi ('Companions') of two kinds: the first consisting of the realm's aristocracy who held large estates upon which they bred the horses necessary for hunting and war; the second, a larger group, consisting of these same Companions and their retainers who together composed the kingdom's cavalry, its only effective military arm (at least through the reign

---

[1] All dates hereafter are BCE.
[2] I have argued this in several articles (see below), but increasingly am supported in the conclusion by other scholars. As samples, I note just two: Butler 2008: 1: 'In this dissertation I argue that Philip and his immediate successors were able to act as transformational leaders by skillfully building a new state out of a society with rich resources but weak institutions'; Anson 2020a: 44: 'The nature of Macedonia prior to the reign of Philip II was that of a backward state with great resources awaiting someone who could overcome the internal division, seize the independent coastal cities that dominated much of the country's trade and achieve defensible borders.'
[3] Hammond 1989c, especially 58–70. Hatzopoulos 1989 and, more recently, 2020. Although Hatzopoulos produces evidence of more advanced political customs and limitations upon a monarch's power, all of these come from either the second half of the fourth century and are initially derived from areas not originally a part of the core Argead kingdom. What international treaties involving Macedon are known to have existed before the late Argead period mention only the king, perhaps an heir, and a few prominent Hetairoi as witnesses. There is no evidence of any assembly ratifying any clause.

of Perdiccas II, who died *c.* 413). Unlike the land of the *polis* (Greek city-state), Macedon was a realm of estates, although a few towns existed, including the primary royal residence: Aegae, the 'hearth of the kingdom' (Diodorus 22 fr. 12 Walton)[4] and the site of the royal burial ground (Justin 7.2.2). Whereas the *polis* was composed of households each owned by citizens who would come together to discuss issues of common concern, to litigate according to established rules, to be judged by accepted jurors, and politically led by elected officials who served (mostly) for set terms (across a broad range of norms, from the ultra-conservative to the radically democratic), Macedon was essentially the household of one family – the Argead – which alone could produce kings. The kings, however, ruled largely in conjunction with the Companions, whom we can think of as Macedon's aristocracy.

Since no one man can rule a kingdom alone, no matter how small that realm is, there were families in Macedon, at least before 360, which were so well established in their roles as royal advisors and near-equal colleagues, that they had to be counted among the Hetairoi whether a particular king wished them to be so or not. Yet, the Hetairoi were not a closed class, ensconced in their perquisites through any known ritual or legal claim, nor did they serve for any defined term. Their number could be and was added to on the whim of a king, who might even choose foreigners to be so designated if they were useful enough or esteemed enough in either a public or private capacity. We know from several literary accounts that a *Hetairos* and even members of his natal family could be demoted or executed for serious offences against the diadem. However, in such cases it behoved the king to explain his punishments lest the Hetairoi as a whole suspect that the monarch was acting so rashly as to call the special relationship he maintained with them as a group entirely into question. The Hetairoi existed to give the king reach and to provide the muscle needed to keep him on the throne against both domestic and foreign threats. In return the king granted his Companions privileges, hunted with them, planned wars with them, worked with them individually, and consulted with them collectively mostly through the institution of the symposium.[5]

Our sources for early Argead history are few, anecdotal and widely strewn, but they are consistent in portraying the royal house as being divinely established, guided, protected, and separated from all others. I do not think that such anecdotes are unique to the

---

[4] For the text, see Walton 1957: 72–73.   [5] Borza 1983: 45–55.

Argeads (at least in the cases of being founded, guided, and protected), when they are put into the context of Greek aristocratic houses and their foundation myths. (I lump the Argead house in with others of Greek origin not to engage in the argument about Macedonia ethnicity, about which I will say nothing in this chapter, but only to introduce an important passage from Herodotus (8.137.1–8.138.3), who associates the founding of the Argead house with Argive, hence Greek, expatriates.) In Herodotus' foundation myth it is recorded that Argead legitimacy began as the result of an astounding series of miracles involving three brothers, the youngest of whom, Perdiccas, was specially chosen by an aspect of Dionysus to establish a new dynasty and to lead it in its earliest conquests. Hence Herodotus, whom I believe visited Macedon in his travels, thought that Perdiccas was the Argead dynasty's founding father.

Herodotus and the Argead Foundation Myth

There is much in Herodotus' foundation myth which smacks of religious ritual and nearby Thracian fire oracles, which I have noted before.[6] It very much looks as if Herodotus came to know of this foundation myth sometime during the reign of Perdiccas II, who ruled Macedon from about 450 to about 413.[7] Thus, at least at the time when Herodotus recorded this foundation myth, the Argeads claimed the dynasty's right to rule from the fact that subsequent kings could trace their roots back to Perdiccas I, although we know collateral branches of the family at times seized the throne from cousins. We also know from this myth that the Argeads did not invariably name the firstborn son of a king as his successor because, right from the start, the *youngest* of three brothers proved to be the most astute and the most charismatic. As noted, associations with divine protection and even claims of divine ancestry are not uncommon among Greek aristocracies, so the essence of this myth is not unique, but, even so, the Argeads enhanced their credentials by claiming Heracles as an ancestor, while Alexander III further strengthened his own stature by tracing his line (through his mother) back to Achilles. What is unique, however, is that, within both the core lands of the Argead dynasty and those added later,

---

[6] Greenwalt 1986, 1994.
[7] Here I am at odds with Vasilev 2016, who dates Herodotus' visit to the reign of Alexander I. I will explain why in the Appendix.

there arose no competing narrative which might allow another family to challenge the Argeads for power within the lands they ruled until after the demise of that dynasty.[8] In the world of the *polis*, aristocrats' claims were rivalled by their peers – not so in Macedon: the Argeads had the exceptional attention and support of the gods. For reasons of space, I will not go into detail with additional anecdotal evidence suggesting this conclusion, but the evidence is there for the early dynasty: Justin (7.1.7 and 7.2.7) and Polyaenus (4.1) both report instances of divine guidance of and protection for the Argead house, with Polyaenus making explicit reference to Dionysus' help.[9]

Royal Rights and Responsibilities

Before considering the importance of the images on Argead coins for this chapter, something should be noted about the king's rights. As the head of the royal *oikos* ('house'), the king expected the loyalty and active support of all of the members of his household in return for his respecting of the ancestral rights of their respective stations. He could also expect to profit from the ownership of that *oikos*, including his monopolies in timber and precious metals, when these latter came under his control. We know little about what taxes were due the king from his subjects, although we know that Alexander abolished the direct taxation of his Macedonian subjects on the eve of his invasion of Asia. We know also that he drew revenues from imports and exports ([Aristotle] *Economics* 1350a.22), and that he profited from the spoils of war. In addition, we also know that he claimed to be the realm's arbiter-in-chief when it came to law, although how he handled that role was occasionally contested. And we also know that he had the rights (and responsibilities) of leading his army into battle (or of assigning the *Hetairos* who would do so) and of leading in the dispensing and receiving of religious piety according to his status as the recipient of the gods' favour or to his own status as a living hero.

Nothing significant is known to have advanced the development of Argead kingship in the fifth century until the reign of Archelaus, except that, after the death of Alexander I, there was for a long time a disputed succession and that, as early as the reign of Alexander I, the

---

[8] Not even the long and much-beset reign of Amyntas III generated a rebellion against Amyntas or his house: see Greenwalt 2011.
[9] Justin's first reference gives an alternative to the foundation myth recorded in Herodotus. In Justin, it is a 'Caranus' not a 'Perdiccas' who founds Aegae and the Argead house.

kingdom could be split up into regions among the sons (or as in the later case of the not-yet-king Philip II, brothers), who exercised day-to-day rule on the king's behalf.[10]

KINGSHIP AND COINAGE

Now we must consider Argead coinage, which was first issued by Alexander I. This is not the place to pursue a detailed numismatic analysis, but it should be noted (because it continues to have relevance until the end of the dynasty) that, as was generally common throughout the Greek world, legitimacy was claimed through the images and legends portrayed on both the obverses and reverses (but especially the former) of coins. Among the most common obverse motifs portrayed on Argead coins from Alexander I through to Archelaus is a rider sometimes on a sedate horse, sometimes on a more animated mount, who frequently carries two spears. During the reigns of Alexander I and Archelaus, these coins frequently bear the inscription of the kings' names in the genitive on the reverse, which suggests that the sole authority for the minting of these coins was that of the kings themselves. (For whatever reason, the coins minted under Perdiccas II's rule bear no inscription.) The point of issuing authority should be emphasized: there is no authority other than the king mentioned. The king *was* the state. The earliest Alexander I issues bear a remarkable resemblance to coins minted by contemporary Thracian monarchs, who ruled regions of Thrace which abutted Argead Macedon.[11] Although we cannot be sure who had minted these images first, the geographical and chronological proximity of these issues suggests that they shared a common meaning. We know that Thracian and Macedonian rulers both assumed the guises of divinities at times in their official capacities and we know that one of the most ubiquitous symbols to emerge from Thrace over a long period of time was the 'Thracian' Rider: I think it likely that the figures on the Macedonian coins share the ideology of this mounted Thracian figure.[12] Hammond thinks that the figure which graces the obverses of Alexander I's coins is that of Alexander himself in the garb of a hunter, since his apparel is not military in nature.[13] This suggestion

---

[10] See Vasilev 2016: 39–41 and n. 6.   [11] Greenwalt 2015, especially 340–343.
[12] Greenwalt 1997, 2002, 2015. It should be noted that religious play-acting was known in the *polis* as well. One of the duties annually delegated to the Athenian *basileus archon* and his wife was to join conjugally under the guidance of Dionysus for the fertility and prosperity of the entire Athenian people.
[13] Hammond and Griffith 1979: 109.

seems more than plausible, and since the obverse of most Greek coins made an overt (to the issuers) reference to some divine protector, it seems likely that Alexander on his coins is not appearing as a mere mortal, but in a religious guise which I would identify as a hero and, as such, bringing to his persona the legitimacy which such a being might command. This conclusion, that the obverse is connected with a proclamation of legitimacy, seems virtually proven by a coin series issued early in the reign of Amyntas III, at a time when his claim to authority was only being settled after almost seven years of civil war. The obverse of this rare issue depicts a rider on a rearing horse with one spear poised to make a downward strike, while the reverse, in a wrap-around fashion, shows a yet-to-be-defeated lion gnawing on a second spear. Thus, this represents quite clearly a hunt in progress and, since Amyntas is the issuing party, one in which he has been successful. I think it can be argued, especially since Amyntas' coin echoes the motif of Alexander's (not to mention that Alexander's type is copied by both Perdiccas II and Archelaus in the interim), that Alexander was linking his legitimacy to an assumed heroic status, one evinced at times in the context of a potent hunt. Here, the king is identified and depicted as protector of his people (I would surmise) not only against the wilds of nature, but also against all enemies to right order, whether they be natural, foreign, domestic, or even metaphysical – even up to and including a hero's role in the afterlife.[14]

The Projection and Maintenance of Royal Power

Since the Argead state had such weak institutions for so long, the projection of the king's legitimacy came not as a result of process, but as a result of ceremonial spectacle. In such spectacles (including the hunt) the king stood for right order, traditionally defined. Thus, just as the king was not bound by legal checks and balances, he *was* bound by tradition, and thus, he was not considered to be an 'absolute' monarch by his subjects, who considered themselves to be free men protected by tradition. If a king went beyond tradition, then his legitimacy could and would be challenged. Even Alexander the Great understood this, and took extraordinary steps to justify his actions by appearing before ad hoc consultative assemblies when he understood that his actions were being

---

[14] Greenwalt 1992.

questioned as being in violation of tradition. Part of a king's holding back of the forces of chaos involved acting as a traditional priest, piously addressing whatever deity had to be addressed at any particular time. Since we have begun to address hunts, let us consider just one such cult, that of Heracles Cynagidas, which did honour (as far as the Argeads were concerned) both to Heracles the progenitor and to Heracles as the master of the hunt. When the king sacrificed to this aspect of Heracles, he almost certainly included at least some of his Hetairoi. When others sacrificed to this deity (and the cult was widespread throughout Macedon), their piety was much the same as the king's, although their attendants would match their social station.[15]

Thus, on one level, the king (and others) acted as a priest in the honouring of his divine ancestor as engaged in an activity of such importance to all Macedonians. In fact, we know a great deal about the Argead king as priest, but limits of space preclude an exhaustive survey.[16] But, beyond such priestly duties, what we are engaged in with the royal hunt takes piety to a new level.[17] The ancient Near East had long seen the royal hunt as a theatre for legitimacy, in which the king symbolically overcame threats (both physical and metaphysical) to his rule and to his realm's existence. Whether the Argeads developed a similar notion independently or not makes little difference, for Argead Macedon was a vassal state of the Persian Empire for about a generation before 479. Thus, the Argead realm would have been exposed to such props for political legitimacy well before Alexander I began minting his (now assumed) hunt obverses. And the tradition seems to have carried down until the reign of Alexander III (on the importance of the hunt to the Pages' Conspiracy, see below, p. 174). In such hunts, the primary hunter – the king – reasserted the potency that led to his legitimacy. As he asserted his royal legitimacy, he did so having assumed a 'heroic' persona, having been enveloped by the charisma of his family. He had become an avatar which transcended his mortality.

ARCHELAUS' REFORMS AND TRADITIONAL JUSTICE

Now let us consider the fortunes of Archelaus (c. 413–399), who benefited greatly from the decline and fall of Athens during the first decade of his reign, which coincided with the Decelean phase of the

---

[15] Hammond and Griffith 1979: 155, 165.
[16] Edmunds 1971; Christesen and Murray 2010 (especially 440–441 for kings), Mari 2011b.
[17] Franks 2012, especially 27–75.

Peloponnesian War. Thucydides (2.10.2) praised Archelaus for having done more to improve the military preparedness of his realm than all of the previous Argead monarchs combined. Among these improvements were the laying out of improved roads and the building of fortifications, which must have affected the countryside of Macedon, and probably involved considerable drainage projects. All of his physical improvements must have affected at least some of the Hetairoi adversely, but even more would have been bothered by the king's policy of centralization and the use of personnel who were not Companions to man his new forts: the Hetairoi excelled in mobile cavalry, not garrisons. In addition to the military improvements noted by Thucydides, we know that Archelaus:

1. Developed Pella as a truly Macedonian (and protected) port, and built a memorable palace there. He probably intended it to become his *de facto* primary residence, because Pella gave access to the sea as Aegae did not, and with its unique placement (somewhat inland but connected to the Thermaic Gulf by a defensible river/canal), was almost as defendable as was the traditional primary residence of Argead monarchs.
2. Placed his well-fortified mint in Pella, while at the same time completely revising and updating his coinage, so as to participate on Macedonian terms in international trade.
3. Negotiated better terms for the export of timber to increase his revenues.
4. Invited notable artists and intellectuals to his court (Euripides came, Socrates did not), who were willing to flee the cultural devastation of Athens in particular and the Greek world in general as the Peloponnesian War wreaked its havoc. What Archelaus received from this patronage was status by association and the resources (along with whatever activities took place in his new palace) to encourage at least some of the Hetairoi to take up residence in Pella for at least a part of the year (during which time Archelaus could keep a closer eye on them than would have been the case if they were dispersed).
5. Founded a Macedonian 'Olympics' at Dion to allow most Macedonians (who were not considered Greeks by the guardians of the major Greek games) to compete in an important sporting venue.

In short, Archelaus took steps to centralize his authority at the expense of the Hetairoi, to financially pay for his upgrades and the germination of a 'middle class' (at least in terms of creating an infantry),[18] to expand Macedon's power in the northern Aegean, and to try to balance his non-traditional power-grab by throwing a few sops to those whose interests he transgressed.

Archelaus was assassinated in 399 during a hunt, leading to a civil war which lasted almost seven years.[19] Aristotle (*Politics* 5.8.11–5.8.12) is the best source for this event. According to the well-informed-in-Macedonian-affairs polymath, three young men named Crataeas, Hellanocrates (of Larisa), and Decamnichus formed a plot against Archelaus because they all felt that Archelaus had unjustly abused them. Aristotle claims that the immediate causes of their anger were sexual in nature, but he goes to say that in at least two of the cases there were underlying political causes, and that their sexual violations had been tolerated to attain certain political ends. When Archelaus eventually refused to fulfil their goals, unjustly in their opinion, they decided to take him down. They did so in the context of the hunt and not the bedroom, not because of their access to weapons, but because they were making a statement: since the hunt was one of spectacles which legitimized a king's power, they would strike the unjust king down in that arena as a protest against his right to rule. Archelaus had morphed into a hubristic Tyrant, he was no longer a law-abiding King. It is not known how much general aristocratic resentment over Archelaus' initiatives lay behind the motives listed by Aristotle, but it is likely that there was at least some sympathy for the assassins, because these expected to get away with murder through the lame excuse that they had hit the wrong target. Archelaus' loyalists, understanding the symbolic nature of the hunt, did not fall for this and, almost certainly through torture (it was good enough for Alexander in the case of Philotas), extracted the truth of the matter.

The Continuing Importance of Royal Display and Symbolic Space

Another hunt also underscores the symbolic nature of the royal hunt – one involving Alexander in Asia and after the issue of his 'orientalization' led many Macedonians to begin to question his loyalty to

---

[18] Greenwalt 2006.   [19] Greenwalt 2019.

Macedonian tradition. A brief summary will suffice here because the events surrounding Alexander after his self-proclaimed adoption of the title 'Great King' (previously held by Darius, Alexander's one-time rival but now an honoured predecessor) are so well known. Facing temporary compliance from most but not all of the Asians he claimed now to rule, Alexander saw the need to graft his previous titles (only one of which was King of Macedon) onto a host of Persian customs. He attempted to introduce *proskynēsis* ('obeisance') into court procedure, to train oriental youths to fight in the Macedonian manner, to raise various Asian notables to political and military positions of importance, to treat those around him, even Macedonians, as the native Persian monarchs had done, and (gasp!) even to dress in the Persian style, all to win popularity among those he knew he needed to maintain his recent conquests. There simply were not enough Macedonians (or Greeks) to rule such a vast empire, even if they all wished never to return home again. Even if he could convince all Macedonians about the propriety of his vision for the future, he knew that the vast majority of his Argead subjects lacked the skill and training to uphold the complex and massively bureaucratic Persian Empire. So Alexander saw the need to change. Many saw his reforms as a violation of Macedonian tradition and thus illegal. As such, many began to question Alexander's right to rule.

One such was a young Macedonian Page, named Hermolaus, who was probably inspired by the tone-deaf Callisthenes. Callisthenes was Alexander's official chronicler of his conquests, an excellent orator and a major, if not necessarily popular, figure at court, who was known to oppose Alexander's oriental initiative. Hermolaus concluded that Alexander, who had once been a legitimate Argead king, had evolved into an oriental tyrant whose rule was illegitimate and whose leadership could no longer be tolerated.[20] In light of this, and knowing the symbolic importance of the hunt, Hermolaus decided to challenge Alexander during a hunt in which he was an attendant. One of the king's obligations during these hunts, in order to establish his legitimate leadership, was to throw first at the object of the hunt. Hermolaus, however, as an act of defiance, stole Alexander's perquisite by launching his spear at the prey first, thus challenging Alexander's status. Alexander knew immediately what Hermolaus had meant by his act and had him punished both physically and through demotion. Imagining these

[20] Greenwalt 2021a and 2021b

punishments as further proof of Alexander's tyranny, he thereafter organized what proved to be an unsuccessful plot to murder the king. Things did not end well for Hermolaus and his co-conspirators.[21]

The king's legitimacy was not only reaffirmed through the spectacle of the hunt. The king also participated in other kinds of public religious festivals so as to legitimize his royal claims. Although I will not go into the details here, two other assassinations fit this bill: the murder of Alexander II at the instigation of Ptolemy of Alorus and the assassination of Philip II, killed by a former lover named Pausanias before thousands of eyewitnesses in what can only be called a religious pep rally before the king was about to head off to his invasion of the Persian Empire. As for the former, I have argued that the same *Hetairos* that had facilitated the smooth accession of Alexander II precipitated his murder less than two years later.[22] Why? I think the quick turnaround came when Ptolemy realized that Alexander II had no intention of maintaining the policies of his father, which had led to a loss of face (Amyntas paid a danegeld to Illyrians), but which had pretty much secured a peace with the Illyrians for well over a decade. If Ptolemy thought Amyntas right not to challenge the Illyrians, and I think he did (primarily because he and Amyntas worked so closely together that Amyntas allowed Ptolemy to marry his daughter), then he would have been aghast at what he would have considered Alexander II's rashness. A rapid change in the relationship between Macedon and an Illyrian king/war-leader powerful enough to pillage that kingdom would have endangered Alexander II's subjects if his initiative failed. This would have sacrificed their well-being to the king's ego in Ptolemy's estimation, not a thing a legitimate protector would do. Hence, I believe that Alexander II was cut down while performing a traditionally validated war dance because Ptolemy thought Alexander unfit to be king. In the case of Philip, whose ambitions and sense of transcendence can only be said to have increased in his last years, he was the object of a carefully planned assassination in a theatre with thousands of onlookers precisely because Pausanias wanted to scream out the magnitude of Philip's injustice in his case. Most of the crowd would not have known of Pausanias' story, but the circumstances of Philip's death, happening as it did just as thousands were viewing Philip apparently presenting himself as a 'thirteenth Olympian', would probably have made many in the crowd sympathize

---

[21] Although he was not a part of the plot, the angry Alexander used it to rid himself of his increasingly tiresome historian.

[22] Greenwalt 2017a: 80–91.

with the slaying of a man who was exhibiting an Olympian-sized and very dangerous hubris before their very eyes. If sacrilege is not some kind of injustice, what is? While Philip was no longer balanced and thinking more of personal glory than of being a shepherd to others, this religious spectacle would have been thought by many an appropriate nemesis for a king who was endangering his realm by his actions (Diodorus 16.93–16.94; Plutarch *Alexander* 10.3).

One more thing must be said about the development of Macedonian kingship. As the power of both Philip and Alexander expanded to reach beyond the core of the traditional Argead kingdom to include many non-Macedonians under their rule, many of whom (like the Greeks and Persians) had much more advanced public infrastructures then did the Macedonians themselves, both rulers understood that they would have to revisit what it would take to be a successful monarch over a broad coalition. It was with this expansion that more formal 'constitutionalism' came to be known within at least part of the territories being ruled. With Philip, as he came to rule more and more Greek cities, he permitted the institutions of these cities, with their elected magistrates and publicly-posted written laws, to continue, at least at the urban level, where they already existed. Alexander did something similar in Asia, and as both kings began to see the nature of their powers grow beyond the customs of their ancestors, the essence of the relationship between king and kingdom began to evolve. Although originally local councils, etc., were limited to the periphery, these began to seep back into Macedon proper. This process only accelerated with the demise of the Argead house, and then Macedon began to 'hellenize', while the Macedonians abroad began to experiment with the political structures that emerged during the Hellenistic Age. Charisma did not entirely evaporate, but the states which emerged were far too large and far too cosmopolitan to be ruled effectively without a far-better-defined state infrastructure.

Appendix: Herodotus and the Founder-Figures

I am not persuaded by Vasilev's argument that Herodotus visited Macedon during the reign of Alexander I.[23] I *do* believe that he visited the realm, but I do so for reasons not considered by Vasilev. Leaving

---

[23] Vasilev 2016; cf. n. 7 above.

aside the arguments of anti-Athenianism and his consideration of chronology, all of which is still up for debate, I think it more likely that Herodotus visited Macedon somewhat after Alexander I had died, because his founder of the Argead house is named Perdiccas, not Alexander. We know that by the fourth century the accepted founder of the dynasty was one 'Caranus', a name we have already seen attested in Justin's alternative foundation narrative.[24] Thus, we know that the Macedonians reconfigured their official king list, certainly for political reasons. Between the time of Herodotus and the acceptance of Caranus, the playwright Euripides had written a play when he was resident at that king's court called *Archelaus*, crediting an 'Archelaus' with founding the dynasty. Euripides, of course, may merely have been flattering his patron in the name he associates with the foundation, but another explanation is possible and I think preferable. Hammond has already posited that the mounted hunter on Alexander I's coins was meant to depict the king himself. If so, then it is quite possible that, before the fourth century, the reigning king merged his identity as hero with the accepted founder of the dynasty, thus reinforcing the ruling king's charisma through a direct connection to the founding of the Argead state. This would mean that with every new king came a new founder. After Archelaus came a civil war which saw several kings rapidly following one another before Amyntas III brought back some stable longevity to the throne. During a period of rapid leadership changes it would have been manifest that none of the short-lived kings possessed the charisma necessary to associate themselves with the founder, or even rule effectively. During such a period there might very well have emerged a consensus around sticking with the name 'Caranus' as the name of the founder, since that name means 'Leader' or 'Chief', a generic, but very acceptable label for the founder of a dynasty. Such a change would have brought some order to the king-list, and to a certain extent taken the name of the founder out of the politics of the day. This is how we can explain how a figure unknown to Herodotus came to displace Perdiccas in the minds of all as the first Argead patriarch.

---

[24] Greenwalt 1985.

Guide to Further Reading

The constitutional approach to Argead kingship should be noted although it is being supplanted in modern scholarship, including my own. The main points of this position are summarized and supported in Hammond 1989c: 58–70 and Hatzopoulos 1996 and 2020. To date, there has been no systematic focus on Argead kingship and especially its evolution, an oversight I soon hope to rectify. But see King 2018 for the latest review of Argead history.

11: COURT AND COMPANIONS

Jeanne Reames

Discussion of Alexander's court demands delineating, both anthropologically (define 'court') and in terms of what will be covered.[1] We have daily functions: what king and courtiers did and where they did it; then the offices, military positions, and institutions; and finally interpersonal connections, or court prosopography. In this chapter, we will consider a few methodological problems, appraise those elite offices and institutions under Alexander, then offer a bibliographic summary. In the following chapter, we will address how Alexander's changes gave rise to personal clashes, conspiracies, and other indiscipline.

DEFINITIONS AND DIFFICULTIES

In Gregor Weber's analysis of the court as a social system,[2] he presents what seems to me a usefully succinct definition: 'an organizational framework for the exercise of power',[3] although he also offers a more complex description[4] akin to Anthony Spawforth's,[5] including delineation of inner and outer courts, and of who comprised each. Of that exercise of power, especially between king and Hetairoi, Wilhelm Völcker-Janssen underscored the informal-negotiation aspect,[6] not unlike Edward Anson's earlier observations.[7] Here, we will preference Weber's briefer version because it allows a broader application without assuming a spatial centre, even a mobile one. All these explanations are indebted to Norbert Elias' iconic *Die höfische Gesellschaft* or *The Court Society*.[8]

---

[1] I dedicate this and the next chapter to the late Eugene N. Borza, who passed away on 5 August 2021 as I was completing edits. It seems fitting to honour the memory of the man who shepherded my own education in ancient Macedonia and is cited liberally throughout.
[2] Weber 2009: 83–98. [3] Weber 2009: 90. [4] Weber 2009: 84–85.
[5] Spawforth 2007b: 84. [6] Völcker-Janssen 1993: 33.
[7] Anson 1985a, updated at Anson 2022; see also Pownall 2022b.
[8] Elias 1969/1983. This was enlarged on by chapters in the edited collection, *Hof und Theorie*: Butz, Hirschbiegel and Willoweit 2004.

When considering Alexander's court and the people in it, three significant hurdles face us. The first is our sources' laser focus on Alexander himself. Even his highest officers move on and off the page in relation to him, making it impossible to know anyone's complete career. Similarly, we can say little about the daily tasks of chancellery, treasury, or court functionaries, nor what division, if any, existed between military and civil offices. Weber notes, 'the administrative and military threads run together in the court';[9] so also Heckel: 'It is ... virtually pointless to differentiate between military status and political power.'[10] While largely true, figures such as Chares, not to mention Callisthenes, seem to have occupied some purely civil roles, and Hephaestion's appointment as chiliarch, if Alexander did resurrect the Persian *hazarapatish* for him, involved as much civil function as military ('the highest civil servant in the state').[11]

Because of our sources' narrow interests, what we learn often comes tucked at the edges of anecdotes, or as window-dressing for significant events. For instance, Olympias sent a special cook to her son in Asia because Pelignas knew, *inter alia*, the proper rites for the royal *patrōia*[12] (Athenaeus 14.659f). These were so important that Alexander still dragged himself up from his deathbed to perform them each morning (Arrian *Anabasis* 7.25.2–7.25.6). Yet what were these *patrōia* beyond generic 'ancestral rites'? We would love to know. And while Macedonian kings acted as a court of appeal,[13] how frequently did this occur? Even *where* did this occur when Philip and Alexander were away from Pella or Aegae, or *in* Pella or Aegae, for that matter? Nor do we know where a king's Hetairoi[14] were housed in the capital: directly in the palace or at townhouses owned in addition to their estates? Were they expected to be in attendance a select number of days like a medieval knight's service for feudal land tenure, or was it up to their discretion, and ambition?[15] These are just three examples. If we look to later Hellenistic courts to make educated guesses,[16] or follow Alan Samuel in comparing the Macedonians with the much later Merovingians,[17] it remains speculation.

---

[9] Weber 2009: 97.　[10] Heckel 2003b: 208.
[11] Dandamaev and Lukonin 1989: 228–229; cf. Briant 2002: 258–261; Collins 2001; Kuhrt 2007: 583; Reames 2010: 203–206.
[12] τὰ ἱερά σου τὰ πατρῷα πάντα.　[13] Adams 1986; Roisman 2012b: 134–136.
[14] For the sake of English clarity, when referring to the social class, I will employ the Greek term, capitalized, while, for the military units, I will employ the translations Companion Cavalry and Foot Companions.
[15] Weber 2009: 87.　[16] D'Agostini, Anson, and Pownall 2021, for a collection of articles.
[17] Samuel 1988.

So, at the outset, we should underscore the paucity of reliable information about the court's daily workings, things our sources consider minutiae.

A second difficulty is the cultural and political overlay of our surviving original sources. Few of these were written by a contemporary of Alexander, and none of them are our biographical histories (Arrian's *Anabasis*, Curtius, Diodorus, Justin and Plutarch's *Alexander*). All have their own agendas, and a good deal of recent work has been done on their Greek and imperial-Roman historiographic overlays. The recognition of such veneers offers important correctives to the ways Macedonian objections to court changes have been repurposed, or misunderstood.

Finally, we lack a baseline. If we wish to consider how Alexander altered his court, it would help to know more about how it functioned before him, or before Philip. Carol King says, 'Problems of succession tell against a highly developed infrastructure ... before Philip II's reign',[18] and Joseph Roisman notes, 'Interest in the nature of the Macedonian monarchy is a modern phenomenon.'[19]

Arguments for a constitutional monarchy generally fall flat.[20] Eugene Borza summed up a king's power so: 'The king could do exactly what he could get away with.'[21] The quip 'what he could get away with' stresses the highly personal nature of each king's reign: freed or limited by his successes, his personal charisma, and his ever-evolving negotiations with powerful Hetairoi families.[22]

In the following chapter, we will explore what current archaeology might suggest regarding early Macedonian royal and elite display. In this chapter, we will review offices and institutions at the court.

Elite Offices and Royal Institutions

We should outline what we know of traditional elite offices and institutions, including Alexander's Persian adaptations. Terminology remains our *bête noire*, not only with sources in Greek and Latin, but also because

---

[18] King 2010: 377–378. [19] Roisman 2012b: 132.
[20] Greenwalt 2010a; King 2010: 390–391 (a bibliographic essay); cf. Hatzopoulos 1996: i.261–i.322.
[21] Borza 1990: 238; also 236–241. [22] Now see also Anson 2022.

of the use of the same word for both social and military units (*hetairos*),[23] or the same one for different military units in differing contexts (*somatophylax*),[24] or Greek words for Persian units (*doryphoroi, melophoroi,* and *rhabdouchoi*).[25]

Terms also changed between kings. Under Philip, the Pezhetairoi were the elite fighting force who became the Hypaspists under Alexander when he extended the honorific Pezhetairoi to what had been the Pezoi (Foot) under Philip.[26] And after 325 BCE, the Hypaspists became Argyraspides.[27] In fact, the army had been in flux for some time, not only under Philip,[28] but also under Alexander II,[29] and back at least to Archelaus (Thucydides 2.100.2).[30]

The Hetairoi, or King's Companions, comprised the Macedonian elite class. When the term emerged is unknown but given archaeological evidence and Vivi Saripanidi's argument that 'heroic' funereal display began *c.* 570/60 BCE,[31] we might imagine it was in use at least by that time, if not earlier. These landed families were wealthy enough to own horses, riding to war or on the hunt with their king.[32] By the reign of Archelaus, a few Greeks may have been added,[33] and we should wonder if Persians such as Bubares, Alexander I's brother-in-law, was made an Hetairos even earlier.[34]

Herodotus' mention of *paredroi* ('those who sit beside') alludes to an informal advisory council as early as Alexander I, a role apparent still in Philip and Alexander's day (8.138.1).[35] Plenty of evidence indicates that the king's interaction with them involved a regular negotiation of power: his and theirs.[36]

---

[23] Heckel 2016: 255–256, 264–268.
[24] Anson 1985b; Hammond 1989c: 148–151; Heckel 2016: 345–346.
[25] Olbrycht 2014: 50–52. Weber (2009: 85) notes similar trouble with Greek words for 'court': *oikia, to basileion, ta basileia,* and *aulē*, with the last being primarily Hellenistic.
[26] Heckel 2016: 254. However, cf. Anson 1985b, 2009 and 2022: 18–22: he argues that the change was instituted by Philip at some point, although he acknowledges that the term had a narrower meaning earlier.
[27] Anson 1985b; Heckel 2016: 272–273. [28] Anson 2020a: 45–71. [29] Greenwalt 2017b.
[30] Greenwalt 2015.
[31] Saripanidi 2017: 96–99, 2019: 178–179. See Chapter 12 for more elaboration.
[32] Kienast 1973: 258; Borza 1990: 125; Völcker-Janssen 1993: 32–37; Paschidis 2006; Greenwalt 2010a. Macedonia was very much a horse culture, with equine importance to elites difficult to overestimate (see Chapter 15 in this volume, by Carolyn Willekes); Müller 2010: 30–31; Carney 2015: 268–269).
[33] Borza 1990:171–177, who suggests perhaps at least Euripides.
[34] Athenaeus 12.538c suggests the term *idioxenoi* was sometimes used for non-Macedonian Friends, but these are not necessarily Hetairoi, whose appointment must have involved some sort of landed settlement: so Nearchus from Crete was granted land around Amphipolis (Arrian *Indica* 18.10).
[35] Borza 1990: 241–242; Heckel 2003b: 205; Weber 2009: 88–89; Greenwalt 2015: 337–338.
[36] Anson 1985a: 316, 2008: 136; Völcker-Janssen 1993: 32–34; Heckel 2003b; Carney 2015: 31–37; Spawforth 2007b: 85–87; King 2010: 378; Sawada 2010: 406–407; Roisman 2012.

The number of hetairoi would have expanded and occasionally contracted across reigns. In Philip's reign, Borza estimates about 100, matching the 100-couch tent Alexander seems to have inherited (Diodorus 17.16.4), but that 100 may refer only to the heads of hetairoi families.[37] Theopompus gives Philip 800 Hetairoi (*FGrH / BNJ* 115 F 225). By the end of Alexander's reign, he had at least 500 with him in Asia (Athenaeus 12.539f).

A few hetairoi families may have enjoyed a semi-hereditary role, as with Antipater, if the Iolaus who acted as regent (*archōn*) for Perdiccas III while he was at Potidaea was Antipater's father (Thucydides 1.62.2).[38] That Antipater wrote *The Illyrian Deeds of Perdiccas*[39] suggests the family had some sort of standing relationship with the crown, and he must already have had a position when Philip became king.[40]

We do not know at what point the seven-man bodyguard unit, the Somatophylakes (bodyguards), and the King's Boys (Paides Basilikoi, sometimes called Royal Pages) came into being. Much current scholarship regards them as extending prior to Philip with probable antecedents at the Persian court.[41] Both offices guarded and cared for the king's person. The King's Boys even performed duties typically reserved for slaves, but being for the king made it an honour – which should encourage us to be cautious about how we understand the king as 'first among equals'. Both units were reserved for the Hetairoi class: the sons of Hetairoi for the King's Boys, and especially favoured Hetairoi for the Somatophylakes. Yet, as demonstrated by the careers of Craterus, or of Philotas before his fall, one could rise quite high at court without being a member of the Seven.

Also called 'bodyguards' (*somatophylakes* again) was the royal unit (*agēma*) of the Hypaspists who protected the king on the battlefield just as the Somatophylakes did off it.[42] For Philip, who fought on foot at least sometimes, the then-Pezhetairoi would have been his personal unit, much as Diodorus describes at Chaeronea (16.86.1).[43] But as Alexander fought regularly in the royal *ilē* of the Companion Cavalry, the royal Hypaspists would have had to run with the cavalry as *hamippoi*.[44]

---

[37] Borza 1990: 255.   [38] Heckel 2016: 33.   [39] Walsh 2012.   [40] Heckel 2016: 34.
[41] Kienast 1973: 243–244; Carney 2015: 207–223; Heckel 2016: 246–251.
[42] Heckel 1986: 245–246, 151–155.
[43] While Diodorus' description of Chaeronea implies that Philip fought there on foot, his wounding in the thigh by a spear in Thrace, which killed his horse under him, tells us he was on horseback there (Plutarch *Moralia* 331c; Justin 9.3.2).
[44] Heckel 2012, 2016: 257.

In short, their primary role was to build social ties – or test them. But the extravagance of these feasts still had performative purposes for the elite, the king foremost of all. Demosthenes bemoaned that, at Philip's supper parties, one could find no moderation in food, wine, or entertainment.[60] Scale clearly mattered, and the palaces at Pella and Aegae, as well as some larger houses, contain multiple dining rooms (*andrōnes*).[61] We also have the 100-couch tent used by Alexander at Dion (Diodorus 17.16.4).

The king might host or be hosted. Agatharchides speaks of the profligacy of parties to which Alexander was invited (*FGrH* / *BNJ* 86 F 2 = Athenaeus 155d), and Ephippus claims the king spent 100 *minai* on each feast, albeit we should understand that as late in his reign (*FGrH* / *BNJ* 126 F 2 = Athenaeus 146c). Giving the best party was a king's job, and descriptions (and complaints) of Philip's or Alexander's profligacy abound.[62]

In light of feasting collections in Macedonian Archaic graves, including expensive metal vessels associated with drinking, such symposia (or at least feasts) had a long history in the region and were strongly associated with elite status.[63] So if the price-tag skyrocketed thanks to Philip's and Alexander's successes, the concept of an extravagant table was longstanding. The tendency to see it as Persian imitation results from unfamiliarity with the archaeological record – not surprising, given the recentness of the finds and their slow publication. Carney has cautioned against viewing fourth- and third-century burials as evincing newly acquired wealth because we have 'less comparable information prior to this period'.[64] Now we have some evidence showing such wealth was not new.

Ergo, if Alexander borrowed some particulars, including a taster (*edeatros*), whom Collins calls 'manager of the royal table' (Athenaeus 2.71b–2.71c),[65] or the seating of preferred guests inside while others ate in a courtyard (Athenaeus 12.538c; Arrian *Anabasis* 7.11.8–7.11.9),[66] we

---

[60] Demosthenes 2.18–2.19; also Athenaeus 3.120e; Pownall 2010; Müller 2016d.
[61] Kottaridi 2011; Akamatis 2011.
[62] Athenaeus 3.120e; 4.166f–4.167c; 6.260d–6.261a (Philip); 1.17f; 4.146c–4.146d; 4.155d; 10.437a (Alexander). The tale of Alexander refusing Ada's chefs with a quip about a night march for breakfast and a meagre breakfast for dinner are part of Plutarch's moralizing and should be ignored (*Moralia* 127b = 180a = 1099c; *Alexander* 22.4).
[63] Saripanidi 2017, 2019; see also the discussion at pp. 192–196 below.
[64] Carney 2015: 249, n .6.   [65] Collins 2012b.
[66] Although, given the evidence of multiple *andrōnes* in both palaces, this may not be a borrowing, or at least not a recent one. Admittedly, the datings of these palaces mean that they represent post-Alexander updates, but we cannot assume Macedonian dining architecture changed significantly.

should not over-read Persian patterns into Macedonian feasting traditions. They had their own, and significant differences existed, such as the regular presence of royal women at Persian dinners.[67] Even late in his reign, Alexander's symposia would not have been alien to Macedonian custom. Carney: 'It is easy to exaggerate or oversimplify the degree of Persian influence on Macedonian court practices.'[68]

Royal hunts, if not nearly as frequent as symposia, served similar functions and also had a long history in Macedonia. Like symposia, the king could use them for semi-political purposes, such as polling opinions or feting dignitaries. They served athletic and military purposes, the pursuit of dangerous prey promoting rivalry in the display of one's courage and skill. We hear of several Hetairoi being wounded while hunting (Lysimachus: Plutarch *Demetrius* 27.3; Craterus: Plutarch *Alexander* 41.3; Peucestas: Plutarch *Alexander* 41.2). Alexander even invited his entire army to hunt with him on one occasion (Curtius 8.1.14).

Macedonians saw successful hunting as proof of excellence (*aretē*), and killing a wild boar without nets was a threshold of manhood that granted one the right to recline at dinner (Athenaeus 1.17f–1.18a). For the king, superiority in the hunt was proof of his right to rule: verification by performance.[69] Depiction of the divine Rider figure as a hunter on coins as far back as Alexander I speaks to hunting's significance for royal presentation.[70] Greenwalt summarizes it as 'a metaphor of order over chaos, justice over hubris, good over evil, bounty over deprivation'.[71] For this reason, none were allowed to outshine the king – even if he were in mortal danger, as Lysimachus learned (Curtius 8.1.14–8.1.19). Carney puts it succinctly: 'the king could not afford to be saved'.[72] Müller even suggests that Hermolaus' decision to strike a boar before Alexander was a form of political protest (Curtius 8.6.7).[73]

Craterus' choice, after Alexander's death, to immortalize in sculpture the hunt wherein he came to Alexander's rescue against a lion, perhaps copied in the Lion Hunt Mosaic at Pella, tells a story of his

---

[67] Kuhrt 2007: 584–586. Carney speculates as to whether royal women did occasionally attend Macedonian *symposia*, but thinks it 'exceptional behavior' if so (1995: 233). If later elite female burials lacked banqueting sets, earlier Archaic burials had them for women and even children, but to indicate their *status and identity*, not their attendance at banquets (Saripanidi 2019: 185, 190).
[68] Carney 2015: 281. [69] Carney 2015: 266, 270–271.
[70] Carney 2015: 266–267, 270–272; Greenwalt 2015: 340–343, 348, and Chapter 12.
[71] Greenwalt 2015: 348. [72] Carney 2015: 271. [73] Müller 2010: 29–30.

Diadoch ambitions (Plutarch *Alexander* 40.4).[74] The *Suda* describes him as exceptionally regal and claims he mimicked Alexander's style except for the diadem (*s.v.* Κρατερὸς ὁ Μακεδών = Arrian *FGrH / BNJ* 156 F 177a). Of all the images he might have selected to donate at Delphi – the most important panhellenic site in all of Greece after Olympia – it was a lion hunt. Not only that, but a hunt in which, because Alexander had been in trouble, he showed himself to be the superior hunter. Together with his choice of dress, we might read this as Craterus' symbolic bid to replace Alexander.[75] He is the bringer of 'order over chaos', as a king should do.

***

The offices and institutions of the Macedonian court were dynamic, changing not only across the reigns of kings, but even within the reign of one king. That reflects the highly personal natural of Macedonian kingship. Again, as Borza said, 'The king could do exactly what he could get away with.'[76] Unsurprisingly, larger changes to the court were inaugurated by the more successful kings, and this is especially true of Alexander's reign. He not only altered the names of army units (Pezoi to Pezhetairoi; Pezhetairoi to Hypaspistai; Hypaspistai to Argyraspides), but he introduced new parallel Persian units (*doryphoroi*, Melophoroi, and *rhabdouchoi / rhabdophoroi*).

Yet in the most traditional, and perhaps oldest institutions – the symposium and the hunt – we see fewer changes. Archaeological evidence suggests an alteration in *scale*, not in the essential understanding of the purpose of these two royal activities. It is perhaps to be expected that the symposium and the hunt became arenas wherein Alexander would experience the greatest push-back against the changes he attempted to institute, discussed in the following chapter.

Guide to Further Reading[77]

Monographs on Macedonia or her kings routinely contain chapters or subchapters on the Argead court and the king's interaction with his Hetairoi. We may point to N. G. L. Hammond's massive, three volume *A History of Macedonia* (i, 1972; ii, with Griffith, 1979; iii, with Walbank,

---

[74] Dunn and Wheatley 2012.
[75] Dunn and Wheatley 2012: 40, 43. That Alexander's probable irritated reaction at the time is omitted in our sources is likely not accidental.
[76] See n. 21 above.   [77] This guide also serves Chapter 12.

1988), as well as his later *The Macedonian State: The Origins, Institutions and History* (1989c); Dietmar Kienast's *Philipp II. von Makedonien und das Reich der Achaimeniden* (1973); J. R. Ellis' *Philip II and Macedonian Imperialism* (1976); Eugene Borza's *In the Shadow of Olympus: the Emergence of Macedon* (1990); Malcolm Errington's *A History of Macedonia* (1993); Wilhelm Völcker-Jannsen's *Kunst und Gesellschaft an den Höfen Alexanders d. Gr. und seiner Nachfolger* (1993); Miltiades Hatzopoulos' *Macedonian Institutions Under the Kings* (1996) and his later *Ancient Macedonia* (2020); Sabine Müller's *Die Argeaden: Geschichte Makedoniens bis zum Zeitalter Alexanders des Großen* (2016b); and Carol King's *Ancient Macedonia* (2018). In 2017 Sabine Müller et al. put out *A History of the Argeads: New Perspectives*. And in 2020, an editorial team of Waldemar Heckel et al. produced a *Lexicon of Argead Macedonia* that includes entries for the court, conspiracies, kings, and courtiers. We must also note the existence of not one but two *Companions* to Macedonia, one from Wiley-Blackwell (Roisman and Worthington 2010) and another from Brill (Lane Fox 2011a).

Prosopography of Alexander's court began with Helmut Berve's 1926 two-volume *Das Alexanderreich auf prosopographischer Grundlage*, which was, for years, the go-to for potted summaries of persons in Alexander's orbit, including helpful citations of relevant ancient sources. Then in 1992, Waldemar Heckel released the original *Marshals of Alexander's Empire*, which evaluated the ties between his officers, some of the more significant with chapters devoted entirely to them. It constituted the most substantial update of Berve that Alexander scholarship had seen, but did not include women or non-military figures. Elizabeth Carney's *Women and Monarchy in Macedonia* (2000) balanced the scales by focusing on elite women from prior to Alexander's reign down into the era of the Successors, as these mothers, sisters, and daughters were potent actors in Macedonian politics and court life.

In 2006, Heckel produced *Who's Who in the Age of Alexander the Great: Prosopography of Alexander's Empire*, which did include women and others not in *Marshals*, albeit with smaller entries for all. Arranged alphabetically, it came closer to Berve's comprehensive original. In 2015, Carney published a convenient collection of her articles that had addressed aspects of the court, often with new postscripts, *King and Court in Ancient Macedonia: Rivalry, Treason, and Conspiracy*.[78] A year

---

[78] When citing any of those articles in this chapter, I use the republished 2015 collection rather than the original because of those added postscripts representing Carney's current thoughts and updated bibliography.

later, Heckel issued a substantially revised version of *Marshals*, retitled *Alexander's Marshals: A Study of the Makedonian Aristocracy and the Politics of Military Leadership* (2016), narrower in scope in terms of who was included, but which incorporated additional information and later publications. In 2021, he expanded his *Who's Who* to include the Successors down to the Battle of Ipsos, retitled *Who's Who in the Age of Alexander and His Successors: From Chaironeia to Ipsos (338–301 BC)*.

In his initial edition of *Marshals*, Heckel opened his second part with 'Career Progress',[79] a review of the Macedonian *cursus honorum* ('career ladder') for a young man of the elite class. The revised edition maintains essentially the same conclusions.[80] In Carney's collection, Part III examines elite institutions from education to the *symposion* and hunting.[81] Also, cited earlier, Gregor Weber's 2009 'The court of Alexander the Great as social system' considers the complex web of negotiations between king and courtiers.

Individual articles and chapters in edited collections are too numerous to list but can be found in bibliographies of the above. We should, however, mention a few that specifically address Iranian aspects of Alexander's court. Brian Bosworth's 'Alexander and the Iranians' in the *Journal of Hellenic Studies* (1980a); Ernst Badian's 'Alexander in Iran' in *The Cambridge History of Iran* (1985); and Ernst Fredricksmeyer's 'Alexander the Great and the Kingship of Asia' (2000) were all foundational. In 2004, Marek Jan Olbrycht published *Aleksander Wielki i świat irański* (*Alexander the Great and the Iranian World*), followed by several articles in English on the court that swim a bit against the current.[82] Maria Brosius' measured 'Alexander and the Persians' in *Brill's Companion to Alexander* (2003a) provides an excellent analysis of Alexander's failures to understand Achaemenid policy; she also wrote an extensive analysis of the Achaemenid court (2007) in the same collection as Anthony Spawforth's 'The Court of Alexander the Great between Europe and Asia'.[83] Spawforth untangles daily functions and how Alexander's court changed, as well as considering his use of physical space. Andrew Collins has written multiple articles on Iranian offices at Alexander's court;[84] and Frances Pownall provides a brief overview of recent

---

[79] Heckel 1992: 237–258. [80] Heckel 2016: 243–280. [81] Carney 2015: 191–279.
[82] Olbrycht 2008, 2014, 2016. [83] Spawforth 2007a, including Spawforth 2007b.
[84] Collins 2001, 2012a, 2012c, 2017.

court studies in her introduction to the edited collection, *The Courts of Philip II and Alexander the Great* (Pownall et al. 2022), a volume in which several chapters address the courts of Philip and Alexander (and the Successors).[85] See also Chapter 6 (Sabine Müller) in this volume.

---

[85] Pownall, Asirvatham and Müller 2022; this volume appeared too late for consideration of its chapters in any significant way.

12: Changes and Challenges at Alexander's Court

Jeanne Reames

Conspiracies and public protest indicate political dissent, factionalism, and a change in perceptions of the ruler by those ruled.[1] In Alexander's reign, conspiracies bunched into two chief groups. We also see several acts of public protest, including two mutinies, perhaps better termed 'indiscipline'.[2] Here, we will focus especially on those clashes that followed his changes to the court in the summer of 330 BCE. In order to better understand the Macedonians' original objections, now hidden beneath our sources' Greco-Roman overlay, we should walk back in time a bit with the aid of recent archaeological discoveries in the north.

As popularly presented, Alexander inserted elaborate Persian ceremonial into a rough-and-ready court – what Anthony Spawforth charmingly refers to as 'homespun', before taking issue with that common view.[3] Our sources exaggerate the court's supposed lack of sophistication to underscore Alexander's eventual Persian seduction, or, conversely, to accentuate Alexander's or Philip's moral purity.[4] Yet recent archaeological evidence suggests that the pre-Philip Macedonians were far from the sheepskin-wearing mountaineers enslaved to their neighbours that Arrian's Alexander describes in his Opis speech (*Anabasis* 7.9.2–7.9.3).[5]

Archaeology and Early Macedon

If few would take Alexander's assessment literally, prior academic discussion of the kingdom Philip inherited tacitly accepted the general appraisal of it as poor, unsophisticated, politically chaotic, and socially

---

[1] Heckel, Heinrichs, Müller and Pownall 2020: 179. [2] Carney 2015: 27–59.
[3] Spawforth 2007b: 90.
[4] For example, Plutarch *Moralia* 178b, 180c; Briant 2015: 320–354; Spawforth 2007b: 88–89; Müller 2010, 2015: 466–469.
[5] Nagle 1996: 167–168.

backward. When Manolis Andronicos uncovered the Royal Tombs at Vergina in 1977, and further work on the enormous Pella palace in particular suggested that Macedonia might not have been so parochial, the mid-fourth century and later dates of the excavated material did not much alter the accepted textual picture of the pre-Philip kingdom.

Greek archaeology of the last few decades no longer permits that illusion. We must radically rethink early Macedon. Philip's rise is better understood as a stabilizing renaissance after a period of weakness. The intermittent nature of Greek/Athenian interest in the region prior to the Persian Wars does not translate into Macedonian primitivism, although it often accidentally does in modern popular thought. New material finds tell a different story.

The best overview in English of recent funerary archaeology is Vivi Saripanidi's 2017 piece, 'Constructing continuities with a "heroic" past: death, feasting and political ideology in the Archaic Macedonian kingdom', followed in 2019 by 'Macedonian necropoleis in the Archaic period: shifting practices and emerging identities'.[6]

In the lowlands, the excavation of Aegae at Vergina demonstrates that the elite class enjoyed no little wealth even early in the Archaic era.[7] So did the elite at Pella, given the Archontiko finds, the bulk of which (over 700 graves) are Late Iron Age and Archaic.[8] Sindos has also produced wealthy Archaic-era burials.[9] Whether the graves at Archontiko, and especially Sindos, belonged to people who would have called themselves 'Macedonian' is under debate, yet Saripanidi notes a uniformity in the material finds between not only Vergina and Archontiko, but also Sindos and Agia Paraskevi post 570/60 BCE that speaks to a uniformity of culture.[10] Whatever the political truth at these sites, they certainly disclose great wealth at an early stage.[11]

Recent excavations at Methone reveal the city to have been a hub of Euboean Greek, Phoenician, and Macedonian trade from the late

---

[6] Copious recent literature, virtually all in modern Greek and much of it published in *Το αρχαιολογικό έργο στη Μακεδονία και τη Θράκη* (*AEMTh*), describes these northern sites. Publications range from yearly archaeological reports to periodic summaries and overviews. I have cited here only a few, mostly in English for the sake of the reader, but some sites are published by the archaeologists only in Greek.
[7] Kottaridi 2011, 2012, 2013; Kottaridi and Walker 2011; Kyriakou 2014.
[8] A. Chrysostomou and P. Chrysostomou 2012, P. Chrysostomou and A. Chrysostomou 2012; del Socorro 2012.
[9] Tiverios 1998; Despini 2009, 2016; Gimatzidis 2010; Ignatiadou 2012.
[10] Saripanidi 2017: 88–92, and 95, 2019: 180, 182–184; Xydopoulos 2017:82–98; cf. Kottaridi 2017: 625–637.
[11] See also Tsigarida and Ignatiadou 2000.

eighth century on, with examples of writing equivalent in date to the famous Nestor Cup from Pithecusae.[12] Tzifopoulos argues that the Macedonian absorption of Pieria and Bottiaea should be backed up into the mid-eighth century,[13] which in turn would require us to backdate the kingdom's founding as well. Pabst wants to place its genesis in the late eleventh or early tenth centuries;[14] if that is surely too soon, somewhere in the eighth century certainly seems reasonable and comes prior to the significant burial changes of 570/60 BCE.[15] It would hardly be the first time archaeology has busted textual testimony, especially of founding myths like that of the Argeads (Herodotus 8.137–8.139).

Archaic and earlier finds at Aiani confirm that Elimeia in the southern highlands was a powerful regional capital long before Philip absorbed it.[16] So also with Tribanishte and Gorna Porta near Ohrid, further north into Lyncestis.[17] Copious amounts of gold such as masks, mouth pieces (*epistomia*), hand coverings, and clothing attachments appear at Aiani and Tribanishte similar to those at Vergina, Archontiko, and Sindos. If the populations were certainly different,[18] the finds evince some shared mortuary practices that used 'princely' wealth to demonstrate vertical status.

Finally, expensive figured tombstones of the late Archaic and Classical eras at sites such as Pydna, Dion, Aegae, Beroea, Pella, and Aiani show that wealth was enjoyed by the elite generally.[19]

If these material finds cannot talk to us the way our texts can, they do make it abundantly clear that luxury displays by the elite were normal in Macedonia as far back as the Archaic era and even into the Late Iron Age. This is not something Philip, much less Alexander, introduced. For example, the tomb of the 'Lady of Aegae' at Vergina, *c.* 500 BCE, contains seventy gold and silver artefacts, including a diadem and sceptre fittings, high-quality glass and bronze vessels, and figurines.[20] We find similar mortuary expenditure in the top two categories of male and female graves from the western cemetery at Archontiko, dating to the same period and earlier.[21] So, too, at Sindos.[22] These include gold *epistomia* and face masks, dress accessories, weapon decorations, even shoe-sole coverings. In addition, other metal and high-value items (ivory, amber, glass) were included.

---

[12] Kasseri 2015; Clay, Malkin and Tzifopoulos 2017; Tzifopoulos, Bessios and Kotsonas 2017.
[13] Bessios, Tzifopoulos and Kotsonas 2012: 20–21.   [14] Pabst 2009: 31–45.
[15] Saripanidi 2019: 189–192.
[16] Karamitrou-Menteside 2008a, 2008b, 2011; Lasslett 2020: 12–13.
[17] Stibbe 2003; David 2018.   [18] Saripanidi 2019: 180–182.
[19] Kalitzi 2016; Haverkost (2023).   [20] Kottaridi 2012; Saripanidi 2017: 95 and n. 84.
[21] P. Chrysostomou and A. Chrysostomou 2012.   [22] Despini 2009, 2016.

If 'princely' burials disappeared in southern Greece and her colonies by the sixth century – money Greeks then put into temples and other public buildings – wealth in Macedonia and other Balkan regions went into the ground in magnificently furnished tombs. Despite the presence of gold *epistomia*,[23] we know too little about the Macedonians' afterlife beliefs to speculate on what these objects meant beyond the obvious: status markers. Greenwalt does reasonably suggest such burial goods were understood as necessary for the afterlife.[24]

Thus, we see that, after 570/60 BCE, heroic spectacle and performance of prestige were expected of royals and the elite.[25] Ergo, if Alexander's and Philip's munificence ran on a grander scale, *it was not functionally different* from that deeply embedded in Macedonian culture for at least two hundred years before Alexander's birth.

Furthermore, the earliest displays are found in graves that predate Persian–Macedonian contact, so they cannot be the result of Persian precedent.[26] Persian forms do appear in silver but not until the end of the sixth century.[27] Nor are these burials influenced by Greeks in the north during the era of tyrants, as we do not find such burials in Greek colonies nearby. Instead, they represent the indigenous adoption and reconceptualization of an idealized 'heroic' past.[28]

These graves, with their evidence of performative status, must alter our understanding of Macedonian responses to court changes introduced in the mid-330s BCE, then expanded on in 324 BCE. The Macedonians' opposition arose not from rustic disdain for or egalitarian horror at extravagant royal pageantry. Their anger stemmed from the adoption of customs of the conquered and, especially, perceived slights to their (elite) standing.

We must also recall that Argead kings were set apart by sacral charisma and a belief in divine descent that Aristotle claims separated their kingship from tyranny (Aristotle *Politics* 1310b).[29] By 336 BCE and probably earlier, Philip had adopted the use of a throne.[30] In Greece, thrones belonged only to priests (or gods); but of course, as king, Philip

---

[23] While gold *epistomia* are associated with 'Orphic' rites later – Edmonds (2011); Tzifopoulos (2010) – or perhaps solar deities among Thracians – Theodossiev 1998, 2000 – we should be cautious about such suppositions so early, *pace* Fol 2009. Theodossiev connects them simply to the wider phenomenon of these 'princely' burials.
[24] Greenwalt 2015: 345.   [25] Saripanidi 2017: 112–113.   [26] *Pace* Touratsoglou 2010: 36–38.
[27] Saripanidi 2019: 185.
[28] Saripanidi 2019: 92–99; also Cohen 1995; *pace* Moloney 2015, who relies mostly on texts.
[29] Fredricksmeyer 2003: 256–257; Greenwalt 2010a: 156–160, 2015: 343–348; Naiden 2019a: 31–45; and Chapter 10 (Greenwalt).
[30] *Oxyrhynchus Papyri* 15.1798; Spawforth 2007b: 91.

was a priest, and we find thrones in Macedonian burials as well.³¹ In his final parade, Philip went so far as to include himself alongside the Hellene Twelve Gods (Diodorus 16.92.5), in the form of a statue (*eidōlon*) 'suitable for a god' (*theoprepes*). The hero-shrine (*herōön*) situated adjacently to and above Royal Tombs I and II at Vergina – regardless of the fraught identification of their occupants – again underscores the unique religious status of the royal family.

If the right to rule extended to the entire Argead/Temenid clan, presentation in our texts of the king as first among equals has been expressed in a way too reminiscent of Greek *polis*-centric ideals, the same ideals that created sumptuary laws to rein in aristocratic exhibitionism. By contrast, the 'heroic' burial style in Macedonia shows lower classes reaching *up*, rather than trying to pull the elite classes down to a more 'subdued' style.³² These graves offer no evidence of democratic equalizing. Royal clusters at Aegae and the top two categories at Archontiko show, instead, flagrant royal and elite splendour.³³ We must, then, reconfigure Macedonian notions of the king as *primus inter pares* in that light. The elite sought not to reduce the king, but to raise themselves *up* – the direction of competitive social display – not down.

The Problem of Anti-Asian Bias

As time went on, so our sources would have it, Alexander succumbed to his passions and put on 'an arrogant spirit' along with Persian clothes (Curtius 6.6.1–6.6.11, *superbiamque habitus animi insolentia sequebatur*; Diodorus 17.77.4–17.77.7; Justin 12.3.8–12.3.12; Arrian *Anabasis* 4.7.4).³⁴ Despotic Alexander played perfectly into the Greek *topos* of the Persian Great King as a tyrant over natural slaves, in contrast to the 'good king' Philip.³⁵ Sabine Müller writes, '*polis*-centred ideology and manner of perception is often an obstacle to the understanding of the Macedonian politics and culture'.³⁶ And Hugh Bowden lays out the Roman *topos* of Alexander's 'acts of hybris' in Bactria.³⁷

---

³¹ Palagia 2018.   ³² Saripanidi 2019: 183–184; cf. Kottaridi 2016: 625–637.
³³ Saripanidi 2019: 175.
³⁴ Müller 2015: 467, for bullet points of the storyline. For the sentiment more generally in Alexander's day, see Xenophon *Cyropaedia* 8.8.9–8.8.12; Isocrates 4.149–4.159; and Aristotle *Politics* 1252b. This attitude is sometimes uncomfortably echoed by modern scholars: Green 1974: 372, 'these same officers whose blunt Macedonian irreverence kept pricking the bubble of his oriental self-aggrandizement'. Later Roman-era examples: Arrian's personal commentary at *Anabasis* 4.7.4 and 4.9.8–4.9.9, and Lucian of Samosata's satirical *Dialogues of the Dead* 12, in the exchange between dead-Philip and dead-Alexander.
³⁵ Müller 2010: 30–32.   ³⁶ Müller 2015: 460.   ³⁷ Bowden 2013: 64–69.

Occasionally, this is reversed with Alexander lifting the Persians out of barbaric squalor, as in Plutarch's *De fortuna Alexandri*, where he claims Alexander 'tamed' (*exēmeroō*) Asia, and that those he conquered were 'civilized by being subdued'.[38] These same attitudes excused slavery on the basis that the slaves were Christianized, and fuelled Richard Henry Pratt's infamous justification for native residential schools: 'Kill the Indian, save the man'.

Blindingly obvious in all this is Greco-Roman prejudice against and hostility to Asian culture. Moralizing on tyranny and vice in favour of freedom and self-control (*sophrosunē*) typically contrasted the free, disciplined, and temperate West against the debauched, enslaved East (e.g. Athenaeus 12.539b). Spawforth explains that bias:

> The preferred solution which suited the moralising tendency in classical historiography as well as reflecting the unwillingness or inability of most ancient authors on Alexander to rationalise royal splendour, was to personalise the issue in terms of Alexander's corruption by his eastern conquests.[39]

Yet in the interest of saying the quiet things out loud, we should emphasize the *ethnic* part, as one can exhibit anti-Asian bias without subscribing to democratic egalitarian political theories. As we have seen, 'royal splendour' was a Macedonian norm. The Macedonians were still biased against Asians.

Similarly, we do not need to excuse Alexander's decision to add Persian protocol to his court by dubbing it simply pragmatic or 'wearing spoils' (Curtius 6.6.5).[40] Almost certainly pragmatism was part of his decision, particularly if he wished his new empire to function, but there is nothing wrong with Alexander deciding he liked Persian things. Diodorus calls him 'an admirer of Persian ways' (18.48.5). To say he imposed Persian court procedural because it appealed to his growing megalomania[41] suggests there is something inherently immoral about Persian traditions. Alexander may not have always understood Persian customs, much less succeeded in his attempts to unite Persian and

---

[38] Plutarch *De fortuna Alexandri*, Moralia 328d, 328f (οὐκ ἂν ἡμερώθησαν, εἰ μὴ ἐκρατήθησαν). This text also lies behind the 'Brotherhood of Mankind' and 'fusion' theories for Alexander's aims that we will discuss towards the chapter's end.
[39] Spawforth 2007b: 88–89 (quote at 89). Briant (2015) details the various ways tales of Persian opulence were understood and employed in Greek and Roman historiography, as well as later Islamic historiography. And both Elizabeth Baynham (1998a) and Diana Spencer (2002) analyse specifically Roman imperial approaches.
[40] Collins 2012c: 372, 375–376, following Bosworth 1980a: 5–10.   [41] Bosworth 1980a: 9.

Macedonian custom,[42] but his wish to do so is not proof of moral decline nor of delusions of grandeur, even if the Greeks and later Romans cast it so.

CHANGES AT THE COURT OF PHILIP AND PRIOR

As noted above, the reign of Philip is better understood as a revival after several decades of weakness. Our archaeological record reveals no little wealth in the kingdom, and its opulent display by the elite, back into the early sixth century. Textual evidence tells us that Alexander I used the Persian invasion to his advantage in order to absorb nearby Paeonia and especially the mines in Thracian Bisaltia, the richness of which is visible in his coinage.[43] The presence of Persians at his court, whatever his later attempts at a pro-Greek spin, probably marked the first introduction of Persian elements (Herodotus 5.17).[44] And he married his sister Gygaea to Bubares, a Persian noble (Herodotus 5.21.2). Their son, with a Macedonian name, Amyntas, later ruled Alabanda in Caria (Herodotus 8.136.1).

Likewise, Perdiccas II's masterful balancing act during the Peloponnesian War should be reviewed through Macedonian, not Athenian, eyes.[45] The archaeological record shows him to be far from a weak king; we find a number of figured tombstones dating to his reign, influenced by Ionic and Athenian style.[46] The elite, and perhaps too a burgeoning merchant class, clearly had money to spend.

Archelaus introduced the most (known) changes prior to Philip. Thucydides recounts his military improvements (2.100.2). In addition, he moved the capital to Pella, likely for better sea trade, then patronized Greek artists to decorate his new palace. He also established at Dion what Badian called a 'counter-Olympics'.[47] All demonstrate that Macedon emerged from the Peloponnesian War in good financial shape.[48]

Archelaus' unexpected assassination in 399 BCE embroiled Macedon in forty years of succession wars amid brief bouts of stability; this weakened her and thinned out the previously burgeoning number of Argeads.[49] No doubt these struggles also reduced the ranks of Hetairoi who supported the wrong candidate, a contraction enormously

---

[42] Brosius 2003a.   [43] Borza 1990: 119–131; Lasslett 2020: 146–154; see also Borza 1982.
[44] Borza 1990: 100–119; Paspalas 2000: 531–532; Müller 2015: 464.
[45] Borza 1990: 132–160; Müller 2017.   [46] Haverkost 2023, concluding chapter.
[47] Badian 1982: 35.   [48] Borza 1990: 162–177.   [49] Borza 1990: 177–197.

accelerated by the crisis at Philip's accession, with over four thousand troops dead on a northern plain near Illyria (Diodorus 16.2.3–16.2.6). Yet this event provided Philip with an unexpected opportunity to introduce, with considerably less objection, non-elite infantry alongside traditional elite cavalry. He also pulled much of Upper Macedonia under his authority and moved around populations, what Ellis calls 'decantation'.[50]

Too little is known of the early battles Philip waged for change, summed up by Diodorus in a few lines (16.2.4–16.3.7, 16.8.1) and by Satyrus' list of his marriages (Athenaeus 3.557b–3.557e).[51] Philip's new kingdom would naturally have created additional layers of competition among the elite. Thucydides calls these Upper Macedonian kingdoms 'allies and dependents', yet they had their own kings and Hetairoi (2.99.2, 4.79.2, 4.83.1). They included Eordaea, Orestis, Tymphaea, and Pelagonia – but especially Elimeia and Lyncestis, which had their own armies and which periodically harboured rival Argeads.[52]

Early Macedonian society seems to have been composed of the royal Argead clan, the Hetairoi class, then commoners, an unknown number of whom were indentured. Post-Philip, this pattern became the royal clan, other royal families, the Hetairoi of all these groups, and commoners, with fewer indentured as Philip expanded the infantry via land grants.[53] These layers of complication can be overlooked, groups assumed to be internally homogenous revealing complexity when examined more closely.[54]

Philip's extensive military acquisitions, which resulted in new land to distribute such as that around Amphipolis (*Syll.*³ 332), would have blunted the edge of resentment, not unlike Alexander's use of gifts to tamp down objections to his introduction of Persian court procedure in mid-330 BCE (Diodorus 17.78.1). Yet we cannot assume that acrimony was entirely allayed, lingering bitterness still being visible even late in Philip's reign, given his banishment of Aëropus and Damasippus for bringing a harp player into camp sometime after Chaeronea (Polyaenus

---

[50] Dell 1963: 62–99; Ellis 1969: 11–12; Borza 1990: 210–211; Anson 2008, 2020a: 73–72, 2022.
[51] Ellis 1969; Borza 1990: 206–216; Carney 2000: 52–76.
[52] The Elimean cavalry was perhaps superior to the Macedonian at one point (Xenophon *Hellenica* 5.2.40–5.3.2), and Thucydides makes it quite clear Arrhabaeus of Lyncestis was a thorn in the side for both Perdiccas II and his son Archelaus (4.83.3, 4.125.1).
[53] Anson 2008, 2022; Greenwalt 2010a: 160–163. It is likely that the Macedonian conquest of Pieria and Bottiaea had included a similar fusion of Macedonians with conquered groups who, textual evidence says, remained in the region (Hatzopoulos 1996: 169–178). So, Philip's forced fusion of neighbours may not have been the first in the kingdom's history.
[54] Heckel 2003b: 197.

4.2.3). The severity of the punishment warns that it was not about the girl, but rather Philip's distrust of Aëropus, as the (probable) former king of Lyncestis.[55]

Alexander's inclusion of Persians at court after 330 BCE had precedent in his father's inclusion of Upper Macedonians, Thessalians, Thracians, and others. So also with Archelaus' inclusion of Greeks earlier.[56] Heckel says, 'To enrol Thracians or Thessalians in ranks of the Hetairoi was far less offensive than to do the same with eastern barbarians.'[57] Yet Victorian British antipathy towards the Irish reminds us that greater familiarity or geographic proximity does not mitigate hostility, and what would have been seen as very alien in one generation was perhaps not so much by the next.[58] The real issue in all cases was increased competition (more Hetairoi) for limited resources (the king's favour and appointments).

Alexander's Court Reforms and Unrest Among the Elite

The first group of conspiracies occurred in wake of Philip's death and might be viewed as alternative bids for the throne. The second group bubbled up in Bactria. Olbrycht says, 'Beginning with the Philotas affair, in all major court scandals ... an important if not crucial point raised was the king's "barbarization"'.[59] Yet the Greco-Roman tailoring of the historiographical accounts of these events for moral effect complicates our attempt to discern the true complaints. In any case, Heckel considers it surprising that there were so relatively few – a point worth underscoring.[60]

After Philip's assassination, the twenty-year-old Alexander's hold on the throne was tenuous, requiring him not only to kill rivals, such as his cousin Amyntas, and silence opposition, but to cut deals.[61] In the end, he survived owing to the support of Antipater on the one hand, and Parmenion on the other.[62] If Parmenion had to sacrifice his son-in-law Attalus, Antipater likely saved his, Alexander of Lyncestis, from sharing the fate of his brothers Arrhabaeus and Heromenes, executed for supposed collusion in Philip's murder.[63] All were sons of Aëropus, likely

---

[55] Heckel 2006: 5, 2016: 19–22.   [56] Borza 1990: 171–177.   [57] Heckel 2003b: 215.
[58] We may also wonder if Alexander I had appointed some Persians to the Hetairoi in the early fifth century.
[59] Olbrycht 2014: 55.   [60] Heckel 2003b: 224–225.   [61] Howe 2015a.
[62] Heckel 2003: 200–203.   [63] Heckel 2006: 19.

the same Aëropus whom Philip had exiled less than two years prior (see above, pp. 199-200). Whether any were actually guilty might be of less interest than the fact Alexander could convince others that they were. Eventually suspicion caught up to Alexander of Lyncestis in Asia Minor, c. 324 BCE, when a letter from Darius was found, offering a bribe if he would kill the king (Arrian *Anabasis* 1.25.3, 9–10; Diodorus 17.32.1–17.32.2; Curtius 3.7.11–3.7.15).[64] Alexander of Lyncestis was taken into custody but not immediately executed:[65] another concession to Antipater?

After this, Alexander faced little opposition. Then again, he was winning. Following the Battle of Issus, he began to style himself 'King of Asia' (Arrian *Anabasis* 2.14.8–2.14.9; Curtius 4.1.10–4.1.14; Plutarch *Alexander* 34.1).[66] What he meant by the title is a vexed question. Fredricksmeyer suggests he intended something beyond Great King, with which Collins agrees.[67] If he had acquired Darius' tent, servants, and family following Issus, these were spoils of war, the charming story of his meeting with the royal family notwithstanding (Plutarch *Alexander* 21.4–21.5; Curtius 3.12.13–3.12.26; Arrian *Anabasis* 2.12.3–12.3.8; Diodorus 7.37.4–7.38.2). Stripped of moralizing and omens,[68] the tale of his use of Darius' dining table as a footstool while seated on the throne may best represent his attitude (Diodorus 17.66.3–17.66.7; Curtius 5.3.13–5.3.15). And whatever Plutarch says of his respect for Darius' wife (*Alexander* 22.3), she died not long before the Battle of Gaugamela, supposedly in childbirth – also related by Plutarch without apparent irony (30.1). Given the timing, the babe could not have been Darius'.

In Susa, after Gaugamela in 331 BCE, following the arrival of substantial reinforcements, Alexander introduced advancement for lower officers on merit and valour rather than heredity, as had earlier been the case (Arrian *Anabasis* 3.16.10).[69] No doubt a popular innovation with those seeking progress, the change also worked to decentre tribal ties and undermine the regional power base of wealthy Hetairoi families. Now fortune lay with impressing the king. Philip's earlier

---

[64] Heckel 2003: 210–214; Carney 2015: 127–137; cf. Badian 2000: 56–63.
[65] His execution, years later, following the trial of Philotas (Curtius 7.1.5–7.1.9; Diodorus 17.80.2; Justin 12.14.1) is remarkable for the amount of time passed and distance covered while he was held prisoner, making one wonder what sort of penal system Alexander's moving army-cum-court had. Another aspect about which virtually nothing is known.
[66] Yet see Hatzopoulos 1997: 44.
[67] Fredricksmeyer 2000: 149; Collins 2012c: 371–372. See Briant 2002: 852–864, on supposed Achaemenid unpopularity.
[68] Baynham 1998a: 117.   [69] Heckel 2003b: 209–210.

creation of infantry with land grants, and Pezhetairoi chosen on merit, had been a similar move with similar goals.[70]

The following spring, after wintering four months in Persepolis and stripping the palace of its movable wealth, Alexander burned parts of it (Diodorus 17.70–17.72; Curtius 5.6.1–5.6.7: Plutarch 38.1–38.8; Arrian *Anabasis* 3.18.10–3.18.12). The Clitarchan tale of drunken revels, embedded in Curtius et al., was for Greek consumption, as what could be more insulting to the Greek male mind than to have an Athenian *hetaira* ('courtesan') lead the destruction of the pinnacle of Achaemenid power? The conflagration also marked, for Curtius, another step along the road of Alexander's gradual loss of self-control and growing decadence.[71]

The archaeological record, however, yields a different story, suggesting a *damnatio memoriae* against Xerxes,[72] and that the burning was not that extensive: 'only certain parts of the terrace were burnt down'.[73] In any case, the razing of Persepolis became a watershed moment, representing an end to the Campaign of Greek Reprisal, perhaps with an eye to appeasing Athens or other Greeks inclined to join Agis' Revolt in Greece, depending on what Alexander knew of the uprising, and when, which is unclear. Now Alexander, as King of Asia, could get on with the business of building a new empire, and, in the months that followed Darius' death, he introduced court changes perhaps conceived of during his months wintering in Persia's greatest city.

Diodorus says, 'he became zealous for Persian luxury and the extravagance of Asian kings' (17.77.4–17.77.7;[74] cf. Curtius 6.6.1; Plutarch *Alexander* 45, 47.3–47.7; Justin 12.3.8–12.3.12). Polyaenus puts the first appearance of Alexander's new receiving tent during his sojourn in Hyrcania (4.3.24), and Diodorus pairs the introduction of *doryphoroi* and *rhabdophoroi* with the surrender of Darius' brother Oxyathres there, following Darius' death in July of 330 BCE; Oxyathres was made a *doryphoros* and Hetairos (17.77.4). About the same time, Persian-style horse trappings and purple cloaks were distributed to his Hetairos as status markers (Diodorus 17.77.5), and Chares of Mytilene probably began to operate then as chamberlain (*eisangeleus*; Plutarch *Alexander* 46.1).[75]

---

[70] Anson 2008, 2009, 2022.   [71] Baynham 1998a: 95–99.
[72] Sancisi-Weerdenburg 1993: 182.
[73] Wiesehöfer 2001: 25; see also Borza 1972; Sancisi-Weerdenburg 1993; Baynham 1998a: 98–99; Bloedow and Loube 1997; cf. Hammond 1992b.
[74] Diodorus 17.77.4: ἤρξατο ζηλοῦν τὴν Περσικὴν τρυφὴν καὶ τὴν πολυτέλειαν τῶν Ἀσιανῶν βασιλέων.
[75] Curtius 6.6.8 and Diodorus 17.7.6 also name a harem and eunuchs, but given the roughness of the coming campaign, we may wonder if it ever left Hyrcania, assuming he had one at all. It may be part of a general theme of growing debauchery.

But the change most remarked on in the sources was Alexander's adoption of partial Persian dress. He donned a long-sleeved purple tunic with a white strip down the middle, a Persian belt (*zōnē*), as well as a diadem of white and purple/dark blue, sometimes tied around a *kausia* or Macedonian hat (Arrian *Anabasis* 4.7.4; Diodorus 17.77.5; Curtius 6.6.4; Justin 12.3.8; Athenaeus 12.535f, 12.537e). There is less agreement as to whether he adopted the upright tiara. Collins argues no, perhaps following Bosworth, but Olbrycht makes a fair case that he did, at least occasionally, although a less solid case for the long-sleeved cloak, or *kandys*.[76] All sources say he eschewed trousers. We are told that initially he wore Persian clothing in court when dealing with Asians, but Macedonian clothing when dealing with Macedonians and Greeks (Plutarch *Alexander* 45.2; Polyaenus 4.3.24; Diodorus 17.77.5 – implied). He even had two seals (Curtius 6.6.6).

If this process is usually described as 'integration', he was, effectively, running two parallel courts – which should be stressed.[77] Initial objections from Macedonians were smoothed over via gifts (Diodorus 17.78.1). If gift-giving was a Persian tradition (Xenophon *Cyropaedia* 8.2.7–8.2.8), it was also a Macedonian one.[78] Both Plutarch (*Alexander* 47.3) and Arrian (*Anabasis* 7.29.4) state that his decision to introduce Persian ceremonial was informed by political concerns, and we should see these changes as a concerted effort at state-building. Unfortunately, he had shot himself in the foot before he even began, by his treatment of Persepolis (Arrian *Anabasis* 3.1811–3.1812),[79] something he seems to have realized only later, if at all. In fact, his failure to grasp cultural fundamentals would continue to dog his attempts to reconcile Persians to his rule.

During the Bactrian campaign that followed these changes, a series of conspiracies and other protests emerged. If our sources blame Alexander's medizing, *inter alia*, in the speeches given by the disaffected figures, we must peel away Greek *polis*-centric and imperial-Roman messaging to discern, if we can, what was the actual *Macedonian* discontent.

The conspiracy of Dimnus, which resulted in the downfall of Philotas and his father Parmenion, proves aggravating. According to our sources, word of the plot was brought to Philotas to warn the king, but Philotas did nothing. Upon realizing no steps had been taken, the

---

[76] Collins 2012c: 392; Bosworth 1980a: 5; Olbrycht 2014: 41–47.   [77] Bosworth 1980a: 5.
[78] Greenwalt 2015: 339–340. Multiple stories can be found in both Athenaeus and Plutarch's *Moralia*, in addition to the primary histories, that demonstrate Macedonian royal concern with gifts. In one such, Philip warns his Theban host not to deprive him of 'invincibility' (*anikēton*) by outdoing him in benefaction (Plutarch *Moralia* 178e), which sums it up quite well.
[79] Brosius 2003a: 181–185.

12.1 Master of the Jardin de vertueuse, *The Execution of Philotas* (c. 1470–1475). Getty Museum: Ms. Ludwig XV 8 (83.MR.178), fol. 149.

informer tried someone else, who did tell Alexander. Philotas was therefore implicated, arrested, tortured, tried, and eventually executed. The actual conspirators committed suicide before arrest or were executed with Philotas (Figure 12.1). Recognizing his danger, with Parmenion back in Ecbatana on his supply lines, Alexander sent agents to murder the old general before he could retaliate for his son's death (Arrian 3.26–27.4; Curtius 6.7–6.11; Diodorus 17.79–17.80; Plutarch *Alexander* 48–49; Justin 12.5.1–12.5.8).

Much ink has been spilt on exactly what happened and to what degree Philotas was complicit, if at all.[80] Badian sees the whole thing as

---

[80] Badian 1960; Heckel 1977; Rubinsohn 1977; Badian 2000: 62–69; Adams 2003; Reames 2008; Carney 2015: 157–158.

Alexander's long-game plot to rid himself of Parmenion's powerful family, a conclusion rejected by most others. Yet discussion then typically turns to why Philotas said nothing, and what were the motives of those Hetairoi who accused him of collusion, especially Craterus, Coenus, and Hephaistion. This is due to our sources' focus on the sensationalism of Philotas and Parmenion's fall, but also to the fact that nothing much is known about the *actual* plot.

If attributed to Dimnus, it included Demetrius, whose status was higher and who, as a Somatophylax, had easy access to Alexander. Why they wanted to kill their king is explained only as a grievance *peri tinōn*, 'concerning certain things' (Diodorus 17.79.1). What are those 'things'? Curtius' (very long) account of Philotas's defence speech (6.10.1–6.10.37) complains of Alexander's divine aspirations and the failure of liberty and free speech at the court – in short, Alexander's slide into Oriental despotism. Yet this reflects Roman imperial anxieties, not Macedonian ones,[81] and so the episode tells us *nothing* except that some members of the court were angry 'concerning certain things'.

In Bactria, the army faced an increasingly brutal campaign against guerrilla insurgency.[82] As far as Alexander's soldiers were concerned, the war was no longer going swimmingly. In addition to court changes and new Iranian guard units, Alexander also began to incorporate native troops into the army as western reinforcements dwindled, owing to unrest back in Greece (Arrian *Anabasis* 4.17.3).[83] Thus, Macedonians had to rub elbows with the very people they had just conquered, or were currently fighting against. Holt says, 'To share their power – or their king – with the conquered peoples was not considered a just reward for all the hazards of war'.[84] Discharged Macedonian veterans, whom Alexander left in hill forts as settlers, resented the arrangement, feeling abandoned at the ends of the earth (Diodorus 17.74.3–17.74.4, Curtius 6.2.15–6.3.18).[85]

Similar resentment at being appointed Satrap of (to him) Nowheresville, plus a lot of wine, fuelled Clitus' harsh words to the king at a symposium in Maracanda, resulting in a brawl that ended with Clitus dead by Alexander's hand (Arrian *Anabasis* 4.8.1–4.9.7; Plutarch *Alexander* 50–2; Curtius 8.1.1–8.2.12; Justin 12.6.3–12.6.11). We must ask whether the words Arrian, Plutarch, and Curtius put into Clitus' mouth reflect anything he actually said, even in gist, but his reported complaints concerned Persians at court, Alexander's divine pretensions,

---

[81] Baynham 1998a: 178–179. [82] Holt 1988, 2005. [83] Olbrycht 2011a.
[84] Holt 1988: 70. [85] Thomas 2008.

and the perceived slight to himself and other generals who fought hard for Alexander without true reward.[86] Arrian says he had made it plain for a while that he disliked Alexander's 'change-over to more barbaric style' (*Anabasis* 4.9.4), words echoed by Plutarch who has Clitus decry Macedonians being beaten by 'Median rods' (discussed above, p. 184) and 'begging Persians for an audience with our king' (*Alexander* 51.1). Curtius adds that Clitus rated Philip's wars in Greece higher than Alexander's victories in Asia because Philip fought 'real men' and Alexander only *Asians* (8.1.30–8.1.31).

Although speaking of the later Hermolaus Conspiracy, Müller argues that Philip's memory had passed into legendary status by that point, reflecting what some Macedonians needed him to be rather than the man he had actually been.[87] Bowden includes Clitus' murder together with *proskynēsis* ('obeisance') and the Hermolaus Conspiracy as part of Plutarch's and Arrian's larger narratives of Alexander's 'three stages of insolence', suited to a second-century CE Roman audience.[88]

That Alexander killed Clitus, likely in a drunken brawl,[89] is established, but what set off Clitus is not.[90] The thematic agendas of later authors have obscured the original dispute. Setting and timing provide better clues. Clitus had been removed from command of half the Companion Cavalry, the most traditional and prestigious of Macedonian units, to become satrap of a very alien place far from home, eliminating any opportunity for his future advancement at court.[91] After saving Alexander's life at Granicus, where was his due *timē* ('esteem')? Clitus' resentment at being side-lined conforms better to Macedonian elite concerns, and his resentment of defeated Asians he perceived as 'gate-keepers' at court would also align. Thinking of the lavishness of Macedonian 'heroic' burials, we must wonder if Clitus feared one such would be denied to him? *In vino whining.*

Sandwiched between Clitus' death and Hermolaus' conspiracy came Alexander's reputed attempt to introduce *proskynēsis*, the traditional obeisance offered to Persian kings. Set at a symposium with friends, or a public event to which Persians had been invited, or both, the starring role in all versions was the bold opposition of Callisthenes,

---

[86] One reported antecedent to the fight involved a poem performed for the king, mocking generals (most now dead) who had recently lost a battle.
[87] Müller 2010: 30–32. [88] Bowden 2013: 63–66, 71.
[89] Müller questions whether the murder of Clitus at a banquet was fabricated as part of a 'drunk Alexander' motif (2009: 218). If I generally agree with her that Alexander's wine consumption became a cautionary trope, rejecting the setting for Clitus' murder, and the alcohol involved, perhaps goes too far.
[90] Carney 2015: 144–146. [91] Carney 2015: 142–143.

court historian and nephew of Aristotle, forcing Alexander to scrap the plan (Arrian *Anabasis* 4.10.5–4.12.7; Plutarch *Alexander* 53.1–55.1; Curtius 8.5.5–8.5.24).

Much of the deb ate about what Alexander hoped to achieve by introducing *proskynēsis* has centred on its religious connections, and the claim that Greeks offered *proskynēsis* only to gods. Yet Bowden's review of Greek literature prior to and contemporary with Alexander proves that assumption to be incorrect and reductive.[92] Still, most scholars line up either on the side of 'he thought he was a god and so wanted to impose veneration', or the side of 'it was a political measure, a continuation of his attempt to regularize court practice'. Which side a scholar chooses often depends on their assessment of Alexander's mental health.

But what if it never happened in the first place?

In two articles published around the same time, Bowden and Müller deconstruct the whole thing.[93] While distinct, their arguments pair in important ways regarding authorial adaptation for thematic ends. In a brief overview as part of a longer argument, Müller explains that *proskynēsis* was used 'to reveal more about the self-definition in contrast to perceptions of the "other", political propaganda, and "nostalgic" tendencies concerning the conservation of models of the Greek literary tradition'.[94]

In a much more extensive article, Bowden not only provides a modern historiographic review and thorough examination of ancient understandings of what *proskynēsis* was,[95] but also explains how both Plutarch and Arrian (who moves the event out of order and does not follow Ptolemy or Aristobulus) have recast Callisthenes (ironically) as standing up for freedom against tyranny,[96] perhaps to echo Seneca and Nero.[97] The result was a retooling of an unmoored or 'transferable' story that had originated with Chares about some sympotic gaff of Callisthenes,[98] crusting it over with anachronistic philosophical debate regarding Alexander's right, or lack thereof, to divine pretensions.[99] Curtius relates the incident immediately before Hermolaus' conspiracy too, pairing it with Callisthenes' downfall and characterizing Callisthenes in the same way as Arrian and Plutarch (8.8.21–8.8.23).

---

[92] Bowden 2013: 56–62, with n. 2 for prior bibliography of the debate.
[93] Bowden 2013 and Müller 2015: 460–463.   [94] Müller 2015: 463.
[95] Including amusing uses for it, such as in response to someone's sneeze (Bowden 2013: 61).
[96] Bowden 2013: 71.   [97] Bowden 2013: 75–76.   [98] Bowden 2013: 70–71.
[99] Bowden 2013: 66–76.

We must recall that this reputed attempt to introduce *proskynēsis* occurred over two years after the 330 BCE court changes which, if staggered across a few months, still came of a piece. One might argue, as Plutarch (*Alexander* 45.1) and Justin (12.7.1) imply, that Alexander held back its introduction because of its controversial overtones. Yet that breaks apart on analysis of how *proskynēsis* was understood by *contemporary* Greek literature.[100] Furthermore, the middle of a gruelling campaign was hardly the time to introduce the most provocative court innovation.

None of this discards *proskynēsis* at Alexander's court; it was quite obviously performed by Persians and other Asians. But that Alexander sought to have *all* perform it is untenable, at least in the way the described event has come down to us.

The final Bactrian political crisis, the Pages' Conspiracy or Hermolaus' Conspiracy, may allow us to get closer to Macedonian opposition if we consider what led up to it as opposed to the speeches invented for the historiographical accounts of the trial. Both Carney and Müller have re-situated events against a Macedonian backdrop of power negotiations and elite status, rather than a philosophic debate on the dangers of tyranny.[101]

On a royal hunt, Hermolaus, one of the King's Boys, speared a boar before Alexander could. Furious, the king had him whipped – a typical, if severe, punishment – but also took his horse, effectively demoting him to the status of a commoner, even if (probably) on a temporary basis.[102] In response, Hermolaus, his lover Sostratus, and several other King's Boys, reputedly encouraged by Callisthenes, conspired to kill the 'tyrant'. Their plans were uncovered, the boys arrested, tried, and executed. Callisthenes was also arrested and eventually died under disputed circumstances (Arrian *Anabasis* 4.13.1–4.14.4; Plutarch *Alexander* 55.2–55.5; Curtius 8.6.1–8.8.23).

As discussed above, royal hunts had symbolic value for Macedonian kings, explaining Alexander's seemingly out-of-proportion anger at anyone who rescued him. If Craterus and Lysimachus acted out of genuine fear for their king's life, Müller suggests Hermolaus was asserting his own status to challenge Alexander's new, more autocratic kingship.[103] This would be exacerbated if Alexander's rage was increased owing to a Persian custom recently inserted into Macedonian royal hunts: a king's right to firststrike.[104] Hermolaus may then be understood to have been objecting to the imposition of the defeated's customs on the

---

[100] Bowden 2013: 56–62. [101] Carney 2015: 269–270, 280 and Müller 2010.
[102] Müller 2010: 30. [103] Müller 2010: 29. [104] Carney 2015: 269–270.

victors. Rather than a Harmodius-like Tyrant Slayer, he becomes, appropriately, an elite young Macedonian offended by threats to his *timē* ('honour'), especially when those threats came from a culture he had been taught to deride.

The Opis Indiscipline and Court Changes in Alexander's Final Year[105]

After the Pages' Conspiracy, resentment over Alexander's medizing appears to fade until 324 BCE in Susa, where he expanded on previous changes, now with less separation between ethnicities in either army units or at court. Take, for instance, the two traditional royal guard units, Persian Apple-Bearers and Macedonian Silver Shields, positioned in the grand audience tent before Alexander, 'King of Asia', in equal numbers of 500 each (Athenaeus 12.539d–12.539f; Polyaenus 4.3.24; Aelian *Varia historia* 9.3).[106] Also, Alexander and ninety-one (so Chares *FGrH / BNJ* 125 F 4) of his top officers married Persian noblewomen, following Persian custom (Athenaeus 12.538b–12.539a; Arrian *Anabasis* 7.4.4–7.4.8; Plutarch *Alexander* 70.2). Of his soldiers, he ordered those who had made what amounted to common-law marriages with Asian women to register them; over 10,000 did so, and even got a wedding present (Arrian *Anabasis* 7.4.8; but cf. 7.12.2).[107]

It was the 30,000 *Epigoni*, Persian youths trained in Macedonian arms, a sort of 'counter infantry',[108] who stoked Macedonian fears most (Plutarch *Alexander* 47.3, 71.1–71.2; Diodorus 17.108.2–17.108.3).[109] Marrying foreign women, or at least keeping them, was the traditional right of the victor. But to see the sons of men they had previously defeated now decked out in armour just like theirs, and using their unique weapons, was another thing entirely.

At Opis, when Alexander discharged a large number of veterans no longer fit for service, after providing them with the ancient version of

---

[105] In the interest of space, I have excluded discussion of the 'mutiny' on the banks of the Hyphasis, as *court* matters were not central to it.

[106] If the inclusion of both in equal numbers is significant, of even more significance is Phylarchus' specification that the Silver Shields stood in front (*proistēmi*; Athenaeus 539e). Bosworth explains that the audience was arranged in concentric rings (1980a: 8).

[107] The order to the soldiers to leave behind their half-Asian children for Alexander to raise and train, something even Arrian calls vague and uncertain (*Anabasis* 7.12.3), amounts to kidnapping a generation. The same was true of his earlier treatment of the *Epigoni* (Bosworth 1980a: 18).

[108] Bosworth 1980a: 17.

[109] Olbrycht 2015 argues that these troops embodied a fusion policy by Alexander, in contrast to Bosworth's earlier argument against fusion (1980a: 17–18).

a golden parachute (Arrian *Anabasis* 7.12.1–12.2; Curtius 10.2.9–10.2.10), a riot broke out that apparently took the king by surprise. Whether we call this a mutiny or indiscipline, it represented Macedonian frustration and disillusionment (Arrian *Anabasis* 7.8.1–7.12.4; Diodorus 17.109.2–17.109.3; Plutarch *Alexander* 71.1–71.5; Curtius 10.2.8–10.4.2; Justin 12.11.1–12.12.10).

Curtius's explanation stresses the soldiers' fear that Alexander intended to recentre his kingship in Asia (which had effectively already happened), and Diodorus suggests it was all about money. Yet Arrian and Plutarch may come closest to the truth, citing a lack of respect on Alexander's part for his oldest, most loyal soldiers. As proof, the men pointed to his adoption of Persian dress and court style, the *Epigoni*, and new Persian *hipparchies* ('squadrons') in the Companion Cavalry (Arrian *Anabasis* 7.6.2–7.6.5), heretofore a wholly Macedonian unit.[110]

To their minds, Alexander had dared to elevate the defeated over the heads of their conquerors, then ejected the men who had won it all for him. Plutarch says they 'were disheartened because the king would give them less attention' (*Alexander* 71.1);[111] and Arrian says they feared themselves objects of contempt (*huperoraō*; 7.8.2). The veterans saw young Persian faces – foreigners – in *their* units and felt replaced. Unimportant. Unheroic.[112]

Alexander's response was to give some sort of speech, if not the one Arrian records (Arrian *Anabasis* 7.9.1–10.7),[113] and then to do exactly what they had accused him of: jettisoning Macedonian guards, replacing Macedonian commanders with Persians, and filling Macedonian-named units with Persian soldiers. His reverse psychology worked, bringing his tearful troops to implore that he take them back, which he did at a reconciliation banquet (Arrian *Anabasis* 7.11.5–7.11.9).

In the end, he still sent them home as he had planned all along. Yet it was never the being discharged that they objected to. It was the being *replaced* by the conquered. When he demonstrated what replacement truly looked like *and*, at the banquet, returned them to what they considered their rightful position as his most cherished troops,[114] the crisis was averted.

Thus, we see how Macedonian objections centred on issues of status recognized or ignored, a sense of displacement and a perceived threat to personal *timē* that endangered their elite status. Given the material

---

[110] But cf. Bosworth 1980a: 15–16.   [111] ὡς ἧττον αὐτοῖς τοῦ βασιλέως προσέξοντος.
[112] Olbrycht 2008 sees something similar but overstresses Alexander's fusion and thus seems to hit only half-on the reasons for Macedonian resentment. The return of 'replacement theory', fuelling right-wing political resentment in many Western countries, carries a similar feel.
[113] Nagle 1996.   [114] Weber 2009: 96.

testimony of Macedonian burials, this is exactly what we should expect. Persian extravagance was never the issue. Indeed, several of Alexander's officers also engaged in lavish lifestyles: Agnon, Clitus the White, Perdiccas, Leonnatus, Menelaus, and Craterus (Athenaeus 12.539c–12.539d; Aelian *Varia historia* 9.3). Similarly, protests over Alexander's divine pretensions found in the speeches of Philotas, Clitus the Black, Callisthenes, Hermolaus, and the soldiers at Opis, reflect Greek and Roman *topoi* ('commonplaces') about hubris. Traditional Macedonian royal style already involved calling attention to the kings' divine descent, as visible in the iconography of earlier Macedonian material culture and coinage.

What got under the Macedonians' skin was a challenge to their belief in their own superiority, which they deemed demonstrated by success on the battlefield. When Alexander appeared to violate that belief by incorporating the vanquished and their customs into his court, they objected. Strenuously.

***

This brings us to the crunch of what Alexander wanted to accomplish with his court revisions: a much-fraught question, the answers to which often slide too far to one side or the other. We cannot resurrect W. W. Tarn's Brotherhood of Mankind, nor any policy of fusion and Hegelian *Aufhebung* ('a melding that translates both components into something more') à la J. G. Droysen. In 'Alexander the Great and the Unity of Mankind', Badian killed the former and in 'Alexander and the Iranians', Bosworth killed the latter.[115]

Yet to dismiss Alexander's court changes as merely pragmatic, a reaction 'to a series of problems',[116] unduly minimizes Alexander's integration of army units, the creation of the *Epigoni*, and his marriage programme. It also diminishes the worth of Asian culture by implying that of course he couldn't actually *like* that stuff, and if he did, it must presage delusions of grandeur.

It was not fusion. Bosworth rightly points out that these units served alongside each other rather than being fully integrated;[117] Macedonian men married Persian women not the reverse; and when Alexander replaced disobedient satraps, he installed Macedonians until

---

[115] Badian 1958a; Bosworth 1980a.
[116] Bosworth 1980a: 20. Bosworth rightly notes how historians of the pre-World War II era, such as Berve, retooled Droysen's idea of fusion into *Herrenvölker* notions of world rule by a master race (1980a: 1). Plutarch's *De fortuna Alexandri*, discussed earlier (p. 197), provided plenty of fodder.
[117] Bosworth 1980a: 14–20. Language barriers no doubt contributed to that. Bosworth sees it as more sinister, calling it 'a policy of division' (14).

only three impeccably loyal Asian satraps remained.[118] Rather than fusion, *parallelism* may be a better term.

One possible way to find a balance is to recognize that if Alexander were struggling with state-building (not unlike his father before him, and Archelaus before that, and even Alexander I when the Persians first came to call), state-building does not require programmatic philosophy. In fact, too much philosophy is antithetical to the sort of hard-ball negotiation successful politics requires. Sometimes one simply throws things at a wall to see what sticks.

Alexander's incorporation of foreign persons and customs at the court was not new, although no king before had tried it on the scale Alexander now attempted. Yet we must also acknowledge that these changes were largely superficial. He failed to understand the fundamental Persian conceptualization of kingship and empire because, as Macedonians tended to do, he 'Macedonized' what he borrowed, and offended Persians in the process.[119] Instead of a '*pax Persica*' enshrined in the Persian ideology of kingship, that of the shepherd king, not unlike other Ancient Near Eastern traditions, Alexander came in like a Macedonian tornado. Brosius says he '"bulldozed" his way' to the centre of Persia, making quite a mess that he never lived long enough to clean up.[120]

It was what his father would have done, after all.

And that is, ultimately, who Alexander was: not King of Asia, but a Macedonian conqueror in a long, white-striped purple robe.

Guide to Further Reading

See the Guide for Chapter 11.

---

[118] Bosworth 1980a: 11–14. [119] Brosius 2003a: 192–193. [120] Brosius 2003a: 193.

13: THE WOMEN OF ALEXANDER'S COURT

Elizabeth D. Carney

Our ignorance of many aspects of the world inhabited by even the most prominent women of Alexander's court (his mother, sisters, and wives) profoundly limits our understanding of their careers and interactions with others. Filling in these gaps in knowledge with assumptions derived from our own world or from the practices of much later royal courts compounds the problem. While ancient sources preserve material about the actions of some of these women, virtually nothing survives about their context. We do not know who was in the room where 'it' happened or indeed if there was a room.

ASPECTS OF WOMEN'S LIVES AT COURT

The Macedonian court was itinerant; it happened not in one place but many. In Macedonia itself, there were two 'palaces,' one at Aegae and one at Pella. The structure at Aegae served primarily for banqueting, with little or nothing in the way of living quarters. The Pella complex (five main structures and with many interconnecting sections or subsections) probably contained many areas for living, as well as administration. Both buildings sat on hilltops above the city.[1] Some court personnel would have followed Philip and, later, Alexander on campaigns; in Philip's day, royal women did not accompany the king on campaign (Satyrus *apud* Athenaeus 557b), but in Alexander's they sometimes did. Even at Pella, it is hard to provide a specific physical location for women of high or low rank. Alexander's mother Olympias or his sisters may have inhabited separate houses or maintained separate households within the palace complex.[2] Once Alexander was travelling in

---

[1] Hatzopoulos 2001; Saatsoglou-Paliadeli 2001; Akamatis 2011; Kottaridi 2011.
[2] D'Agostini 2021: 20–23.

Asia, his quarters and those of any women with him must have been, at times, temporary, likely splendid tents.[3]

All these royal women may have been surrounded by servants and advisors, but only rarely do we hear about them. Were some of these attendants, like Alexander's wet nurse, Lanice, of relatively high social rank?[4] Molossian women, including some of Olympias' kin, may have accompanied her; certainly, some male relatives participated in Philip's court (Justin 8.6.5; Plutarch *Alexander* 5.4; Arrian *Anabasis* 2.27.6, 3.5.5). Indeed, royal wives may customarily have arrived at court with female companions. Many servants were likely slaves, supplied by Macedonian conquests (e.g. Olynthus whose entire population was enslaved; Diodorus 16.53.3). Enslavement and rape were norms for women on the losing side in ancient warfare.[5] The attendants of Alexander's wives were probably largely Asian, though captives came in many ethnicities. Some staff members of Alexander's female kin were male. Olympias had a male slave who helped to perform ritual and whom she wanted to sell to Alexander (Athenaeus 559f–660a) and his sister Cleopatra employed a musician (Pausanias 1.44.6). His niece Adea Eurydice had a male counsellor (Diodorus 19.11.3) and she later acted in political concert with elite males, one of whom seems to have been her secretary (Arrian *FGrH / BNJ* 156 F9.30–33).[6]

It is difficult to assess how often men and women saw each other at court, partly because we do not know if they regularly dined or drank together.[7] Sources do not usually mention their presence, but that does not guarantee they were not there. Royal women appeared in public on some occasions. Alexander's grandmother Eurydice met publicly with the Athenian admiral Iphicrates (Aeschines 2.26–2.29). His sister Cleopatra confronted the old general Antipater in person (Arrian *FGrH / BNJ* 156 F11.40). Olympias appeared at the head of an army (Diodorus 19.11.2–19.11.4). Alexander's wife Roxane, Olympias, and other royal women travelled with armies. Did Alexander's closest companions personally know his mother and his sisters or did they simply know about them? Plutarch (*Alexander* 10.1–10. 3) describes his friends and his mother giving him the same (as it turns out) bad advice, but it could have been rendered serially and separately. Did royal women hear petitions in public or simply read them? Rather than assuming these

---

[3] Spawforth 2007b: 94–120; Alonso Troncoso and Álvarez Rico 2017: 113–124.
[4] See Asirvatham 2021 for a discussion of her role and connections.   [5] Gaca 2015.
[6] Carney 1987: 496–502; Carney 2000: 132–137 on her career.
[7] Herodotus 5.18.3 seems to be a dubious anecdote intended to stress the Hellenicity of the Macedonians.

women lived the somewhat sequestered life of an upper-class Athenian woman, the more useful parallel would be the women in the families of tyrants.[8] Orators referred to Eurydice and Olympias by personal name in the Athenian assembly, something they would never do to an Athenian citizen woman. Eurydice and other royal women participated in local and international *philia* networks,[9] suggesting that male and female court elites did know each other. These women were public figures.

The court in which Alexander grew up was a complicated place, changing rapidly as his father Philip's successes and ambitions increased.[10] There were visiting embassies, artists, and intellectuals in longer-term residence, and increasing numbers of non-Macedonian royal Companions. Philip was often away on campaign, intensifying Alexander's connection to his mother Olympias, his only full sister, Cleopatra,[11] and possibly to his paternal grandmother, Eurydice, who may have lived well into Philip's reign. Within a few years of becoming king, Philip had probably married five women. Later he married two more; there were also his male lovers, possibly including Olympias' brother, Alexander I of Epirus (Justin 8.6.6–8). In the absence of consistent practices about royal succession and in the presence of polygamy, mothers acted as succession advocates for sons.[12] It is difficult to know how much Alexander would have seen of Cynnane (Philip's daughter by his Illyrian wife Audata) and Thessalonice (Philip's daughter by the Thessalian Nicesipolis). Thessalonice could have had more contact with Alexander than Cynnane because she was likely brought up by Alexander's mother whereas Cynnane, apparently trained as a warrior, may not have been. Apart from Olympias herself, perhaps as many as five other wives of Philip could still have been alive at the time Alexander became king.[13]

After 334, Alexander never saw his mother or sisters again, but they apparently remained well-informed about and to some degree involved in events at his court in various parts of Asia and the Near East;[14] this implies they had means of acquiring information, despite the considerable distance, and that they corresponded with various elite

---

[8] Carney 1993b; Mitchell 2012. [9] Carney 2019: 71–74.
[10] On Philip's court, see Spawforth 2007b: 90–92.
[11] On the sisters of Alexander, see Carney 1988.
[12] Ogden 1999: 3–40; Carney 2000: 82–113. Strootman 2021 focuses on women in Hellenistic courts, but is helpful for the Argead period.
[13] Ogden 1999: 17–40; Carney 2000: 40–46, 51–81, 155–8; Müller 2021b.
[14] Spawforth 2007b: 87 considers his mother and full sister part of the 'outer court' because they were so far away (and implies that Alexander's wives might be part of the inner court), but this interpretation focuses on geography at the expense of politics. See also Weber 2009.

males. Our sources refer to letters or correspondence between his mother and Alexander and imply correspondence with his only full sister, Cleopatra, though one must recall the ancient fondness for writing (and reading) fictional correspondence between famous people. Alexander's courts must have been full of spies or, to put it more politely, informants. Some would have been, in effect, foreign agents, sending information back to hostile or potentially hostile powers like Athens, but others would have worked for members of the royal family. Some of these spies would have been women. For instance, Antigone, from Macedonia, captured first by the Persians and then by the Macedonians, was apparently made a slave mistress to Philotas, commander of the Companion cavalry. One of Philotas' rivals, however, forced her to spy against Philotas; her information apparently contributed to Philotas' downfall and death (Plutarch *Alexander* 48.3–49.1, *Moralia* 339e).[15]

As Philip's fame and the prestige of his court grew, so, not coincidentally, did the prominence of the women of his family: his seven marriages mirrored and facilitated his political/military expansion and demonstrated the *truphe* (luxury) of his court, even in respect to wives. The building he ordered constructed at Olympia after his great victory at Chaeronea, the Philippeum, included statues of himself, Alexander, his father, his mother, and Olympias, thus highlighting the importance of Argead women as well as men.[16] He transformed the wedding of his and Olympias' daughter Cleopatra into an international event (Diodorus 16.91.4–16.92.5), setting a precedent for Hellenistic kings to follow, including Alexander himself.[17] Even before Philip, however, Argead women were part of *basileia*, not apart from it, often serving as the reserve troops of the dynasty, as did Philip's mother Eurydice (Aeschines 2.26–2.29); they were called into action when events warranted and males were unavailable to represent the royal *oikos* (house, household).[18]

The Career of Olympias

Among the women of Alexander's court,[19] Olympias was the most prominent.[20] She was the daughter of the Molossian king Neoptolemus I. Her uncle Arybbas (sole king since the death of his

---

[15] Müller 2021c: 88–93. [16] Schultz 2007. [17] Ager 2017. [18] Carney 1995.
[19] Ogden 1999: 41–51; Carney 2000: 82–113.
[20] Carney 1993a, 2006; Müller 2021d. O'Neil 1999 offers a very different perspective.

brother) had arranged her marriage to Philip c. 357, probably as part of an alliance against the Illyrians. Her brother, Alexander I of Epirus, later arrived at Philip's court and, c. 342, Philip forced Arybbas off the throne of Molossia, replacing him with this brother. Philip treated Olympias' son Alexander as though he was the heir, thus giving her the highest status of his wives. Though Philip had married at least one other woman after Olympias, it was his seventh marriage to Cleopatra, niece of Attalus, that threatened to jeopardize the position of Alexander and thus his mother. At the wedding feast for his niece, Attalus asked the guests to toast to the possibility of a legitimate heir to the throne, implying that Alexander was not legitimate; Alexander was enraged but Philip countenanced the insult, possibly even supported it. Consequently, Alexander and his mother departed for her native Molossia, though reconciliation with Philip soon followed (Plutarch *Alexander* 9.3–9.6; Satyrus *apud* Athenaeus 557d; Justin 9.7.5–9.7.7). Olympias and a number of Alexander's advisers convinced him to interject himself into marriage negotiations Philip was conducting with the satrap of Caria on behalf of Alexander's half-brother Philip Arrhidaeus; when Philip discovered Alexander's involvement, he was outraged and exiled Alexander's advisers (Plutarch *Alexander* 10.1–10.3). As part of this somewhat shaky reconciliation, Philip arranged the marriage of his daughter Cleopatra to Olympias' brother, Alexander I of Epirus. He planned a grand wedding festival to impress the world with the renewed stability of his kingdom and the stability of royal succession on the eve of his departure for war against the Persian Empire. Instead, an assassin struck him down during these festivities (Diodorus 16.94.1–16.94.4). Alexander (after suppressing turmoil at home in Macedonia and revolts by some of the Greek powers in the league Philip had created) led the Macedonian/Greek expedition to Asia in the spring of 334. Before he left for Asia, Alexander arranged the death of Attalus (author of the wedding insult; Diodorus 17.2.4–17.2.5, 17.5.1–17.5.2) and Olympias effected that of Philip's last wife, Cleopatra and her baby or babies (Justin 9.7.12; Pausanias 8.7.5; Plutarch *Alexander* 10.7). Plutarch seems to have Alexander reproach his mother for this violent action,[21] though it is hard to believe that he was either ignorant of it or actually disapproved. As we will see, Alexander's wife Roxane did something similar after Alexander's death; murders, even of children, were hardly unprecedented in the course of Argead succession

---

[21] Howe 2015a hypothesizes that Alexander was angry at her because he himself had wanted to marry Cleopatra.

struggles (Diodorus 14.37.6, 15.71.1, 16.2.2–16.2.4). Plutarch (*Alexander* 2.5–2.6) portrays Olympias as an enthusiast for snakes and cults employing them. He also recounts that some sources claimed that she told her son that his father was divine, but others insisted that she repudiated the notion (*Alexander* 3.1–3.2).[22]

Olympias and Cleopatra never saw Alexander again. Cleopatra accompanied her husband to Molossia and when he too departed on a military expedition in 334 (to southern Italy), she seems to have functioned as a regent there and continued to do so after her husband was killed in Italy in 331.[23] Olympias remained in Macedonia until about 331 and then went home to Molossia where she remained until 317, years after her son's death in 323. Her brother's death may have been the formal excuse for her return to Molossia (Livy 8.24.17), but her increasingly acrimonious dealings with Antipater, the man Alexander had left in military and administrative control of Macedonia and the Greek peninsula, were probably the actual cause. She and Antipater complained about each other by letter to Alexander (Arrian *Anabasis* 7.12.6), but initially Antipater seemed to be winning the dispute (Diodorus 18.49.4; Pausanias 1.11.3). Once back in Molossia, however, Olympias' fortunes improved; she and her daughter may have ruled Molossia together. Both Olympias and Cleopatra appear on the Cyrene grain lists as recipients of grain in a time of famine; the list refers to them in a fashion typically used to refer to heads of state (*SEG* ix 2). Cleopatra also sold grain to Athens (Lycurgus *Leocrates* 26). These activities may have been done in concert with Alexander the Great or independently of him. Alexander sent Olympias and Cleopatra splendid gifts, presumably from his plunder (Plutarch *Alexander* 25.4). Olympias planned a golden dedication at Delphi (*Syll.*³ i 252 N 5–7) and made a dedication of a *phiale* (cup) to the cult of Hygieia (goddess of health) in Athens, probably for the cult statue itself (Hyperides *Euxenippus* 19). This last Athenian speech associates her with Alexander and also with the Macedonians; it also reveals that, angry about Athenian renovations of the sanctuary at Dodona in Molossia, Olympias asserted that the country of Molossia belonged to her (19–25). Cleopatra and Olympias both attempted to influence Alexander's decision-making, Cleopatra on behalf of the tyrant of Heraclea (Memnon *FGrH* / *BNJ* 434 F4.37) and

---

[22] Ogden 2011a:14–28 discusses Alexander's serpent sire, finding no certain evidence that these stories originated with Olympias. Carney 2006: 102–103 concludes that Olympias was not their originator.

[23] On her career, see Carney 2000: 75–76, 89–90, 123–128; Meeus 2009b; D'Agostini 2021; Müller 2021d.

Olympias on many issues, often warning Alexander against various figures at court (Curtius 7.1.36–7.1.40; Diodorus 17.32.1–17.32.2, 114.3; Plutarch *Alexander* 39.5). Antipater's influence declined after 330 and in 324 Alexander ordered him to give up his position to Craterus and report to Babylon with reinforcements (Justin 12.12.9; Arrian *Anabasis* 7.12.4); Antipater, however, had not followed Alexander's orders by the time of the king's death and Craterus had not left Asia Minor.

In this period of the last year or two of Alexander's reign, after his return from India, affairs in his empire, particularly in the Greek peninsula, became quite unstable. Plutarch (*Alexander* 68.3) asserts that in this troubled period Olympias and Cleopatra formed a faction against Antipater, with Olympias taking rule of Molossia and Cleopatra of Macedonia. Since Antipater was clearly still in position as *strategos* immediately after Alexander's death (he organized Macedonian resistance to the Greek revolt; Diodorus 18.12.1–18.12.3, 16.4), Plutarch cannot mean that Antipater had been removed from his position, but he does seem to mean that mother and daughter took over some more overt aspects of rule in the two kingdoms. Alexander, after all, had been gone for ten years and their royal blood, their partaking in *basileia*, had come to matter more than it had in 334. This complicated situation may explain why both Antipater and Olympias tried to extradite Alexander's runaway treasurer from Athens (Diodorus 17.108.7).

Had Alexander not died in 323, it is impossible to know what might have happened. As it was, after Alexander's death, his mentally challenged half-brother Philip III Arrhidaeus and his posthumous son Alexander IV became nominal co-kings, with various of the Successors in actual command. In 319 Antipater brought both the kings (and Philip Arrhidaeus' wife Adea Eurydice and Alexander IV's mother Roxane) back to the Greek peninsula, but died soon thereafter, supposedly warning against the rule of a woman, presumably a jab, if authentic, against Olympias (Diodorus 19.11.9). Olympias remained in Molossia until 317, cooperating with her nephew Aeacides, who now functioned as Molossian king. The latest regent, Polyperchon, asked her to return to Macedonia (Diodorus 18.49.4, 18.58.3–18.58.4). After some hesitation, apparently worried about the long-term future of her grandson, she did eventually return in front of an army led by Polyperchon and Aeacides; the Macedonian home army immediately went over to her forces and she captured and killed Philip Arrhidaeus and Adea Eurydice, as well as a number of the supporters of Cassander, Antipater's son, the ally of Adea Eurydice and Philip Arrhidaeus (Diodorus 19.11.1–19.11.9;

Justin 14.5.8–14.5.10). In the end, thanks to Cassander's military prowess, he defeated Olympias and had her killed by the kin of those she had eliminated (in 316 or 315). He also imprisoned Alexander IV and Roxane, though he postponed their murder until *c.* 310 (Diodorus 19.50.5, 51.2–51.6; Justin 14.14.6.1–14.14.6.13). Cleopatra lived longer than Olympias, to about 309, but ultimately fared no better. Many of the Successors wanted to marry her but none ultimately did so. When she attempted to escape what amounted to prolonged house arrest, apparently hoping to marry Ptolemy, she too was murdered (Arrian *FGrH / BNJ* 156 F11.40; Diodorus 20.37.3–20.37.6).[24]

The fate of Alexander's half-sisters was equally bloody. Cynnane had married Philip II's nephew and had a daughter by him, Adea Eurydice. Alexander killed Cynnane's husband (Alexander's cousin) soon after he took the throne, allegedly for plotting against him (Polyaenus 8.60; Justin 12.6.4). Early on, Alexander planned to remarry Cynnane to a barbarian ally, but the prospective groom died (Arrian *Anabasis* 1.5.4–1.5.5) and Cynnane seems to have spent the rest of Alexander's reign training her daughter in military matters. After Alexander's death, Cynnane managed to escape the control of Antipater's forces and leave for Asia with her daughter and a small force. When she approached the Macedonian army in Asia, however, the regent Perdiccas had her killed. The army, furious that a daughter of Philip had been murdered, insisted on the completion of the marriage Cynnane had apparently planned, that of her daughter to Philip Arrhidaeus (Polyaenus 8.60; Arrian *FGrH / BNJ* 15, F 9.22–9.23). Adea Eurydice's brief but bold career ended, as we have noted, when Olympias forced her death.

Thessalonice lived longer than her sisters but came to an equally violent end. In 316 or 315, Cassander captured her along with the rest of Olympias' entourage and, as part of a series of acts meant to indicate that he was a legitimate successor, married her and had three sons with her (Diodorus 19.52.1–19.52.2; Justin 14.6.13; *Heidelberg Epitome*, *FGrH / BNJ* 155 F2.4). After the death of Cassander and his oldest son (both of natural causes), one of her remaining sons believed she was favouring the other and so killed his own mother, an action that led ultimately to the deaths of both brothers in turn (Diodorus 21.7.1; Plutarch *Demetrius* 36.1–36.6; Justin 16.1. 1–16.1.4, 9; Pausanias 9.7.3–9.7.4).[25]

---

[24] Carney 2021: 322–325; Müller 2021d. [25] Landucci Gattinoni 2009.

The Court in Asia

Let me now turn to women involved in Alexander's court in Asia. Only briefly 'at court' was Ada, a member of the ruling Carian dynasty; she had struggled with her brother for rule and when Alexander, in the course of his campaign, arrived in Caria, he favoured her against her pro-Persian brother and treated her as a kind of second mother, thus acquiring a kind of local legitimacy (Arrian *Anabasis* 1.23.7–1.23.8; Diodorus 17.24.2; Strabo C657).[26]

The spotlight must, however, be on the Persian or partly Persian women who were compelled to become part of Alexander's court. Barsine was the daughter of the Persian satrap Artabazus (who was of royal Achaemenid descent) and of a sister of two Rhodian Greek mercenary generals, both employed by the Persians, Mentor and Memnon. Barsine had been married to at least one of her uncles, if not (serially) both, but she was a widow with a number of children when Alexander, after his victory at Issus, took many elite Persian women captive. Soon after her capture, Alexander began a sexual relationship with her but never married her, despite her high birth and important family. Parmenion supposedly urged Alexander to begin this relationship (Plutarch *Alexander* 21.4, *Eumenes* 1.3); whether or not that is true, despite the absence of a marriage, Alexander's relationship with Barsine had important political aspects.[27] In 327, Barsine had a son by Alexander, called Heracles (Pausanias 9.7.2; Lycophron *Alexandra* 801–4; Plutarch *Eumenes* 1.3; Diodorus 20.20.1; Curtius 10.6.10–10.6.12; Justin 13.2.7, 15.2.3).

Alexander's reluctance to marry a member of the Persian elite, despite his very real interest in involving the Persians in running the empire that once had been theirs, was not limited to Barsine. Among the other elite Persian women who came into his control after Issus were also the mother (Sisygambis), wife (Stateira), and two daughters of Darius III (Stateira II and Drypetis; Curtius 3.12.17, 21, 25, 4.11.3; Diodorus 17.37.6, 38.1; Justin 11.9.16, 12.6–12.7). At the time, Darius was a long way from being defeated, so it is not surprising that Alexander (and Darius) used them as a kind of bargaining chip (Arrian *Anabasis* 2.25.3). Darius tried repeatedly to ransom his family (Diodorus 17.39.1, 54.2; Curtius 4.11.5–4.11.6, 12–15; Justin 11.12.1–11.12.3; Plutarch *Alexander* 29.7). Darius was supposedly surprised when he learned that

---
[26] Ruzicka 1992: 135–155.
[27] Müller 2021c. See also Carney 1996: 571–576; Ogden 1999: 41–43.

his wife Stateira had not been raped (Curtius 4.10.31–4.10.34). She may, however, have died in childbirth (Plutarch *Alexander* 30.1; Justin 11.12.6),[28] a possibility that challenges the story of Alexander's sexual restraint. Still, Alexander gave her a splendid funeral, one that matched her earlier status as king's wife rather than her more recent one (Curtius 4.21.4; Diodorus 17.54.6; Plutarch *Alexander* 30.1–30.3; Justin 11.12.6–11.12.8). The sources' admiration of Alexander for his sexual self-control is queasy-making today, but his actions cleverly combined the traditional value of captive women as symbols of victory with a less traditional interest in incorporating them into a new sort of monarchy.[29] Some sources describe a quasi-mother-son relationship between Sisygambis and Alexander, a more long-lasting and elaborated version of his dealings with Ada. Alexander's treatment of Sisygambis apparently replicated the importance of the king's mother in the Persian monarchy.[30] Even while he had gone further east, Sisygambis may have been able to advocate for those she favoured (Curtius 5.3.12–5.3.15). When Darius was finally dead (the victim of one of his own satraps), Alexander sent the body back to Sisygambis for burial (Plutarch *Alexander* 43.7). Supposedly, on news of Alexander's death she starved herself to death (Diodorus 17.118.3; Curtius 10.5.19–10.5.25; Justin 13.1.5–13.1.6). One might attribute her suicide to her relationship with Alexander, but it could as easily have been the consequence of her gloomy view of her prospects (and especially those of her granddaughters) once Alexander was gone. If so, it was a realistic assessment.

When Alexander departed for points east in 330, he left behind Darius' two daughters (and Darius' son) at Susa, in the care of their grandmother, to be instructed in Greek (or perhaps Greek culture generally; Diodorus 17.67.1). Alexander had promised to arrange dowries for Drypetis and Stateira, but in fact he married one (Stateira II) and Hephaestion the other, at the mass weddings in 324 (Arrian *Anabsasis* 7.4.5; Diodorus 17.107.6). He probably also married Parysatis, the daughter of Artaxerxes Ochus (Aristobulus *FGrH / BNJ* 139 F52). Both sisters (or possibly Stateira II and Parysatis) were murdered, probably by Perdiccas and Roxane, soon after the death of Alexander in 323 (Plutarch *Alexander* 77.4). Thus, a long delay occurred between when Alexander initially controlled the sisters (333) and when the marriages happened in 324.

---

[28] Curtius 4.10.8 says she died of travel fatigue and Diodorus 17.54.7 gives no cause.
[29] Carney 1996: 567–568. [30] Brosius 1996: 21–24; Llewellyn-Jones 2013: 111–113.

In between Alexander's initial encounter with the royal Persian women and his much-delayed marriage to one of the daughters of Darius and to one of the daughters of the earlier Persian king, Ochus, he married Roxane in 327. She was the daughter of Oxyartes, a Bactrian noble. Alexander encountered and married her during his campaign to capture the region; the marriage, though described by ancient authors as a love match, was clearly part of his attempt to control Bactria (Plutarch *Alexander* 47.7–8; Curtius 8.4.21; Arrian *Anabasis* 4.18.4, 4.19.4–4.19.5, 8.2.26–8.2.29). Roxane travelled east with him and may have born him a son who died at birth or soon after (in 326; *Metz Epitome* 40, 70). Not surprisingly Alexander rewarded her father with a satrapy (Arrian *Anabasis* 6.15.3; Curtius 9.8.9–9.8.10).[31]

In 324 Alexander finally married Darius III's daughter Stateira as well as Parysatis, daughter of Ochus, all part of the mass marriages at Susa. On this occasion Alexander staged a grand ceremonial banquet in which many of his important officers married members of the Persian elite: Hephaestion married Darius' daughter Drypetis; Craterus married Amastris, daughter of Darius' brother; Perdiccas wed a daughter of the satrap of Media; Ptolemy and Eumenes married two daughters of Artabazus (i.e. sisters or half-sisters of Barsine); Nearchus a daughter of Barsine and Mentor; Seleucus the daughter of Spitamenes (a late Bactrian leader) Apama; and there were other marriages as well (Diodorus 17.107.6; Justin 12.10.9–12.10.10; Plutarch *Alexander* 70.2; Arrian *Anabasis* 7.4.4–7.4.8). By these marriages, if long-delayed, Alexander intended to show that the new ruling class of his empire would be a combination of the Persian and Macedonian elite. To some degree the elite marriages paralleled the solemnization of relationships between ordinary soldiers and women they had encountered along the way.

Alexander's two Achaemenid marriages would ordinarily have rendered Roxane insignificant, were it not for these events. Late in 324 Roxane became pregnant, though she had not yet borne a child when Alexander died in June of 323 at Babylon (Justin 13.2.5; Curtius 10.6.9). Soon after Alexander's death, Roxane murdered Stateira and her sister Drypetis (supposedly and not implausibly with the help of the first regent, Perdiccas, thus eliminating any possible half-Achaemenid, half-Argead babies; Plutarch *Alexander* 77.4).[32] In the end Roxane's fate was no better than that of the women she'd eliminated. The Successors

---

[31] Müller 2012b: 295–309.
[32] Parysatis, Alexander's other Persian wife, may have been the victim instead of Drypetis.

showed no interest in marrying her.³³ It was her status as mother of Alexander IV that enabled her to live until *c.* 309, not the fact that she was Alexander's widow.³⁴ A succession of regents dragged her and her son around to various spots; the pair ended up with Olympias, then were arrested, imprisoned, and ultimately murdered by Cassander (Diodorus 19.52.4, 105–112; Justin 14.6.13, 15.2.2–15.2.5; Pausanias 9.7.2).

While the cumulative effect of the content of this chapter may make the reader feel like an audience member at the end of *Hamlet,* with good reason, that is not the whole story. We used to think that all the Persian brides from the mass marriages were rejected except for Seleucus' wife Apama (Arrian *Anabasis* 7.4.6; Plutarch *Demetrius* 31.5; Memnon *FGrH / BNJ* 434 F 1.4.4), who became the founding mother of the Seleucid dynasty. While Craterus did reject Amastris in favour of a marriage to Phila, daughter of Antipater (Arrian *Anabasis* 7.4.5), we simply do not know how many other elite Persian women were rejected, particularly since many of the Successors practised polygamy. Moreover, Amastris went on to marry another successor, Lysimachus, and to found a city and name it after herself before, admittedly, she was murdered by her sons.³⁵ Roxane may not have fared well, removed from family connections in the west, but some of the Persian women who remained in the east may have done better.

In terms of the notion of symbolic capital, an important way to assess the influence of wives in polygamous marriages, it is easy enough to see why Roxane's influence and thus importance did not stand up to that of surviving elite Macedonian women,³⁶ but it is much harder to explain the fate of Barsine and her son, particularly the rejection of his candidacy at Babylon. It is true that neither he nor his mother (Justin 13.2.7) was on the spot (not that Alexander IV, still a foetus, was either), and that Nearchus, who had become Barsine's son-in-law, was his succession advocate and was disliked by many members of the Macedonian elite, as his inglorious post-Alexander career confirms (Curtius 10.6.10–10.6.12). After the murder of Alexander IV, Heracles was briefly a candidate but Cassander and Polyperchon had him (and probably his mother as well) killed, though he was the only male Argead left alive (Diodorus 20.20.1–20.20.2, 28.4). It is significant that he also had Achaemenid blood. Doubtless both Heracles and Alexander IV

---

³³ Müller 2012b: 301.   ³⁴ Harders 2014.   ³⁵ Van Oppen de Ruiter 2020.
³⁶ Müller 2013 applies the idea of symbolic capital to Argead women and those of the Successor era. In terms of Roxane, the lesser prestige (compared to the Achaemenids) of her family, her distance from them, and her lack of support in court circles are relevant.

would always have been killed as they edged to adulthood since their mere existence threatened the Successors' gradual move towards their own kingships, but the initial preference for an unborn baby over an existing male child can only mean that the very fact that he was not only part Persian but also part Achaemenid was the issue, the disadvantage.

Conclusion

It should be apparent how interwoven women of various ranks and ethnicities were into the politics of Alexander's court. We see men and women working together, not infrequently for violent ends. Women's access to information, implying their participation in information networks covering great distances, their attempts to influence events and decisions, and their ability to exercise patronage to their own ends is striking. Their violent deaths resemble those of male Argeads and many of the Successors. They were, in the end, killed because they somehow constituted a problem, a threat to others, just as the men did.

Guide to Further Reading

For women in the Macedonian and Hellenistic courts in general see Macurdy 1932; Carney 2000 (with several of the essays also in Carney 2015); Coşkun and McAuley 2016; and Kunst 2021. Müller 2021b focuses more specifically on the Argead women. For biographies of Alexander's mother Olympias and grandmother Eurydice, see Carney 2006 and 2019 respectively; useful prosopographical biographies of the other women around Alexander are provided in Heckel 2021. For the dynastic systems in which the women of these courts found themselves players, see Ogden 1999; Weber 2009; Strootman 2021 and, with a broader purview, Dunn and Carney 2018. For weddings, see Ager 2017. For the physical contexts of the royal women in their palaces, see Hatzopoulos 2001 and Kottaridi 2011.

14: RELIGION

Hugh Bowden

Over recent decades there has been a series of transformations in approaches to the study of ancient Greek religion. It is understood that religion was fundamentally about relationships. The actions taken by Greek communities and individuals in respect of the gods were determined by the need to seek help, or to avoid harm from them. From this perspective there was no fundamental distinction between the nature of relationships with gods and of relationships with other communities and individuals. Cities could honour human benefactors with the benefits which ranged up a scale from relief from taxes, free meals (this was a common honour given to victors of panhellenic games), to gold crowns and honorific statues, and even cult buildings, as for example at Amphipolis in the fifth century (Thucydides 5.11.1). All of these things might be offered to the gods as well. It is now also recognized that human knowledge about the gods was very limited. There were no authoritative sources of information about the gods, and no certain way to know which god to seek to propitiate if misfortune struck. The consultation of oracles and other forms of divination could be used to seek answers in some circumstances, but human–divine relationships were always constrained by uncertainty. The central texts of Greek literature, the Homeric poems, depicted a world in which the gods remained invisible to mortals, and would appear to them only in disguise. For Alexander and his contemporaries, the world of gods was one to be negotiated with due caution. There were no hard and fast rules about behaviour, or clear notions about the gods to assent to. And those who seek to make sense of Alexander's own religious positions need to be cautious in drawing too many firm conclusions from evidence which is often unreliable.

Religious activity was a fundamental responsibility of Alexander in his roles as king and as general, and his relationship with the communities he ruled over was mediated through religion. This chapter will explore these aspects of his life. The writers of the Roman imperial period whose narratives provide much of our evidence for Alexander's actions give us only limited information about this regular religious activity, and show more interest in presenting Alexander as a forerunner of some Roman emperors in making extravagant claims to divinity. Modern scholarship has tended to follow their lead, so this chapter will also examine questions relating to Alexander's religious self-presentation.

Alexander as King and Commander

In the Eastern Mediterranean and the Near East in the first millennium BCE, where states had kings, they acted as intermediaries between the gods and the community. While this is clear in the iconography of Egypt and Persia, it is also clear from accounts of Macedonian and Spartan kingship as well. Alexander is said to have offered established sacrifices at Aegae or Dion in the winter of 335/4 BCE before he started his campaign (Arrian *Anabasis* 1.11.1; Diodorus 17.16.3). At the end of his life, in Babylon, we are told that, according to the Royal Diaries, he continued to offer the customary sacrifices each morning even when he was too ill to do much else (Arrian *Anabasis* 7.25; Plutarch *Alexander* 76).

Alexander spent relatively little of his reign actually in Macedonia, but he grew up there, and the religious culture of the region will have been an important part of his inheritance. Macedonia had had cultural links with the Greek cities to the south since the late sixth century, and Macedonian rulers had taken part in panhellenic festivals from that period. Cults to the Greek gods were well established in Macedonia, and festivals included Greek elements such as athletic competitions.[1]

While on campaign Alexander, like all generals, would have been particularly reliant on the support of the gods to ensure his military successes. The ancient narratives, especially Arrian, present Alexander as benefitting from the skills of his *mantis* (seer) Aristander of Telmessus. As is clear from the works of Xenophon (whose own *Anabasis* was a model for Arrian's), a good general would sacrifice before engaging in any significant action, whether starting a march, crossing a border, or starting a battle or siege.[2] It was the role of the *mantis* to read the entrails of the sacrificed animals, and also to interpret the flight and calls of birds, astronomical signs, and any other phenomena deemed ominous. Roman writers sometimes expressed scepticism about non-Roman

---

[1] Mari 2002, 2011b.   [2] Bowden 2004.

forms of divination (even though there was not a great deal of difference between Roman practices and those of their contemporaries), and this explains why Curtius in particular accuses Alexander of succumbing to superstition (e.g. 7.7.8) in employing Aristander. There is however no reason to doubt that Alexander would have consulted *manteis* whenever it was appropriate, and that his entourage would have included not only Greeks, but also Babylonian scholar-priests (called 'Chaldaeans' by Arrian, e.g. *Anabasis* 7.16), Persian Magi (Curtius 5.1.22), and possibly even Egyptians (Curtius 4.10.4).

In the course of campaigns, Alexander marked the limits of his empire through religious ritual. He is said to have erected an altar by the Jaxartes river (Pliny *Natural History* 6.18), having asserted his authority over the Scythians beyond it (Arrian *Anabasis* 4.4.9; Curtius 7.8.1–9.19). Similarly, he erected a series of altars on the banks of the Hyphasis, marking the extent of his claim to territory in the Indus valley (Arrian *Anabasis* 5.29.1; Curtius 9.3.19; Diodorus 17.95; Plutarch *Alexander* 62.4; Strabo C171). When, at the end of his march down the Indus valley, Alexander reached the Indian Ocean, he sailed out and offered elaborate sacrifices from his ship (Arrian *Anabasis* 6.19.4–6.19.5, *Indica* 20.10). These ritual activities, marking the eastern extent of his campaigning in Asia, can be connected to significant activities at the start of his expedition, when Alexander set up altars on either side of the Hellespont, and made sacrifices during the short voyage, and then at Troy (Arrian *Anabasis* 1.11.6–1.11.8). None of these ritual activities would have been considered particularly unusual by Alexander's Greek contemporaries (nor indeed by the other peoples within his empire). They are worth noting as a reminder that for Alexander, no more or less than for any other commander, working with the gods was a necessary precondition for military success.

Relations with Greek Cities

What we would call Alexander's diplomatic relationships with the Greek cities were conducted through activity at religious sanctuaries. The major 'panhellenic' sanctuaries of Delphi, Olympia, and Isthmia were key sites of communication between Alexander and the Greek cities allied to him, and the sanctuaries and temples of individual cities were locations which could be used by the cities to express their attitudes towards the man who would have been in the eyes of some their liberator, and perhaps in the eyes of others their oppressor.

The Delphic Amphictyony and the League of Corinth

As heir to his father, Alexander effectively inherited the leadership of two groupings of Greek cities: the Delphic Amphictyony and the so-called League of Corinth. The origins of the former dated back at least to the sixth century BCE. It was in essence a group of Greek communities, mainly from the region around the city of Delphi, which took responsibility for looking after the fabric of the sanctuaries of Demeter at Anthela and of Apollo at Delphi. Delphi was a wealthy sanctuary (and had been more so before the destruction of the temple in an earthquake, and the loss of much of its portable wealth during the Sacred War of 356–346 BCE). It was the home of the Delphic oracle and of the four-yearly Pythian Games, second in importance only to the Olympics. Taking a leading role in overseeing the work of the sanctuary would have brought prestige to Alexander, as it clearly did to Philip II before him. Some scholars have argued that the Amphictyony had a significant political role in the Greek world, and Diodorus (17.4.3) does state that the Amphictyons granted Alexander the leadership of Greece. However, this is the same phrase that Diodorus had used to describe what was granted to him by the Thessalian League, and there is no evidence for the Amphictyony being engaged in the broader military or political concerns of the Greek world in this period. The Amphictyony's activity was always related to its responsibility for the sanctuaries of Delphi and Anthela. Alexander's involvement in the Amphictyony was about accepting a religious responsibility: to honour and propitiate Apollo at one of his most important sanctuaries.

The League of Corinth was rather different in its purpose, but that does not mean that its religious dimension should be ignored. It was an alliance set up by Philip II to campaign against the Persians. Delegates met initially at the sanctuary of Poseidon at Isthmia, near Corinth, and this location was clearly chosen because this is where delegates from the Greek cities met to plan their resistance to Xerxes' invasion of 480–479 BCE (Herodotus 7.172). It was a permanent alliance, which continued to exist after the aims of its initial campaign had been achieved with the destruction of Persepolis. Delegates would convene annually, with meetings coinciding with the major Panhellenic Games, and it would have been at such a meeting at Olympia in 324 BCE that the 'exiles decree' would have been presented to the Greek cities. The context of these meetings, the celebration of victories in athletic competitions overseen by the gods, would have made an important contribution to the character of the deliberations.

Individual Cities

Alexander's relations with individual Greek cities were also frequently mediated through sanctuaries. After his victory at the River Granicus, Alexander sent 300 panoplies (suits of hoplite armour) to Athens, to be dedicated on the acropolis. This action can be compared with the dedication of 300 panoplies in sanctuaries in Attica by the Athenian general Demosthenes after victory over the Ambraciots during the Peloponnesian War (Thucydides 3.114). The panoplies may well have been part of Alexander's personal share of the spoils, as was the case with Demosthenes. This was the first booty won on Alexander's campaign, so his choice to send it to Athens must be recognized as a sign of respect for the city, and for Athena, the goddess of the acropolis.

This use of religious sanctuaries as sites for building relationships between Alexander and the Greek cities can be seen even more clearly in Asia Minor, and we can see that this was a two-way process: Alexander wanted to present himself as a liberator and a benefactor to the cities, while the leading citizens of the newly liberated cities had strong motivation to show honour to Alexander, so that his support for them would be maintained. Arrian (*Anabasis* 1.18.2) refers to Alexander ordering the overthrow of oligarchies and the installation of democracies in these cities. This would have meant removing from power the leading citizens who had been working with the Persians, and replacing them with other members of the elite, often returning exiles, who would be loyal to Alexander. From the perspective of the newly restored citizens, Alexander could be seen as a new founder (*oikist*) of their city, deserving of the kind of honours that were traditionally given to founders. This would include festivals in his name, and the installation of cult with priests of Alexander appointed. There was nothing radically new in this, and similar honours had been awarded, or at least offered, to 'liberators' such as Lysander at Samos and elsewhere (Plutarch *Lysander* 18) and Agesilaus in Thasos (Plutarch *Spartan Sayings* 210c–210d) in the late fifth and earlier fourth centuries. The motivation for this would have come primarily from the leading citizens themselves: it was a way of recognizing the good that Alexander had done for the cities, including for example the suppression of factional violence in Ephesus (Arrian *Anabasis* 1.17.12).[3]

It is important to understand actions like the creation of festivals and even priesthoods of Alexander as types of honours, expressing the nature of the relationship between those granting the honours and

---

[3] Habicht 2017: 1–17.

Alexander as recipient. But Alexander honoured the cities that honoured him. We have already noted that Alexander chose to dedicate part of his spoils from the battle of the Granicus in Athens, indicating the existence of a positive relationship between Alexander and the city. This would still have been the case in 324 BCE, when Alexander had just returned to the Persian heartland from his successful campaigns in central Asia and the Indus valley, and when we know from a speech of Hyperides (5.31–5.32) that the Athenians voted to erect a statue to 'King Alexander, Unconquered God'. It has been argued that this decision must have been a response to a specific request for divine honours from Alexander himself. The evidence for such a request is very weak. A number of anecdotes are recorded, mainly by Plutarch, referring to debates in Athens and Sparta about plans to offer cult to Alexander (Plutarch *Moralia* 187e, 219e, 842d; Diogenes Laertius 6.63; Aelian *Varia historia* 2.19, 5.12). The only ancient source actually to report such a demand is the late and unreliable Aelian (*Varia historia* 2.19), and it should be noted that the decision to set up a statue does not amount to offering divine cult. Considerable weight has been put on the fact that Hyperides' *Funeral Oration*, dating to 322 BCE, when Athens had revolted from Macedonian power after Alexander's death, presents offering honours to Macedonians as distasteful to the Athenians:

> These [the dangers of Macedonian rule over Greece] are clear from what we are forced to do even now: sacrifices made to men; statues, altars and temples to the gods disrespected, while those to men are treated with respect, and we are forced to treat the servants of these people as heroes.
>
> Hyperides 6.21

There is clear exaggeration here, as would have been considered appropriate for the rhetoric of the annual funeral oration, and it would be an error to read back the mood of this speech onto the situation two years earlier, when those Athenian politicians who saw the advantages of working with Alexander were in the ascendant in Athens. We should therefore see this statue as an element in an exchange of honours between Alexander and the Athenians.

In Asia Minor Alexander also paid attention to religious sanctuaries. He is said to have set up an altar and planned a temple to Olympian Zeus at Sardis (Arrian *Anabasis* 1.17.5–1.17.6); he dedicated the new temple to Athena at Priene; he probably sponsored the restoration of the oracular sanctuary of Didyma near Miletus (implied by Strabo 814c). At Ephesus, he redirected tribute previously paid to the Persians to the temple of Artemis (Arrian *Anabasis* 1.17.10). It is in this context that we should understand another representation of Alexander with divine attributes. We are told that there was a famous painting of Alexander made for the temple of Artemis at Ephesus by Apelles, depicting him wielding a thunderbolt (Pliny *Natural History* 35.92; Plutarch *Moralia* 335a, *Alexander* 4.1).

We have no indication of the date at which this painting was made, but since it was by Apelles it must have been contemporary with Alexander, and the most plausible time for the work would be when he was in Ephesus in 334 BCE. The thunderbolt was an attribute of Zeus, and so this portrait is presenting Alexander as god-like in some way. The fact that it was displayed in a temple, and remained there, we may assume, many years after Alexander's death, should encourage us to recognize that such an image was not considered offensive. The thunderbolt can be seen as something given to Alexander by Zeus. It is arguably similar to the sceptre that Agamemnon is described as holding in the *Iliad* (1.100–1.109), which was made by Hephaestus for Zeus, and handed down by him until it was inherited by Agamemnon. It is a symbol of the authority he has as king, granted by Zeus. We have a later image of Alexander holding a thunderbolt on the so-called Porus decadrachms, or Elephant medallions, which were minted after Alexander's successful campaign in the Indus valley. The obverse of these large silver coins depicts a horseman in combat with an elephant with two riders on its back, presumed to be Alexander fighting the Indian prince Porus. The reverse shows a figure in armour, with a plumed helmet, a sceptre in his left hand and a thunderbolt in his right; a winged figure holds a garland above his head. This is clearly once again Alexander with the attributes of Zeus: the god is depicted seated with a similar sceptre in his left hand on other coins of Alexander. It is not clear whether this coin image would have been known to the Athenians at the time when they voted to award him an honorific statue, but the image, with its combination of thunderbolt and crowning by Victory could be seen as a representation of Alexander as an 'unconquered god'. These images are not evidence that Alexander wanted to be worshipped as a god, but rather a means of showing the closeness between Alexander, as king, and Zeus, as king of the gods. And this is how the Greeks would have understood them.[4]

---

[4] On both the images of Alexander with a thunderbolt see Stewart 1993: 191–209. Some of Stewart's points are made less well than they could have been, because he is too ready to take the later literary traditions about Alexander at face value, but he recognizes that the image of Alexander as god should be taken as 'metaphorical'.

Alexander in Egypt, Babylon, and Persia

Egypt

Alexander entered Egypt in November 332 BCE, facing no resistance from the Persian satrap Mazaces, or the Egyptians themselves. He left the kingdom in the spring of the following year. Inscriptions from Karnak, Luxor, Hermopolis, and Bahariya present Alexander with a complete Pharaonic titulary, indicating that he was considered to be the legitimate ruler of Egypt. None of the Alexander historians say that Alexander was formally crowned as pharaoh while there, but their silence should not be taken as proof that he was not. There was time for him to have taken part in appropriate rituals, and Arrian mentions a series of festivals during his time there.[5]

Where we have representations of Alexander in Egyptian religious contexts, he is presented as a typical Egyptian pharaoh. For example, in a sequence of reliefs in the Barque Shrine in the temple at Luxor he is shown in a ritual attitude in the presence of a number of Egyptian gods. At the same time there are elements of Greek religious practice presented alongside the Egyptian activity. So, for example, according to Arrian, Alexander held athletics contests in the Greek style in association with the festivals he celebrated at Memphis to Egyptian gods (*Anabasis* 3.1.4, 3.5.2). A temple was constructed for Alexander in the Bahariya oasis in the western desert in Egypt, and a stone pedestal there, which may have been a statue base, is inscribed with the complete set of his pharaonic titles:

> Horus, 'the ruler of the rulers of the entire land'; Two Ladies, 'the lion, great of might, the one who takes possession of mountains, lands, and deserts'; Horus of Gold, 'the strong bull who protects Egypt, the ruler of the sea and of what the sun encircles'; King of Upper and Lower Egypt, 'beloved of Re, the chosen one of Amun'; Son of Re, 'son of Amun, Alexander'.

On the same stone is a much shorter Greek inscription, reading 'King Alexander, to his father Ammon'.[6] This is a typical Greek form of dedicatory text, next to a typically Egyptian one, so that Greek and Egyptian visitors to the site would be able to make sense of what they saw on their own terms. We will return to the significance of the phrase

---

[5] Bowden 2014a. [6] Bosch-Puche 2008, 2013, 2014.

'son of Amun/Ammon' later. Like the festivals at Memphis, this is an example of Alexander presenting himself bilingually, making his commitment to the gods comprehensible to two audiences.

Babylon

Documents from Babylon demonstrate that Alexander took seriously the expectations of kingship there too. Again, the Alexander historians do not mention any coronation ritual, but Alexander is presented as taking on the role of the king, including working closely with the Babylonian priestly elite (Arrian *Anabasis* 3.16.5). An astronomical diary from the time of his entry into the city indicates that he promised to restore the temple of Marduk – something expected of all Babylonian kings – although Arrian suggests that he was not able to achieve a great deal (Arrian *Anabasis* 3.16.4, 7.17.1–7.17.4). He appears also to have taken part in a 'substitute king ritual' in 324 BCE on his return to Babylon. The Greek authors give accounts of a strange set of events, which involved a prisoner or a madman sitting on the royal throne, and being dragged off and subsequently executed (Arrian *Anabasis* 7.24; Diodorus 17.116; Plutarch *Alexander* 73). These stories have been recognized as garbled descriptions of a Mesopotamian ritual in which, in response usually to astronomical signs, the king would abdicate temporarily, so that the danger would fall on a substitute, usually a prisoner, who would be executed once the crisis had passed.[7] Whether the historians (or their sources) were confused about this ritual, or whether they chose to rewrite it in terms their readership would understand (presenting the actions of the prisoner or madman as omens predicting Alexander's imminent death), we cannot tell. It is, however, clear that Alexander himself took the Babylonian rituals entirely seriously.

Persia

We do not have contemporary evidence for Alexander's religious activities in Iran itself. There are far fewer Persian royal inscriptions overall, and none from the reign of Darius III. Those that do exist from earlier tell us little about the religious activities of kings, so the absence of evidence about Alexander is not significant. Diodorus (17.66.3–17.66.8) and Curtius (5.2.13–5.2.15) report a story about Alexander sitting on the

---

[7] Van der Spek 2003.

royal throne at Susa, causing the attendants to react strongly. The story is reminiscent of the stories about the man sitting on the Babylonian throne, with a similar focus on its significance as an omen. It is possible that behind it was an actual coronation ritual at Susa. Alexander's subsequent actions, including his adoption of Achaemenid court protocol, suggest that he would have taken on the religious functions of the king in Iran, as far as this was possible while he was on campaign, in the same way that he took on the responsibilities in Egypt and Babylon.

Heracles, Dionysus, and the Matter of *Proskynēsis*

Stories about Alexander's adoption of one particular element of Persian court protocol have become entangled in arguments about whether Alexander requested to be worshipped as a god, and this is worthy of some exploration. Curtius (8.5.5–8.5.24), Arrian (*Anabasis* 4.10.12) and Plutarch (*Alexander* 54) all tell stories about Alexander's attempt to require Persians and Macedonians alike to prostrate themselves before him, on the basis that he deserved this honour because of his god-like achievements. As Curtius puts it, introducing his account of the episode, Alexander 'wanted not only to be called the son of Jupiter, but to be believed to be so' (8.5.5). In Arrian's version of the story (*Anabasis* 4.10.6), the sophist Anaxarchus is put up to argue that on the basis of his achievements there was a better case for the Macedonians to regard Alexander as a god than for them to consider Heracles or Dionysus as gods. Curtius (8.5.10–8.5.11) gives a very similar version, referring to Hercules and Father Liber (Roman equivalents to Heracles and Dionysus) and identifying the speaker as a different Greek sophist, Cleon. The argument is based on the idea that both these gods were mortals who had been eventually granted immortality as a result of their achievements. While this may have been a widely held idea about Heracles in Alexander's time, it is less clear that this held for Dionysus.[8]

Although modern scholars have tended to believe that the debate depicted by Curtius and Arrian must have happened, there are good reasons to doubt this. The story is based on a misunderstanding of what the practice of *proskynēsis* involved. The word was used by Greek

---

[8] Arrian (*Anabasis* 5.1–5.3) discusses the historicity of the stories circulating about Dionysus and Heracles in Alexander's time, expressing scepticism about them, but suggesting that they were used to win favour from Alexander.

writers to describe the formal practice of Persians in greeting each other, which varied depending on the social distance between the two actors, ranging from a mutual kiss on the lips to prostration, according to Herodotus (1.134.1). These gestures never implied any worship of the Persian king. For the Alexander historians writing centuries later, the word always means prostration, and they equated this with the worship of gods, although there is little evidence for Greeks normally prostrating themselves before cult statues. The story told by Arrian and Curtius was an embellishment of other stories about Alexander's symposia which had nothing to do with Alexander wishing to be worshipped himself.[9]

Given the significance of Heracles and Dionysus in this story, it is worth considering how far Alexander was concerned to emulate these gods. They are paired together quite often by the Alexander historians as Alexander's precursors, or as individuals whom he might seek to rival (e.g. Arrian *Anabasis* 2.16.1, 4.10.6, 5.26.5, *Indica* 5.8–5.10, 7.4–8.10; Curtius 3.10.5, 8.5.8, 8.5.11, 8.5.17, 8.10.1, 9.2.29, 9.4.21). There is also contemporary evidence for their cult in Macedonia in Alexander's time and earlier.

Heracles

The Argead dynasty of Macedonia claimed descent from Heracles. Alexander followed the practice of his predecessors by issuing coins which depicted the beardless head of Heracles wearing a lionskin on the obverse: the bronze coins had images of Heracles' club and bow on the reverse, while the silver coins depicted Zeus seated on a throne with a sceptre in his left hand and an eagle on the right. A number of stories told about Alexander present him either as having particular devotion to Heracles, or being particularly determined to emulate, and to surpass, the achievements of his ancestor: for example his siege and conquest of Tyre is presented as the consequence of the Tyrian refusal to allow him to sacrifice to Heracles at his temple within the city (Curtius 4.2.2–4.2.5; Arrian *Anabasis* 2.16), and his desire to visit the oracle of Amun at Siwah is said to have been because his ancestor had visited it (Arrian *Anabasis* 3.3.1–3.3.2). Heracles was presented in myth as having travelled across the world in the course of his labours, including east into the Caucasus, where he shot the vulture that fed on Prometheus' liver

---

[9] Full discussion in Bowden 2013.

(Arrian *Anabasis* 5.3.2). However, it is very likely that these stories represent the interests of the historians who reported them, rather than accurately representing Alexander's personal motivations.[10]

Dionysus

Dionysus was, like Heracles, the son of Zeus by a mortal mother, and like Heracles he was said to have travelled widely, particularly in the east. Stories about Alexander's emulation of Dionysus are set in the later part of his career, during and after his campaign in the Indus valley. One example is his visit to Nysa in the upper Indus valley, a city said to have been founded by the god, where the Macedonians were inspired to frenzy (Arrian *Anabasis* 5.1–5.2; Curtius 8.10.7–8.10.18). Another is the story of Alexander's return from the Indus through Carmania, where he is supposed to have engaged in a wild Bacchic procession (Arrian *Anabasis* 6.28.1–2; Curtius 9.10.24–9.10.29). Arrian expresses scepticism about both stories. There is much evidence for the cult of Dionysus in Macedonia in the fifth and fourth centuries BCE, and Euripides' *Bacchae* was written for performance there, when Euripides was at the court of Alexander's ancestor Archelaus. Plutarch (*Alexander* 2) describes Alexander's mother Olympias as particularly involved in rites associated with Dionysus, although since this is mentioned in the specific context of a snake being seen sleeping next to her, this may be Plutarch rationalizing that phenomenon. But there are other explanations for why the narratives include these stories relating to Dionysus. Cult of the god was particularly important in Alexandria, the city from which several of the earliest accounts of Alexander emerged (Ptolemy, Clitarchus, the Greek *Alexander Romance*). It may therefore be that, as with Heracles, episodes where Alexander is closely associated with Dionysus have more to do with the interests of later historians rather than reflecting the historical Alexander.[11]

ALEXANDER AND AMMON

One episode more than any other has drawn the attention of scholars interested in the topic of Alexander's religious self-understanding. That is his visit to the oracle of Amun at the Siwah oasis in the Libyan desert. A re-examination of all the elements of this story will provide a useful

---

[10] Djurslev 2021b. [11] For fuller discussion, see Stoneman 2021a.

case-study in the interpretation of Alexander and religion. Some of the issues involved in this re-examination have been touched on earlier in this chapter, and this will act to bring them together.[12]

The sanctuary of Amun in the Siwah oasis was probably founded under the 26th dynasty, that is in the seventh or sixth century BCE. According to Herodotus (4.181.2; cf. 2.42) the oracle was founded from Egyptian Thebes, where there was a long-established oracle of Amun.[13] The oracle was well known to Greeks by the first half of the fifth century, and this is probably in part because of the relationship to the shrine developed by the Greek settlement of Cyrene, which was celebrated by Pindar (*Pythians* 4; cf. Pausanias 9.16.1).[14] Amun was represented in Egyptian iconography as a ram-headed god, and in his Greek form, as Ammon, he was depicted as a man with ram's horns. The site at Siwah has been excavated, and this has revealed the presence of two temples, the earlier built by Amasis (570–526 BCE), and the later by Netanebo II (360–342 BCE), the last ruler of an independent Egypt, and a processional way between them. The functioning of the oracle involved the carrying of the cult image of the god on a barque along the processional way, a process described by Curtius (4.7.23–5.7.24) and Diodorus (17.50.6).[15]

Being in the western desert, over 500 km west of Memphis, the oasis of Siwah was not often visited by Egyptian pharaohs. There are a number of reasons why Alexander might have chosen to visit it. The reputation of the oracle in the Greek world may have been a significant factor (Arrian *Anabasis* 3.3.1; Diodorus 17.49.2). According to Arrian (*Anabasis* 3.3.1–3.3.2) he also wanted to emulate his ancestors, Heracles and Perseus, but, as we have seen, this is likely to be a later invention. Another figure with whom comparisons can be drawn is the Persian king Cambyses, the leader of a previous successful invasion of Egypt. Herodotus (3.26) describes a disastrous expedition sent by Cambyses against 'the Ammonians' that ended with his army being buried in the desert sands. Stories about Alexander almost becoming lost in the desert, but being rescued by divine intervention (Arrian *Anabasis* 3.3.3–3.3.6; Curtius 4.7.10–4.7.16; Diodorus 17.49.3–17.49.6; Plutarch *Alexander* 27.1–27.3) were arguably told to contrast Alexander's expedition with his predecessor's, but the comparison is likely to have been of interest to the historians rather than to Alexander himself. A desire to visit a site associated with two pharaohs who ruled Egypt when it was not under

---

[12] For background, see Bowden 2014a: 43–53. [13] Černý 1962.
[14] For further information about Greek contact with the sanctuary at Siwah, see Classen 1959.
[15] For a full description of the site, see Kuhlmann 1988.

Persian control might be a more plausible reason. It is also quite likely that he wanted to establish relations with the Greek cities of Cyrenaica, and used a visit to the sanctuary as a way of doing this, just as his activities at sanctuaries in Asia Minor had been part of his development of relationships with the Greek cities there. Certainly he was met on the way by ambassadors from Cyrene bearing gifts (Curtius 4.7.9; Diodorus 17.49.2).

The suggestion that has been taken up by modern scholars, however, is that of Curtius (4.7.8), who suggests that he wanted to demonstrate that Jupiter was his father. As we have already seen, in his royal titulary Alexander included in some cases the personal name 'son of Amun, Alexander'; elsewhere he is described as 'son of Re, Alexander', or simply 'Alexander'. The use of 'son of Amun' has precedents from earlier periods, but is not very common: it tended to be used by foreign rulers, for example Darius I, and usurpers. This was reason enough for Alexander to adopt the form, but it may also have appealed because Amun/Ammon was the Egyptian god best known outside Egypt.[16] We have seen that Alexander made a dedication in Greek at the Bahariya temple to 'his father Ammon', indicating that he saw significance in being 'son of Amun'.

The association between Alexander and Amun/Ammon was emphasized by Alexander's successors. Several of his former companions issued coins with Alexander's head on them, with a range of divine attributes. Ptolemy I issued silver tetradrachms sometime in the period 316–312 BCE with the head of Alexander on the obverse, wearing an elephant headdress and, emerging from beneath it, a pair of ram's horns. The elephant is taken to represent Alexander's victories in India, but it may also have been associated specifically with Dionysus, whose importance in Ptolemaic Alexandria was demonstrated in particular by a great festival procession in the reign of Ptolemy II Philadelphus, of which a description can be found in the *Deipnosophistai* of Athenaeus (197c–203b).[17] The rams' horns are, as we have seen, attributes of Amun/Ammon. The horns are not very prominent on these Ptolemaic coins but are much more visible on the coins of another of Alexander's former companions, Lysimachus, who issued coins showing Alexander on the obverse with somewhat larger horns and no elephant headdress. Clearly Alexander's successors saw benefits in drawing attention to their relationship with Alexander, and at the same time his relationship with Amun/Ammon. It was not a cause of

---

[16] Bosch-Puche 2014: 89–98.   [17] See Rice 1983.

embarrassment, which is important to bear in mind when considering the representation of the relationship in later literary sources.[18]

The earliest description of Alexander's visit to Siwah comes from Callisthenes, Alexander's court historian, who was present with him there, and whose account is reported by Strabo (C814). His version of events was probably drawn upon by Ptolemy, when he wrote his history decades later, and Arrian made use of Ptolemy's narrative: certainly, Arrian's version of events is fairly close to Callisthenes' as found in Strabo, and it is ultimately from Callisthenes that Arrian took the statement that Alexander decided to visit the oracle because he had heard that Heracles and Perseus had done so. Callisthenes says that the priest of the oracle told Alexander that he was the son of Zeus. The surviving fragments of Callisthenes make it clear that he consistently used the names of Greek equivalents for non-Greek gods, so this can be taken to mean that the priest described Alexander as son of Amun. Callisthenes does not suggest that this was part of any oracular response, and we can take it at face value – as no more than the priest addressing Alexander with his pharaonic title. Arrian omits this part of the story altogether, but the other Alexander historians (Curtius 4.7.25; Diodorus 17.51.1; Plutarch *Alexander* 27.3) make much of it. In all cases the priest is described as addressing Alexander spontaneously, rather than answering a question or following any oracular process, and Alexander explicitly accepts this as a message from the god. In Greek tradition, such spontaneous responses at an oracular sanctuary were considered to be particularly significant: for example the oracle given to the Athenians about the wooden wall (Herodotus 7.140) was uttered before the ambassadors had a chance to put their question, and Plutarch (*Alexander* 14.4) tells a story of how Alexander himself was the beneficiary of another such spontaneous remark by the priestess at Delphi when he tried to force her to prophesy. These three authors then emphasize the significance of the priest's greeting by having Alexander ask the oracle whether his father's murder has been avenged: in response the priest warns Alexander that his father cannot die, but that Philip's murderers have been punished. In contrast Callisthenes (followed by Arrian) does not say anything about what Alexander asked.

In Greek poetic contexts, heroes could have a human father as well as having Zeus as their father. Heracles could be described as son of Amphitryon and of Zeus in the same poem (e.g. Homer *Iliad* 5.392 and 14.266; Bacchylides *Epinicians* 5.57–5.58 and 85). Although prose

---

[18] For a full discussion of the coin evidence, see Dahmen 2007.

writers attempted to offer rationalizations for these apparent contradictions (e.g. Herodotus 2.145–2.146), the idea of dual paternity seems not to have been considered problematic. For Alexander to be son of Ammon would not have required him not to be son of Philip. The suggestion of a conflict between divine and human paternity is most explicitly brought up in the Roman moralizing tradition, as a way of presenting Alexander as a negative *exemplum*. So the Roman moralist writer Valerius Maximus, who wrote during the reign of Tiberius, but was presumably drawing on an established tradition, said of Alexander:

> The virtue and fortune of king Alexander became uncontrollable through three very clear stages of insolence: for out of disdain for Philip he adopted Jupiter Hammon as his father; tired of the customs and manners of Macedonia, he assumed Persian dress and practices; out of scorn for the mortal condition he emulated divinity. He was not ashamed to conceal his nature as a son, a citizen, and a mortal man.
> Valerius Maximus. 9.5.ext.1

Curtius, who describes Alexander in accepting the priest's greeting as 'forgetful of his human condition' (4.7.25), is explicitly following this tradition. In the accounts of Diodorus and Plutarch it is the priest, not Alexander, who is denying that Philip was Alexander's father.

There is another Egyptian version of events that casts doubt on Alexander's paternity, but in a way that is partly comic, and wholly unreliable. The so-called Greek *Alexander Romance* is recognized as having its roots in Egypt in the third century BCE. In this tradition, Alexander is said to have been the son of the last pharaoh of Egypt, Nectanebo II, who was a magician, and who seduced Olympias by disguising himself as the god Ammon in the form of a snake. Importantly, however, Alexander's birth is accompanied by thunder, lightning and earthquakes, suggesting that he is not a mere mortal. The development of the stories in the *Alexander Romance* did not take place in isolation from the other traditions about Alexander. So Plutarch's story that Philip once saw Olympias in bed with a snake, which was actually the god Ammon (*Alexander* 2.4, 3.1) is related to this version, and the story in the *Alexander Romance* only makes sense if the idea that Alexander was son of Ammon/Amun was already in circulation.

What emerges from this analysis is that Alexander was recognized in Egypt as son of Amun, as his pharaonic titulary announced. This idea could be played with in different ways by those who wrote about Alexander. But we cannot conclude from the evidence that Alexander understood this title in any way other than as being part of his role as pharaoh. Nor can we find evidence that Alexander used this title outside Egypt, or made any special claims to divine paternity in the other territories of his empire.

Guide to Further Reading

A good book-length study of the religion of Alexander the Great remains to be written. Most older scholarship about Alexander shows a failure to grasp the nature of Greek religion, and therefore misunderstands the religious assumptions shared by Alexander and his contemporaries. The best most useful recent guide to Greek religion in general is probably Larson 2016. Despite its title, and the author's expertise in Greek religion, Naiden 2019a is a traditional biography of Alexander, embellished by descriptions of ritual activities he may have engaged in. For the Macedonian background see Mari 2011b, and for the relationship between the Argead kings and Greek cities see Bowden 2017 and Mari 2002. The evidence of honours for Alexander in Greek cities is well summarized in Habicht 2017. For a revealing discussion of the evidence from Priene in particular, see Thonemann 2012. The evidence for Alexander's role in Egypt as pharaoh is discussed in several chapters of Grieb et al. 2014. For Alexander's engagement with Babylonian religion, see Van der Spek 2003. For the fullest discussion of the issue of *proskynēsis*, see Bowden 2013.

15: ARMY AND WARFARE

Carolyn Willekes

THE ARMY PRE-ALEXANDER

When Alexander took the throne in 336, he inherited an impressive legacy courtesy of his father Philip II, who had placed Macedonia at the centre of Greek affairs by instigating a series of reforms that would serve as the foundation for his son's conquests.[1] Philip was not starting from a *tabula rasa* in terms of Macedonian warfare, but this was a land of cavalry not infantry. References to Macedonian troops in Herodotus and Thucydides name them as horsemen; likewise, Xenophon makes reference to the presence of the Macedonian cavalry in the army of the Spartan Teleutias at Olynthus.[2] In 424 and 423, Perdiccas II relied on a hired Spartan army to divert Athenian interests away from the north.[3] Thucydides does note that Perdiccas had established a force of hoplites, but these are described as 'Hellenes dwelling in his country' – presumably resident Greeks rather than native Macedonians.[4] Thus, the mainstay of the Macedonian military rested on its horsemen, the most notable of which were the Companion cavalry who rode into battle alongside the king.[5]

The prominence of the cavalry in Macedonian history is largely the result of topography and social structure. One reason given for the absence of a strong native hoplite presence in Macedonia is the largely rural nature of the region.[6] The mainstay of the rural economy was a form of transhumant pastoralism, rather than sedentary farming, and the majority of the land was owned by members of the elite,

---

[1] For works on the life and career of Philip II, see Anson 2020a; Gabriel 2010; Worthington 2008b; Hammond 1994; Hatzopoulos and Loukopoulou 1980; Cawkwell 1978; Ellis 1976.
[2] For references to Macedonian cavalry in Herodotus, see *Histories* 7.185, 9.31.5, 9.44.1. For Thucydides see 1.61.1, 1.62.4, 1.63.2, 4.124.1. For Xenophon see *Hellenica* 5.2.40.
[3] Thucydides 4.124–4.128, 4.124.1 and Anson 2010: 53.
[4] Thucydides 4.124.1 and Anson 2010: 53.
[5] Hammond 1998 for Macedonian cavalry recruitment. On the Companions and their relationship with the king, see Hammond 1989c: 140–148. Wrightson 2010: 83–84 discusses the possibility that Alexander's generals and senior officers fought on horseback.
[6] Anson 2020a: 18–19. For the *polis* and hoplites, see Hanson 1999, van Wees 2004: 47–57 and Sears 2019: 31–59.

creating not only a social structure in which many were part of a dependent population of tenants and pastoralists, but also ideal conditions for horse breeding as the animals could be cycled through different grazing areas throughout the year.[7] Substantial numbers of horses would have been required to maintain the cavalry, thus breeding programmes must have been established by the period of Alexander's reign.[8] Philip II also made a practice of gifting horses to Athenian ambassadors to gain their favour, suggesting that Macedonia was breeding good-quality horses.[9] Further evidence for established breeding programmes can be found on Athenian *dokimasia* ('muster') tablets from the fourth and third centuries BCE. Several of these tablets reference the caduceus brand which has been connected to Macedonia, as horses marked with this symbol appear on coins of Alexander I, Pausanias and Amyntas III.[10]

Philip's Reforms: The New Macedonian Army

The death of Perdiccas III in battle against Bardylis and the Illyrians in 359 brought with it the loss of 4,000 soldiers;[11] yet within the first year of his reign Philip defeated Bardylis with a force of 10,000 infantry and 600 cavalry.[12] This was made possible through his creation of a well-trained, state-maintained force, one which allowed him to secure, even extend Macedonia's borders.[13] Diodorus and Polyaenus imply that Philip began his reforms shortly after becoming king, but it is not implausible to suggest that he had been considering these ideas for some time, particularly given the speed with which they were implemented.[14] Philip's time as a hostage in Thebes from 368–365 BCE likely provided some of the impetus for his ideas. The Theban army of this time was known for its use of combined arms, something which Philip likewise incorporated

---

[7] For urbanization and sedentary agriculture and interrelations with pastoralism, see Howe 2008b: 34–40.
[8] Diodorus 17.17.4 states that Alexander had 1,800 Macedonian cavalry with him when he crossed the Hellespont in 334. If we allow that each cavalryman would have travelled with at least two trained horses, this places the number of Macedonian mounts at a minimum of 3,600. For Macedonia and horse breeding see Blaineau 2015: 81–83 and Karunanithy 2013: 64–66.
[9] Demosthenes 19.265; cf. Howe 2008b: 47.   [10] Chandezon 2014: 159, Kroll 1977: 86–88.
[11] Diodorus 16.2.1, 16.2.4–16.2.5.   [12] See Hammond 1989b.   [13] Diodorus 16.3.1.
[14] Diodorus 16.2.1–16.2.2; Polyaenus 4.2.10. Philip's 'inspiration' may have come from neighbouring territories: Howe 2017; Hammond 1997a; Griffith 1981; Best 1969: 110–119. On the *sarissa*, see Anson 2010; Connolly 2000; Manti 1994, 1992; Hammond 1980a–1980c; Markle 1977 and 1978. There may also have been a Iphicratean connection: Wrightson 2019: 164; Sekunda 2014a; and Best 1969: 102–110.

into his battlefield strategies, and Alexander became a master of executing combined arms tactics.[15]

Key to Philip's reforms was the introduction the *sarissa*, a 4.5–5.5 metre-long pike with a foot-long metal spearhead and butt spike, weighing approximately 6 kg.[16] The length of the *sarissa* allowed for minimal armour, typically consisting of a Phrygian-style or *pilos* helmet and greaves, though a linen or leather breastplate could also be added to the mix. The two-handed grip required to manoeuvre the *sarissa* negated the use of the large hoplite *aspis*.[17] Instead, a small, round shield, approximately 0.6 m in diameter, was strapped to the upper left arm.[18] Philip was thus able to outfit these men at state expense, creating his own professional infantry force, who could fight year-round. The *sarissa* may have lowered costs, but it was an unwieldy and awkward weapon to come to grips with, hence Diodorus' reference to the drills and training exercises used by Philip.[19] The *sarissa* phalanx, whose troops became known as the *pezhetairoi*, formed an essential component of the Macedonian army, creating a formidable appearance as it anchored the centre of the line and advanced menacingly against the enemy. Through constant training these men could execute various turns, manoeuvres and formations in response to changes in terrain and the movements of both the enemy and the other units on their own side. At Chaeronea, for example, the *pezhetairoi* ('foot-guards') of the *sarissa* phalanx pivoted deftly to hold its ranks between the feigned retreat on the Macedonian right, and the cavalry charge on the Macedonian left.[20]

In addition to the creation of this new style of infantry Philip added allied troops to the Macedonian army – both through conquests and diplomacy. This included the famed Thessalian cavalry, who came to serve as the lynchpin on the left wing of Alexander's army.

The Composition of Alexander's Army

The army with which Alexander crossed the Hellespont in 334 was not of great size, estimates ranging from 30,000 foot and 4,000 cavalry to 43,000 foot and 5,500 cavalry, but it was well suited to the use the

---

[15] For combined arms in early fourth-century Theban combat, see Wrightson 2019: 150–158 and Sears 2019: 133–136; Van Wees 2004: 195–197.
[16] Further analysis about the components of the *sarissa* can be found in Sekunda 2001, Manti 1992: 36–37, Markle 1977: 325–326.
[17] For armour and equipment, see Karunanithy 2013: 100–115 and Juhel 2009.
[18] Asclepiodotus 5.1.
[19] Diodorus 16.3.1. See also Curtius 3.2.13–3.2.14. For training drills and practices, see Karunanithy 2013: 19–39. Asclepiodotus 5.1–5.2 for the appearance of the phalanx.
[20] Polyaenus 2.2. See also King 2018: 120 for the mobility of the Macedonian phalanx.

combined arms tactics that would become a hallmark of his battles.[21] The Granicus, Issus, Gaugamela and Hydaspes battles all followed a pattern of attack that relied on the cohesive deployment of different styles of infantry and cavalry to achieve victory. Alexander's strategy can be likened to cracking a bullwhip: the handle remains relatively stationary, but its action is central to grounding the entire reaction of the whip crack. The further you move from the handle, the more energy there is there is until you reach the tip of the whip which moves the quickest and with the greatest amount of force. For the action of the crack to be effective, each part of the whip influences and responds to the other. Using this imagery, we can break Alexander's battle line down into the following components. The tip of the whip crack was the right wing. The troops stationed here included the Macedonian Companion cavalry led by Alexander and they served as the primary offensive arm, moving swiftly and decisively to instigate an engagement.[22] The Companions numbered 1,800 men and were organized into eight *ilai* ('bands'): seven regular *ilai* and the *agēma* ('Guard'). There were also five *ilai* of *prodromoi* ('advance guards') and Paeonians.[23] To the left of the Companions were the 3,000 Macedonian infantry known as the *hypaspists*. The exact appearance of their armament is the topic of debate, but they were viewed as the elite infantry of Alexander's army. Based on the evidence in Arrian, we can surmise that the *hypaspists* were split into three *chiliarchies* ('corps') of 1,000 men each, one of which was the *agēma*.[24] The *hypaspists* held the line between the Companion cavalry on the right and the *pezhetairoi* in the centre.[25] They were versatile troops, and one of their primary tasks was to fight as *hamippoi* ('infantry mixed with cavalry').[26] At centre of the line were the 9,000 *pezhetairoi*, split into six *taxeis* ('contingents'). This title was originally designated for the elite infantry who served as the king's guard, but during Philip's

---

[21] For a breakdown of his forces, see Diodorus 17.17.3–17.17.5; Arrian *Anabasis* 1.11.3–1.11.5; Plutarch *Alexander* 15.1.

[22] Moreno Hernandez 2004; Hammond 1998; Griffith 1963; and Brunt 1963 discuss cavalry composition. For cavalry formations and tactics, see Aston and Kerr 2018: 8–11.

[23] The Companion cavalry are typically classed as 'heavy' cavalry based on their equipment and fighting style, while the *prodromoi* are often viewed as 'light' cavalry who served a variety of functions, including scouting and skirmishing. Gaebel 2002: 172–9 examines the purpose of the *prodromoi*.

[24] King 2018: 121. Arrian *Anabasis* 3.29.7, 4.24.10, 4.30.5–4.30.6, 5.23.7.

[25] For debate about the *hypaspists*, their armament and purpose on the battlefield, see Anson 2020a: 62; Sekunda 2010: 454–456; Hammond 1989c: 151; Heckel 1986: 285–288; Anson 1985b; Milns 1971, 1967.

[26] See Xenophon *The Cavalry Commander* 5.13 and Spence 1993: 58–59 on the use of *hamippoi*. Hypaspists as *hamippoi*: Heckel 2012.

reign it came to refer to the soldiers of the *sarissa* phalanx.[27] This shift may reflect Philip's practice of providing land grants to his citizens, thereby creating a new class of landowners who derived their property from the king. These landowners now gave their loyalty to the king, rather than the aristocracy, a relationship Philip highlighted by naming them as *pezhetairoi*.[28] They connected the two halves of the line as the army advanced forward, fighting offensively or defensively as the situation required. The left wing, anchored by 1,800 Thessalian cavalry and 600 allied cavalry, typically fought in a defensive role. The action of this wing tends to be glossed over by the sources in favour of the right, but the essential part this wing played on the battlefield should not be overlooked.[29] Their task required consummate skill, as it is challenging to fight defensively from horseback. Alexander also incorporated different units of light infantry. These troops were regularly used to cover the wings of his line, but their mobility and agility lent their skills to a range of situations, particularly the Agrianes who were viewed as the best of the javelin men.[30] Finally, he had 7,000 allied Greek infantry courtesy of the League of Corinth. At Issus and Gaugamela these men were held in reserve behind the *pezhetairoi*, but they could also be placed on the left with the Thessalian and allied cavalry.

Combined Arms in an Equestrian Tradition

The military genius of Alexander rested on the ways in which he was able to deploy a diverse array of troops as a cohesive whole that worked together seamlessly and efficiently.[31] Alexander's successful use of combined arms on campaign – whether in pitched battles or more *ad hoc* scenarios – relied on a thorough understanding of the strengths and weaknesses of each set of troops to ensure that they were deployed in the most effective manner, creating a fluid series of manoeuvres. This is a deceptively difficult thing to do as it requires knowledge of the infantrymen, cavalrymen and the horses, and how they behave both as individuals and in unison. Alexander was uniquely placed to accomplish this because of Macedonia's long equestrian tradition. The pervasive

---

[27] See Anson 2020a: 86–91; Anson 2009; Hammond 1989c: 148–151; Sekunda 2010: 447–448 and 456–8; Erskine 1989.
[28] Anson 2020a: 76–7, also Anson 2009: 88–90.
[29] See Aston and Kerr 2018: 6–8 for the Thessalian cavalry in general; Strootman 2012 for the Thessalian cavalry in Alexander's army.
[30] Devine 1986: 268 suggests that the Agrianes may also have fought as *hamippoi*.
[31] Demosthenes 9.47–9.52 on Philip's diverse forces.

presence of the horse in Macedonian society created a familiarity with this animal, and this was key in building the required unity between infantry and cavalry.

First, we can consider the strength and skill of the Macedonian cavalry. Alexander used his knowledge of equines and their behaviour to alter the nature of cavalry combat, using his horsemen to engage in hand-to-hand combat with enemy cavalry and infantry, rather than focusing on skirmishing and harassing his opponents from a distance.[32] This was a brilliant move as the primary weakness faced by a phalanx is its exposed flanks, which are vulnerable to the much swifter cavalry. Although the phalanx presents a seemingly solid formation, this is not actually the case. When approaching a phalanx from the flanks or rear (and at times, even the front), there are small gaps that appear which a horse and rider can use to their advantage if they are skilled enough. Hence Alexander's preference for the wedge formation: it created a narrow point to push into a gap. By placing the boldest horses at the front of the formation, Alexander's Macedonian cavalry was able to break open minor gaps. The devastating effect of a well-trained cavalry force against a phalanx is exemplified by Alexander and the Companion cavalry at the battle of Chaeronea, where they obliterated the Theban Sacred Band. At Chaeronea, Philip and Alexander made evident the deadly effectiveness of horses and cavalrymen trained to fight in close combat.[33]

Infantry who are familiar with horses are more likely to hold firm against an oncoming charge and, given the prevalence of the horse in Macedonian society, this was likely the case for the Macedonians. Further, knowledge of equine behaviour can play to an infantryman's advantage. At Gaugamela, the cavalry of Mazaeus was thrown off their charge when the *pezhetairoi* beat their *sarissas* upon their shields, causing the Persian horses to shy away from the phalanx.[34] Even with this familiarity, however, the phalanx might still find their rear and flanks at risk. This is where the use of combined arms becomes key, as both infantry and cavalry could come to the aid of the phalanx. In all of Alexander's major battles, his infantry faced large numbers of cavalry and, although gaps did appear, this seems have been due more to the topography of the battlefield and the speed at which the right wing advanced, rather than the lines breaking before equine charges. Most

---

[32] Willekes 2015.
[33] For Chaeronea, see Diodorus 16.86.1–16.86.6; Plutarch *Alexander* 9; Polyaenus 4.2.2; also Sears and Willekes 2016.
[34] Diodorus 17.58.3.

importantly, however, the familiarity with horses was essential to creating the cohesion between the Companion cavalry, *hypaspists*, and *pezhetairoi*. The Macedonian infantry understood how cavalry moved and responded to events on the battlefield, and this allowed them to maintain a connection down the line.

THE GRANICUS (336 BCE)[35]

At the Granicus (Figure 15.1) Alexander arranged his forces in a manner that would become a template for his other battles.[36] The 9,000

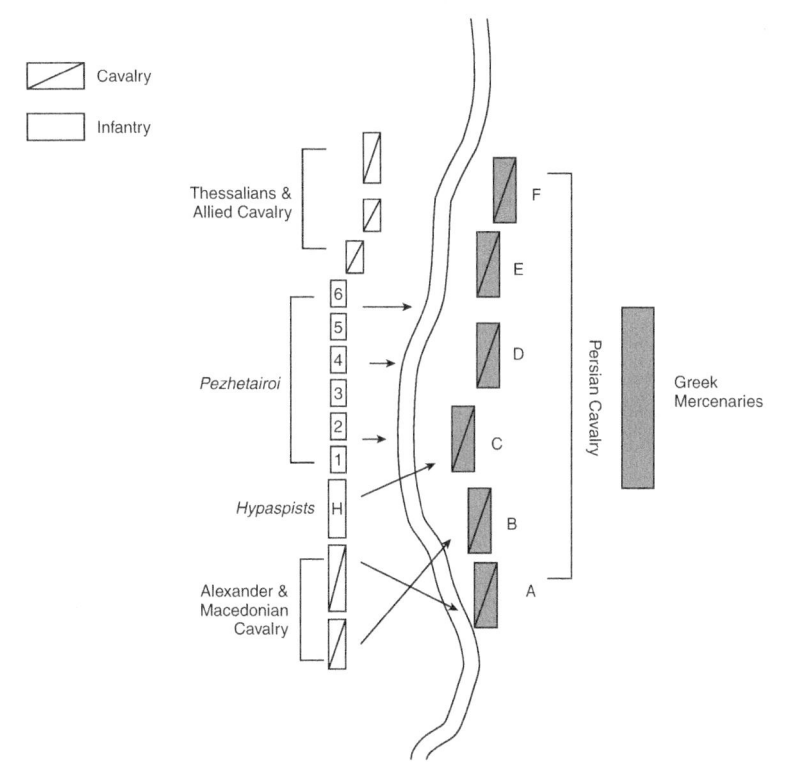

15.1 The Battle of the Granicus: initial battle order; reprinted, with modifications, from Heckel 2008: 47.

---

[35] Primary sources: Arrian *Anabasis* 1.13.1–1.16.7; Diodorus 17.18.2–17.21.6, Plutarch *Alexander* 16.1–16.11.
[36] For discussions of this battle, see Fuller 1958: 147–154; Hammond 1980b; Devine 1986; Bosworth 1988a: 35–44; Badian 1977; Nikolitsis 1974.

pezhetairoi were placed at the centre of the line. To their right were the 3,000 *hypaspists* and the Companion cavalry led by Alexander. On the left wing were the Thessalian and allied cavalry. The Persians placed their cavalry on the steep eastern bank of the river, with the Greek mercenary infantry drawn up behind them in reserve. The ensuing engagement was primarily a cavalry battle, and the Macedonians made their own equestrian abilities known. In what would become a familiar practice, Alexander took the initiative as he '... leaped on his horse and encouraged his entourage to follow him and show their courage'.[37] First, he sent across the *prodromoi* as these lighter and more mobile cavalrymen could serve as pathfinders through the river while also drawing the Persians out from their position on the bank.[38] Alexander then followed with the rest of the Macedonian cavalry, engaging in fierce hand-to-hand combat in what Arrian describes as an infantry battle fought on horseback.[39] The Macedonians gradually gained the upper hand, not only through mounted combat skills, but also on account of the 'light infantry interspersed among the cavalry'.[40] This comment of Arrian's may refer to the *hypaspists* fighting as *hamippoi* pulling down enemy horsemen, all the while moving between the ranks of their own attacking cavalry and keeping a link to the *pezhetairoi*. The *pezhetairoi* also made their way across the river, and here the length of the *sarissa* may have proved an advantage as it allowed the men to reach up and push back against the Persian horsemen on the bank. The ability of the *pezhetairoi* to cross the river while holding formation in the face of a cavalry attack speaks to their skill, training and confidence around equines. The force of the Macedonian cavalry charge combined with the pressure provided by the *hypaspists* and *pezhetairoi* caused the Persian centre to give way, at which point the Persian cavalry broke and fled, abandoning the Greek mercenaries who now found themselves surrounded without having engaged in the main battle at all. Throughout the battle it seems that the Thessalian and allied cavalry remained of the far side of the river, maintaining their defensive position.

---

[37] Arrian *Anabasis* 1.14.5. A cavalry charge from the Macedonian right would become a hallmark of Alexander's battles.
[38] Devine 1988 refers to Alexander's strategy here as a 'pawn sacrifice'.
[39] Arrian *Anabasis* 1.15.4.   [40] Arrian *Anabasis* 1.16.1.

Issus (333 BCE)[41]

This battle took place in the region of Cilicia on the shores of the Gulf of Issus at the Pinarus River.[42] The choice of battlefield negated any numerical advantages Darius held, sandwiched as his forces were between the mountains and the sea (Figure 15.2). Nonetheless, he tried to match his battle line to the topography in the hopes of using the rocky terrain to disrupt Alexander's strategy. Darius, who held the Persian centre, placed a large portion of his cavalry on his right wing, directly against the sea, as, according to Curtius, he 'chose to make it a contest of cavalry'.[43] Next to these were part of the *kardakes* ('foreign mercenaries'), then a portion of the Greek mercenaries.[44] To the left

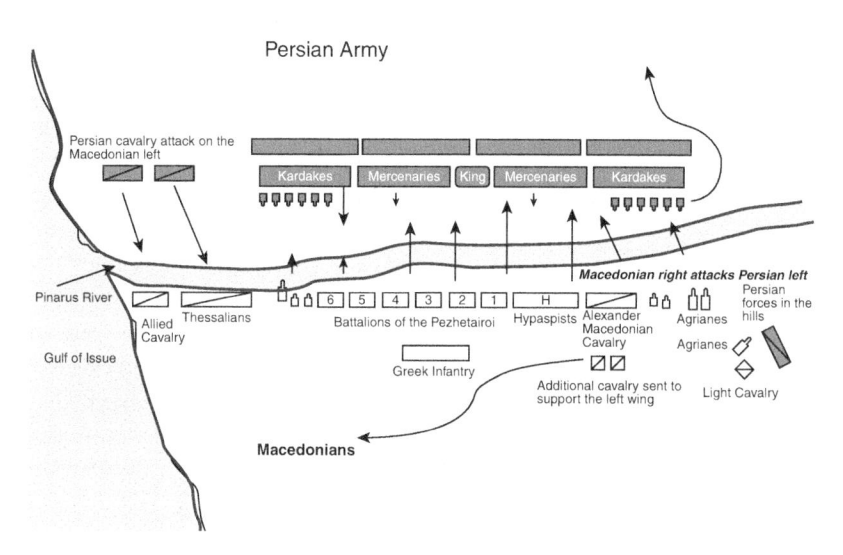

15.2 The Battle of Issus: initial battle order; reprinted, with modifications from Heckel 2008: 62.

---

[41] Primary sources: Arrian *Anabasis* 2.7.1–12.8; Diodorus 17.33.1–17.34.9; Plutarch *Alexander* 20; Curtius 3.8.13–11.20; Polybius *Histories* 12.17.21.

[42] The exact location of the Pinarus has been much debated with the Deli Çay, Payas and Kuru Çay all being put forward as possible contenders. For analyses of the location and battle, see: Heckel 2020b: 89–97; Heckel 2008: 57–65; Lendon 2005: 115–139; Hammond 1992a; Bosworth 1988a: 58–62; Devine 1985a, 1985b; Engels 1978: 131–134; Murison 1972; Fuller 1958: 154–162.

[43] Curtius 3.11.1.

[44] The *kardakes* fought as infantry, but the exact nature of their origins and armament is a topic of some debate. Heckel states that they were 'armed in the hoplite fashion' (2020b: 95) while Charles 2012: 11–14 suggests that they followed the style of Iphicratean *peltasts*.

of the Persian king were the additional mercenaries, and then the remainder of the *kardakes*, with additional men placed up in the hills. Alexander's allied cavalry were stationed on the left next to the sea, but when he realized that the bulk of the Persian cavalry had been arrayed opposite, he sent the Thessalian cavalry over to join them as well as two *ilai* of the Companion cavalry. This was done to prevent the Persian cavalry from outflanking him. The *pezhetairoi* held the centre, with the Greek infantry behind them. The *hypaspists* took up their crucial position between the cavalry of the Macedonian right and the *pezhetairoi*. To immobilize the troops Darius had stationed in the hills, Alexander placed the Agrianes and some of the light cavalry on the edge of his right flank. As at the Granicus, Alexander led an opening charge from the right with the Companion cavalry and *hypaspists* aiming for Darius in the Persian centre as they forced their way through the *kardakes* and Greek mercenaries on the Persian left. Arrian writes that Alexander urged the right into a rapid charge once they were within bowshot of the Persians so as to minimize the damage caused by the Persian archers.[45] The difficulty of maintaining a single cohesive front was made evident here: a gap appeared between the *taxeis* of the *pezhetairoi* as they surged forward to keep up with the *hypaspists* over difficult terrain. This gap was exploited by a portion of Darius' Greek mercenaries, who caused significant damage to the split ranks of the Macedonian phalanx. In the meantime, the cavalry of the Persian right charged across the river to attack the Thessalians and allied cavalry, who maintained their defensive position, engaging in a fierce battle that continued even after the Persian line began to collapse.[46] On the Macedonian right, Alexander's bold charge broke through the Persian lines, causing Darius to abandon the battlefield. Once the Persian cavalry realized that their king had fled, and that the Greek mercenaries had been routed, they too wheeled into retreat with the Thessalian cavalry in hot pursuit.[47]

Gaugamela (331 BCE)[48]

In his final battle against Alexander, Darius selected a broad plain that suited the numerical superiority of his army as well as his cavalry and

---

[45] Arrian *Anabasis* 2.10.3.   [46] Arrian *Anabasis* 2.11.2; Curtius 3.11.13–3.11.15.
[47] Hammond 1978 provides an interesting analysis of the cavalry pursuits in Alexander's battles.
[48] Primary sources: Arrian *Anabasis* 3.11.1–3.15.7; Diodorus 17.56.1–17.61.3; Plutarch *Alexander* 33.8–33.11; Curtius 4.12.1–4.16.9.

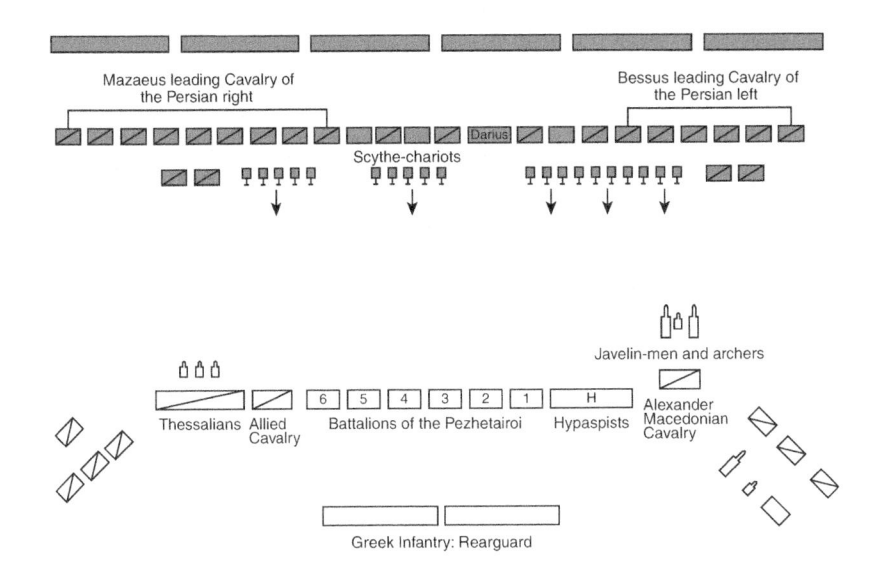

15.3 The Battle of Gaugamela: initial battle order; reprinted, with modifications from Heckel 2008: 76.

chariotry.[49] On the day of the battle Alexander drew up his forces in a manner that echoed Issus: the *pezhetairoi* held the centre with the Thessalian and allied cavalry in their defensive position on the left wing, while the *hypaspists* and Macedonian cavalry took the right wing. The Greek infantry was once against stationed to the rear of the *pezhetairoi*. In addition, he placed light infantry in front of the cavalry on both wings, while also stationing additional cavalry in an oblique position on the furthest end of each wing to prevent encirclement (Figure 15.3).[50] Darius' strategy relied on different forms of horsepower to overwhelm Alexander's line – including scythed chariots, which were tasked with mowing down the infantry. This did not work entirely as planned: the light infantry Alexander had placed in front of the cavalry pelted the chariots with javelins. Arrian makes a key statement when he says:

> A number did in fact manage to pass through the Macedonian ranks, for these, following their instructions, parted where the chariots attacked. As a result, the chariots

---

[49] See Arrian *Anabasis* 3.8.7. For analysis of the battle, see Sears 2019: 171–14; Heckel 2008: 75–80; Bosworth 1988a: 74–85; Griffith 1977; Devine 1975a, 1975b; Marsden 1964; Fuller 1958: 163–180.
[50] Diodorus 17.57.5.

passed through intact and without harm to the men at whom they were aimed ...

Arrian *Anabasis* 3.13.6

This observation highlights two key things about the *pezhetairoi*: first, the importance of their rigorous training and the fact that they could perform intricate manoeuvres in response to a battlefield situation; second, it speaks (again) to the familiarity of the Macedonians with horses. If Arrian's account is to be believed, it indicates that the *pezhetairoi* held their nerve in the face of charging chariots as they were able to step in a clear and ordered manner out of their way, creating clear paths for the chariots to charge through. Curtius' account differs in some details from Arrian, having the front ranks of the phalanx part to allow the chariots through to the centre before turning to surround them, stabbing at them with their *sarissas*.[51] Diodorus also describes the chariot charge. Here the infantry beat their *sarissas* against their shields to spook the horses before opening lanes to allow the remaining chariots through.[52] Both Curtius and Diodorus mention that the phalanx did not remain unscathed and the scythes cut down several men.[53] Though these three accounts differ in the details, the overall impression suggests that Darius' chariots were not the success he had intended as they failed to create overwhelming terror and panic in the Macedonian infantry.

As per custom, Alexander instigated the action from the Macedonian right. His charge was challenged by the Scythian cavalry, who had been ordered forward to outflank Alexander's cavalry. A fierce engagement took place, with the Macedonian cavalry finally forcing their way through. This action created a gap on the Persian left which Alexander immediately exploited, arcing the Macedonian cavalry, the *hypaspists*, and part of the *pezhetairoi* into the Persian lines, surging towards Darius at the centre. Showing the advantage of combined arms tactics, the *pezhetairoi* held the Persians in place as the *hypaspists* and Macedonian cavalry worked in unison to collapse the Persian line in on itself. The plan was not seamless: as at Issus, a gap appeared between two *taxeis* of the *pezhetairoi* as they tried to keep up with the swifter action to their right. The gap was spotted by part of the Persian and Indian cavalry, who burst through and made for the Macedonian camp before being brought down

---

[51] Curtius compares the appearance of the formation to a rampart: 4.15.14–4.15.17.
[52] Diodorus 17.58.2–17.58.5.
[53] There is some debate as to where exactly these attacks occurred, and it seems that they may have happened on both the Macedonian left and right, see Heckel et al. 2010: 109.

by the troops Alexander had placed in reserve. Darius, as at Issus, fled the battlefield when he realized that his line was falling apart.[54] In the meantime, a furious battle once again played out on the Macedonian left, where Parmenion directed the allied and Thessalian cavalry against the Persian cavalry.[55] The Thessalians and the allies once again showed their mettle and skill, pushing the enemy cavalry into flight.

The conquests of Alexander are an iconic part of ancient history. His genius on the battlefield has been thoroughly analysed from antiquity to the present day. Alexander's use of combined arms tactics and his success in utilizing a diverse range of troops highlights his adaptability and ingenuity. Moreover, the role of the cavalry in serving as the primary offensive and defensive arm, as well as their ability to work in conjunction with different forms of infantry, speaks strongly to Macedonia's long-established equestrian identity.

Guide to Further Reading

On Philip II, see, most recently, Anson 2020a as well as his 2009 article; see also Lane Fox 2011b and Worthington 2008b for biographical and military elements of Philip's life. For Greek warfare in general, see Sears 2019; Wrightson 2019 focuses primarily on combined arms; Van Wees 2004 provides an excellent analysis of different elements of Greek warfare. On the Macedonian army, see Heckel 2016 for the people and politics; Karunanithy 2013 for a detailed examination of the many components within the Macedonian army; and Hatzopoulos 2015 and Hammond 1989c for structure and organization in particular. For Alexander's army, see Heckel 2020b and 2008, with two interesting perspectives on Alexander's conquests; note also Bosworth 1988a; Sekunda 2010 offers a good introduction to the components of Alexander's army; see Wrightson 2010 for command structure. On equines in ancient Greece, see Aston and Kerr 2018 for Thessaly, Blaineau 2015 for the Greek warhorse, and Howe 2008b for aspects of horse breeding and rearing in Greece, while Gaebel 2002 and Spence 1993 provide useful discussions of cavalry. On the Macedonian cavalry, see Sears and Willekes 2016 for aspects of cavalry at Chaeronea; Willekes 2015 for equine elements in the Macedonian cavalry; Chandezon 2014 for cavalry logistics; Moreno Hernandez 2004 for theoretical elements; and Hammond 1998 for recruitment.

---

[54] Diodorus 7.60.1–7.60.4.
[55] Arrian *Anabasis* says, 'This was the hardest cavalry fighting of the engagement' (3.15.2).

16: ALEXANDER'S MODERN MILITARY REPUTATION

F. S. Naiden

European military writers took up the subject of Alexander in the sixteenth century, joining a field already crowded with Latin poets and epitomizers, philosophers writing in ecclesiastical Latin, and versifiers in German and the Romance Languages. These previous authors had drawn upon just one important Alexander Historian, Curtius Rufus; Arrian, Plutarch, and Diodorus Siculus were little known. Sixteenth-century writers drew on all four to ask whether Alexander set a positive or negative example for later commanders and statesmen.[1]

If positive, Alexander would establish a tradition, one that in the sixteenth century began to be called the Great Captains, that gallery of conquerors beginning with Alexander, always including Caesar, and, after a gap of a thousand years, resuming with moderns such as Gustavus Adolphus, Turenne, Marlborough, Frederick the Great, and Napoleon.[2] Unlike most of these men, Alexander was born to the purple, and thus set a second example, one concerning grand strategy as well as the combat operations that were the measure of Great Captains. Gustavus and Frederick were hereditary rulers, too, but neither of them wore several crowns, as Alexander did by being Pharaoh and King of Babylon as well as King of Macedon.

If Alexander set a negative example, modern writers would need to explain why Alexander's extensive conquests were somehow a failure. Since Alexander won his battles, a negative example would have to concern grand strategy. The Macedonian might be compared to Hitler as well as Napoleon.

---

[1] The role of *exempla* in Ancient historiography, and in later writing on Ancient history: Grethlein 2010: 330–331, noticing Alexander. All translations are the author's.

[2] A survey: Wheeler 2012. The most influential American contribution to the genre: Dodge 1890. The best-known book to make numerous, mutually complementary references to all these commanders remains Clausewitz 1832. The most recent work: Lonsdale 2007, with Naiden 2008.

Many familiar names in modern military literature have viewed Alexander as an example, beginning with the French noble Rohan, passing down to Frederick, the only Great Captain who doubled as a writer on the subject, then to Clausewitz and others influenced by Napoleon, and recently to the British General Fuller, who envisioned Alexander in terms of twentieth-century, armoured warfare, and to the Israeli military historian Van Creveld, who has envisioned Alexander in terms of twenty-first century, asymmetrical warfare.[3] If the phrase 'Great Captain' is now dated, the study of Alexander, like that of other canonical military leaders, remains important in a post-imperial era.[4]

Perhaps the Captains are dated because they seem static, like so many statues in a hall of fame. Some military writers, however, regarded the tradition that Alexander inaugurated as evolutionary. The measure of his success would be not his conquests, but his effect down through the centuries. These writers tended to be civilians. The first was Machiavelli, who wanted his programmatic Prince to imitate Alexander by uniting many states. Next came Montaigne, who applied Greek, civic standards to Alexander, and then Montesquieu, the first to describe Alexander's conquests as an attempt to spread civilization. One effect of these conquests was the rise of Christianity. Later, Sir William Tarn gave a British, imperial accent to this view. Fuller and Van Creveld figure in this group, too, but as dissenters. Their Alexander is a revolutionary rather than Tarn's imperialist, and his effect has been happily negative.

For all these writers, one ancient author is especially relevant, but not any of the Alexander Historians. Julian the Apostate set forth the difficulties of comparing Great Captains and sovereigns in his *Caesares*, a dialogue in which Alexander competes with sundry Romans for the honour of being the greatest ancient leader. In addition, the medieval literature that modern writing superseded – a literature epitomized by Alexander's being a mere warrior, one of nine canonical Worthies – also deserves notice. After touching on these two topics, this chapter will review leading writers in chronological order, noting the kind of example Alexander sets, but also noting tensions between the roles of commander and political leader, and thus between military operations and national or imperial strategy.

---

[3] Montecuccoli 1998, 1973; Fuller 1958; Van Creveld 1991. Frederick on Alexander: Frederick II 1787.
[4] An example of the cult of Alexander in American business schools: Steenkamp 2020 chapter 16, comparing Alexander to de Gaulle, *si parva licet componere magnis*.

The Ancient and Medieval Background

Julian's *Caesares* lets Alexander and six Romans tell an Olympian jury which of them was the best leader. Zeus presides, but he and the other gods also sponsor the contenders. Alexander receives the support of Heracles; Augustus, of Apollo; Marcus Aurelius, of Zeus and Cronus; and so on. The contestants are to speak in chronological order, Zeus says, so Alexander has pride of place. The terms of debate are Greek, not Roman, for the seven are to be regarded as athletes, judged by wins and losses and the quality of their opponents. (To no objection from Zeus, the Roman speakers introduce two triumphal criteria, the number of casualties inflicted and cities captured.) Before letting the contestants speak, Zeus asks them to state their aims succinctly. Alexander says, to conquer all people; Caesar, to be foremost; Trajan, to be better than Alexander; and Marcus Aurelius, to imitate the gods. As these answers imply, Marcus wins, but only by a plurality. Polytheism would seem to prevent unanimity. Constantine, sponsored by Jesus, finishes last.

As suits his aim, Caesar insists on speaking first, usurping Alexander's place, and proceeds to condemn Alexander for fighting Darius, an Oriental, and not a worthy, European opponent such as Pompey; for pretending to be a god in Egypt and elsewhere; and for sparing enemies while killing his own associates. With these charges, Caesar raises issues of Orientalism and of the balance to be struck between clemency and cruelty. The reference to killing associates who were Alexander's companions, such as Clitus and Philotas, raises the related issue of Alexander striking a balance between his duties to his companions and his needs as a king. In his reply to Caesar, Alexander says he was both a king and a warrior, a pair of roles that demand more balancing. Alexander proceeds to deny that Asian opponents are inferior and asserts that conquerors resemble gods. He says he marched farther than Caesar, reaching India, a claim that raises the issue of the limits to be set to conquests. After Alexander finishes, Augustus will assert that remote conquests, such as Germany, are unretainable.

Two more issues emerge not from the debate, but from Julian's handling of Alexander as a *dramatis persona*. The young Macedonian – less than half the age of nearly all the others – is impetuous throughout, the quality that he displayed in conquering the Persian Empire in just eight years. Granted that his god-like celerity was a military plus, how could anyone imitate it? For that matter, what other general could have Heracles, a demigod, as a sponsor, ancestor and model? Alexander had an aura all his own, explaining why so many of his enemies surrendered without a fight, as in Egypt and Babylon, and why even Caesar, proud to be first among the

Romans, feels obliged to belittle him. Alexander's uniqueness is one of Julian's themes.

These themes have modern echoes. Alexander's swiftness was an operational advantage that appealed to modern generals from Napoleon onwards, whereas balancing the duties of king and companion, or king and warrior, was a matter of state policy, and so it would matter mainly to sovereigns until the professionalization of army command in the nineteenth century. In the twentieth century, this issue reappeared in another way, as more and more layers of command separated generals from increasingly alienated troops. The moral issue of clemency and cruelty has been ever-present in military operations, but it has affected strategy because it affected the fate of conquered populations.

Alexander's claim of going farther than others was a matter of limits placed on warfare as an instrument of policy – limits that involved the 'Orient' as modern Europeans understood it. As for Alexander's uniqueness, it involved his self-deification, which might seem irrelevant to later writers, but not so: writers who denied Alexander a unique touch of the divine called him a genius instead. From the Napoleonic era onwards, genius became an accolade that chiefly Napoleon attained, but that strategists like Hitler might aspire to. The genius was a secular god-king.

If Julian offers guideposts for later writers, the Alexander of the Middle Ages does not. This period, lacking any phrase such as 'Great Captain', regarded Alexander as one of the Nine Worthies first appearing in a fourteenth-century chivalric morality tale.[5] The nine fall into religious groups, pagans (the other two being Hector and Caesar), Jews (Joshua, David, and Judas Maccabee), and Latin Christians (King Arthur, Charlemagne, and first King of Jerusalem, Godfrey of Bouillon). Hector shows that military success was not requisite and that the Worthies did not need to be kings or emperors, still less conquerors. In this literature, military operations are simple, brutal, and sometimes magical, and strategy is mostly providential. The Alexander we take for granted did not yet exist. We had to invent him, and we can choose to dispose of him.

Alexander During the Renaissance and Reformation

Machiavelli was the first among a number of modern writers to give an ambivalent, even contradictory response to Alexander, whom he could study in all the Alexander Historians, not just the ecclesiastical and

---

[5] Jean de Longuyon, *Les Voeux du paon*, c. 1310, as at Casey 1956. One Christian chronicler of this period reckoned Alexander as only 92nd among notable monarchs: Deuchler 1996, surveying this subject.

vernacular sources that inspired the Nine Worthies.[6] The Florentine preferred amateur, militia soldiers, as shown by his *Discourses on Livy*, and unhappily realized that Alexander was virtually a professional. Professionals tended to overthrow governments, Machiavelli thought, or lobby them for useless wars. If professional soldiers lacked a strong-willed commander, they were all the more likely to become disruptive, 'as was the case with the Macedonian army after the death of Alexander'. Alexander had insisted on serving his own purposes, not theirs, or those of the Macedonian people or the Greek allies. These flaws perversely recommended him as a model for the Prince, who would bully or seduce Italians into uniting.[7]

Machiavelli praised Alexander as an unencumbered ruler, governing through appointees and hirelings, not through or alongside a landed aristocracy. Darius happened to be a ruler of the same kind:

> If we look at the nature of the government of Darius, we shall find that it resembled Turkish rule. The Turkish realm is governed by one master, all others being his servants. Dividing his kingdom into sanjaks, he dispatches administrators to them, and shifts and changes them as he likes.

When Alexander sought to conquer the Persian Empire, he could not expect

> ... to be summoned by the princes and lords of the kingdom, or to be helped by any popular revolts. He who attacks [such a kingdom] ... must expect to find the enemy united ...; but once the ruler [of this kingdom] has been conquered and routed in the field and as a result his armies cannot be replaced, there is nothing to fear but the royal family.

Alexander had to attack Darius head on and drive him from the field. After this victory and Darius' death, he kept possession of the kingdom (*Il principe* 4).

Machiavelli had lit upon an enduring theme in the study of Alexander's strategy – the conqueror's aim was to replace his enemy, and it was thus, in some sense, to metamorphose into his enemy. This strategy was possible because Near Eastern rulers were not hobbled by

---

[6] Stadter 1975; Monfasani 2016; Giustiniani 1961.
[7] Machiavelli 1546 chapter 1, 1531 chapter 3.13, 1532 chapter 19. Amateur, but not citizen, since peasants without citizenship make better soldiers than the urban population of a city-state (as was true in the armies of Alexander and Philip): Rahe 2022.

restive populations and treacherous officials, two banes of politics in Renaissance Italy.

Some fifty years later, a very different writer took a similar stance towards Alexander. Asking himself which few, outstanding men surpassed the rest of humanity, Montaigne named Homer, Alexander, and Epaminondas of Thebes.[8] Aside from picking the best war poet, the essayist had picked a Republican general who was, and remained, a magistrate, and a royal general who was a Balkan king turned intercontinental despot. Montaigne may seem to have chosen the latter two for their operational successes, yet he may also have picked them for a strategic similarity: both remade political landscapes. Epaminondas used federalism to change Greece and Alexander used Greek colonies to change the Levant and parts of Central Asia. In the long run, Epaminondas' project failed and that of Alexander succeeded.

Could commanders like these two emerge from among the *condottieri* and soldiers of fortune of the fifteenth and early sixteenth centuries? These men lacked troops matching the Thebans or the Macedonians. Better armies, and a new standard for military leaders, that of the Great Captain, emerged a little later, outside both Italy and France. The first improved army was Spain's and the first commander to be called a 'Great Captain' was Córdoba, who united much of Italy, as Machiavelli wished, but under a foreign prince, Ferdinand of Aragon. Córdoba organized the first effective infantry carrying firearms as well as the pikes for which the Swiss were famous (and for which the Macedonians had been). The use of firearms transformed artillery, cavalry, and siege trains, and with them standards of generalship. The generals of this era also had a new master, the national states that came to dominate Europe, Spain first among them. One of these states, the Netherlands, was home to advances in both military science and Protestant political power.[9]

The most influential military writers of the seventeenth centuries, the generals du Rohan and Montecuccoli, adapted Alexander to this new paradigm. The Duke du Rohan was the leader of the Huguenot armies in the French Wars of Religion in the early seventeenth century, but also fought in the Low Countries. He contrasted Alexander with the 'delicate captains' of modern warfare and used both him and Caesar to illustrate 'principles of war' that were chiefly principles of operations.[10]

---

[8] Montaigne 1875 book ii, chapter 36.
[9] The leading Dutch military writer Maurice of Nassau mentions Alexander repeatedly (1616), but only to illustrate principles found in the ancient military handbook of Aelian.
[10] Delicacy: Rohan 1640: 125.

One, 'employing several good general officers', evoked Alexander's relying on Philotas, Craterus, and other companions to conduct sorties. Yet a general should never leave the command of his whole army to subordinates – 'not if he wished to be Alexander'. Other remarks in Rohan's 1636 *Traité de la guerre* touched on army morale and grand strategy. Like Alexander, a commander must share risks and privations with his men. In victory, he must show 'the height of humanity' towards those who surrender. He must likewise allow autonomy to all the defeated. If the conqueror could not trust the defeated, he should limit their autonomy by sending colonies among them, as Alexander did.[11] Rohan's Alexander was a king who did not forget his companions or his troops, and who did not regard his enemies as inferiors.

For Rohan, Alexander was a nostalgic figure, making cavalry charges that were now becoming less common than infantry engagements and sieges. At a time when Alexander and the rest of the Nine Worthies were still faces on soldiers' playing cards, Rohan and his expert readers thought of the king as a figure of unattainable glamour.[12] Yet Rohan's Alexander also taught lessons in managing troops and subject peoples. The king had a common touch as well as despotic power.

Montecuccoli, a professional soldier in the Austrian service, improved linear infantry, one of the Dutch contributions to seventeenth-century warfare. This renowned commander fought Swedes, Frenchmen, Turks, and Cossacks – a circuit that led him to focus on supply lines and strategy as well as combat. Alexander appealed to him on all these counts. Montecuccoli praised him mistakenly for introducing the first army pensions, but correctly for making his soldiers shave, so that they would be harder to clutch in battle.[13] When Alexander burned all the army's baggage, so that troops would move swiftly, he set an example by burning his own first – Rohan's common touch. Yet Montecuccoli praised Alexander for spying on his own men by reading their letters home. Similarly, he praised Alexander for threatening to kill the survivors of a defeat if they told the rest of the army how many casualties they had suffered. Montecuccoli's Alexander is the first to be a propagandist as well as a hero leading by example.[14]

---

[11] Rohan 1640 chapter 7. Other advice: chapters 4, 18, 20.

[12] Rohan 1640 chapter 7, where the Turks and Persians are praised as fighters of battles, not sieges – the same pro-Orientalism as in Machiavelli. The Worthies survived in popular literature down through the end of the seventeenth century, much in the way that the Great Captains survive in war-gaming today.

[13] Alexander was apparently the first leader of a national army to pay wages to all his men, as opposed to paying mercenaries only. For the costs, see Holt 2016: 112–119.

[14] Montecuccoli 1988: 280, 199, 294, 301, 269, originally published in 1652.

Montecuccoli's king is both a cynic and an imperialist. The policy of self-divinization is thus no longer a regrettable impiety or an incidental aberration, but part of a more important, secular policy of exaggerating Alexander's reputation. Montecuccoli approves the words attributed to Alexander by Curtius Rufus, but not the other Alexander Historians, 'May the Indians, too, think me divine.'[15] For Alexander, Montecuccoli went on to say, pitched battles were not sought because they were glamorous or even productive. They saved time and lives because enemies would refuse to fight once Alexander established his god-like invincibility.[16] Montecuccoli's is the first contrived Alexander, dependent on his reputation.

Unlike Rohan and Montecuccoli, Montesquieu took it for granted that a Great Captain might not be a monarch. If so, the Captain would need to influence one. For British readers of Montesquieu's time, the best example of such a captain was Marlborough, whose war-making depended on having a leading cabinet minister, Godolphin, persuade Queen Anne to adopt the general's plans. As important as Godolphin was Marlborough's wife, the Queen's favourite. Marlborough's hoped-for balance of power, one that would put England in a pivotal position, had to make sense to Anne in terms of Whig and Tory, social life and court ceremonial, and Sarah Marlborough accomplished this petty part of grand strategy. When she fell, her husband did as well.

With examples like this before him, Montesquieu envisioned Alexander as a commander who, thanks to training by Aristotle, thought somewhat like a minister – Godolphin and Marlborough in one person, or even Louis XIV and Richelieu. Reading the Alexander Historians for evidence of long-range policy, not sieges, battles, or campaigns, he reconceived his hero, so that operations were the tools of strategy, and strategy served macroeconomic purposes. Alexander, Montesquieu argued, wished to unlock the wealth of Asia and give both Greek and Semitic entrepreneurs the chance to expand and prosper. The king minted the first widely used Asian currency, built vast new infrastructure, and established colonies attractive to investors as well as settlers. All this would take centuries, so the king was developing a strategy for his dynasty as well as himself – or, in the event, for his generals and their descendants. This was strategy as Richelieu would understand it, except

---

[15] Curtius Rufus 8.8.15, where the statement justifies the condemnation and torture of Hermolaus.
[16] Montecuccoli 1988: 191 and 1973: 224, the latter originally published in 1703.

Alexander did not need to tolerate the machinations of any such subordinate.[17]

Like Machiavelli's, Montesquieu's Alexander was pro-Oriental. Machiavelli preferred Oriental empires to European feudal kingdoms; Montesquieu preferred a larger, more richly endowed civilization to a smaller, poorer, less sophisticated one.

These two intellectuals did not affect broad swathes of opinion. French kings stuck with the Alexander of Bossuet, the worldly clergyman who said Alexander's trouble was not his being a pagan, but his being so improvident as to leave an infant and an idiot as heirs.[18] French and other military men followed the lead given by the most famous military writer of the eighteenth century, Frederick the Great of Prussia, who saw Alexander as a king whose successes were a model to reject. Frederick explained that one of the best generals of the era, Charles XII of Sweden, had gone astray by trying to imitate Alexander through overly ambitious plans, through undue reliance on his own reputation for victory and on speed rather than strength. Unlike Caesar, Alexander was inimitable.[19] Frederick himself merited comparison to Alexander's father, the circumspect Philip of Macedon, but not to Alexander.[20]

Frederick's views reflected the development of linear infantry and also military engineering, both of which made battles bloodier, sieges longer, and conquests smaller. Heavy cavalry, Alexander's chief arm, became a showpiece and camaraderie among troops, which was perhaps Alexander's chief asset, became less important than discipline and training. Eighteenth-century European warfare also lacked the religious motive of the previous century. For an Enlightenment ruler such as Frederick, Alexander's claim to divinity was absurd rather than impious and his desire for universal empire was ignorant rather than arrogant.

Frederick surely read Julian's *Caesares*, but did not mention it in his own voluminous writings. He shared Julian's opinion of Alexander as lacking a certain Roman *gravitas*. Only a few decades after Frederick's death, the advent of Napoleon Bonaparte would make this opinion seem captious. The greatest of Great Captains would make Alexander's operations and ambitions newly and frightfully relevant.

---

[17] This thesis, but minus Godolphin and Richelieu: Briant 2012. The chief source: Montesquieu 1748 vol. x, 13–14; vol. xxi, 8.

[18] Bossuet 1681 vol. i, 564–575.

[19] For Charles XII, see n. 3 above. Luvaas 1966 includes a chapter on 'Strategy', but for Frederick and for Frederick's contemporaries, strategy was a matter of statecraft; Frederick 1741 chapter 4 says that Machiavelli underestimates cultural and social differences between Orient and Occident.

[20] Gillies 1789. Philip is not mentioned in any list of Great Captains known to me.

Alexander, Napoleon, and Two World Wars

Napoleon associated himself with Alexander far more than Frederick or any other previous Captain had. In his one long work on warfare, *Dix-huit notes sur l'art de la guerre*, he ranks Alexander ahead of Hannibal, Caesar, Turenne, Gustavus Adolphus, Prince Eugene and Frederick.[21] This is a list of invaders, the biggest invader coming first; the implied criterion is that the best invasions are those that succeed against the odds. Alexander, Hannibal and Frederick exemplify this sort of success; leaving aside the Civil Wars, Caesar does in Gaul; Gustavus does in the Baltic and northern Germany, a less important if not smaller theatre of operations. Napoleon alone equals Alexander. He went to Egypt, too, and he went to Russia instead of India.

Napoleon's boast was as true politically as militarily, for he was the only modern to become an emperor dominating a region comparable to the Ancient Near East. At this point, however, the comparison lapses. Napoleon did not leave generations of successors on several thrones – only the descendants of a renegade marshal, Bernadotte, on the throne of Sweden. The fundamental political factor of Napoleon's era was the French Revolution, not any individual ruler, and so the kinds of changes that Alexander wrought in the Ancient world, at least according to Montesquieu, were not the work of Napoleon and could not have been. Napoleon thus could not match the Enlightenment conception of Alexander's strategy. His movements across the face of Europe were comparable only on a map, and ended, as Alexander's had not, in retreat and defeat.

Although the Captains in Napoleon's list are mostly sovereigns, the list nevertheless suggests interest in operations. In the *Dix-huit notes* Napoleon singles out Alexander and Caesar for concentration of forces, rapid movement towards objectives, successful psychological warfare, including demoralizing and deterring enemies, and political dexterity in dealing with allies and subjects. Above all, Napoleon praises them for focusing on battlefield victory and all the preparations needed to achieve it. Meanwhile, he avoids political comparisons between the two of them and himself. The *Dix-huit notes* are a work of exile, and at this time Napoleon feared lest political comparisons make it harder for him to woo French opinion and be allowed to return home. His critics were well aware that among all the positions that ancient or modern Captains might

---

[21] Napoleon I 1858–69 vol. xxxi, 365–489; Alexander, 415–417; Hannibal, 418; Caesar, 419–422.

hold – Marshal, Consul, King, and Emperor – Napoleon alone had held them all. He had been unduly successful.

His true, but unacknowledged, strategy had been personal, not revolutionary or national. In this, too, he resembled Alexander, who may be described as seizing crowns for himself, not for Macedon – first Egypt's by dint of cooperation with the country's priests, then Babylon's by dint of the victory at Gaugamela, and then India's, by dint of divine sponsorship, as in Montecuccoli.[22] India, however, had never had a national ruler. The subcontinent confronted Alexander with a cultural as well as a topographical limit. Failure in Russia and Egypt confronted Napoleon with similar limits.

A contemporary of Napoleon's, the Catholic conservative Chateaubriand, saw Napoleon's Alexandrian qualities as being among the Emperor's worst. Chateaubriand complained that Napoleon had turned himself into a legend during his own lifetime, as Alexander had done, and woefully predicted that the delusive self-portrait achieved by Napoleon would outlast all other impressions of him – a case of a commander exploiting his own reputation both before and after death. Another insult of Chateaubriand's was that Napoleon had returned the art of war to its mobile, impulsive infancy, again meaning Alexander. The aristocratic Chateaubriand contrasted Napoleon with Alexander in just one respect – Napoleon was a parvenu, not a prince. As this learned but wry author put it, if Alexander was the son of Zeus, Napoleon was the son of Jupiter *Scapin*. Corsica, Chateaubriand went on, was to France what Macedon was to Greece in the time of Alexander and Demosthenes.

In another remark about Alexander's religious policy, Chateaubriand adopted an evolutionary stance inspired by Montesquieu. Alexander's being a god suited that time and place and let him rely less on force and more on manipulation. The king's religious policy was a part of a policy of economy of force, one rarely attributed to Alexander.[23] Napoleon, though, was born 2,000 years too late for this kind of posturing. It offended both his Republican soldiers and the Christian soldiers of the new army being established under the Restoration.[24]

---

[22] Not Persia's, as explained at Naiden 2019a chapter 7, 'A Vacant Throne'. The contrary view, making this the only important throne for him to seize: Machiavelli 1532, as above, and recently Briant 2012, as above, regarding Alexander as the last Achaemenid, whereas seizing several thrones *seriatim* suggests a comparison with the first Teispid, Cyrus the Great.

[23] To my knowledge, only by a scholastic, Roger Bacon, in his *Compendium studii philosophiae* (2013 [originally 1271] vol. i, 395), who says that Alexander had one soldier for every twenty-six of the enemy. This is the only statistical description of Alexander's campaigns before the nineteenth century.

[24] Chateaubriand 1849 vol. i, 811 and 1815: 28–29, adding the complaint that Napoleon was a mere fighter of battles, not a strategist: 1849 vol. ii, 242, 295. Another view: Fulińska 2018.

Chateaubriand's critique touched on a theme latent since Machiavelli and Montaigne, who both felt torn between civic and royal models for generalship. To refer to Montaigne, could any nation make use of both an Epaminondas and an Alexander? A commander like Marlborough could finesse this question, influencing his Queen through a minister responsible to Parliament. Later commanders in both Britain and post-Revolutionary France would have to submit to the authority of Parliament or the President of the Republic, or to a Godolphin serving as Secretary of the Army. Strategy would become these politicians' business, operations remaining that of the generals. A new question, that of the relation between civil and military authority, would arise in both France and Britain, and then arise elsewhere, only to be answered juridically: civil authority would be supreme. Marlborough had been a duke who lived like a king in a country where kings lived like dukes. Post-Napoleonic generals would be *employés* ennobled after they retired, like Viscount Montgomery of Alamein.

Employé was a new word, and there was another, *strategy*, which as late as Frederick's time had only meant leading armies to and on the battlefield, but now came to mean the whole conduct of war. Partly to lay claim to this new field of endeavour, armies established general staffs. The German Clausewitz was perhaps the first staff officer to address the subject of Alexander's reputation. He listed Alexander first among Great Captains, Napoleon second, and the rest far behind. Under Alexander, he explained, the art of war reached perfection and did not recover this quality until Napoleon. This was the highest praise Alexander had received since Julian put the king in the company of Heracles.

Clausewitz proceeded to undermine this praise by introducing a qualification that was as new as his evolutionary, Hegelian notion of the perfection of an art.[25] This qualification was that an army's performance depended on 'military character', or *kriegerische Tugend*. Without it, what could even Alexander have accomplished?[26] Clausewitz was implying that Alexander needed not only to recruit, train, maintain, and, of course, lead his army, but also to create and maintain a certain national temper, a task that went beyond maintaining morale and might better be called laying the social and political foundation for morale. This temper or character was most important for officers, who ought to be

---

[25] Clausewitz 1832 §§8.3.a, b = 1976: vol. i, 580, 587, 590, listing Gustavus, Charles XII, and Frederick the Great, only to damn them with faint praise.
[26] Clausewitz 1832 §3.3.5 = 1976 vol. i, 189.

members of a kind of guild [*Innung*] . . . an individual steeped in the spirit and essence of war; who trains the capacities that it demands, rouses them, and makes them his own; who applies his intelligence to every detail; who gains ease and confidence through practice; and who immerses his personality in the appointed task.[27]

Every Macedonian officer needed to be something of an Alexander (compare Napoleon's reported remark that every French soldier carried a marshal's baton in his knapsack).[28] This theme hearkened back to the role-playing by Alexander in Julian, where the king doubles as a companion and also as a common soldier. Clausewitz, however, adds that a leader needs to teach others to play roles, and to play them as well as the leader does. Insofar as possible, his personal merits need to be institutionalized. This was a new, Clausewitzian rationale for general staffs, that nineteenth-century innovation that had only a modest ancient forebear in Alexander's circle of royal *hetairoi* or in a Roman commander's *amici*.

Clausewitz also addressed Alexander's double identity in another connection. To explain why he conquered more lands faster than later Europeans did, Clausewitz said he was a king who was also his own *condottiere*.[29] Other commanders, alas, had to leave strategy to civilians, and that hindered them. In the next century, Alexander would attract military writers who wanted generals to break with convention and develop strategies of their own, as Napoleon had done, as well as more numerous (and influential) writers who regarded Alexander as a paragon of operational excellence in a now familiar gallery in which no one yet realized Napoleon occupied the last available niche.[30]

---

[27] Clausewitz 1832 §3.5.5 = 1976 vol. i, 187, but translated somewhat differently. Another view of this passage: Naiden 2007, arguing that Philip II, not Alexander, established a comparable standard in Macedon. Shifting credit for Macedonian success from Alexander to Philip or Parmenion is a theme missing from Julian, but not from the Alexander Historians; it reappears at Beloch 1912–1927 vol. iii.1, 226.

[28] Blaze 1837 vol. i, 5.

[29] Clausewitz 1832 §8.3b = 1976 vol. i, 587. A definition of strategy: 'it borders on political science, or rather . . . the two become one', §2.5 = vol. i, 167.

[30] For example, Chairman of the Joint Chiefs of Staff 2006: App. A, 'Principles of War', listing nine such principles, most traceable to Clausewitz, but only at his most conventional, an 1812 composition appended to *Vom Kriege*. Only Chairman of the Joint Chiefs of Staff 2018, a revision of 2006, dated 22 October 2018, adds potentially strategic concerns, listing three, 'restraint, perseverance, and [concern for] legitimacy'.

Alexander in Recent Decades

One of the unconventional writers, J. F. C. Fuller, wrote the best military biography of Alexander, *The Generalship of Alexander* (1958). This book grew out of two developments, one Fuller predicted and one he failed to condemn. The first was the mobility achieved by armoured and aerial warfare, an innovation that Fuller advocated in the 1920s, only to find that German generals learned more from him than the Allies did. Fuller regarded Alexander as the past master of this kind of warfare, a view similar to Napoleon's praise for Alexander's swiftness.

On this score, Fuller resembled his collaborator, the British soldier B. H. Liddell-Hart, but Liddell-Hart objected to Alexander on other grounds. In his book on Great Captains, Liddell-Hart dismissed him as a 'sepoy general' fighting against Asians, not Europeans.[31] Liddell-Hart also conceived 'an indirect approach' that differed from Alexander's onslaughts in big battles like Issus and Gaugamela. Liddell-Hart did not grasp that by directly attacking the Persian army, and in particular by directly attacking the person of Darius, Alexander was attempting to gain control of the Persian Empire indirectly, an example of Liddell-Hart's method. Alexander wished to avoid extensive or intensive wars resembling the Western Front in World War I. Fuller and Liddell-Hart both were reacting to this waste of men and materiel.

Fuller's preference for lightening strokes to laborious occupation was the reason he noticed the other development – the Nazi blitzkrieg in the first years of World War II. Fuller attributed this success to Hitler's acumen as well as to mobile warfare. Hitler was, he wrote, a strategist who excelled at assessing the military potential of his opponents. He had known not only that the French lacked their vaunted *élan*, but also that the British would dither until too late. In the case of the Soviet Union, Hitler needed to grasp the political potential of the Ukrainians and other subject peoples and turn them into Nazi allies. Alexander had done the like during the invasion of the Persian Empire, gaining civilian support by being crowned Pharaoh in Egypt and then securing military resources by marrying Scythian and Persian princesses.

Alas, Hitler proved to be no Alexander, but Stalin and the other Communist leaders of the era were Alexanders of a sort, for they grasped that they could prevail by wooing foreign peoples more than by defeating foreign armies. Fuller cited Tito's helping Stalin on the Eastern

---

[31] Liddell-Hart 1926: 250–251, where he echoes Julius Caesar in Julian. So also Liddell-Hart 1927, to this writer's knowledge the only list of Great Captains that omits Alexander.

Front and Mao's helping Stalin in 1945, when the Soviets invaded China. Western generals were mere nationalists in comparison.

Before the war, Fuller had sympathized with the British Fascists. Now his critics realized that his political aberrations were one of several offences. He had already lost faith in the big battles and national surrenders that Clausewitz and the World War II Allies took for granted. Now he had lost faith in Western leadership, preferring Hitler's. With Hitler gone, he preferred Stalin's. Fuller admired Sir William Tarn, the most influential Alexander biographer of the twentieth century, but Fuller rejected two themes found in Tarn and many other writers – Alexander's operational mastery and the theme of beneficent conquest due to Montesquieu.[32] Fuller thought mastery mattered less than orchestrating allies and that beneficence did not matter.

Fuller had even worse news for Western field commanders than he did for his critics. As if seizing on Clausewitz' language of *kriegerische Tugend*, he revived the theme of Alexander's role-playing, but to sanguinary effect: British generals would continue to be mediocre until more of them braved death at the front. That alone would let them get the best out of their men. And they should die young – 50 or 60, the modern norm for top commanders, was too old.[33] Better Alexander, worn out at 33. Yet Fuller was Romantic as well as bloody-minded. As weapons became more mechanical, 'the spirit that controlled them' needed to become less so. Generals needed to cut heroic figures, as they had in previous centuries, and Alexander was the most heroic of generals, as Julian had noticed.[34]

Fuller's complex reaction to Alexander anticipates the last writer in this survey, the Israeli, Van Creveld. Van Creveld praised Nazi fighting power in World War II in the most shocking possible way: the Wehrmacht was morally superior to the Allies, thanks to its egalitarian spirit and its stress on individual initiative.[35] The antithesis to this German virtue of *Auftragstaktik* was American bureaucracy. The Israelis imitated German qualities in the Six-Day War against the Arab states in 1967, only to discover in later years that the Arab turn to tactics such as suicide-bombing had rendered this kind of warfare obsolete.

The Israeli kind of warfare, like that of World War II, distinguished between soldiers and civilians. The new kind did not. Did this change make Alexander as obsolete as roving armoured divisions?[36]

---

[32] He may have found his way to Montesquieu through the latter's most important English follower, Tarn 1948, whom he often cites in his own biography, published twelve years later, as at n. 3 above.
[33] Fuller 1936: 11–22. [34] Fuller 1936: 27. [35] Van Creveld 1982. [36] Van Creveld 2007.

No, answered Van Creveld. His Alexander made conquests 'divorced from any kind of "realistic" policy'. Instead the king fought for the sake of burnishing his military reputation, a traditional theme, or for a new reason, which was that fighting became an end in itself. With Alexander, and only with Alexander, 'Means take the place of ends.'[37] In this kind of warfare, soldiers and civilians gave way to predators and prey. Van Creveld's is the first Alexander to be primitive – the first to put the expectations and experiences of his soldiers ahead of the concerns of generals or political leaders.

This conclusion is illuminating for late twentieth- and early twenty-first-century warfare in which small bands of soldiers are supremely important, including both Western soldiers designated as commandos and Islamists designated as terrorists. Alexander provides a model for the terrorists and other non-state military actors, not, of course, because he ceased to be a king, or rather, not because he ceased to hold several crowns, but because he and his army were a pride or a pack. The difference between Alexander's forces and Alexander's government effectively collapsed.[38] The primitive was a kind of anarchist.

Van Creveld was repudiating many old themes, but he revived a theme found in the medieval writers who thought of Alexander as one of the Nine Worthies. The king and his men acted in the name of a shared ethos, just as Judas Maccabee or a crusader did. Alexander spared Porus, for example, for the very reason that the sources give, and that modern writers have found mistaken or inadequate – chivalric admiration for the enemy.[39] Van Creveld might have added that Alexander made Porus one of his companions, as if to erase the cultural difference between the Macedonian invaders and the rulers of the Indus Valley.[40]

Van Creveld also drew attention to a quality of Alexander's that the author of this chapter has briefly noted elsewhere – his contempt for the value of his own life. No other mass killer has put himself at such great risk so often. Sacrifice for a cause does not explain this conduct, for Alexander often took risks for trifling reasons. Belief in his own godhead does not explain it. When wounded, he joked about the blood, not *ichor*, flowing from his veins.[41] Guilt does not explain it. He scarcely felt any. This paradigmatic soldier was very much at odds with familiar rationales for combat. That will keep him interesting to other soldiers, whether

---

[37] Van Creveld 1991: 188.   [38] Van Creveld 1991: 111, 199.   [39] Van Creveld 1991: 213.
[40] Naiden 2019a: 194.   [41] Plutarch *Alexander* 28.2. See Naiden 2019b: 57.

they regard him as a Caesar, a Worthy, a Great Captain, or a *beau idéal* for Hitler or Mao. Like the Alexander of Julian, the Alexander of tomorrow will be the exception that defeats every rule – the mortal god, shallow genius, comradely egotist, or commanding anarchist. Contradictions will keep him alive.

Guide to Further Reading

Most recent scholarship on Alexander the Great deals with political and social aspects of his reign; some focuses on the Roman reception of Alexander, and some on Alexander's reaction to Persia and to the most important parts of the Persian Empire, notably Egypt; less deals with warfare, be it strategy, operations, tactics, or equipment, which were more important subjects in scholarship down to World War II. Smallest of all is the body of writing by commanders and military historians seeking to evaluate Alexander in modern terms. Among the most recent is Lonsdale 2007, which devotes chapters to grand strategy, operations, and the use of force, and provides references to recent work on warfare in Alexander's era; Naiden 2019b cites recent Alexander scholarship relating to grand strategy, while Naiden 2008 situates Lonsdale among other recent interpreters of Alexander's failings and achievements. Wheeler 2012 follows another avenue into Alexander *comparanda*, by comparing Alexander's modern reputation to that of other ancient commanders and exploring how such comparisons became a theme in modern military writing. Van Creveld 2007 is the most probing and radical of recent views on Alexander's generalship, but the broadest and best survey of the subject remains Fuller 1958, a book that links Alexander's reputation to developments in twentieth-century politics. Fuller's is the most compelling imperialist Alexander, in contrast to Van Creveld's anarchic if not anti-imperialist version of the conqueror.

For the related (and much studied) subject of the modern reputation of Alexander's top subordinates, several of whom became Near Eastern kings after his death, the best introduction is Waldemar Heckel, 2016, *The Marshals of Alexander's Empire: A Study of the Makedonian Aristocracy and the Politics of Military Leadership*.

17: Finance and Coinage

Kyle Erickson

> Indeed, that was an apt and true reply which was given to Alexander the Great by a pirate who had been seized. For when that king had asked the man what he meant by keeping hostile possession of the sea, he answered with bold pride, 'What thou meanest by seizing the whole earth; but because I do it with a petty ship, I am called a robber, whilst thou who dost it with a great fleet art styled emperor.'
> Augustine *City of God* 4.4.25 (Dods trans.)

On his deathbed in Babylon in 323 BC Alexander was likely the richest man in the world. This chapter will investigate the extent of wealth at his disposal and summarize some of the key aspects of the financial and monetary world of the latter half of the fourth century. Although Alexander appears to have pleaded poverty on the eve of his invasion of the Persian empire,[1] he was far from poor. His father's expansion of the Macedonian kingdom increased the tribute and manpower available to the king; furthermore, the expanded exploitation of the Macedonian silver mines increased the supply of monetizable silver. Nor were Philip and his son hesitant to utilize this wealth to make ostentatious displays of Macedonian power both at home and abroad. In fact, Alexander's famous steed, Bucephalas, is said to have cost the young prince thirteen talents from his own resources.[2]

It is these resources that formed the initial core of Alexander's wealth and provided the ability for Alexander to launch his invasion. Before turning to Alexander's finances as king in Asia, it is perhaps worth considering the potential range of Macedonian sources of wealth. Alongside this, it is necessary to briefly examine the role of warfare and institutional state violence as a means of capturing and disrupting

---

[1] De Callataÿ 2012: 91.
[2] Plutarch, *Alexander* 6.1. By comparison, the daily wage for an Athenian skilled labourer was about 2–3 drachms per day, so Bucephalas would have cost somewhere in the region of 50–75 years' worth of wages for a skilled labourer.

wealth. The Augustinian comparison between Alexander and the pirate that starts this chapter serves to highlight the disparities in how we discuss the famed conqueror's sources of wealth and their acceptability.[3] At the core of both Alexander's and Philip's conquests and riches lay a vast human toll, not only the deaths of combatants or the transfer of wealth from Persians to Macedonians, but also the countless women and children sold into slavery, their homes and cities burned. Alexander and his army, while more successful than many, were not unique in antiquity in their ruthlessness in conquest; in fact, for his Roman biographer Plutarch, only a very small number of his actions were beyond what could be expected from such a conqueror.[4] This seizure of resources was also a double-edged sword in financial terms, as Alexander's vast 'fleet' took considerable resources to maintain and to pay his soldiers. This constant need for increased treasures to pay the army led to the perceived need for continual conquest and new sources of income. In fact, much of the newly conquered territory and its taxation would have been absorbed by the expenses of the army;[5] as a result, we cannot separate the army from the economy or from Alexander's own finances.[6]

Alexander's wealth, both his supposed lack thereof as he set foot in Asia and his riches at his death, is commented on by Alexander historians, ancient and modern. Detailed analyses of Alexander's finances and revenue are somewhat less frequent. However, Holt and Le Rider have both recently provided holistic overviews of Alexander's wealth and its lasting influence.[7] There is one aspect of Alexander's finances that has received a number of detailed surveys: his coinage. Through his act of conquest and the subsequent Greco-Macedonian settlements throughout the Near East, the typical Greek form of money, coinage, came to dominate across the former Persian empire. Through his unparalleled coin production, his coinage defined much of the monetary standards for the next several centuries, and his distinctive coin types remained a standard design until the Roman conquest.[8] As Price sets out in his preface to the now standard *The Coinage of Alexander the Great and Philip Arrhidaeus*: 'it had been previously reported to the Trustees of the Museum, on 11 June 1910, that a catalogue of this section of the

---

[3] Augustine *De civitate Dei* 4.4.25, which likely derives from Cicero, *De republica* 3.14.24.
[4] See, for example, Plutarch *Alexander* 13. For modern assessments of Alexander as a warlord see, for example, Bosworth 1996b.
[5] Milns 1987: 254–256. [6] Millett 2010: 475. [7] Le Rider 2007; Holt 2016.
[8] Posthumous Alexander coinage continued to be produced until the early first century BC, although by then coinage was largely civic in origin: Price 1991: 24.

collection was in preparation, but the complexity of the series prevented that publication'.⁹ In the intervening ninety years before the publication of Price's survey, considerable work had been done on untangling the correct attribution and chronology of this coinage which allowed Price to build a system that has become the standard classification system for Alexander's coinage. In the 2000s and onwards the wider adoption of open data has allowed work to be done to bring major collections of coinage around the globe together digitally. For Alexander's coinage, this framework has been built on Price's classifications and the PELLA project has worked to digitize the Alexander corpus and also undertake a catalogue of Argead coinage.¹⁰ This project (and so too the wider Hellenistic Royal Coinages project) both allows the accurate identification of any particular coin of Alexander and simplifies the synthesis of the large corpus of material in a broader framework. Before returning to his coinage, this chapter will first attempt to calculate Alexander's wealth, then consider how he utilized and distributed it. Finally, we will attempt to assess the impact of Alexander's conquest in financial terms.

Calculating Alexander's Wealth

Alexander's wealth was not solely confined to gold and silver but incorporated the wide array of assets possessed by the Macedonian kingdom. In exploring Alexander's finances, a key principle to take into account is the difference between liquid assets and non-liquid assets. While the concept of liquidity, by which I mean the ability to convert assets into a readily useable form, may not have been understood by Alexander or his contemporaries within a modern framework,¹¹ it remains useful for understanding some of the claims of Alexander's poverty. It is perhaps therefore useful to classify the types of assets in which Alexander and his father's wealth was collected and its varying degrees of liquidity.

The most liquid of Alexander's assets was his coinage and bullion, which went extensively to military pay and expenditures.¹² At the beginning of his reign, it is these assets in which Alexander was

---

⁹ Price 1991: 8. See Dahmen 2018 for a brief overview of the various local coinages within Alexander's empire.
¹⁰ http://numismatics.org/pella/
¹¹ This chapter will resist any attempt to place Alexander as a 'board-room warrior' or the like, as the comparison is both unhelpful and inaccurate. See Holt 2016: 154–157 for the dismissal of this approach.
¹² For estimates on the cost of the army, see Meadows 2014. For the uses of coinage in a military context, see Aperghis 2004; de Callataÿ 2016.

undoubtedly short. Unlike modern paper or electronic money, gold and silver in large quantities were not always entirely mobile or accessible to Alexander and the army when he needed them. For example, Engels proposed that when Parmenion was ordered to transport the captured bullion and coins (180,000 talents worth) from Persepolis, Susa and Pasargadae to Ecbatana it took as many as 20,000 mules and 5,000 camels.[13] With this volume of treasure, it is unlikely that all or even the majority travelled with Alexander and the bulk of the army.[14] This logistical problem could also become a financial one, as Alexander's demand for money from his companions in India shows.[15] The fact that at the furthest reaches of his campaign, having already conquered the wealth of Persia, Alexander lacked access to ready money demonstrates that a lack of liquid assets was not necessarily indicative of his total wealth.

The next most liquid or readily useable assets would have been livestock, cattle, sheep and goats but also particularly horses, of which an extensive supply would have been necessary for the extended cavalry campaign. This stock would have been supplemented by either purchase or seizure from local populations to replace that which was either consumed by the army or which was no longer fit for battle throughout the campaign. As a result, it is unlikely that during the campaign Alexander would have been able to derive additional income from this commodity.

In addition to wealth in gold and silver, Alexander inherited from his father control over a number of estates and control over the silver mines at Philippi. Alexander would have also had access to a range of other sources of income that would have included taxes, rents, revenue from royal estates and control over Macedonian timber and the other mines and industries in Macedonia.[16] This wealth was not as useful for immediate payments, but it could either be liquidated or used in a variety of ways by Alexander to finance his kingship.

The final type of asset that Alexander possessed is perhaps the hardest to quantify, the prestige and status connected to his role as

---

[13] Engels 1978: 79. Holt 2016: 86–88 argues that Engels' calculation of the weight is too high, as it does not differentiate between value in gold and silver, but that the number of animals proposed by Engels would be suitable for the volume of treasure.

[14] Holt 2016: 137–141 convincingly argues against Le Rider's assertion (2007: 234) that the treasury moved with Alexander.

[15] Plutarch *Eumenes*, 2. See also Holt 2016: 41.   [16] Kremydi 2011: 161; Holt 2016: 181.

king.[17] The ability of Alexander to distribute offices, land or other material rewards among his subordinates could often be substituted for direct payments in money. This had the additional benefit of tying the recipient into Alexander's system. Both the Macedonian and Persian economic structures that Alexander inherited relied heavily on this payment through authority, which allowed the recipients the opportunity not only to enhance their status but also their own wealth.

Let us now attempt to ascertain Alexander's wealth as it developed throughout his campaign. At the start of his reign, Alexander not only possessed but used some substantial assets to buy loyalty to his new regime; this included not only command positions in the army but also gifts of land and territory. His ability to distribute the royal estate between those loyal or potential allies serves as a useful reminder that the wealth of the Macedonian kings was not limited only to moveable assets but also tied heavily to land, people and resources. Holt calculates that, in addition to the 60–70 talents held in the Macedonian treasury, Alexander was also able to draw on approximately 1,000 talents per year from the mines at Philippi, and more than 200 talents from other sources of income. As Alexander conquered the former Persian territory, his ability to distribute land and offices and to collect tribute and other forms of revenue increased exponentially.

Additionally, Alexander was able to use slaves both as workers and as a source of income as they were sold. The slave trade, particularly following the capture of new cities, would form a core component of Alexander's ability to raise income along the campaign. The human cost from ancient warfare could be measured not just in the battlefield losses or the destruction of crops and livestock, but also in the capture and sale of civilians, usually women and children. Alexander was not unique and tapped into an ongoing market throughout the eastern Mediterranean, but the scale of his conquests dramatically altered the market. By counting only the slaves taken in mass at Thebes (30,000), Damascus (30,000), Bajaur (40,000) and Sangala (70,000),[18] we arrive at a total of 170,000 individuals taken. However, the number will have been substantially higher, as there are twenty-four reported instances of Alexander enslaving a population, but again these are likely to have been only the more notable incidents, where a large portion of the population was taken, with smaller raids not being taken into account.

---

[17] See, for example, Carney 2002; 2015: 191–282, or even Callisthenes' remark that he 'left poorer by a kiss': Plutarch *Alexander* 54.3, Arrian *Anabasis* 4.12.5. See Bowden 2013: 70–71.
[18] Holt 2016: 181–183.

While it is impossible to estimate with any certainty, it seems likely that upwards of 350,000 people would have been enslaved over the course of the twelve-year campaign.[19] Only Diodorus in his account of the sack of Thebes gives an economic equivalent for the conqueror, where 440 talents were raised by the sale of the 30,000 enslaved inhabitants.[20] While the increase in the number of slaves captured had an impact on their price, Alexander was still able to raise substantial sums from their sale.

Slavery or death were not the only potential consequences for the civilians in the face of the Macedonian armies. Plutarch highlights another potential consequence in the context of his narrative of the sack of Thebes:

> Among the many and grievous calamities which thus possessed the city, some Thracians broke into the house of Timocleia, a woman of high repute and chastity, and while the rest were plundering her property, their leader shamefully violated her, and then asked her if she had gold or silver concealed anywhere.
>
> Plutarch *Alexander* 12.1 (trans. Perrin)

The ancient authors consistently draw attention to other items of value taken by Alexander and his men, while they are enumerated only when they were rare, of exceptional value or highlighted an aspect of Alexander's character. In addition to the looting of cities, towns and villages, the baggage of defeated armies was clearly distributed among the army, with the best of the spoils saved for Alexander himself:

> Straightway, then, Alexander put off his armour and went to the bath, saying: 'Let us go and wash off the sweat of the battle in the bath of Dareius.' 'No, indeed,' said one of his companions, 'but rather in that of Alexander; for the property of the conquered must belong to the conqueror, and be called his.' And when he saw the basins and pitchers and tubs and caskets, all of gold, and curiously wrought, while the apartment was marvellously fragrant with spices and unguents, and when he passed from this into a tent which was worthy of admiration for its size and height, and for the adornment of the couch and tables and banquet

---

[19] Holt 2016: 183. [20] Diodorus 17.14.1–17.14.4.

prepared for him, he turned his eyes upon his companions and said: 'This, as it would seem, is to be a king.'

Plutarch *Alexander* 20.7–8 (trans. Perrin)

Alexander's troops committed acts like this across Europe and Asia, with the king only forbidding them on rare occasions and more often than not actively encouraging them (the most famous example being the sack of Persepolis).

Holt estimates the amount of wealth that Alexander captured during his campaign as within the wide range of 300,000 and 400,000 talents (1.8–2.4 billion drachms).[21] This capture of wealth by Macedonians was enormous by previous Greek scales. For comparison, roughly a century earlier, Thucydides stated that the Athenians received 600 talents a year as tribute from the Delian league.[22]

Spending Alexander's Fortune

Having acquired the wealth of the Persian kings, Alexander was not shy in spending it. As noted above, the output of Alexander's mints increased substantially towards the end of his life. While, as we will see, this likely corresponded to an increase in expenditure, Alexander had consistently utilized his wealth.

Holt divides Alexander's expenditure into several categories, these including religious ceremonies, burials, temple financing, gifts, rewards, tax remission, art, bridges, canals, cities, docks, ships and the military, in addition to other losses or abuses by his subordinates.[23] These categories obviously relate to a variety of different types of political and economic activity, with some recognizable from modern governmental functions. Alexander's largest expenditure was undoubtedly pay for the two Macedonian armies, the one with Alexander himself and the other with Antipater in Macedonia. However, attempting to establish the figures for regular army expenditure has met with failure. None of our ancient sources record the rates of pay for all the various contingents in the army. From Arrian's discussion of the enrolment of Persians into the army at Babylon in 323 BC,[24] it is clear that there was a progressive pay scale depending on the location of troops within the phalanx. This only gives us information about one part of the army. The range of estimates

---

[21] Holt 2016: 185. For our hypothetical worker earning two–three drachms a day, the wealth captured would equal roughly 2.7 million years' worth of work.
[22] Thucydides 2.13.3.   [23] Holt 2016: 96; see appendix 3 for a breakdown of the expenditure.
[24] Arrian *Anabasis* 7.23.3–7.23.4.

for overall pay is fairly wide: Andréadès, at the high end, estimated an expenditure of between 5,000 and 7,000 talents annually up until 330 BC and up to 15,000 talents thereafter;[25] Meadows, however, estimated an annual expenditure merely of 6,000 talents, which assumes a base pay of one drachm a day.[26] Milns, in his study of Alexander's pay, cautioned against any firm conclusions, but suggested that by the end of his reign expenditure on the army was consuming the entirety of the Macedonian king's annual income.[27]

Gift-Giving and the King

One of the most important social functions of the Macedonian kings was the distribution of resources among the elite, for there was nothing worse than a miserly king.[28] At this, Alexander excelled, his ancient biographers consistently praising his generosity.[29] One of the important aspects of Alexander's generosity was that it was not only limited to the distribution of coinage or land but rather encompassed the full range of captured treasure. For example, he returned the statues of the Tyrannicides to Athens and paid for a bronze sculpture of those who fell at Granicus.[30] This also allowed Alexander to exploit the political implications of bestowing gifts to foster changes within the court: for example, as he began to adopt Persian garb, by gifting high-status (purple) Persian style clothing to his commanders.[31] The rewards of Alexander's conquests did not only go to Alexander's companions, but also to the increasing number of hangers-on (*parasitoi*) who benefitted from the generosity and their proximity to the king. Further, the king sponsored an increasing number of competitions, particularly athletic competitions,[32] in which large prizes went to the victors.

The most famous of these gifts is Alexander's attempt to pay off the debts accrued by his soldiers on their return from India. But Alexander's attempt was exceptional, as was the amount of the debt in question, 9,870 talents, on the basis of which Holt calculates that the debts could have averaged as high as 6,580 drachms per debtor.[33] At the same time, Alexander offered dowries and gifts to those who were married alongside him at the mass wedding in Susa.

[25] Andréadès 1929.   [26] Meadows 2014: 171.   [27] Milns 1987: 254–256.
[28] Mitchell 1998: 167–177; Massar 2004.
[29] Plutarch *Moralia* 181e; Plutarch *Alexander* 39.1; Arrian *Anabasis* 7.28.3.
[30] Plutarch *Alexander* 16.17–16.18; Finn 2014.
[31] Diodorus 17.77.4–17.77.5; Plutarch *Alexander* 39.10; Holt 2016: 97–99.   [32] Adams 2007b.
[33] Holt 2016: 125.

Religious Ceremonies

Alexander was steadfast in his obligations to the gods. Holt counts nearly 5,000 offerings made during his campaign.[34] These ranged from small to large, from dedications after the crossing of each river to the establishment of altars and payments for temple construction. For each of these, Alexander's treasury would have paid the costs. The most expensive of these would have been the financial support for temple construction and refurbishment. This did not always go as Alexander hoped: at Ephesus Alexander offered to pay for the reconstruction costs of the temple of Artemis so long as he received a dedicatory inscription; the Ephesians declined the offer.[35] At Priene, Alexander got his way. The dedicatory inscription now in the British Museum begins, 'King Alexander dedicated this temple to Athena Polias.'[36] This is one of the undoubtedly large number of dedications by Alexander that are not included in the literary records. It was not only in the Greek realm that Alexander paid to reconstruct temples, he also did so in Egypt, notably Alexandria, and Babylon. Shortly before his death, Alexander also promised to underwrite the construction of temples at Delos, Delphi, Dodona, Dion, Amphipolis and Troy; these donations, had they ever been carried out, would have cost upward of 10,000 talents.[37]

Infrastructure and City Foundations

Perhaps the most productive use of Alexander's wealth was the investment in the creation of new settlements,[38] tax exemptions for temples and the initiation of large building projects. The number of cities founded by Alexander himself is disputed as many of the settlements attributed to him are more likely to have been developed by his successors. Nevertheless, even to establish a dozen or so new cities and a host of other smaller settlements would have required significant expenditure. As van der Spek has argued, 'In the long run, any growth in prosperity in the Hellenistic period may have been caused by the fact that the Seleucid kings, apart from wasting money in wars, also invested money in the foundation of cities, which must have been incentives for economic activity: increased food production, production of building materials and hence industry and

---

[34] Holt 2016: 107.   [35] Arrian *Anabasis* 7.25–26.3; Plutarch *Alexander* 76.
[36] *CIG* 2904 = *IK Priene* 149.
[37] Plutarch *Moralia* 343d; Diodorus 18.4.4–18.4.5. See Holt 2016: 109.
[38] Fraser 1996: 240–243; Cohen 1995, 2006, 2013.

trade.'³⁹ The same was undoubtedly true of Alexander and also the other Successors. At the very least, a new city would have required engineers and labourers to build walls, a gymnasium, homes, roads and a water supply. The total cost, not all of which would have been paid for by the king's coffers, would have been tremendous. This does not even include the numerous grants of seized land to the increasing array of colonists and settlers who came to populate the new cities.⁴⁰

As we have seen, between the military, gifts and payments Alexander had constant need of ready liquid assets. As a result, Alexander produced a massive number of new coins, which were distributed throughout the empire. We now turn our attention to these.

Counting Coins

When Alexander took over from his father, Macedonia already had a long-standing tradition of minting coinage. In fact, Philip's coin production had expanded considerably in line with his successes and became the model for a significant portion of Celtic coinage.⁴¹ Alexander would eventually establish his own mark on ancient coinage.⁴²

The date and the original location of Alexander's new coin-type designs remain a matter of debate. Price followed Newell in arguing that Alexander began to mint his own gold and silver coin types immediately at the start of his reign, in 336 BC, in Pella.⁴³ Le Rider, de Callataÿ and many others have argued that the production of these types did not commence until Alexander had reached Tarsus in Cilicia and that production began in 333/2 BC (silver) and 331/30 BC (gold).⁴⁴ One compelling argument for the later transition to his own types lies in the transition of Macedonian coinage from the Thraco-Macedonian standard ($\pm$ 14.70g for a tetradrachm) to the Attic standard ($\pm$ 17.20g).⁴⁵ This change to a heavier coin standard seems unlikely when Alexander was already short of coined money and bullion.

Using the PELLA project database, we can get an overview of the production of Alexander's coinage throughout the campaigns. As we can see, silver made up the greatest proportion of his coinage. And, of that, the majority was produced as tetradrachms (Figures 17.1 and 17.2).⁴⁶

---

³⁹ Van der Spek 2006: 287–288.   ⁴⁰ See Billows 1995.   ⁴¹ Kremydi 2011: 165–167.
⁴² The production of Phillip's types continued in Macedonia throughout Alexander's lifetime and down into the 290s, see Le Rider 2007: 37–43, 107–109; Dahmen 2018: 159.
⁴³ Price 1991: 27–28.
⁴⁴ See Le Rider 2007: 2–15 for a comprehensive overview of the debate.
⁴⁵ De Callataÿ 1982.   ⁴⁶ Charts derived from the PELLA Project (30.05.2021).

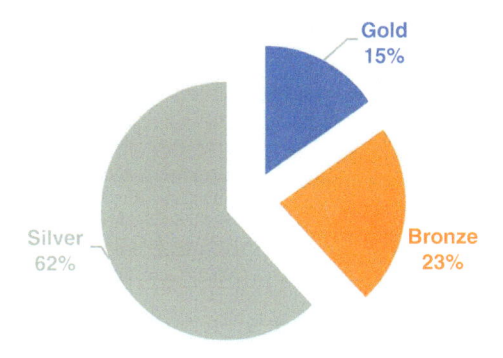

17.1 Percentage of Alexander's coinage by metal.

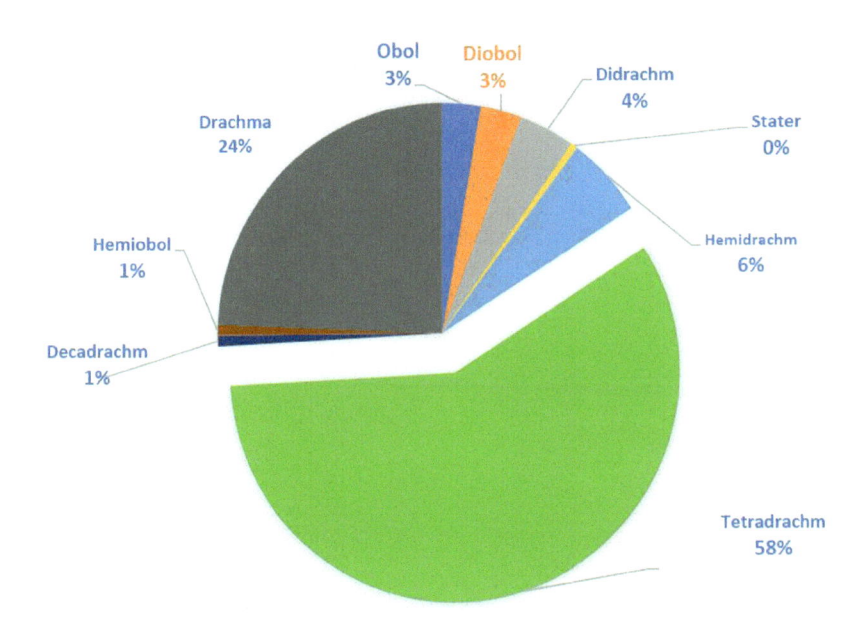

17.2 Percentage of Alexander's silver coinage by denomination.

Furthermore, the production of coinage was not uniform across the campaigns. Dahmen identifies a significant increase in gold and silver coin production in the last three years of his reign, particularly in Macedonia, Asia Minor and Babylon.[47] This production does not

---

[47] Dahmen 2018: 163.

match Alexander's acquisition of new treasures, but does align with Alexander's increasing pay obligations, payments of soldiers' debts and perhaps his preparations for new campaigns after his return to Babylon.

Designs of Coinage

Alexander's coinage was produced in three metals: gold, silver and bronze. Bronze coinage was likely designed for more local circulation or use within the army itself on a daily or weekly basis, while silver and gold were substantially more valuable and circulated more widely. The bronze coinage shows the widest variation in type, whereas the silver and gold coinage each have a single main type. Alexander's gold coinage was produced largely in staters and half staters and depicted the head of Athena facing the right in a crested Corinthian helmet, normally decorated with a coiled snake on the obverse and Nike standing facing the left, holding a wreath in her right hand and a stylis in her left hand on the reverse (Figure 17.3).[48] At the mints of Pella, Lampsacus, Miletus and Sardis, quarter starters with the same obverse and a bow and club reverse were produced (Figure 17.4), and eighth staters with a thunderbolt reverse.[49]

17.3 Gold stater, 8.57 g. Obv.: helmeted Athena. Rev.: Nike standing, facing left, holding a wreath in her right hand and a stylis in her left hand; legend, ALEXANDROU. Magnesia Mint. Yale Numismatic Collection, 2001.87.9969.

---

[48] Price 1991: 29. The coiled-snake motif decorating Athena's helmet is not always consistent and other creatures (eagle-headed griffin [Asia Minor]; lion-griffin [East]; seated sphinx [Babylon/Susa]; a duck or dove [Susa]) also decorate the helmet at the various mints, and sometimes it is left without decoration.

[49] Price 1991: 30.

17.4 Gold quarter stater, 2.15 g. Obv.: helmeted Athena. Rev.: lightning bolt; legend, DROU; bow and club; legend, ALEXAN. Pella Mint. Yale Numismatic Collection, 2001.87.9971.

The silver coinage was produced in a number of fractions from decadrachms to fractions of drachms, with the tetradrachm the most prominent type. The silver obverse shows the beardless head of Heracles facing to the right, and the reverse shows Zeus seated on a throne or stool facing left, holding an eagle in his outstretched right hand and a sceptre in his left (Figure 17.5).[50]

Alexander's gold and silver coinage shows a clear preference for the traditional Macedonian gods of Zeus, Athena and Heracles. The gold coinage has a particular emphasis on victory, and the naval elements of the reverse likely allude to the battle of Salamis and the Greek victory over the Persians.[51] The smaller gold fractions, silver and bronze coinage are dominated by images connected to Zeus and Heracles, with the beardless head of Heracles serving as the obverse image and a range of reverse images including various combinations of bow, quiver and club, or the eagle standing on the thunderbolt. Other common variations include the bust of a young, diademed male on the obverse and a horse running on the reverse, which appears to derive from older fourth-century Macedonian types, or a round Macedonian shield obverse and a Macedonian helmet reverse.[52]

Price divided Alexander's coinage into three distinct groups: 'imperial' – that produced by the imperial court at mints around the growing empire; 'local coinage' – produced by Alexander or his satraps or

---

[50] Price 1991: 30. There are some variations within the reverse image, with developments particularly in the position of the legs throughout Alexander's lifetime.
[51] Price 1991: 29–30.   [52] Price 1991: 31–32.

17.5 Silver tetradrachm, 17.15 g. Obv.: beardless head of Heracles, facing right. Rev.: Zeus seated on a stool, facing left, holding an eagle on his outstretched right hand and a sceptre in his left; legend, ALEXANDROU. Damascus Mint. Yale Numismatic Collection, 2007.182.343.

local officials for local circulation; and finally 'posthumous coinage' – continuations of Alexander's imperial coinage produced by his Successors and then by civic authorities.[53] Meadows has questioned the divisions, asserting that a division between 'Macedonian' and 'imperial' is more useful for the lifetime issues and that the production of posthumous coinage was more complicated that has been previously asserted. For example, the later use of Alexander's coin types ('Alexanders') has often been seen as civil resistance to other Hellenistic royal coinage but may have in fact been royal and produced by the Hellenistic kings.[54] Both the volume of coins produced by Alexander and their longevity as a type offer a useful backdrop for understanding the economic impact of Alexander.

Assessing Alexander

How one views Alexander and his conquests depends, more often than not, on one's cultural milieu. The pirate Alexander from Cicero, the destroyer of Zoroastrianism, to the hero who walled in the unclean nations – no view of Alexander is ever simple and straightforward.[55] The rise of the European colonial empires allowed scholars to see in Alexander the model for the use of the untapped wealth of the orient.[56]

---

[53] Price 1991: 24. [54] Meadows 2001, 2018: 65–70.
[55] For the most useful overview of the Alexander legends, see Stoneman 2008.
[56] See, *inter alia*, Rostovzeff 1941: 129–135; Green 1990: 360; Billows 1995: 215.

For the obsessed CEO in the latter half of the twentieth century, Alexander could become the idealized modern wolf of Wall Street.[57] These approaches tend to gloss over Alexander's flaws or successes as much as they often skip over the historical context. However, it is useful to assess, finally, if the significant spending and accumulation that we have covered in this chapter made a significant financial impact on the world following Alexander's death. There is one indisputable fact in assessing this: Alexander produced a vast number of new coins that entered circulation.[58] As we have seen, this production only represented a portion of Alexander's wealth (de Callataÿ estimates about one-tenth of the available gold was converted to coins in the Hellenistic period),[59] but it is the easiest aspect of Alexander's wealth to assess in terms of its impact.

Holt proposes an interesting counterfactual for the assessment of Alexander's monetary impact. He asks what the impact would have been had Alexander taken Parmenion's famous advice to accept Darius' offer of the lands west of the Euphrates and c. 30,000 talents as ransom for his family, thus ending the war in 331 BC.[60] Holt calculates that the amount of plunder and ransom Alexander had already taken, when added to this ransom, nearly equates to the 90,000 talents de Callataÿ calculates as the total output of Alexander's mints.[61] From an economic perspective, this calculation calls into question the value of the further eight years of plunder, death and destruction brought about by the rest of the campaign.

As we've seen, Alexander began his reign largely following the minting policies of his father, both in type and in scale. It was not until he was more firmly established and had achieved some victories that he began to mint his own coinage. This was largely silver, and the majority was produced as fairly valuable tetradrachms. The modern observation of Alexander's minting practices is in a not insignificant way driven by analysis of coin hoards. Coin hoards represent simultaneously not only the wealth of an individual, family or group, but also the realized threat of loss. We can likely see one of the drivers for this in Samuel Pepys'

---

[57] See Meyer 1989.
[58] See de Callataÿ 2011: 20–23; Holt 2016: 166. See Olivier et al. 2018 for the analysis of the metallic content of Alexander's mints. Interestingly, only Amphipolis, the most productive of Alexander's mints, appears to be using a new supply of bullion.
[59] De Callataÿ 2011: 22.
[60] Diodorus 17.54.1–17.54.5, Curtius 4.11.1–4.11.22, Plutarch, *Life of Alexander* 29.7–29.8, Justin 11.12.9–11.12.15. For the purposes of the counterfactual, the precise moment of the offer is irrelevant.
[61] Holt 2016: 166–167.

diary for 13 June 1667, when, fearing a Dutch invasion, he took a number of steps, including burial, to protect his wealth.[62] The remaining coin hoards only represent those who, unlike Pepys, were unable to collect their stored wealth. The significant uptick in coin hoards buried and recovered from the later half of the fourth and early third century demonstrate the economic uncertainty of the post-Alexander period.[63] What is also apparent from the concentration of Alexander coins in the hoards found further east is that the increase in monetization occurred only with his successors, the Seleucids and Diodotids.[64] As van der Spek has argued, rather than releasing the stored potential of Persian wealth, '[t]he conquests of Alexander the Great brought serious devastation and destruction to the whole of Western Asia; the sudden minting of such an enormous amount of bullion (approximately the weight of the gold housed in Fort Knox) led to inflation for thirty years'.[65] It was the new cities founded by Alexander and his successors that created new sources of wealth.

However, as I have attempted to highlight, Alexander's wealth was not purely monetary, but also included new lands. Here, from the Macedonian perspective, considerable new opportunities arose. The settlement of Macedonian soldiers across the Near East and the establishment of new cities created opportunities for a new Greco-Macedonian elite to capitalize on Alexander's success. Those favourites of Alexander who received donations of land and who were able to retain them through the tumultuous aftermath of his death were undoubtedly wealthier than prior to the conquest. The final and greatest beneficiaries of this new system were the new kings that arose from the wars of the Successors: they took the spoils of Alexander's gains and used them to build their own empires. While Alexander's conquest of the Persian empire did not radically transform the economy of the Near East, for the Macedonians who followed him, he created a new world in which any of them could be king.

Guide to Further Reading

Overall, the work of first resort for Alexander's finances is now Holt 2016, which supersedes Le Rider 2007. For Alexander's coinage, the standard remains Price 1991, with important updates by Le Rider

---

[62] Pepys 1893, 13 June 1667.
[63] See Olivier et al. 2018: 135 for the distribution of hoards and the general movement of Alexanders from eastern mints westward.
[64] Holt 2016: 170–172. [65] Van der Spek 2006: 287.

2007 as well as the ongoing work of the PELLA project (http://numismatics.org/pella/). For calculating the total volume of Alexander's coinage, see De Callataÿ 2011 and Olivier et al. 2018. For Alexander's army's pay regime, see Milns 1987, which in this regard supersedes Engels 1978.

18: THE ADMINISTRATION OF ALEXANDER'S EMPIRE

Maxim M. Kholod

The Asian expedition of Alexander the Great, which lasted almost ten years, resulted in the emergence of a new world empire, more extensive than its predecessor, the Achaemenid empire. This new empire spanned a vast area – from Macedonia in the west to western India in the east. Apart from that, there existed a number of territories which, though technically not part of Alexander's empire, fully acknowledged his supreme authority (Phoenician city-states, the Cypriot kingdoms, the Indian kingdoms of Porus and Abisares). Thus, in this regard, the status of these territories and the lands actually constituting the empire were similar: although the former retained a certain autonomy, they, just like the latter, had to submit to Alexander as monarch. Greece, unified into the Corinthian League, and the Greek cities in Asia Minor, freed from Persian domination by the king, were not part of his empire either. Officially the relationships of Alexander, the *hegemon* of the Corinthian League, with its members as well as with the Greek cities in Asia Minor (even if they were not enrolled in it) were considered ones of alliance. Despite the fact that the Greek cities were *de facto* dependent on Alexander, a situation which grew even more pronounced towards the end of his rule, it never came to the point where they were subjugated to his monarchical power.

Alexander was the central figure in the empire's administration. Although his most trusted confidants formed a sort of unofficial council that Alexander could discuss pressing issues with, including those pertaining to governance (e.g. Arrian *Anabasis* 6.2.1), the king always had the final say. He was the one to take decisions on all the key administrative matters and in the latter years of his life the autocratic principle in the decision-making process concerning these – or, indeed, any other – issues became stronger. Regarding administration, Alexander was assisted by his immediate circle or, more broadly, representatives of the Macedonian and later Persian nobility who were appointed by the king to different posts – both staff positions such as satraps (see below, pp. 300-314) or extraordinary ones created for the sake of executing a specific task.[1] Such appointees reported directly to their monarch. Alexander expected all his officials to comply fully with their obligations, and when the king found that they did not do their job properly, he normally dismissed them (e.g. Arrian *Anabasis* 3.6.8) or even punished them if crimes had been committed (see below, p. 313).

Macedonia held a special position in Alexander's empire. Although it was the birthplace of both the king and his soldiers, the locus of power was soon shifted by Alexander from there to his newly acquired territories in Asia, and Macedonia effectively turned into the periphery of his empire. Before setting off on his Asian expedition, Alexander left Antipater to supervise Macedonia and deal with the Greek cities of the Corinthian League as well as the North Balkan tribes in his stead, duties which Antipater discharged until his king's death (Diodorus 17.17.5, 17.118.1, 18.12.1; Arrian *Anabasis* 1.11.3; Curtius 4.1.39; Justin 11.7.1).[2] The practices of governance employed by Alexander in Asia (see below, pp. 292-315) were not transplanted back to Macedonia, and hence, as far as we can tell, the pre-existing administrative system there underwent no changes during his rule.[3]

The bulk of Alexander's empire was made up of the conquered territories in Asia. He did not introduce significant change in the administration of this part of his empire at the regional level, generally retaining the system inherited from the Persians. The satrapy remained the basic administrative division, headed, as under the Achaemenids, by the satrap (both terms – 'satrapy' and 'satrap' – were kept by the Macedonians as well).[4] Alexander's unwillingness to implement an administrative system different from what had previously existed in these lands is understandable. Changing the administrative model which had long proved its effectiveness and which local people were familiar with was inadvisable under the conditions of war. In addition,

---

[1] For example, in the spring of 331 Alexander placed Coeranus in charge of the collection of tribute (*phoros*) in Phoenicia, and appointed Philoxenus to collect both tribute in Asia Minor 'west of the Taurus' and most probably financial contributions (*syntaxis*) from the Greek cities located there (Arrian *Anabasis* 3.6.4; Kholod 2017: 141–146). Besides, it seems that in the winter of 331/0 Menes was entrusted with the task of taking control of sea communications with the coast of Syria, Phoenicia and Cilicia, and that of keeping them open and in good order (Arrian *Anabasis* 3.16.9–3.16.10, 3.19.6, 4.7.2; Kholod 2021).
[2] Berve 1926: ii.46–ii.51, no. 94; Heckel 2006: 35–36 (§1).
[3] On Macedonia in the absence of Alexander, see, in particular, Berve 1926: i.224–1227; Gilley and Worthington 2010: 199–204; Lane Fox 2011c: 385–391.
[4] For the Achaemenid satrapies and satraps, see for example Dandamayev and Lukonin 1989: 96–111; Jacobs 1994: 89–116, 2006; Klinkott 2005.

Alexander could not offer a viable alternative in this connection: the administrative practices tailored for the Macedonian kingdom itself were clearly ill-suited for his Asian domain.

In the present chapter I intend to focus, accordingly, on the regional administration of the Asian lands in Alexander's empire (at the satrapal level),[5] bearing in mind that this issue is of particular importance for our understanding of the empire's nature.

Satrapies

Insofar as we are able to judge, during Alexander's reign the total number of his satrapies amounted to thirty-one, of which twenty-one still remained by the time of the king's death (Map 18.1).

The other satrapies had either seceded from the empire in the meantime, like Greater Cappadocia (with Paphlagonia) and Armenia (see below, pp. 299-300), or were abolished by Alexander. Some were added to other provinces, being absorbed into them, like the satrapy of the Tapurians, Lycia and Pamphylia and probably Drangiana.[6] Others were unified, which led to the emergence of qualitatively new satrapies. Syria should be identified as one of the latter, since Alexander most likely first divided it into two satrapies – the northern and the southern one, but later restored it within the boundaries of the former satrapy of 'Beyond-the-River' (although already excluding Phoenicia).[7] This was also the case with the satrapy of Arachosia and Gedrosia: when the positions of the heads of Arachosia and Gedrosia, two vast provinces of equal importance, happened to be vacant almost simultaneously, the king unified them, appointing a single person as the satrap.[8]

Table 18.1 contains the list of the satrapies of Alexander's empire, indicating what changes they underwent and when.

The overwhelming majority of the satrapies that became part of Alexander's empire were the former Achaemenid satrapies. Apart from

---

[5] General overviews of Alexander's satrapies: Berve 1926: i.253–i.273; Seibert 1985: 206–217; Bosworth 1988a: 229–241; Jacobs 1994: 52–88; in addition, see Klinkott 2000; Wheatley and Heckel 2011: 86–105, 108–119.

[6] I share Bosworth's opinion that Drangiana, separated from Arachosia by Alexander, was not immediately added to Areia, but existed as an independent satrapy (headed by a certain Persian Arsames) from the autumn of 330 to the winter of 328/7. See Bosworth 1981: 22–23, 1988a: 237.

[7] On the administration of Syria under Alexander, see Kholod 2021. For the point that Phoenicia was withdrawn by the king from satrapal jurisdiction, see Berve 1926: i.285; Badian 1965a: 169; Bosworth 1988a: 232.

[8] The evidence of the changes happening both for above-mentioned satrapies and for those that will be discussed below is provided in Table 18.1.

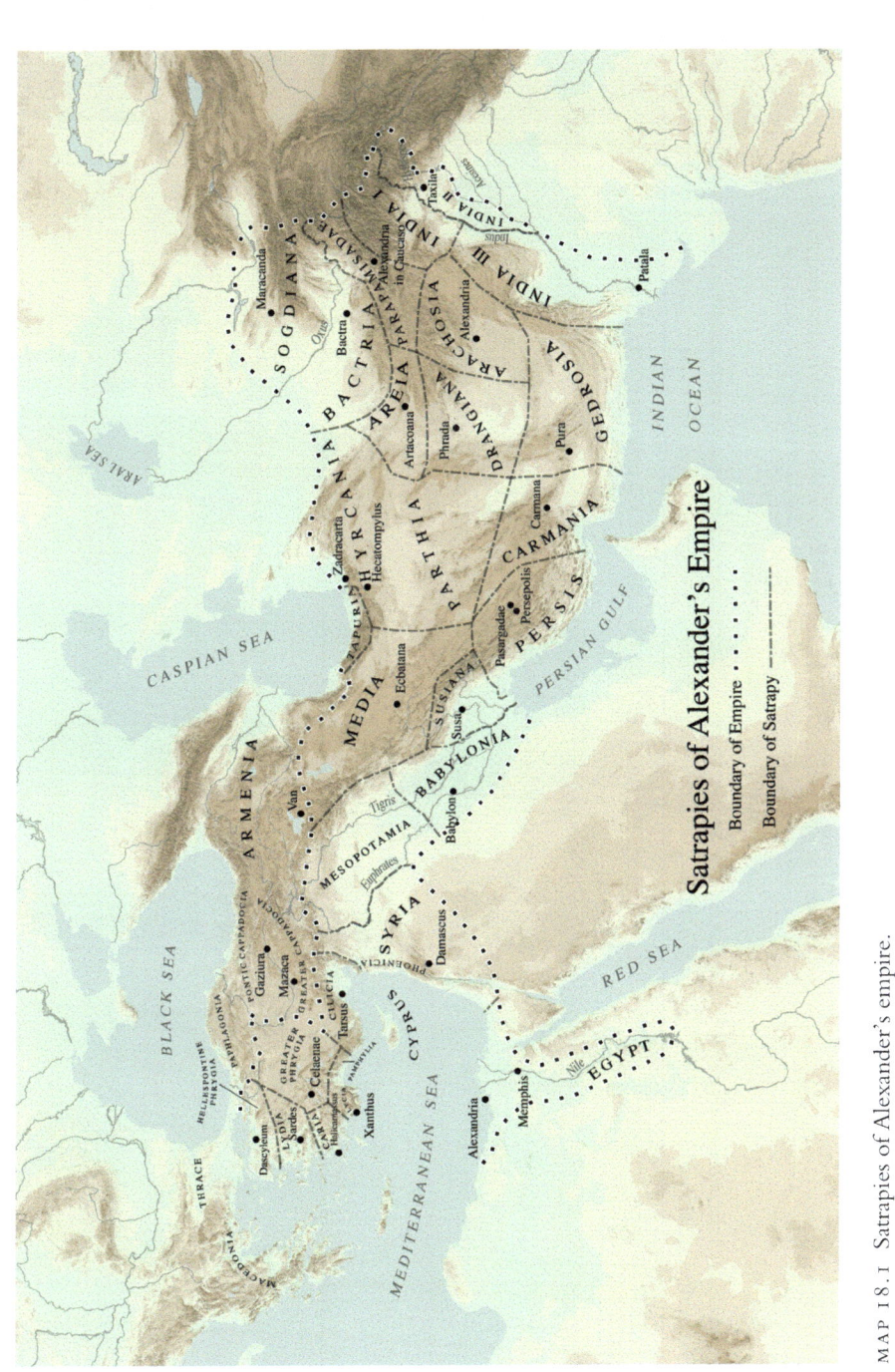

MAP 18.1 Satrapies of Alexander's empire.

Table 18.1 *Alexander's satrapies*

Alexander's satrapies	Changes
1. Hellespontine Phrygia(*)	• + Paphlagonia (summer 333 to winter 333/2) [Arrian *Anabasis* 2.4.2; Curtius 3.1.24; in addition, see below]
2. Lydia(*)	
3. Caria(*)	
4. Lycia and Pamphylia(+ ×)	• − Lycia (winter 334/3) [see below]. • winter 334/3 to most probably 329 [Arrian *Anabasis* 1.27.4, 3.6.6, 4.7.2] • added to the satrapy of Greater Phrygia (most probably 329) [Diodorus 18.3.1, 18.39.6; Arrian *Successors* 1.6, 37; Dexippus *FGrH / BNJ* 100 F 8.2; Curtius 10.10.2; cf. Justin 13.4.15]
5. Greater Phrygia(*)	• + Lycaonia (332) [Curtius 4.5.13] • + Lycia and Pamphylia [see above]
6. Greater Cappadocia(−)	• summer 333 to winter 333/2 [Arrian *Anabasis* 2.4.2; Curtius 3.4.1; cf. Plutarch *Alexander* 18.5; Appian *Mithridatic Wars* 8] • independent, together with Paphlagonia (from winter 333/2) [Diodorus 17.48.5–17.48.6; Curtius 4.1.34–4.1.35; in addition, see Nepos *Eumenes* 2; Diodorus 18.3.1, 18.16.1–18.16.3, 18.22.1, 31.19.3–31.19.5; Plutarch *Eumenes* 3.2, 3.6; Arrian *Successors* 1.5, 1.11; Dexippus *FGrH / BNJ* 100 F 8.2; Curtius 10.10.3; Appian *Mithridatic Wars* 8; Justin 13.4.16, 13.6.1–13.6.3] • − Paphlagonia [see above] • − Lycaonia [see above]

7. Cilicia(*)
8. Northern Syria(+ ×)
   - winter 333/2 to probably 329 [Arrian *Anabasis* 2.13.7, 3.6.8]
   - united into one satrapy with southern Syria (probably 329) [see below]
9. Southern Syria(+ ×)
   - late 332 to probably 329 [Curtius 4.1.4, 4.5.9, 4.8.9–4.8.11]
   - united into one satrapy with northern Syria (probably 329) [see below]
   - Phoenicia (332) [see below]
10. Syria(*)
    - probably from 329 [Diodorus 18.3.1; Arrian *Successors* 1.5; Dexippus *FGrH / BNJ* 100 F 8.2; Curtius 10.10.2; Justin 13.4.12; in addition, see Arrian *Anabasis* 4.7.2; Curtius 7.10.12]
11. Egypt(*)
12. Armenia(−)
    - early autumn 331 to sometime after late autumn 331 [Diodorus 17.64.6; Arrian *Anabasis* 3.16.5; Curtius 5.1.44].
    - independent (from sometime after late autumn 331) [Strabo 11.14.9 = C529; absent from all the lists of the satrapies distributed in Babylon in 323; in addition, see Plutarch *Eumenes* 4.1, 5.2; also Diodorus 19.23.3; Polyaenus 4.8.3]
13. Babylonia(*)
    - Mesopotamia (most likely at the end of Alexander's reign) [see below]
14. Mesopotamia(+ *)
    - most likely from sometime at the end of Alexander's reign [Diodorus 18.3.3; Dexippus *FGrH / BNJ* 100 F 8.6; Justin 13.4.23]
15. Susiana(*)
    - + the land of the Mountain Uxians (winter 331/0) [Curtius 5.3.16]
16. Persis(*)
17. Carmania(*)

Table 18.1 (cont.)

Alexander's satrapies	Changes
18. Media(*)	• + possibly the land of the Cossaeans (winter 324/3) [cf. Diodorus 17.111.4–17.111.6; Strabo 11.13.6 = C524; Plutarch *Alexander* 72.3; Arrian *Anabasis* 7.15.1–7.15.3; *India* 40.6–8; Polyaenus 4.3.31]
19. Tapuria(×)	• + the land of the Mardians (spring 330) [Arrian *Anabasis* 3.24.3; Curtius 6.5.21] • added to the satrapy of Parthia and Hyrcania (either winter 329/8 or winter 328/7) [Arrian *Anabasis* 4.18.2; Curtius 8.3.17]
20. Parthia and Hyrcania(*)	• + the satrapy of the Tapurians and Mardians [see above]
21. Drangiana(+ ×)	• autumn 330 to winter 328/7 [Diodorus 17.78.4, 17.81.1; Arrian *Anabasis* 3.28.1; Justin 12.5.9] • added to the satrapy of Areia (winter 328/7) [Arrian *Anabasis* 4.18.3, 6.27.3; Curtius 8.3.17; in addition, see Diodorus 18.3.3; Dexippus *FGrH* / *BNJ* 100 F 8.6; Justin 13.4.22]
22. Areia(*)	• + the satrapy of Drangiana [see above]
23. Arachosia(×)	• – Drangiana [see above] • united into one satrapy with Gedrosia [see below]
24. Gedrosia(×)	• + the land of the Oreitae (autumn 325) [Arrian *Anabasis* 6.22.2–6.22.3] • united into one satrapy with Arachosia [see below]
25. Arachosia and Gedrosia(+ *)	• from late 325/early 324 [Arrian *Anabasis* 6.27.1; Curtius 9.10.20; in addition, see Diodorus 18.3.3; Dexippus *FGrH* / *BNJ* 100 F 8.6; Justin 13.4.22]
26. Parapamisadae(+ *)	• from spring 329 [Arrian *Anabasis* 3.28.4, 4.22.5, 6.15.3; Curtius 9.8.9–9.8.10; in addition, see Diodorus 18.3.3; Dexippus *FGrH* / *BNJ* 100 F 8.5; Justin 13.4.21]
27. Bactria and Sogdiana(*)	

28. 'India I' (Indian lands west of the Indus, Pers. Gandhara)^(+ ×*)	• autumn 327 to autumn 326 [Arrian *Anabasis* 4.28.6] • united into one satrapy with 'India II' (autumn 326) [Arrian *Anabasis* 5.20.7, 6.2.3, 6.14.3, 6.15.2, 6.27.2; Curtius 10.1.20] • restored as a separate satrapy (the end of Alexander's reign) [Diodorus 18.3.3; Dexippus *FGrH* / *BNJ* 100 F 8.5; cf. Justin 13.4.21] • [on the Indian satrapies in general at the time of the settlement in Babylon in 323, see Diodorus 18.3.2–18.3.3; Dexippus *FGrH* / *BNJ* 100 F 8.5; cf. Arrian *Successors* 1.36, for Triparadisus]
29. 'India II' (Indian lands east of the Indus)^(+ × *)	• spring 326 to autumn 326 [Arrian *Anabasis* 5.8.3] • united into one satrapy with 'India I' [see above] • restored as a separate satrapy (the end of Alexander's reign) [see above]
30. 'India I and II'^(+ ×)	• autumn 326 to sometime at the end of Alexander's reign [see above]
31. 'India III' (Indian lands of the lower Indus)^(+ *)	• from late winter 325 [Arrian *Anabasis* 6.15.4; in addition, see above]

Key to symbols: ⁽⁺⁾ satrapies created by Alexander; ^(−) satrapies seceding from Alexander's empire; ^(×) satrapies abolished by Alexander; ^(*) satrapies existing at the time of Alexander's death.

Syria, which, as said above, though initially divided into two separate provinces, was restored several years later, no more than three Persian satrapies were abolished by Alexander, and even this only happened with time. Among these provinces were the satrapy of the Tapurians, which (along with the land of the Mardians annexed to it earlier) was absorbed into Parthia and Hyrcania, as well as the satrapies of Arachosia and Gedrosia, which, as we have seen, Alexander unified into one province by the end of his reign. Although Alexander chose to retain the Persian satrapies, it does not follow from this fact that they remained within their former boundaries: most of them underwent some territorial changes.

In addition to the former Achaemenid satrapies, Alexander's empire included provinces that were new administrative divisions. Some of them were created by the king in the territory of the former Persian empire. Of these Lycia and Pamphylia, the two Syrian satrapies and probably Drangiana were later abolished, while Mesopotamia,[9] Arachosia and Gedrosia, and Parapamisadae too continued to exist at the time of Alexander's death. The others were established in the conquered Indian territories – those that had long been beyond the sphere of Persian control, such as the lands of the satrapy of 'India I'[10] (the former Achaemenid province of Gandhara), and those that had never been part of the Persian empire, such as the lands of the satrapies of 'India II' (between the Indus and the Hydaspes) and 'India III' (from the confluence of the Indus and the Acesines as far as the ocean). Nor did Indian satrapies escape changes to their boundaries. Indeed, after the revolt of the Assacenians in 'India I', suppressed by the heads of the neighbouring satrapies, Parapamisadae and 'India II' (Arrian *Anabasis* 5.20.7), Alexander unified it with 'India II'. However, this new satrapy that resulted from the merging of two previously separate provinces proved to be short-lived: at some point at the end of the king's life, 'India I' and 'India II' again became independent satrapies.

It is obvious that all Alexander's decisions about creating or abolishing provinces and redrawing their borders had their reasons. Undoubtedly, the common reason was his natural desire to strengthen control of the region the satrapies belonged to, and to make administration of the provinces as efficient as possible. Apart from that, such changes were also occasioned by special reasons in each case. These

---

[9] On this satrapy, see now especially Kholod 2021: 512–514.
[10] The names I use here for Alexander's Indian satrapies ('India I, II, III') are not historical, but chosen for the sake of convenience.

reasons could differ, but it is clear that all the territorial changes were determined by current needs. For example, it should be assumed that the initial division of the Persian satrapy of 'Beyond-the-River' into two provinces – the northern (winter 333/2) and the southern (latter half of 332) – was dictated by the specific progression of the subjugation of the Syrian region. While its northern part fell under Macedonian power soon after the battle of Issus, the process of conquering the rest of Syria took months. Besides, creating two satrapies in Syria allowed Alexander to control its vast territory better, which was essential in the light of the then turbulent military situation in the vicinity of the region. The subsequent unification of Syria (probably 329) was also logical: given that by that time the whole of Syria was completely pacified, and there were no external threats either, Alexander did not have grounds to keep the province divided.[11]

Among the satrapies that managed to secede from Alexander's empire were Greater Cappadocia and Armenia. When the king was making a forced march through the southern lands of Greater Cappadocia, in a hurry to engage Darius' army, the local population recognized Alexander as their ruler (summer 333).[12] He placed a certain Sabictas in charge of Cappadocia (see below, p. 310). But after the battle of Issus part of the Persian army retreated to Cappadocia (and Paphlagonia) and from there, cooperating with the local forces, launched a counter-offensive in the spring of the following year (Diodorus 17.48.5–17.48.6; Curtius 4.1.34–4.1.35).[13] Despite the military successes achieved by the Macedonian satraps of Asia Minor, Greater Cappadocia (with Paphlagonia) was able to retain its independence from Alexander, albeit with the loss of Lycaonia, which was annexed by Antigonus the One-Eyed, the satrap of Greater Phrygia. Nothing is known of Sabictas during these events. At this point Greater Cappadocia fell under the control of Ariarathes, the satrap of Pontic Cappadocia, who had not been subjugated by the Macedonians. He ruled it, along with his own province (and Paphlagonia), for all the subsequent years of Alexander's reign.[14] As for Armenia, it is reasonable to believe that it, or at least a part of it, surrendered to Alexander when his troops were operating in its southern lands shortly before the battle of Gaugamela (early autumn 331). Moreover, when Alexander was in

---

[11] Kholod 2021.
[12] Bosworth 1980b: 189; 1988a: 231; Jacobs 1994: 56–57; Debord 1999: 456.
[13] On this Persian counter-offensive, see, in particular, Anson 1988: 472–475; Billows 1997: 43–45; Debord 1999: 462–465.
[14] Berve 1926: ii.59–ii.60, no. 113; Heckel 2006: 44.

Babylon, he sent the Persian Mithrenes to Armenia as its satrap (late autumn 331; Diodorus 17.64.6; Arrian *Anabasis* 3.16.5; Curtius 5.1.44). This person was never heard of again. Therefore, it is unclear whether he was able to assert control of the satrapy entrusted to him and, if he was, whether he ruled the entirety of it. However, regardless of the results of Mithrenes' mission, by the time of Alexander's death the satrapy of Armenia was obviously not controlled by the Macedonians. Apparently, at some point before the king's death, Orontes, the former Persian satrap of the province, managed to regain this territory.[15]

Satraps and Satrapal Administration

As far as can be judged from our sources, over the whole period of Alexander's reign the total number of satraps placed in charge of the various provinces was fifty.[16] Every single one of them was personally appointed by Alexander. Some were chosen from among the prominent Macedonians (or Greeks) serving in his army, some were representatives of the oriental nobility, predominantly Persians, who joined his side: twenty-nine known satraps belong to the first group, while twenty-one belong to the second.

Table 18.2 provides a list of the heads of Alexander's satrapies, including the period of their tenure. The satraps of Asian descent are in italics.

Presumably, while choosing satrapal candidates from among the Macedonians (or Greeks), Alexander was guided mainly by general considerations about whether they would be able to perform their duties in due fashion, since none of his subjects had either the relevant experience or knowledge of the provinces entrusted to them (with the exception of Calas, the satrap of Hellespontine Phrygia, who was one of the commanders of the Macedonian expeditionary corps operating in this territory in 336–335).[17] Alexander must also have taken into account a candidate's military abilities, but they did not play a key role. It is telling that only a handful of satraps of Macedonian origin (Calas, Antigonus the One-Eyed and Clitus the Black) had previously held important posts in the army. Alexander clearly did not want to

---

[15] Cf. Bosworth 1980b: 315–316; Anson 1990: 125–128; Hammond 1996a: 130–137.
[16] Here I set aside Cleomenes of Naucratis, regarding whom it is unclear whether he did officially become the satrap of Egypt at the end of Alexander's life, and the Persian Orxines, who usurped the province of Persis after the death of its satrap Phrasaortes. On these persons, see below, pp. 313–315.
[17] Kholod 2018: 413–415.

Table 18.2 *Alexander's satraps*

Alexander's satrapies	Satraps
1. Hellespontine Phrygia	• Calas (spring 334 to sometime before 328/7) [Arrian *Anabasis* 1.17.1, 1.17.8, 2.4.2; Curtius 3.1.24, 4.5.13; Memnon *FGrH* / *BNJ* 434 F 12.4] • Demarchus (from sometime before 328/7) [Arrian *Successors* 1.6]
2. Lydia	• Asander (summer 334 to spring 331) [Arrian *Anabasis* 1.17.7, 2.5.7, 4.7.2; Curtius 3.7.4, 7.10.12] • Menander (from spring 331) [Arrian *Anabasis* 3.6.7, 7.23.1, 7.24.1; Curtius 6.6.35; Dittenberger 1915–24 no. 302. ll. 4–30 2.II.6; in addition, see Diodorus 18.3.1; Arrian *Successors* 1.6; Dexippus *FGrH* / *BNJ* 100 F 8.2; Curtius 10.10.2; Justin 13.4.15]
3. Caria	• *Ada* (autumn 334 to *ca.* 326) [Arrian *Anabasis* 1.23.7–1.23.8; cf. Diodorus 17.24.2–17.24.3; Strabo 14.2.17 = C657; Plutarch *Alexander* 22.4] • Philoxenus (from *c.* 326) [Ps.-Aristotle *Economics* 2.31 = 1351b–1352a; Arrian *Anabasis* 7.23.1, 7.24.1]
4. Lycia and Pamphylia	• Nearchus (winter 334/3 to 329) [Arrian *Anabasis* 3.6.5, 4.7.2] • Antigonus the One-Eyed as satrap of Greater Phrygia (from 329) [Diodorus 18.3.1, 18.39.6; Arrian *Successors* 1.6, 1.37; Dexippus *FGrH* / *BNJ* 100 F 8.2; Curtius 10.10.2; cf. Justin 13.4.15]
5. Greater Phrygia	• Antigonus the One-Eyed (from spring 333) [Arrian *Anabasis* 1.29.3; cf. Curtius 4.1.35, 4.5.13; in addition, see Diodorus 18.3.1; Arrian *Successors* 1.6; Dexippus *FGrH* / *BNJ* 100 F 8.2; Justin 13.4.14; cf. Curtius 10.10.2]

Table 18.2 (cont.)

Alexander's satrapies	Satraps
6. Greater Cappadocia	• *Sabictas* (summer 333 to winter 333/2) [Arrian *Anabasis* 2.4.2; cf. Curtius 3.4.1, 'Abistamenes']
7. Cilicia	• Balacrus (autumn 333 to c. 326) [Diodorus 18.22.1; Arrian *Anabasis* 2.12.2; Curtius 4.5.13; cf. Curtius 4.5.9, 'Socrates'] • Philotas (probably from late summer/early autumn 324) [Diodorus 18.3.1; Arrian *Successors* 1.5; Dexippus *FGrH* / *BNJ* 100 F 8.2; Curtius 10.10.2; Justin 13.4.12, 6.16]
8. Northern Syria	• Menon son of Cerdimmas (winter 333/2 to early spring 331) [Arrian *Anabasis* 2.13.7] • Arimmas (early spring 331 to late summer 331) [Arrian *Anabasis* 3.6.8] • Asclepiodorus (late summer 331 to winter 329/8) [Arrian *Anabasis* 3.6.8, 4.7.2]
9. Southern Syria	• Andromachus (autumn 332 to winter 332/1) [Curtius 4.5.9, 8.9–8.11] • Menon son of Cerdimmas (early spring 331 to winter 329/8) [Curtius 4.8.11, 'Memnon', which is most likely a corruption of 'Menon']
10. Syria	• Menon son of Cerdimmas (?) (probably from winter 329/8).
11. Egypt	• Cleomenes (?) (from sometime at the end of Alexander's reign) [Ps.-Aristotle *Economics* 2.33 = 1352a–1352b; Pausanias 1.6.3; cf. Ps. Demosthenes 56.7]
12. Armenia	• *Mithrenes* (late autumn 331 to sometime before Alexander's death) [Diodorus 17.64.6; Arrian *Anabasis* 3.16.5; Curtius 5.1.44]
13. Babylonia	• *Mazaeus* (autumn 331 to 328) [Arrian *Anabasis* 3.16.4, 4.18.3; Curtius 5.1.44, 8.3.17] • Stamenes (winter 328/7 to sometime at the end of Alexander's reign) [Arrian *Anabasis* 4.18.3; cf. Curtius 8.3.17, 'Ditamenes']

- Archon (from sometime at the end of Alexander's reign) [Diodorus 18.3.3; Justin 13.4.23; in addition, see Rhodes and Osborne 2003 no. 92. block a §i.l.3; cf. Dexippus *FGrH / BNJ* 100 F 8.6]

14. Mesopotamia
- Arcesilaus (from sometime at the end of Alexander's reign) [Diodorus 18.3.3; Justin 13.4.23; cf. Dexippus *FGrH / BNJ* 100 F 8.6, 'Archelaus']

15. Susiana
- *Abulites* (late 331 to spring 324) [Arrian *Anabasis* 3.16.9, 7.4.1; Curtius 5.2.17; Plutarch *Alexander* 68.7]
- *Oropius* (spring 324 to late 324/early 323) [Dexippus *FGrH / BNJ* 100 F 8.6]
- *Coenus* (from late 324/early 323) [Dexippus *FGrH / BNJ* 100 F 8.6; Justin 13.4.14]

16. Persis
- *Phrasaortes* (early 330 to c.326) [Arrian *Anabasis* 3.18.11, 6.29.2, 6.30.1]
- *Orxines*, usurper (c. 326 to early 324) [Arrian *Anabasis* 6.29.2, 6.30.1–6.30.2]
- *Peucestas* (from early 324) [Arrian *Anabasis* 6.30.2–6.30.3, 7.6.3, 7.23.1, 7.23.3, 7.26.2; cf. Diodorus 17.110.2; in addition, see Diodorus 18.3.3; Dexippus *FGrH / BNJ* 100 F 8.6; Justin 13.4.23]

17. Carmania
- *Astaspes* (early 330 to late 325) [Curtius 9.10.21, 9.10.29]
- *Sibyrtius* (over a short time in late 325/early 324) [Arrian *Anabasis* 6.27.1]
- *Tlepolemus* (from late 325/early 324) [Arrian *Anabasis* 6.27.1; cf. Arrian *Indica* 36.8; in addition, see Diodorus 18.3.3; Justin 13.4.23; cf. Dexippus *FGrH / BNJ* 100 F 8.6, 'Neoptolemus', which is most likely a corruption of 'Tlepolemus']

18. Media
- *Oxydates* (summer 330 to winter 328/7) [Arrian *Anabasis* 3.20.3, 4.18.3; Curtius 6.2.11, 8.3.17]
- *Atropates* (from winter 328/7) [Arrian *Anabasis* 4.18.3, 6.29.3, 7.4.1, 7.4.5, 7.13.2, 7.13.6; Curtius 8.3.17, wrongly calling him 'Arsaces'; in addition, see Diodorus 18.3.3; Justin 13.4.13; cf. Arrian *Successors* 1.5; Dexippus *FGrH / BNJ* 100 F 8.2; Curtius 10.10.4]

Table 18.2 (cont.)

Alexander's satrapies	Satraps
19. Tapuria	- *Autophradates* (summer 330 to either winter 329/8 or winter 328/7) [Arrian *Anabasis* 3.23.7, 3.24.3, 4.18.2; Curtius 6.4.24–6.4.25, 6.5.21, 8.3.17, 10.1.39, 'Phradates'] - *Phrataphernes* as satrap of Parthia and Hyrcania (from either winter 329/8 or winter 328/7) [Arrian *Anabasis* 4.18.2; Curtius 8.3.17]
20. Parthia and Hyrcania	- *Amminapes* (summer 330 to sometime before early 329) [Arrian *Anabasis* 3.22.1; Curtius 6.4.25, 'Manapis'] - *Phrataphernes* (from sometime before early 329) [Arrian *Anabasis* 3.28.2, 4.7.1, 4.18.1–4.18.2, 5.20.7, 6.27.3, 6.27.6, 7.6.4; Curtius 8.3.17, 9.10.17; in addition, see Diodorus 18.3.3; Justin 13.4.23; cf. Dexippus *FGrH / BNJ* 100 F 8.6, 'Rhadaphernes']
21. Drangiana	- *Arsames* (autumn 330 to winter 328/7) [Curtius 8.3.17] - *Stasanor* as satrap of Areia (from winter 328/7) [Arrian *Anabasis* 4.18.3; Curtius 8.3.17]
22. Areia	- *Satibarzanes* (summer 330) [Arrian *Anabasis* 3.25.1–3.25.2, 3.25.5; Curtius 6.6.13, 6.6.20] - *Arsaces* (late summer 330 to summer 329) [Arrian *Anabasis* 3.25.7, 3.29.5, 4.7.1; cf. Curtius 7.3.1] - *Stasanor* (from summer 329) [Arrian *Anabasis* 3.29.5, 4.7.1, 4.18.1, 4.18.3, 6.27.3, 6.27.6, 6.29.1; Curtius 8.3.17; cf. Diodorus 17.81.3; in addition, see Diodorus 18.3.3; Dexippus *FGrH / BNJ* 100 F 8.6; Justin 13.4.22–23]
23. Arachosia	- *Menon* (winter 330/29 to late 325/early 324) [Arrian *Anabasis* 3.28.1; Curtius 7.3.5, 9.10.20] - *Sibyrtius* as satrap of Arachosia and Gedrosia (from late 325/ early 324) (see below, Arachosia and Gedrosia)

24. Gedrosia	- Apollophanes (autumn 325) [Arrian *Anabasis* 6.22.2–6.22.3, *Indica* 23.5; cf. Arrian *Anabasis* 6.27.1]
- Thoas (late 325/ early 324) [Arrian *Anabasis* 6.27.1]
- Sibyrtius as satrap of Arachosia and Gedrosia (from late 325/ early 324) (see below, Arachosia and Gedrosia)
25. Arachosia and Gedrosia	- Sibyrtius (late 325/early 324) [Arrian *Anabasis* 6.27.1; Curtius 9.10.20; in addition, see Diodorus 18.3.3; Dexippus *FGrH / BNJ* 100 F 8.6; Justin 13.4.22]
26. Parapamisadae	- Proexes (spring 329 to summer 327) [Arrian *Anabasis* 3.28.4]
- Tyriespes (summer 327 to late winter/early spring 325) [Arrian *Anabasis* 4.22.5, 5.20.7, 6.15.3; Curtius 9.8.9, 'Terioltes']
- Oxyartes (from late winter/early spring 325) [Arrian *Anabasis* 6.15.3; cf. Curtius 9.8.9–10; in addition, see Diodorus 18.3.3; Dexippus *FGrH / BNJ* 100 F 8.5; Justin 13.4.21; cf. Curtius 10.10.4]
27. Bactria and Sogdiana	- *Artabazus* (summer 329 to summer 328) [Arrian *Anabasis* 3.29.1, 4.15.5, 4.16.2–4.16.3, 4.17.3; Curtius 7.5.1, 7.11.29, 8.1.10, 8.1.19]
- Clitus the Black (summer to autumn 328) [Curtius 8.1.19; 8.2.14]
- Amyntas (autumn 328 to possibly 325) [Arrian *Anabasis* 4.17.3, 4.22.3; Curtius 8.2.14; in addition, see Diodorus 17.99.5–17.99.6, 18.7.1; Curtius 9.7.1–9.7.11; cf. Justin 13.4.23]
- Philip (from sometime at the end of Alexander's reign) [Diodorus 18.3.3; Dexippus *FGrH / BNJ* 100 F 8.6; cf. Curtius 10.10.4; Justin 13.4.23]
28. 'India I' (Indian lands west of the Indus, Pers. Gandhara)	- Nicanor (autumn 327 to 326) [Arrian *Anabasis* 4.28.6; cf. 5.20.7]
- Philip son of Machatas, as satrap of 'India I' and 'India II' united in one province (see below, 'India I and II')

Table 18.2 (cont.)

Alexander's satrapies	Satraps
	• Peithon (from sometime at the end of Alexander's reign) [Diodorus 18.3.3; Dexippus *FGrH / BNJ* 100 F 8.6; cf. Curtius 10.10.4; Justin 13.4.21; in addition, see Diodorus 18.39.6; Arrian *Successors* 1.36]
29. 'India II' (Indian lands east of the Indus)	• Philip son of Machatas (spring to autumn 326) [Arrian *Anabasis* 5.8.3, 5.20.7; cf. Plutarch *Alexander* 60.16]
	• Philip son of Machatas, as satrap of 'India I' and 'India II' united in one province (see below, 'India I and II')
	• no satrap (from 325) [Arrian *Anabasis* 6.27.2; cf. Curtius 10.1.21]
30. 'India I and II'	• Philip son of Machatas (autumn 326 to 325) [Arrian *Anabasis* 6.2.3, 6.4.1, 6.14.3, 6.15.2, 6.27.2; *Indica* 19.4; cf. Curtius 10.1.20–10.1.21]
31. 'India III' (Indian lands of the lower Indus)	• Peithon (from late winter 325 to sometime at the end of Alexander's reign) [Arrian *Anabasis* 6.15.4, 17.1–17.2; Curtius 9.8.16]
	• (?) (from sometime at the end of Alexander's reign) (see above, 'India I')

deprive his troops of the best commanders by scattering them across the regions, and it appears that they themselves had no intentions of becoming the head of a satrapy either.

The situation was somewhat different when Alexander appointed Persians as satraps. In this case loyalty to the king was of great importance as well as the ability to discharge one's duties efficiently and honestly (although, as evidenced by later events, at first Alexander would sometimes make a wrong assessment in this regard; see below, p. 313). Likewise, the monarch had to bear in mind that some of the Persian nobility had already had experience in governing provinces, and therefore they could be of service while occupying similar positions under the new ruler.[18] Moreover, in the cases of those Persians that were retained (or reappointed later) as satraps by Alexander, he could not but consider their knowledge of the corresponding regions and the connections they had forged there as advantageous. That must be the principal reason why Alexander soon reappointed Phrataphernes, the satrap of Parthia and Hyrcania under Darius (Arrian *Anabasis* 3.8.4, 3.23.4; cf. Curtius 4.12.9, 4.12.11), and Atropates, who had governed Media in the same time period, to their positions (Arrian *Anabasis* 3.8.4).

However, prior to the battle of Gaugamela (1 October 331) Alexander chose satraps almost exclusively from among the Macedonians. The reason for this is easy to understand: their devotion was unquestionable, which was crucial in the precarious military situation that persisted before the total defeat of the Persian king.

As far as we are able to judge, the satraps of Macedonian (or Greek) origin had full authority in the provinces they were in charge of. They were both *de jure* and *de facto* in general command of the occupation troops Alexander left with them (e.g. Arrian *Anabasis* 1.17.7, 2.13.7, 4.22.3; Curtius 7.3.5) as well as the mercenary units they formed themselves (Diodorus 17.106.3, 17.111.1). The Macedonian garrisons stationed in their territories were, if not fully, then at least partly dependent on them too (see below, p. 309). Besides, these satraps had local forces at their disposal that could be drafted if necessary (e.g. Arrian *Anabasis* 2.20.2).[19] Doubtless they also held authority in the civilian

---

[18] Apart from the Persians who were retained as satraps, Artabazus, appointed satrap of Bactria and Sogdiana, had governed Hellespontine Phrygia (Berve 1926: ii.82–ii.83, no. 152; Heckel 2006: 55), while Mazaeus, nominated satrap of Babylonia, had been in charge of Cilicia and the province of 'Beyond-the-River' (Berve 1926: ii.243–ii.244, no. 485; Heckel 2006: 156–157). The evidence for these two persons and the others mentioned below as Alexander's satraps is indicated in Table 18.2.

[19] In this passage, note the mention of several Lycian warships sent correspondingly by Nearchus, the satrap of Lycia and Pamphylia, to Alexander at Tyre.

sphere in their satrapies, and most likely they were in charge of the administration of finance too. Indeed, even if special financial officials, regularly appointed, really existed in the provinces,[20] they must have been subordinate to the Macedonian satraps (see below, p. 309), just like all the other administrative functionaries left with them. Little is known about such functionaries, Macedonian or Greek (Arrian *Indica* 33.8, 34.1–34.5, 36.1–36.2, 37.1), but it is certain that every satrapy had them and they in turn had subordinates – the representatives of the local traditional administration that continued to exist under Alexander. Balacrus, the satrap of Cilicia, was in charge of coinage in his province. This is evidenced by two series of silver staters (of the Persian weight) with the name of Balacrus in their legend, produced at the Tarsus mint. This fact, however, distinguishes him from the other provincial heads: apart from the Persian Mazaeus when he was satrap of Babylonia under the Macedonian king, they did not use the prerogative to mint coins bearing their names.[21]

In this context it is appropriate to consider how Alexander organized the administration of Lydia. Arrian writes that after seizing Sardis, the capital of the satrapy, the monarch made Asander, son of Philotas, satrap, leaving him sufficient forces. Alexander also appointed Pausanias, one of the Companions, commandant of the fortress of Sardis, giving him soldiers for the garrison, and a certain Nicias to assess and collect tribute (*phoros*) in the province (Arrian *Anabasis* 1.17.7). Thus, in Lydia Alexander divided the administrative functions between several officials. However, it does not follow from this fact, as scholars often believe,[22] that such a measure was intended to limit the power of the satrap, especially in the financial sphere. Indeed, it should be assumed that Nicias' appointment was primarily occasioned by Alexander's intention to organize the collection of tribute efficiently in such a wealthy and structurally complex satrapy as Lydia. In view of this, it was reasonable to give the job to a special official rather than to Asander who, being occupied with various matters, including military affairs, could not be expected to pay close attention to the work of his satrapy's fiscal mechanisms. Moreover, it cannot be ruled out that Nicias was also entrusted with the collection of the financial contributions (*syntaxis*)

---

[20] However, apart from Egypt (which cannot be compared to the satrapies because of its special position, that is, it had no satrap for a long time, if at all), only two such financial officials – Nicias in Lydia (see below) and Asclepiodorus in Babylonia (Arrian *Anabasis* 3.16.4) – are attested, a fact which rather suggests that these appointments were exceptional. See Bosworth 1988a: 241–242. On Egypt, see below, pp. 314–315

[21] On these coins of Balacrus and Mazaeus, see now especially Le Rider 2007: 153–156, 206–209.

[22] See, for example, Griffith 1964: 23–30; Jacobs 1994: 53; Anson 2013: 141–143.

from the Greek cities in Asia Minor,[23] apparently those in the vicinity of Lydia. It is unknown whether Nicias was subordinate to Asander, but it follows from Arrian's account of his appointment that Nicias had no military unit at his disposal and hence was bound to depend on Asander, should the satrap consider it necessary to intervene in his activities. In addition, it is clear that Asander himself, not Nicias, was responsible for transporting the money collected to Alexander, for only the satrap was in position to provide soldiers for a convoy.[24] Unlike Nicias, it seems that, as the fortress' commandant, Pausanias was more independent. But even in this case – as in any similar cases – his independence should not be overestimated. Formally reporting directly to Alexander, in reality Pausanias must have been dependent on the satrap of Lydia for a number of matters, at least for such an important thing as supplying the garrison with food and money. Furthermore, it appears logical that, should Sardis come under threat owing to a worsening of the military situation, Pausanias would have had to seek help from and perhaps even subordinate himself to a certain extent to Asander, who, having more substantial forces, would naturally then take centre-stage.[25]

Before the battle of Gaugamela there had been only two cases of Alexander appointing orientals as satraps. They were Ada in Caria and the above-mentioned Sabictas in Greater Cappadocia. Ada, the last member of the Hecatomnid dynasty, was ousted from power by her younger brother Pixodarus as early as 341/0. She was, furthermore, unable to regain her position after his death in 335.[26] When Alexander arrived in Caria in 334, Ada chose to side with him and was recognized by the king as the ruler of Caria (Diodorus 17.24.2–17.24.3; Strabo 14.2.17 = C657; Plutarch *Alexander* 22.4; Arrian *Anabasis* 1.23.8) and, after the capture of Halicarnassus, as its satrap too (Diodorus 17.24.2–17.24.3; Strabo 14.2.17 = C657; Plutarch *Alexander* 22.4; Arrian *Anabasis* 1.23.8). In turn, Ada adopted the king as her son (Plutarch *Alexander* 22.4; Arrian *Anabasis* 1.23.8), which made him a legitimate heir to the Hecatomnids. Placing Ada in charge of the province allowed Alexander to secure the support of the local population during the continued fight for Caria. In addition, Alexander could hardly doubt Ada's loyalty, since she, having no strength, desperately needed the Macedonians' support, especially in the current situation. Moreover, Alexander left his own officer with Ada, the Macedonian Ptolemy, in

---

[23] Kholod 2013: 83–92.   [24] On Nicias' position and functions, see Kholod 2017: 140, 146.
[25] Cf. Heckel 2006: 193 (§1). However, see Bosworth 1988a: 229; Anson 2013: 141.
[26] Hornblower 1982: 41–50; Ruzicka 1992: 111–137; Debord 1999: 404–406.

whose hands was concentrated real military power in Caria: he was in command of sizable forces stationed in the area by the king for the struggle against the Persians (Arrian *Anabasis* 1.23.6, also see 2.5.7; Curtius 3.7.4). It is thus not surprising that Ada, posing no threat to Alexander, could keep her position up until her death (*c.* 326).[27] As for the appointment of Sabictas as satrap of Greater Cappadocia, the reasons for it are not as obvious as in Ada's case owing to our insufficient knowledge about what was happening in this area at that time. It is possible to suppose that Sabictas was either a member of the Cappadocian nobility dissatisfied with the Persian rule, or (less likely) a Persian bearing a grudge against it, who somehow managed to convince Alexander of his significance and, naturally, loyalty. Besides, it seems that such an appointment was advantageous to the king himself at that point. Indeed, the presence of a Macedonian as satrap in Greater Cappadocia would have meant assigning troops to him, which would have had the undesirable effect of weakening Alexander's army before the upcoming battle against Darius. Be that as it may, subsequent events surrounding the retreat of part of the Persian army into Greater Cappadocia after the battle of Issus (see above, p. 299) showed that Sabictas was unable to retain the post given to him by the king.[28]

If before the battle of Gaugamela Alexander's appointments of orientals as satraps were exceptions due to special circumstances, later this situation changed. After Mazaeus, a prominent Persian noble, who had fled from the battlefield at Gaugamela to Babylon, surrendered the city to Alexander without a fight, he was made satrap of Babylonia (autumn 331). From now on, over the next few years, the satrapal posts in the newly conquered provinces were given or confirmed by Alexander almost exclusively to representatives of the Persian aristocracy that offered submission to him: right after Mazaeus, in the same Babylon, Mithrenes was placed in charge of Armenia (see above, p. 300); soon afterwards Abulites received the position of satrap in Susiana (late 331); Phrasaortes in Persis (early 330); Astaspes in Carmania (early 330); Oxydates and later Atropates in Media (summer 330 and winter 328/7 respectively); Autophradates in Tapuria (summer 330); Amminapes and then Phrataphernes in Parthia and Hyrcania (summer 330 and sometime before early 329 respectively); Satibarzanes and after his rebellion Arsaces in Areia (summer 330); probably Arsames in Drangiana (autumn 330); Proexes and

---

[27] See for example Berve 1926: ii.12, no. 20; Ruzicka 1992: 155; Wheatley and Heckel 2011: 101.
[28] Bosworth 1980b: 189; Heckel 2006: 243, 338, n. 661; cf. Berve 1926: ii.348, no. 690.

subsequently Tyriespes in Parapamisadae (spring 329 and summer 327 respectively); and Artabazus in Bactria and Sogdiana (summer 329). The only Macedonian Alexander nominated as satrap in this period was Menon, whom the monarch chose to be the head of Arachosia, apparently mainly for military reasons (winter 330/29).[29]

The new policy of predominantly appointing Persians as satraps, adopted by Alexander after the battle of Gaugamela, is quite understandable. Now that the future of the Achaemenid empire was sealed, as its new ruler he badly needed the support of the Persian aristocrats who, despite the defeat, remained a strong influence over the local Asian and especially Iranian population. It was thus crucial for Alexander to win them over *inter alia* by means of giving various high positions, including satrapal posts, to those representatives of the Persian nobility that showed loyalty to him.

However, while placing the Persians in charge of provinces, Alexander always took measures to limit their power, especially in the military sphere, and to keep them under control. Indeed, the real military power in the satrapies belonged to the Macedonian commanders of the occupation forces left there (e.g. Arrian *Anabasis* 3.16.4, 3.16.9, 3.19.7, 3.26.3; Curtius 5.1.43, 5.2.16, 7.2.19–7.2.32). Although these commanders were officially considered subordinate to their respective satraps, in reality they could act, when they saw fit, independently (e.g. Arrian *Anabasis* 2.5.7; Curtius 3.7.4).[30] As for the commanders of Macedonian garrisons in the fortresses located in the provinces, they were all the more independent from Alexander's Persian satraps (e.g. Arrian *Anabasis* 3.16.9; Curtius 5.1.43, 5.2.16, 5.6.11). If they, reporting directly to the king, could cede some of their power, they would do so only in a very complicated military situation and then cede it to the Macedonian commanders of the occupation forces rather than to the satraps of Persian origin. The responsibility of Alexander's Persian satraps to recruit troops from among the natives in their provinces, when the king found it necessary, and to command them (e.g. Arrian *Anabasis* 4.17.3, 7.6.1, 7.6.3–7.6.4) did not significantly increase their actual military power. Indeed, if these recruited natives joined Alexander's army, they fell under the supreme command of the king (or his marshals), while if they remained in their satrapy and participated in local military operations (e.g. Arrian *Anabasis*

---

[29] Bosworth 1981: 22–23, 1988a: 237.
[30] In this context the example of Media is telling too. The fact that the commanders Alexander left there were practically independent from the satrap Atropates is confirmed by their numerous abuses against the local population (Arrian *Anabasis* 6.27.3–6.27.5; Curtius 10.1.1–10.1.9).

3.28.2, 4.7.1, 4.18.2, 6.29.3; Curtius 8.3.17), their contingent was hardly considerable in number: Alexander certainly could not allow the numerical superiority or even equality of these troops, whose loyalty was unproven, to the provincial Macedonian forces. Usually the presence of Macedonian officials, especially military ones, in the provinces was enough to control their satraps of Persian origin. However, sometimes Alexander took additional steps in this direction. It is known that in Parthia and Hyrcania, as well as in Parapamisadae, Alexander assigned special overseers (*episkopoi*) to their satraps (Arrian *Anabasis* 3.22.1, 3.28.4). Regardless of whether or not these appointees exercised military functions, it is clear that they reported directly to Alexander, and their main duty was to supervise the satraps, playing the role of the king's watchdogs.

Despite the restrictions, the Persian satraps did, however, wield a fair amount of power. Hence, the close attention Alexander paid to their activities, especially after the uprising of Satibarzanes, the satrap of Areia, which was suppressed only with great difficulty (summer 330–spring 329). Alexander gradually abandoned the policy of appointing predominantly Persian satraps, finding it more advantageous to replace them with Macedonians (and Greeks). The first such example was the case of Stasanor of Soli, who was ordered by the king to arrest Arsaces, previously made satrap of Areia in place of Satibarzanes, and to take his place (summer 329).

Nevertheless, prior to the Indian campaign Alexander still did not show an obvious preference for Macedonians (or Greeks) over Persians as heads of provinces. At least, the satraps of Persian origin, including those whose loyalty he found questionable, were replaced by both Macedonians and other Persians. The situation with the appointment of satraps began to change when Alexander was in India. In this period only one Persian was placed in charge of a province, and even in that case it was the king's father-in-law Oxyartes: he succeeded Tyriespes, the satrap of Parapamisadae, who, like his predecessor Proexes, was accused of misgovernment (late winter/early spring 325). In the rest of the cases – all three Indian provinces and Gedrosia – Alexander appointed Macedonians as satraps. His choices at this point can be explained by the highly turbulent nature of the Indian region and of Gedrosia (in part), which required the concentration of power in the Macedonians' own hands, but the subsequent replacements of the Persian satraps with the Macedonians clearly demonstrate that Alexander abandoned his previous stance on the matter.

These replacements occurred after Alexander returned from the Indian campaign and began to restore order to his empire, punishing the high-ranking officials that in his absence had shown insubordination and had been involved in numerous abuses of power and even obvious crimes.[31] Among those Alexander found guilty at that time were a number of his Persian satraps. On arrival in Carmania, Alexander ordered the execution of its head Astaspes, suspecting him of disloyalty (late 325). In his place he appointed the Macedonian Sibyrtius and a little later Tlepolemus, another Macedonian. In Persis, Orxines was put to death by Alexander too. While the king made war in India, Orxines had usurped the vacant post of satrap after the death of Phrasaortes. He was accused of plundering temples and royal tombs as well as of executing many innocent Persians. It was the Macedonian Peucestas that now became the satrap of Persis (early 324). The head of Susiana, Abulites, was charged with neglecting his duties and, contrary to Alexander's orders, failing to send supplies to the army during its march through the Gedrosian desert. Abulites was put to death along with his son Oxathres, the ruler of Paraetacene (spring 324), and succeeded by a certain Oropius, possibly a Persian (if so, his name has survived in a corrupted form).[32] However, Oropius was soon deposed on suspicion of inciting rebellion and fled, and so Coenus, a Greek or more likely a Macedonian, was made satrap of Susiana (late 324/early 323). At some point shortly before Alexander's death a new satrap was assigned to Babylonia as well: Stamenes was replaced by the Macedonian Archon. In all likelihood, it was at this point that another Macedonian, Arcesilaus, was placed in charge of the newly created satrapy of Mesopotamia.

If most of the satraps of Persian origin thus failed to meet Alexander's expectations, he clearly did not have grounds to think the same about his Macedonian (and Greek) satraps: otherwise, punitive actions would certainly have been taken against them at that time too.[33] It seems that it was the devotion the Macedonian satraps demonstrated to their monarch during his absence (or at least, their non-involvement in any serious wrongdoing, which would suggest the opposite of devotion) that finally convinced Alexander that satrapal positions from that time onwards should be given, as previously, to the Macedonians. As a result, at the time of Alexander's death only a handful of his Persian satraps continued to retain

---

[31] Badian 1961: 16–25. For a more balanced view of the events, see Higgins 1980: 139–152.
[32] Heckel 2006: 186; cf. Berve 1926: ii.57, no. 107.
[33] Calas, the satrap of Hellespontine Phrygia, and Apollophanes, the satrap of Gedrosia, should hardly be viewed as victims of this great purge, as Badian has suggested (1961: 17–18). See Heckel 2006: 75, 41–42.

their posts, namely Phrataphernes, the satrap of Parthia and Hyrcania, and Atropates, the satrap of Media, both of whom had been able to prove their loyalty to the king beyond any doubt; there was also Oxyartes, the satrap of Parapamisadae, whom Alexander naturally trusted as Roxane's father.

Among the provinces of Alexander's empire there was one he did not assign a satrap to, at least initially. This was Egypt. It is certain that Alexander was wary of entrusting control over this special country to a single person. Instead of a satrap Alexander appointed two governors (according to Arrian, 'nomarchs'), Doloaspis and Petisis (either both of them were Egyptians or it may be that only Petisis was Egyptian, whilst Doloaspis might have been Persian). These persons were in charge of two parts of the country, these apparently coinciding with Upper and Lower Egypt. Although they were formally the highest officials in the country, their authority was most likely limited to civilian administration alone. This double governorship, however, did not last long. When Petisis asked to be released from his position, Doloaspis became the sole governor of the country. Military commands in Egypt were entrusted by Alexander to his officers, and it is they that actually exercised the real power there. But the king took steps to divide this power between several commanders, doubtless to prevent its dangerous accumulation by a single man. Peucestas and Balacrus were placed in charge of the two main groups of the occupation forces, located probably in Upper and Lower Egypt. Polemon was given command of the Nile flotilla. The most important Egyptian fortresses, Memphis and Pelusium, were given into the charge of Alexander's commandants Pantaleon and Polemon. Likewise, a separate command was established for the mercenary troops: the king appointed Lycidas the Aetolian as their commander, Eugnostus as secretary (*grammateus*) and Aeschylus and Ephippus as overseers (*episkopoi*). The neighbouring areas of 'Libya' and 'Arabia around Heroopolis' were transformed by Alexander into two special administrative districts. They were placed under Apollonius and Cleomenes of Naucratis respectively. Simultaneously, Cleomenes was put at the head of the financial administration of the whole of Egypt, the administration of which accordingly became separate too. Above all, he was responsible for collecting tribute from the nomarchs that were ordered to exact it in a traditional manner at a local level (it appears that in this case the word 'nomarchs' was used by Arrian to denote not the two governors of Egypt but rather the heads of its traditional territorial divisions; Arrian *Anabasis* 3.5.2–3.5.6; cf. Curtius 4.8.4–4.8.5).[34]

---

[34] On the administration of Egypt under Alexander, see, in particular, Bosworth 1980b: 275–278; 1988a: 234; Huß 2001: 72–75; cf. Jacobs 1994: 58–63; Burstein 2008: 183–194.

Such functions, as well as some others he carried out in relation to finance (note that he discharged these responsibilities with great skill and even ingenuity) allowed Cleomenes to turn himself over time into the most influential person in the civilian administration of Egypt. Besides, the fact that he supervised the construction and peopling of Alexandria, that is the implementation of the king's 'personal project', greatly contributed to his power as well. Whether Cleomenes was officially nominated satrap of Egypt at the end of Alexander's reign or whether he merely occupied a leading position there in effect, is unclear.[35]

In conclusion, although Alexander borrowed the system of regional administration from the Achaemenids, he introduced changes to it, adapting it to the new circumstances. Alexander's actions in the administrative sphere were not aimed at the realization of some abstract ideal. They were taken to meet the particular needs arising before him. At the same time, it is obvious that all the king's actions were in pursuit of one main goal: that of creating an effective administrative system for the imperial lands that would allow better control and exploitation of the subjugated peoples. Did Alexander succeed in achieving this goal? It appears that to a certain extent he did. At least, at the time of the king's death his power over the entire empire looked rather stable (though not without reservations). Undoubtedly, if Alexander had not died then, he would have continued to perfect the organization of the administration of his empire. But as fate would have it, the process of state-building was left unfinished by him.

Guide to Further Reading

The empire's administration is described to one extent or another, if not in all, in almost all general works on Alexander. At the same time, there are quite a few studies dealing more particularly with this issue or its aspects, including the regional/satrapal administration of Alexander's imperial lands in the East. Apart from the works indicated above in note 5, on the regional/satrapal governance under Alexander in general, see Badian 1965a: 170–182; Higgins 1980: 138–152; Anson 2013: 141–152. In addition, still useful, though now somewhat dated, are Julien 1914 and Lehmann-Haupt 1921. Of relevance to some separate satrapies of the empire are, in particular, Leuze 1935: 407–465; Bosworth 1974, 1981, 1983; Holt 1988: 52–86; Hammond 1996a; Panichi 2018; Lerner 2018;

---

[35] For Cleomenes, see for example Le Rider 1997: 71–93; Ladynin 2012: 92–98; Baynham 2015: 127–134. In addition, see the works indicated in the previous note.

Kholod 2021. For general information about each of Alexander's satraps, Berve 1926: ii and Heckel 2006 are indispensable. Also of note are the relevant sections in major commentaries on the principal historical texts cited above. Among such commentaries, those on Arrian's and Curtius' writings by Bosworth (1980b, 1995) and Atkinson (1980, 1994, 2009) are of particular importance. For the empire's financial administration, the article by Griffith 1964 remains valuable, although a number of his conclusions seem controversial. On Alexander's garrisons, see, for example, Thomas 1974.

19: Geography, Science and Knowledge of the World

Antonio Ignacio Molina Marín

According to many historians, Alexander was not so much a conqueror as a romantic explorer and a scientist.[1] The main aim of this article is to give a third view. In my opinion Alexander was neither an explorer and scientist nor a simple conqueror; he was rather a king, an Argead king, and the whole question of his approach to his expedition must be studied from the perspective of the ideological foundations upon which the legitimacy of the Macedonian kings' rule was based. In other words, to debate whether Alexander was either a conqueror or a scientist is an approach that is absolutely anachronistic, given that, as I hope to show, there was no clear distinction between the two in antiquity.

How Did the Greeks Conceive of the World Before and After Alexander?

The Greeks before Alexander had reached the conclusion that the world was not a flat disk but a sphere (Geus 2003: 232), and was divided into three continents. However, although the sphericalness of the earth was a commonly accepted fact, the Greeks never rejected the concept of the edges of the earth. As P. Janni (2000: 36) notes, a sphere is a finite space, but unlimited. Greek thinkers could never bring themselves to deny the existence of spaces or places that delimited the ends of the earth, because without periphery there could not be a centre, and the centre of *kosmos* was traditionally, of course, on Greek soil. Centre was an important element of Hellenic thought, because the term equated to civilization and culture. The superiority of the Greeks to other peoples was based on their central position in the *oikoumenē*, the inhabited world (Molina Marín 2011: 57).

---

[1] E.g. Bodson 1991: 130; Alvar 2000: 83–84. For the notion that he was rather a pragmatic king, see Kraft 1971.

Following on from this, the limits of civilization were identified not only by geographical features but also by monsters, which marked and guarded the boundaries between both realms, of the civilized and the uncivilized. In this view of the world, mythical and scientific schemes blended and coexisted. The mind of Alexander the Great is a real conundrum for us, but we have no reason to believe that his understanding of world space differed from this common conception. He thought that the world was spherical but also that it was limited and surrounded by the Ocean.

The Greeks' vision of the world was captured in their maps. However, a Greek map was not merely a scientific product, it was also considered a work of art. Indeed, the Greek word for a map was *pinax*, which actually meant 'picture'. Paradoxically, geometrical patterning and symmetry were common elements of artwork and maps alike. Greek maps were not merely representations of reality, they were also symbols of power.[2] Just as Phidias created images as they should be, Greek geographers shaped a world as they wished it to be. The map of a Greek cartographer aspires not only to represent reality objectively, but also to order and control the world he imagines. Concomitantly, geography was never a pure science, because it was also a branch of literary endeavour.[3]

It is frequently said that after the fall of Persian Empire the world and science changed, and that Alexander played a significant role in this process. It is true that the Greek world knew Asia much better as a result of the conquest.[4] The new information allowed the intellectuals of Alexandria to write their books. However, neither Alexander nor his staff ever elaborated a new map of the world. The man who did this was Eratosthenes of Cyrene. He began his *Geographika* with a reference to Alexander's conquests (Strabo C47) and asserted that his work was a valuable contribution to the thought of his time, because the world had been expanded by Alexander. His claim has been accepted by many scholars.[5] However, the historians of Alexander's expedition are usually criticized for being over-dependent on earlier geographical traditions and on geographical themes established prior to the expedition,[6] which challenges the notion that it established new geographical and intellectual horizons.

---

[2] Arnaud 1983: 692 observes that there was a 'monopole impérial de la cartographie'.
[3] Nicolet 1991: 66; Romm 1992: 3; Molina Marín 2011: 18–21.
[4] Gerkhe 2015: 97: 'Alexander had not fundamentally changed the Greek vision of the world. Mentally, it was already directed towards the whole. But after his campaigns, infinitely more was known regarding many details.'
[5] Albaladejo Vivero 2005: 55; Bucciantini 2015a: 98.
[6] Pearson 1960: 13; Albaladejo Vivero 2005: 56; Bucciantini 2015a: 98.

Traditionally, ancient geographers and historians based their knowledge on their *autopsia*, that is direct observation in the field, but Eratosthenes was not a traveller and he therefore depended on other authors for all his data. Thus, his affirmation of the scientific benefits of the Macedonian conquest of Asia could be his way of disguising his lack of empirical knowledge. Many years afterwards, Strabo also adopted Eratosthenes' point of view about the connection between military and geographical progress (Strabo C14). The reasoning was identical: he wanted to surpass Eratosthenes by correcting him (*diorthosis*), and in order to do that he had to indicate that he had more data than his rival, this by virtue of the conquests of the Roman Empire. The connection of military conquests to the advancement of science was a *topos* that served to exalt an author's work over that of his rivals.

Curiously, Eratosthenes also censured the historians of Alexander because they changed the map of Asia in order to promote the Macedonian king's fame (Strabo C509, 689; Arrian *Anabasis* 5.3.1–5.3.4). Apparently, Alexander himself had no interest in mapping his domains or reproducing them faithfully as a geographer would do. However, he did commission surveyors, the bematists Diognetus and Baeton, to measure the distances travelled by the army in steps. It has generally been considered that the work of the bematists was a purely scientific and metrological work (Berve 1926 nos 99 and 198). However, in the fragments of their work that have been preserved they speak about fantastic creatures such as the Antipodes ('feet-turned-backwards') of Abarimon (Pliny *Natural History* 7.11; Aulus Gellius 9.4.6).

Everyone is aware that this decision was made for logistical reasons. However, there are also other explanations. A thing measured is a thing subjugated. The man who measures the world is the one who controls it, but that does not necessarily indicate a true desire for knowledge. We may compare this act of measurement with the claim that in Julius Caesar's time four men were ordered to travel around the world to measure it (Julius Honorius *Cosmographia* 1; Aethicus Ister *Cosmographia* 1a). Indeed, one of the most beautiful Greek myths tells that Zeus wanted to measure the surface of the world, and in order to do so released two eagles, one from the East, another from the West. Finally, the two birds met at Delphi (Pindar fr. 54 SM). Zeus is the lord of the world because he measures it; Alexander, son of Ammon-Zeus, could not be less than his divine father.

Was Alexander the Great an Intellectual and an Explorer?

Several passages of Plutarch could be considered as evidence of Alexander's interest in science (*Alexander* 7, 35, 41, 52–53, 57.5–57.9, 64–66). For Plutarch his thirst for knowledge was genuine and he assumes it to be the result of Aristotle's influence upon him.[7] Moreover, Plutarch presents him as a great reader (*Alexander* 8), although he and Ptolemy Chennus (*Strange History* 5 *apud* Photius *Bibliotheca* cod. 190, 151a) are the only sources to mention the readings of the Macedonian king. Nonetheless, it is a commonly accepted opinion among the Alexander historians that Alexander was an intellectual, a *philomathēs*, friend of wisdom. We find this view, for instance, projected by Onesicritus of Astypalaea, a student of Diogenes who represented Alexander as a philosopher in arms.[8] In this way Alexander became a philosopher who liked to speak to foreign sages, an explorer who wanted to see the end of the world with his own eyes (Gómez Espelosín 2010: 61). Like Plutarch, modern scholars cannot resist the temptation to link the student Alexander with his mentor Aristotle. Some scholars build on this relationship to assume that Alexander would have read almost all of the significant Greek writers: Hesiod, Hecataeus, Scylax, Pindar, Herodotus, Ctesias, Hippocrates, Xenophon, Plato and Isocrates (cf. Molina Marín 2022). The advocates of this view of Alexander maintain that he was truly interested in every field of knowledge. Although it is generally thought that he never wrote anything, letters aside, some researchers have actually attributed the creation of theatrical plays to him.[9] If all these theories were true, Alexander could be worthy indeed of the epithet 'Great', given that he read more Greek writers even than most Classical philologists do. No doubt Alexander's education was above average, but this does not entail that he read everything.

It is also held that Aristotle inculcated in Alexander a deep longing for knowledge and the desire to go beyond the unknown, a desire encapsulated in the application of the word *pothos* to the Macedonian king. *Pothos* is mentioned by Aristotle in the *Hymn to Virtue* he dedicated to Hermias of Atarneus and composed during his stay in Macedonia. We do not know the precise significance of this word, but it is considered indicative of Alexander's true nature as an explorer. However, although

---

[7] Pédech 1980: 135; Bosworth 1988a: 21; Stoneman 1997: 14; Alvar 2000: 84.
[8] Onesicritus *FGrH / BNJ* 134 F 17a = Strabo C715-16: ἐν ὅπλοις φιλοσοφοῦντα.
[9] Stoneman 2015: 29: 'Alexander was a great reader, and perhaps even an author.'

Ehrenberg (1938: 56) argued that Alexander was the only Macedonian to use this word, we find his grandmother Eurydice already using it in an inscription famously recorded by Plutarch (*Moralia* 14 b–14c). The term *pothos* is also linked to Heracles, the supposed ancestor of the Royal Macedonian house, and also has various meanings associated with Alexander's emulation of and rivalry with his mythical ancestors (Molina Marín 2017: 22–23). It cannot, therefore, be regarded simply as signifying a longing for knowledge.

Nonetheless, Aristotle undoubtedly did have some impact on Alexander's mental image of the world, the image upon which his plans for conquest were contingent. As Tarn (1948: ii.369) once said, 'he had Aristotle's geography in his head'. Aristotle emphasized the importance of maps in his works (*Rhetorica* 1360a, 33–35; cf. *Meteorologica* 362b, 12–15), and it is assumed that he knew and made use of Eudoxus' map (Jacob 2008: 125). The only trace of an Aristotelean map, or at least one that can be called such, is to be found in a diagram that adheres closely to Ephorus of Cyme's scheme, in that it uses the winds to locate the cardinal points and places Greece in the centre (*Meteorologica* 363a; Molina Marín 2011: 116). However, it is not clear whether Aristotle considered geographical charts as the most suitable tool for the training of a general and a king, or, accordingly, how often actual maps (*gēs periodoi*) were present during Alexander's lessons at Mieza. Nonetheless, we may be confident that Aristotle created at least a mental map in Alexander's mind, that is to say, a personal worldview on the basis of which the king designed his plans for conquest, and that this must have been very similar to Aristotle's diagram.

The world that the philosopher taught to his most famous student was spherical, with three continents (Europe, Asia and Africa) and several inner seas (*Meteorologica* 354a, 1–5). Unlike the bematists, Aristotle did not see the mountain ranges that extended from the Taurus to the Caucasus as a continuous whole (Arrian *Anabasis* 5.5.3; *Indica* 2.1–2.3, 3.3–3.4). He considered that the Indus was the greatest river of Asia (later on, the same would be thought of the Ganges). He held that one of the arms of the Araxes (Aras?) was the Tanaïs (Don), which ultimately led to Alexander's presumption that the Jaxartes (Sir Daria) was the upper part of the Tanaïs. The presence of elephants in Africa and Asia led Aristotle to believe in a connection between the Red Sea and the Pillars of Hercules (*De caelo* 298a 10–15). Consequently, a leitmotiv of Alexander's campaign was a geographical hypothesis supported by zoological observation, the most famous case of which being the identification of the Nile with the Indus owing to the similarity of its flora (the lotus) and fauna (the crocodile).

In any case, the Macedonian king constantly had to redefine what he had learned from his mentor. In other words, Alexander ever compared Aristotle's worldview with the reality before his eyes. He was not a theorist like his teacher, but a man of action who based his knowledge on his autopsy, and this knowledge was crucial for him and his people, because he was the leader and guide of his army (Jacob 1991). It was always he that chose the route and road to follow, and for the Macedonians he was the ferryman into an unknown world.

Sovereign of the Four Regions: Alexander and the Boundaries of the Earth

The Macedonian mission had been completed with the death of Darius III in summer of 330 BC. Although the war was over, Alexander then took the decision to invade India. The explanation given by scholars is usually romantic, and is bound up with the idea of Alexander as an explorer rather than a conqueror (Stoneman 2019: 37) and his relationship with the so-called edges of the earth. According to Adams (2007a: 34) 'Alexander can be seen as a "frontiersman" in the classical sense.' To many scholars his campaign in India was due only to his desire to see the Ocean that defined the limits of the world in Greek geographical thought.

Aristotle considered that the Ocean was very close to 'Parnassus' (i.e. the Taurus–Hindu Kush ranges), unlike Herodotus, who had talked about desert lands in those places (Herodotus 3.98). When we think of the search that Alexander carried out for the Ocean, we must bear it in mind that, thanks to the teachings of his mentor, he believed it to be very close to India. Accordingly, he would probably not have driven his troops so far if he had had a true idea of the distances that separated him from his target (cf. Gómez Espelosín 2014, 2017).

It seems certain that Alexander thought that he was close to the end of the world. This is confirmed by the name given to his new foundation, Alexandria Eschate ('Alexandria the Furthest'). Roman authors considered Alexander's search for the Ocean as evidence of his longing for conquering everything: 'Let Alexander be content with having conquered that portion of the world where the sun is content to shine ... Beyond everything is the Ocean, beyond the Ocean nothing' (Seneca *Suasoriae* 1, trans. Edward 1928). In a similar context

Curtius says that Alexander had 'embraced the infinite in his mind' (*animo infinita complexus*, 10.1.17).

The arrival of the Macedonians at the Hyphasis River, the last tributary of the Indus to the east, resulted in a confrontation between the king and his army (Plutarch *Alexander* 62.2–62.6; Justin 12.8.10–12.8.11; Diodorus 17.94.3–17.94.5; Arrian *Anabasis* 5.25.3–5.27.9; Curtius 9.3.3–9.3.5). The reason was the army's refusal to cross the river. Among their anxieties was the belief that they were coming to an unknown land, to another world. Faced with this situation, tired and scared, the Macedonians refused to continue the advance, and this led to a dialogue between the educated king and an army scared by the old stories about the edges of the world. A similar incident had occurred during an eclipse, when the king had had to calm his army (Curtius 4.10.5–4.10.6). In his speech Alexander talks about his expansion plans, namely to cross the Hyphasis and Ganges rivers and to sail around the Ocean from the Persian Gulf to Libya, and from there as far as the Pillars of Hercules, so that 'to this empire there will be no boundaries, but what the god has made for the whole world' (Arrian *Anabasis* 5.26). As Bosworth has shown, this speech is a reworking.[10] It is impossible that Alexander had so detailed and precise a geographical conception, given that he thought the Caspian was a gulf, not a landlocked sea. We do not even know whether he had heard of the Ganges.[11] We see once again how the geographical boundaries are used by our sources to create the image of a supreme conqueror. But at any rate, his soldiers did not share Alexander's geographical knowledge. In the speech given to him by Curtius, Coenus confesses his fear at entering another world (*alius orbis*): '*In alium orbem paras ire et Indiam quaeris Indis quoque ignotam*' (Curtius 9.3.8). Although the Macedonian soldiers were an essential element in the conquest of Asia, they could not be considered as conquerors on a par with their king, because, unlike Alexander, they never dominated and knew the space. The true conqueror is the one that does not allow himself to be dominated by the fear of geographical features.

In these circumstances, Alexander brought an end to the expedition, building altars that marked the limit of his empire. This marked the true conclusion of the expedition, since it was from this point that the return began. According to Plutarch (*Alexander* 66.2), Alexander asked the gods that no one should cross beyond the limits of his empire.

---

[10] Bosworth 1988b: 133: 'But there is nothing in the context that is demonstrably not Arrian's invention, while there are demonstrable anachronisms and a considerable body of material adopted from other parts of the work.'

[11] Bosworth 1996b: 186.

Given this context, the question that arises is this: Where did Alexander the Great plan to stop? Even he must have put a limit on his craving for glory. Reaching the eastern Ocean is an accomplishment the symbolism of which escapes us. Possibly, in this way, his empire took on a universal quality, because it extended from one part of the world to another. He emulated other rulers of the ancient world who had washed their weapons in the sea (e.g. Sargon). In other words, perhaps he was following the Eastern tradition that associated the borders of empire with the limits of the world (Miltner 1952: 549), and thus became the new lord of the four regions of the *oikoumenē*.

In any case, it seems clear that at that time Asia was equated with the domains of the Achaemenid Empire, and consequently any project of conquest in this direction implied the possibility of reaching such extremes (Gómez Espelosín 2017: 372). In other words, it is very probable that Alexander considered India as a part of the Persian Empire (cf. Badian 1998), and therefore a territory that should be included among his domains.

Heroes who reached the limits did so with the help of the gods, and Alexander himself was no exception. Strabo (C170) says that Alexander raised altars at the limits of his expedition in imitation of Heracles and Dionysus. These altars can be related to the Pillars of Heracles and understood to signal that Alexander had equalled Heracles' exploits.

The voyages of exploration that Alexander commissioned shortly before his death[12] and the so-called last plans have led many ancient and modern authors to suppose that Alexander wanted to dominate the entire world (Curtius 10.1.17–10.1.18; Arrian, *Anabasis* 7.1.2–7.1.3). Indeed Aristobulus says that Alexander wished to be the master of everything (πάντων εἶναι κύριον: *FGrH* / *BNJ* 139 F56 = Strabo C741). Furthermore, we must not forget that many of these expeditions were commissioned precisely in order to gain information about Arabia, and, as Högemann (1985) has conclusively argued, the king of Babylon traditionally had the mission of dealing with the Arabian tribes. Nevertheless, this view conflicts with other passages that affirm that Alexander refused the proposal of Pharasmenes that he should conquer the territories bordering on Chorasmia (e.g. Arrian *Anabasis* 4.15.4). This last claim is incompatible with the aspiration to create a universal empire. But the issue cannot be resolved. Arrian (*Anabasis* 7.14) was correct when he said that no one could be sure of what Alexander's plans were.

---

[12] 'Heraclides': Arrian *Anabasis* 7.16.1–7.16.2; 'Androsthenes': Arrian *Anabasis* 7.20.7; Strabo C765; 'Archias': Arrian *Anabasis* 7.20.7; 'Hieron's: Arrian *Anabasis* 7.20.7, *Indica* 18.9; 'Anaxicratides': Strabo C767.

Lord of Animals: Zoology

During their campaign the Macedonians had the opportunity to encounter a large number of creatures, some real, others fantastic, but since what we are pursuing here is science and not paradoxography, we will focus on the former: poisonous serpents (Arrian *Indica* 15.11), crocodiles (Curtius 8.9.9), the dogs of India (Curtius 9.1.31– 9.1.34), lions (Curtius 8.1.14–8.1.15), tigers (Curtius 9.8.2), oxen (Arrian *Anabasis* 4.25.4), rhinoceroses (Curtius 8.9.17, 9.1.5), hippopotamuses (Arrian *Indica* 6.8), camels (Curtius 5.2.10), baleens (Arrian *Indica* 30.1– 30.1.9, 39.4–39.5), parrots (Arrian *Indica* 15.8–15.9), apes (Arrian *Indica* 15.10) and elephants (Arrian *Anabasis* 4.30.8) powerfully attracted the attention of Alexander historians. Often, we are told how other rulers gave Alexander some of these animals as a present or how he himself tried to collect them. For many scholars this has been evidence for the curiosity of Aristotle's student and his interest in the animal world. According to Pliny, the Macedonian king would have sent some of these species to his teacher in order to study them, which gave Aristotle the opportunity to dissect an elephant and write his treatises on zoology:

> When Alexander the Great became inflamed with a desire to learn the nature of the animal world, and assigned this pursuit to Aristotle, a man who excelled in every field of study, then it was ordered to the many thousands of men in the territory of all Asia and Greece to obey him: All those to whom hunting, birding, and fishing gave sustenance, and all who were in charge of pens, flocks, beehives, fishponds, and aviaries, were not to let any living thing escape his notice. And by questioning these men he laid the foundations for those nearly fifty brilliant volumes on biology.
> Pliny *Natural History* 8.17.44

Authors such as Jaeger advocated this notion,[13] but today we know that the relevant works of Aristotle were published before he became Alexander's teacher, during his stay in Asia Minor.[14] Romm has rejected the veracity of this text, since the objective is to make

---

[13] Jaeger 1948: 330: 'It can scarcely be true, as has sometimes been asserted, that the *History of Animals* would be conceivable apart from the discoveries made by Alexander's expedition.'
[14] Lee 1948: 61 highlights that most of Aristotle's descriptions derive from his stay in Assos and Mytilene.

Alexander the patron of his teacher's investigations.[15] It has also been denied that Aristotle could have dissected an Indian elephant, given that he did not know the difference in size between an Indian one and an African one.[16] Besides, Aristotle expressed annoyance that his nephew Callisthenes had not sent him scientific information as he had promised. This could therefore be taken as evidence that there was no elaborate organization at work between Alexander and Lyceum (Fraser 1994: 175).

The presence or absence of these animals enabled the Macedonians to establish original geographical theories (albeit erroneous ones). One such theory held, as we have seen, that the Nile and the Indus were the same river owing to the presence of crocodiles.

However, kings could collect animals for purposes that had nothing to do with science. The dogs of India were highly esteemed for their hunting skills. Elephants became the favourite weapon of war for the Hellenistic kings, Alexander being one of the first to collect large contingents of the pachyderms (Arrian *Anabasis* 3.8.6; Diodorus 17.89.2). We know that he also kept lions as pets (Plutarch *Alexander* 73.6–73.7): this animal was a symbol of power and majesty for both Greeks and Persians. Alonso Troncoso (2013: 255) has shown that the monarch's taming of a wild animal was advertised as his power over the forces of nature. The taming of Bucephalas by Alexander and a wild bull by Seleucus are further examples of this gesture. Ptolemy I minted coins on which Alexander appeared in a chariot drawn by four elephants. Certainly, the animals were not merely a way of representing the monarch's curiosity and his thirst for knowledge; they were also a means of demonstrating his control over the forces of nature.

Royal Gardener: Flora

The expedition was a great incentive for botany. New species such as the banyan or *Ficus Bengalensis* (Diodorus 17.90.5; Pliny *Natural History* 7.21, 12.22–12.23; Curtius 9.1.10) were studied by the Alexander historians. Proof of this progress was the publication of Theophrastus' studies on plants. But was the work of Theophrastus

---

[15] Romm 1992: 108: 'But what Strabo had tried to do by linking Alexander with Patrocles, Pliny here accomplishes even more effectively by attaching Alexander to a collaborator of unimpeachable authority: Aristotle himself. In this way he gives new substance to the vision of Alexander's conquest of the East as a scientific crusade.'

[16] Romm 1989: 574; Bigwood 1993: 550.

written because of the direct contribution of Alexander the Great? Hugo Bretzl (1903) concluded that it was, more than a century ago. In his opinion, Theophrastus would not have been able to write his studies on botany if the Macedonians had not conquered Asia and sent the plant species they were finding along the way to the Lyceum. Bretzl based his theory both on the common points between Theophrastus and the Alexander historians and on the profound scientific differences in the information they supply. This last was to be explained by Theophrastus' dependence upon a report that incorporated all the data conserved on the expedition (Strabo C69); this was why, according to Bretzl, he does not quote Alexander's historians. However, Theophrastus does indeed quote one of the expedition's historians, Androsthenes of Thasos (*Causes of Plants* 2.5.5 = Androsthenes *FGrH* / *BNJ* 711 F3) and, in the opinion of Fraser (1994: 177), he must have listened to the accounts of the expedition's veteran soldiers. Oral sources could have included tales to the effect that Alexander prohibited his soldiers from eating certain types of fruit because they caused diarrhoea (Theophrastus *History of Plants* 4.4.5,12, 8.4.5). These stories are not found in any of our other sources, and for this reason they could have derived from soldiers returning to Greece.

On the one hand, knowledge of plants was vital for a contingent of thousands of men and animals that was always searching for food and supplies,[17] devouring everything in its path (cf. Arrian *Anabasis* 4.21.10, *Indica* 19.7; Curtius 6.4.21, 6.19, 9.9.8). On the other hand, we must not forget that Alexander had knowledge of medicine (Plutarch *Alexander* 8.1, 41.5–41.8). It has always been said that he learned it from his teacher Aristotle (Plutarch *Alexander* 8.1; Kern 1938: 43), but in recent years it has been argued that Alexander's interest in medicine needs to be explained rather through his imitation of Achilles. Apparently, it was normal for members of the Aeacid royal house to have some healing skills.[18] Likewise, the Argead kings seem to have taken a great interest in physicians. We can see this, for example, in Perdiccas II's patronage of the most famous physician of antiquity, Hippocrates of Cos (*Suda* s.v. Ἱπποκράτης).[19] Amitay (2010) has claimed that Alexander could have travelled to Jerusalem owing to his personal interest in balsam, a medicinal plant typically found in this zone. A knowledge of plants

---

[17] On the different kind of plants mentioned by the Alexander historians, cf. Pédech 1980: 148–151.
[18] Plutarch *Pyrrhus* 3; cf. Antela Bernárdez 2019.
[19] Antela Bernárdez and Sierra Martin 2018: 38.

and their qualities was in the interest of a king who wanted to present himself to his subjects as a healer king, almost as a thaumaturge.

Moreover, we know that balsam used to be planted in royal gardens, *paradeisoi*. A *paradeisos* was an artificial enclosure, an architectural space for plants, a luminous and lush place, the existence of which symbolized the power of the king as creator and universal ruler (in Greek, *kosmokratōr*). This was the role played by the Persian *paradeisoi* before the conquest. It was not uncommon for the kings of Mesopotamia to be projected as gardeners. We must not forget that when Hephaestion chose Abdalonymus as king of Sidon, he was, we are told, in a garden.[20] Harpalus is said to have made many attempts to adapt species from different climatic regions to other places (Theophrastus *Historia plantarum* 4.4.1). Libanius relates that Seleucus planted cypresses at Daphne, following, possibly, in the footsteps of Heracles (Ogden 2017b: 149–150): '... Soon the grove was flourishing' (*Orations* 2.94–8). Planting a foreign species and getting it to germinate was a beautiful metaphor for the establishment of power, and a symbol that the gods endorsed the monarch's legitimacy. In a word, a garden was a symbol of conquest and power, and only a true king could create such a thing.

Conclusion

As this study has shown, a synergy obtained between geographical knowledge and conquest, given that the former was an essential to military campaigns, while the campaigns expanded geographical data. In other words, without scientific knowledge there was no conquest; without conquest there was no progress in Greek science. Therefore, a general often became a geographer or explorer.

Alexander was no exception. Alexander the explorer was only one aspect of Alexander the conqueror, a consequence rather than a cause. Alexander was not an explorer *strictu sensu*, but rather a conqueror of space. His longing to dominate everything led him to try to understand the geographical space. This is evidenced in the mutiny of Opis: Alexander was not alarmed by the stories about the end of the world, because of his understanding of geography: his knowledge rendered him the one true conqueror of Asia, in distinction to his Macedonians

---

[20] Burstein 2007: 148, for the motif of the gardener-king being widespread in Mesopotamia. Ctesias may have made it known in the Greek world and Clitarchus may have incorporated it into the story of Abdalonymus of Sidon.

soldiers. Evidence of what we say is to be found in the encounter between the young Alexander and the Persian ambassadors:

> He once entertained the envoys from the Persian king who came during Philip's absence, and associated with them freely. He won upon them by his friendliness, and by asking no childish or trivial questions, but by enquiring about the length of the roads and the character of the journey into the interior, about the king himself, what sort of a warrior he was, and what the prowess and might of the Persians. The envoys were therefore astonished and regarded the much-talked-of ability of Philip as nothing compared with his son's eager disposition to do great things.
> Plutarch *Alexander* 5.1 (Perrin 1919 trans.)

This story demonstrates that Alexander was not only interested in the geography of the Persian Empire, but also that he wanted to know it in order to conquer it. His thirst for knowledge was very much subordinate to his eagerness for glory.

A conclusion cannot be avoided: Alexander wanted to know the *kosmos* in order to make it easier to conquer. Alexander the explorer was another facet of the Argead king that wished to surpass his mythical models, and the way to do that was not through reading and writing, but by the spear.

Guide to Further Reading

For Alexander as an explorer and a man of science, see Bodson 1991 and Alvar 2000. Fraser 1994 and Molina Marín 2011 offer more critical views. Favourable assessments of Alexander's contribution to geography are supplied by Gehrke 2015 and a series of publications by Gómez Espelosín: 2010, 2014, 2017, 2023, with the last being the most exhaustive monograph on the subject to date. Two important general studies on the Alexander historians are Pearson 1960 and Pédech 1980. Useful for zoological and botanical issues are the works of Bretzl 1903; Bigwood 1993; Fraser 1994; and Romm 1992.

Part III

The Historical and Biographical Tradition

20: Arrian's Alexander

Daniel W. Leon

Introduction: Authorship and Source Criticism

No ancient author has extended as much influence over modern studies of Alexander's life as Arrian. There is a nearly universal consensus that the quality of Arrian's work surpasses that of other extant accounts and a similar conclusion seems to have been reached in antiquity. The flurry of new analytical literature on Alexander that appeared in the late first and early second centuries ended when Arrian's work began to circulate, most likely in the 120s.[1] Ancient readers admired the depth of his erudition and medieval critics appreciated the quality of his writing so much that one declared Arrian superior even to many Classical historians, high praise from an intellectual community devoted to the active creation of a canon.[2] Still, modern readers have generally been less impressed by Arrian's intellect and literary ability, possibly as a result of the now-debunked view that Greek literature in the Imperial Period was of a lower quality than in earlier periods.[3] Focus has instead fallen on Arrian's use of sources. Because Arrian based his Alexander material on

---

[1] Late-first to early-second-century treatments of Alexander include Dio's *Kingship Orations*, Curtius' *Histories of Alexander the Great*, Plutarch's biography and orations *On the Fortune or Virtue of Alexander*, and possibly Justin's epitome of Pompeius Trogus. For the disputed date of Justin, see Yardley and Heckel 1997: 8–13. The little-known Amyntianus (*FGrH / BNJ* 150) attempted to rival Arrian in the later second century but was unsuccessful; his history survives only in Photius' brief and harsh summary (*Bibliotheca* cod. 131). For the date of the *Anabasis*, see Leon 2021: 115–121; cf. Leroy 2022.

[2] Lucian *Alexander* 2 calls Arrian 'a man among the most prominent Romans and someone who spent his whole life in learning' (ἀνὴρ Ῥωμαίων ἐν τοῖς πρώτοις καὶ παιδείᾳ παρ' ὅλον τὸν βίον συγγενόμενος). Photius *Bibliotheca* cod. 92 says that anyone comparing him to Classical authors 'could see that even many of the ancients were his inferiors in composition' (πολλοὺς καὶ τῶν ἀρχαίων ἴδοι τῆς αὐτοῦ τάξεως ἱσταμένους ταπεινότερον) and a bit earlier says, 'the man is second to none of those writing history best' (ἔστι μὲν ὁ ἀνὴρ οὐδενὸς τῶν ἄριστα συνταξαμένων ἱστορίας δεύτερος.).

[3] For evolving scholarly views of literature in this period with a focus on historiography, see Asirvatham 2017.

eyewitness accounts, scholars have perceived an attractively low level of interference between historical events and themselves.[4]

Source criticism has therefore dominated the study of Arrian's work, often to the point of ignoring Arrian's own contributions to the tradition in which he was working. Many scholars have instead used his work to pursue the goal of reconstructing the lost Hellenistic histories upon which he based his accounts.[5] The characters of the reconstructed histories, in turn, have been used to illuminate parts of Arrian's narrative where he makes no explicit reference to his sources. This is a dangerously circular process, particularly in the case of Ptolemy, whose fragments are drawn almost exclusively from quotations in Arrian's *Anabasis*. In a real sense, the only Ptolemy we know is the Ptolemy Arrian wants us to know, which makes it next to impossible to discuss Arrian's adaptation of the 'original version'.[6] What is more, Arrian repeatedly demonstrates his awareness that eyewitnesses – including his preferred sources – manipulated traditions for their own purposes, and he declares that a central part of his mission is to correct the falsehoods that have entered the tradition in this way.[7] As a result, it is important to devote more attention to elucidating the logic of the coherent texts that survive.

Views of Arrian's relationship to his sources have evolved considerably in the past 100 years. Whereas earlier scholarship tended to see Arrian primarily as a conduit of information, over time it has become evident that his interventions were extensive.[8] Recent studies of Arrian have built

---

[4] Primarily Ptolemy and Aristobulus for the *Anabasis* and Nearchus for the *Indica*. All three campaigned with Alexander and so had direct access to the events they described. Compare the remarks of Liotsakis 2019a: 1–8.

[5] The two most recent commentaries on Arrian's *Anabasis*, Bosworth 1980b and 1995 and Sisti and Zambrini 2001–2004 apply source critical methods on nearly every page.

[6] Upwards of 80 per cent of the fragments of Ptolemy come from Arrian, although some are repeated in other sources. See Howe's commentary in *BNJ* for details (2018b). In cases where we have an external corrective, the character of Ptolemy's history does not seem to be what we would expect from Arrian, that is, entirely consumed with military matters. For example, Pliny the Elder draws on Ptolemy's apparently extensive discussion of botany (*FGrH / BNJ* 138 T 2 = Pliny *NH* 1.12.13). Apart from this reference in Pliny, the only other uses of Ptolemy's history are brief geographical notices (FF 5 and 31–33) and one short discussion of a cultural tradition (F 11). It is impossible to judge the surrounding context but Ptolemy's evident interest in geography, botany and culture suggests a more comprehensive approach than what we see in Arrian's use of him.

[7] His scathing critique of Callisthenes (*Anabasis* 4.10.1–4.10.2) is the best demonstration, for which see Leon 2021: 27–32. For his comments on inexplicable disagreements between Ptolemy and Aristobulus, see *Anabasis* 3.4.4, 4.3.5, 4.14.3, and 5.20.2. Truth-seeking is of course a traditional goal of historical authors, but traditional need not mean disingenuous and different authors approach this goal through different methods which must be carefully observed; cf. Asirvatham 2017: 479–482.

[8] Kornemann 1935 treats the *Anabasis* largely as a verbatim transcript of Ptolemy. Montgomery 1965: 162–233 argued that Arrian was somewhat independent of his sources. Bosworth 1988b

on this realization and shown large-scale elements of compositional design that could never have arisen by chance if Arrian were merely pulling chunks of his narrative fully formed from earlier histories.[9] It is now clear that Arrian's studies of Alexander's life make arguments that must be understood on their own terms. The rest of this chapter will demonstrate how some of those arguments work and lay out a few ways of approaching Arrian's characterization of Alexander. The longest of Arrian's works on Alexander, the *Anabasis*, will form the core of my discussion, but I will touch briefly on other works that illuminate Arrian's vision. As we will see, Arrian was especially interested in exploring the relationship between an individual's innate abilities and the exterior circumstances that constrain or nourish those abilities.

The Structure of the *Anabasis*

To understand how Arrian presents Alexander in the *Anabasis*, it is necessary first to come to grips with how the character of the narrative itself changes over the course of the work. While Arrian has often been seen as an encomiast of Alexander, there is a strong strain of criticism that runs through the history, especially in the last three books. Part of what makes the *Anabasis* interesting is its willingness to confront Alexander's humanity, 'warts and all'. Still, the design of the work conceals the more troubling aspects of Alexander's character in some segments while highlighting them in others, and sorting out the reasons for this practice illuminates the argument Arrian was trying to make.

The *Anabasis* falls into two unequal halves devoted to distinct phases of Alexander's career. In the earlier half, Arrian presents Alexander as a unifier of the Greeks and an avenging hero bent on the destruction of the Persian Empire. Alexander's childhood and education, his troubled relationship with his father, rumours of his involvement in Philip's death and his uneven record of diplomacy after taking the throne all go unmentioned. Arrian goes out of his way to submerge behaviour and circumstances that would disturb his initial characterization. For example, the destruction of Thebes was a famously brutal power move designed to intimidate those *poleis* inclined to resist Alexander's authority, but Arrian presents it as a tragic accident brought about by Theban intransigence and the mistakes of one of Alexander's

demonstrates Arrian's active adaptation of source material and develops a sophisticated methodology for undoing it.
[9] Burliga 2013: 104–128, Liotsakis 2019a: 14–80 and Leon 2021: 75–84, 105–108; cf. Leon 2019.

subordinate officers (*Anabasis* 1.7.4–9.10). Through such means Arrian establishes a straightforwardly laudatory (and somewhat boring) portrait of Alexander to begin the work.

The second half of the *Anabasis* introduces a more nuanced character as Arrian begins to explore the moral implications of Alexander's behaviour. Opinions differ on precisely where the change takes place, but all agree that Arrian's long digression covering several of Alexander's most infamous actions (*Anabasis* 4.7.4–4.14.4) plays an important role in dividing the narrative.[10] After this point, Arrian criticizes Alexander more freely and more often. The shift from a textbook Panhellenic hero to a complicated historical personage in need of more rigorous analysis helps Arrian contextualize Alexander's notoriously erratic behaviour so that it becomes clear how much change (political, financial, geographical, personal) he experienced over the course of his short life. As Alexander's circumstances grow more complex, the simple motivations of his early career no longer suffice to explain the course of events. His growth as a person arises in response to challenges he did not anticipate and Arrian uses these learning experiences as a way to dramatize what is useful about studying history for those of his readers who consider themselves agents of historical change. Alexander, in turn, becomes a case study in numerous difficult historical problems pertaining to issues of both politics and intellectual culture current in Arrian's own time.

Development and Change in the Narrative

The shift discussed above has numerous demonstrable effects on the narrative that provoke sophisticated questions about Alexander's character. Arrian often marks these questions through the technique of narrative patterning, a device borrowed from Herodotus.[11] Episodes from Alexander's early career set up episodes later in his life by opening key analytical themes that will recur throughout the work. Through these patterned narratives, Arrian identifies changes in Alexander's

---

[10] Rightly noting that the digression occurs at the exact centre of the work and introduces themes that recur in the later books, Stadter 1980: 83 suggests that the digression itself is the pivot point. Liotsakis 2019a: 14–80 argues for an even sharper division between the two halves of the *Anabasis* occurring precisely at the break between the third and fourth books. My own view is that Arrian elaborates a more gradual transition beginning in the aftermath of Gaugamela (*Anabasis* 3.16.3–3.18.12) and continuing to the death of Spitamenes (*Anabasis*. 4.17.7), for which see Leon 2021: 69–84.

[11] For Herodotus and narrative patterning, the fundamental works are Immerwahr 1966 and Lateiner 1989: 163–186. For the use of this technique as a connection to Herodotus, see Leon 2019.

character that develop over time.[12] He is especially interested in how new geopolitical scenarios (such as his accession to the throne of Persia) pose challenges to established character traits.

A clear example of this technique centres on the theme of fame, which Arrian elaborates by repeatedly returning to the question of name recognition as it connects to Alexander's ambition. In a programmatic statement early in the *Anabasis*, Arrian claims that Alexander had not yet received his due measure of fame (*Anabasis* 1.12.2–1.12.5). However implausible this may seem, it is true that no 'standard' Alexander history existed when Arrian composed the *Anabasis*, and by linking his literary fortunes to this question of Alexander's fame Arrian sought to establish himself in that role. His prefatory remarks find their echo in the closing of the work when Arrian assesses the end-point of Alexander's career by saying that there was no one left in the world who had not frequently heard Alexander's name (*Anabasis* 7.30.2). With this concluding note, Arrian suggests that he has achieved the goal he set for himself in the first book while telling the story of Alexander's rise to fame. However, he has not simply asserted Alexander's success. Rather, he has made the argument in the narrative itself. Two episodes involving Alexander's reception of foreign embassies and narrated in parallel reveal the processes that led to Alexander's acquisition of fame.

Both episodes centre on the question of name recognition, and Arrian links them through parallel narration.[13] In so doing he foregrounds the growth of Alexander's fame between two divergent moments in his career. The embassies come from the Celts and the Romans, the former after the first campaign narrated in the *Anabasis*, the latter after the last. These moments present an obvious opportunity for comparison which Arrian exploits. In both cases, after a successful military campaign, non-Greek peoples who were not directly involved in the preceding events send embassies to Alexander. Arrian records these embassies in catalogue form but caps each one with an elaborate interaction between Alexander and the strongest of the ambassadors. Those interactions involve ethnographic investigations in which Alexander himself asks questions of the ambassadors.

---

[12] The nature of characterization in Greek literature has been the subject of a long debate and scholars have sometimes denied the possibility of true character development. De Temmerman and van Emde Boas 2017: 6–11 discuss a number of ways to approach this problem. McVey 2019: 2–8 gives a comprehensive history of scholarship on the question. At least in the case of Arrian, I hold with those who see character in Greek literature as something that develops and changes over time.

[13] The material on embassies appears in expanded form in a different context in Leon 2021: 51–57.

The concluding interviews explicitly measure the growth of Alexander's fame. Arrian tells us that Alexander asks the Celts what they feared most because he hopes that 'his own great name had reached the Celts and beyond' (*Anabasis* 1.4.7).[14] Alas for Alexander, it had not, and the Celts, who see no reason to fear him, respond by mentioning their fear of a falling sky, evidently a reflection of their religious beliefs.[15] Alexander, in turn, sends them away, disappointedly 'mumbling something about Celts being boastful' (*Anabasis* 1.4.8).[16] After his first set of impressive feats, Alexander's name had barely travelled beyond the Balkan Peninsula. By comparison to the vast stretches of territory he would later cover, this theatre of fame seems rather small and Arrian has thus defined a starting point for a change that would be fully realized later in the narrative.

The Roman embassy contrasts sharply both in the scope of the episode and the result. It is a part of a second series of embassies coming from the edges of the known world and the issue of name recognition appears again in inverted form. Here, everyone involved has clearly heard of Alexander but, Arrian tells us, some of their names were previously unknown to his company (*Anabasis* 7.15.4). The Romans come last and Alexander commends their virtues while predicting their future greatness. Arrian then lingers to discuss whether they really did send an embassy. To say that the Republic would willingly seek friendship from a foreign king runs counter to Roman ideology and although Arrian names two Greek historians as sources, he laments that he was not able to find a corroborating Roman account of the event. Arrian frequently uses uncertainties like this one to provoke active evaluative responses in his readers, and the effect here is particularly strong. Even if the event turns out to be fabricated, Arrian has given us reasons to pause and consider it as a real possibility. Only Alexander could make it seem plausible. In contrast to the Celtic episode in which an insignificant group treated Alexander dismissively, now we can legitimately wonder whether his fame was so great as to displace the cultural values of Rome's Republican elite. Alexander's ambition, evident already but unfulfilled in the Celtic episode, has finally achieved its goal.

There is a similar growth process involved in tracking Alexander's formal political position. Until the Battle of Gaugamela, Alexander's primary motivation in the narrative was a war of retribution against the Persian Empire in response to the invasions of 490 and 480/79, but once

---

[14] ἐλπίσας ὅτι μέγα ὄνομα τὸ αὑτοῦ καὶ ἐς Κελτοὺς καὶ ἔτι προσωτέρω ἥκει.
[15] Rankin 1987: 59–60, 252. [16] τοσοῦτον ὑπειπὼν ὅτι ἀλαζόνες Κελτοί εἰσιν.

he has defeated Darius that motivation disappears and must be replaced. Arrian is emphatic on this point when Alexander burns the palace at Persepolis. He explicitly denies that retribution could suffice as an explanation for Alexander's actions any longer (*Anabasis* 3.18.1–3.18.12). After this moment, Arrian develops a series of new motives for Alexander as his connections to Persian history grow ever more intertwined. An earlier adversarial relationship with the kings of Persia gradually gives way to the reality that Alexander must now rule as one of them. Arrian begins to frame his narrative with Persian exempla made famous to Greeks by Herodotus. Such exempla were widely accessible to Arrian's contemporary audience through their rhetorical training, itself largely dependent on Herodotus for the period of the Persian Wars.[17] We have already seen how Arrian uses Herodotean narrative techniques to make his point, and now he adds Herodotean content to complicate his presentation of Alexander's performance as a king.

Arrian calls attention to Persian exempla quite explicitly at times. He frequently does so in his own narrative voice, as when he compares Alexander's mutilation of Bessus to stereotypical behaviour of Persian and Median kings. According to Arrian, brutality was a standard part of kingship for Persians and Medes and so to be expected of their kings, but not of Alexander and so some change must have occurred (*Anabasis* 4.7.4). On other occasions, he attributes such comparisons to the historical actors themselves. Thus, in narrating Alexander's expedition into Scythia, Arrian includes a speech in which Alexander declares that he wishes to perform better than Darius I had when he failed to conquer the Scythians many years before (*Anabasis* 4.4.3). This is no casual reference, since Arrian is the only extant source to describe Alexander's invasion of Scythia as a failure. The mention of Darius, also unique to Arrian, aligns Alexander's actions in this short campaign with Darius' earlier and more extensive operation, encouraging a comparison with humiliating results for Alexander, who is forced by severe diarrhoea to end his expedition without achieving anything of value. In addition to this explicit comparison, Arrian weaves in subtle intertextual references to Herodotus' accounts of the expansionist reigns of Darius I and Cyrus, picking up on the earlier historian's interest in the greed and arrogance of powerful individuals.[18] In so doing, he illustrates that Alexander, like Darius I and Cyrus before him, struggles to understand the limits of his power. By drawing on exempla most familiar from the Persian parts of Herodotus' *Histories*, Arrian puts Alexander into

---

[17] Gibson 2004: 126–127.   [18] Leon 2019: 553–559.

a world Herodotus created and asks his readers to assess Alexander's role within it, thus reorienting his narrative following Alexander's accession to the Persian throne.

Through such elaborate engagements with Herodotus, Arrian moves Alexander into a new context that entails a more complex relationship with Persian history and thus a wider range of potential interpretations of his character. Alexander's paranoia and uncontrollable rage are more prominent in Arrian's account of the latter portion of his career, and the growing number of scandals and challenges to Alexander's authority thus appear to have a rational basis. Arrian deploys Greek stereotypes of Persian kings in order to argue that changing political circumstances such as those Alexander experienced can fundamentally alter a person's character. Arrian gives no explicit guidance as to how we should evaluate Alexander's career in light of such changes, however. By offering multiple perspectives, he urges readers to think through the full complexity of Alexander's life and times.

Arrian's focus on circumstance is important to his understanding of individual character. He allows for the possibility of change, whether for good or ill, as a person passes through different stages of life. In his final assessment of Darius, for example, he concentrates on things Darius could not control that led him to behave poorly in a leadership role (*Anabasis* 3.22.2–3.22.6). The timing of Alexander's invasion and a number of other factors hampered his development, although Arrian also maintains that he could potentially have grown into an even worse king. While Darius served largely as a foil for Alexander in the *Anabasis*, some of the same issues come into play in Arrian's final evaluation of his protagonist (*Anabasis* 7.28.1–7.30.3). His assessment is fundamentally positive, but he acknowledges that he has often criticized Alexander and cites Alexander's youth, preternatural success, and a series of bad advisers as mitigating factors. As such, changeable situations do not simply allow a person's character to show through but can alter its development in detectable ways. Alexander's circumstances changed dramatically and repeatedly throughout his life, resulting in a mercurial quality in the character that emerges from Arrian's narration.

Alexander the Philosopher?

Although Arrian is somewhat charitable to the folly of youth, his portrait of Alexander also includes a genuine struggle to learn from wiser people. The idea of Alexander as a philosopher king, popular in other accounts, is largely absent from Arrian's work and Arrian says next to nothing about Alexander's vaunted education. In fact, when Alexander interacts with philosophers in the *Anabasis,* he often comes across as a reluctant learner. This facet of Arrian's characterization of Alexander may owe something to Arrian's own interest in exploring the ideal of the good king. He frequently describes the problem of monarchs who listen to bad advice and ignore good advice, and he seems to have found in Alexander a congenial exemplum with which to explore the pitfalls of monarchy as a system of government.[19]

The best example of this flaw in Alexander's character occurs in the seventh book of the *Anabasis*. The book opens with a series of famous philosophical episodes, all of which raise the question of whether material gain and political power provide true benefits to a human being, two major themes of the book.[20] The episodes involve the ascetic philosophers in India who call Alexander's ambitions pointless (*Anabasis* 7.1.5–7.1.6), an earlier encounter with Diogenes the Cynic, who only wanted Alexander to get out of his light (*Anabasis* 7.2.1), and finally Alexander's attempt to enlist a philosopher into his entourage (*Anabasis* 7.2.2–7.3.6). Each episode in its way critiques Alexander's unquestioning pursuit of power, and Alexander ignores the lessons presented to him without ever offering a serious rebuttal. Arrian openly states that Alexander chose to ignore good advice because he was 'governed by renown' (*Anabasis* 7.2.2).[21] Through other people's perspectives on Alexander's goals and priorities, Arrian identifies a key point in understanding his subject. He was a terribly stubborn man who struggled to adapt when presented with sensible objections to his way of thinking. This feature simultaneously explains his ability to achieve seemingly impossible goals and his inability to consider the ramifications of his actions.

The most extensively treated episode records Alexander's efforts to recruit an Indian philosopher to travel with him. Plutarch (*Alexander* 65.1–65.4; 69.3–69.4) and Strabo (C714–C718) also give extended accounts of these events, but Arrian's version is unique in a number of important ways. First, while both Plutarch and Strabo stress that Alexander used Onesicritus and Nearchus as intermediaries to contact the philosophers, Arrian says that Alexander himself saw them (*Anabasis* 7.2.2). Second, Plutarch and especially Strabo emphasize the cultural

---

[19] See for example 2.6.4, 4.8.3, 4.9.8, and 7.29.1.
[20] Stadter 1980: 86–88; cf. Liotsakis 2019a: 139–143. On the difference between Arrian's account and other versions, see Muckensturm-Poulle 1998: 195–213.
[21] ἐκ δόξης ... ἐκρατεῖτο.

differences between Greeks and Indians and use them to explain why Alexander and his entourage found the philosophers so astounding, but Arrian does not. Instead, he casts their virtues in terms entirely familiar to Greek audiences, stressing issues of self-control and firmness of mind that were especially important in Arrian's lifetime. Finally, Plutarch and Strabo both refer to misunderstandings arising from language differences but Arrian never mentions the languages used for communication between the parties. Thus, although all three authors appear to have drawn from at least some of the same sources, Arrian's manipulation of this source material results in an account with greater immediacy and less exoticism than the other two while also furthering his characterization of Alexander as largely immune to the lessons of philosophy.

The point of Arrian's account becomes clear when he contrasts the two most famous of the Indian philosophers, Dandamis and Calanus. The contrast appears in Plutarch and Strabo as well, but Arrian's interventions again yield a unique result. For Plutarch, Dandamis is mild while Calanus is harsh and wise. For Strabo, Dandamis (whom he calls Mandanis) is noble while Calanus is servile. In both accounts the two men appear to operate without any clear hierarchy. In Arrian's version, Dandamis is presented as the leader of the philosophers (*Anabasis* 7.2.2) and so it makes sense that Alexander tries to recruit him first. Dandamis refuses, using words that are absent from Plutarch's and Strabo's versions but which pick up key themes of Arrian's history. When Arrian says that Dandamis does not desire (*pothein*) anything from Alexander, he echoes the recurring motif of Alexander's famous *pothos*, a quality that Dandamis does not share.[22] He also explicitly denies that Dandamis fears (*dedienai*) Alexander in any way. Ultimately Alexander is forced to concede that Dandamis was truly free (*Anabasis* 7.2.3–7.2.4). These two motivations, fear and benefit, appear in Arrian's prefatory remarks where he reminds his readers that such motivations can interfere with a historian's freedom to produce truthful accounts (*Anabasis* 1.praef.2). Other instances of fear and benefit in the *Anabasis* include Arrian's critique of Callisthenes (4.10.1–4.10.2) and his parallel narration of the Celtic and Roman embassies to Alexander discussed above (pp. 337-338). This accumulation of episodes shows that fear and benefit are thematically important qualities for Arrian as he examines Alexander's reign. In each of these episodes Arrian has used related terminology to emphasize the freedom of people who could easily have been overwhelmed by Alexander's power. The exchange with Dandamis includes

---

[22] On Alexander's *pothos*, see Brunt 1976–1983: 1.469–1.470 and Montgomery 1965: 191–217.

overt references to fear of death, thus tying this theme to Alexander's inability to overcome death, the central concern of the seventh book. Dandamis' lack of interest in Alexander's ambitions underscores the contrast between a fulfilling life of asceticism and the insatiable hunger for external approval that was forever driving Alexander. Alexander's acknowledgment of Dandamis' freedom shows the legitimacy and perhaps the supremacy of a way of life other than the one he has chosen. Stubborn as ever, Alexander acknowledges the lesson without accepting it and he seeks to enlist an inferior philosopher, Calanus, instead.

The sequel to this exchange is Alexander's successful recruitment of Calanus, whose actions must be understood in light of the backdrop established by Dandamis. There is a sort of dissonance involved in Arrian's story of Calanus, since he introduces him by saying that his own people viewed him as especially lacking in self-control (*hautou akratora*, *Anabasis* 7.2.4) but then immediately begins to narrate a tale of extraordinary feats in that very field of virtue. Calanus becomes suddenly ill but refuses to change anything about his daily routine (*diaita*), knowing that he would die. Unable to stop his friend's health declining, Alexander orders a celebration involving a massive funeral pyre prepared for Calanus' inevitable end (*Anabasis* 7.3.2). At this celebration Calanus climbs onto the pyre and allows himself to be burned to death as he remains calm and motionless (*Anabasis* 7.3.5). Calanus' ability to conceal or ignore pain involves plenty of self-control and, what is more, concealment of outward signs of vulnerability was especially important to Arrian's contemporary audience and so the story speaks directly to their values.[23] Calanus' rapidly declining health blatantly prefigures the illness Alexander himself will soon experience, and Arrian's concluding remarks show that he means this story to represent an ideal response:

> ταῦτα καὶ τοιαῦτα ὑπὲρ Καλάνου τοῦ Ἰνδοῦ ἱκανοὶ ἀναγεγράφασιν, οὐκ ἀχρεῖα πάντα ἐς ἀνθρώπους, ὅτῳ γνῶναι ἐπιμελές, [ὅτι] ὡς καρτερόν τέ ἐστι καὶ ἀνίκητον γνώμη ἀνθρωπίνη ὅ τι περ ἐθέλοι ἐξεργάσασθαι.

> Competent men have written these things and others like them about Calanus the Indian that are not entirely useless to humanity, not for anyone who wants to know that human will to accomplish whatever it may wish is a strong and invincible thing.
> (*Anabasis* 7.3.6)

---

[23] See especially Gleason 1995.

The emphasis on human will here is important because it explicitly forbids us from viewing Calanus' actions as superhuman or unattainable. His philosophical background was not so unlike anything that Arrian or his immediate readers would recognize and his virtues, likewise, are intelligible. Thus, the benefits of philosophical training, particularly in having a calm attitude towards death, become clear to readers even as it becomes equally clear that Alexander does not yet understand the lesson. Calanus' low standing in the eyes of his fellow philosophers shows that even his exemplary behaviour could be surpassed. Through the spectrum of Indian philosophers, Arrian has created a framework for evaluating Alexander's own self-control. He does not compare well.

Alexander's stubbornness led to both positive and negative results. His refusal to accept defeat allowed him to achieve seemingly impossible victories, as when he captured the Rock of Aornus through sheer force of will (*Anabasis* 4.28.1–4.30.4). Nevertheless, this same quality repeatedly imperilled Alexander's life and, because of his central position in his military and political system, his entire empire as well. For example, Arrian reports Alexander's rash actions among the Mallians (*Anabasis* 6.9.5–6.11.1) and includes the censure of a group of his highest-ranking friends, who feared for the empire in the event of his death (*Anabasis* 6.13.4). Significantly, Arrian adds the weight of his own authority to these criticisms, stating that Alexander was not strong enough to overcome the pleasure of battle (*Anabasis* 6.13.4). It is important to note that Arrian's complaint is about Alexander's self-indulgence and lack of strength, precisely the issues the Calanus episode explores. His pleasure is more important to him than his responsibilities as a ruler. For all that Arrian may have trusted Alexander to lead him into battle, it is an open question whether he would wish for Alexander as his king.

Thoughts from the *Discourses* and the *Indica*

While bearing in mind that authors approach problems differently in different genres and works, it would be short-sighted to limit our discussion entirely to the *Anabasis* when Arrian wrote so much about Alexander in other works. Here, two works in particular are relevant to us. The *Indica* is another extended historical narrative centred on Alexander's campaigns, although it focuses on a narrower set of events than the *Anabasis* and so offers an alternative perspective. The *Discourses of Epictetus* touch on Alexander several times and pick up on one of the key themes of the *Anabasis* discussed above: the relationship between political power and personal freedom.

To begin with the *Discourses*, Alexander appears four times.[24] All the references are brief but they share a common interest in defining the limits of Alexander's power. In each case Alexander appears as a prime example of a powerful person, and in each case his power is circumscribed as the anecdote plays out. Alexander gets angry because he does not understand why the will of the gods sometimes subverts his own (2.22.17), he tries unsuccessfully to force private individuals to act in accordance with his will (3.24.70, 2.13.24), and he takes on too much responsibility to be truly happy (3.22.92). These stories partake of the same characterization we saw in the *Anabasis*, where Alexander routinely fails to appreciate the lessons of philosophy and the importance of curbing his own strong will. He is not a deep thinker, however brilliant he may have been on the battlefield.

The Alexander of the *Indica* too shares important elements with the Alexander of the *Anabasis* but its different focus allows a complementary reading of Alexander's character to emerge. Whereas the *Anabasis* begins with a military narrative and follows Alexander closely for almost the entire text, the *Indica* opens with a long ethnography occupying nearly half the work. When it does shift to narration of Alexander's campaign, it chiefly follows the coastal voyage of Alexander's fleet, undertaken by Nearchus while Alexander was leading a disastrous march through the Gedrosian desert. Arrian is thus giving us a sideways look at Alexander's leadership abilities and relationship with his subjects by focalizing the narrative through a subordinate.

Arrian's presentation of Nearchus' journey displays a tension between Alexander's obvious talent as a military commander and his questionable priorities as someone responsible for thousands of other people's lives.[25] As he introduces the voyage, he highlights Alexander's judicious selection of capable officers and careful attention to logistical matters (*Indica* 18.1–19.9), leaving an unsurprising impression of military skill. As soon as the narrative shifts to Nearchus' perspective, however,

---

[24] *Epicteti dissertationes* 2.13.24, 2.22.17, 3.22.92, 3.24.70. Brunt 1977 and Burliga 2013: 80–103 reach opposite conclusions on the extent of Epictetus' influence over Arrian's historical outlook; cf. Mathéus 2022.

[25] Liotsakis 2019b reads this tension more charitably, arguing that Arrian has used it to create suspense for a successful mission that ultimately reflects well on Alexander's character. For the relationship of Nearchus to Alexander in the *Indica*, see Schunk 2019: 111–188.

Alexander's personal motivations come to the fore, specifically his desire for glory (*Indica* 20.1–20.2). Nearchus refuses special treatment and volunteers to lead the expedition, but his conversation with Alexander relates more to dispelling fear in the ranks than to the wisdom of the plan or the safety of the men. Much military genius follows, and the safe arrival of Alexander's fleet is clearly the result of Nearchus' capable discharging of his duties. In the *Indica*, as in the *Anabasis*, Alexander's greatest concern is for his own reputation while high-level subordinates like Nearchus are left to manage the human costs of his ambition.

Conclusion

Arrian's Alexander is difficult to pin down because Arrian has designed him that way. The complexity of the historical contexts to which Arrian repeatedly appeals while explaining his behaviour shows the importance of external factors in formulating a person's character. Alexander's choices in each phase of his life lead to new challenges. Sometimes he responds well and sometimes he does not. He is at his best when reacting in the moment, but often struggles to conceive of the long-term effects of his actions. Ultimately, Arrian's Alexander comes across as an impressive individual whose greatest faults lie in his failure to understand his responsibilities to other individuals. Haunted by an unquenchable thirst for glory and perhaps a little too happy to get blood on his hands, he presses at the boundaries of virtue and invites Arrian's readers to think seriously about whether Alexander's model of heroic leadership works in the real, complicated world in which they themselves live.

Guide to Further Reading

Studies of Arrian's work have proliferated in the past ten years, resulting in a wealth of resources for exploring his literary output. The essays collected in Rollinger and Degen 2022 introduce various contemporary approaches to Arrian's work on Alexander, although this volume appeared too recently to be fully considered here. Liotsakis 2019 investigates the narrative logic of the *Anabasis*, while Leon 2021 and Burliga 2013 situate the *Anabasis* within Arrian's *oeuvre*. Burliga also examines the influence of Stoicism on Arrian's historiography. Arrian's main Stoic influence was Epictetus, for whose philosophy see Long 2002. The most complete commentary on the *Anabasis* is the Italian edition by Sisti and Zambrini 2001–2004. For readers of German, Schunk 2019 is the best comprehensive treatment of the *Indica* available. Those without German can still learn much from the introduction and appendices to Brunt's Loeb edition, 1976–83. Stoneman 2022b makes connections with other second-century Greek writing about India. All recent work on Arrian draws on the work of A. B. Bosworth, particularly his historical commentary on the first five books of the *Anabasis* (Bosworth 1980b, 1995) and his *From Arrian to Alexander* (1988b). Other older works also remain influential. Stadter 1980 treats Arrian as a public figure in the Roman empire. Tonnet 1988 offers many valuable discussions of stylistic and intellectual features of Arrian's writing; this book is particularly helpful for the so-called minor works. Pearson 1960 gives a detailed introduction to some of Arrian's source material. Studies of Greek literature from the Imperial Period have exploded recently, particularly with relation to the cultural phenomenon known as the Second Sophistic, to which Whitmarsh 2005 and Gleason 1995 give excellent introductions. To learn about Arrian's work in connection to the historiography produced in this context, see Asirvatham 2017.

21: Plutarch's Alexander

Philip Bosman

Introduction

The reasons for Plutarch's Alexander being the most influential of the ancient literary presentations are not difficult to fathom:[1] Plutarch wrote a manageable birth-to-death narrative of Alexander as part of a series of biographies of famous Greeks and Romans that maintained their popularity over the ages. His *Life of Alexander* is packed with intriguing events and anecdotes, some of them found nowhere else in the ancient sources. It is both inspiring and eventually tragic, skipping tedious detail but including personalized comments. In two speeches, Plutarch presents Alexander as a philosopher, even the best of them for putting into practice what the others only taught. The unity of humankind Plutarch's Alexander supposedly envisioned found considerable traction during the early twentieth century and retains some credence even today.[2]

Plutarch (c. AD 50–120) was a prolific author: some 128 works from his pen survive, by itself testimony to his popularity in later antiquity. But he wrote much more than that: 227 works are listed in the Lamprias catalogue.[3] His *oeuvre* is usually divided into two groups. On the one hand, a miscellany of writings referred to as the *Moralia*, on a great variety of topics of interest to the intellectual circles in which he moved. The other group are his biographies (or *bioi*, as the ancients called them), 46 of which form part of the *Parallel Lives*. Plutarch embarked on this ambitious project later in life (from the early reign of Trajan to his death under Hadrian); in it he paired eminent, mostly political, figures with one another, always a Greek with a Roman (or vice versa). For 19 of these pairs a *synkrisis* ('comparison') survives, in which Plutarch points out why he considered them together.

Alexander was important to Plutarch. The *Alexander–Caesar* pair is among the longest and best researched. Furthermore, the two epideictic

---

[1] Cf. Asirvatham 2018: 355.   [2] Asirvatham 2018: 356 n. 3.
[3] Lamprias was a family name, so the catalogue most probably derived its name from a relative.

orations devoted to Alexander aside, he is the most frequently mentioned figure in the *Moralia*, and features in other *Lives* as well.[4] We can also say that Plutarch was important to Alexander. Ancient biography found its definitive form with him;[5] with the *Life of Alexander* he was particularly successful in fashioning a rich crop of source material into an intriguing whole. A naturally curious scholar, Plutarch was evidently keen to display his impressive erudition on Alexander. Finally, his aversion to malicious historiography worked in favour of the Macedonian's legacy.

We need not be surprised that Alexander featured prominently in the mind of Plutarch. While the Macedonian sparked literary and historical interest ever since his spectacular campaign, what survives is mainly from the Roman era.[6] He was a contentious topic among the Romans already in the late Republic but became even more so in imperial times among authors, philosophers and imperial elites (including the emperors themselves).[7] Plutarch wrote a century into the Roman empire, where – like Alexander – a single person held sway over the realm. He was from a wealthy, educated family in his native Boeotian town of Chaeronea and mingled with high-placed officials and politicians both Roman and Greek. He dedicated the *Parallel Lives*, *Table Talk* and *Progress in Virtue* to Q. Sosius Senecio, twice *consul ordinarius* and confidant of Trajan and Hadrian, but also, apparently, on intimate terms with Plutarch.[8] Already as a young man, Plutarch accompanied his teacher, the politically engaged philosopher Ammonius; in his old age, the emperor Hadrian awarded him the *ornamenta consularia*.[9] Political figures dominate the list of those in the *Parallel Lives*, and the *Moralia* includes various titles indicating his interest in kingship, leadership and politics. He viewed the education of those participating in politics as perhaps the most important part of being a philosopher.

During Plutarch's adult life, Greek culture gained renewed appreciation through the public appearances and profiles of learned orators like Dio Chrysostom. He experienced the early stirrings of a movement

---

[4] Asirvatham 2018: 357. On Alexander in the rest of the *Lives*, see Mossman 1992; Buszard 2008; Stadter 2010; Monaco Caterine 2017.
[5] The opinion of the authorities Stadter 2007: 536 and Pelling 2009: 613.
[6] Cf. Wallace 2018b: 162.
[7] Brief bibliographies on the Roman Alexander and the *imitatio Alexandri* in Welch and Mitchell 2013: 98 n. 1 and Wallace 2018b: 162 n. 1.
[8] See Stadter 2002a: 4–13, 2014: 13–17 on Plutarch's connections with Greek and Roman elites; on his status as philosopher and literary figure, Dillon 2002: 29–40; Bowie 2002: 41–56.
[9] That is, at least according to the *Suda*, II 184–5 (*s.v.* Πλούταρχος).

scholars refer to as the Second Sophistic.[10] Among others, there was an upsurge in displays of intimate acquaintance with the classical Greek past as a mark of erudition. While Plutarch's *Lives* are not limited to the era typically approved for reference by the Second Sophistic, Alexander figured at the later margin of Greece's glory, not least because his monarchical (albeit Macedonian) inheritance had something to say to life in the empire. Plutarch, furthermore, had reason to take a personal interest in Alexander. He grew up where a 16-year-old Alexander commanded the cavalry in the decisive battle of Chaeronea (338 BC) against combined Greek forces, and knew where 'Alexander's Oak' still stood near the mass grave (*polyandrion*) for the Macedonian fallen (*Alexander* 9.2). Halfway from Chaeronea to Athens, his second home, was the ancient city of Thebes, which Alexander razed to the ground as a final warning on Greek soil that resistance would be fatal.

Plutarch's writings on Alexander have mostly been considered for the potential insight they can give into the historical figure.[11] Recent decades have seen the pendulum swinging to Plutarch the author. The researcher's challenge is to account for the author's genres and purposes. In such an account the sophistication of the ancient author should be matched by a subtlety of formulation. Given the intricacies involved in deciphering Plutarch's Alexander, the current study can only provide some pointers by discussing Plutarch's orations together with the *Life*.

On the Fortune or Virtue of Alexander the Great

Plutarch wrote two speeches on the topic of whether Alexander's achievements were the result of *tychē* ('fortune', 'luck', an external force for better or worse)[12] or *aretē* ('excellence', 'virtue', a collective term for good moral qualities). The speeches are part of a small group of four epideictic orations[13] in the *Moralia*, and sometimes regarded as closely related to the *Fortune of the Romans*, in which Alexander indeed appears briefly at the text's corrupted end (fortune caused his death, 326a–326c). The relationship between the two speeches on Alexander is not clear either: the second speech refers to what the speaker neglected 'yesterday' (*chthes*, 333a), so that the hypothesis that they were delivered

---

[10] On Plutarch and the Second Sophistic, Schmitz 2014.   [11] Hamilton 1969: lxvi.
[12] Cf. Swain 1989: 273.
[13] To Aristotle *Rhetoric* 3, epideictic does not judge past actions or direct future actions, but praises or blames, i.e. influences values and beliefs, cf. Kennedy 1994: 4.

on two consecutive days is not altogether far-fetched.[14] The first speech starts by referring to the speech on Fortune (either the *Fortune of the Romans* or some other, lost speech), and ends rather abruptly, either owing to manuscript corruption or to performance-related factors. Plutarch maintains a lively tone throughout the speeches with numerous rhetorical ornamentations and sleights of hand, and the odd literary quotation. The argument that Alexander owes his success not to Fortune but to his personal abilities is backed by evidence Plutarch adduces from the broad range of sources at his disposal.

The first speech counters, on behalf of Philosophy, or rather, of Alexander, Fortune's claim that Alexander is her 'work' (*ergon*), as his achievements were the result of his own virtuous efforts even despite the regular adversity of Fortune (326d–326e). The link between virtue and philosophy derives from the fact that the latter generates the former, and the various virtues are demonstrated to have fortified Alexander against the onslaughts of Fortune. Alexander therefore put philosophy into effect, so that he may be counted an even greater philosopher than those usually regarded as such: Pythagoras, Socrates, Arcesilaus, Carneades, even Zeno, who only wrote down his vision of cosmopolitanism, and Plato, who wrote the austere and ineffectual *Laws* (328a–329b). Philosophers, Plutarch argues, can claim the title on the basis of their teachings, sayings and deeds (328b), and he continues by furnishing evidence under these three headings that Alexander was a great philosopher and that his practical implementation of the virtues was the cause of his greatness.

The second speech starts by referring to what was omitted the day before, namely Alexander's promotion of the arts, which he left to those equipped for the task, focusing himself on his military prowess (333d–334d). The speech leaves behind the idea of Alexander as philosopher-in-action and focuses on the virtues that distinguish Alexander from other rulers whom Fortune afforded the same advantages but who did not attain the same level of accomplishment. Fortune, in fact, was (made) great while Alexander ruled (336f), because she was reinforced by martial skill, ambition, self-mastery, boldness and mildness, all employed at the opportune moments. Greatness lies in the use of the good, not its mere possession (337c–337d), and Alexander was great in exercising his authority honourably and 'in kingly fashion'. If he was great because of Fortune, he was even greater in how he dealt with Fortune and how he

---

[14] Discussion in Gilley 2009: 88–105.

prevailed despite Fortune (339a), as his many wounds, toils and troubles bear witness (341a–345b).[15]

Though often referred to, the speeches have received surprisingly little dedicated attention.[16] They are usually considered to be among Plutarch's earlier works, at least earlier than the *Life*, with which interesting correspondences and differences can be traced.[17] Some of the issues surrounding them are whether Plutarch's arguments are in earnest or merely rhetorical, whether he directs them at a certain philosophical school, and whether they are about making a philosophical point or about defending Alexander specifically. Arguments that Plutarch leaves hints specifically aimed at Trajan have not found general acceptance.[18]

Plutarch's purpose with the speeches requires careful formulation. Gilley argues that the speeches are concerned more with Plutarch's philosophy than with Alexander. She reads Speech 1 as a paradoxical encomium because of the depiction of Alexander as a philosopher; the author in fact exploits the well-known information of Alexander's life in order to denigrate him as a glory-seeking megalomaniac, while arguing for philosophy as both a theoretical and a practical enterprise.[19] However, the more straightforward reading, that Alexander's depiction as the philosopher-in-action is not the chief aim of the speech but a means to an end, remains more convincing.[20] Plutarch borrowed the idea of philosopher-in-arms from Onesicritus, a pupil of the Cynic Diogenes. While Onesicritus may have applied the notion of the philosopher-by-action to Alexander, this use of the term philosophy goes back to at least the late-fifth-century mythographer Herodorus, who claimed that Heracles 'philosophised until his death' (*FGrH / BNJ* 31 fr. 14). Antisthenes no doubt developed the theme in his (lost) books on Heracles, while its most famous practitioner was Diogenes, who cast aspersions on philosophy as a mere intellectual activity. The parallels between Heracles and Alexander as civilizers of the world run through Plutarch's speeches, while the parallel with Diogenes is famously made explicit: 'If I were not Alexander (i.e. implementing philosophy through great deeds), I would be Diogenes (acting out philosophy through self-sufficiency)' (331f–332a). Plutarch's civilizing Alexander, the cosmopolitan idealist and unifier of mankind, has found a stellar but

---

[15] For a more detailed synopsis of the speeches, see Hamilton 1969: xxiii–xxix.
[16] See Hamilton 1969: xxiii–xxxiii; Cammarota 1998; and Gilley 2009 on the first and D'Angelo 1998 on the second speech. Asirvatham 2005 notes that the Alexander of the speeches reflects Roman imperial ideals.
[17] Gilley 2009: 137–342 provides commentary on Speech 1, including Plutarch's use of sources.
[18] Hamilton 1969: xxix n. 1.   [19] Gilley 2009.   [20] Hamilton 1969: xxix.

brief revival in Tarn's attempt to transpose it as a serious vision of the historical figure.²¹ In Speech 1 this is memorably expressed as bringing both the persuaded and the conquered together, 'uniting and mixing them in one great loving-cup' (329c).

There have been attempts to cast Plutarch's orations as polemical against particular philosophical schools, whether Cynics and Stoics or Peripatetics, but recent scholarship has shown that no school advocated a consistent attitude towards Alexander, with some philosophers using him as a positive example and others from the same school as a negative one.²² It is important to note that Plutarch does not side in principle with *aretē* against *tychē*, but argues the case of Alexander specifically, who benefitted from but also struggled and prevailed against Fortune, owing to his character having been formed by philosophical education.²³ Most scholars would preclude a serious philosophical purpose for the argument on the basis of Plutarch's genre: epideictic oratory is about praise and blame, but as much about display, inspiring the audience, entertaining and dazzling them with rhetorical skill and ready knowledge.²⁴ The encomiastic speeches are less about salvaging Alexander from bad press than about Plutarch impressing his audience with his ability to adduce appropriately and to apply an incredible array of proofs from his Alexander repository.²⁵

The Life of Alexander

*Plutarchan Biography*²⁶

In comparison with the speeches, Plutarch follows a more considered approach in his *Life*. This can be seen in the treatment of the fortune–virtue theme, which is reduced to a few carefully phrased authorial comments. Before relating Alexander's stay in Egypt, Plutarch notes:

> By yielding to his [= Alexander's] assaults, Fortune had strengthened his determination, and his passionate nature

---

[21] Tarn 1933; countered by, in particular, Badian 1958a.
[22] Hamilton 1969: xxix, xl–lxii; Fears 1974.
[23] Asirvatham 2012: 316 notes that, in Plutarch, 'philosophy in general is good for Alexander because it is good for kings'.
[24] Plutarch's speeches may not have been *extempore* declamation (cf. Penella 2019), but the style and purpose seem similar.
[25] Arguments for a reading as rhetorical display already in Hoffmann 1907: 8–96; Badian 1958a: 437; Hamilton 1969: xxix, xxxiii. On epideictic oratory, Carey 2007.
[26] Generally on Plutarchan biography: Duff 1999; Beck 2014: 249–528; Jacobs 2018.

boosted his ambition until he became invincible against things, and not only his enemies, but even places and opportunities succumbed to his will.

Plutarch *Alexander* 26 (trans. Waterfield 2008: 337)

Plutarch wrote the *Life of Alexander* in the genre of the *bios*, which has roots in prose encomium and historiography. The original instance of the former, Isocrates' *Evagoras,* has a birth-to-death structure with a basic premise of praise (of achievements and moral character) for the purposes of inspiration and education.[27] The requirement resonated with Plutarch's own view of responsible history-writing.[28] From history-writing it inherited the narrative form and the requirement of truthfulness.[29] Biographical subjects are most often political figures, though over time philosophers and authors, orators, martyrs and saints were added. Time also added critical appraisals of a subject, and a choice between thematic and chronological treatments of a subject's achievements. By the late first century AD, biography had come to be considered the appropriate form for treating imperial history.[30] In Plutarch, the genre reached a previously unattained level of maturity. Like his contemporary Suetonius, Plutarch also tried his hand in writing a *Lives of the Emperors* before turning to a novel project of his own, namely writing biographies of eminent Greek and Romans in tandem. While the equal distribution between Greek and Roman figures on its own reveals an attempt by Plutarch to put the cultures on a par, close analysis shows a complex relationship between the pairs, with little if any preference for the Greek figures. Rather, Plutarch's bias lies with (Hellenic) *paideia*, which some Romans can apply (though from the outside, as it were) better than their Greek counterparts.

Much of the finer points of Plutarchan biography lie beyond the scope of this chapter, such as the question as to why a productive moral philosopher would have turned to writing *bioi*.[31] Perhaps he found the open-endedness and nuance of historical narrative and aphorism a subtler form for the *mimesis* (emulation) he had in mind. Plutarch

---

[27] Cf. Hägg 2012: 10, 30–41.
[28] On Plutarch's relationship to history, Pelling 2002a. Of Plutarch's 'traces' of malicious historiography in *The Malice of Herodotus*, the following seem most applicable: including disreputable and irrelevant material; suppressing the good and noble; preferring the worst version when alternatives are available; preferring or inventing ungenerous interpretations; ascribing success to fortune rather than to courage or wisdom; cf. Chrysanthou 2020: 50.
[29] Polybius 10.21   [30] Stadter 2007: 543 on Tacitus and Suetonius.
[31] See Desideri 2017 for more profound reasons behind the move to biography.

expresses his goal and his personal involvement in the project in the proem of the *Aemilius Paulus–Timoleon* pair as follows:

> I began writing my *Lives* for the sake of others, but I find that I am continuing the work and delighting in it now for my own sake also, using history as a mirror and endeavouring in a manner to fashion and adorn my life in conformity with the virtues therein depicted. For the result is like nothing other than daily living and associating together, when I receive and welcome each subject of my history in turn as my guest, so to speak, and observe carefully 'how great he was and of what demeanour' and select from his career what is most important and most beautiful to know.
>
> Plutarch *Aemilius Paulus* 1.1 (trans. adapted from Perrin 1919: 261)[32]

Plutarch thus states his interest in the virtues and noble deeds of the figures he presents, but also the fact that these aspects of their lives are material for reflection for himself even though he meant them for others. These others appear to be mostly, though not exclusively, potential readers from the governing classes, whether in local politics (mainly) or in the upper echelons of imperial power, such as the dedicatee Senecio. The *Lives* may indeed be associated with kingship literature, but more specifically with the moral formation requisite for being a successful ruler/politician/leader. It is with this in mind that he selects his material. His paradigmatic statement in the proem of the *Alexander* may have the specific pair of Alexander and Caesar in view, but the criteria of selection, namely the revelation of character, applies throughout.[33] Finally, his chosen format allows him, instead of prescribing, to engage his readers in the process of moral discernment, of deciphering the mimetic value of the presented material. In doing so, Plutarch presents himself as a model of how such moral discerning should be done.[34]

---

[32] Other self-reflecting remarks in, among others, *Pericles* 2.4, *Nicias* 1.1 and, indeed, *Alexander* 1.1–1.3.
[33] On the proems, see Duff 1999: 13–51; see also Schneeweiss 2007.
[34] See the discussion in Chrysanthou 2020: 71–73. The notion of 'ethical decipherability' is from Kirkland 2019: 506–507; on Plutarch's self-presentation as moral authority, Van Hoof 2010: 66–80.

Structure and Content[35]

The *Alexander* follows for the most part the chronological order of Alexander's life, starting just before his birth and ending just after his death. The main building blocks of his *bios* are episodic material, mainly in summary style, often providing context for an anecdote or direct speech, and occasionally interrupted by authorial comment. The relatively simple method conceals considerable complexity which results in a 'layered' depiction of Alexander. In the proem (1.1–1.3), Plutarch explains his methodology for the pair: with the sheer amount of their great deeds, he limits himself to those incidents that reveal character as the genre of the *bios* requires.

The *bios* proper starts with Alexander's ancestry (Heracles and Aeacus, 2.1) and birth narratives (2.1–3.5), as prerequisites for a full-blown biography. The section includes a number of portents to emphasize the importance of the figure and to introduce some narrative themes (e.g. fire, lion, Dionysus). The young Alexander's (4.1–5.3) physical appearance, warm body and fragrance are linked to his hot temperament, which explains his fondness for drinking and his inner drive (he is *thymoeidēs*). The young protagonist's physical make-up already displays and explains the character and behaviour of the adult: despite being violent and excessive in some ways, he has control over his appetitive urges and his ambition directs his mind towards higher ideals (4.4). Alexander's *epimeleia* ('care', 'attention', 'education') is dealt with in 5.4–8.4. Brief episodes (e.g. the taming of Bucephalas) and comments illustrate the characteristics of the young Alexander. At 7.1, Philip observes his son's resistance to compulsion but openness to reason and to education. His mentors are Leonidas and Lysimachus, and then the great Aristotle. Plutarch stresses Alexander's philosophical inclination, which is both innate and the product of his education (8.4).

The next section deals with the start of Alexander's political and military career in Greece, the internal troubles in the royal household and Philip's assassination. Alexander inherits a kingdom threatened on all sides by jealousy, hatred and danger (11.1) which he stabilizes by boldness and great-mindedness (*tolmē kai megalophrosynē*, 11.2). The razing of Thebes is followed by mildness towards Athens, whether

---

[35] Waterfield 2008: 306–307 divides the *Life* into the following sections: 1–10 (from birth to the death of Philip); 11–23 (from accession to his notion of kingship); 24–28 (from Egypt to his claims to divinity); 29–42 (from Gaugamela to the death of Darius); 43–56 (from Persian dress to the Pages' Conspiracy); 57–66 (India); 67–77 (from his return to Susa and to Babylonia to his death).

owing to psychology (like a lion with its *thymos*, 'inner drive', sated) or to strategy (13.2). Alexander now readies himself for the Asian campaign, before which Plutarch relates two meetings for their character-revealing capacity: with Diogenes the Cynic and with the Delphic Pythia. The campaign is preceded by portents and Plutarch provides the meagre resources for the campaign to hint at the odds for success, but also at Alexander's magnanimity and piety (15.2–15.3). Apart from the Granicus river, the military engagements (Sardis, Halicarnassus, Miletus) are dealt with in passing. The biographer relates omens predicting success (Xanthus, Gordium), but tones down exaggerated reports, rather opting for the sober account of a letter by Alexander himself about a lucky escape along the Pamphylian coast. Alexander's trust in his physician Philip receives detailed attention (19). Fortune gifts Alexander with a favourable location at Issus (*hē tychē pareschen*, 20.4), but is overshadowed by his military skills during the battle (dealt with in a single line). The battle is followed by the longest digression on Alexander's character in the whole work, which stresses his self-mastery and his honourable and humane (*philanthrōpa*) treatment of the conquered (21.3–21.4). Plutarch finds stories of Alexander's proclivity for heavy drinking exaggerated (23.3) but concedes that it made him boastful and susceptible to flattery.

Major events between Issus and Gaugamela include the siege of Tyre, the foundation of Alexandria and the trip to Siwah. Plutarch explains Alexander's claims to divinity as strategic. Before Gaugamela, Darius concedes the magnificence of his rival, and Alexander gets his *aristeia* (a Homeric-style arming scene followed by a sequence of personal military prowess, 32). The outcome of the battle dissolves (*katalelysthai*) the Persian empire; Alexander is declared 'king of Asia' and celebrates with sacrifices and munificence and by assuring the Greeks of their future autonomy (34).

A slight change of tone sets in after Alexander's entrance into Babylonia and his acquisition of the great wealth of the Persian empire. Plutarch focuses more on court politics and becomes less forgiving. Alexander orders a slaughter in Persis and is complicit in the burning of the palace, though he soon repents. Though luxury cannot redirect his ambition, honour or 'great goodwill' (37–41), he becomes harsh in judgement and loses rational discretion owing to his love for *doxa*, 'glory' (42.2). Alexander's policy of 'cultural fusion' and his dealing with inner court tension (Hephaestion and Craterus) get attention. The following section deals in relative detail with the Philotas conspiracy (48–49), the murder of Clitus (50–52), the *proskynēsis* issue (54), the

Conspiracy of the Pages and the demise of Callisthenes (55). Plutarch is circumspect about the first and even-handed about the second, but puts Callisthenes in a favourable light as representing a positive influence rejected by Alexander. His rival Anaxarchus' Calliclean philosophy strengthens the king's vanity and disregard for law.

During the Indian leg of the campaign (57–66) Alexander becomes more implacable, personally killing both a Companion (Menander) and a Persian commander (Orsodates) when they defy orders (57; note also the case of Oxyartes, 68.4). This section, which includes the last action sequences, starts with an ominous portent followed by a good one; Plutarch comments that Alexander 'aspired to overturn fortune with boldness and power with excellence' (58). The sequence of sieges and conquests (Nysa, Taxila, Porus, the Malli) includes the Macedonians' refusal to continue beyond the Ganges (62) and the river trek down to the coast. Plutarch devotes some time to the gymnosophists and the meetings with Dandamis and Calanus, but barely mentions the disastrous trip through the Makran (66.3).

The final section (67–74) starts with an extravagant week-long Dionysian *kōmos* ('revel') through Carmania, Plutarch's signal of the unravelling of Alexander under the sway of Liber, god of delusion. A drunken Alexander is depicted at festivals and planning expeditions he is too weak to undertake. Rumours of his weakness instigate outbreaks of rebellion and criminality, turmoil and instability throughout the conquered territories and back home (68). En route through Persia the tomb of Cyrus reminds him of uncertainty and change, Calanus immolates himself, and Alexander calls for a drinking contest of which the victor, Promachus by name, dies with 41 other contestants. The mass marriage of the Companions with Persian brides in Susa is followed by an enormous wedding feast where all guests receive a golden *phialē* (a drinking or votive bowl), and the 30,000 trained Persian boys cause jealousy among the Macedonians, though they finally submit to the will of the king. Alexander's unreasonable grief when Hephaestion dies leads him to slaughter the whole nation of the Cossaeans. By the time he reaches Babylon, Alexander is despondent, despairing and suspicious of gods and men (74.1), troubled (*tarachōdēs*), fearful (*periphobos*) and superstitious. The immediate occasion of the fever that leads to his death is a drinking bout, though Plutarch gives two accounts of the death sequence: a brief one from Aristobulus, and a verbatim medical case report from the *Diaries*. The surviving text, probably incomplete, ends with Plutarch dismissing speculations of poisoning.

Sources

For the present volume, the issue of Plutarch's use of sources is pertinent: seeing that the *Life of Alexander* is secondary and late, what does it offer to a study of the figure of Alexander? To state simply that Plutarch mentions 24 sources is misleading, as 17 of them are mentioned only once and 10 of these in a single passage (the Amazon story, 46.1–46.2). His most regularly mentioned authorities are Aristobulus, Chares and Onesicritus, though a good case can be made for familiarity with Clitarchus, as some episodes (e.g. the Persepolis burning, the trek through Carmania) correspond to the vulgate accounts.[36] It appears that Plutarch often relied on memory when he quoted his sources and occasionally made use of an intermediate compiler (Hermippus in particular), but dismissive views of Plutarch's knowledge of his sources have receded: most scholars would now accept that he read the important works himself and did a thorough investigation of Alexander even before writing the declamations. The favoured arrow in his quiver was no doubt a collection of letters to and from Alexander, which he mentions some 30 times and the authenticity of which he was so convinced of as to let them drown out other voices.[37] For the most part, however, Plutarch does not mention sources, resorting rather to the indefinite 'they' or the impersonal 'it is said'.[38]

Hamilton notes that Plutarch's main contribution lies in the court intrigues of chapters 48–55. Plutarch is reticent about his sources here, often reverting at this point to *legetai* ('it is said') or *phasin/legousin* ('they say'; cf. 48.1, 52.5, 53.3; 49.6, 50.4, 55.5). He mentions using the late-third-century BC biographer Hermippus in the story told to Aristotle about Callisthenes, but probably relied on Clitarchus and on Chares, who are quoted mainly on the events surrounding Callisthenes's falling out with Alexander (54.3, 55.5). Plutarch also refers to letters Alexander wrote to Craterus, Attalus and Alcetas (55.3), and also to Antipater (55.3–55.4), the latter on his intended revenge on Callisthenes and Aristotle. The use of letters here corresponds with the rest of the *Life*, where reference to a letter gives reported events a more personal and often more realistic appearance (e.g. on his passage down the coast of Pamphylia, 17.3–17.4; the oracle of Ammon; 27.5 – see also Alexander's own words at 28.2 to the same effect; the story of the Amazon queen,

---

[36] Cf. Hamilton 1969: xlix–lxii. Other sources mentioned more than once are Callisthenes, Eratosthenes, Duris and the *Diaries*.
[37] Cf. Monti 2016.   [38] See Cook 2001 on Plutarch's use of *legetai* in the *Alexander*.

46.2). In general, Plutarch tones down the more outrageous or contentious accounts of his sources. On Alexander's death, for instance (75.4–76.1–76.4), he gives a brief account of Aristobulus (that Alexander had a fever, then drank wine, became delirious, then died), then juxtaposes it with the dispassionate (and therefore haunting) quotation from the *Diaries* (*Ephemerides*). An interesting use of this technique occurs in the other special contribution of Plutarch's work, namely the birth and childhood narratives (2–8), in particular on Alexander's divine sire. Plutarch names Eratosthenes as his source that Olympias told Alexander 'the unspoken truth about his begetting', but then refers to 'others' who imply that it was actually Alexander himself who spread the rumour and that Olympias protested about him potentially bringing the wrath of Hera down on her (3.2).

The Alexander of the Life

Scholarship has suggested several avenues for the interpretation of Plutarch's *Life of Alexander* against the contextual circumstances of the author at the time of its writing. It has been argued that the *Life* is apologetic, responding to the predominantly critical appraisal of Alexander among philosophers and Roman authors, in particular his despotic rule and his general corruption by the Persian empire, by wealth and luxury, by his success and *typhos* ('delusion', 'vanity', 'arrogance'), or by his rejection of Aristotle's tutorship.[39] It has been argued that the complexity of the Alexander of the *Life* reflects Plutarch's own ambivalence towards the liminal Macedonian identity of Alexander.[40] It has been argued that the *Parallel Lives* should be read as a form of resistance literature against Roman power in the manner provided by the Second Sophistic.[41] Recently, Asirvatham argues that Alexander is Plutarch's most typical Greco-Roman hero, and that Plutarch deliberately divorces Alexander from his Macedonian connection, his successors and his Roman interpreters to set him up as the supreme world conqueror.[42] Plutarch's Alexander is often seen as a response to the attempts at *imitatio Alexandri* among Roman rulers in particular, among whom are counted not only Pompey and Caesar, but also Trajan. For the latter, the Alexander of the *Life* is meant to function as a *schēma*, an indirect warning that his emulation should be undertaken neither lightly

---

[39] Cf. Wardman 1955: 96; Gilley 2009: 83.   [40] Whitmarsh 2002: 174–175, 191.
[41] See discussion in Buckley-Gorman 2016: 60–70.   [42] Asirvatham 2018.

nor uncritically.[43] Not all of the suggested avenues are equally promising. If, for instance, its parallel life may serve as a clue, Pelling claims that Plutarch in the *Caesar* deliberately shies away from specific references to the contemporary, in order to give the *Life* a timeless relevance.[44] Trajanism in Plutarch, as Whitmarsh notes, goes largely unexpressed.[45]

Plutarch's Alexander in the *Life* is in the first instance a product of his writerly strategies. These include, as I have argued here and elsewhere, his choice of genre, the selection, interpretation and emphases in his use of source material, his personal philosophical assumptions, his narrative design and the themes in accordance with which he fashions the biography. A ground-up approach should better reveal the ideal reader, if indeed Plutarch had a specific reader-profile in mind.

In Plutarch's famous encapsulation of the genre in the *Alexander* proem, a *bios* spends time on the 'signs of the soul' just as a portrait painter pays careful attention to 'the face and the lines around the eyes, by which character is shown' (1.3). We may assume that Plutarch's Alexander emerges from the relative attention paid to specific episodes. It is unfortunate that we do not have the *synkrisis* ('comparison') with the *Caesar*, if it ever existed, though some similarities are straightforward: they are the great, divinely assisted conquerors of the Greeks and the Romans, both are ambitious and daring, generous, eager to accomplish great things and indeed successful in doing so with great military skill. Both are prone to despotic and excessive behaviour later in life, seduced by flatterers more than defeated by enemies. A further connection is of course the fact that Caesar emulates Alexander (and finds himself wanting; *Caesar* 11.5–11.6; *Antony* 6.3). Buckley-Gorman argues that Caesar's imitation was defective insofar as it only aspired to Alexander's great achievements, and did not look close enough for the causes of his successes and failures.[46] There can be little doubt that, for Plutarch, Alexander was the greater of the two.[47]

While appreciative of military skill, Plutarch shows little interest in military affairs. Alexander's strategic acumen and battle tactics, his legendary endurance and speed, ability to assess and leadership skills are all subsumed in the more general virtues of courage and daring. Alexander's successes are the results of his greatness of mind and his ambition to achieve great things.[48] Plutarch is more interested in Alexander's people-management skills, with one set applying to his

---

[43] Monaco Caterine 2017. For the *imitatio Alexandri* among Romans in general, Spencer 2002, Kühnen 2005.
[44] Pelling 2002b.   [45] Whitmarsh 2004.   [46] Buckley-Gorman 2016: 59.
[47] Stadter 2010: 200–208.   [48] Strauss 2003: 134–142.

troops and another to those with whom he is on more intimate terms. Towards the women of the Persian court and even towards his enemies he acts with moderation and kindness, and with great generosity towards his Companions. In court conflicts he has varied success, resolving tension between Hephaestion and Craterus, but being unable to contain insurrection and personal animosity peacefully.

Plutarch shapes his biography with a sense of overall design. He introduces a number of themes at the start that colour the narrative throughout. Philip dreams of putting a lion-shaped seal on Olympias' womb; the animal then becomes a running metaphor for Alexander's Herculean/Achillean character: aggressive, predatory and finally ruined, as we are told of a lion being kicked to death by a donkey (2.3, 40.3, 73.3). Olympias dreams of a thunderbolt causing a runaway fire; Alexander is scared by an experiment with naphtha, burns down Persepolis and is in the end consumed by fever (2.2, 35, 37, 75–76). Omens portend great things, or are forcibly interpreted as doing so, but they become obscure and foreboding as the narrative unfolds. Alexander treasures and trusts philosophers (7.1–8.1, 14.1–14.3) and doctors (19.2–19.5) at the outset but rejects and executes them later in the *Life* (53–55, 64–65; 72.2). Alexander holds the *Iliad* dear (8.2), enacting the role of his forebear Achilles in military matters (15.4–15.5), just has he does that of his forebear Heracles in his travelling, conquering and civilizing aspects. Dionysus threatens from the start (2.5) and breaks through in the whirling finale.

The inner dynamo of the biography, as has often been noted, is the soul of the protagonist, or rather the interplay between elements of Alexander's *mixis* ('mixture').[49] Plutarch's Alexander is, to start with, endowed with a 'great nature' (*megalē physis*)[50] that is choleric (hot and dry), to the extent that it can be smelled. This gives rise to an overactive *thymos*, 'inner drive' (and a great thirst) which again translates to an overpowering *philotimia* (ambition).[51] In Plutarch's Aristotelian conception of the soul, the irrational part is habituated by reason to form *ēthos* (character), and the required input to reason comes through education, in particular philosophy, which teaches the virtues. Alexander has little issue with the irrational part of the soul as long as his ambition keeps his mind fixed on achieving great things. Mostly, his *thymos* works to his advantage, manifesting in courage and achievement, but there are the

---

[49] Cf. Wardman 1955; Sansone 1980; Duff 1999: 72–100; Buckley-Gorman 2016: 8–12.
[50] *On the Delays of the Divine Vengeance* 552c.
[51] On Alexander as *thymoeidēs*, Wardman 1955: 97; Hamilton 1969: lxiii–lxiv.

occasional lapses in self-restraint even as a boy (4.4–4.5), manifesting in audacity, anger and violence. Alexander needs the mental straightjacket (aspiration to virtue) that philosophy provides, but when the hold of reason slackens (through drinking, flattery, *hybris*), ambition flips over to love of glory, cruelty and anger appear, and Alexander becomes overly emotional, despondent and prone to superstition.

Conclusion

In sum, Plutarch's Alexander is not merely an exemplum for philosophical truths: the author is interested in the figure of the great conqueror, though committed to the selection of appropriate material. The *Life* is less an apology than the result of Plutarch's generous interpretation. Alexander's moral life functions as Plutarch's hermeneutical key to unlocking the life-story. The biography aims at educating the politically inclined by offering inspiration and warning, but above all by illustrating the role of personal morality in the art of governance. Plutarch writes within a long Roman tradition that saw Alexander as a contentious figure, but also as worthy of imitation. Whether he had Trajan himself in mind when writing the *Alexander* is uncertain; more certain is that he presents himself as competent to offer valuable advice.

Guide to Further Reading

On the general topic of ancient biography, the reader can go to Hägg 2012 and the more recent compendium of contributions in De Temmerman 2020. The volume of literature on Plutarch and Plutarchan biography is daunting. Solid recent treatments of both under various headings can be found in Beck 2014 (especially 1–60 and 249–528). On the *Lives* specifically Duff 1999 stands out, but see also Jacobs 2018. Two studies devoted to Plutarch's epideictic speeches on Alexander are D'Angelo 1998 (on the first) and Cammarota 1998 (on the second); a handy synopsis and insightful treatment is provided in Hamilton 1969 (xxiii–xxix). Hamilton is also still the standard work on the *Life of Alexander*, including an introduction with discussion of the main issues and detailed commentary, with Asirvatham 2018 offering newer perspectives and a more up-to-date bibliography. Waterfield 2008 has a six-page introduction to his English translation of the *Life*.

22: CURTIUS' ALEXANDER

Elizabeth Baynham

INTRODUCTION: CURTIUS' ERA, SOURCES AND CURTIAN RECEPTION

Perhaps we may begin by asking 'Who was Curtius?' The manuscripts ascribe the authorship of the *De gestis Alexandri Magni regis Macedonum* to a Q. Curtius Rufus,[1] but the short answer is that nobody knows who this man was. We do hear of several Curtii, including a Roman senator and proconsul of Africa (cf. Tacitus *Annals* 11.20–11.21; Pliny *Letters* 7.27), as well as a rhetorician who is mentioned by Suetonius (*De grammiticis* 2.395),[2] but it is uncertain whether the historian was either of these men, or even whether all the Curtii in question were one and the same individual – which seems unlikely. It is also unusual in extant Latin historiography for a Roman to have written a specialist and detailed history on a non-Roman subject.[3]

No other ancient writer mentions a Curtius in connection with a specialist Latin history of Alexander the Great – although Curtius' work is not alone in apparently being overlooked – but given that we only have a fraction of the literature which was produced in the ancient world, we cannot use the silence of our extant sources as an indication of lack of impact or popularity.[4] Bosworth made a convincing case that Curtius' history was better known among Romans than was previously thought in recent times, and that it may have profoundly influenced Tacitus – not just in terms of borrowed phraseology, but in parallel characterization. In particular, Curtius' Alexander provided a useful foil for Tacitus' portrayal of Germanicus.[5]

---

[1] The surviving codices of Curtius' text derive from a single archetype from the ninth century AD; see Baynham 1998a: 2–3 with n. 8.
[2] Cf. *PIR*² C1618, C1619; Atkinson 1980: 50–57; cf. Atkinson 2009: 2–17; Baynham: 1998a: 217, n. 52; Power 2013: 117–120.
[3] Baynham 2007: 428–429.   [4] Bosworth 2004: 551–552.
[5] Bosworth 2004: 551–567, with nn. 1–2 on previous scholarship, noting parallel passages between Curtius and Tacitus.

The first two books of Curtius' work were lost, which means that any preface that would have very likely given the historian's identity and date was lost with them. Curtius was clearly a Roman author who wrote during the Imperial period, as apart from identifying with Rome throughout his history, he includes a famous excursus (10.9.1–10.9.6) in which he celebrates Rome's new emperor (whoever he was) for saving the Roman people from either an internal crisis or civil war.[6]

If we reasonably assume that Curtius had named his emperor in the opening of his history, most likely in dedication of the history to him, the historian probably saw no need to give the emperor's name again in the digression which honours him – Curtius' immediate audience and the honorand himself would have been well aware for whom the digression was meant. So by pure chance we are left with one of scholarship's great mysteries. There are some other contemporary references within the text; one is to Tyre's current enjoyment of the *Pax Romana* (Curtius 4.4.21), while two other passages (Curtius 5.7.9, 5.8.1) mention the current cities of the Parthian kings; however, neither of these is particularly helpful in pinning down a precise context.[7] More broadly, Curtius' use of Latin and his literary style appear to place him in the first or early second centuries AD.[8]

It is not this chapter's purpose to revisit the problem of Curtius' identity or when he wrote; suffice to say here that the evidence can support a case for several emperors, but more strongly for just three – Augustus, Claudius and Vespasian – and perhaps convincingly for one of the latter two. Recent scholarship has re-affirmed a Vespasianic date;[9] however, the puzzle is also academic. While certainty about Curtius' date may help clarify certain issues of interpretation, it does not affect the historian's presentation of Alexander. What matters is that Curtius wrote under one-man rule, and that the vast empire of which he was but a small part was governed by someone who was effectively a king – as powerful as any Persian monarch, or Hellenistic dynast. Yet although Curtius may have been well aware of certain parallels between Alexander's reign and past emperors – like the trials which follow the fall of Alexander's powerful general Philotas, and the fall of Tiberius' minister, Sejanus – it is unlikely that he intended the entire history as

---

[6] The scholarship on Curtius' date is considerable; for older summaries, see Koch 2000: 13–16; for more recent bibliography, Power 2013: 113, n. 1; also Müller in Wulfram 2016a: 13, n. 1.
[7] On the Parthians, Atkinson 1980: 23–24. See also Lerouge-Cohen at Mahé-Simon and Trinquier 2014a: 199–210.
[8] Atkinson 1980: 43–50; Spencer notes the 'transitional' nature of Curtius' prose in language and theme; Spencer 2002: 80–82.
[9] Bosworth 2004: 566 with n. 94; Power 2013: 117–120.

a crypto-allegory of the Roman principate.[10] Curtius was writing on Alexander – that was probably enough.

Curtius' history was surprisingly popular in subsequent ages, particularly among the elite classes from the fifteenth to the nineteenth centuries – a span offering a kind of *aetas Curtiana* as Wulfram has termed it.[11] Two recent, specialist volumes are testimony to growing scholarly interest in Curtius. They include (among many themes), investigations of modern Curtian reception ranging from several European monarchs' fascination with the text – usually for their own dreams of military glory – to Juan Ginés Sepúlveda's use of Curtius' history as a template for his own history of Hernán Cortés and the conquest of Mexico.[12]

The great German philologist and editor of Curtius, Carl G. Zumpt, who produced a volume of Curtius' text for a British market shortly before his death, ended his preface with comments highlighting Alexander's campaigns in countries where in recent times 'British valour has won such brilliant victories' – probably alluding to the successes of the First Afghan War in 1839, such as the capture of Kandahar and Ghazni – while graciously omitting any reference to the disastrous British retreat from Kabul in 1842. No doubt Zumpt intended to flatter his intended audience at the time, but the irony of such a statement today can only lend a contemporary resonance to his reflections on Curtius' Roman history of Alexander – not just for subsequent British history, but for the history of any country which has tried to conquer Afghanistan.[13]

Zumpt's remarks highlight one minor area which makes Curtius' history curiously relevant. The text fell into disfavour in the first half of the twentieth century, possibly owing to scholars' preferences for Arrian and Plutarch over Curtius, their distaste for the highly rhetorical nature of the work and the history's connection with the so-called 'Vulgate' tradition – or the main source used by Diodorus in Book 17, Justin/

---

[10] Baynham 2009: 295. One of the most striking Roman contemporary parallels is the speech of Amyntas in Curtius 7.1.19–7.1.40, defending his former friendship with Philotas, which recalls the Roman *eques* Marcus Terentius' speech about his connection with Sejanus (Tacitus *Annals* 6.8); cf. Baynham 1998a: 34, n. 59; Bosworth 2004: 564–565. See also Pausch's excellent discussion of Curtius' use of Roman contemporary updating in Wulfram 2016a: 73–98.

[11] Wulfram 2016b: 11.

[12] See Mahé-Simon and Trinquier 2014a; Wulfram 2016b, with Koch 2017: 67–69. On Curtius' influence upon Christine of Sweden, Louis XV, Charles XII and Philippe V, see Grell at Mahé-Simon and Trinquier 2014a: 265–304; on Juan Ginés Sepúlveda and the portrayal of Cortés, see Thurn at Wulfram 2016a: 411–426.

[13] Zumpt 1849: v; on the British and other modern invasions of Afghanistan, see Holt's thoughtful observations in his Introduction, Holt 2005: 1–22; also Warren at Moore 2018: 739–753.

Trogus in Books 11–12 and the *Metz Epitome*.¹⁴ This likely common source was identified as Clitarchus of Alexandria, a historian of uncertain date.¹⁵ Although this man was not an eyewitness of Alexander's campaigns, he was the son of Dinon, a historian of Persia (Pliny *Natural History* 10. 136 = *FGrH / BNJ* 137. T2), while other evidence suggests he was also attached to the Ptolemaic court as a tutor to the young Ptolemy Philopator (great grandson of the dynasty's founder and Alexander's general, Ptolemy Soter).¹⁶

So Clitarchus came from a highly literary background, and at Alexandria he had access to one of the best libraries in the ancient world. Also, if he had grown up at Ptolemy Philadelphus' court, he could well have talked to some aged veterans of the expedition during his youth.

However, Curtius almost certainly used other sources besides Clitarchus – whom he criticizes for inaccuracy (9.5.21). Within the same context, he is critical of Ptolemy Soter's history as well as Timagenes, although the extent to which he used either is debatable. He may have also drawn on a range of earlier work including eyewitness accounts like Callisthenes, Aristobulus, Chares, Nearchus and Onesicritus,¹⁷ but what mattered to him was his own presentation of the Alexander story. In this aspect he would have been influenced just as much if not more by great literary figures of the past like Herodotus, as well as writers like Livy who were much closer to his own time, along with the paradigms offered by Roman rhetorical *exempla*.¹⁸

We need to remember that the age of Curtius' presumed *floruit* was not just a highly oral culture in which an elite education placed high value on the spoken word – regardless of whether the context was politics, the law courts, war or entertainment. It was also an age of grandiose spectacle – mass entertainment offered by Imperial *munera* like gladiatorial games, or club-syndicated chariot racing or minor blood sports like cock-fighting and bear-baiting. Less violent displays included

---

¹⁴ On modern criticism of Curtius, see Baynham 1998a: 5–6.
¹⁵ On Clitarchus' date scholars are divided between *c*. 310–300 BC or *c*. 280–260 BC; on the former, see Prandi 1996: 69–71, 77–79; Baynham 2003: 10–11. Parker 2009: 28–55 argues for the third century BC; but cf. Zambrini 2007: 216; Prandi 2012b: 15–26, supporting the earlier date, a position more recently reaffirmed in her introduction to Clitarchus, *FGrH / BNJ* 137 (cf. also Chapter 24 in this volume).
¹⁶ So *P.Oxy.* lxxi 4808, but the part of the text which discusses Clitarchus is incomplete; see Prandi's analysis, 2012b: 15–26.
¹⁷ On Curtius' sources, Atkinson 1980: 58–59; Baynham1998a: 81 with n. 88; see also Mahé-Simon at Mahé-Simon and Trinquier 2014a: 91–108.
¹⁸ Baynham 1998a: 25–30; on Herodotus, 139 with n. 12; on Livy, most recently, Braccesi at Mahé-Simon and Trinquier 2014a: 109–118; James 2023: n. 1 documents earlier scholarship.

the theatre, along with public and private diversions like professional mime, or dancing troupes. Yet composing literature, particularly poetry and history, was a hobby for the elite classes as well as a profession, particularly for grammarians and rhetors.[19] In addition to live performances in the splendid homes of literary aficionados,[20] civic architecture also offered *odea* (little theatres), which were also often part of Imperial Baths complexes. Live readings of contemporary history could also have a political impact – as with the probable public dissemination of Caesar's propagandist *memoranda* on his campaigns in Gaul to a largely uneducated Roman audience.[21]

Pliny the Younger enthusiastically proclaims his own love of literature and philosophy, as well as his pleasure in composing himself – when, as he implies, given his own importance to the Imperial machine, his busy schedule allowed him to (cf. Pliny *Letters* 1.10, cf. 1.9). But he also describes (Pliny *Letters* 1.13) members of his own class sending their slaves in to listen to *recitationes* (live performances) in order to let their owners know if the speaker was saying something worth listening to – at which point, claimed Pliny, the elite would come 'sauntering in'.[22]

Although, as we noted earlier, some twentieth-century scholarly perceptions of Curtius' history criticized the work as a sloppily inaccurate, overblown, sensationalist 'pop history', such opinion tends perhaps to overlook both the context and audience expectation of the historian's day. It is significant that Curtius' debt to earlier predecessors is consistently demonstrated through intertextuality. While an educated audience would also play a role in this, in the sense that recognition of literary allusions to an earlier work would offer an engaging point of common reference for them – much in the same way that a modern audience today recognizes a 'quotation' from one film in another – intertextuality was not just out of reverence for the literary *maiores*, or great writers of the past. It was also the stamp of genre, imparting *gravitas*, and part and parcel of the tools of the historian's trade.[23]

The early Roman empire also produced pro-Imperialist historians like Velleius Paterculus, as well as giants like Livy and Tacitus – and we know the names of many more – including significant figures like

---

[19] On ancient appreciation of the importance of historiography as a literary genre as well as its role in education, see Nicolai at Marincola 2007: 13–26, especially 20–21.
[20] Marincola at Feldherr 2009a: 14 with nn. 21–22.
[21] Flower at Feldherr 2009a: 67; the publication of Caesar's *De bello Gallico* is a much debated area, but see Wiseman 1998: 1–9.
[22] On the *recitatio*, see Sherwin-White 1966: 115.
[23] Bosworth 2004, especially 552–554, which explores the question of a specific echo of a text as opposed to a writer drawing on earlier material common to both texts.

Asinius Pollio – whose works have been lost. We cannot be sure who would have 'received' Curtius' history, but any Roman citizen with an education in rhetoric and history would have probably been all too familiar with Alexander the Great as a benchmark of military excellence, as well as an *exemplum* of great *virtus* and *vitia*. They would be looking for a grand and dramatic story, coloured with rousing speeches and epic narrative. Several decades ago, the so called 'Wiseman–Woodman revolution'[24] established that Roman historiography was essentially a blend of information and rhetorical construction, and that a Roman audience would have accepted this as such. The question of historical 'truth' and of the extent to which accuracy may have been sacrificed for literary priorities is far more complex, and probably indeterminable.[25] For example, in the famous meeting between Alexander and the defeated Indian rajah Porus after the battle on the Hydaspes River in 326 BC, Alexander supposedly asked Porus how he would like to be treated, to which he replied 'Like a king' (Arrian *Anabasis* 4.19.2; Plutarch *Alexander* 60.7, cf. *Metz Epitome* 61). The tradition is fairly consistent in extant Alexander historiography with the exception of Curtius, who has Porus warn Alexander about the fragility of Fortune (Curtius 8.14.41–8.14.43).[26] Curtius has the same scenario as the other sources, and although the variant could well have derived from Clitarchus, it is likely that the actual words were Curtius' own composition to enhance his literary development of the theme of *Fortuna*.[27]

The extant Alexander historians, while they may have had access to eyewitness or near-contemporary accounts which are lost to us, were nevertheless still dependent on earlier writers whom they were in turn 'receiving', and upon whose value they had to exercise their own judgement as they tell us themselves. Arrian explains his historical methodology in his preface and his preference for Ptolemy and Aristobulus – two eyewitness historians of Alexander – as his principal sources, but adds that he would also regularly include additional material as *logoi* – or 'tales' – and hence remove the need for verification.[28] Audience expectation as well as the evident abundance of Alexander histories is perhaps why Arrian explicitly stated his choice of primary

---

[24] Feldherr 2009b: 6–8.
[25] But see Bosworth 2003: 167–197, who highlights the awareness ancient writers had for the principle of historical truth.
[26] Bosworth 1995: 308–309.
[27] Baynham 1998a: 123–124; cf. Stoneman at Wulfram 2016a: 301–322 on the unique aspects of Curtius' depiction of Alexander's *Fortuna*.
[28] On Arrian's use of *legomena*, see Bosworth 1980b: 20–22, elaborated further in Bosworth 1988b: 61–93; cf. Stadter 1980: 66–76.

sources in his Preface as well as his challenge to his audience to read any history of Alexander before his own, thereby giving his confident imprimatur to the quality of his own work.

In the twenty-first century, scholarly appraisal of Curtius' history has become more positive. As we noted earlier, recent investigation has explored the work's sophisticated narrative, its literary structure and its use of sources, speeches, depiction of characters and themes, as well as interest in geography, ethnography and medicine.[29]

THE EXTANT TEXT OF CURTIUS: ITS RANGE AND SCOPE

One important aspect to keep in mind when reading Curtius is the state of the text. Arrian's specialist history in seven books, although shorter than some of his other works, survived mostly intact;[30] there is a large section missing from Diodorus Book 17, and the historical part of the *Metz Epitome* covers only part of Alexander's reign, roughly 330–326 BC.[31] But Curtius' history is quite lacunose. We do not know how long the missing books and book sections were, or what they may have unfolded. Freinsheim's substitute books, which were derived from the other extant Alexander texts, can also be misleading, as brilliant as they are.[32] Essentially, Freinsheim was trying to offer the reader a summary of the events which Curtius' lost books would have probably covered and although he tries to imitate something of the Curtian élan, he could not reproduce the lost books any more than we can.[33] Out of the history's *decad* (ten books), we have Books 3–5 in their entirety, but the ending of Book 5 is lost, as well as the beginning of Book 6.

---

[29] On Curtius' narrative, literary structure and characterization, see Porod 1987; Moore 1995; Baynham 1998a; Spencer 2002; also Yakoubovitch at Mahé-Simon and Trinquier 2014a: 125–138; Galli at Wulfram 2016a: 159–170; Pausch at Wulfram 2016a: 73–98; Porod at Wulfram 2016a: 99–126; Wulfram at Wulfram 2016a:127–158. On Curtius' interest in medicine, see Schulze at Wulfram 2016a: 209–218; also Macherei at Wulfram 2016a: 219–238. For Curtius' geography, see Rapin at Mahé-Simon and Trinquier 2014a: 139–186; Mahé at Mahé-Simon and Trinquier 2014a: 187–198; Behrwald at Wulfram 2016a: 263–276; on Curtius' ethnography and literary narrative, see Lerouge-Cohen at Mahé-Simon and Trinquier 2014a: 199–210; Trinquier at Mahé-Simon and Trinquier 2014a: 211–264.
[30] Stadter 1980: 60.
[31] The large lacuna in Diodorus 17 takes out narrative from 328/7 BC, resuming at around 327/6; see Welles 1962: 361, with n. 5. The missing events are briefly described in the text's Table of Contents. On the scope of the *Metz Epitome*, see Baynham 1995a: 64–65.
[32] On Johannes Caspar Freinsheim, a seventeenth-century editor of Curtius, see Baynham 1998a: 4; Siemoneit at Wulfram 2016a: 369–387.
[33] There have been scholarly attempts at 'recreating' lost texts largely derived from extant sources which appear to be using them; for example, Kornemann 1935 tried to resurrect Ptolemy, and more recently Andrew Chugg has tried to reproduce Clitarchus (Chugg 2015); on the difficulties of this method, see Baynham 2003: 20.

Books 7–9 are largely extant, and so is probably close to a half of Book 10. What does this mean in real terms?

We do not have Curtius' possible account of Alexander's childhood, including his early education, or instruction by Aristotle in his adolescence. We do not have the narrative of Philip's death – or know whether the historian (cf. Justin/Trogus 9.7.1) thought Alexander knew about the conspiracy to murder Philip. Likewise, the narratives of Alexander's early campaigns against the Triballi and other tribes across the Danube; the sack of Thebes; the advance into Asia and the first victory over the Persian satraps at the Granicus; and the path of conquest down the coast of Asia Minor, including the siege of Halicarnassus, as well as Alexander's relationship with the mature Hecatomnid princess, Ada of Caria, are all lost. Instead, Curtius' extant account begins with the Great King's preparations for the next engagement at Issus. The first *pentad* (group of five books) evidently concluded with the death of Darius, but the actual ending is gone, and the commencement of Book 6 along with it – in which Curtius had turned his attention back to Greece and the unsuccessful war that the Spartan king Agis III waged against Antipater, Alexander's regent in Macedonia, in 331 BC. Book 10 is also heavily undermined, with lacunae taking out Curtius' account of much of the events of 324 BC, including unrest in Greece, Alexander's command to his satraps to disband mercenaries, the flight of his treasurer Harpalus, the Susa weddings and the death of Hephaestion. The text breaks off during the soldiers' mutiny at Opis (Curtius 10.2.12–10.4.3), and resumes when Alexander is on his deathbed, thus dropping out the description of the circumstances which put him there.

These gaps not only mean the loss of information, but also potentially compromise the overall narrative structure, and hence our own interpretation. For example, Curtius was undoubtedly interested in the theme of kingship. He not only explores Alexander's exercise of royal power but in Books 3–5 draws a robust comparison and contrast with the Persian Great King, Darius III – in fact Curtius gives more attention to this figure than any of the other Alexander historians, including Arrian.[34] In the second *pentad*, Curtius focuses on the deterioration of Alexander's *regnum* and his corruption by his own success or *Fortuna*, not just in terms of the king's adoption of Persian dress and customs, or in terms of his excessive alcohol consumption and *ira* (rage), but also in terms of his manipulation (in Roman eyes) by prostitutes or low-status

---

[34] On Curtius' portrayal of Alexander and Darius, see Baynham 1998a: 132–164; Müller at Wulfram 2016a: 13–48; cf. Galli at Wulfram 2016a: 159–170.

creatures like the Persian eunuch, Bagoas, Darius' former lover – whose spiteful machinations result in the death of Orsines (Orxines), an eminent Persian satrap and the descendant of Cyrus, founder of the Persian Empire (Curtius 10.1.22–10.1.42).[35]

It is also possible that, in the lost first two books, Curtius may developed a nuanced portrait of Philip II and his relationship with his son, which would have balanced the Alexander/Darius diptych – so there may well have been three kings highlighted in Curtius' history, rather than two. We will probably never know. But, like Banquo's ghost, Philip II remains a haunting, if inconvenient, presence for Alexander in Curtius' text, with several references to the reverence in which he was held by the Macedonians, especially the older generation (cf. Curtius 6.6.9).[36] There is also some evidence that Curtius was well aware of Alexander's rivalry with his father (Curtius 8.1.24–8.1.26, 8.1.52).

It is true, however, that Curtius' necrology of Alexander (Curtius 10.5.26–10.5.37) focuses on Alexander alone, rather than comparing him with Philip, as we find in Justin/Trogus (9.8), although that text also offers an additional obituary of Alexander (12.16). Also, Curtius offers explanatory information about individuals as they occur in his text who were important to Alexander, like Hephaestion, who was a boyhood friend (Curtius 3.12.16), and Bucephalas, Alexander's horse (Curtius 7.5.18–7.5.19). It is perhaps unlikely that he would have duplicated such statements about either if they had already appeared earlier, but, given the history's length, and the likelihood of live readings, audience 'reminders' as to who these characters were are also possible.

One figure who is largely absent from Curtius' text – at least as we have it – is Alexander's mother Olympias. To some degree her absence reflects historical reality, as Alexander never saw his mother again after 334 BC, although they seem to have corresponded as regularly as distance and communications would allow.[37] Yet her correspondence with Alexander appears to have been influential (cf. Curtius 7.1.12, 36–40), and the historian's awareness of Olympias' importance for the king is shown by his stated intention to consecrate her at her death (Curtius

---

[35] On Alexander's 'moral' deterioration, Baynham 1998a: 165–200; Yakoubovitch at Mahé-Simon and Trinquier 2014a: 125–138; on manipulation by a concubine, Atkinson 2009: 102, who notes parallels with Livy and other sources; on Bagoas, Ogden 2009b: 203–217; Ogden 2011a; Baynham and Ryan at Moore 2018: 615–639.
[36] On the Macedonians' regard for Philip II, cf. Curtius 3.10.7, 4.10.3; also 6.11.24, 8.1.27, 8.1.33, 8.1.36, 8.7.13.
[37] See Carney 2006: 53–59.

9.6.26, cf. 10.5.30). This may well reflect Curtius' nod to contemporary Roman Imperial family policy,[38] but it would also not have been historically implausible, given Alexander's request to Ammon to bestow hero cult status, if not godhead, upon his favourite, Hephaestion (Arrian *Anabasis* 7.14.7, 7.23.6; cf. Plutarch *Alexander* 72.3; Diodorus 17.115.6). However, as we shall see, Olympias' role as a mother-figure is also replaced by someone else – namely Sisygambis, the mother of Darius.

Curtius and Alexander

We may now turn our attention to Curtius' depiction of Alexander. The historian's admiration for Alexander's military genius, his capacity to inspire devotion and his personal *felicitas* (good luck) is not in doubt. But it may be helpful to examine what Curtius himself highlights as standout features of the king's personality. In keeping with the conventions of Greco-Roman historiography, Curtius' history, as we noted earlier, is permeated with speeches, which in addition to imparting information, differing perspectives and commentary on events, are also convenient vehicles for developing characterization.[39] But Curtius gives his own appraisal – or rather he appears to be speaking *in propria persona* – in several key digressions: just after the king's meeting with Sisygambis, the Persian queen mother (Curtius 3.12.18–3.12.23); just prior to the burning of Persepolis (Curtius 5.7.1–5.7.2); just after Alexander's meeting with Thalestris, the queen of a tribe of Amazons (Curtius 6.6.1.–6.6.12); after the death of Orsines (Curtius 10.1.39–10.1.42); and following Sisygambis' suicide (Curtius 10.5.23).

Each digression on the king's character occurs either in relation to a woman, or a eunuch, negative in the case of those who are considered prostitutes and hence women 'whom it would not be a crime to violate' (Curtius 5.7.2; Thais), women whom a Roman audience would consider 'barbarians' (Thalestris) or 'males who made females of themselves through *stuprum* (sexual depravity)' – namely, Bagoas (Curtius 10.1.26).

Women receive more attention in Curtius' history than in Arrian's *Anabasis*, although, as we noted previously, the Roman historian's treatment of Alexander's relationship with Ada of Caria is lost. Like Sisygambis, this woman seems to have acted as a kind of substitute mother to the king.[40] Curtius also gives some attention to Alexander's

---

[38] Atkinson 2009: 163.
[39] The seminal study on speeches in Curtius is Helmreich 1927; for more recent treatments, see above, n. 29.
[40] See Carney 1996: 563–583; Carney 2006: 166 n. 97; cf. Carney 2003b: 248–249.

interaction with Cleophis, mother of the Indian ruler, Assacenus (Curtius 8. 10. 22–8.10.36), whom the king also restores as queen of the region, using similar terminology that features in the treatment of Sisygambis' family: *decus pristinae fortunae*, 'the glory of her former status' (Curtius 8.10.35, cf. 3.12.23).[41] Women are more prominent in the Vulgate generally, but only in Curtius are women specifically linked with the historian's excursuses on Alexander's character.

Curtius' description (5.7.1–5.7.7) of the destruction of the royal palace of Persepolis portrays it not as an act of deliberate policy as in Arrian's account (*Anabasis* 3.18.11–3.18.12), but as a mistake, an impulsive decision which was made and acted upon amid an alcohol-soaked binge. Alexander's *ingentia animi bona* (huge natural talents), like his bravery, his military efficiency, his *clementia* (mercy) and usual self-restraint are compromised by an excessive *cupido* (lust) for wine (Curtius 5.7.1). To make matters worse, the king allowed himself to be influenced by an *ebrium scortum* (drunken tart). For Curtius, Alexander' Thais and Bagoas are tarred with the same brush: they are both *scorta* who are allowed to interfere in matters of state – which reflects badly on Alexander.[42]

Thalestris, described as a queen of the Amazons, or a tribe of warrior women from Themiscyra in the area of the Thermodon river, and drawn by the king's fame, visits Alexander in order to conceive a child by him, promising to return a son to his father, but to keep a daughter for herself.[43] Significantly, Alexander's tryst with the Amazon also immediately follows the arrival of Bagoas (*in ipso flore pueritiae* – 'in the very bloom of youth'), who had been presented by the Persian noble (and regicide) Nabarzanes as a peace-offering to Alexander. It is within this context that Curtius introduces the theme of Alexander's orientalism (Curtius 6.6.1–2), namely his adoption of Persian costume and customs, as an indication of the deterioration of his kingship, in so much as he was exchanging *continentia* (continence) and *moderatio* (self-control) for *superbia* (arrogance) and *lascivia* (wantonness).

This was clearly a *topos*, since similar sentiments are reflected in the other extant Alexander histories, with Arrian going so far as to defend Alexander's adoption of Persian ways in his necrology (*Anabasis* 7.29.3– 7.29.4). But Curtius also brings in a twist in perspective in this excursus by bringing in the Macedonians' response to Alexander's behaviour and

---

[41] On Curtius' treatment of Cleophis and Alexander, see Baynham 2012: 27–37.
[42] Atkinson 2009: 102; Ogden 2009b: 216: Baynham and Ryan 2018: 633–635.
[43] On Thalestris, Baynham 2001: 115–126; Mayor 2014: 320–323, 328–331.

the nature of its impact on them (Curtius 6.6.9–6.6.12, cf. 6.2.2–6.2.4); in short they feel that 'they are the vanquished not the victors'. The description of their discontent and resentment also sets the scene for the coming threats to Alexander's life and reign from within his own army – first from the fall of the powerful generals, Philotas and his father Parmenion (Curtius 6.7.11–7. 2.1.34), who were accused of plotting to murder Alexander, and second, and more dangerously, from Hermolaus and a group of noble Macedonian youths who personally attended the king (Curtius 8.6.2–8.8.23).

In view of the apparently negative depiction of Alexander's orientalism, Curtius' portrayal of the king's relationship with Darius' family as an example of commendable behaviour may seem surprising. Yet Curtius' depiction of Alexander's honourable treatment of Darius' family, who were taken captive after the battle of Issus, was likely shaped by an episode of Alexander-*imitatio* by Scipio Africanus, and by his famous *continentia* in relation to the high-status, captive female family members of the Iberian chieftain Indibilis and the Celtiberian prince Allucius. This tradition is represented in several Roman writers, including Livy, Seneca the Elder and Aulus Gellius.[44]

Curtius relates the incident of Sisygambis' mistaken act of obeisance towards Hephaestion, believing him to be Alexander – which Arrian (*Anabasis* 2.12.6–8) also records as a *logos*[45] – and Alexander's magnanimous response in lifting the Persian queen mother to her feet himself, and addressing her from the outset as *mater* (Curtius 3.12.17). However, Sisygambis, uncertain of her new status and, as Curtius notes, lacking *fiducia* (confidence), calls herself Alexander's *famula* (servant). Curtius comments that if Alexander had only been able to maintain such self-control, he would have been *felicior* (happier) in that he would have been able to control his *superbia* (arrogance) and *ira* (anger) – faults that he was otherwise never able to contain. An even more intriguing – and distinctive – episode that Curtius highlights in relation to Alexander's character is the king's faux pas in relation to offering Sisygambis a present of Macedonian garments, along with the women who had made the clothing, and a large quantity of purple cloth. These commodities had already been sent to Alexander 'as a gift' (Curtius 5.2.18). We are not told who had originally sent this expensive present, but both the purple fabric (a royal colour) and the gender-specific nature of the gift – in that textiles and weaving were both heavily associated with women – suggest Olympias, in a gesture which would remind

---

[44] See the discussion in Spencer 2002: 172–173. [45] Bosworth 1980b: 220–222.

Alexander both of his homeland and of her. If so, Alexander was re-gifting a present from his biological mother to his 'adopted' one.

But this was no slight – the king was offering Sisygambis the highest compliment he could and, as with his marriage to the Bactrian princess Roxane, which was conducted according to Macedonian ritual (Curtius 8.4.28), this is one of the few instances where Alexander was trying to incorporate Persians directly into his own family, by applying his own cultural customs to them rather than by adopting Persian customs. He thought that Sisygambis and the other female members of her family would be able to make him clothes, just as his mother Olympias and his sisters had done for him at home (cf. Curtius 5.2.20).

Unfortunately the attempt backfired. In elite Persian society, only slave women worked in wool, and Sisygambis believed that Alexander was treating her like a menial – ironically fulfilling the very description she had applied to herself. When the king heard of her distress, he came to see her personally and to explain his intentions; he admitted to cultural ignorance in relation to the present of the wool, but also pointed out that he had been respectful of Persian family customs, such as not sitting in a mother's presence unless permission had been granted (Curtius 5.2. 22). He finished their meeting by reassuring Sisygambis that she was his mother, and on the same footing as Olympias.

It is true that historically Alexander – at least in terms of his own propaganda – seems to have presented himself as a descendant of Perses, eponymous founder of the Persians, and so as coming to claim ancestral lands, in which case treating the Persian royal family as his own was appropriate, as well as helping to reconcile the Persian nobility.[46] Also, if Richard Stoneman is right, Curtius' text may reflect the influence of Dinon's *Persica*, most likely through the intermediary Clitarchus, as Diodorus' history also records information about Sisygambis, although not to the same degree.[47] Sisygambis exercises her privileged position by interceding on behalf of others on two other occasions: she pleads for mercy for Medates, her son-in-law, and the governor of the Uxii, a people who put up strong resistance to Alexander in the mountainous country between Persia and Susa (Curtius 5.3.12–5.3.15). That Persian royal mothers could and did exercise influence over their sons is attested elsewhere, along with evidence for some kind of formal right of intercession;[48] Curtius comments that even if had it been Darius himself

---

[46] Baynham 2022: 152–153.   [47] Stoneman in Wulfram 2016a, especially 313–319.
[48] Baynham 2022: 165–166.

who had been the victor, his mother would not have obtained a better outcome (5.3.15).

However, it is with Alexander's death that the final chapter in the relationship between the Persian queen mother and the Macedonian king is played out. With Alexander's protection gone, and the question of a successor uncertain amid ambitious marshals contesting power, Sisygambis believed she would be an inevitable casualty. She decided to take matters into her hands, refusing food and dying after an interval of five days. Sisygambis' death is symbolic: it links the final passing of the Persian empire along with Alexander's. As the historian notes (Curtius 10.9.1), *insociabile est regnum* ('royal power is indivisible') and, as events were to prove, not one of Alexander's remaining marshals was able to succeed him: his empire broke apart into separate kingdoms after his death. And Curtius' necrology, like Arrian's, celebrates the extraordinary in Alexander.

In conclusion, Curtius' Alexander is no whitewash, but nor is he a cardboard cut-out of a ruthless tyrant. Ironically, neither is the Alexander of the *Historiae's* great counterpart, Arrian's *Anabasis*, against which Curtius' text has been unfavourably compared for so long. But, equally, Arrian's apologia is more striking, and his criticism more subtle.[49] Curtius presents a multi-faceted, complex king: the Alexander who murders his friend Clitus at a banquet (in cold blood) at Maracanda (Curtius 8.1.50–8.1.52) is the same king who rouses his hypothermic soldiers during a snowstorm in the Hindu Kush (Curtius 7.3.17). Curtius' narrative promotes the epic nature of Alexander's story, which is one reason why the history continues to resonate with a modern audience.

Guide to Further Reading

Accessible texts of Curtius are Bardon 1961–1965 (Latin and French); Rolfe 1946 (Latin and English); and Müller and Schönfeld 1954 (Latin and German). The last was used by Atkinson 1998–2000 in his Italian edition with notes for the Mondadori series. The best English translation is Yardley 1984, with maps, notes and appendices by W. Heckel.

There are three commentaries by J. E. Atkinson: 1980, 1994 and 2009. The first covers Books 3–4, while the second covers Books 5–7.2. The 2009 Commentary for the Oxford Clarendon Ancient History

---

[49] Bosworth 2007: 452–453.

series focuses on Book 10 and contains an English translation as well as detailed analysis.

Holger Koch published an extensive bibliography on Curtius in 2000 which is still an indispensable reference collection for older bibliography on Curtius. Important doctoral dissertations with a predominantly literary focus include Porod 1987 and Moore 1995. There is also a specialist monograph on Curtius by Baynham 1998a and extensive discussion of the Roman historian in Spencer 2002. Mahé-Simon and Trinquier 2014a and Wulfram 2016a are a pair of European edited collections with a particular interest in Curtian reception, especially in Renaissance and modern Europe.

23: PTOLEMY AND ARISTOBULUS

Frances Pownall

Ptolemy and Aristobulus occupy a privileged position in the historiographical tradition because Arrian, who is usually considered the most reliable authority on Alexander,[1] identified them as his principal sources. Arrian opens his history of Alexander's expedition as follows (*Anabasis* praef. 1): 'In the places where Ptolemy the son of Lagus and Aristobulus the son of Aristobulus reach a consensus about Alexander, the son of Philip, I record what they say as entirely true.' He then adds that while many writers have offered a wealth of often-contradictory details on Alexander, he has chosen to base his narrative upon Ptolemy and Aristobulus as the 'more trustworthy' (*pistoteroi*) sources on the grounds that they both participated in Alexander's campaign; in addition, it would have been shameful for Ptolemy to lie, as he too was a king. Furthermore, they composed their histories once Alexander was already dead, and so neither was motivated by either fear or flattery to record anything other than what really happened (praef. 1–2).

Unfortunately, the eyewitness accounts of Alexander's campaign by Ptolemy and Aristobulus are no longer extant (apart from scattered citations by later authorities that have been stripped from their original narrative contexts). Nor can we simply assume that we can recover their lost histories from Arrian's narrative. Despite his dismissal of what had become the standard tradition on Alexander by the second century AD (pithily summarized by Philip Stadter as 'flattery, gossip, the marvelous, the romantic and novelistic'),[2] Arrian did in fact draw on it frequently to supplement the narrative of his principal sources, as he states explicitly in the very next section of his prologue (praef. 3).[3] It is also becoming increasingly apparent that he did not mechanically reproduce his

---

[1] See, for example, the influential assessment of Bosworth 1988b: 13: 'His work is the most complete and the most sober account of Alexander's reign.'
[2] Stadter 1980: 67.   [3] On Arrian's engagement with a variety of sources, see Pownall 2022a.

sources, but painstakingly shaped his narrative in accordance with his own literary agenda and very much in response to his political and intellectual *milieu*,[4] adding yet another layer of possible distortion between what Ptolemy and Aristobulus actually wrote and his own account that was composed hundreds of years later. Therefore, an examination of how Ptolemy and Aristobulus portrayed Alexander must be grounded in what can be gleaned from the ancient biographical testimonies and the snippets that remain from their historical works.

Ptolemy

Ptolemy presents a difficult case as a source for Alexander. In addition to the almost complete loss of his history, the surviving fragments (*FGrH / BNJ* 138) suggest that the work was conceived as a work of propaganda intended to justify Ptolemy's foundation of a new royal dynasty in Egypt, which ultimately hinged on his ability to spin himself as a legitimate successor to Alexander.[5] As a result, what remains from his history tells us at least as much about Ptolemy himself as about Alexander.

Ptolemy's early life and career remain shadowy, perhaps deliberately so for, as Waldemar Heckel has observed, his previous political and military experience was not nearly as extensive as others' in Alexander's inner circle.[6] According to a late source (Pseudo-Lucian *Macrobii* 12), Ptolemy was born in 367/6 BC, a date that has sometimes been questioned because it appears incompatible with the popular belief that he was a boyhood friend of Alexander (whose birth was ten years later). But Philip II's banishment of Ptolemy, along with other advisers of Alexander, in the wake of the Pixodarus marriage negotiations fiasco (Plutarch *Alexander* 10.3; cf. Arrian *Anabasis* 3.6.4–3.6.6) suggests that he was in fact older,[7] and it would have been important for Ptolemy's dynastic aspirations to stress the length as well as the intensity of his bond with Alexander. Similarly, the fictions that Ptolemy's mother Arsinoë was a member of a minor branch of the Argead royal family

---

[4] On Arrian's literary and cultural aims, see Burliga 2013; Liotsakis 2019a; Leon 2021; the papers in Rollinger and Degen 2022; cf. Leon in this volume (Chapter 20).

[5] On Ptolemy's 'quest for legitimacy', see Bingen 2007: 15–30. Although the self-serving nature of Ptolemy's history has been challenged (Roisman 1984 and Worthington 2016b: 213–219), it remains the scholarly consensus: see, for example, Zambrini 2007: 217; Müller 2014: 78–90 and 2020d; Howe 2015b and 2021; Heckel 2016: 230–239 and 2018.

[6] Heckel 2018: 3.

[7] On this point, see Heckel 2016: 231–232 and 2018: 3–6; Worthington 2016b: 10–11.

(Satyrus *FGrH / BNJ* 631 F 1) and that Ptolemy was an illegitimate son of Philip II (Pausanias 1.6.2; cf. Curtius 9.8.22) were invented to provide him with a blood link to Alexander's line.[8]

Although Ptolemy almost certainly served with Alexander from the very beginning, likely as a member of the Companion cavalry, his first attested command does not occur until 331 BC. According to Arrian (*Anabasis* 3.18.9), Ptolemy was entrusted with 3,000 troops at the Persian Gates, with which he successfully prevented the enemy's retreat to the Achaemenid heartland, routing and destroying most of the Persian forces. This command is not mentioned in any other source, and Ptolemy seems to have appropriated the role in the battle that was actually played by Philotas (cf. Curtius 5.4.30).[9] In the wake of Philotas' condemnation in 330 BC, Ptolemy was appointed as one of seven royal bodyguards (Arrian *Anabasis* 3.27.5), a prestigious office that apparently catapulted him into Alexander's inner circle. While it cannot be denied that Ptolemy henceforth played an increasingly prominent role, his self-promoting agenda makes it difficult to assess the true extent of his contributions to Alexander's campaign.[10] Ptolemy claims sole responsibility for the capture of Bessus, who had murdered Darius and usurped his throne (Arrian *Anabasis* 3.29.6–3.30.5 = *FGrH / BNJ* 138 F 14); Alexander's apprehension of Bessus therefore represents a critical step in his recognition as the legitimate successor to the Achaemenid empire. In Aristobulus (*FGrH / BNJ* 139 F 24), by contrast, Ptolemy plays only a minor role, and he does not appear at all in the accounts of the other sources (Diodorus 17.83.7–17.83.9 and Curtius 7.5.19–7.5.26 and 7.5.36). Not only does Ptolemy exaggerate his own part in the capture of Bessus, but the dramatic chase scene in Arrian's narrative is deliberately reminiscent of Alexander's earlier pursuit of Darius from the Caspian Gates (Arrian *Anabasis* 3.21.2–3.21.10), and is intended to portray Ptolemy as a second Alexander, thus legitimizing him by proxy.[11] Similarly, Ptolemy takes all the credit for informing Alexander of the so-called Pages' Conspiracy (Arrian *Anabasis* 4.13.7), whereas according to Curtius (8.6.22) the plot was divulged to both Ptolemy and his fellow bodyguard Leonnatus.[12] Ptolemy appropriates from a minor official the discovery at the Oxus River of spontaneous

---

[8] On the legitimizing function of Ptolemy's mythology, see Ogden 2013c.
[9] So Bosworth 1980b: 328–329; cf. Howe 2015b; Heckel 2016: 232 and 2018: 8; Worthington 2016b: 38–39.
[10] A useful chart of Ptolemy's own claims in Alexander's campaign versus the evidence from other sources can be found at Heckel 2018: 16.
[11] So Howe 2021; cf. Bosworth 1980b: 376–377.
[12] Bosworth 1995: 97; Heckel 2016: 235; Worthington 2016b: 52.

springs of water and oil,[13] signifying divine assent for Alexander's conquests, but also (perhaps more crucially) attaching it to the future Ptolemaic dynasty.[14] Arrian's narrative of the campaigns in Bactria and Sogdiana in 328 and the conquest of India in 327 highlights Ptolemy's actions, at the continuing expense of Alexander's other commanders (particularly Perdiccas, Leonnatus and Craterus, who were all conveniently dead by the time that he was composing his history), and even occasionally Alexander himself.[15] The spotlight on Ptolemy culminates in his leading role in Alexander's victories at the Rock of Aornus (Arrian *Anabasis* 4.29.1–4.29.6; cf. Curtius 8.11.5, who mentions only a certain Myllenas)[16] and Sangala (Arrian *Anabasis* 5.21.1–5.24.8 = *FGrH / BNJ* 138 F 35). Ptolemy alleges that he engaged in single combat with an Indian commander (described in Homeric terms by Arrian *Anabasis* 4.24.4–4.24.5 = *FGrH / BNJ* 139 F 18), relegating even Alexander to an auxiliary position;[17] possibly he invented a *monomachia* for himself to rival the (apocryphal) tradition of a duel between Alexander and Porus that may have been circulated by Alexander himself.[18] By 324 BC, according to Ptolemy, he (rather than Perdiccas) became Alexander's right-hand man after the death of Hephaestion.[19]

Whatever the true extent of Ptolemy's contributions to Alexander's conquest of the east, there is no doubt that he began to emerge from the pack in the immediate aftermath of Alexander's sudden death in 323 BC. He asked for and received the satrapy of Egypt in the Settlement of Babylon,[20] a canny choice as the natural defensibility of his new territory allowed him to fend off with relative ease any attempt of his rivals to unseat him in the ensuing Wars of the Successors. It did not take long for Ptolemy to bolster his position on an ideological as well as a physical level. In 321 BC, he made the bold move of hijacking the funeral cortège conveying the embalmed corpse

---

[13] Arrian *Anabasis* 4.15.7–4.15.8; cf. Plutarch *Alexander* 57.4–57.5; Curtius 7.10.13–7.10.14.
[14] Müller 2018.
[15] Howe 2008a; cf. Errington 1969; Bosworth 1980b: 26 and 1996b: 46; Heckel 2016: 234–236; Worthington 2016b: 47–56; Howe 2018b, commentary on *FGrH / BNJ* 138 F 18.
[16] On the identity of Myllenas, see Heckel 2018: 11 and n. 61.
[17] Bosworth 1995:161–163; cf. Worthington 2016b: 54–55.
[18] Lucian *Quomodo historia conscribenda sit* 12 = Aristobulus *FGrH / BNJ* 139 T 4, with commentary by Pownall 2013.
[19] For example, Arrian *Anabasis* 7.15.1–7.15.3, where (as Heckel 2016: 237 n. 39 observes), Ptolemy is in charge of contingents that are normally under Alexander's own command; cf. Errington 1969: 239–240.
[20] Arrian *FGrH / BNJ* 156 F 1.5; Diodorus 18.3.1; Curtius 10.10.1; Justin 13.4.10–13.4.11; Pausanias 1.6.2 (who emphasises Ptolemy's own agency in the division of territories among the Successors).

of Alexander to the royal Argead necropolis in Macedonia,[21] and diverting it to Memphis,[22] the capital of his satrapy, where he buried it with elaborate honours. Burial of the previous king conferred legitimacy upon the burier according to Macedonian tradition,[23] and Alexander's body continued to hold potent symbolic importance for Ptolemy,[24] even as he began to transition from securing his position in Egypt to laying the foundations for a new dynasty that would overshadow all of his rivals. By 311 BC, Ptolemy transferred the seat of his satrapy to Alexandria,[25] where he turned the fortress settlement originally founded by Alexander into an impressive capital city (reburying the embalmed corpse of Alexander in elaborate splendour at its centre) and founded a cult to the deified Alexander,[26] paving the way for his own eventual apotheosis and that of his successors. Ptolemy's empire-building efforts culminated in his assumption of the title of king (*basileus*) and coronation as pharaoh in 304 BC.[27] He laid the groundwork for his succession by associating his son Ptolemy II in his rule two years prior to his death (Porphyry *FGrH / BNJ* 260 F 2.2) and died in his own bed in 282 BC, having founded what ultimately became the most successful of the Hellenistic kingdoms.

Ptolemy's history of Alexander's expedition was the ideal vehicle to build a case for himself as his rightful successor in Egypt. As we have seen, Ptolemy exaggerated his own achievements (both in terms of the significance of his role and the strategic importance of the campaigns in which he was involved), and minimized the role of his fellow officers (and future rivals) in Alexander's victories. Not surprisingly, Ptolemy's appropriation of sole credit for military successes is counterbalanced by his efforts to elude personal responsibility for defeats and other unfortunate events. Thus, he appears to have glossed over his role in the murder of Clitus, when his inability to protect Alexander from Clitus' violent confrontation and his subsequent failure to restrain the king from impetuously running him through with a spear reflected rather badly

---

[21] Arrian *FGrH / BNJ* 156 F 9.25 and 10.1; Diodorus 18.2–18.5; Strabo C794 = 17.1.8; Pausanias 1.6.3; Aelian *Varia historia* 12.64.
[22] So *Marmor Parium FGrH / BNJ* 239 B 11; Curtius 10.10.20; Pausanias 1.6.3; Pseudo-Callisthenes 3.34.5; other sources conflate Alexander's original burial at Memphis with his permanent resting place at Alexandria (see Ogden 2014b: 20–22).
[23] Lianou 2010: 127–128; Caneva 2016: 35–42; Worthington 2016b: 93–95 and 129–133.
[24] Erskine 2002 and Holton 2018.
[25] On Ptolemy's mythmaking efforts in creating a suitable backstory for the foundation of Alexandria, see Howe 2014.
[26] Hölbl 2001: 94; Worthington 2016b: 132–133.
[27] On the date of Ptolemy's declaration of kingship, see Caneva 2016: 68–75; cf. Worthington 2016b: 160–162. On Ptolemy's coronation, see Hölbl 2001: 21–22.

on Ptolemy as a royal bodyguard.[28] Likewise, by Ptolemy's own account, he was not present at the disastrous siege of Malli, where Alexander suffered a near-fatal wound. The tradition that he saved Alexander's life on this occasion appears to be a later Ptolemaic invention circulated by Clitarchus[29] and Ptolemy goes to great lengths to refute any impression that he failed to protect Alexander, not only on the grounds that he was commanding a different campaign elsewhere (Arrian *Anabasis* 6.11.8 = Ptolemy *FGrH* / *BNJ* 128 F 26a and Curtius 9.5.21 = Ptolemy *FGrH* / *BNJ* 128 F 26b), but also hinting that Perdiccas was responsible for the military failure that led to Alexander's brush with death (Arrian *Anabasis* 6.9.1–6.9.2).[30] Because military victory was the key to legitimate rule for the Argead rulers and later for the Successors,[31] it was crucial for Ptolemy's dynastic aspirations that he should portray himself as a successful commander, equal to or even surpassing Alexander himself, and to distance himself from any reverses.

Another strategy in Ptolemy's ultimate goal of legitimizing his position as ruler of Egypt was to highlight his personal connections (real or invented) to Alexander. But for this strategy to be successful, the figure of Alexander had to be above reproach. Thus, in addition to Ptolemy's personal glorification in his history, a strongly apologetic slant is apparent, which likely goes back to Alexander himself (possibly through the intermediary of Callisthenes, who was embedded in the expedition as the official historian)[32] and is particularly visible in the deflecting of responsibility for military defeats from Alexander to others. For example, Ptolemy (whose account is preserved in Arrian *Anabasis* 4.5.2–4.5.9) attributes the debacle at the Polytimetus River to the incompetence of the Macedonian commanders rather than to Alexander's misjudgement of the threat posed by Spitamenes (cf. Plutarch *Alexander* 50.8),[33] presumably in accordance with the official version of the event.[34] Similarly, Ptolemy minimizes the extent of local resistance against Alexander as he pushed farther east, whereas

---

[28] On Ptolemy's role in events leading to the death of Clitus, see Curtius 8.1.45 and 8.1.48; Arrian *Anabasis* 4.8.9 (explicitly based on Aristobulus *FGrH* / *BNJ* 139 F 29, rather than Ptolemy); cf. Worthington 2016b: 48–49.
[29] Clitarchus *FGrH* / *BNJ* 137 F 24, with commentary by Prandi 2016; on Clitarchus, see also Prandi in this volume (Chapter 24).
[30] Müller 2020d: 452; cf. Worthington 2016b: 62.   [31] Müller 2020b.
[32] On Callisthenes, see Djurslev in this volume (Chapter 25) and Pownall 2020b.
[33] Although Arrian does not explicitly name Ptolemy as his source, immediately following this passage he switches to Aristobulus for an alternative account (discussed below, p. 389).
[34] Bosworth 1995: 25 and 34; cf. Pownall 2013, commentary on *BNJ* 139 F 27.

Aristobulus and Curtius portray the Sogdian campaign as difficult, protracted and bloody.[35]

This apologetic tendency is even more evident in Ptolemy's take on the cluster of somewhat unsavoury episodes highlighted in the later tradition as the canonical crimes of Alexander.[36] Ptolemy (Arrian *Anabasis* 3.26.1–3.26.4 = *FGrH* / *BNJ* 138 F 13) downplays Alexander's role in the condemnation and execution of Philotas (and his father Parmenion), making no reference to the extenuating circumstances found in the much more detailed accounts of the other sources nor offering any suggestion that Philotas was innocent of the charge of conspiracy.[37] Instead, he offers a seemingly straightforward account of how clear evidence of Philotas' guilt was brought to light, and he was convicted and summarily executed by the assembled Macedonians, which was presumably the officially sanctioned version of the incident. So too Alexander's own legitimizing message explains why Ptolemy is the only source who refrains from relating the gruesome details of the torture, mutilation and execution of Bessus carried out on Alexander's orders in accordance with the standard Achaemenid punishment of usurpers.[38] Similarly, Ptolemy's main concern in his account of Callisthenes' trial and condemnation appears to have been to absolve Alexander of responsibility, for he states explicitly that Callisthenes was in fact guilty of inciting the Pages to conspiracy, in stark contrast to the contention in the later tradition that Alexander took the opportunity to eliminate a vocal opponent of his incorporation of Achaemenid court ceremonial.[39] In contrast to the other contemporary authorities (Aristobulus and Chares of Mytilene), who absolve Alexander of responsibility for Callisthenes' death by attributing it to natural causes,[40] Ptolemy emphasizes the legitimacy of his punishment,

---

[35] Arrian *Anabasis* 4.3.5 = Ptolemy *FGrH* / *BNJ* 138 F 15 and Aristobulus *FGrH* / *BNJ* 139 F 26; Curtius 7.6.17–7.6.23; cf. Bosworth 1995: 21–22 and the commentaries *ad loc.* of Howe 2018b and Pownall 2013.

[36] Dio Chrysostom 64.20; cf. Livy 9.18; Valerius Maximus 9.3 *externis* 1. Even in the more idealizing narratives of Arrian (*Anabasis* 4.7.4.14–4.14.4) and Plutarch (*Alexander* 48–55), these episodes that did not reflect well upon Alexander are grouped together to minimize their impact; Bosworth 1995: 45–47.

[37] Diodorus 17.79–17.80; Curtius 6.7.1–7.2.38; Justin 12.5.1–12.5.4; Plutarch *Alexander* 48–49.

[38] Arrian *Anabasis* 4.7.3–4.7.4; cf. Diodorus 17.83.7–17.83.9; Curtius 7.5.19–7.5.26 and 36–43; Justin 12.5.10–12.5.11; Plutarch *Alexander* 43.6.

[39] Arrian *Anabasis* 4.14.1 = Ptolemy *FGrH* / *BNJ* 138 F 16; cf. Curtius 8.6.1–8.8.23; Plutarch *Alexander* 55; Justin 12.7.1–12.7.3. On the reflection of contemporary propaganda in the accounts of Ptolemy and Aristobulus, see Pownall 2018: 61–62 and Squillace 2018: 127–129.

[40] Arrian *Anabasis* 4.14.4 = Aristobulus *FGrH* / *BNJ* 139 F 17 (see discussion below, pp. 387–388) and Plutarch, *Alexander* 55.5 = Chares of Mytilene *FGrH* / *BNJ* 125 F 15 (with discussion of Müller 2017b *ad loc.*).

claiming that on Alexander's orders he was tortured and hanged, a form of execution (as in the case of Bessus) reserved for rebels and usurpers.[41]

The distinctive spin that Ptolemy took in his history is best illustrated by the variations that he introduced into the existing tradition (ultimately based on the account of Alexander's court historian Callisthenes FGrH / BNJ 124 F 14) of Alexander's pilgrimage to the shrine of Ammon at Siwah. One element unique to Ptolemy's version is the substitution of snakes for crows as divine guides escorting Alexander and his army through the desert to the oracle and back again (Arrian Anabasis 3.3.5–3.3.6 = Ptolemy FGrH / BNJ 138 F 8). These snake guides are likely Ptolemy's own invention in order to legitimize his dynastic claim to Egypt, where the snake played an important role in royal ideology.[42] Ptolemy is also the only authority to claim that Alexander returned to Egypt via the more arduous desert route to Memphis instead of retracing his steps along the Mediterranean coastline (Arrian Anabasis 3.4.5 = Ptolemy FGrH / BNJ 138 F 9). With this substitution, Ptolemy directly associates Alexander's divine filiation proclaimed by Ammon at Siwah with Memphis, the ancient capital of the pharaohs, the seat of Ptolemy's satrapy and the site of his original burial of Alexander's body, once again emphasizing Alexander's legitimacy (and by extension his own) in traditional Egyptian terms.[43]

It is not clear at what point in his long and eventful reign Ptolemy composed his history, a work of at least three books (FGrH / BNJ 138 F 31). Nevertheless, the blatant self-promotion in the extant fragments and the emphasis upon his close association with an Alexander who has been rebranded as a Ptolemaic predecessor suggest that he wrote it at an earlier point in his rule, when his need for legitimation in Egypt was the greatest.[44] Although Ptolemy's portrayal of Alexander largely represents his own creation, the first-hand account of a high-ranking officer provides invaluable insight on the military events of the campaign, and also offers some tantalizing hints of how Alexander wished to be viewed by his contemporaries.

---

[41] Arrian Anabasis 4.14.4 = Ptolemy FGrH / BNJ 138 F 17.   [42] Ogden 2009c esp. 161–162.
[43] So Pownall 2021; cf. Howe 2014.
[44] As I have argued in Pownall 2021: 36 (with earlier references). On Ptolemy's 'Egyptian Identity', see Howe 2018a.

Aristobulus

While we know a great deal about Ptolemy (even if most of it emanates from his own self-fashioning), Aristobulus (*FGrH / BNJ* 139) is much more of an enigma. Arrian identifies him as the son of another Aristobulus (who is otherwise unattested),[45] and later sources state that he was from Cassandreia,[46] located on the site of the former Greek city of Potidaea. But because Cassander did not found the city until 316 BC, Cassandreia (under that name, at least) cannot have been his place of birth, which remains unknown. Nor do we have any information on Aristobulus' date of birth, but his participation in Alexander's expedition (Arrian *Anabasis* praef. 2 = *FGrH / BNJ* 139 T 6), and reference to the Battle of Ipsus in 301 BC (Arrian *Anabasis* 7.18.5 = *FGrH / BNJ* 138 F 54) suggest that he was born in the second quarter of the fourth century BC. Unlike Ptolemy, Aristobulus held no known military commands and does not appear to have been part of Alexander's inner circle. Although it is often assumed on the basis of his appointment to oversee the restoration of the plundered tomb of Cyrus the Great (*FGrH / BNJ* 139 F 51) and his presence on a commission in India (*FGrH / BNJ* 139 F 35) that his mandate in Alexander's expedition was to provide technical expertise, neither of his known missions involved any special engineering or architectural skills.[47] Furthermore, the extant fragments of his history include painstaking discussions of diverse topics including omens (and their interpretation), monuments, technology, agriculture, ethnography, botany, zoology, climate and topography, attesting to a wide range of interests as well as attention to detail. The most that can be said is that his role on the expedition does not appear to have been primarily a military one.

The extant fragments suggest that Aristobulus offers a generally apologetic treatment of Alexander, as can perhaps be seen most obviously in his narrative of the high-profile eliminations of some of his most senior officers. Like Ptolemy, Aristobulus absolves Alexander of responsibility for the deaths of Philotas (Arrian *Anabasis* 3.26.1 = *FGrH / BNJ* 139 F 22) and Callisthenes (*Anabasis* 4.14.1 = *FGrH / BNJ* 139 F 31), claiming that both were justly condemned for complicity in conspiracies against the king's life. Similarly, Aristobulus offers an exculpatory account of Alexander's murder of Clitus, for he omits the antecedents

---

[45] Arrian *Anabasis* praef. 1 and 6.28.2 = *FGrH / BNJ* 139 T 6 and T 1 (= F 50).
[46] Plutarch *Demosthenes* 23.6 = *FGrH / BNJ* 139 T 2; Pseudo-Lucian *Macrobii* 22 = *FGrH / BNJ* 139 T 3; Athenaeus 43d and 251a = *FGrH / BNJ* 139 F 6 and 47.
[47] So Bosworth 1980b: 27 and Stadter 1980: 69.

to the unfortunate incident (*Anabasis* 4.8.9 = *FGrH* / *BNJ* 139 F 29). By failing to mention the cause of Clitus' angry outburst, Aristobulus glosses over the highly contentious changes that Alexander was introducing to the traditional Argead conception of kingship. He may also have wanted to downplay Alexander's inebriation, which was certainly an aggravating factor in his violent response to Clitus' accusations, just as he minimizes Alexander's alcohol consumption on other occasions (*FGrH* / *BNJ* 139 F 30, 59 and 62). Instead, Aristobulus lays all the blame on Clitus (simultaneously throwing Ptolemy under the bus by underscoring his failure to act as an effective bodyguard), claiming that when Ptolemy forcibly removed him from the scene, he returned to the symposium expressly to antagonize Alexander, with tragic results.

Although Aristobulus and Ptolemy both adhere to the official version of events that was presumably endorsed by Alexander himself, there are some slight (but telling) differences in their accounts. While Ptolemy emphasizes the legitimacy of the execution of Callisthenes on Alexander's orders, Aristobulus claims that he was paraded around in front of the army in chains, and subsequently died of an illness.[48] By insisting that Alexander spared Callisthenes' life, Aristobulus portrays him as acting with clemency. A similar motive may also lie behind the variant tradition in Aristobulus on the identity and fate of the perpetrator of the destruction of the tomb of Cyrus the Great (and unless he is exaggerating his role in the tomb's restoration, Aristobulus was in a position to know). Aristobulus (Arrian *Anabasis* 6.29.11 = *FGrH* / *BNJ* 139 F 51a) states that Alexander tortured the priests who were guarding the tomb but, when they refused to implicate anyone, he set them free. His further comment (cited by Strabo C730 = 15.3.7 = F 51b) that the plundering of the valuable contents of the tomb but not of the corpse points to an act of grave robbers, rather than the satrap, betrays that he is aware of the official version circulated (likely by Ptolemy) that Orxines, the self-appointed satrap of Persia (Arrian *Anabasis* 6.29.2; cf. Curtius 10.1.22), had been hanged on Alexander's orders for despoiling sanctuaries and royal tombs (Arrian *Anabasis* 6.30.1–6.30.2). True to form, while Ptolemy (assuming he is Arrian's source) emphasizes the legitimacy of Orxines' execution by alleging that he was guilty of sacrilege rather than insubordination,[49] Aristobulus highlights Alexander's clemency. The parallel episodes involving the

---

[48] Cf. Chares of Mytilene (*FGrH* / *BNJ* 125 F 15), who claims that Callisthenes died of natural causes while awaiting trial by the allied *synedrion*.

[49] Badian 1958c:147–150.

Phoenician sailor who retrieved the royal diadem after it became entangled in some reeds (Arrian *Anabasis* 7.22.3–7.22.5 = *FGrH* / *BNJ* 139 F 55) and the 'substitute king' who sat on Alexander's throne (Arrian *Anabasis* 7.24.3–7.24.5 = *FGrH* / *BNJ* 139 F 58) provide further evidence of Alexander's merciful nature, for once again Aristobulus is the only authority who does not state that they were immediately executed.[50] It is tempting to suppose that Aristobulus is responsible for the identification of clemency as a trademark quality of Alexander by the later tradition.

Another apologetic tendency is revealed in Aristobulus' refusal to portray Alexander as characteristically acting with impulsive rashness. In his rendition of the famous episode of the Gordian knot, Aristobulus alleges (*FGrH* / *BNJ* 139 F 7) that Alexander released the knot by carefully removing the axel pin holding it in place, instead of dramatically slicing through it with his sword, as in the version that became dominant in the later tradition.[51] So too he is the only source to claim that Alexander became ill from exhaustion upon his arrival at Tarsus rather than from jumping recklessly into the frigid Cydnus River (*FGrH* / *BNJ* 139 F 8).

Although the overall tenor of Aristobulus' history is apologetic, there are places where he is overtly critical of Alexander. Unlike Ptolemy, Aristobulus makes no effort to absolve Alexander of responsibility for the failed assault on Spitamenes at the Polytimetus River. In his version (*FGrH* / *BNJ* 139 F 27) it is not the Macedonian commanders who are ultimately responsible for the disaster but Alexander himself, for failing to communicate effectively the chain of command.[52] He also appears less willing than Ptolemy to sanitize the brutality of Alexander's campaign, particularly as he moved farther east. His assertion (*FGrH* / *BNJ* 139 F 26) that Alexander captured the seventh Sogdian fortress by force and slaughtered all of its defenders stands in stark contrast to Ptolemy, in whose narrative the city was peacefully surrendered to Alexander (as noted above, pp. 384-385). Nor does Aristobulus condone Alexander's growing megalomania. When he mentions Alexander's professed intention to conquer the Arabian peninsula, Aristobulus criticizes his relentless imperialism and

---

[50] Diadem: 'most of the other Alexander historians' (Arrian *Anabasis* 7.24.4); throne: Diodorus 17.116.4 and Plutarch *Alexander* 74.
[51] So Arrian *Anabasis* 2.3.7; Plutarch *Alexander* 18.3; Curtius 3.1.18; Justin 11.7.16. On the propagandistic importance of this episode for Alexander, see Squillace 2018: 124–126.
[52] So Carney 1981: 155–156; see also Pownall 2013, commentary on F 27.

hints that he was motivated to embark on this proposed campaign by the desire to be recognized as a god.[53]

The copious detail preserved in many of the extant fragments, as well as the (probably apocryphal) anecdote of his reading aloud from his history to Alexander on the Hydaspes (*FGrH / BNJ* 139 T 4), suggest that Aristobulus took extensive notes during the campaign. Nevertheless, his history is attested (even if by a late and unreliable source) to have been a work of old age,[54] a statement corroborated by a reference to the Battle of Ipsus in 301 BC (*FGrH / BNJ* 139 F 54). The long gestation period may explain the apparent inconsistency of Aristobulus' willingness to put a eulogistic spin on some of Alexander's actions based on the official version of events, but to deviate from it in others, where he offers a much more negative interpretation. By the time that Aristobulus was composing his history some thirty years later, the memory of Alexander had already become hotly contested and open to manipulation as the Successors jockeyed for position in the new world order.[55]

Conclusion

Arrian defends his selection of Ptolemy and Aristobulus as the principal sources for his history on the grounds that they offered eyewitness accounts of Alexander's expedition, which could be presumed to be reliable because they were composed after his death. Nevertheless, his confidence in their supposed freedom from bias is at the very least misplaced and possibly even disingenuous. The narratives of both Ptolemy and Aristobulus, particularly in the notorious episodes that were later remembered as iconic stains on Alexander's character, are manifestly exculpatory and apologetic, in accordance with the official version that was propagated (presumably on Alexander's orders) at the time. Furthermore, both sources had their own agendas in composing their histories of Alexander's campaign. Ptolemy's chief concern was to lay the ideological foundations for his own future dynasty in Egypt by highlighting the legitimacy of Alexander's rule and representing himself as a worthy successor. Aristobulus' relative obscurity in comparison with Ptolemy makes his agenda more difficult to discern. But the insertion of explicitly critical passages into his generally idealizing

---

[53] Aristobulus is cited by both Arrian (*Anabasis* 7.19.6–7.20.1 = *FGrH / BNJ* 139 F 55) and Strabo (C741 = 16.1.11 = F 56), who are clearly drawing on the same passage.
[54] Pseudo-Lucian *Macrobii* 22 = *FGrH / BNJ* 139 T 3.   [55] As noted by Zambrini 2007: 218.

history suggests that he too shaped this larger-than-life figure in response to contemporary events during the decades of turbulent rivalry between the Successors in the wake of Alexander's unexpected death. Despite the tendentious subtexts to their narratives, however, Ptolemy and Aristobulus preserve detailed eyewitness accounts of the events of Alexander's expedition which can serve as a useful check against the sensationalizing accounts and flights of fancy of the later tradition.

Guide to Further Reading

The testimonia (T) and fragments (F) of Ptolemy and Aristobulus have been collected by Jacoby, *FGrH / BNJ* 138 and 139 respectively, now updated with full historical commentaries and English translations in the *Brill's New Jacoby* (*BNJ*) entries of Howe (Ptolemy) and Pownall (Aristobulus). On Ptolemy's career, see Heckel 2016: 230–240; Worthington 2016b; the essays in Howe 2018c; and Müller 2020d. On Ptolemy's history, see Müller 2014: 78–90; Howe 2018a (with earlier bibliography); and Pownall 2021. Unlike Ptolemy, Aristobulus has not enjoyed a flurry of interest in current scholarship. The most comprehensive overviews of Aristobulus' life remain the (now outdated) contributions of Pearson 1960: 150–187 and Pédech 1984: 331–405; see now Pownall 2013: Biographical Essay. On Aristobulus' history, see Zambrini 2007: 218–219; Müller 2014: 95–98; and Squillace 2018.

24: CLITARCHUS' ALEXANDER

Luisa Prandi

The opportunity to examine Clitarchus once more is both intriguing and challenging, because this writer is a real Scarlet Pimpernel.[1] I see it anyway as a further opportunity to review with a critical eye what I have previously written on this topic[2] and to express some new insights.

GENERAL BACKGROUND

First, I give some basic and essential information concerning the *Testimonia* and *Fragmenta* of Clitarchus (*FGrH / BNJ* 137). This twofold approach dates back to Jacoby and has the well-known result of splitting and dismembering sentences and statements. I will continue to use it, although it is necessary to move beyond such a view if we want to understand the writers who mentioned Clitarchus.

His popularity as an Alexander historian and a fine writer is the more prominent topic because many passages deal with his style or fame, not with his life and work. If we want to understand why Clitarchus became so popular, we need to appreciate the importance of the Fragments, the principal and most reliable way to approach his work. We have to focus on the reason for each mention of him and not neglect the network of intermediaries. This evidence as a whole may then be combined with the few known biographical details in order to establish Clitarchus' chronology, which is still uncertain. Not without reason, the last two sections, dealing with chronology and his portrait of Alexander, have a question mark at the end of the title; I hope they will encourage readers to reflect.

---

[1] Bosworth 1997 entitled his dissenting but friendly review of my book *In search of Cleitarchus*.
[2] See (also for previous bibliography): Prandi 1996, for an overview; Prandi 2012b, for chronology; Prandi 2016, for commentary. I follow the *BNJ* numbering and tacitly refer to it for the commentaries on each Alexander historian mentioned here.

Despite more than 10 *Testimonia*, his biographical details are scarce and puzzling.³ Clitarchus followed a family tradition because his father was Dinon (T2), known as the author of a history of Persia (*FGrH / BNJ* 690). Diogenes Laertius says that he attended two philosophical schools, that of Aristoteles of Cyrene followed by that of Stilpo of Megara (T3). Finally, two pieces of information connect Clitarchus to Alexandria. Philodemus of Gadara refers to him as *Alexandreus* (T12) and the anonymous author of *P. Oxy.* 4808 (T1b, early second century AD) calls Clitarchus *didaskalos* (preceptor) in a passage, unfortunately incomplete, where the term *Philopatoros* ('of *Philopator*') also appears (see pp. 396–400).

Also in relation to the Fragments, not all 52 of them are equally important, because at least a third of them have little meaning; most are gnomic sentences (Jacoby considered F35 and FF38–FF52 *zweifelhaftes*).⁴ Sometimes his name appears in lists of various writers (e.g. F15, in a *status quaestionis* compiled by Plutarch on the subject of Alexander's Amazon). Little more than 30 Fragments contain useful information (see pp. 395–396) Only one of these, F21 from Aelian, closely concerns Alexander (see pp. 401–404).

Clitarchus' work was entitled *Peri Alexandrou historiai* ('Histories about Alexander'), according to writers of the Hellenistic period (Clearchus, F1, F3 and F30; Dionysius *Scytobrachion*, F17), and it probably occupied 14 or 15 books.⁵ Another title, *Peri Indikēn* ('On India'), recorded by Aelian (F18), is worthy of consideration (see pp. 395–396).

Popularity

Clitarchus is definitely the Alexander historian most mentioned by ancient writers. His popularity had two evident phases, the first in Alexandria in Egypt, and the second in Rome. Traces of his Hellenistic popularity may be detected in later writers such as Strabo, Pliny, Athenaeus, Diogenes Laertius and the scholiasts. Their references to Clitarchus depend on writers who lived and studied in Alexandria during the Hellenistic age: Clearchus of Soli, Chamaeleon, Sotion,

---

³ T1 is a *Suda* entry without any content.
⁴ It may be noted that Clitarchus may have included some moral statements in his own work but we do not have any examples among the fragments. These aphorisms are quoted separately.
⁵ Book 12 deals with the Indian Gymnosophists (F6).

Eratosthenes, Dionysius *Scytobrachion*.[6] They usually provide brief and limited information. The only one who expresses an opinion – a very critical one – is Eratosthenes (F12, F13). He argues against Clitarchus as regards the geography of Hyrcania (the Caucasus region).[7] However, the above-mentioned authors are the earliest witnesses to his popularity because they read his work, which was evidently available in the Alexandrian Library. Another voice from Egypt, although later, is worthy of consideration. The anonymous author of *P.Oxy.* 4808 (T1b, ll.11–T1b, ll.12) says that Clitarchus wrote 'boastfully' (*kompō[dōs]*) but also says of him that he was 'blameless in his arrangement' (*amem[pto]s d'estin ten diathe[si]n*).

A wide range of Greek and Latin writers who lived in the first century BC and/or first century AD expressed opinions on his work: Philodemus of Gadara, Sisenna, Cicero, Posidonius of Apamea, Dionysius Longinus, Demetrius, Pliny, Curtius Rufus and Quintilianus. They mention Clitarchus to praise or criticize him, as an unavoidable cultural reference. Philodemus left Alexandria in 70 BC to move to Italy and appears to be the best candidate for having introduced Clitarchus to the Roman cultural world.[8]

The men who represented Roman culture expressed opinions about Clitarchus that mostly concerned his writing, at a time when debate over the virtues and defects of the Asian style was lively. They seem to consider him a standard of reference, positive or negative, more with regard to style than content. According to Philodemus, there was such a thing as a Clitarchean way of writing (T11). We know from the critical remarks of Cicero (T13≈F8) that Coelius Rufus and Sisenna were fond of Clitarchus (the second was a historian who appreciated a colleague). Cicero, though, did not appreciate Sisenna's style and was therefore ready to blame his favourite author (T13≈F8). He regards Clitarchus as a poor model and blames him for lying and writing 'with all the pomp of rhetoric and a tragic air' (*rhetorice et tragice*, T7≈F34). Posidonius disagrees with him for scientific reasons about the ocean tides (F26), and also has issues with his geography (F13). Both Longinus and Demetrius criticize him for his startling style and bad choice of terms ('shallow', *phloiodes*, T9; 'unsuitable wording', *acharin logon*, T10).

---

[6] Clearchus in Athenaeus (F2, F11, F30); cf. Zecchini 1989: 202–208; Chamaeleon and Dionysius in scholia (F17); Sotion in Diogenes Laertius (F6); Eratosthenes in Strabo and Pliny (F13, F16).

[7] A survey of the main geographical problems is given in Rapin 2014.

[8] The historian Timagenes, having made the same journey, possibly knew Clitarchus' work (T8≈F24; see pp. 396–400) and could also have played a similar role.

Quintilian, in his canon of historians,[9] says very pointedly of Clitarchus that 'his cleverness is praised but his reliability is criticised' (*probatur ingenium sed fides infamatur*, T6), as if his fascinating style overstepped the content of his writings. None of them depend on him as a source. Curtius attributes to him the vices of careless selection of material and credulity (*securitas* and *credulitas*, T8≈F24).[10] It was perhaps Pliny, who mentions Clitarchus within a small group of Greek historians concerned with Rome (F31), that found the most felicitous description for him: 'renowned' (*celebratus*, T2).

Unfortunately, almost none of the extant fragments are *verbatim* quotations or long enough to allow us to perceive Clitarchus' mode of writing. A clear view of Clitarchean style is thus beyond our reach. However, his style was appropriate to a certain type of audience and had no small part in his popularity. From Cicero, Quintilian and Curtius we can conclude that Clitarchus was not a reliable historian and that his aim was to astonish his readers. This judgement fits in with his involvement in geographical and scientific controversies. All this evidence shows that Clitarchus was the best-known Alexander historian when Diodorus Siculus, Pompeius Trogus and Curtius Rufus were writing their works.[11]

Relevance of the Fragments

A wide range of writers refer to Clitarchus, but in many cases without any real bias or indeed first-hand knowledge. First, Clitarchus's name is sometimes given in lists, alongside those of other writers of varying genre, importance and popularity, in such a way that we are not permitted to understand precisely what he wrote. Examples are the lists of Pliny's sources (T14a–T14c), of the opinions about long-lived men in India (F23), the lengthy list of writers who recounted the Amazon's visit to Alexander or disbelieved it (F15), and ancient opinions regarding Themistocles and the Persian king, Xerxes, or his son (F33), as well as the different counting systems used by Greek historians with regard to the chronology of Alexander's expedition (F7). It must also be remembered that some authors do not depend directly on Clitarchus, but trustingly quote another writer who, in turn, had read and quoted Clitarchus before: we have, as it were, a series of Russian

---

[9] Cf. Matijašić 2018: 20–21 and 113–115.   [10] Cf. pp. 396–400.
[11] Cf. the following section and pp. 401-404. Cf. also Coppola 2015: 24–26 who argues persuasively for an impact on Virgil.

dolls.[12] Some mention his name only because they found it in debates or controversies.[13] Other writers refer to Clitarchus only once, without any criticism and in connection with information of some importance, such as Harpocration (F4) and a scholiast (F9). However, this is not enough to demonstrate strong interest on their part or first-hand knowledge.[14]

Diodorus and Curtius are particular cases because they wrote extensively on Alexander and supposedly depended on Clitarchus, although they mention him only once or twice.[15] Nobody but Aelian, who has preserved for us five fragments and the longest quotations – with special regard to the country of India (FF18–22) – seems to show a strong and personal interest in Clitarchus. In fact, all his fragments concerning India, a considerable number, were particularly popular. Strabo, Curtius, Pliny and Aelian in particular quote him on India, seemingly without any intermediaries or any criticism. Since Aelian refers to the title *Perì Indikēn* (F18), we may suppose that the relevant section of Clitarchus's *Histories* had an independent life.

Table 24.1 is a summary table[16] of the narrative material attributed to Clitarchus: The overall results are not abundant but deserve careful attention. Roughly speaking, all the pieces of information, except F4 and F9, are very brief and limited. The same number of entries are devoted to the whole of Alexander's campaign and to the Indian section. In the first category, FF12–FF16 are linked together by reference to Hyrcania: they appear as a cluster, which further reduces the number of individual items. Half as many relate to the past, be it Greek or (mainly) barbarian.[17]

Which Ptolemy?

The chronology of Clitarchus is still a most puzzling matter. Taking into account his Alexandrian background, we may wonder who,

---

[12] Cf. 'General Background' section, above, note 6. F30 on Harpalus and the *hetairai* may be a paradigmatic case: Theopompus is the author quoted, but at the end we read that Clitarchus wrote the same.
[13] Cf. the following section on FF12–FF16.
[14] Harpocration mentions, by contrast, the historians named Marsyas six times (*FGrH / BNJ* 135, 136), who were less popular than Clitarchus. There are only three quotations of Clitarchus by the scholiasts (also F5, F17).
[15] Cf. pp. 401–404. [16] A different way to show the evidence.
[17] We can presume the influence of his father Dinon, most evident in F21.

Table 24.1 *Narrative material attributed to Clitarchus*

Alexander's Asian campaign	India	The past
F1 Theban wealth	F6 Gymnosophists	F2 Sardanapalus
F4 Spartan hostages	F17 Mt Nysa and *skindapsos*	F3 Theia and Myrrha
F7 chronology of the *diabasis*	F18 snakes	
F8 Alexander's win at Issus	F19 monkeys	F5 Persian tiara
F11 Thais at Persepolis	F20 processions	F9 sardonic laugh
F12 Euxinus and Caspian	F21 birds and mermaids	F10 Babylonia
F13 Euxinus and Caspian	F22 birds	F32 sanction of adultery
F14 Hyrcanian bee	F23 Mandi	
F15 Amazon queen	F24 Ptolemy in India	F33 Themistocles
F16 Amazons	F25 kingdom of Sambus	F34 Themistocles
F26 Macedonians and tides	F27 Ichthyophagi	
F30 Harpalus and *hetairai*	F28 salt mines	
F31 Roman embassy	F29 isles in the Persian Gulf	

among the first Ptolemies, was contemporary with the historian,[18] perhaps Ptolemy Soter, king from 305 to 282 BC and himself an Alexander historian, as claimed by a *communis opinio*,[19] or Ptolemy Philadelphus (282–246 BC), or even Ptolemy *Philometor* (246–222 BC) and the very young Ptolemy *Philopator* (from 222 BC).[20] We have the following information:

- Clitarchus was son of Dinon, writer of the literary genre of *Persika*, known to have lived during the fourth century, which might suggest a high birth date,[21] although this is not a conclusive factor.
- Philodemus puts *Alexandreus* next to Clitarchus name. If this adjective refers to his residence in the city of Alexandria, Clitarchus could have been born elsewhere and (long) before its foundation. If, instead, it refers to his birthplace, Clitarchus must be younger, born (perhaps long) after 331 BC.

---

[18] Caneva 2013: 194–199 remarks that the cultural environment varied widely over the decades. In my opinion Pearson 1960: 212–242 provides a careful and balanced analysis of the evidence for this topic, still valid today.
[19] Among others Jacoby 1923: II.B; Badian 1965b; Goukowsky 1976: xx–xxvi; Baynham 2003; Heckel 2008; Prandi 2012b.
[20] A late date, variously nuanced, has been advocated by Tarn 1948; Hazzard 1992 and 2000: 7–17; Parker 2009; Caneva 2013: 194–199; Schorn 2013: 106–110.
[21] Cf. Lenfant 2009.

- His attendance at Stilpo's lessons is also an ambiguous piece of evidence. The philosopher is associated in various ways with Ptolemy I,[22] but a disciple is usually younger. Furthermore, we do not know when or where, whether in Athens or in Alexandria, Clitarchus attended his lessons.
- There is no indisputable proof of his involvement in the Asiatic campaign. Concerning the walls of Babylon, Diodorus points out the divergence between the old guard represented by Ctesias and the newcomers represented by the Alexander historians (T5–F10). Among them only Clitarchus merits a mention, perhaps because he was his source. The passage may suggest that Clitarchus was not a member of the campaign but that he was close to the time of the first Alexander historians. Clitarchus refers to an embassy sent by the Romans to Alexander (F33) and some scholars consider this a proof of his presence at least in Babylon in 323 BC, where many embassies reached the king. The *aliter ignoti* Aristos and Asclepiades (*FGrH / BNJ* 143 F2 and *FGrH / BNJ* 144 F1, quoted and rejected by Arrian) mentioned such a Roman embassy, while Memnon of Heraclea (*FGrH / BNJ* 434 F18) talks about some diplomatic exchanges between Alexander and the Romans, these, however, dating from the first years of his reign.
- Three not-so-small divergences exist between Clitarchus and Ptolemy, about the burning of Persepolis, the visit of the Amazon and Alexander's rescue in India. According to Clitarchus, Thais was responsible for the burning (F11). This agrees with Diodorus (17.72.2), who narrates that the Athenian courtesan (*hetaira*) had a leading role and acted, without a previous plan, in a symposium atmosphere with a view to avenging the Persian Wars. Conversely, Arrian (*Anabasis* 3.18.11–3.18.12, who depends on Ptolemy) attributes to Alexander a deliberate project to set fire to the palace. Clitarchus is foremost among the writers who narrated the encounter between Alexander and the Amazon (F15); Ptolemy is one of those who denied it. Finally, both Clitarchus and Timagenes[23] say that Ptolemy took part in the attack on the Indian town where Alexander risked his life and was lucky to be rescued (T8≈F24). Ptolemy instead stated in his work that he was busy at the time with another task (Curtius 9.5.21). Either Clitarchus wrote before Ptolemy, or

---

[22] Diogenes Laertius 2.115 and 3.111.   [23] Cf. 'Popularity' section above, and further below.

afterwards and chose not to agree with him. Clitarchus was living in Alexandria and his behaviour shows independence, not flattery, and does not appear appropriate for an official historian.[24]

If we want now to interpret Homer from Homer, we may notice that many ancient writers agree in mentioning Clitarchus as being very close to some authors living in the fourth century BC. Pliny lists writers who had said something about Rome (T4–F31) and says that Clitarchus was closest (*proximus*) to Theopompus. Quintilian in his canon of historians puts Clitarchus right after Ephorus, adding that 'after a long interval' (*longo post intervallo temporis*) Timagenes was born (T6). Diodorus associates him with the Alexander historians who took part in the expedition (T5–F10). Within Plutarch's *status quaestionis* about the Amazon's visit (F15), the first names on both lists, together with Clitarchus, are all members of the Asiatic campaign. Clement of Alexandria mentions Clitarchus right after Phaenias of Eresus and Ephorus, and before Timaeus, Eratosthenes and Duris (F7). As we saw above (pp. 393–396), later writers found mention of Clitarchus in works by Hellenistic-period authors. The case of Athenaeus, who mentions Clitarchus in Book 13 (F2, F11, F30), depending extensively on Clearchus (fourth/third century BC),[25] is worthy of attention, I think.

Futhermore, the evidence favouring the age of Ptolemy *Philadelphus*, or even those of his successors, may be questionable:[26]

- The anonymous author of the papyrus *P. Oxy.* 4808 (T1b)[27] notes in a passage unfortunately compromised by some *lacunae* (ll. 13–17) that Clitarchus had some position of responsibility (*epi tou*, 'over the') and was a *didaskalos* ('preceptor'). The only name nearby, although not contiguous, is *Philopatoros* (of *Philopator*). This is the epithet of Ptolemy IV, born around 244 BC and on the throne from 222 to 205 BC. If we accept that Clitarchus was given the task of educating the future king, we have to conclude that the historian was alive, and active, at the beginning of the thirties and to assume that he was born at the end of the fourth century (*c.* 320–310). We know of some long-

---

[24] The mention of the Amazon is perhaps forgivable: we all remember the anecdote about Onesicritus being mocked by king Lysimachus for his inventiveness on this topic (Onesicritus FGrH / BNJ 134 T8). Other information related to Ptolemy himself and to a woman, Thais, who was very intimate with him. We may consider this, so to speak, sensitive data.
[25] Cf. Tsitsiridis 2013: 1–8.   [26] I discuss here only the best-grounded data.
[27] The text looks like a series of statements concerning the sources for the history of the eastern Mediterranean Sea, from Alexander the Great to the Roman conquest (Onesicritus, Chares, Clitarchus, Hieronymus and Polybius). The author appears to be a cultivated man. Cf. Landucci Gattinoni and Prandi 2013: 94–96.

lived historians, although nothing tells us that Clitarchus' life resembled their cases. If the suggestion that the authoritative Hermippus is the source of the papyrus' information about Clitarchus was right, the case for a low chronology would be strengthened. However, the papyrus is very fragmentary.[28]

- Clitarchus and Patrocles agree, though without giving any measurements, that the Black Sea and the Caspian Sea are the same size (F12; cf. Patrocles *FGrH* / *BNJ* 712 F7). Patrocles travelled from 284 to 280 BC on behalf of Seleucus Nicator to explore the Caspian Sea,[29] so some think that Clitarchus must have written after that point.[30] However, FF12–16 of Clitarchus deal with Hyrcania and the arrival of the Amazon queen, and are all related to a Hellenistic-era geographical debate. Thus Polyclitus, who reported this episode and was involved in the same controversy about the Black Sea and the Caspian (*FGrH* / *BNJ* 128 F7), may be a good candidate as well for Clitarchus' source here, and an earlier one.

- Some scholars assume that the historian wrote at the time of Ptolemy Philadelphus.[31] They believe that Clitarchus focused on the origin of the surname *Soter* credited to Ptolemy I and traced it back to his presence in the Indian town where Alexander risked his life (T8≈F24), although this was denied by Ptolemy himself. In fact, there is no evidence that Ptolemy I attributed any particular importance to this surname, while his son Ptolemy II gave it a bureaucratic and religious significance. For my part I would note that Curtius accuses Clitarchus of the careless selection of material and of credulity, not of undue invention. His account may imply that according to Clitarchus, Ptolemy had a role in rescuing Alexander, but it is very brief. So, we have no reliable evidence that Clitarchus dealt with the origin of the surname *Soter*. Moreover, this origin is in any case doubtful.[32]

To conclude, I wonder whether a high date remains the more compatible with the greater quantity of the independent data.[33]

---

[28] Cf. Schorn 2013: 107. We can read only the ending of the name, -*pos*, while the initial part is dubious.

[29] Recently, Williams 2016.   [30] Cf. Parker 2009: 36–37 who summarizes earlier hypotheses.

[31] Likewise Hazzard 1992 and Hazzard 2000: 7–17, but see the remarks of Johnson 2000; Caneva 2013: 194–199.

[32] Arrian *Anabasis* 6.11.8 resolutely denies that Ptolemy rescued Alexander; Pausanias 1.6.1 accepts it, while maintaining at 1.8.6 that the Rhodians gave him this surname. There is detailed discussion about its origin in Muccioli 2013: 81–94. A remarkable new hypothesis, unrelated to Alexander, is proposed by Worthington 2016a.

[33] I mean that a high date does not clash with Clitarchus being the son of Dinon, being *Alexandreus*, attending Stilpo's lectures or possibly joining the expedition. It is not inconsistent with Ptolemy's different recollections, because these had not yet been committed to writing. It fits

Who Is Clitarchus' Alexander?

Among the fragments, only one preserves a brief remark on Alexander's behaviour, F19 from Aelian, concerning the king's fear at the sight of apes that he mistook for Indian soldiers.[34] To better appreciate this remark, we can compare the passage with Strabo C699, possibly depending on Onesicritus,[35] where the Macedonians, and not Alexander, are the protagonists. Though mistaking the monkeys for a hostile army, they appear unafraid and get ready to attack them. The Indian king Taxiles then gave an explanation and put an end to any fight. The story is the same, in Aelian from Clitarchus and in Strabo from Onesicritus, and typical of the encounter with a new world. The focus, however, is different: on Alexander's fearful reaction on the one hand, and on the Macedonians' brave one on the other.

This constitutes a typical situation in Alexandrography and we may imagine that the episode was initially more complex. After both the king and his army experienced fear at the sight of beings that looked human but were difficult to see among the trees, all the men decided to fight with all their strength. But if the Macedonians got ready to fight, someone must have given them orders and ultimately these could only have come from Alexander. Aelian's account refers to the beginning, and Strabo's to the end, of the same scene. Since Strabo says that Taxila was together with their (the Macedonians') king, perhaps Onesicritus also said something about Alexander. Did Clitarchus add some further detail that was neglected by Aelian? Perhaps so, I now think; thus, we cannot safely say that Clitarchus was negative towards Alexander, because it depends on the king's actual behaviour. However, we can say that the historian was not flattering. Alexander appears very human in his fear before the unknown and the monstrous.

Many scholars have confidently maintained that Clitarchus offered a negative portrait of Alexander, and many others that this portrait was positive. Ancient writers who mention Clitarchus do not furnish any evidence on the matter.

---

with the lifetime of Clearchus, who seems to know the work of Clitarchus. It does not contradict the collocation of Clitarchus with writers living in the fourth century BC, as attested by Diodorus, Pliny, Quintilian, Plutarch and Clement.

[34] Aelian *De natura animalium* 17.25 (first part) reads as follows: 'Clitarchus says that there are monkeys of a mottled hue and immense size in India. Moreover, he says that in mountainous districts they are so numerous that Alexander son of Philip and the army under his command were also quite terrified at the sight of their massed numbers, imagining that they saw an army marshalled and waiting in ambush for them. The monkeys happened to be standing upright when they appeared.'

[35] *FGrH / BNJ* 134 T10≈F21.

I have dealt extensively with the fragments (pp. 395–400) precisely because I think that a good awareness of their real contents may be the best starting-point for evaluating the influence of Clitarchus' work on the Alexander historians who lived in the Roman age. The popularity of Clitarchus (see pp. 393–395) leads us to believe that he may have been a reference author for Diodorus, Trogus and Curtius.[36] However, Table 24.1 shows how little evidence we have to identify Clitarchus within later writers' work, lacking quotations of it as we do. So, the modern trend to trace every report of uncertain authorship back to Clitarchus, and, typically, every account that seems astonishing and unreliable,[37] is poorly founded.

The widespread belief that Clitarchus is the cornerstone of the so-called *Vulgata* or 'Vulgate Tradition'[38] is based on a series of similar episodes in Diodorus, Trogus/Justin and Curtius, but it is in conflict with their portraits of Alexander, which show marked differences. Diodorus praises him and regards him as an ideal *trait d'union* between Heracles and Julius Caesar. In Trogus/Justin we read a dense portrait of Alexander, contrasting with that of Philip, as a king unable to master his wrath or drunkenness. Curtius usually reports the darker side of each episode, outlining Alexander's evolution towards tyranny.[39] Hence, we have great difficulty in tracing these back to an account that could, with confidence, be called Clitarchean.

Diodorus, allegedly the closest to Clitarchus, only partially depends on him because he also borrows from another source, possibly Duris of Samos.[40] For their part, Trogus/Justin and Curtius are more similar to each other than to Diodorus and also depend on other writers. The peace talks between Darius and Alexander provide a paradigmatic

---

[36] Diodorus devotes all of Book 17 to Alexander, one of the longest in his *Bibliotheca*, Trogus/Justin Books 11–12.

[37] By way of example cf. Wüst 1953; Sohlberg 1972; Heckel 1980 and 2007; Zahrnt 1996; Burstein 1999; Baynham 2001.

[38] Raun 1868; Schwartz 1901; Jacoby 1921; Schachermeyr 1970: 11–24; Goukowsky 1976: x–xix; Bosworth 1976a. Contra, Tarn 1948, with a peculiar hypothesis about a mercenary source and poetasters (discussed in depth by Brown 1950); Hammond 1983; Prandi 1996; Wirth 1993b (see also below, p. 404). Balanced remarks by Mahé-Simon and Trinquier 2014b: 15–20.

[39] Cf. Prandi 2018 on Diodorus: the passage at 17.38.4–17.38.7, where Diodorus says that Alexander was able to cope with success, is very enlightening. Prandi 2015 on Trogus/Justin: the comparison between Alexander and Philip (9.8.11–9.8.21) is mirrored in the narrative; cf. also Worthington 2010. Baynham 1998a on Curtius: the treatment of Philotas' affair is very representative of his *forma mentis*.

[40] Cf. Landucci: 1995, Landucci 1997: 189–194 and Prandi 2013: xviii–xxx for a hypothesis, with documentation, that the content of Book 17 may be traced back to Clitarchus and Duris.

case. All the ancient writers we can read agree only on who was responsible for the offer, always Darius, and who was responsible for the talks' failure, Alexander. The times, places and number of the diplomatic exchanges are different. Diodorus (17.39 and 17.54) and Arrian (*Anabasis* 2.14 and 2.25) mention two attempts, although they differ regarding time and place.[41] Trogus/Justin (11.12.1–11.12.4 and 11.12.9–11.12.16) and Curtius (4.1.7–4.1.14, 5.1–5.8 and 5.1.11) instead report three similar attempts. Their narrative appears to derive from the same outline given by Diodorus and Arrian, but with one exchange duplicated. We can reasonably assume that Trogus and Curtius depended on the same source, while Diodorus followed another account, less elaborate and perhaps more reliable. What was the role of Clitarchus in this frame?

Some supposedly promising leads that reveal the influence of Clitarchus on Roman-period historians are not always satisfactory. Clitarchus attended the lectures of the Cynic philosopher Stilpo and we can expect to find in later writers some evidence of this way of thinking. The story of Abdalonymus of Tyre, a gardener who became king, seems an appropriate litmus test. Some other differences aside, Diodorus (17.47) recounts it as a providential change of destiny, while Curtius stresses the qualities of the man himself, suggesting a Cynic reading (4.1.16–4.1.26), and Trogus/Justin is similar to him (11.10.8). However, another Alexander historian, Onesicritus, is known to have had Cynic inclinations. It is difficult to say whether the account of Abdalonymus in Curtius and Trogus/Justin should be traced back to Onesicritus or to Clitarchus.

His stay in Alexandria (T12) enabled Clitarchus to become closely acquainted with the religion and politics of Egypt. Hence, for example, we might expect that the description, lengthy although not fully reliable, of the pilgrimage to Siwah could be traced back to him.[42] Callisthenes says that only the king was admitted to the temple and, as for Ptolemy and Aristobulus, no details are preserved.[43] However, we read in Diodorus, Trogus/Justin and Curtius similar and longer accounts dwelling on a procession with the *xoanon* (wooden idol) of Ammon in a golden vessel, carried by the priests and followed by singing

---

[41] Plutarch *Alexander* 29.7 narrates only the second attempt.
[42] Diodorus 17.49–17.51; Justin 11.11.2–11.11.13; Curtius 4.7.5–4.7.32. Cf. the overview in Howe 2013. A very conventional approach is given by Collins 2014a.
[43] Callisthenes *FGrH* / *BNJ* 124 F14; Ptolemy *FGrH* / *BNJ* 138 F8; Aristobulus *FGrH* / *BNJ* 139 F14.

women, as well as three verbal questions and oracular answers. The boat closely recalls the rite outlined on a papyrus predating Alexander's time (*Pap. Brooklyn* 47.218.3, 651 BC), in which the vessel of Ammon in Thebes moves in response to the *ostraka* of the worshippers.[44] Our accounts cannot depend on eyewitnesses – because the nearly complete silence of Callisthenes, Ptolemy and Aristobulus shows that Alexander chose not to speak about the consultation – but rather blend Egyptian rituals and Greek oracular practices. The result is not quite consistent but very impactful.

I still believe that G. Wirth[45] was right in suggesting that, very soon after Alexander's death, a range of events, places and people became an essential part of the story of the greatest enterprise ever undertaken. Initially this was not always a written story. We know very little about the veterans, including non-combatants, and their talks. However, it is clear that they all popularized their experiences, stressing positive or negative sides of Alexander's behaviour. So, if we still want to maintain the term *Vulgata*, we should think in terms of a number of essential episodes, open to different interpretations, rather than search for a single written work at its core.

Clitarchus is indeed an elusive writer. Perhaps he was a collector of these very reports, partly spoken and partly already written,[46] and aimed to produce a wide-ranging, magnificent and multifaceted work,[47] even a stunning one as ancient writers testify. With these premises, however, the Scarlet Pimpernel remains Alexander himself.

Guide to Further Reading

On Clitarchus' father Dinon the best study is Lenfant 2009. On the possibility that the Indian section of Clitarchus' *Histories* had an independent circulation see, extensively, Prandi 2016, both the Commentary to FF18–23 and the Biographical Essay. A date even as late as the first century BC has been proposed for Clitarchus: this by Gitti 1953, a hypothesis nowadays superseded. The portrait of Alexander and the memory of him did not remain constant across the decades: besides Pearson 1960 and Caneva 2013, see also Dreyer 2009. For a detailed commentary on the three divergences between the fragments of

---

[44] Cf. Parker 1962 and Prandi 2013: 76–9. [45] Cf. Wirth 1993b: 8 and 15–19.
[46] Some points in common with the fragments of Nearchus and Onesicritus are consistent with Clitarchus knowing their work.
[47] Cf. also Wiemer 2011: 192–195.

Clitarchus and Ptolemy, see Prandi 1996: 79–83 and Prandi 2016, on FF11, 15 and 24. The different evaluation of these data by Bosworth 1997 proves the difficulty of our evidence for Clitarchus. All aspects of the question of the Roman embassy to Alexander the Great are reconsidered by Humm 2006.

25: CALLISTHENES, CHARES, NEARCHUS, ONESICRITUS AND THE MYSTERY OF THE *ROYAL JOURNALS*

Christian Thrue Djurslev

Waldemar Heckel's prosopography of Alexander's age includes an entry for the protagonist to prevent the book from reading 'like Hamlet without the prince'.[1] The account ends with a summary of the principal literary sources:

> The most important of the writers who accompanied the expedition and knew the King personally deserve mention. Eumenes of Caria and Diodotus of Erythrae were said to have been the authors of the *Royal Journals* or *Ephemerides*, but the authenticity and nature of the Journals are hotly disputed. Chares of Mytilene was the court chamberlain and an eyewitness source for some of what went on 'behind the scenes'. Callisthenes of Olynthus accompanied Alexander as the 'official historian' and sent reports back to Greece at the end of each campaigning season, serving thus as both propagandist and war correspondent. Onesicritus and Nearchus described the progress of the fleet from the Hydaspes to the Tigris and their fragments deal with India, but the former may have written a work on Alexander closely modeled on Xenophon's *Cyropaedia*.[2]

Heckel goes on to add three names to the polyptych: Ptolemy, Aristobulus and Clitarchus of Alexandria, who are covered in the previous chapters of this volume. In this chapter, the aim is to expand upon Heckel's portrayals of the first five significant historians of

---

[1] Heckel 2006: vi.   [2] Heckel 2006: 18, *s.v.* 'Alexander [2]'.

Alexander.³ I offer a brief biography of each author, as well as an impression of what they wrote. Any outline, however, must begin with a notice of the problematic nature of the evidence and, consequently, the elusiveness of the subject.⁴

One does not simply walk into the morass of the earliest historiography at Alexander's court. Not only is the scholarship vast, but the perils are also great because none of these Alexander historians' works remains extant. What content survives is reworkings by later writers, often operating centuries apart, sometimes writing in other genres, styles, idioms and even languages.⁵ For instance, as evidenced in previous chapters of this part of the volume, self-conscious authors rewrote material to varying degrees for the benefit of their own narratives, as in the case of Plutarch's biography and Arrian's or Curtius Rufus' histories (the last in Latin).⁶ Unfortunately, we only possess the words of these intermediary sources. It is, therefore, impossible to test reliably how the intermediaries compare to the originals without sufficiently large samples of the originals available.⁷ The originals simply cannot be cut from the cloth of later rewritings, sometimes even with extensive recontextualization of the latter.⁸

Of course, absence of evidence is not evidence of absence. Later sources document the existence of these named historians. However, as already indicated, possible shortcomings are legion. For instance, ancient biographical literature is known to be notoriously incongruous because later biographers typically embellished accounts of their subjects. In this case, then, the available data about the Alexander historians allow little to no certainty. The 'facts' are, therefore, an open invitation to interpretation, and even reinterpretation.⁹

---

³ See also the balanced accounts of Bosworth 1988b: 242–247 and Baynham 2003.
⁴ See, for example, Müller 2019: 11.
⁵ Scholars have traditionally divided the 'preservation' into two categories: (1) references to the lives of the Alexander historians, the so-called *testimonia* (T); and (2) fragments (F), which are snippets of text, such as direct citations, that may or may not be faithful. The task of identifying T and F has previously been conducted first in lavish editions by Karl Wilhelm Ludwig Müller (1813–1894; see in particular Müller 1846) and later by Felix Jacoby (1876–1959). Even though both resources have received new life online, the latter remains the standard point of reference. It is, however, important to realize that such reconstructions remain modern constructs with considerable methodological idiosyncrasies in selection, organization and interpretation. Cf. Baron 2013: 9–14.
⁶ This is to say nothing of the other extreme, when authors refer to material superficially or without even having read it. See, for example, the discussion of Diogenes Laertius' Onesicritus biography below (pp. 416–419).
⁷ This is possible with other historians like Herodotus, Xenophon and Polybius – see, for example, Hau 2021: 239.
⁸ Lenfant 2013.   ⁹ For his revised views on Callisthenes, see Heckel 2020a.

These opening remarks are not meant to deny any responsibility for what follows, but rather to emphasize the shaky foundations on which the following sketches are based.

CALLISTHENES OF OLYNTHUS (c. 370–327, FGrH / BNJ 124)[10]

The first historian under discussion was a northern Greek with ties to members of Philip's court,[11] most famously Aristotle,[12] for or with whom he may have conducted historical research.[13] It is clear that Callisthenes served as a man of letters at Alexander's court.[14] History may have been his primary occupation, since he had acquired fame for his pro-Macedonian history of contemporary Greece until the birth of Alexander.[15] The sequel may have been another history,[16] or a freestanding monograph on the Asiatic campaign, for a few texts attribute to him an 'Alexander's deeds', *Alexandrou praxeis*.[17] Unfortunately, it is a late title for a work of unknown textual form and parameters. There is no evidence of the publication details, although many believe, as Heckel once did, that the work was published in instalments to relay reports to Greek readers during the initial phase of the campaign, perhaps to support the immense visual displays of Alexander's victories.[18]

---

[10] Bibliography on Callisthenes until 2015 at Molina Marín 2018: 32–33. Cf. Gilhaus 2017: 30–37.
[11] Heckel 2006: 76–77, *s.v.* 'Callisthenes [1]'.
[12] Despite the rich biographical tradition linking them with familial ties (cf. T1, T2, T6, etc.), the exact nature of their relationship remains contested.
[13] T23 = *Syll.*³ 275 suggests that Callisthenes did historical research with or for Aristotle on the Pythian victor lists.
[14] T23 *bis* preserves Callisthenes' only known 'official' title, *epistolographos*, which may indicate that he was in charge of Alexander's correspondence for a time.
[15] Diodorus 14.117.8, 16.14.4 (= T27a–T27b) writes that Callisthenes' *Greek History* filled 10 books and chronicled the period from the King's Peace (387) to the outbreak of the Phocian War (356). A tentative list of Callisthenes' *oeuvre* is compiled at Rzepka 2016 (biographical essay).
[16] Note, for example, that F12a = John Lydus *On Months* 4.107 (p. 146) mentions that Callisthenes also wrote about his experiences with Alexander in the fourth book of his *Greek History*, *Hellenica*. Cf. F57 on Philip's eye injury in a *Macedonian History*.
[17] T18c '*gesta Alexandri*' (a scholion to Ovid's *Ibis*); T26: ''Ἀλεξάνδρου Πράξεις' (*Gnomologium Vaticanum*, fifteenth century AD).
[18] Pedersen 2015: 120–122 proposes that Callisthenes – as represented by Arrian *Anabasis* 1.13–1.16 and Plutarch *Alexander* 16 – is the authority for the story concerning the epic charge into the riverbed of the Granicus which paved the way for Macedonian victory (cf. the less dramatic account at Diodorus 17.19–17.21). The event is commemorated in Alexander's subsequent dedication of a lavish war monument in Dion, which comprised of an incredible group of 25 equestrians in bronze executed by the court artist Lysippus; see Stewart 1993: 123–130.

Of the c. 70 fragments ascribed to Callisthenes, only a handful refer explicitly to Alexander.[19] There may be many more, as it appears that other first-generation historians exploited Callisthenes' material. It seems that Callisthenes was responsible for describing many of the early events until the battle of Gaugamela (331 BC; cf. F37) or the death of Darius.[20] In any case, it is certain that Callisthenes could not have narrated events beyond the spring of 327 because of his demise in that year.[21]

It is difficult to assess the exact nature of Callisthenes' writing,[22] because of the reuse of Callisthenes in other authors' reworkings of yet more lost sources.[23] Common patterns in what remains are: chronological synchronisms of events, and therefore comparisons to other great 'panhellenic' wars, mostly the Trojan War (e.g. F10b) and the Persian War (e.g. F30); heavily embellished battle narratives, despite Callisthenes' eyewitness status (e.g. T29); and strong mythologization of Alexander as a hero (e.g. F36) or god (e.g. F31). We know of the latter feature because it was criticized extensively by another famed Hellenistic historian, Timaeus of Tauromenium (c. 350–260 BC), fragmentarily preserved in Polybius' *Histories* (c. mid-second century).[24] Polybius himself took umbrage with Callisthenes' ostensible ineptitude in military matters.[25]

Despite later historians' polemics,[26] the general impression of the fragments suggests that Callisthenes' history, whatever its form, competed with Homer and Herodotus, the most famous accounts of Greeks warring against eastern enemies. A passage that ties all the above themes together is Callisthenes' account of the visit to the Siwah Oasis,[27] which casts Alexander in Herodotean and Homeric roles. The king is divinely supported by various omens, Greek cities and nature (crows); competes with Hellenic champions of international background (Heracles and Perseus); gains unique access to information of godly descent at

---

[19] FF2, 10b, 14a–14b, 30, 31, 35–37.
[20] Jacek Rzepka argues that Callisthenes may have polished the battle narrative after Parmenion's removal at Ecbatana (winter 329). This is but one indication that Callisthenes did indeed keep his powder dry rather than sending bulletins back to Greece.
[21] Heckel 2020a: 207–208 revises his previous view, arguing that the burning of Persepolis was the last event narrated. Cf. Müller 2019: 20.
[22] The explicit testimonia and fragments derive mainly from Plutarch, as well as the *Geography* by Strabo (c. AD 20s).
[23] See, for example, Arrian *Anabasis* 3.3.1–3.3.2, who silently attests F14a through an intermediary (Aristobulus?); cf. *FGrH / BNJ* 134 F13–15, with Pownall 2013.
[24] T20 = Polybius 12.12b.   [25] T29 = Polybius 12.17–12.22.
[26] Commonplace in Greek historiography – see, for example, Marincola 1997: 218–36.
[27] FF 14a–14b. Cf. Gilhaus 2017: 37, n. 39.

Homeric-style oracles, incidentally supported by independent seers (the Sibyl); reverses the effects of the Persian War at Apollo's oracle; and learns of the prophecies about his imminent victories in Persia.[28] This heroic representation of Alexander – the son of Zeus who spearheaded a divinely ordained mission against Persia on behalf of the Greek states – seems to have been the thrust of Callisthenes. Such an image is perhaps surprising when we consider that Callisthenes had first-hand knowledge of the campaign and privileged access to Alexander. However, the literary flattery is perhaps equally unsurprising, given the fact that Alexander was Callisthenes' patron and the initial scope of the campaign as a 'panhellenic crusade'.[29]

Callisthenes wrote the first truly contemporary history of Alexander, insofar as he died before the king. However, his repute is inevitably linked to his paradoxical fall from grace. Three stories outline his defiance against the Macedonian warlord:[30] Callisthenes refused to perform obeisance or *proskynesis* to the king; he belittled or berated the Macedonian leaders in public (baited by Alexander's request for an anti-Macedonian argument after a laudatory speech given at an unspecified symposium);[31] and he became associated with the instigation of a conspiracy.

Callisthenes' resistance is out of character for someone paid to perform flattery in writing.[32] Later sources' representation of an epic stand-off between an enlightened Greek and 'barbarian' despot simply does not add up. Incriminating stories only begin to circulate after 329, indicating Callisthenes' cooperation until that time. The sheer length of the spiralling conflict (winter 329–spring 327) indicates that Callisthenes' fall was not an impulsive removal on the king's part, as was his brutal murder of Clitus at a symposium (summer 328). According to Lara O'Sullivan, Callisthenes rather fell prey to court intrigue. After Alexander moved into Afghanistan, western resistance

---

[28] Note also that the Milesians warn Alexander of future threats in Sparta (the revolt of Agis and the battle at Megalopolis?), the only city outside the Corinthian League reinvented by Philip and Alexander.

[29] Yates 2019: 202–248. The notion of a revenge war against Achaemenid Persia proliferated in the elite environments of fourth-century Macedon and Greece, but the Greek loss at Chaeronea (338) prompted King Philip II to revamp the project as a crusade led by Macedon (Spring 337). Upon seizing power after his father's death in 336, Alexander rehashed the policy at the symbolic sites of the Hellespont and Troy (334); for the latter, see Briant 2018.

[30] Summarized in the central digressions on Callisthenes' downfall at Plutarch *Alexander* 52–55 (T7) and Arrian *Anabasis* 4.10–14.3 (T8). Cf. Curtius 8.5–8.8.

[31] Plutarch *Alexander* 53.3–53.6.

[32] This is brought out well by O'Sullivan 2020 in her analysis of the *proskynesis* episode.

dissipated and the need for a Greek-oriented narrative receded.[33] As Callisthenes' role became compromised, the intellectual balance at court shifted, opening the floor to rivals, whom Callisthenes was ultimately unwilling to ally with or unable to oust.[34] His attempts to counter their lobbying had disastrous results in the hands of his competitors, who made sure that negative versions of his sayings not only reached the attention of the king, but also the close circle around him, such as Hephaestion. Court schemes thus sealed the fate of the Greek 'traitor'. It seems fitting that the circumstances surrounding the death of the first major historian are obfuscated by contrasting reports, even among the eye-witnesses (T18a–f).[35]

Chares of Mytilene (*FGrH* / *BNJ* 125)[36]

The second historian under discussion was one such witness (FF14– FF15). Plutarch gives him the last word when highlighting the inconsistencies of those who recorded the cause of Callisthenes' death:

> Chares reports that after Callisthenes' arrest, he was kept imprisoned for seven months in order to be tried by a *synedrion* in the presence of Aristotle. However, during the days when Alexander was wounded among the Mallians and Oxydracae in India, Callisthenes died from obesity and the disease of lice.[37]

The account exudes an apologetic tendency, which seems representative of Chares' massive *Histories concerning Alexander* (in ten books or more).[38] The king is markedly absent and blameless, for he is given no agency; he is even absent at the time of death, impaired, ostensibly, by one of the worst injuries he sustained during the campaign. In Alexander's absence, things simply happen to Callisthenes. He is to be

---

[33] O'Sullivan 2019: 618–619.
[34] A case in point is the episode during which flatterers competed to console Alexander after the killing of Clitus: Plutarch *Alexander* 52.3–52.7 (Callisthenes, Anaxarchus); Arrian *Anabasis* 4.9.7–4.9.9 (Callisthenes, Anaxarchus, Agis); Curtius 8.5.8–8.5.20 (Callisthenes, Agis, Cleon). Justin 12.6.17 mentions only Callisthenes.
[35] A rather suspicious fact noted by Gilhaus 2017: 32.
[36] Bibliography for Chares: Molina Marín 2018: 35. Cf. Cagnazzi 2015, Gilhaus 2017: 79–81, Müller 2017 (biographical essay) and 2019: 21.
[37] Plutarch *Alexander* 55.8 ~ F15 (trans. Müller, adapted). Cf. Plutarch *Sulla* 36.5, who prefers to follow Aristobulus (*FGrH* / *BNJ* 139 F33).
[38] Athenaeus (50 per cent of the corpus) maintains across most fragments that Chares wrote Περὶ Ἀλέξανδρον Ἱστοριῶν (514e ~ F2). Cf. Athenaeus 93c (F3), 538b (F4), 575a (F5), 437a (F19a). Athenaeus 171c (F1) mentions the *Histories* without Alexander.

tried by Greek law – a lawsuit which includes Aristotle (!) – at the council of Corinth, which deflects blame from Macedonian institutions (it is not mentioned that Alexander presided over the Corinthian League). Chares' note of the long duration of Callisthenes' imprisonment suggests a wish to give him a fair trial, and a rather sensational one at that, had the prisoner not expired. Finally, the cause of death is highly suspicious, not only an unknown illness suffered by other significant characters in Plutarch's *oeuvre*,[39] but also obesity, which is not normally associated with prisoners of war.

Chares' carefully crafted narrative represents an 'official' version that exculpates the king and restores faith in court protocol. This is significant since Plutarch refers to Chares as 'chamberlain' or 'master of ceremony' (*eisangeleus*), a role that perhaps pertained to court ceremonial of Macedonian and/or Achaemenid origins.[40] In this context, I note Giustina Monti's suggestion that some fragments concern Alexander's letters, which may indicate that the title, whatever its meaning, also made Chares responsible for written communications.[41] The fragments of Chares generally take an interest in court affairs, from cultural politics (e.g. F4: the mass marriages at Susa) to social engagement (e.g. F9: a so-called *mēlomachia*, a staged naval battle during which contestants pelted Babylon's best apples at each other). However, as Sabine Müller reminds us,[42] it is important to recognize that the vast majority of fragments stem from Plutarch's biography and Athenaeus' *Sophists at Supper*, a notorious third-century 'cover text',[43] which deals exclusively with socio-cultural matters. It is therefore crucial that some fragments, including the ones concerning Callisthenes, betray an overt political agenda, whereas others present material that never came to dominate the narratives of the campaign, such as Chares' uniquely attested story about the wound that Alexander suffered in single combat with Darius at the battle of Issus (F6).

Yet, these alternative tales were circulated. Chares wrote them, despite his eyewitness status and his privileged access; the case of Callisthenes' flatteries may be compared. Perhaps Chares' fragments can be read as a good illustration of the sort of storytelling with which

---

[39] Müller 2017, commentary on F15.
[40] Plutarch *Alexander* 46.1. Müller 2017, commentary on T2, judiciously evaluates the vast amount of scholarly literature written on a uniquely attested title.
[41] Monti 2016: 30 n. 56. Did Chares succeed Callisthenes as *epistolographos*?
[42] Müller 2017 (biographical essay).
[43] That is, 'the text in which the fragment is contained': Hau 2021: 239. Cf. Baron 2013: 4, 'the multiple senses of "cover" (to protect, but also to obscure) neatly convey the functions performed by the preserving author'.

Callisthenes competed for favour at court. Since Chares' work seems to flatter Alexander the most, it is unclear what immediate purpose it would have served, had he published it after Alexander's death. It is possible that writing such a history was a way to curry favour with the Macedonian leaders of the post-Alexander world in which war veterans regularly relied on previous connections to the successful king.[44] Authors could do the same with words.

Unfortunately, we know next to nothing of Chares himself,[45] not even his entry into or exit from the Macedonian court. His Mytilenian origins are equally obscure. It is unknown when Chares penned his *Histories*, although the work must have been one of the first in the field and appeared before that of Aristobulus.[46] It may have appeared around the time of Onesicritus' (discussed below, pp. 416–19).[47] If Athenaeus is indeed correct in calling the work a history, it is possible that Chares was writing a type of text we know from other Greeks who ventured east, most famously Ctesias of Cnidus, Artaxerxes II's court physician.[48] This might explain the novelistic features integrated into the political history, together with the intensive focus on eastern ethnography (FF16–FF17). A context of alterity discourse (in which 'the other' is projected) is particularly well suited to explaining or excusing Macedonian customs, including excessive drinking. Chares associated this with Indian society instead, describing the debauchery at the wine celebrations after the suicide by self-immolation of Calanus, an Indian sage (F19a–F19b). Forty contestants died, including the winner Promachus. Calanus' death at Pasargadae (324 BC) also ignited the imagination of the next two historians,[49] Nearchus and Onesicritus.

NEARCHUS OF CRETE (*FGrH* / *BNJ* 133)[50]

Following Jacoby's order of Alexander historians and histories, there are eight minor entries between Chares and the third historian under

---

[44] Wallace 2020: 132–143. [45] Heckel 2006: 83 *s.v.* 'Chares [2]'. [46] Gilhaus 2017: 80 n. 4.
[47] Gilhaus 2017: 383, commentary on F12: the dating depends on when the story of the Amazon queen began to circulate. It may have originated with Onesicritus *FGrH* / *BNJ* 134 T8 and F1.
[48] Like Ctesias in his *History of Persia*, Chares reports a host of stories of *orientalia*, including a supposedly Persian love-romance of Zariadres and Odatis (F5 ~ Athenaeus 575a–575f). If Monti is right that Chares was in charge of letters, another Ctesian parallel consists in the fact that Ctesias relayed epistolographic correspondence in the negotiations of Artaxerxes and the Athenian general Conon in 399–397 BC.
[49] Nearchus F4 ~ Arrian *Anabasis* 7.3.6; Onesicritus *FGrH* / *BNJ* 134 F18 ~ Lucian *Death of Pelegrinus* 25.
[50] For bibliography on Nearchus, Molina Marín 2018: 34–35.

discussion. Nearchus distinguishes himself from all the previous Alexander historians subsequent to Callisthenes in being a well-known person and author,[51] not only by virtue of his prominence in Macedonian politics, but also because of the extensive 'quotations' of Nearchus in the *Indica* (*On India*) of the Romano-Greek historian of the imperial period, Arrian.[52] Quantitatively speaking, Arrian preserves almost half of the corpus of Nearchan fragments (43 per cent), which makes understanding Nearchus an exercise in reading Arrian as an intermediary.

The task may seem straightforward at first. Arrian's *Indica* provides a detailed summary of Nearchus' eyewitness account of the arduous naval expedition down the Hydaspes river and into the Indus delta (autumn 326 BC), from which the Macedonian fleet journeyed to Susa in Mesopotamia (arriving March, 324) after a stop in Carmania (December, 325). However, Arrian also rewrote Nearchus' account for another text, his *History of Alexander* (or the *Anabasis*), and the respective versions of the sea voyage do not add up, as Henning Schunk has shown.[53] Moreover, we have yet another 'control source',[54] namely the revision of Nearchus in the imperial geographer Strabo (25 per cent of the Nearchan corpus). Strabo's reading of Nearchus helps to confirm that Arrian was indeed rewriting Nearchus for his own purposes in both the *Anabasis* and the *Indica*.

As already said, Arrian's adaptations matter for our understanding of Nearchus. First, Arrian's choice of the Ionic dialect for the *Indica* does not seem to match the original language in which Nearchus wrote (possibly Attic), but rather reflects Arrian's homage to Herodotus.[55] Second, scholars have often noted that Nearchus evoked Homeric (F1.30) and Herodotean (F8) antecedents in terms of content,[56] but this may once again be Arrian flexing his literary muscles rather than Nearchus himself.[57] Third, in terms of Nearchus' role, it is clear that Arrian's *Indica* is rather partial towards Nearchus' own achievements,

---

[51] Heckel 2006: 171–173 *s.v.* 'Nearchus'.
[52] Especially F1 = Arrian *Indica* 18–42. For Arrian, see Leon (Chapter 20) in this volume. Cf. Goukowsky 2022.
[53] Schunk 2019: 111–188.
[54] A term employed by Bosworth 1988b: 56; he used it to check information in Arrian through a source that covered the same piece of information, such as Strabo.
[55] *Pace* Whitby 2012 (biographical essay), who accepts the suggestion of Pearson 1960: 122. Cf. Schunk 2019: 60–63.
[56] See e.g. Bucciantini 2015b:125–137.
[57] Schunk 2019: 189–240 on Arrian and Homer. For this topic in Arrian's *Anabasis*, see also Liotsakis 2019a: 163–225.

insofar as it primarily mediates his deeds by drawing parallels with those of the king himself: the Cretan led a significant expedition on the waterway, while the king led the army on land.[58] However, Schunk's comparison of the *Indica* and the *Anabasis* demonstrates that Nearchus is always made subordinate to Alexander, and this may be of Arrian's devising, with a view amplifying the focus on Alexander in both works at the expense of Nearchus.

On this last point, it is unclear to whom Nearchus was promoting himself. It was probably not Alexander, who had trusted him ever since adolescence.[59] Although Plutarch claims that the *Royal Diaries* (discussed below) said that Nearchus read his account of the sea voyage to Alexander on his deathbed,[60] it is generally agreed that Nearchus wrote after the king's passing. Ernst Badian argued that Nearchus was trying to vindicate himself against charges levelled by Onesicritus,[61] whereas, for Gerhard Wirth, Nearchus was, rather, attempting to ingratiate himself with Antigonus Monophthalmus after 315 BC.[62] Andrea Zambrini offers a darker take, arguing that Nearchus cast himself as close to Alexander in order to silence whispers of his implication in the poison plot (T10d).[63] For Anna Gadaleta this self-defence may have occurred in 317 BC.[64] Whatever the truth of the matter is, Nearchus did play an active role in post-Alexander politics, staging a short-lived attempt to seize power through his connection to Alexander's son Heracles, the brother of his wife (T11). Thereafter he consigned himself to remain with the Antigonid faction, seemingly until his death (after 313/12 BC).[65]

This level of uncertainty is uncomfortable when one considers that Nearchus enjoyed a political career and that his account is probably the text from the days of Alexander himself that we know best. How difficult is it, then, to say something with confidence about the historians and histories we know even less about? Nevertheless, we

---

[58] In this sense, Nearchus appears to anticipate Ptolemy's history in which the future king of Egypt heavily embellished episodes of his campaign experience to promote himself as a legitimate successor to Alexander at the expense of everyone else. Cf. Pownall in this volume (Chapter 23).

[59] Nearchus was close enough to the pre-campaign Alexander to be banished in the Pixodarus affair (336 BC): Arrian *Anabasis* 3.6.5; cf. Plutarch *Alexander* 10.4.

[60] Plutarch *Alexander* 76.3 ~ *Ephemerides* FGrH / BNJ 117 F 3b. Cf. Arrian *Anabasis* 7.25.4 ~ FGrH / BNJ 117 F3a, who claims that Nearchus was listening to Alexander's plans for Arabia. *Pace* Bearzot 2017, commentary on F3b, the conflicting stories can be reconciled if Nearchus read his 'official' log in preparation for the next campaign.

[61] Badian 1975, reprinted at Badian 2012: 193–210.

[62] Wirth 1988, endorsed by Whitby 2012 (biographical essay).

[63] Zambrini 2013, proposed in Zambrini 2007: 481–482.   [64] Gadaleta 2008.

[65] T13a–c places Nearchus' last political activities in Syria, as advisor to Demetrius Poliorcetes. Wheatley and Dunn 2020: 70 maintain the position that Nearchus survived the battle of Gaza and produced his writing thereafter.

can say with some confidence that Nearchus kept some form of logbook of the pivotal sea voyages that could be consulted by much later researchers (Arrian and Strabo). Although the title of the text is lost, and its parameters are unknown, it may – perhaps – have contained a narrative that extended from Nearchus' return journey from India up until the mass marriages at Susa, when Nearchus married into Alexander's family.[66] Moreover, the available fragments indicate that Nearchus may have thought about writing a complete history of the whole campaign in the style of Callisthenes, Chares or Onesicritus, but it does not seem that he ever got the opportunity. At any rate, Nearchus' navigation of choppy waters is an apt allegory for a Greek officer's decade-long experiences at the Macedonian courts.

ONESICRITUS (FGrH / BNJ 134)[67]

Strabo famously referred to the fourth historian under discussion as 'the chief helmsman of the incredible', *archikybernētēs tōn paradoxōn* (T10) but, in the same passage, conceded that Onesicritus provided some reliable information on India. In fact, even though Strabo rated Nearchus and Onesicritus at a similar level of trustworthiness (T11), he reused Onesicritus' text more regularly than Nearchus' (preserving 30 per cent of the Onesicritan corpus). Pliny also preferred Onesicritus (20 per cent of the known corpus),[68] citing him for local data on places where there were no shadows (T13a), on people with remarkable bodies (13c), on the nature of trees (13e) and on fruit-bearing trees (13f).[69] Plutarch relied solely on Onesicritus of the two throughout his works, seemingly having no knowledge of (or access to) Nearchus. In his preference for Nearchus, Arrian is the only Roman-era author to distort this one-sided picture.[70]

It is common to detect a rivalry between Nearchus and Onesicritus based on their similar content. For instance, both chronicled

---

[66] Gilhaus 2017: 120.   [67] For bibliography on Onesicritus, Molina Marín 2018: 33–34.
[68] It is possible that Pliny read Onesicritus through the Greek writings of King Juba II, who was also a prominent historian.
[69] Pliny cites both Nearchus and Onesicritus for information about places and people, T13b.
[70] For the fact that Roman readings of Alexander-related texts distort our view of Alexander, see now Finn 2022. As for Arrian, did he simply trust in the historical authority of Nearchus, or did Nearchus' work provide a less maligned literary predecessor for Arrian's own Trajanic travelogue of the Black Sea? We ignore Arrian's choice of source material at our own peril. Cf. Carlsen 2014.

the events of the same voyage.[71] However, the former was highly critical of the latter,[72] not only berating Onesicritus for misunderstanding the policy behind the mission,[73] but also omitting mention of him when they received the same honours for their joint expedition.[74] Scholars have seized upon this conflict to determine the priority of their works.[75] If Onesicritus had written before Nearchus, he had written a work that invited correction from a superior officer. If Onesicritus wrote after Nearchus, he may have tried to assert his own role against the indictment. There is no straightforward solution to this problem. On the one hand, Onesicritus' (extant) narrative is imprecise and void of criticism of Nearchus, which may indicate that Onesicritus wrote in a vacuum and, therefore, first. On the other hand, if Nearchus wrote a self-aggrandizing narrative at the expense of Onesicritus (and others), it stands to reason that the text should elicit a reaction from other members of the crew, which it did. In this context, it is not helpful to point to Arrian's critique of Onesicritus' lying about his title,[76] which required correction, for Arrian clearly took no offence at the inconsistencies of Nearchus. Moreover, as we have seen, every Alexander historian wrote in a self-promoting fashion.

Another interpretation is to read Nearchus' (singular) criticism in the style of the exchanges between Alexander and Parmenion: Onesicritus made a proposition that Nearchus rebuffed, thus saving the day and, therefore, gaining the full crowning glory. That reading would be fully in line with Nearchus' self-validating narrative, while not requiring Onesicritus to have written first. It follows that, if the exchange between Nearchus and Onesicritus in Nearchus' work is merely incidental, Nearchus and Onesicritus (and others)[77] could have written in any particular order. They could have done so independently of each other in the period after Alexander's death. On this reading, we are no closer to a solution of the dating issues, but we are less restricted in the way we may read the works of Nearchus and Onesicritus.

As for the rest of the work, which comprised at least four books (T8), scholars typically accept the title attested in Diogenes Laertius'

---

[71] Onesicritus *FGrH* / *BNJ* 134 F28 ~ Pliny *Natural History* 6.96–6.100.
[72] In a word, 'Intimfeind' (Müller 2019: 20).
[73] Nearchus *FGrH* / *BNJ* 133 F1 ix ~ Arrian *Indica* 32.9–12. Cf. F1e ~ Arrian *Anabasis* 7.20.9.
[74] Arrian *Indica* 42.9 ~ Nearchus *FGrH* / *BNJ* 133 T9a, in which Nearchus receives a gold crown from Alexander at Susa. Cf. Arrian *Anabasis* 7.5.6 ~ Onesicritus *FGrH* / *BNJ* 134 T6, in which both Onesicritus and Nearchus receive a crown.
[75] Gilhaus 2017: 119.   [76] Arrian *Anabasis* 6.2.3 ~ Onesicritus *FGrH* / *BNJ* 134 F27.
[77] A certain Orthagoras (*FGrH* / *BNJ* 713) wrote yet another (lost) account of the voyage.

biography of Onesicritus (T1),[78] 'How Alexander was raised' (Πῶς 'Αλέξανδρος ἤχθη).[79] Diogenes goes on to compare the work to Xenophon's *Anabasis* and *Cyropaideia*. However, the (extant) fragments do not meet the title's promise. Although they concern the campaign narrative, none of them deal with Alexander's youth.[80] Scholars have accordingly begun to assign much of the childhood content of Plutarch's *Alexander* to Onesicritus, as well as the culture-hero narrative of the Plutarchan *Fortune or Virtue of Alexander*,[81] but Plutarch never refers to Onesicritus in those contexts. As for quasi-philosophical content, some fragments do indeed contain that (e.g. F5), but the vast majority reflect the typical content of the Alexander histories, such as politics, ethnography and geography.

Arrian offers the alternative title of *Contemporary History* or *syngraphē*, used twice in the same passage (T9b = F27).[82] We know this title from the first line of Thucydides, and Onesicritus was certainly a *syngrapheus*. As Sabine Müller argues,[83] the work integrates many of the features of the historians after Callisthenes, including an increased emphasis on Asiatic spaces, such as the tomb of Cyrus (F34). Of course, Onesicritus' level of severity may not meet expectations of the *syngramma* genre, given the fact that Onesicritus accepted (or even invented) the mythologizing story of Alexander's liaison with the Amazon queen.[84] The work also amplifies Onesicritus' own worth, not only during the naval expedition, but also in terms of his association with Alexander writ large. For instance, he is selected to meet Calanus and the Brahmans (F17a–F17b). Nevertheless, it is a serious possibility that Onesicritus' work was contemporary history rather than a philosophical romance.

Onesicritus the person is, however, a mystery.[85] There is a very insistent tradition linking him to the Cynics (e.g. T1, 2, 3, 5a),[86] but the pre-campaign stories seem apocryphal. He only appears to have

---

[78] See, for example, Müller 2019: 20.   [79] Whitby 2011, commentary on T1.
[80] Gilhaus 2017: 178. The launch of the campaign is probably the earliest point of reference (F2, 38).
[81] See, for example, Pédech 1984: 78–80.
[82] I suspect that in this passage Arrian (*Anabasis* 6.2.3) paid due attention to terminology, as he was accusing Onesicritus of lying about his professional title. Arrian receives support from an unusual source, Lucian (*Macrobii* 14 ~ T9a), who uses a cognate verb, *syngraptō*.
[83] Müller 2012a.
[84] Onesicritus *FGrH* / *BNJ* 134 F1 ~ Plutarch *Alexander* 46.1–46.3. Plutarch's long list of authors recording this story does not include Nearchus.
[85] Heckel 2006: 183–184, *s.v.* 'Onesicritus'.
[86] In contrast to the *communis opinio* noted in Gilhaus 2017: 177 n. 4, I share in the scepticism of Winiarczyk 2007.

gained prominence after his participation in the campaign – we do not know when he joined – and he may have acquired opportunities in the absence of Callisthenes. We can imagine a scenario in which the Cynic school seized upon his writings of utopian societies, such as the kingdom of Musicanus (F 11, 22, 24–25), or he may have joined them precisely because he had had such experiences abroad. A post-campaign encounter with Diogenes of Sinope would not be an anachronism, for the Cynics' founder lived until 321 BC.

To date Onesicritus' composition, scholars have refused to use the dubious anecdotes proposing that he wrote during Alexander's lifetime (T10) or read his work at the court of King Lysimachus (after 306, T8).[87] However, it is not impossible that Onesicritus wrote at an early date and revised over the years, in a similar fashion to Nearchus. If so, his account offered one of the first full-scale campaign narratives (alongside that of Chares). An indication of an early date appears in a late source (F37), which suggests that Onesicritus had to censure his account of Alexander's death; he refrained from naming the individuals attending Alexander's party in which the king was rumoured to have been poisoned. Such a *recusatio* only makes sense during a time at which such information was sensitive, that is, in the aftermath of Alexander's death.[88]

Ephemerides: The Royal Diaries (*FGrH* / *BNJ* 117)[89]

The final work under discussion is perhaps the most remarkable document among all the early histories of Alexander. It purports to be Alexander's royal diary, compiled by the Greek secretary Eumenes of Cardia (or little-known collaborators),[90] who had apparently held the office for seven years under Philip and served Alexander for the full campaign (T2b).[91] The document presents a straightforward day-to-day outline of the king's activities, not only political events, such as war councils, but also cultural and personal matters such as religious sacrifice or bathing. It is a tantalizing thought that a diary of the king's own

---

[87] See, for example, Pearson 1960: 85.
[88] Similar concerns in, for example, Nicobule *FGrH* / *BNJ* 127 F1 and Medius of Larissa *FGrH* / *BNJ* 129 T4–T5.
[89] For bibliography on *Ephemerides*, Molina Marín 2018: 44–45.
[90] For Eumenes' title, TT2a–TT2c give respectively (a) ὁ γραμματεὺς ὁ βασιλικός; (b) *scriba*; and (c) ἀρχιγραμματεύς. As for Eumenes' collaborator, T1 ~ Athenaeus 434b supplies the name of the unknown Diodotus of Erythrae.
[91] It is not clear how the responsibilities of the secretary position relate to the duties of Callisthenes (*epistolographos*) or Chares (*eisangeleus*).

movements during the entire campaign may have been available, had Eumenes' tent not burned down in 326 BC.[92] The fragments that remain all relate to the period after that incident. In their current form, the extant fragments refer to three distinct events: (1) Alexander hunting for fun (F1); (2) a month of drinking activities, probably in the winter of 324 (F2a); and (3) the events leading up to Alexander's death (FF3a–3b).

The vast potential of the document as a historical source has naturally prompted scholarly discussion. Cinzia Bearzot, the most recent editor of the few fragments, maintains Felix Jacoby's verdict that the journal presented an image of Alexander that he himself wanted to leave behind for posterity. However, other scholars, including Brian Bosworth,[93] insisted that the document was a later forgery designed to benefit the circle of Eumenes, who, like Nearchus and other named individuals in Alexander's entourage, stood accused of conspiring against the king at that fateful banquet at Medius'. Most other scholarly positions on the document's authenticity vary between these extremes.[94]

Unfortunately, there is no single piece of evidence that decides the issue, but the arguments from the camp of Bosworth appear more plausible to my immediate view. There are simply too many oddities in the present fragments, including the appearance of Sarapis as a Babylonian deity. Our principal sources of the *Ephemerides'* account of the death, Arrian (F3a) and Plutarch (F3b), consistently report different information in places where one would expect harmony if they had indeed had the text before them. Other issues pertain to authorship and content. For instance, if Jacoby's camp is right that the diary left an unspoiled image of Alexander, it does not compute that most fragments could be used as evidence for the extreme drinking habits of the Macedonians (e.g. F2c). Even if later sources tend to intensify the focus on drinking, it still seems like an obvious matter to have removed from the original, especially if the diary was maintained by a Greek who was aware of the heavy-drinking *topos* like Chares.[95] In terms of simple credibility, it is not plausible that an account of Alexander's last days should be unbiased; too much was simply at stake in the Successor Wars, as everyone was forced to renegotiate their position in the post-Alexander power vacuum. This tendency is also true for the previous three Alexander histories and their historians.

[92] Plutarch *Eumenes* 2.6–2.7.   [93] Bosworth 1988a: 299.
[94] Bearzot 2017 (biographical essay) provides a summary of scholarship since Ulrich Wilcken (1862–1944).
[95] Of course, the matter of who actually wrote it, if not Eumenes, remains.

Guide to Further Reading

The main collection of the earliest Alexander historians remains the work of Jacoby 1923–(*FGrH*), especially the Greek text of the fragments (volume II.B) and the German commentary (volums II.D and III.D). Jacoby's collection has received new life online through the editions, commentaries and English translations edited by Ian Worthington (*BNJ*). The Dutch publishing house Brill has committed to maintaining and updating this resource – now rebranded *Jacoby Online* – for years to come, and it will no doubt generate even more insight into ancient historical writing in general, as well as the Alexander historians in particular. Unfortunately, *Jacoby Online* is behind a paywall, and so is not widely accessible. English-language alternatives exist, but they are not up to date: there is a complete translation of the fragments in Robinson 1953–1963 and a scholarly synthesis of all the relevant authors in Pearson 1960. Scholarship in other languages continues apace, most prominently that of Gilhaus 2017, which provides introductions, German rendering of the fragments and commentary. In French, the fullest collections of the historians are Pédech 1984 and Auberger 2005. In Italian scholarship, which seems to be the current home of source-critical research into the fragmentary historians, numerous detailed studies of individual historians continue to appear, such as Cagnazzi 2015 on Chares.

Part IV

The Ancient World's Memory of Alexander

26: The Successors and the Image of Alexander

Daniel Ogden

The physical image of Alexander flourished across the *disiecta membra* of the empire he created and far beyond it. Every purse of the Hellenistic age will have contained a coin emblazoned with his profile, minted by one of his successors.[1] No doubt his image was prominent too in other, less durable media, such as frescos and tapestries. But here we will consider the appropriation of his image in the broader sense — and principally through the medium of texts — in relation to the founders of the greater two of the Successor dynasties, that of the Ptolemies and that of the Seleucids. If his image was similarly appropriated by the Antigonids, little evidence survives for it, for all Plutarch's reference to Demetrius Poliorcetes as a 'stage Alexander'.[2] We can be sure that Ptolemy himself was the ultimate source of the association of the figure of Alexander with himself, but we cannot divine the degree to which Seleucus was an active agent in his own association with that same figure, even more prolific though it came to be.

Ptolemy

Ptolemy's appropriation of the figure of Alexander was as literal and as tangible as it could be. In 321 BC the regent Perdiccas finally released Alexander's embalmed body, two years after his death, to begin its long journey from Babylon back to the Argead cemetery at Aegae (Vergina) in a magnificent hearse. Ptolemy, now satrap of Egypt, suborned the officer presiding over the cortege, Arrhidaeus (not to be confused with

---

[1] See Dahmen 2007 *passim*, Wheatley and Dunn 2021 and Chapter 30 of this volume. Images of Alexander on his own coinage are rare, with the famous 'Porus medallions' the most signal exception to this rule. For a rather different approach to the subject of 'Alexander's image in the age of the Successors', see Meeus 2009a.
[2] Plutarch *Demetrius* 41.

Philip Arrhidaeus), to divert the train to his own Egypt. In a version of this tale projected into legend, Aelian has Perdiccas escorting the body in person, and Ptolemy in turn stealing it from him in person. Perdiccas gives chase, fights him for the body and recovers it, leaving Ptolemy to return to Egypt. Only too late does he realize that Ptolemy has substituted a dummy for the real thing.[3] Ptolemy initially housed the body in Memphis 'for a few years', as Curtius tells, before transferring it to Alexandria: perhaps it was intended from the first to bring the body back to the new city, once the construction of the splendid palace complex of which the new tomb was a part was sufficiently well advanced.[4]

A popular tradition that doubtless developed in early Ptolemaic Egypt, though one that we are hardly able to tie to Ptolemy himself, magnified the implications of his appropriation of the body: this is the opening tale of the *Alexander Romance*, a document that itself – in the earliest version of it to which we have access, the alpha recension – appears to be of the early third century AD (see Chapter 28). According to this, Alexander was in effect returning home in death, for he was not the blood son of Philip of Macedon, but the child of the last legitimate pharaoh of Egypt, Nectanebo II, who had fled before the Persians to take refuge at Philip's court. In this way, Ptolemy's Egypt was repositioned as the *fons et origo* of Alexander's empire, and its significance within the new world order boosted far beyond that of a mere wealthy and conveniently detachable outlier amongst his former conquests.[5]

If we follow the line strongly argued by Timothy Howe, most recently in this very volume (Chapter 5),[6] that the city of Alexandria was to all intents and purposes the foundation of Ptolemy rather than of Alexander himself (and I am increasingly inclined to do so), then in naming the city Alexandria – or even just in retaining the name of Alexandria from a vestigial predecessor – for his grand new city and capital, Ptolemy yoked himself firmly and physically to the memory of the king.

The version of the city's foundation myth preserved in the alpha recension of the *Alexander Romance* is seemingly a confused affair. It implies that the hero shrine Alexander established for the great Agathos

---

[3] Strabo C794; Pausanias 1.6.3; Arrian *Successors* FGrH / BNJ 156 frr. 9.25, 10.1; Aelian *Varia historia* 12.64. Discussion: Erskine 2002, Ogden 2014b: 19–25.
[4] Curtius 10.10.20; Parian Marble FGrH / BNJ 239 B11; Pausanias 1.6.3 and 1.7.1 (who alone defers the transfer of the body to the age of Ptolemy II); cf. Fraser 1972: i.15–i.16, ii.31–ii.3 nn. 79–80.
[5] *AR* (A) 1.1–1.14. [6] So too Howe 2014.

Daimon serpent (*drakōn*), which he had ordered to be slain at the site as the first houses were being constructed, and which was transformed in death into a host of smaller *agathos daimōn* serpents that were to serve the new householders as protective 'house snakes', was in some way associated also with Alexander himself. But this confused position finds endorsement, surprisingly, in the archaeological record: we know that the 'Alexander Aegiochus' ('Aegis-wearing') statue-type was developed in Alexandria as early as *c*. 320–300 BC, and we may assume that it was approved by Ptolemy: in it the figure of Alexander is accompanied by the Agathos Daimon serpent, winding itself around a tree trunk beside his left leg.[7]

This Ptolemaic association of the figure of Alexander with a serpent is of interest when we come to consider the historical (or at any rate historiographical) traditions of Alexander's trip to the Siwah oasis. We know that the general tradition held that his army, after getting lost in the desert, was rescued by a pair of crows, but that Ptolemy alone, in his own *History of Alexander*, turned the saviour-pair into serpents (*drakontes*). It looks as though Ptolemy was trying to build a broader context for his pairing of Alexander with the Agathos Daimon serpent here.[8]

A serpent also binds the figures Ptolemy and Alexander together in a marvellous tale of the siege of the Brahmin city of Harmatelia in 326/5 preserved in a number of sources.[9] According to this, Ptolemy had suffered a mortal wound during the siege, this from an arrow tipped with a venom extracted from the local snakes. Alexander was distressed by Ptolemy's plight more than that of any other of his men, for he loved him best. Sleeping by his side, he had a vision of a serpent (*draco*) with a herb in its mouth: the serpent demonstrated that this was a cure for Ptolemy, and showed him where to find it. On awakening, he sent men to fetch it, and Ptolemy was duly restored (the imagery of the healing serpent is – *inter alia* – Asclepian). The tale's projection of this unique and exceptional bond between Alexander and Ptolemy is striking

---

[7] *AR* (A) 1.31–32; cf. Phylarchus *FGrH* / *BNJ* 81 F27 = Aelian *Nature of Animals* 17.5. For Agathos Daimon in general, see Dunand 1969, 1981; Ogden 2011a: 34–39, 2012, 2013a: 286–309, 2013b, 2014a; Barbantani 2014; Djurslev and Ogden 2018. For the Alexander Aegiochus, see Stewart 1993: 246–253, 421–422, with figs. 82–83.

[8] Ptolemy *FGrH* / *BNJ* 138 fr. 8, *apud* Arrian *Anabasis* 3.3.4–3.3.6; cf. Callisthenes *FGrH* / *BNJ* 124 fr. 14, *apud* Strabo C814; Diodorus 17.49.5; Curtius 4.7.15; Plutarch *Alexander* 27, *Itinerarium* 21. Discussion at Ogden 2011a: 33–34.

[9] Cicero *On Divination* 2.135; Diodorus 17.103.4–17.103.8; Justin 12.10.2–12.10.3 (Trogus); Strabo C723; Curtius 9.8.22–9.8.28; Orosius 3.19.11. Discussion at Eggermont 1975: 105–137; Ogden 2011a: 30–32.

indeed. The fact that it features in the works of both Diodorus and Curtius (and also Justin) points to an origin for it in the lost history of Clitarchus of Alexandria. The date at which Clitarchus wrote has always been controversial, and the controversies have recently been given a fresh fillip by the discovery of a new papyrus (see Chapter 24). If we cling to the earlier date suggested for the composition of his work, c. 310 BC, that is, under Ptolemy himself (as I myself am inclined to do), then it is hard to believe that Clitarchus composed the tale without his approval. If we prefer the later suggested date for his work, some point during the reign of Ptolemy III, then no doubt he hoped to gratify that king with graceful flattery of his grandfather. But, either way, it remains a fair possibility that, before Clitarchus, it originated with the first Ptolemy himself, most probably in his own *History of Alexander* (if that had been completed by the time at which Clitarchus himself wrote), or at any rate in other ideological projections. If we fear that such a tale would have been impossibly narcissistic in Ptolemy's own mouth, we have only to look to recent events in Britain and America alike to reassure ourselves that narcissism and an abject lack of self-awareness travel easily with despotism.[10]

Finally, there are two groups of tales that celebrated a particular bond between Ptolemy and Alexander that we have no means of tying to Ptolemy himself (though the possibility that they originated with him or his entourage remains open). First, in the *Alexander Romance* again, in the course of his dealings with Candace in the third book, Alexander decides, for reasons frankly underexplained, to conceal his identity from the queen, and so he temporarily transfers his diadem to the head of Ptolemy, his right-hand man, whilst he himself adopts the role of another of his distinguished officers, that of Antigonus (one thinks of Prince Charming and Dandini).[11] We understand of course that, in the grander scheme of things, the action predestines Ptolemy to be Alexander's successor — an interpretation that becomes particularly clear when we compare the tale with a similar one associated with Seleucus (below, p. 431). Were this motif confined to the *Romance*, it would hardly be worth mentioning at this point, but it is also attested, fragmentarily, outside it. The *Suda* tells of Alexander, without offering any further context, that: 'Arriving at the lake in Alexandria [sc. the Mareotic lake], he lost his diadem when an enormous downpour burst forth, and he was only just able to swim to land.'[12] We can extrapolate

---

[10] For Clitarchus' 'eulogy' of Ptolemy, see Hamilton 1977: 143–144.
[11] *AR* (A) 3.19; discussion at Ogden 2017a: 39–40. [12] *Suda* s.v. Ἀλέξανδρος.

the rest: it must have been retrieved by Ptolemy (either at the time or at some later point), and in this way too symbolized the transfer of kingship between the two men. The water context of this version of the motif corresponds tightly with the water context of the Seleucus tale, and in both cases the two Successors receive their diadem at the place that is to become the seat and origin-point of their own power. But the *Suda*'s fragmentary narrative also invites comparison with a second Seleucus tale in accordance with which his loss of his special signet ring – another circlet – in the Euphrates explicitly destined the adjacent city of Babylon as the origin-point of his own vast empire (again, see below, pp. 432–3). This parallel might suggest that Alexandria – as opposed to Macedon – is being projected as the true origin-point of Alexander's vast empire; this would be wholly consonant with Alexander's projection as the son of Nectanebo.

Secondly, Ptolemy's birth myth. A tale preserved in its fullest form by a fragment of Aelian tells that Ptolemy was not after all the son of his supposed father, the obscure Lagus, but rather the son of Philip II, who had had an affair with Ptolemy's mother Arsinoe, and left her pregnant before passing her on to Lagus to become his wife. The baby Ptolemy was exposed in a (suitably martial) shield, where he was found and protected by an eagle, the thunderbolt-bearer of Zeus himself, of course, protector of kings, and subsequently to feature in particularly splendid from on Ptolemy's coin-issues (cf. Figure 26.1); the eagle kept the baby watered with the (also suitably martial) blood of the quails it caught for him.[13] As a weird origin-tale, this story *ipso facto* legitimated Ptolemy as king or at any rate explained him in this role, just as Alexander himself was legitimated (etc.) by the tale that he was sired by a gigantic serpent (cf. Chapter 1 of this volume), and as Seleucus was legitimated by the tale that he was sired by Apollo (see below, p. 432).[14] But, more specifically, this tale made Ptolemy not merely Alexander's best friend but his actual half-brother – so long, that is to say, as we turn a blind eye at this particular point to the tales that Alexander was himself sired by someone other than Philip, be it the serpent or Nectanebo.

---

[13] Curtius 9.8.22; Pausanias 1.6.2, 1.6.8; *AR* (A) 3.32; *Suda* s.v. Λάγος, incorporating Aelian fr. 283 Domingo-Forasté. Discussion at Lianou 2010; Ogden 2013c, 2017b: 346–350.

[14] Alexander's siring by a giant serpent: Cicero *On Divination* 2.135; Antipater of Thessalonica at *Greek Anthology* 9.241; Livy 26.19.7–26.19.8; Justin 11.11 (i.e. Trogus); Plutarch *Alexander* 2–3; Ptolemy Chennus *apud* Photius cod. 190, §148a; Aulus Gellius 6.1.1; Lucian *Dialogues of the Dead* 13; Pausanias 4.14.7; Alexandrian choliambic epitaph at Fraser 1972: ii, 950; *AR* (A) 1.6–1.8, 10, 12, 14, 24, 30, 35, 2.13, 21, 3.33; Solinus 9.18. Discussion at Ogden 2022a (superseding 2009c, 2011a: 29–56, 2015).

26.1 Gold pentadrachm of Ptolemy Soter. Obv.: Ptolemy. Rev.: Zeus-eagle carrying thunderbolt. Harvard Art Museums: 1.1965.2740.

There is no doubt much embroidery over the centuries here, but we can at least be sure that the determination that his figure and his city should be associated in popular imagination with that of Alexander originated with Ptolemy himself.

SELEUCUS

The tales binding Alexander with Seleucus are richer and more copious than those binding him with Ptolemy, but in this case the documentary trail goes cold, and we are not in a position to affirm that the connection must have gone all the way back to and begun with Seleucus himself, though we may well suspect that it did.[15]

The tales associating Seleucus with Alexander fall into two broad categories: those in which Seleucus enjoys a syntagmatic association with the king, in other words, tales in which he is shown to interact with him directly; and those in which he enjoys a paradigmatic or typological relationship with him, which is to say, tales in which he is engaged in a pattern of action that parallels that in which Alexander is also shown, separately, to be engaged. Some tales straddle both types.[16]

The syntagmatic tales first. It eventually came to be believed that the Seleucid dynasty drew its descent from Alexander: at any rate, in the inscribed stelae of his great tomb-sanctuary atop Nemrud Dağ, Antiochus I of Commagene (r. c. 69–36 BC) traced his own descent back to Alexander and even Heracles through the Seleucids. Presumably

---

[15] For the legend of Seleucus in general, see Ogden 2017b, now supplemented by Ogden 2020 and 2022b.
[16] For typology, see Ogden 2022b, especially 79–80.

he held that Alexander was Seleucus' father (a historical nonsense in terms of their respective ages, of course). Seleucus himself can hardly have entertained this notion.[17]

But other syntagmatic tales could, in theory at least, go back to Seleucus himself. Pausanias speaks of an omen predicting Seleucus' future greatness shown at a significant point when Seleucus was in the company of Alexander: 'For, when he was setting out from Macedonia with Alexander and sacrificing to Zeus at Pella, the wood that had been placed on the altar approached the cult image of its own accord and was kindled without the application of fire.'[18] We have already anticipated the tale of Alexander's diadem. According to Appian and Arrian, when Alexander was sailing in the Babylonian marshes in 323 BC, just prior to his death, the wind caught his diadem and blew it off. It caught on some reeds growing from the tomb of an ancient Assyrian king. Seleucus dived into the water to swim to rescue it, and so as not to get it wet, brought it back on his own head, thereby inadvertently destining himself for kingship and the role of Alexander's successor (whilst the resting of the diadem on the tomb could be considered an omen of death for Alexander).[19] In his *Res gestae*, published *c.* AD 390, Ammianus Marcellinus twice tells that Alexander had actually designated Seleucus his successor to the kingdom of Persia, at any rate, in his will.[20] In a final syntagmatic episode with Alexander, the ghost of the king visited Seleucus in his sleep, as Diodorus reports, to tell him of the rulership that was destined to be his.[21]

And so to the paradigmatic or typological tales. It is important to stress from the start that when a pair of tales of Alexander and Seleucus mirror each other, it need not always be the case that, just as Alexander preceded Seleucus, the development of the Alexander tale preceded that of the Seleucus one. Indeed, in many cases it seems best to think of the tales as evolving in parallel.

Like Alexander and indeed Ptolemy, Seleucus had his own weird birth myth, which made play with the anchor imagery that the historical Seleucus promulgated on his coins from 311 BC (Figure 26.2), as Justin reports:[22]

---

[17] For the inscriptions and their context, see Sanders 1996: i.254–i.377. Seleucus was probably two years older than Alexander: Justin 17.1.10, with discussion at Ogden 2017b: 11–12.
[18] Pausanias 1.16; cf. Appian *Syriake* 56.284; discussion at Ogden 2017b: 54–56.
[19] Arrian *Anabasis* 7.22; Appian *Syriake* 56.287–57.292 (both authors refer to variant versions of this tale excluding Seleucus); discussion at Ogden 2016, 2017b: 33–40.
[20] Ammianus Marcellinus 14.8.5, 23.6.8; discussion at Ogden 2017b: 63–64.
[21] Diodorus 19.90; discussion at Ogden 2017b: 64–66.
[22] For discussion of the coins, Ogden 2017b: 270–275.

26.2 Silver tetradrachm of Seleucus I. Obv.: Alexander. Rev.: Zeus with eagle and the Seleucid anchor mark. Harvard Art Museums: 1.1965.2557.

Seleucus' martial valour too was distinguished and the circumstances of his birth were remarkable. For when his mother Laodice had married Antiochus, a man of distinction amongst Philip's generals, she saw a vision as she slept in which she conceived after sleeping with Apollo. Impregnated, she received from the god as recompense for the congress a ring upon which an anchor had been engraved. She was commanded to give it to the son she was to bear. The vision was rendered remarkable by the ring with the same engraving that was discovered in the bed the next day, and also by the shape of the anchor which was on Seleucus' thigh from the moment the tiny child was born. Therefore, as Seleucus was setting out on his Persian campaign with Alexander, she gave it to him, and explained to him about the circumstances of his birth ... The proof of the circumstances of his birth endured also amongst his successors, since in fact his sons and grandsons bore an anchor on their thigh, as if it were a natural mark of their stock.

Justin 15.4.2–15.4. 9[23]

Appian supplies a further detail, to which we have already referred: 'His mother had a dream in which she was told to give whatever ring she found to Seleucus to wear, and that he would be king wherever he dropped it. She found an iron ring with an anchor engraved on it, and he

---

[23] Discussion at Ogden 2017b: 23–40.

lost this signet ring in the Euphrates.'[24] The imagery of Seleucus' birth myth nicely refracts that of Alexander's (see Chapter 1 again): Apollo, as a divine sire, salutes the notion that Zeus had struck Olympias' womb with a thunderbolt, thereby impregnating her;[25] so too the notion, once again, that Alexander had been sired by a gigantic serpent evidently a manifestation of a deity of some sort; and so too the more general notion that Alexander was somehow the son of Ammon.[26] The motif of the signet ring also salutes another version of Alexander's birth myth in accordance with which Philip had dreamed that he had sealed Olympias' womb with a signet ring emblazoned with a (Heraclean?) lion.[27]

Of all the legendary material bearing upon him, it is this birth myth that we are able to bring closest to the time of the historical Seleucus, albeit not very close even so. It appears to have been known to Euphorion, who worked at the court of Antiochus III (r. 223–187 BC), and who, indeed, could be considered a good candidate for the generation of much of the legendary Seleucus material as we have it: 'Laodice, Seleucus' mother, foresaw a kingdom in Asia for him before she had even given birth to him: Euphorion bruited this abroad.'[28]

Appian has the following tale of Seleucus' consultation of the Oracle of Apollo at Branchidae-Didyma near Miletus, which, if historical, would have taken place at some point between the years 334 and 331 BC: 'It is said that whilst he was still a soldier of the king [Alexander] and participating in his campaign against the Persians, he received an oracle at Didyma as he made enquiry about his return to Macedon: "Hurry not to Europe; Asia is much better for you."'[29] This refers to the fact that Seleucus would make himself master of Asia, but die at the very point when, in old age, he at last crossed back into Europe (i.e., into Thrace), en route to taking possession of Macedon itself, which had just fallen to him by virtue of his defeat of Lysimachus.[30] In Diodorus'

---

[24] Appian *Syriake* 56.284–56.285.   [25] Plutarch *Alexander* 2–3.
[26] Alexander as the son of Ammon: Ephorus *FGrH* / *BNJ* 70 F217; Callisthenes *FGrH* / *BNJ* 124 F14 (*apud* Strabo C814); Diodorus 17.51; Antipater of Thessalonica at *Greek Anthology* 9.241; Justin 11.11 (i.e. Trogus); Curtius 4.7.8.25–4.7.8.27; Plutarch Alexander 2–3, 27; Lucian *Dialogues of the Dead* 13; Pausanias 4.14.7; Alexandrian choliambic epitaph at Fraser 1972: ii.950; *AR* (A) 1.6–1.8, 10, 12, 14, 24, 30, 35, 2.13, 21, 3.33.
[27] Plutarch *Alexander* 2–3.
[28] Euphorion F119 Lightfoot = Tertullian *De anima* 46.6 p. 63.25 Waszink; discussion at Ogden 2017b: 278–280.
[29] Appian *Syriake* 56.283; Diodorus 19.90; cf. also Libanius *Orations* 11.99; discussion at Ogden 2017b: 56–58, 261–264.
[30] Justin 17.2.1–17.2.5, Memnon *FGrH* / *BNJ* 434 F8, Appian *Syriake* 62.334, Pausanias 1.16.1–1.16.2, 10.19.7, Eusebius *Chronicle* Arm. g344 = p. 117 Karst = Porphyry *FGrH* / *BNJ* 260 F32.2–F32.4.

account of the same consultation, the oracle addressed him as 'King Seleucus'. This episode mirrors episodes from the Alexander tradition in two ways. First, it exhibits a general resemblance with Alexander's own consultation of the Oracle of Ammon at Siwah, in which he was supposedly addressed as the son of the god. Second, the structure of the prophecy as conveyed by Appian mirrors that implied by an omen received by Philip in relation to Alexander in the *Alexander Romance*. Here, a bird lays an egg on Philip's lap; it rolls off and breaks open on the floor; a tiny serpent (*drakontion*) is released, circles around the egg shell and dies as it attempts to return within it. This, we are told, foretells both Alexander's encirclement of the world and then also his death 'before he lays his head down in the fatherland that gave him birth'.[31] Indeed, it is a striking fact that this prophecy corresponds rather better with the circumstances of Seleucus' death than it does Alexander's.[32]

Diodorus and Appian tell the tale of Seleucus' king-making flight from Babylon before Antigonus, pursued by enemy riders. This mirrors a tale in the *Alexander Romance* in which Alexander himself made a king-making flight from Persia (here conceived of as a city, just like Babylon) before Darius, again pursued by enemy riders.[33]

The several tales of Seleucus' city-foundations mirror the city-foundation tales and other episodes of the Alexander tradition in numerous ways. Some points of comparison may be telegraphically indicated. The sites for the cities of the Syrian Tetrapolis, Seleucia-in-Pieria, Antioch-on-the-Orontes, Laodicea and Apamea, are identified when, in each case, Zeus's eagle seizes body parts from a sacrificial altar and deposits them at the site chosen by the god. This motif mirrors the *Alexander Romance*'s tale of Alexander's rediscovery of the lost sanctuary of Sarapis at the site of Alexandria and his refoundation of it: again Zeus's eagle swoops down and seizes entrails from the altar at which Alexander is initially making sacrifice and deposits them on the altar of the lost sanctuary. Furthermore, we are told that Seleucus marked out the circuit of Antioch with grain (whilst using his famous elephants to indicate the positions of the towers), and marked out the circuit of the walls for Laodicea with the blood of a boar that attacked him at the site, while the eagle itself marked out the circuit of Apamea's walls by

---

[31] *AR* (A) 1.11.
[32] Discussion at Ogden 2017b: 261–264, 318 and 2018. On the Alexander side, see now also di Serio 2020.
[33] Diodorus 19.55–19.56; Appian *Syriake* 53.266–53.269; *AR* (A) 2.13–2.16 ≈ *AR* Arm. §§174–188 Wolohojian. The significance of this important pair of narratives – and their several further analogues – does not admit of meaningful exposition in short compass: see the expansive discussion at Ogden 2017b: 68–98.

allowing blood to drip from the animal heads (those of a bull and a goat) it was carrying. The motif of the marking-out of the circuit of the walls corresponds with that of the widely attested tale in accordance with which Alexander marked out the circuit of Alexandria's walls with grain that a flock of birds promptly ate, this being seen as a good omen.[34]

The site for Seleucus' foundation of the Oracle of Apollo at Daphne is identified when his horse stalls as he is out hunting and paws out of the ground a golden arrowhead inscribed with the name of 'Phoebus': this was one of the arrows that Seleucus' own Apollo had been hunting with when he had come across Daphne and pursued her, and she had evaded his advances by transformation into a laurel tree. As Seleucus picks the arrowhead up a serpent (*drakōn*) charges at him, rampant and seemingly on the attack, but when it gets close enough to recognize him, it gives him a gentle look and disappears. This episode mirrors two from the Alexander tradition, specifically the *Alexander Romance* again in both cases: first, that in which a great serpent intervenes in the early stages of the foundation of Alexandria (as discussed above, pp. 426–7); and, second, that in which Alexander founds Paraetonium. Like Seleucus, Alexander is hunting with his retinue, and refers to an arrow misfired (and presumably ending up lodged in the ground) as 'mis-strung' (*paratonon*): this word is then taken as a *klēdōn* (an omen derived from an involuntary sound or utterance), and made the source of the name of the city Alexander founds at the place.[35]

We may draw attention to a pair of legendary tales associated with Seleucus that relate to the figure of Alexander in both syntagmatic and paradigmatic fashions. The tale of Seleucus' foundation of Antioch should be compared with an interesting tale preserved by Libanius, in accordance with which Alexander himself in the course of his campaign had been impelled to found a city at its future site. He had thrown up a fountain house and a few buildings, but had then been called back to

---

[34] Seleucus' foundation of the Syrian Tetrapolis cities: John Malalas *Chronicle* 198–203 Dindorf = Pausanias of Antioch *FGrH / BNJ* 854 fr. 10.1–11; Libanius *Orations* 11.85–11.93. The tradition of Seleucus' foundation of Seleucia-on-the-Tigris also shares some of this imagery: Pliny *Natural History* 6.122 tells that the shape of the circuit of its walls was said to resemble an eagle with its wings outspread, which is suggestive in light of the Apamea tale in particular. Alexander's refoundation of the sanctuary of Sarapis: *AR* (A) 1.33. The birds at Alexander's foundation of Alexandria: Strabo C792; Valerius Maximus 1.4 ext. 1; Curtius 4.8.6; Plutarch *Alexander* 26.5–26.6; Arrian *Anabasis* 3.2.1–3.2.2, *AR* (A) 1.32 ≈ *AR* (Arm.) §85 Wolohojian; Stephanus of Byzantium s.v. Ἀλεξάνδρειαι, Amyntianus (?) Fragmentum Sabbaiticum *FGrH / BNJ* 151 §11; *Itinerarium Alexandri* 49; Ammianus Marcellinus 22.16.7; Eustathius *Commentary on Dionysius Periegetes* 254. Discussion at Ogden 2017b: 99–173, von Reden and Strootman 2022.

[35] Daphne: Libanius *Orations* 11.94–11.100; cf. Justin 15.4.7–15.4.8. Alexandria and Paraetonium: *AR* (A) 1.31. Discussion: Ogden 2017b: 138–151 and 2019.

the Asian interior by his compulsion for conquest. So Seleucus' foundation of Antioch corresponds paradigmatically with Alexander's own abortive city-foundation at the same site, but it also connects with it syntagmatically insofar as Seleucus' foundation can be seen as the completion of the project initiated and endorsed by Alexander.[36]

Finally, Appian gives us a further tale foreshadowing Seleucus' future greatness: '[Seleucus] was big and strong in body. Once, when Alexander was sacrificing a wild bull, the creature bucked out of its bonds, but Seleucus held it fast, alone and with only his bare hands. This is why they add horns to his statues.' So here Seleucus and Alexander stand side-by-side again, and Seleucus evidently makes an all-important impression upon the king, but the tale's greater force is in its paradigmatic mirroring of the Alexander tradition's famous tale of the boy Alexander's taming of the wild Bucephalas, his 'Bull-head' horse, an achievement directly parlayed into a prediction of future greatness for the lad, in Plutarch's account of it at any rate.[37]

Conclusion

The legend of Seleucus was richly bathed in the imagery of Alexander, and this imagery was focused, in different ways, on the person of Seleucus himself. Some of the tales are of his personal interaction with the king, whilst he yet lived, and indeed in one case even after he has died. Others serve to establish a typological parallel between the actions of Alexander and those of Seleucus (and some seek to do both). The case of Ptolemy is slightly different: whilst there is again a certain amount of focus on Ptolemy's personal interaction with Alexander (the Harmatelia tale; the birth narrative, perhaps, by implication), much of the legend-generation in this case focuses rather on Alexander's relationship with Ptolemy's city of Alexandria, the glory of which was the king's tomb. So long as Ptolemy remained ensconced in the city, he could afford to bask in a more reflected form of glory. In saying this, I of course attribute intention to Ptolemy, not unfairly: we can be sure that some at any rate of the Alexander imagery associated with his kingdom emanated from him or his retinue. We cannot be sure that the same was true of the Alexander imagery in the case of the Seleucid kingdom, given that none

---

[36] Libanius Orations 11.72–11.76; discussion at Ogden 2017b: 110–114.
[37] Appian Syriake 57.294; cf. Suda s.v. Σέλευκος; discussion at Ogden 2017b: 58–63. Bucephalas: Plutarch Alexander 6, AR (A) 1.17 (cf. 1.15); for discussion of the Bucephalas episode more generally: Anderson 1930, Baynham 1995b, Ogden 2020.

of it is attested until roughly a century after Seleucus' own death. We may wish to imagine, nonetheless, that much of the relevant Alexander imagery did originate with Seleucus or his court, and we may even wish to imagine Seleucus, perforce, focusing this imagery on his own person given that, unlike Ptolemy, he had no body of Alexander to display and venerate in Antioch or Seleucia-on-the-Tigris.

We should be cautious in assuming that, where there is a nice correspondence between a tale of Alexander and a tale of one of his Successors, the former was created first and inspired the latter. The creation of the tale of Seleucus' foundation of Antioch (following historical fact) must, for example, have preceded the tale of Alexander's abortive foundation of a city at the same site. It is tempting always to speak of such imagery as 'legitimating', and it surely was, though this concept can be a little reductive and can imply a certain cynicism behind the generation of the imagery; even more so the term 'propaganda'. It could well be, in the cases of both dynasties, that a good amount of the Alexander imagery, whatever its initial catalysts, was created by people who, happy enough to speak in supportive terms of the kings or dynasties under which they lived, were keen, above all, to tell a good story, and to explain the acquisition and retention of monarchical power in terms and in codes, particularly narrative codes, that their immediate audiences would understand and appreciate.

Guide to Further Reading

For Alexander's image on coins, see Dahmen 2007; Stewart 1993; Wheatley and Dunn 2021. For Ptolemy's capture of Alexander's body, see Erskine 2002; Ogden 2014b. For the city of Alexandria, see Fraser 1972; McKenzie 2007; for the historical circumstances of its foundation, see Howe 2014 and Chapter 5 in this volume. For Agathos Daimon, see Dunand 1969, 1981; Ogden 2013b; Barbantani 2014; Djurslev and Ogden 2018. For the Harmatelia episode, see Eggermont 1975. For the foundation myths of the Seleucid cities, see Ogden 2017b; Visscher 2020; von Reden and Strootman 2022. For Alexander's birth myth, see Chapter 1 in this volume, with further bibliography. For Ptolemy's birth myth, see Lianou 2010; Ogden 2013c. For Seleucus' birth myth, see Ogden 2016, 2017b, 2022b. For possible interaction between the city-foundation myths of the Ptolemies and the Seleucids, see Ogden 2014a.

27: ALEXANDER AND THE ROMAN EMPERORS

Sulochana Asirvatham

INTRODUCTION

The Alexander most visible to us today is one that was created and recreated in the Roman period. There are no extant narrative sources for him that predate Polybius, and our main narratives on the king's character and exploits belong to Diodorus Siculus, Quintus Curtius Rufus, Plutarch and Arrian, with other late Republican and Imperial writers providing assorted anecdotes. The relevance of Alexander's conquests and perceived personal characteristics to Roman discourses involving imperialism and ethical one-man rule make his continued presence in Roman literature an irresistible focal point for Roman historians and Alexander-reception-scholars alike. There is enough of a response in literature that we can reasonably describe the trajectory of intellectual interest in Alexander during the Roman period: while a handful of Greek writers like Arrian see him as a Greek culture hero, almost all Latin writers (as well as many Greek writers) tend to diminish him as a mere king in contrast to philosophers; dismiss him as a violent madman and tyrant; and, most importantly, characterize his empire as ephemeral as compared with that of the Romans.[1] These writers suggest an awareness that Alexander could be a model for powerful Romans, but that he is better taken as a cautionary tale.

More difficult is pinning down the degree to which powerful Romans engaged in conscious *imitatio Alexandri*, which generally involves squaring literary hints with material evidence that does not always speak to us as directly as we would like. Very often, for example, *imitatio Alexandri* includes imitation of someone else, either of Hellenistic kings or of earlier Romans. Are the noble, undefeated elephants on Caesar's coinage only a reference to Alexander, who defeated elephants in Porus' army but never employed them himself

---

[1] For some recent literary readings see Spencer 2002; Asirvatham 2010; Peltonen 2019.

on the battlefield, or did it include the Hellenistic kings who did employ them?[2] Or, in the case of Caracalla, did it include Dionysus?[3] Which influences are more important? Similarly, does the appearance of Augustus, Trajan or Commodus wearing an *aegis* (a 'magical protective goatskin')[4] on a cameo or a coin reference Alexander directly or, rather, the line of Hellenistic rulers who adopted it into their iconography?[5] If Germanicus, Caligula and Nero imitate Augustus imitating Alexander,[6] which figure is more important – Augustus or Alexander? Trajan, Commodus and Caracalla are notable for imitating Hercules, but his worship was ancient for both Greeks and Romans. Must it importantly also indicate Alexander-*imitatio*?[7] The majority of studies have dealt with one or more figures involved in the first-century BCE civil wars – Pompey, Caesar, Mark Antony and Octavian – with significant disagreement on how much inspiration each man took from Alexander.[8] Another focus is Augustus, whose relationship with Alexander has been treated with scepticism over the past half-century.[9] We possess less evidence for *imitatio* among the Flavians and Antonines and the emperors in between (except for Trajan). The Severans, and especially Caracalla, show the most evidence overall of *imitatio*, but even there the credibility of the literary evidence is somewhat compromised by anti-Severan bias (Cassius Dio) and sensationalism (*Historia Augusta* = SHA). Scholars are thus usually forced to determine whether or not *imitatio* is happening in a particular case based on 'common-sense' understandings of where we might expect to see imitation. Namely, Alexander-as-model makes best sense for emperors who seek eastern

---

[2] See Dahmen 2007: 8–9; Nousek 2008: 298–299.   [3] Lichtenberger 2011: 40–43.
[4] Williams 2009: 135.
[5] On the famous Blacas cameo depicting Augustus (probably commissioned after his death to avoid the implication of living divinity), see Williams 2009: 135–136, who notes that the pose is found on Hellenistic coins and on a small cameo perhaps depicting Philip V. Kühnen notes that the nude back shown on the cameo was long-imitated by Augustus's successors from Tiberius onwards (2005: 25–27), which would make their *aegis* portraits primarily imitations of Augustus, secondarily of Alexander.
[6] Kühnen 2005: 162–180.
[7] Beaujeu 1955: 99–101 thinks not. Hekster thinks it was a reaction to Domitian (2005: 205–207). Both Cassius Dio 73|72|.2 and Herodian 1.14.8 mention Commodus' imitation of Hercules without reference to Alexander (see Loar 2021: 514–515). As for Caracalla, Baharal 1994: 551–552 and Lichtenberger 2011: 40–43 stress the fact that Heracles is one of the patron gods of Lepcis Magna, the birthplace of Septimius Severus, and appears on the latter's coins as well. Severus is not associated by any source with Alexander.
[8] One important dialogue was initiated by Peter Green (1978), who argued, against scholars like Meyer (1919), Taylor (1931), DeWitt (1942) and Michel (1967), that Caesar's *imitatio* has been exaggerated in the modern era; Gruen 1998 and Martin 1998 similarly doubt Pompey's *imitatio*. A recent counterargument by Welch and Mitchell 2013 posits that Alexander was an important part of the rivalry between Pompey and Caesar.
[9] Earlier studies include Kienast 1969; Weippert 1972; and Wirth 1976.

expansion. But even here there are problems. The emperors had continual trouble beating back the Parthians (who could be conceptually mapped onto Alexander's Persians). On the other hand, Alexander famously failed to defend his empire once he conquered it. And, of course, the army proved itself superior to the Macedonian army over a century and a half before Augustus.

Despite all this, the idea that the emperors regularly imitated Alexander is taken for granted in popular and often even in scholarly literature. But what do 'regularly' and 'imitated' mean, exactly? We face major hurdles in definition and quantification when we generalize about Alexander-*imitatio* in the empire. Even if we were to take the most positivistic approach to the evidence, what exactly counts as *imitatio*, and how much evidence do we need to say that a Roman was interested in, obsessed with or modelled himself after Alexander? Instead of adding my two cents to the scholarly back-and-forth on individual emperors, I chart a path between overly credulous and overly sceptical conclusions by tightening our definition of *imitatio*, which in turn allows us to see more clearly how emperors used Alexander differently before western and eastern audiences.

Greek Imitation, Roman Emulation

According to Peter Green's formulation, we can manage our perceptions of how the ancient sources connect Romans to Alexander by making distinctions between pure *imitatio* and *aemulatio*, both of which refer to the public personae of Roman would-be Alexanders.[10] A third term, *comparatio*, refers to comparisons between Alexander and Romans in literary sources that may or may not correspond to those Romans' real-life *imitatio* or *aemulatio*. (I do not deal substantially with *comparatio* here.)[11] While *imitatio Alexandri* is the default terminology for any level of copying, I would argue that almost all of what we see at Rome, at any rate, is probably better described as *aemulatio*,[12] since imitation alone

---

[10] Green 1978. These Latin terms are modern coinages, but strike me as capable of encapsulating the range of ways in which Roman emperors and writers dealt Alexander. We see something close in the SHA *Alexander Severus*: discussing his education in Greek and Latin texts, the author says that the emperor 'also read a biography of Alexander, whom he especially imitated' (*legit et vitam Alexandri, quem praecipue imitatus est*, 30.2).

[11] It is possible to argue, of course, that literary comparisons were motivated by outside encouragement from powerful Romans and their supporters, as has been well done by Welch and Mitchell 2013 for Pompey and Caesar. But the subtlety necessary for such arguments itself points away from the idea of a general Roman fixation on Alexander.

[12] In agreement with Stewart 2003: 56.

presupposes the superiority of the one that is imitated – think *imitatio Christi* – and it is difficult to imagine who of the emperors would want to present himself as inferior to Alexander under any circumstance.[13] Thus, while Green notes that there is a grey area between imitation and emulation, we could also say that Roman imitation of Alexander for a Roman audience likely always contains a measure of competitive emulation.

The situation in the east, where *imitatio* of Alexander was a Hellenistic tradition at least for some ruling families, appears to be different.[14] There is evidence, for example, for the integration of cults of Alexander (and his family members) with those of the Ptolemies, Seleucids and perhaps the Antigonids, whose members at various times claimed Alexander's mantle; Alexander-cult also seems to be revived later during the time of the Severans.[15] We also see in the Roman period Greek cities claiming falsely to have been founded by Alexander. To the extent that city leaders may see themselves or their city 'embodying' a long-dead figure – in the same way Julians could claim to embody Aeneas by advancing their civilization, or any ruler might see himself as a new Hercules – we might call this *imitatio Alexandri*. Local leaders sometimes seem to be the prime movers of Roman receptiveness to Alexander. To give an example from Republican history: Shane Wallace suggests that the city of Amisus' claim to Lucullus, that Alexander had given them democracy, was meant to encourage Lucullus to imitate Alexander's example.[16] Here it would be Greek interest rather than a 'natural' Roman affinity for Alexander that acts as a motor: a Greek city self-identifies with Alexander (as lovers of democracy) in such a way that encourages, or taps into a latent possibility, of Roman *imitatio*. This is not to say that there are no instances in which the opposite may have happened (a Roman's admiration of Alexander results in Alexander-*imitatio* in an eastern city), but it seems advisable to take each case individually.

---

[13] Peltonen 2018: 494 notes that some Church fathers promoted *imitatio Alexandri* on the model of *imitatio Christi* especially in the east – validating my sense that pure admiration of Alexander is generally directed at Greek sensibilities rather than Roman.
[14] On Hellenistic Alexander-imitation see Bohm 1989; Stewart 1993; Trofimova 2012.
[15] For an overview of the cults from the Hellenistic through Roman periods, see Wallace 2018b: 182–187.
[16] Wallace 2018b: 168.

Alexander in Imperial vs Provincial Coinage

In Fergus Millar's oft-cited phrasing, inscriptions and coins were 'the most deliberate of all symbols of public identity' in the ancient world: they were commissioned by those in power and inevitably designed for public circulation.[17] The word 'identity' is important here, as it emphasizes the commissioning agent's intimate self-association with what he puts into public circulation. Identity is best gleaned in written texts, and an inscription or coin heralding a connection to Alexander is a relatively uncomplicated way of making a public and positive verbal self-association with Alexander. It makes sense, then, that we look here first for emperors' public declarations of being 'like Alexander'. Since we know of no inscriptions that explicitly link Alexander to Rome or to specific Romans, our starting point for determining the presence and relative intensity of self-identification with Alexander is coinage,[18] which also happens to be uniquely useful as we possess examples from practically every minting in Greco-Roman antiquity. Furthermore, the fact that Imperial Roman coinage can be usefully divided into the categories of 'imperial' (coins struck on imperial authority in centrally controlled mints and circulated throughout the empire) and 'provincial' (coins produced under local authorities for local circulation) allows us to see whose propaganda is being promoted through the connection with Alexander (that of the emperors, or that of the local authorities, with or without response to emperors?) and who the audience might be (the empire as a whole, or local audiences?).

Imperial coinage, then, would in theory make the loudest proclamation that an emperor wished to be publicly associated with Alexander. But we possess no Imperial coins that depict Alexander or that are embossed with a legend that indicates Alexander.[19] A search through the 10 volumes of *Roman Imperial Coinage* (*RIC*) and the *Online Coins of the Roman Empire* (*OCRE*) database finds nothing Alexander-related, but two Imperial coins that depict Hadrian facing personified Macedonia, who wears a traditional native hat (*kausia*) and short tunic and carries a whip; these are part of Hadrian's *adventus* series of coins

---

[17] Millar 1995: 230, quoted by, for example, Howgego 2005: 1 and Dahmen 2007: 3.
[18] Howgego 2005: 1: 'What coinage most obviously provides is an enormous range of self-defined and explicit representations of public/official/communal identities, principally civic in nature. The material thus largely allows us to avoid the thorny problems associated with externally defined, implicit, and private identities.'
[19] There is no external evidence for the SHA's claim (*Alexander Severus* 25.9) that Alexander Severus depicted himself on *electrum* or gold coins in the costume of Alexander the Great.

showing his arrival at various provinces.[20] There is one seeming exception to the lack of Imperial Alexander-themed coinage: a series of late-antique (fourth- and fifth-century) contorniates (hollow-holed medallions) that were struck at Rome. But their pagan content (Alexander the Great, for one, appearing among the earlier examples, in some cases with the Latin labels *Magnus* and *Macedon*) as well as their depictions of images connected with the circus games, suggest that they were not regular products of the mint but created for more limited audiences.[21] A basic conclusion we can draw from Alexander's absence from the vast body of Imperial coinage is that whatever seeming *imitatio* an emperor engaged in, he stopped short of advertising his desire to be associated with Alexander to the whole world. This strikes me as a relevant data point to pit against modern generalizations about Roman Alexander-mania, especially considering the frequency with which references to Parthia, by contrast, occur in Imperial coinage from Trajan through to Macrinus, during which time period three emperors campaigned in the east: Lucius Verus, Severus and Caracalla. As Jason Schlude has recently demonstrated, these men modelled themselves in their imperial propaganda on Trajan:[22] that is to say, they participated in *imitatio Traiani* rather than *imitatio Alexandri*.

On the other hand, in the provincial coinage of the Greek east – what Ann Johnston has called the 'small change of the system', as it was produced only in silver and bronze, with gold reserved exclusively for imperial coinage[23] – Alexander is a non-negligible presence. The quantity of locations in which Roman provincial Alexander-coinage is found is relatively limited: Alexandria kat'Isson and Aegeae in Cilicia; Nicaea in Bithynia; Alexandria in the Troad; Smyrna in Ionia; Abila and Capitolias in Syria Palestina; Gerasa in Arabia; Apollonia Mordiaeon and Sagallassos in Pisidia; Caesarea ad Libanum in Phoenicia; Macedonian *Koinon*; Caesarea in Cappadocia; Heliopolis in Syria. We can add here the famous third-century hoards of Tarsus in Cilicia and Aboukir in Egypt that produced medallions (apparently mimicked by the above-mentioned contorniates) which were used for contest prizes rather than for money.[24] Alexander's appearance on provincial coinage reflects what Sophia Kremydi-Sicilianou calls the 'double "belonging" to a local community and to the dominant Roman state'.[25] But it is also sporadic, sometimes lining up with the reigns of emperors typically

---

[20] *RIC* ii 454–455 and 466.   [21] For a brief history of interpretations, see Mittag 2015.
[22] Schlude 2020: 156–185.
[23] Johnston 1989 in her review of Klose 1987, one of the first major studies on this body of coinage.
[24] See Touratsoglou 2008.   [25] Kremydi-Sicilianou 2005: 96.

connected to Alexander in literary sources, other times lining up with emperors *not* typically connected to Alexander. For some figures who are associated with Alexander in the literary sources, like Octavian-Augustus,[26] Caligula[27] and Nero,[28] we find no contemporary provincial Alexander-coinage.

Of the two major provincial coin types in which Alexander appears, the first presents Alexander as (fictive) founder of a city (*ktistes* or, in Capitolias, *genarches*), and thus emphasizes the city's ancient pedigree.[29] The Cilician cities Alexandria kat'Isson (the biggest repository of provincial Alexander-coins, second only to that of the Macedonian *koinon*) and Aegeae together provide a good snapshot of the variety of emperors – reputational Alexandrophiles as well as ones without that association – under whom Alexander-as-*ktistes*-coins were commissioned. (Interestingly, Alexander never visited these cities; their pride in him would have stemmed from the fact that Alexander had defeated Darius nearby, at Issus.) The most popular coin at Alexandria kat'Isson was a bearded and diademed Alexander first appearing in 43/44 in the reign of (the non-Alexandrophile) Claudius and revived at the time of (the Alexandrophile) Severus Alexander.[30] At Aegae, it is in the reign of (the non-Alexandrophile) Hadrian[31] that we find the first coin depicting an emperor with Alexander on the reverse, but we do not see coins explicitly connecting emperors and Alexander until the third century with Macrinus, who appeared with Alexander as well as his son Diadumenian on a series of coins (these men are not elsewhere associated with Alexander). On the other hand, a coin from Alexandria kat'Isson that depicts Alexander as *ktistes* (a male figure robed and performing a sacrifice) appears during the reign of Trajan and is revived under Caracalla, both of whom are associated with Alexander in the sources.[32] We also see Alexander-as-founder in three cities under Marcus Aurelius and Commodus (Nicaea, Alexandria in the Troad

---

[26] Suetonius *Augustus* 18.1 presents Augustus showing respect to Alexander's corpse; Cassius Dio 51.16.5 shares a similar story, with the added detail that he broke off Alexander's nose.

[27] Suetonius *Caligula* 52.1 says that Caligula often wore the garb of a triumphing general even prior to campaigning, and sometimes donned the breastplate of Alexander, which he stole from the king's tomb.

[28] Pliny *Natural History* 34.63; see below, pp. 447–448.   [29] See Ziegler 2014.

[30] Dahmen 2007: 123–124.

[31] Hadrian may have preferred Alexander's father as a model, at least at Athens. SHA, which routinely notes Alexander-*aemulatio*, says that Hadrian had himself initiated into the Eleusinian mysteries following the examples of Hercules and Philip II (not Alexander) (*Hadrian* 13.1). For further parallels between Hadrian and Philip in terms of both portraiture and philhellenic aims, see Kouremenos 2022.

[32] On Trajan, see Cassius Dio 68.29–68.30 and SHA *Hadrian* 4.9. On Caracalla see Cassius Dio 78.7–78.8 and SHA *Caracalla* 2.

and Capitolias) with some reiusses and a few additions during the Severan Period. Neither Antonine emperor is known for an attachment to Alexander, but Nicaea may be a case in which a city's self-identification with Alexander coincides with an emperor's positive attitude towards that city. Karsten Dahmen, for example, proposes that Nicaea created Alexander-as-*ktistes* coins with Commodus on the obverse in order to flatter the young emperor, perhaps in thanks for the help he gave the city after an earthquake and/or to curry favour with him in competition with their longtime rival Nicomedia, which had fallen out of favour with Commodus.[33]

The second major Alexander-type is that of the Macedonian *koinon*, which does not arise until the third century under the Severans. Coins referring to the 'Macedonians' from the time of Philip V and Perseus show that the *koinon* existed before the Romans but was incorporated into the imperial cult (as were all the *koina*).[34] The cult was celebrated in a series of festivals, among which was an 'Alexandreia' in the provincial capital Beroea, first attested in the reign of the Alexander the Great's namesake Alexander Severus in 229 CE,[35] and perhaps intended to honour him.[36] Here we may be able to surmise a correspondence between imperial activity against the Parthians and an expression of local pride in Macedonia's best native son.[37] Even earlier, in the reign of Elagabalus (204–222 CE), we find Alexander-coins on site that usually bear his portrait and the legend *ΑΛΕΞΑΝΔΡΟΥ*, and feature the largest variety of references to Alexander's legend, ranging from his parentage by Zeus Ammon as a snake (a feature of both Plutarch's *Life of Alexander* and the *Alexander Romance*) to his military accomplishments, as well as a set of Olympias coins.[38] The short-lived Elagabalus was not known as an Alexandrophile; we can only guess, as Dahmen has, that this activity related to his desire to be seen as Caracalla's offspring. The idea of a general 'Alexander-complex' among Severans, especially after Caracalla, is validated by the appearance of Alexander-coins during the Severan age outside of the Macedonian *koinon*. The most direct evidence for Caracalla's self-identification with Alexander is in a coin found in both Caesarea in Cappodocia and Heliopolis in Syria, around the time of Caracalla's approach to Parthia (215 CE), that depicts the

---

[33] Dahmen 2007: 126–127. [34] Kremydi-Sicilianou 2005: 101–102.
[35] See SHA *Severus Alexander* 5.1–5.2; 13.1.
[36] Kremydi-Sicilianou 2005:102 and n. 87, citing Gounaropoulou and Hatzopoulos 1998, nos. 68, 69.
[37] Kremydi-Sicilianou 2005: 102–103; see also 102 n. 91 (with epigraphical references) for the increased use of the name Makedon in second- and third-century Beroea and Thessaloniki.
[38] Dahmen 2007: 33.

emperor holding a shield with Alexander's image on it. Caracalla is the only emperor to present himself on a coin in this way, with Alexander-as-protector, during his lifetime.[39] Other Severan-era coins may allow us to perceive local sensitivity to the Severans' pro-Alexander sentiment, such as the coins of Gerasa in Arabia, the majority of which were minted between Trajan and Septimius Severus. This is indicated by the choice of name used on the coins, as the city had two: the first, Gerasa, was based on the Greek word *geras* ('old age'), and refers to the legend that it was founded by Alexander's veterans; the second, Antioch on the Chrysoroas, references its actual historical foundation under Antiochus III or IV.[40] Alexander-coins were minted in this city under Septimius Severus, Caracalla and Elagabalus,[41] with the Severus and Caracalla coins using the (Alexander-related) city name Gerasa.

It is worth noting, however, that Septimius Severus is not otherwise associated with Alexander. We can contrast this with Trajan, whom the sources label an Alexandrophile. Trajan is the first emperor under whom the first Roman coins at Gerasa were produced[42] and also tangibly benefitted the city by linking it to trade routes,[43] but there are no Alexander-coins in Gerasa during his reign. The exact connection between perceived *imitatio* on the part of emperors and Greek provincial coinage, then, is not always clear. But (returning to Millar): if we take coinage seriously as a strong indicator of public identity, the absence of Alexander from imperial coinage, contrasted with his significant presence on provincial coinage, sometimes even in the company of emperors, suggests that an emperor might find positive use for Alexander in the east.

Other Alexander-Images and Alexander-Actions in Context

Emperors had other means of associating themselves with Alexander's portraits beyond coinage. Alexander-portaiture had a profound influence on Hellenistic and, in turn, Roman portraiture, and art historians have made specific cases for such features as the *imitatio* of Alexander's Lysippan head-tilt to the left, for example, in the cases of Augustus and

---

[39] Dahmen 2007: 34.   [40] Dahmen 2007: 131.
[41] See Dahmen 2007: 29 and 86 n. 222–224; on the coins of Roman Gerasa in general see Lichtenberger and Raja 2020.
[42] Lichtenberger and Raja 2020.   [43] Kraeling 1938: 47 and n. 94.

Caracalla.[44] But ancient literature provides us with some strange and even rather violent examples of Alexander-*imitatio* and *aemulatio*, for example, in the manipulation of Lysippan and Apellan Alexander at Rome and also in Alexander's presence as part of war booty. The situation is inverse to what we see with Alexander-coinage, which is invisible in the west and visible in the east. Alexander-art, by contrast, becomes part of the Roman landscape – and proportionately less so in the geographical periphery from which it had been pilfered. The level of imperial self-identification with Alexander-images at Rome, however, may be lower that what is often imagined based on the use and presence of Alexander-statuary there. Furthermore, *imitatio* manages to find its way east after all, not in physical objects so much as in physical acts performed by emperors for local audiences.

Imperial manipulation of Alexander's image: if we can believe Herodian, Caracalla provides us with the most obvious instance of *imitatio*-as-self-identification, a 'statue-type worthy of ridicule' (χλεύης ... ἄξιαι εἰκόναι, 4.8.2) whose head featured Caracalla's face on one side and Alexander's on the other. Other reported actions involving Alexander-statues are better described as purely emulative/ competitive. For example, Suetonius (*Augustus* 50.1) tells us that Augustus had a seal with Alexander's face on it, but then changed Alexander's face to his own face. (The original, however, had a sphinx on it: *imitatio Sphingis*?) The poet Statius (*Silvae* 1.1.84–1.1.88) also mentions a Lysippan statue of Alexander riding a steed that had been placed in the Forum Julium opposite the temple of Venus Genetrix, its head replaced with that of Julius Caesar. We also learn from Pliny the Elder of Nero's gilding of another Lysippan work, a bronze statue of the infant Alexander (*Natural History* 34.63). The manipulation might be done by one emperor in another's honour: Augustus put Apelles' portrait of Alexander in his Forum, but Claudius replaced Alexander's face with that of Augustus (*Natural History* 35.95).

The last anecdote raises the question of how significant Alexander's visage was at Rome. The literary contexts in which these anecdotes are embedded show that the Romans' primary interest was the acquisition of Greek art, not the acquisition of Alexander. The fact that these Alexander-images existed in the public spaces of Rome suggests a whole other order of *aemulatio* – if we can properly call it that – in which Alexander's figure is just one part of the general art-appropriation resulting from conquest. Most acquisition took place

[44] See most recently Kiilerich 2017.

during the Republic by civil war heroes who wished to aggrandize their war prowess in the public square (an exception being Nero, who, according to Pausanias 10.7.1, carried off 500 statues of gods and men from Greece), and turned Rome into what Catharine Edwards says functioned 'in some ways ... as a museum city'. The first 'museum' for plundered Greek art was most likely the Porticus Metelli,[45] constructed by Quintus Metellus in 148 BCE after the defeat of the Macedonians, who installed there another Lysippan monument – one of Alexander and his companions who fell at the Granicus (Pliny *Natural History* 34.4). Augustus' aim, in the words of J. J. Pollitt, to 'convert private collections into public exhibitions'[46] only further integrated Greek art into the civil landscape. Tellingly, the stories of Metellus' Alexander-monument and Nero's statue-gilding both occur in a Pliny passage whose main subject is not Alexander but Lysippus of Sicyon himself (in a book of the *Natural History* devoted to the natural history of metals). Pliny lists all the statues the sculptor was famous for, including several Alexander-related works but much else: a statue of a man using a strigil, a drunken female flute-player, dogs and a huntsman, a chariot of the sun with Rhodian-style rays on its crown as well as numerous other chariots and a satyr that was now at Athens. Lysippus, furthermore, exists in Book 34 as just one member (albeit an exalted one) of a large number of Greek sculptors. Pliny also indicates that Alexander was not the only member of a defeated nation to be represented. Among the first works of art commissioned by outsiders, three statues of Hannibal stood in Rome 'within whose walls he alone of Rome's enemies hurled a spear' (*cuius intra muros solus hostium emisit hastam*: *Natural History* 34.15). Plutarch, too, mentions the dedication of gilded figures of Jugurtha surrendering to Sulla (*Sulla* 6), and, according to Cassius Dio, Augustus filled Rome with commemorations of Actium and even a glorified Cleopatra (51.22.1–51.22.3).[47] As Edwards emphasizes, individual works of art were not always treated with honour or seen in the spirit of unambiguous triumphalism. While someone like Metellus may have gazed upon Alexander and exclaimed to himself, 'I have defeated the legacy of Alexander!', the presence of Alexander-statues alongside myriad other figures is hard to describe, overall, as a direct manifestation of the

---

[45] Edwards 2003: 51. See also Loar, MacDonald and Padilla Peralta 2018 on Rome's 'cargo culture'. On public and private collecting culture at Rome, Tivoli and Pompeii, see Neudecker 2015.

[46] Pollitt 1978: 165. There were also worries over the corrupting influence of Greek art on Rome and the violence of despoliation (what Pollitt calls the 'Catonian' attitude found in Livy's description at 25.40.1–25.40.3).

[47] References found in Wallace 2018b: 182.

widespread Roman desire to emulate Alexander, especially given potentially negative associations with him.

As for the east: some pre-Imperial Alexander-sculpture remained on site – an exquisite example being the reliefs on the Alexander-sarcophagus, which was discovered in 1887 near Sidon, Lebanon. There is also evidence that Alexander-sculpture was still being produced in the Imperial period: for example, small bronze statuettes that may have been used for cult purposes, like a second-to early third-century CE Lysippan one found in early twenty-first-century Constantinople.[48] But the most important image disseminated throughout the empire was that of the emperor himself. This is famously the case for Augustus,[49] and as Andrew Stewart notes Trajan set up his own portrait – not Alexander's – on the shores of the Persian Gulf, even as he was purportedly following in the latter's footsteps.[50] But there is some evidence of emperors wanting to present themselves as Alexander's successor when they travelled to places of special significance to him. Perhaps only Trajan voices his desire at Rome to be compared to Alexander.[51] Augustus is reported to have visited Alexander's tomb in Alexandria and may have also subtly referenced Alexander to the Athenians.[52] Troy was the city where Rome and Alexander were best able to meet ideologically, and not just as descendants of men on opposing teams: Strabo (C594–595) makes Alexander a proto-Roman by stressing his matrilineal descent from the Molossian Aeacidae, who he notes once had (Trojan) Andromache as queen, rather than his connection to Achilles. According to Livy, both Gaius Livius Salinator and Lucius Cornelius Scipio visited the site in 190 BCE and individually sacrificed to Minerva, as Alexander had to Athena.[53] There is also inscriptional evidence for Augustus' visit to Ilium on his 20 BCE travels,[54] but the visit is not mentioned in the literary sources. Conversely, there is no material evidence for Caesar's visit to the site, but it appears in Lucan, who

---

[48] Harvard Art Museums 1956.20 = Nelidov 1911, lot 43. For speculation on cult-purpose, see the item's webpage at https://harvardartmuseums.org/collections/object/312306. Cited here as well are a mid–late 2nd-c. CE large-scale Roman bronze portrait of Alexander (Kunze 2000); and a mid–late 1st-c. CE Roman bronze statuette of Alexander as Zeus (Kunze 2007: 197–201).

[49] See, for example, Boschung 1993 and Smith 1996.

[50] Stewart 2003: 59 and n. 66, citing Jordanes *Romana* 268 for the statue. For the latter, see also Olajos 1981.

[51] Cassius Dio 68.29–68.30 has Alexander directly compare himself to Alexander in the Senate, which leads Kühnen 2005:195 to surmise that this is coming from Trajan's own writings. If historical, this would be a rare instance of verbal self-*comparatio* indicating *aemulatio* directed to a Roman audience.

[52] For the visit to Alexander's tomb, see Cassius Dio 51.16.3–51.16.5; Suetonius *Augustus* 18.1; Plutarch *Antony* 80.1; for Athens, see O'Sullivan 2016.

[53] Livy 37.9.7, 37.37.3; see Wallace 2018b: 179.   [54] *IGR* iv 203; see Halfmann 1986: 158.

depicts him tromping around the site (anachronistically depicted as burned down) – a scene which numerous scholars have seen as a purely literary response to Aeneas' movements in the *Aeneid*.[55] (In the above-cited passage, Strabo also says that Caesar gave benefactions to the city because he was an Alexandrophile and because the Romans believed they were descended from Aeneas and he himself directly from Achilles's son Iulus, but does not mention the visit.) The highly poetic and intertextual nature of Lucan's account is a reminder that what we take as literary evidence for *imitatio Alexandri* may be merely an act of authorial *comparatio* instead (in this case, deeply unflattering to Caesar).

Conclusion

If a Roman emperor imitates Alexander alone in a forest, did the imitation really happen? It is hard to imagine what imitation would mean outside of the context of someone – anyone – noticing it. And who that someone is, 'the audience', appears to make a significant difference. Of course, generals, emperors, and city leaders are not the only individuals whose interest in Alexander is worth studying (and we can consider their separate audiences as well). There is plenty of evidence for Alexander's presence among the elite in the west and both the elite and the non-elite in the east[56] – and the last of these categories may provide the purest examples of *imitatio*, with men claiming to have been soldiers in Alexander's army.[57] Their basis for self-identification with Alexander would presumably be related, uncomplicatedly, to his achievements on the battlefield: there, he is truly someone to imitate. Scholars will continue to find Alexanders throughout the empire. At the risk of dwelling in over-familiar territory, I have focused on the question of *imitatio* among emperors and provincial leaders in possible interaction with them. My approach accepts that a handful of Roman emperors may have been 'interested in' Alexander but seeks to better establish what interest actually looks like by reconsidering the concepts of *imitatio* and *aemulatio* and drawing distinctions between Roman and provincial

---

[55] Most recently, McRoberts 2018 has argued that the scene parallels *Aeneid* 6 in its entirety.
[56] For just a few examples from the wealthy: as to Italy, Stewart 2003: 56–60 lists the famous Battle of Issus mosaic found in Pompeii's House of the Faun as well as privately owned statuary (such as the Azara Alexander-herm and bronze Herculaneum equestrian statuette) and some reliefs and paintings near Rome. In the east, Wallace cites, for example, Alexander's 'breastplate and spear', which was seen by Pausanias (8.28.1) in Gortys, as a possible fake belonging to a private home (2018b: 169).
[57] See Wallace 2018b: 165 (for Theophrastus) and n. 10 (for inscriptions and papyri).

Greek audiences. Without dismissing the world of ways in which various aspects of the Alexander-myth may have been subtly exploited by powerful Romans, this study tends to reinforce the conclusions of scholars who warn against overstating Alexander's popularity as a conscious 'model' for rulers. The fact that the first-century BCE Pompey and the third-century CE Caracalla were easy to mock for their imitations shows that obvious *imitatio* at Rome was disadvantageous.It seems that this would not have bothered anyone in the east, especially one who took pride in Alexander as their city-founder or progenitor.

Guide to Further Reading

The majority of studies of Alexander-imitation in the Roman period have focused on the Republic, for which see Green 1978; Spencer 2002; and most recently Welch and Mitchell 2013. Kühhen 2005 remains the best starting point for the Imperial period, as it gathers both literary and material references for each emperor's reception of Alexander. Particularly helpful when comparing eastern and western imperial responses to Alexander are Dahmen 2007, which surveys Alexander's image on Greek and Roman coinage, and Wallace 2018b, which cites numerous examples for Alexander's civic use in the Hellenistic and Roman periods both in Rome and the periphery.

28: THE ALEXANDER ROMANCE

Christian Thrue Djurslev

This chapter introduces the most widely read text about Alexander from the ancient world, the so-called *Alexander Romance* (*AR*).[1] This title does not indicate a 'romance novel' in a modern sense, but refers rather to the older French sense of a novel, or *roman*, that is a lengthy prose narrative of complex and fictional character.[2] The *AR* has a biographical frame, narrating Alexander's life, deeds, and death. The prose narrative, embedded with about 280 lines of verse, is bookended by stories of the king's conception (1.1–1.14) and funeral (3.34).[3] While the biographical core may immediately suggest a parallel to Plutarch's *Life of Alexander*, the *AR* offers an imaginative rewriting of Alexander history replete with fantastical features, including unicorns (*AR* Arm. §224 Wolohojian). Even a cursory comparison with other Graeco-Roman historical writing on Alexander reveals that the *AR* stands out in at least three ways.

First, whoever wrote the *AR* does not seem to present a coherent portrait of Alexander. The initial impression of inconsistency also radiates from the apparent lack of moulding. Many scenes are demonstrably excerpted wholesale from other texts; in fact, even independent texts are included in unaltered or very lightly modified form,[4] such as a Hellenistic pamphlet purporting to chronicle Alexander's last days (3.30–3.32) and even his will (3.33). Accordingly, the stringing together of heterogeneous parts creates a sense of incongruity and unevenness when conflicting sources clash.[5] At first blush then, the *AR* gives the impression of bricolage because it consists of disparate materials that have been assembled and patched together. Moreover, the plot itself (see below, pp. 457–463) feels like a storyboard because of its highly episodic form.

---

[1] The following expands Djurslev 2017.
[2] Of course, the *AR* concerns a real person, but this did not deter ancient authors: cf. Hägg 2014.
[3] There is no preface but the anonymous author adds an epitaph, *AR* 3.35.
[4] Nawotka 2017: 23–25.   [5] Jouanno 2020: 211 points to Alexander's unstable genealogy.

Secondly, because the flexible narrative permits the addition and subtraction of scenes seemingly at will,[6] each revision engendered an independent version of the *AR*. For instance, to highlight the diversity and originality of the adaptations in Byzantine Greek manuscripts, modern scholars have assigned a Greek letter to each variant (in chronological order: *alpha, beta, lambda, epsilon, gamma*). The variants differ in language, length, form, function, and content. Some invent engaging scenes, such as stories about Alexander in a diving bell (Figure 28.1) or a flying machine (*lambda*). Others provide windows onto the developing story-worlds of the Abrahamic religions: they preserve Alexander's ostensible preaching of Judaism in Alexandria or his enclosure of the unclean nations, Gog and Magog (*epsilon*).

Thirdly, the fluidity of the text – the adaptable narrative and its constant revision – enabled the wide circulation of the *AR* in the premodern period.[7] There are instantiations in more than twenty languages from Icelandic to Ethiopian and Malay. Evidently, engaging readers across Africa and Eurasia, the *AR* differs from other ancient accounts of Alexander, such as Arrian's *History*,[8] which left fewer traces outside the Greek sphere.[9] In this respect, the anonymous text can be compared not only to the Bible, but also to the manifold manifestations of the *Life of Aesop*, the *Life of Ahikar*, the *Life of Homer*, the *Life of Moses*, and the *History of Apollonius, King of Tyre*.

Such divergences have also helped to make the *AR* an immensely important text, comparatively. The importance goes beyond it being an engaging and entertaining story. Scholars have considered it one of the best examples of Greek fiction and perhaps even among the first novels in world history.[10] Moreover, the *AR* preserves multiple significant documents for the study of the historical Alexander, as scholars increasingly recognize. It is also worth noting that, besides being well received in antiquity, the text became popular and influential in its own right. Not only is the *AR* one of the most circulated texts next to the Gospels, but it was also for a long time the only version of the 'historical' Alexander known to readers outside the European continent.

---

[6] Accordingly, Konstan 1998: 127–128 classified the *AR* as an 'open text', a highly unstable and anonymous type of text that encouraged further redistribution and independent rewriting.
[7] Selden 2010: 14 claims that the 'text networks' in which the *AR* participated disappeared in the fifteenth century.
[8] Of course, the texts are similar in other ways: see, for example, McInerney 2007.
[9] The Romano-Greek Alexander historians (Diodorus, Plutarch and Arrian) were naturally read widely in Byzantium, as demonstrated by Jouanno 2018a and 2018b.
[10] See already Stoneman 1994a; cf. Stoneman 2018b.

28.1 Alexander is lowered into the sea. Folio from a Khamsa (Quintet) of Amir Khusrau Dihlavi, illustrated by Mukunda (attributed), 1597–1198. Metropolitan Museum of Art, 13.228.27.

Accordingly, the *AR* has stimulated an incredible amount of cultural production across spaces that the historical Alexander never saw.

Scholarship on this text has been a venerable and vibrant enterprise, in some periods even eclipsing the study of the protagonist himself.[11] Despite the richness of the *AR*, however, the text has hardly been taken seriously in traditional studies of the historical Alexander. But the tide is turning, as is evident in this volume and elsewhere.[12] In what follows, I continue the ongoing trend of retrieving the *AR* 'from ignominy',[13] recontextualizing the *AR* as a literary text.[14]

In Search of an Alexander Romance

While New Philology and Reception Studies redirect attention to the later instantiations of the *AR*, traditional philological practice has explored their origin, namely the lost Greek original, the *alpha* version. The reconstruction of this archetype, or the *Ur-text*, represents a challenging task. Consider only the paratextual information provided by the chief manuscript witness and its 'translations':

- An anonymous Greek text in three books contained in Codex A (BnF par. graec. 1711, AD 1013–1124), entitled Βίος Ἀλεξάνδρου τοῦ Μακεδόνος, *The Life of Alexander of Macedon*;
- A Latin adaptation of a very similar text to the one in Codex A by Julius Valerius (possibly the consul of AD 338), entitled *Res gestae Alexandri Macedonis translatae ex Aesopo graeco, The Deeds of Alexander of Macedon translated from Aesop the Greek*;[15]
- An Armenian rendition extant in several manuscripts with the descriptive title, *A History of the Great World Conqueror, Alexander of*

---

[11] The most instructive example of the immense operation is a library collection, now digitized and online, which belonged to the teacher Heinrich Christensen (1849–1912). The website, hosted by Belgrade University, contains *c.* 150 scholarly monographs and articles about the *AR* published in the nineteenth century or earlier, for which see http://ubsm.bg.ac.rs/engleski/zbirka/knjiga/posebna-biblioteka-dr-hajnriha-kristensena-1849-1912 (accessed 22 March 2022). More recently, Richard Stoneman (particularly Stoneman 1991) has invigorated interest in the *AR*, feeding into the surge of broader scholarly interest in imperial Greek prose, including the Greek novel, and into scholarly recognition of wider cultural interaction in the ancient Mediterranean.

[12] See, for example, Carney 2015: xix–xxii, discussing *inter alios* Bowden 2014b: 143. Cf. Müller 2019, referring to the *AR* sixteen times.

[13] Ogden 2017a: 252.   [14] Encouraged by Arthur-Montagne 2019: 72.

[15] The Teubner edition of Rosellini 2004 is complemented by a French translation, commentary, and apparatus in Callu 2010. Gavin Kelly informs me that an unpublished translation of Julius Valerius into English was undertaken for Cecil Rhodes in the 1890s, and there is an initiative to digitize this and other translated texts at the Groote Schuur estate in Cape Town, South Africa.

Macedon – A Life of Bravery and Heroic Deeds, and also a Death Marked with Marvels.[16] The text appears to have been a source for a national history of Armenia by Moses of Khoren (d. *c.* AD 490) and so is traditionally dated to the fifth century. It is pseudonymously attributed to Alexander's teacher, Aristotle.

Based on this survey, there is no immediate agreement as to the author or the genre to which the earliest version of the *AR* belonged, nor as to its title. Take the authorship of the original text, for instance: Byzantine authors, including John Tzetzes (*c.* 1110–1180), attributed the Greek version to Callisthenes, an established historian at the historical Alexander's court.[17] However, Callisthenes died before Alexander and, therefore, could not have written the bulk of the third and final book of the *AR*.[18] Accordingly, subsequent scholarship referred to the author as 'Pseudo-Callisthenes'. With this early modern label, Pseudo-Callisthenes joins a catalogue of hypothetical authors proposed by ancient tradition: famous names were appropriated with a view to garnering authority or popularity for texts,[19] such as Aristotle, Aesop, and even Ptolemy I, who did in fact compose an Alexander history.[20] To stress this anonymity, I refer to the author of the original Greek version as the 'romancer'.[21]

Alpha derives its name from being the first archetypal instantiation, but also the text from the Codex A. The constitution of the *alpha* text itself is difficult because the manuscript is a poor witness. Modern attempts at restoration have primarily been a compromise between the mangled Greek text and the ostensible authority of the Armenian version. In the *editio princeps* from 1846, Karl Müller (1813–1894) recognized the potential of the Armenian, which had been discovered four years previously,[22] but he did not incorporate it. In 1896, Richard Raabe released a retroversion into ancient Greek to 'facilitate' access to the Armenian text. In 1926, Wilhelm Kroll (1869–1939), who also wrote the comprehensive *RE* entry on the *AR*,[23] published an interpretation of *alpha* that he called 'the most ancient version', *recensio*

---

[16] Wolohojian 1969 offers a convenient English translation.   [17] See Chapter 25.
[18] As was first recognized by the Renaissance humanist Isaac Causabon (1559–1614) in a letter to Joseph Scaliger (1540–1609), dated 15 August 1605; their Latin correspondence is printed in Pfister 1976: 20. Cf. Nawotka 2017: 2–3.
[19] Twelve (!) potential author names, together with evidence, are discussed in Pfister 1976: 31–34.
[20] See Chapter 23.   [21] Following the exemplary Garstad 2018a.
[22] Müller 1846: x ('Pseudo-Callisthenes: *Introductio*'). Further insight into the history of the earliest scholarship in Wolohojian 1969: 5–8. Cf. Pfister 1976: 24–25.
[23] Kroll 1919.

vetusta,[24] which integrated Raabe's retroversion of the Armenian.[25] This edition, and the comparative methodology it exemplifies, still speaks to researchers.[26]

It is evident, however, that an exclusively philological approach cannot stand on its own. Aside from the problems of positivism and irrevocable loss of the original, the privileged position of the Armenian text is problematic because the text remains under-studied; in fact, the Armenian seems much closer to the Byzantine *beta* recension of the *AR*, not only in content, but also in approximate date (fifth century AD). Discoveries of papyri and other material evidence have offered variant readings and even complete episodes that may have informed the original romancer. One may find a more inclusive approach to textual variation in the most recent edition, which – like Harvard's 'Homer Multitext' project – collates the principal texts and presents them separately for individual and collective interpretation.[27]

Content and Structure

All versions of the *AR* comprise three books of varying lengths and content. They also follow a similar narrative pattern loosely organized around biographical practice, brilliantly reflected in the Latin rendition. Julius Valerius, or his medieval editor, provides the subheadings 'rise' or 'birth', *ortus*, for book 1; 'actions', *actus*, for book 2; and 'death', *obitus*, for book 3. The plot of *alpha* may be outlined thus:

Book 1

Origins and the Nectanebus narrative (1–14):

- Nectanebus, Egypt's last indigenous Pharaoh, divines his country's doom at Persian hands and escapes to Macedonia (1–3);
- Nectanebus gains prestige and the attention of Olympias, whom he seduces (4–7);

---

[24] The title page of Kroll 1926 prints *Historia Alexandri Magni: recensio vetusta*. Haight 1955 translates Kroll's text into English.
[25] Kroll 1926: vii–viii justifies the use of Raabe 1896.
[26] See, for example, Ory Amitay's project, 'Origins and composition of the *AR*' (Israel Science Foundation), which foregrounds Greek and Armenian.
[27] Stoneman 2007 (book 1) and 2012 (book 2). The third and final volume of this edition has yet to appear.

- To avoid suspicion of Olympias' infidelity, Nectanebus casts multiple spells on Philip, who also witnesses a serpentine portent of Alexander's greatness (8–11);
- Nectanebus' horoscope for Alexander and his birth (12);
- Alexander's looks (13.3), education (13.4), and early exploits (13.5–13.7);
- The revelation of Alexander's parentage and Nectanebus' death (14).

The rise of Alexander (15–19):

- Alexander's breaking-in of Bucephalas, a man-eating horse (17), which act, according to the oracle at Delphi, is the sign of Philip's successor, a new Heracles (15);
- Aristotle predicts Alexander's future greatness (16);
- Alexander participates in the Olympic Games, winning the chariot race (18–19).

The fall of Philip (20–24):

- In Alexander's absence, Philip divorces Olympias and marries Cleopatra (20), whose wedding Alexander disrupts by killing the wit Lysias with a cup and injuring other guests with Philip's sword (21);
- Alexander reconciles his parents (22);
- Alexander momentarily takes over Philip's tasks, dealing in diplomatic fashion with Methone (23.1), Persian envoys (23.2–23.4), and an unnamed city (23.5);
- Pausanias, a Thessalian nobleman, desires Olympias and plots to kill Philip, whom he attacks, but does not immediately kill, whilst Alexander is away. Alexander returns and assists Philip in exacting revenge on Pausanias. Philip dies from his wound and is buried (24).

The conquest of the north and the west (25–26):

- Alexander persuades Philip's soldiers to support him (25);
- The new king assembles a huge force (26.1–26.2) with which he retakes Thrace and Lycaonia (26.3). They then journey to Sicily and Italy, where Rome surrenders and pays tribute (26.4–26.6).

Consolidation of the south (30–34):[28]

- In Africa, Alexander refuses to assist the Carthaginians against the Romans (30.1);

---

[28] Book 1 of *alpha* lacks the chapters 27–29.

- Alexander visits the oracle of Ammon in Libya, asking questions about his parentage (30.3–30.4) and founds Alexandria (30.5–30.7);
- Alexander founds Paraetonium (31.1) and travels to the tomb of Osiris (31.2), after which he arrives at the building site of Alexandria, named Rhacotis (31.3–31.8);
- Interlude in the foundation-narrative of Alexandria: it is compared to other great cities and found to be the greatest (31.9–31.10);
- The foundation of Alexandria continues (32);
- Alexander seeks out Sarapis, ostensibly the chief Egyptian divinity of the area, and encounters many signs of Egypt's great antiquity, including Sesonchosis' obelisk (33.6);
- Sarapis and Alexander interact, after which the king dedicates a temple to the god (33.13);
- Alexander travels to Memphis and embraces his status as Nectanebus reincarnate (34).

The sack of Tyre (35).
The first battle against Darius (36–41):

- Diplomatic exchanges with the envoys of Darius (36–38), Darius' consultation of his governors (39); and the last pre-battle exhortation from Darius to Alexander (40);
- A major battle ended by Darius' flight (41).

The conquest of the Greek world (42–47):

- Darius prepares for the next encounter (42.1–42.3), but Alexander goes against Achaea (42.4);
- At Bebrycia, Alexander sees a statue of Orpheus sweating, which interpreters consider a sign of imminent victory (42.6–42.8);
- Alexander at Troy (42.9–42.13);
- Alexander at Abdera (43);
- Alexander's conquest of northern Greece and the Black Sea area (44);
- Alexander is declared as strong as Heracles at Delphi (?) (45);
- Alexander's sacking of Thebes (46) and its rebuilding (47).

Book 2

The aftermath in Athens (1–5) and Sparta (6):

- Conflict between the Athenian general Stasagoras and Alexander over the pro-Macedonian prophecy of a priestess (1);

- Various responses to the conflict by the orators Aeschines (2.5–2.7); Demades (2.8–2.10); and Demosthenes (3–4), with whom Alexander eventually agrees (5);
- Alexander seizes Sparta (6).

The second war against Darius (7–16):

- Darius discusses the upcoming war with his generals (7);
- Alexander suffers a near-fatal illness after swimming in the Cydnus River and is saved by his doctor, Philip (8);
- Alexander returns to the action, subduing Media and Armenia (9.1), and reaches the Tigris, where he fights Darius' governors (9.8) and survives an assassination attempt by a Persian (9.9–9.11);
- Epistolary exchanges (10–11); Darius also alerts the Indian king Porus to Alexander's campaign (12);
- After consulting Ammon in a dream (13.4–13.6), Alexander visits Darius as his own messenger (14), steals gold cups from his table (15.1–15.5), is recognized (15.6–15.8), and makes a narrow escape with the booty (15.9–15.10);
- Darius' final defeat at the battle on the icebound river Stranga; Darius flees but his army is destroyed when the soldiers fall into the river, which suddenly unfreezes itself (16).

The demise of Darius (17–20):

- Darius finds himself isolated after the battle at the Stranga (17);
- Alexander visits various sites in Persia, including the tomb of Cyrus (18);
- Darius makes a new attempt to muster forces by writing again to Porus (19.1–19.5), but is betrayed and injured by his own ally, Bessus (20.1–20.5);
- Alexander finds the wounded Darius in the palace and embraces the Persian as a father, the moment he dies in Alexander's arms (20.6–20.12).

Alexander's revenge and the restoration of Persia (21–22):

- Alexander orders the burial of Darius (21.1–21.2), makes an extensive eulogy detailing his plans for Persia (21.3–21.21), and punishes the killers of Darius (21.22–21.26);
- Some Persians rebel against Alexander (22.1), who wins them over by taking care of the women of Darius' family (22), including Roxane, Darius' daughter (22.14–22.16);
- The Macedonian army marches on India (22.17).

Book 3

Prelude to the Indian campaign (1):

- Having marched through a great desert and ravines (1.1), Alexander's weary army quits (1.2–1.5); Alexander persuades them to continue, but sends the veterans home (1.6–1.8).

The Indian campaign (2–4):

- Alexander and Porus exchange letters, which sets up the conflict (2);
- Alexander outwits Porus' stratagems and war-beasts (3.3–3.4), and a regular fight ensues in which Bucephalas dies (3.6);
- Having fought for twenty-five days (4.1), Alexander's army begins to surrender, wherefore Alexander challenges Porus to a duel, which he wins (4.2–4.4).[29]

The philosophical discourse among the Gymnosophists (5–7).
Alexander's letter to Aristotle about India (17).
Conflict with the descendants of Semiramis (18–23):

- Alexander corresponds with Candace, queen of Meroe (18);
- Candace commissions a painter to capture the image of Alexander (19.1–19.2);
- Candace's son, Candaules, is manipulated by Ptolemy into thinking that Alexander is the messenger Antigonus (19.3–19.11), and the incognito Alexander assists Candaules in retrieving Candaules' stolen wife (20);
- Candaules acts as tour guide to 'Antigonus' and points out the cave of the gods (21.4);
- 'Antigonus' meets Candace and sees Semiramis' palace (22.1–22.8);
- Candace outwits Alexander by showing him his own picture, but promises to keep his identity secret because he has assisted Candaules (22.9–22.15);
- Candace's youngest son wants to kill 'Antigonus', but Alexander resolves the conflict and impresses Candace, who wants to adopt him; Alexander departs unharmed (23);

Alexander's encounter with the now god-like dead Pharaoh, Sesonchosis, in a cavern (24);

---

[29] Kroll 1926 omits 3.4.8–3.4.16.

Alexander's epistolary exchanges with the Amazons (25–26), Aristotle (26.8), and Olympias (27–28);
An ill omen presaging Alexander's death in Babylon (30);
The poison plot (31–32):

- Antipater, Alexander's regent in Macedonia, has an enmity towards Olympias, so when Alexander seeks to do something about it, Antipater engages his son Cassander in an elaborate plot to kill the king (31);
- Cassander conveys a poisonous draught in a mule's hoof to Babylon, and his accomplice Iolaus (Iollas) manages to serve Alexander the drink twice for rapid effect; the assassins make their escape (31.10–32.3);
- At night the dying Alexander attempts to throw himself into the Euphrates to disappear in the fashion of a god, but Roxane prevents him (32.4–32.10);
- Alexander wants to settle his affairs and summons Ptolemy in particular (32.11–32.15).

The will (33.1–33.25) and death of Alexander (33.26–33.27):

- Holcias reads Alexander's will (33.1), which confers major possessions upon Ptolemy;
- Ptolemy asks to whom Alexander bequeaths his kingdom (33.26), and the king dies (33.27).[30]

The burial (34):

- A quarrel breaks out about Alexander's burial, but Ptolemy consults the oracle of the Babylonian Zeus, who sends the king to Memphis, Egypt (3.1–3.3);
- Ptolemy escorts Alexander's body to Memphis, where the deceased is greeted as a new Sesonchosis (34.4), but the Archpriest redirects the procession to Alexandria, where Ptolemy builds a tomb (33.5–33.6).

An epitaph recording Alexander's biographical details, campaigns, and city foundations (35).

The above summary has glossed over the many geographical and historical inaccuracies of the *AR*. For instance, one may point to obvious distortions of chronological order, such as the placing of the first battle against Darius before the conquest of Greece, or the glaring error that Roxane was a daughter of Darius.[31] In the past, emphasis on such infelicities has so

---

[30] Kroll 1926 inserts the Ptolemy-centred material from *AR* (Arm.) 33.26–34.6 into the Greek text.
[31] Stoneman 1991: 1.

often led to scholarly value judgements of the *AR*'s historical worth, but historical accuracy was not necessarily the chief aim of the text, as we shall see below. Nevertheless, the romancer did incorporate important existing materials, and these have attracted attention.

Sources

Certain tales and documents in *alpha* have been used by past scholars to attempt to identify the earliest constituents of the text.[32] To this end, scholars have typically employed one of the traditional tools of historicism, source-research or *Quellenforschung*. The main proponents of this were Adolf Ausfeld (1855–1904)[33] and Reinhold Merkelbach (1918–2006).[34] The former had his arguments about an early Hellenistic date for the *AR* invalidated by discoveries of various papyri,[35] whereas the latter used said papyri to argue that the original romancer had collected and edited a text based on much existing material. Such documents were principally Egyptian tales (focusing on the foundation of Alexandria, etc.); regular Alexander history; and a collection of letters or a *Briefroman*,[36] a continuous narrative of Alexander's life narrated through letters.[37] To Merkelbach, these materials stemmed from various points in the Hellenistic period, primarily the second century BC, a supposition he supported by his comprehensive source-criticism or *Quellenkritik* of *alpha*.[38] Merkelbach's conclusions have been contested, not least his negative views of the romancer's compositional ability.[39]

Readers of this volume will not be surprised to learn that source-criticism and research on the *AR* have attracted scholars of the historical Alexander. Common procedures have been to single out the disparate historical episodes, as well as entire independently circulated documents;

---

[32] See, for example, Fraser 1996: 205–226.
[33] See, for example, Ausfeld 1894, 1907. As a schoolteacher, he had also turned the Alexander legends into a book for his students, posthumously published as Ausfeld 1909.
[34] Merkelbach 1954, updated by Jürgen Trumpf and re-published in 1977.
[35] Cf. Merkelbach and Trumpf 1977: 11–13. Documentary evidence has been found in the form of papyri (Trumpf 2006), inscriptions (e.g. Burstein 1989), and other material (e.g. Hatzilambrou 2019, concerning an *ostracon*).
[36] The *AR* contains *c.* thirty-five letters, primarily to and from Alexander, and Merkelbach claimed that they represented an 'epistolary novel'. This is a type of text otherwise witnessed solely by the series of seventeen letters attributed to Chion of Heraclea (d. 353 BC), which explain how Chion put the theory of Plato's Academy into practice by slaying the tyrant Clearchus in his hometown.
[37] Merkelbach and Trumpf 1977: 226 offer a schematic overview.
[38] Merkelbach and Trumpf 1977: 108–155.
[39] See, for example, criticisms at Gunderson 1970, Berg 1973; Samuel 1986; cf. Nawotka 2017: 19, 24.

to extricate them from the *AR*'s narrative; and to recontextualize them on their own terms. For example, modern historians, including Brian Bosworth (1942–2014), have debated the form and function of Alexander's will (3.33.2–33.25),[40] an independent document of uncertain Hellenistic date.[41] The original version of the will was integrated into the *AR*'s narrative at an uncertain point,[42] probably by a Rhodian entity; the current version in the *AR* is often referred to as the 'Rhodian interpolation' because, according to it, Rhodes stood to gain major concessions and the prestige of caring for the bereaved queen mother, Olympias (3.33.12).[43]

DATE

These scholarly activities have, unfortunately, not led to any conclusive dating of *alpha*. A long list of chronological arguments has been advanced with the result that *alpha* could have appeared during a window of about six hundred years.[44] The *terminus post quem* is determined by Alexander's death, and the *ante quem* is the fourth-century AD translation of the *AR* into Latin. In Richard Stoneman's view, it is possible that the romancer, perhaps a Hellenistic Alexandrian, composed an *AR* in the third century BC.[45] Other scholars maintain the traditional dating in the third century AD.[46] A key argument for a late date is the Roman vocabulary of A,[47] which includes late military terminology and a host of Greek glosses of Latin words. A diplomatic 'solution' is to consider *alpha*'s linguistic expression as emblematic of an imperial Greek revision of a Hellenistic original.[48] Of course, this solution does not preclude the possibility that more than one revision of *alpha* was made during the same time span[49] or that *alpha* emerged only in the imperial period.

---

[40] Overview at Nawotka 2017: 244–245.
[41] The autonomy of this document can be inferred from the inclusion of the will in a parallel Latin version, known as the 'book of the death and testament of Alexander the Great', *Liber de morte testamentoque Alexandri Magni* (*LM*), appended to a separate late antique work, the so-called *Metz Epitome* (*ME*). For the former, see the edition of Thomas 1966, with an updated text at Callu 2010 appendix 3 and Ravazzolo 2012; Heckel and Yardley 2004: 281–289 offer a complete translation into English. For the latter, see still Baynham 1995a.
[42] According to Nawotka 2017: 244, *P. Vindob.* 31954 from the first century BC (or AD) transmits a similar text as *AR* 3.3.11–3.3.12; cf. *LM* 116.
[43] See Baynham 1998b.   [44] Reviewed by Stoneman 2007: xxv–xxxiv.   [45] Stoneman 2009.
[46] See, for example, Jouanno 2002: 26–28, maintained in Jouanno 2020: 210. Cf. Nawotka 2017: 3–5.
[47] Wyss 1942 (*non vidi*), discussed by Nawotka 2017: 29. Cf. Whitmarsh 2018: 150.
[48] Stoneman 2018a.   [49] Suggested by, for example, Trnka-Amrhein 2018: 28.

Place of Composition

Perhaps the least contested issue with *alpha* is its Egyptian roots.[50] Egypt plays a prominent role throughout the text, not only as a site of Alexander's origins, but also of his life and legacy. One may point to the elaborate narrative about Nectanebus, the founding of Alexandria and Alexander's city as his final resting place. Recurring appearances of North African characters, such as Ammon, Sarapis, and Sesonchosis, contribute to this slant. The romancer routinely refers to Egypt's national lore, customs, language, religion, etc., and he is the only ancient author willing to proclaim Alexander Pharaoh (1.34.2),[51] the logical consequence of his Nectanebus redivivus narrative (*AR* 1.35). The overwhelming amount of Aegyptiaca suggests an originally Egyptian context of composition, perhaps Ptolemaic Alexandria, according to Stoneman's theory,[52] or the traditional view, now rejuvenated, that the *AR* was written in Severan Alexandria (or later in the third century AD).

Unfortunately, we may be failing to see the desert for the dunes. Tim Whitmarsh has urged caution,[53] arguing that the alleged 'Egyptianizing' is as artificially constructed as the text's Hellenocentric view of Alexander. The rich Egyptian features are pre-existing materials reworked by the romancer; they are playfully integrated to reflect on the issue of cultural dominance, and the romancer effortlessly discusses many other models of cultural power from Greece, Rome, Africa, Mesopotamia, and India. For Whitmarsh, it is rather cultural hybridity that makes up the *AR*.[54]

If Whitmarsh is right, we are less restricted in the way that we may think of the composition of *alpha*. Jacqueline Arthur-Montagne has made a very attractive hypothesis based on the less-known papyrological and anecdotal evidence for the declamations of the rhetorical schools of the Roman Empire.[55] She argues that Alexander regularly appeared in

---

[50] See, for example, Braun 1938: 31–43; Pfister 1976: 35–52 ('ägyptische Volksbuch'); Stephens 2003: 64–73; Nawotka 2017: 25–27.

[51] Ptolemy *FGrH* / *BNJ* 138 F9 (= Arrian *Anabasis* 3.4.5) comes closest.

[52] Stoneman 2009: 150–152. Cf. the conclusion of Koulakiotis 2006: 232–234, the most wide-ranging study of intellectual references to Alexander, which claims that much of the *AR* materials come from 'the non-historiographical tradition' of the Greek and Hellenistic worlds. Peltonen 2019: 6, 219–220, argues that the *AR* itself does not seem to have made a mark on the major literary texts of the imperial period, stressing the absence of the *AR*'s fantastical stories.

[53] Whitmarsh 2018: 149.

[54] Whitmarsh 2018: 135–144 (cf. his cosmetic title, 'Alexander in Kohl').

[55] Arthur-Montagne 2016. I thank the author for making chapter 5 of her dissertation available to me, as well as the revised discussion from her much-anticipated monograph (chapter 4).

pedagogical exercises that required students to revise the biographical narrative rather than that of the military campaign, necessitating creativity and imagination so as to compose letters like Alexander,[56] speak like him, or resolve conflicts caused by him (especially in Greece). The rhetorical handbooks contain school exercises, from *chreiai* ('sayings') and *paradeigmata* ('examples'), that incorporate themes, content, and forms familiar from *alpha*.[57] Such exercises are not fully-fledged compositions, but rather foundational pieces or writing-prompts for rehearsing rhetorical arguments anchored in a historical setting. The sheer volume of material attested in papyri from the first centuries BC and AD indicates the massive scale of the writing of 'revisionist Alexander fiction' across the Roman school system. In my view, it is not impossible to imagine that one such student, or his schoolmaster, one day decided to compose an elaborate retelling combining these standard exercises and filling in the blanks with pre-existing materials like Alexander's will. Accordingly, the composition of *alpha* could have been done anywhere in the urban schools of the Hellenophone part of the Roman Empire.

CLASSIFICATION

The identification of a text's genre normally signals the modes of interpretation appropriate to it, but the *AR* flouts every convention.[58] Including the text under a broad label like 'novel' has not satisfied critics,[59] and some have actively situated the *AR* on the 'fringes' of ancient historiography, biography, and novelistic writing,[60] inadvertently contributing to its marginalization. A few scholars prefer the label 'pagan hagiography', a catch-all term typically used to explain the lives of philosophers and holy people in the late antique period.[61] These categories ultimately imply a more serious content or purpose, such as a religious significance, than the *AR* admits of.

---

[56] Arthur-Montagne 2014.
[57] In Djurslev 2020, I proposed to view the discourse on Alexander, or *Alexandrology*, as reflecting the building blocks of rhetorical materials, an approach which – I contend – complements Arthur-Montagne's position on the declamations. According to Briant 2020: 111, these avenues of exploration show much promise.
[58] The *AR*'s kaleidoscopic nature also makes the text difficult to classify: cf. Jouanno 2020: 209.
[59] The *AR* features, in the form of Dowden 1989, in Reardon's collection of the Greek novels in English translation.
[60] Nawotka 2017: 13–18 sketches the relevant positions. [61] Becker 2013: 51–77.

Yvona Trnka-Amrhein is currently developing a promising concept, the 'ruler novel'.[62] This proposes a genre of legendary stories about world-conquering royalty, such as the Assyrian 'power couple' Ninus and Semiramis,[63] and the Egyptian Sesonchosis.[64] This kind of prose fiction accommodates the rather entertaining narrative of the *AR*, with all its intriguing imitations and its crossover encounters with international 'superheroes'.[65] Furthermore, it also helps to explain all the 'spin-off' episodes, preserved on papyri.[66] This interpretation also explains the archetypal representation of Alexander, because superhero portraits often replay popular tales or character types to convey an engaging story.

Approached as an inventive prose narrative, the *AR* offers a completely new take on the life story: Alexander's circuit of the Mediterranean is 'history as it should have been', with this half-Egyptian king consolidating his main possessions, namely Egypt, Macedon, and the western Mediterranean, before launching the expedition against Greece and the East.[67] Book 2's narrative of the Persian restoration can be read in a similar fashion: the stories legitimize Alexander's rule of Persia by writing the usurper into the royal family's acceptance and into kinship with it. Book 3 amplifies the drama of otherworldly war, wonder, and death, whilst also providing a full explanation for how things turned out after Alexander. It is easier to appreciate such readings if we are inclined to see the *AR* as an attempt to rewrite Alexander (and early Diadoch) history rather than to parrot it.

The Alexander Romance as a Literary Text

Given the increased focus on the textual qualities of the *AR*, the scholarly community is experimenting with many forms of literary analysis. For example, comparison of episodes in the different-language versions of the *AR* has yielded rich results.[68] Concerning *alpha*, scholars have sought to emphasize a structurally oriented 'author'

---

[62] Trnka-Amrhein 2018: 26, convincing Arthur-Montagne 2019: 71 (verdict: 'superlative contribution').
[63] Ninus and Semiramis are not in Bielman Sánchez 2019, but the couple may be proposed for a next instalment.
[64] Trnka-Amrhein 2020.
[65] Alexander is no stranger to such fiction – see, for example, Taylor 2015.
[66] Trnka-Amrhein 2018: 45 (cf. her title, 'the fantastic four', alluding to the Marvel franchise).
[67] Garstad 2018a: 129; cf. Garstad 2016.
[68] See, for example, Paschalis 2007; Konstantakos 2015; and Djurslev 2021a.

rather than a compiler or redactor. Corinne Jouanno highlights the use of supernatural signs to generate story structure, so that the events predicted happen in a divinely ordained way. This in turn confers a 'meaningful destiny' upon the protagonist,[69] whose life might otherwise appear to have had a premature end. Another structural element examined by Jouanno is that of thematic doublets that infuse the narrative with a sense of 'seriality'; that is, events recur in similar ways, such as Alexander's encounters with Darius and Porus. The doublets imbue the narrative with a sense of familiarity and direction under the guidance of a higher power or providence (*pronoia*).

As for the characterization of Alexander, the portrait is simplistic, insofar as it lacks extensive character development or complex features, such as inner monologue.[70] Some scholars regard the representation as idealized and encomiastic, which is common in biographical writing.[71] Others view Alexander more as a type of folk hero, and they have accordingly explained the representation along the lines of stock characterizations in other ancient literature.[72] Corinne Jouanno explores a number of biographical models, such as the *basilikos logos* ('royal treatise'), but prefers to consider the romancer's Alexander a trickster figure, whose solitary nature adds to his characterization as such a type.[73] The trickster theme features in the king's speeches and correspondence, but also in the extraordinary episode in which Alexander disguises himself as Hermes to dine with Darius (AR 2.14–2.15).[74] In this respect, the king acts in a fashion similar to that of his father Nectanebus, substituting magic tricks for the power of *paideia* ('learning'). These initial results demonstrate the potential of appreciating the *AR* as a literary narrative.

Conclusion

This chapter has introduced the *AR* in its first hypothetical instantiation, or *alpha*, outlining how people have tried and try to understand the text.

---

[69] Jouanno 2020: 217.
[70] It is, of course, a historiographical trait to characterize individuals mainly through their actions, speeches, and other lines of communication.
[71] This is due to the positive personal traits of the king, such as cleverness, as well as the complete absence of Alexander's vices and canonical crimes, such as the killings of Clitus and Callisthenes. Cf. Nawotka 2017: 27–28.
[72] See, for example, Konstan 1998: 137, arguing that 'The *AR* is . . . an ego fantasy in which a small man . . . stands up to haughty kings and giants and succeeds as much through scrappiness as force.' Cf. Karla 2012.
[73] Jouanno 2020: 211–216; cf. Jouanno 2013: 69–70.   [74] Garstad 2018b.

We have considered the work as a literary text in its own right rather than as a lacklustre compilation or a source of spurious material.[75] In terms of interest in the historical Alexander, this is an important first step for appreciating how the *AR* fits in with the much more familiar Alexander histories of Greece and Rome, texts that we have only recently begun to take seriously as literary narratives. In terms of classical scholarship, consideration of an alternative text like the *AR* helps us to challenge the canon and encourage interdisciplinary research into how stories about a significant 'classical' character fuelled the cultural imagination of many peoples across the ancient world. And this is not to mention how the *AR* tradition as a whole looks ahead to the rich cultural production from the Middle Ages to Modernity: the text's role in shaping world culture across time and space cannot be denied.[76] These are all important directions for current work on the *AR*.

Guide to Further Reading

The best place to start is with the text itself. Stoneman 1991 offers a concise and lucid translation of the main versions of the *AR*, with selected supplements from other texts. Haight (1955) translates *alpha* faithfully from Kroll 1926, but the translation is dated, as is Kroll's text. The advanced reader may wish to consult Stoneman's Mondadori edition, which may one day appear in English (in the hopes of the author). This book does not include the Armenian text, for an English translation of which see Wolohojian 1969. Stoneman's edition does, however, provide an extensive Italian commentary on many matters. For a modern English commentary, mainly on *alpha*, consult Nawotka 2017.

The next stop ought to be Stoneman 2008, which remains one of the most accessible and engaging introductions to the *AR* tradition as a whole. The bibliography covers the relevant scholarship, whether it is the study of *alpha* or the Danish *AR*. The four volumes of Gaullier-Bougassas 2014 offer specialist studies of the entire European tradition. Jouanno 2002 remains the fullest treatment of the Greek tradition, especially in Byzantium. For traditions further east, see Aerts 2010 and Manteghi 2018.

---

[75] Cf. the opinion of Elizabeth Hazelton Haight (1872–1964), 'the Alexander Romance is the greatest historical romance I have ever read' (Haight 1955: x).
[76] Stoneman 2022c.

Nowadays, much work on the *Romance* is published in diverse edited volumes loosely based on conferences, which can render it hard to gain an overview of the field. One pedagogical collection of papers is Zuwiyya 2011, which is organized in terms of time, space, and theme.

29: Alexander in Jewish and Early Christian Literature

Aleksandra Klęczar

Introduction

The present overview concentrates on the periods in the history of Judaism and Christianity roughly coinciding with the traditional definitions of classical antiquity. Thus, most topics covered in this chapter deal with the writings from the Second Temple and from Rabbinic Judaism (also using the Talmudic writings, despite the complicated issue of their dating), as well as with the Christian writings from the Patristic era. Special exception will be made for the development of the *Alexander Romance*, since the texts belonging to this category are notoriously difficult to date, as far as their origins are concerned, and while certain versions can be dated securely, the stories and narratives included in them are often of much older origin. This choice of chronological framework is motivated by the fact that it allows us to see the images of Alexander within the traditions of Judaism and Christianity against the framework of their development within the pagan Graeco-Roman sphere of culture, if indeed such a sharp division can ever be made.

In case of the Jewish and Christian literature from the periods under discussion certain preliminary remarks are necessary. In short, whatever conclusions one draws, they will always be debatable and tentative, owing to at least two reasons. The first is the scarcity and the state of preservation of the material, a problem well known also to students of other ancient cultures. The second is the unspoken assumption that when we are talking about the Jewish or Christian image of Alexander, or of any other figure or topic, we mean the image as produced, discussed, and proliferated by a small percentage of the community in question, namely by its intellectuals and writers; in a limited number of cases, also by its artists and/or their patrons. We have no feasible ways of knowing what a Jewish merchant from the second-century BCE or a Christian servant girl in fourth-century CE Rome thought about Alexander, if they ever even did think about him. Still, certain popular opinions can be inferred from the authoritative writings, especially if one considers the practices of education, which spread and normalized certain sets of opinions and excluded others. For the Alexander legend some degree of popular knowledge, as opposed to intellectual speculations and debates, can also be extrapolated from the development of the *Alexander Romance*(s) in particular cultural milieus. Whatever the pre-origins of the *Romance*,[1] one should assume a certain period of oral transmission and development for the texts, even if the original was a written, elite-produced document, as many scholars believe. This is a partial justification of the inclusion of the *Romance* in the present chapter, despite the extant texts of it often exceeding the selected chronological boundaries.

The main conceptual problem for the students of the Jewish and Christian receptions of Alexander is that of continuity and change, both within the traditions themselves and in their relations to the broader cultural and political context of the reality of the Hellenistic and Roman empires. Indeed, it would be difficult to talk about their Alexander — especially the Jewish Alexander — if one were to exclude the political dimension of these retellings and their meanings for the actual power-relations. The Alexanders whom we encounter in Jewish and Christian texts of the period are, on the one hand, the results of the appropriation of a historical Macedonian military leader and king, re-created with these origins in mind by the cultures and religions in question, for whom Macedonia was a more or less distant place (in geographical, historical and cultural terms). On the other hand, however, these re-imaginings of Alexander are a product of these new cultural milieus, created and reworked with the given culture's specific needs, values and interests in mind. In this general way, the tactics and methods of dealing with Alexander within the Jewish and Early Christian traditions are not dissimilar to those of other cultures, such as Persian or Arabic.[2] What will interest us most in the following chapter are the specifics of reading and re-writing Alexander in the religious and cultural contexts of Judaism and Christianity.

It is also worth remembering that both the Jewish and especially the Christian reception of Alexander are far from uniform. Quite the opposite: the geographical, historical, social and linguistic differences, the ethnic and cultural diversity and the various identities added to those of 'Jewish' or 'Christian', in the case of the authors, must have

---

[1] Merkelbach and Trumpf 1977; Stoneman 1991; Nawotka 2004; Chapter 28.
[2] Persian: Wiesehöfer 2011; Nabel 2018. Arabic: Doufikar-Aerts 2010.

influenced their works and created varied, dynamic patterns in the reception of Alexander. Surely an intellectual of the Alexandrian Diaspora under the early Ptolemies would have had a different outlook to that of a liberated ex-prisoner of war in Vespasian's Rome or a rabbi in fifth-century Iraq?

In the case of the term 'Christian writers' used in this chapter, its meaning is limited to the group of authors concentrating mainly on apologetic themes, within Eastern and Western Christianity, during the first formative centuries of Christian thought and literature. The reasons for such a limited approach are connected with the sheer number of relevant Christian texts of various characters and genres: in order not to turn the paper into a mere list of mentions, some criteria must be set.

The early Christian reception of Alexander has recently been re-evaluated by Christian Djurslev.[3] While the traditionally prevalent view has been that the Christian tradition, especially the apologetic and theological texts, had a rather hostile opinion of Alexander and in general differed in its representations of Alexander from the pagan ones,[4] closer analysis of the sources now suggests that there was not a significant difference, but rather that there was a careful and varied selection and re-evaluation of Alexander material, sometimes in tune with the depictions in Greek and Roman pagan traditions, sometimes stressing other episodes and motifs and assessing them in accordance with the Christian set of values and ideas.

The following chapter compares these visions and looks at how certain inherited images of Alexander were adapted and changed, at what was kept, lost and added. It focuses on the crucial motifs and ideas, the presence of which was of special significance for the Jewish and Christian traditions. Instead of ordering the material chronologically, topics and motifs present in both Jewish and Christian depictions of Alexander are singled out so that both the similarities and differences, as well as the peculiarities of the representations, may come sharply into comparative focus. This topic-centred approach, to quote Djurslev's phrase, gives the reader a chance to observe certain processes in the reshaping and reworking of Alexander stories within the two traditions discussed here, while at the same time showing more clearly the interconnection and inspirations between the cultural spheres in question.

---

[3] Djurslev 2020.   [4] Cary 1956.

The Jerusalem Episode

The story of Alexander's visit to Jerusalem, first preserved in Josephus (later first century CE), but possibly dating from an earlier period, is the most crucial and important of the episodes specific to the Jewish Alexander tradition, while at the same time it was repeatedly exploited also by Christian authors.

In Josephus' version (*Jewish Antiquities* 11.304–11.347) the story is in two parts, one strand discussing the relations between the Jews and the Samaritans and the history of an elite Jew, Manasseh, allied by marriage to the Samaritans and responsible for some of their actions against the Jews of Jerusalem. The other strand (or rather a combination of a few sub-stories) is the narrative of Alexander's threat to the city, his recognition of the High Priest Jaddus as a figure known to him from a prophetic dream (in this dream the great God had spoken to Alexander in Jaddus' form) and his subsequent acceptance in the city. Later, Alexander bestows a number of political privileges on the Jewish populace of his kingdom and enables the Jews to triumph politically over their Samaritan neighbours (see Figure 29.1).

A number of variations of the story exist. In the Talmudic treatise *Megillat Ta'anit* (§9) the political story is simplified: the reason for the Jewish–Samaritan debate is not a single person's ambition, but rather it is part of the general wicked scheme of the Samaritans who want the Temple destroyed and are trying to use Alexander to achieve that. More importantly, however, the ending is much more dramatic: for their duplicity the Samaritans get destroyed and their city is *ploughed under and sowed . . . with vetch*, not unlike the biblical Shechem in Judges (9:45). This description of the ultimate Jewish triumph fits into the context of the broader work well, given that it often concentrates on important military successes of the Jews.

A large part of the scholarship on the episode consists of two strands: first, the relationship between the various accounts and, secondly, its possible historicity and the question of the models underlying the various versions of the story.[5] What seems especially interesting, however, are the ways in which these stories are invested with new meanings with every appearance, as they are reworked and retold.

In Josephus' account the main importance of the story may lie in its possible political interpretation. The Jews in this account are pious,

---

[5] Amitay 2006.

29.1 Italian, active first half sixteenth century, *Alexander and the High Priest of Jerusalem*. National Gallery of Art, Washington, DC: 1968.18.20.

loyal and trusting in God. Alexander is presented as a world leader who is beneficent towards the Jewish populace and willing to give them a privileged place in his empire. Thus, he might be treated as a model of behaviour for other political leaders, which would fit well with

Josephus' general outlook on Jewish–Roman relations.⁶ The retellings in Talmudic and *Romance* versions seem to have a more general meaning: the Jewish–Samaritan conflict is still there, but its dimensions become more epic and its outcome more dramatic.

The Jerusalem narrative became particularly important for Christian literature as it grew. In Origen's *Against Celsus* (5.50) the scene, shortened and devoid of details, is used mainly to prove the power of God over humans, even pagans.⁷ Djurslev suggests that Alexander's friendliness towards the Jews should be treated as a model for the Roman treatment of Christians in the future: that would make Origen's aim in using the story similar to that of Josephus.⁸ In Eusebius' *Demonstratio evangelica* (8.2.67) the story of Alexander in Jerusalem is also presented in a shortened way, in a form suitable for the author's apologetic purpose. Its importance lies mainly in the fact that its popularity, combined with the authority of Eusebius, resulted in the inclusion of the Alexander-in-Jerusalem story in Christian historical works and world chronicles.⁹

Alexander as the Universal King / the Time-Marking Figure

Among the most frequent motifs making use of the character of the Macedonian king within the Jewish cultural milieu is the concept of the time before and after Alexander. In other words, the lifetime of Alexander is used to mark a certain crucial change: a new era, a new beginning, the end of some phenomenon – most commonly, the end of prophecy in Israel.

Often coinciding with the latter is the concept of Alexander's universal kingship. A universal king, or, as he is sometimes called, world emperor (*kosmokratōr*) is a ruler whose dominion encompasses the entirety, or the larger part, of the known world. His rule is often, but not always, sanctioned by God, even though universal kings in Jewish tradition are, in general, foreign rulers (which can be explained by the fact that the very idea of kingship is problematic, if viewed in the context of the concept of God as the ultimate master of the Jewish people).¹⁰ Their lists

---

⁶ Klęczar 2019: 82–33.   ⁷ Demandt 2009: 189.   ⁸ Djurslev 2020: 132–133.
⁹ Jouanno 2016.   ¹⁰ Lorberbaum 2011.

have at some point been semi-canonized in Jewish tradition: the names of the same universal kings are often repeated in various sources. Up to a certain point in time Alexander is, invariably, the last of them before the coming of the Messiah; later, Roman emperors replace him as the last ones, but this does not eliminate the name of Alexander from these lists.

One of the earliest accounts of Alexander in Jewish tradition, and at the same time one of those that had a lasting impact on later stories focusing on the Macedonian king, can be found in 1 Maccabees 1–10. The narrative concentrates on one crucial, from a Jewish point of view, facet of Alexander's biography, namely on his role as a founder of Hellenistic dynasties. Specifically, the story of Alexander is used to frame the history of a character of the utmost importance for the text: the arch-enemy of the Jews, Antiochus IV Epiphanes. While nowhere in the text is Alexander explicitly called an evil ruler, certain correspondences between him and Antiochus suggest that the kingship of both can be described in similar terms: on the one hand, universal and encompassing the majority of the known world, on the other, characterized by pride and a hubristic desire to conquer and control everything, disregarding both the needs of the conquered and the will of God.

The Alexander narrative in 1 Maccabees describes, in a concise form, the king's life story, covering his rise to power and his career. It opens the narrative of the book in its currently known Greek form, serving as a preface to the main topic (the war with Antiochus and the emergence of the Maccabee family). The history of Alexander is told here in terms which set his life and mission within the paradigm of a universal king. Its significant feature is the role of Alexander in delineating the events: specifically, the figure of Alexander is used to mark a beginning of a new era. With his conquest, a new epoch of rule and rulers starts, one that would see new challenges and new dangers for the Jews. The role of Alexander is stressed by the fact that, in contrast to the prevailing Graeco-Roman tradition, 1 Maccabees shows him on his deathbed dividing the empire between successors and deciding the sequence of kings, and progresses from him to the root of all evil, Antiochus Epiphanes.

Such a reading of 1 Maccabees became important also in Christian circles. For Christian authors, the story of Alexander's rise and fall represented the ultimate fulfilment of Daniel's prophecies and thus the incontestable proof of their veracity. That also meant that the pieces of information provided there – such as the story of Alexander himself dividing his kingdom between the Successors – were treated as established historical facts.

The important exception is Eusebius' *Chronicle*, lost in its original form, but preserved in a variety of versions (the Syriac and Armenian translations; Book II as reworked in Latin by Jerome) and Greek quotations. The work's innovative form — Book I was an excerpt-based summary of the history of the nations, Book II a chronographic table presenting lists of dates and events — made it a crucial point of reference for the later Christian historians. The presence of Alexander in the *Chronicle* is quite important: the presentation of his life is fuller than in the majority of Christian sources, starting with his birth as a son of Philip and Olympias (no divine origins here, obviously!), goes on through his military campaigns, from the sack of Thebes to his entry into India, and finishes with his death in Babylon; the narrative, predictably, includes the visit to Jerusalem and the defeat of the Samaritans. The selection of events from Alexander's life is ample if idiosyncratic,[11] and the details differ slightly between the translations and Jerome's modernized version.

Alexander and Prophecy

The theme of Alexander as marking the end of prophecy is another important one in Jewish tradition. It may be read into 1 Maccabees (14:41, 44–46; in both these passages prophecy is said to have ceased some time before the Maccabean wars) and it is explicitly mentioned in the treatise *Seder Olam* (second century BCE). In both these sources Alexander functions as a character delimiting a certain period in history: before him, Israel had prophets who led the people, but after the times of Alexander this era ended, and sages replaced prophets. Alexander's kingdom is thus the final one: its fall would mean the end of the old world and the commencement of Messianic times.

The most influential text describing Alexander as a world ruler and at the same time as part of a sequence of monarchs/kingdoms, leading to the end of times, is undoubtedly the Book of Daniel. Of the three visions that might be connected with him and the Macedonian empire (Daniel 2, 7, and 8) it is the third one that is of crucial importance. It describes a fight between a ram and a he-goat, the latter symbolizing Alexander as well as his kingdom and the kingdoms of his Successors. The actions of the ram are presented as hubristic and cruel, and, ultimately, destined to cause the fall of the he-goat, or rather of the

---

[11] Djurslev 2020: 168.

smallest of his horns, representing the Seleucid state. The proud and ruthless empires will replace one another and ultimately all will fall, because such is the will of God – this seems to be the main conclusion of the vision.

It would be difficult to overstate the importance of Daniel's vision for the further development of Alexander's image, both in Jewish and Christian literature. But it was not the only text incorporating Alexander into a prophetic context. A similar vision of the Macedonian king can be found in notoriously difficult *Sybilline Oracles* (difficult owing to the variety of possible interpretations and the complicated origins of the collection). Here Book III is of special importance, as it presents the oracles concerning the Macedonians and their kings. The Sybilline vision shares significant aspects of its images with Daniel (Diadochi as horns, the sequence and succession of kingdoms), but, interestingly, it presents Alexander and his ancestors as descendants of Cronus (euhemeristically presented as a mortal universal king). The children of Cronus are proud, hubristic, and war-like, and the same qualities apply to Alexander. It is clear that the author(s) of this passage were familiar with the main points of the history of Alexander: mentions of his purple cloak, of him being begotten by thunder and of the fate of his son would suggest that Alexander here is primarily the war leader, provoking cruel conflicts that would finally end by the will of God.

The idea of Alexander as a king associated with prophecy and with the repressive states of the Successors, in other words the Alexander mainly taken from the Book of Daniel, became crucial for the Christian vision of his conquests and for the ways his figure was interpreted within Christian literary and theological spheres. Of special importance here is Jerome, whose image of Alexander is intricately connected with his analyses of the Old Testament prophets.[12] But Jerome was not the first Christian writer to comment on the Book of Daniel; it was already an object of interest for authors such as Origen and Eusebius (whose commentaries are lost). The direct identification of Alexander as a he-goat was apparently well established in the Christian tradition, as was the identification of the last horn with Antiochus IV Epiphanes, a feature shared with the Jewish literature of the period.[13] The eschatological dimension of Daniel's prophecy, however, was not as important for Christian literature as the fact that Alexander's conquests and his Graeco-Macedonian army's triumph over Persia could be understood and interpreted as a living proof of Daniel's veracity and the fulfilment of

---

[12] Djurslev 2020: 123–128.   [13] Djurslev 2020: 100–101.

his prophetic visions. Thus, Alexander became a part of the Christian Biblical narrative. The motif of Alexander's association with prophecy was continued by Lactantius, who mentions Alexander twice (*Institutiones Divinae* 1.6.8, 2. 7. 18, *c.* 303–311 CE), once in the context of the Sybil's prophecy foretelling his deeds, and a second time when discussing the false existence of pagan gods (the episode with the blinding of the soldiers who plundered Proserpina's temple, known also from Valerius Maximus, 1.1 ext. 5).

Another aspect of Alexander's association with prophecy and prophets is the story of the bones of Jeremiah, which the king had brought to the newly founded Alexandria to protect the city from the plague of snakes (*Midrash Haggadah Numeri* 30, 15; third- or fourth-century CE). The story of the snakes in Alexandria is known also from the *Romance* tradition, where the snakes are benevolent and non-aggressive, more in accordance with the Greek meaning of the omen.[14] Their dangerous aspect is probably a feature inherited from the Jewish tradition. The protection conferred by the Jewish prophet points at a possible political meaning, stressing the importance of the Alexandrian Jewish Diaspora (Klęczar 2014). A similar tale appears, in a Christian context, in John Moschus' *Pratum spirituale* (77; sixth-century CE).

ALEXANDER THE KING CHOSEN BY GOD, THE RIGHTEOUS FOREIGN RULER

One of the most fascinating and complex problems within the corpus of Jewish writings on Alexander is the question of the conqueror's relation to God and, conversely, God's plans for Alexander. The sources give us a plethora of possible answers: in Josephus (*Jewish Antiquities* 11.329–11.339), Alexander had been chosen by God and instructed in a prophetic dream about the proper actions towards the Jews. In the same passage, he is presented as the one finding the Book of Daniel in the Jerusalem Temple; he later reads and interprets passages pertaining to himself. While this scene does not present Alexander as a believer, nor does it prove his full incorporation into Jewish society, he is clearly shown as a sympathizer towards Jewish faith and tradition. Similar representations of Alexander leaning towards Judaism and Jewish culture are quite popular in ancient and medieval Jewish writings. These strategies of assimilating and appropriating the figure of Alexander are

---

[14] Ogden 2013a.

not unique to Jewish narratives. A special feature, however, is the range of possibilities presented in the texts and the numerous ways in which the character of Alexander and the teachings of Judaism are made to combine and intersect. As a righteous foreign king, is Alexander sometimes indirectly compared to other important rulers, Jewish or foreign? Of special importance among the latter is Cyrus the Great, of the former Solomon (*Targum Sheni* 1.2).

In Christian literature a slightly similar idea appears in Clement of Alexandria's writings (*Stromata* 1.24.158.3–1.24.159.6), where a typology of kings is supplied. Alexander is placed among the powerful rulers, together with Heracles; while they are not presented as divinely inspired, they are nevertheless neither criticized nor presented in a negative light. Conversely, Tertullian (*Against the Jews* 7.7) presents a list of universal kings, similar to some extent to the lists known from the Jewish tradition and containing the names of Solomon, Darius the Great, Nebuchadnezzar, the pharaohs of Egypt and Alexander, together with the Romans and their Germanic neighbours. His aim, however, is different to that of the compilers of Jewish lists: rather than show the sequence of empires stretching to the foretold end of days, Tertullian uses the list to show the limitations of the kings mentioned and their inferiority in comparison with Jesus Christ, the only king to rule over the entire earth.

Gog and Magog: The Gate of Alexander

The general outline of the story of the Gate of Alexander and the Unclean Peoples as it is known from the majority of sources consists of three main elements: (1) Alexander travelling to the far corner of the world; (2) the Unclean Peoples (often called Gog and Magog, which is a clear Biblical inspiration) posing a threat to the peaceful existence of the world; and (3) Alexander defeating the Unclean Peoples and building an impenetrable wall (usually between two mountains) to keep the world safe from their incursions and attacks. The notion of the breaching of the wall and Gate may be connected with millenarist ideas and apocalyptic or eschatological interpretations.

This outline is a later development: the first mentions of the Gate of Alexander (Josephus *Jewish War* 7.244–7.245) do not ascribe any eschatological meaning to the act of building it,[15] nor do they combine

---

[15] Djurslev 2018; Klęczar 2019.

the Gog and Magog (originally known mainly from Ezekiel 38:1–4, in the form of *Gog of the land of Magog*) with the Unclean Nations and the Gate. This combination of motifs becomes an important motif in the *Alexander Romance* (recension γ) and, owing to its biblical associations and its monotheistic overtones, it reappeared in numerous retellings of Alexander legends.[16]

THE HUBRIS AND EXCESSIVE PRIDE OF ALEXANDER

A set of Talmudic narratives, describing episodes often overlapping with stories from various versions of the *Romance*, present Alexander as excessively proud, hubristic and thus earning, at some point, either a lesson from one of his interlocutors or some kind of punishment.

Within the Jewish Alexander tradition there are relatively few narratives presenting the king as inherently evil. If he happens to be characterized thus, it is usually due to his connection with the spread of Hellenism and with the persecutors of the Jews. Such a vision is sometimes included in the Maccabean narratives, where it plays into their propagandistic aims. The figure of Alexander falls close to this kind of representation in 1 Maccabees, where he is projected as a precursor of Antiochus IV.

Another group of texts in which the motif of the conqueror's hubris can be detected is the Talmudic material. In *Tamid* 32a–32b Alexander is denied entry into the Garden of Eden and this denial is presented in a narrative saturated with Biblical allusions. The intertextual relation between this passage and Psalm 118 suggests, typically for the Talmudic method, additional possible readings, in this case connected with ideas of kingship and rule. Together with his exclusion from the Garden of Eden, Alexander gets a gift in a form of human eye, one that *is never satisfied*. The quotation used here once again alludes to a Biblical intertext, this time Proverbs 27:20, and its aim is to present Alexander as someone who is lacking certain necessary qualities (namely, being a *tsaddiq*, a righteous man in all respects) necessary to enter Paradise: these qualities are symbolized by the eye that wants to see, and thus to possess everything. Because he cannot put a stop to his *pothos* ('longing'), as the Greeks would say, and his ambitions, Alexander will have, finally, to die. In this image of the king denied entry to the Garden of Eden one can also detect a hint of a debate crucial for the

---

[16] Anderson 1932.

Christian image of Alexander: the problem of his auto-deification and the ways in which a monotheistic culture should to react to it.

Another story used for similar purposes and present in a number of Talmudic writings (*Avodah Zarah* 3.1.42c) and Midrashic writings (*Numbers Rabbah* 13, 14; a slightly different version in Rabbinic writings, *Pirke de Reb-Eliezer* 11.28b–11.29a, *Yalkut Shimoni* on 1 Kings, 211) is the narrative of Alexander's flying. The story has clear parallels in Greek *Alexander Romance* and is one of the stories most often retold and continued in later cultures. Here, the idea of Alexander's flight is used to convey the sobering message: whatever Alexander sees from above and tries to possess, he could never be equal to God. He might be the ruler of the entire world, but political power, even over territories so vast, is incomparable with the power of God, ruler of all the lands who sees all the hidden places of the earth.

In Jewish literature we can also find a series of scenes in which Alexander participates in a debate, often with a Jewish personality, and loses the argument. Such is the story of Alexander's meeting with King Kazia, transmitted in three slightly different versions. They are known from several Talmudic tractates and Rabbinic works (*Baba Mezia* 2.5.8c; *Genesis Rabbah* 33; *Pesikta de-Rav Kahana* 9.24; *Leviticus Rabbah* 27.1; *Midrash Tanhuma Emor* 6; *Yalkut Shimoni* Ps. 36.727). The stories describe the deeds of Alexander at the court of Kazia, who rules beyond the Land of Darkness. The Macedonian is shown observing a judicial dispute between two of Kazia's subjects and the king's ruling on it. Kazia and his subjects are described as righteous and uninterested in financial gain, while Alexander proves himself to be both greedy and quite uncivilized in his ways. The follow-up, with the scene of Alexander being served a golden meal, precious but inedible, hints once again, critically, at the conqueror's greed.

Similarly, in a much earlier work, pseudo-Hecataeus' treatise *On the Jews*, preserved fragmentarily in Josephus' *Against Apion*, Alexander again engages in argument, this time twice: the first time with the Jewish soldiers sent to repair the pagan temple of Bel, the second time with a Jew called Mossalamus. In the first one, Alexander finally relents and allows his Jewish subjects a reprieve from rebuilding an offensive pagan temple. In the second, the soldier Mossalamus seems to be a careful variation of Alexander himself. When the army stops its march because of an omen, Mossalamus solves the problem with an action quite reminiscent of the Gordian Knot anecdote: he simply shoots down the supposedly prophetic bird, thus proving himself less naïve and less superstitious than Alexander and his army. This image of Alexander

Appendix: The Hebrew Romance of Alexander

Among the numerous versions of the *Alexander Romance* is a group of texts created within various Jewish milieus, dated from the twelfth to the fifteenth centuries. While these texts might have, ultimately, a common source (a version of the Alexander narrative that may have originated in Egypt in Hellenistic times: see Chapter 28), they are not derived directly from it, nor are they connected to the Talmudic tradition, despite often retelling the same stories. Some of these texts (MS Héb. 671.5, Bibliothèque Nationale, Paris; MS. 145, Jews' College, London; MS. Heb.1087, Biblioteca de Rossi, Parma) are translations either directly from the Greek version or from versions translated first into other languages; Arabic is here of special importance. They also exhibit some affinities to the text of Yosippon (for which see below). Another group contains possibly the best-known and most popular of Jewish versions of the *Romance*, namely *Sefer Toledot Aleksandros Ha-Makdoni*, adapted from a number of sources by an eminent Jewish intellectual Immanuel ben Jacob Bonfils (c. 1300–1377 CE); also in this group was the Turin manuscript, currently lost, but known from preserved descriptions to be very similar to *Sefer Toledot*. These versions seem carefully constructed, using not one model, but several, with a creative use and re-working of their material. The third group consists of MS. Heb. D11, Bodleian Library, MS 53 Estense Library (Modena) and the lost Damascus manuscript, of which only the Russian translation of Harkavy exists. These versions concentrate on fanciful, adventurous, fairy-tale elements; they also often contain both material not known from other sources and motifs and stories of typically Jewish character. Saskia Dönitz, who proposed this typology, suggests also the existence of a fourth group, represented by a single fragment (MS Codex Hebr. 419xx, Bayerische Staatsbibliothek, Munich), probably adapted from Old French Romance.[17]

The text sharing a great deal with the *Alexander Romance* is the Alexander narrative in *Sefer Yosippon*, a medieval Hebrew chronicle composed in Biblical style and dealing with universal history from Adam to the Roman-Jewish war. Despite the main source for Yosippon being a Latin translation of Josephus' *Jewish War* and *Jewish Antiquities*, the material concerning Alexander is probably based on the Latin *Historia de preliis* (J2 redaction).[18]

---

[17] Dönitz 2011.   [18] Wallach 1947: 190–198.

These Jewish *Alexander Romance* texts, despite their differences, share a significant part of their material and some of their attitudes, among which two are of interest here. First, they generally present Alexander in a positive light, even though some scenes (like the dispute with the Gymnosophists) can be read as slightly critical or even humorous. Secondly – and this is a quality they share with other versions of the *Romance* – they often appropriate the figure of the Macedonian conqueror, presenting him either as a strong sympathizer and supporter of the Jews or as someone who is at least symbolically part of the culture in which the given version of the *Romance* has been created.

Guide to Further Reading

For Alexander in Jewish literature, see Dönitz 2011 and Klęczar 2019. For Alexander in early Christian literature, a topic of considerable recent interest, see Peltonen 2019 and especially Djurslev 2020 (cf. also 2018). For Alexander in Muslim literature, see Doufikar-Aerts 2010 (Arabic) and Wiesehöfer 2011 (Persian). For the Alexander Romance tradition, see Cary 1956; Jouanno 2002; and Stoneman 2008.

30: ALEXANDER IN ANCIENT ART

Agnieszka Fulińska

In modern art the main motifs of Alexander's imagery are easy to recognize. The histories and the *Alexander Romance* provided artists with attractive scenes that allowed the combination of historical subject matter, highly valued by the various academies, with moral instruction in the virtues of a ruler, or with a mythological dimension. Thus, clemency towards the family of Darius or towards king Porus, the taming of Bucephalas, the founding of Alexandria, the meeting with the Amazon queen, etc., have become popular topics, while Alexander has frequently been deployed as a mirror, metaphor or allegory for modern rulers and their virtues.[1] These themes are not, however, found associated with Alexander in ancient art before the third century CE, when some legendary topics begin to appear on Roman coins.

In his own lifetime, as well as in the Hellenistic and Roman ages that followed, Alexander was represented in complex scenes only relatively rarely and such scenes, being the domain of painting, have barely survived to our time. In the preserved corpus, portraits are prevalent, intended to serve as the king's symbolic presence in the conquered lands, and subsequently as the divine presence of the ultimate founder of the Hellenistic dynasties, or the hallowed hero of the past for the Romans. Yet even these portraits, which share common traits, traits mentioned in the literary sources as the king's characteristic features, pose a problem, because in the Hellenistic period they became the model for ideal male imagery, and therefore they proliferate as a *type*, frequently associated with heroes and divinities, while not necessarily intentionally representing Alexander himself.[2] In R. R. R. Smith's words, '[Alexander's image] entered the common stock of Greek

---

[1] One of the best-known and most ambitious projects in this vein is the series of paintings by Charles le Brun executed for Louis XIV of France.
[2] On 'Alexander' as a sculptural type, see Hölscher 1971; 2009; and Trofimova 2012.

iconography (...) and was absorbed into a whole series of images, divine and mythological.'[3]

Corpora of Alexander's portraiture have been compiled since at least the mid-nineteenth century, but of major impact have been those from the early- to the mid-twentieth century, which, however, were prone to see Alexander in every sculpted head that exhibited any resemblance to the characteristic traits.[4] This in turn provoked hypercriticism, which resulted in doubts concerning a considerable number of the former identifications. A most reasonable catalogue of Alexander's actual portraiture has been drawn up by Andrew Stewart.[5] However, in discussing Alexander's image we must not neglect the influence of the ideal model, nor Alexander's syncretizations and associations with gods and heroes, since affinities of this kind augmented his 'visibility',[6] and gave rise to a discrete but deeply charismatic omnipresence for Alexander in the Mediterranean world.

IN SEARCH OF ALEXANDER'S FACE

The face of Alexander was at a time one of the best-known images in the world: this was due to the numerous representations of him that circulated around the whole of the ancient Mediterranean and beyond. These representations mostly originated in sculpture and were replicated on coins. Paradoxically, though, we cannot say that we know Alexander's appearance: as in many cases of prominent individuals from the pre-photographic past, we are confronted with the public image these persons chose to propagate. Therefore, the story of 'Alexander in ancient art' is the story of an artistic and political creation, which evolved over time to suit changing political requirements and aesthetic tastes, and yet preserved iconic traits that still allow for easy identification of the subject and the assessment of its influence on artistic canons and fashions. Irrespective of the question of actual likeness, the intention of representing Alexander – or the model based on Alexander – is clear in these images.

Our knowledge of Alexander's physical appearance, as derived from textual sources, is scarce and not very detailed; moreover, the preserved texts are later than Alexander's lifetime, and so even if their

---

[3] Smith 1988: 59.
[4] De Ujfalvÿ 1902; Schreiber 1903; Bernoulli 1905; Gebauer 1938/39; Bieber 1964.
[5] Stewart 1993, Appendix 4.
[6] Hölscher 2018: 2, 73 for Alexander's 'theatrical mentality' in self-presentation.

authors had access to original testimonies, they may have embellished or modified the descriptions to suit their own ends and exalted the mythicized king.[7] Nevertheless, several traits are recurrent in our sources, and we can assume that there is some truth to them, especially in that in many respects they go against the Greek ideal of beauty.

According to ancient authors Alexander was relatively short, and had the mannerism of tilting his head;[8] he was also clean-shaven.[9] The latter habit raises a question of whether the king wanted to emphasize his youth and make it eternal – the fourth century BCE being the period when many gods and heroes lost their mature aspect and became more and more frequently represented as youths[10] – or whether he had simply failed to grow a beard. The writers also agree on longish hair, probably fair. However, blond hair is a trait of beauty according to Greek tradition, and therefore could have been falsely accorded to the divinized king for that reason. More important is the emphasis given to his characteristic hairstyle, allegedly resembling a lion's mane (another idealizing trait), and described as the *anastolē* ('putting back'). Yet another trait, mentioned in relation to sculpted portraits, continues to perplex modern researchers: the 'melting gaze' or 'limpid eyes'.[11] Finally a comparison of Alexander with his closest friend and companion, Hephaestion, tells us that the latter was 'more handsome'; the anecdote about Darius' wife taking the more impressive man for the king made its way not only into biographies, but also into modern art, for example such masterpieces as Veronese's *The Family of Darius before Alexander*. The image that comes down to us, therefore, is not very flattering, and we can assume that when Plutarch says of the sculptor Lysippus that he was the only one properly to 'bring out [Alexander's] essential genius [*aretē*] and preserve his virile and leonine demeanour', he has in mind Alexander's commanding presence and his other personal traits, that is, his *ēthos* ('moral character'), rather than the king's physical appearance.[12] Plutarch believes this task to be more important than the other sculptors' attempts to 'represent his crooked neck and melting, limpid eyes', that is, the detail of the physical features.

---

[7] For a comprehensive selection of excerpts from ancient sources, see Stewart 1993, Appendix 1; cf., however, the discussion on their reliability and on invented Alexanders at 38–41.
[8] For whether this had a medical origin or was a personal mannerism, see Stewart 1993: 75–76.
[9] Discussion of the significance of this at Boardman 2019: 38 and Smith 1988: 46.
[10] Interestingly, it applies in the first place to Dionysus and Heracles, both major figures in the Macedonian pantheon, and in the Argeads' own dynastic 'mythology'.
[11] ὑγρότης τῶν ὀμμάτων: Plutarch *On the Fortune of Alexander* 2.2 (cf. *Alexander* 4).
[12] Plutarch *On the Fortune of Alexander* 2.2.

Several of the aforementioned physical traits found their way into artistic representations, and they very often serve modern scholars as guidelines for the identification of Alexander's portraits or their influence on the general model. Most commonly, when looking for Alexander, four of these characteristic features are taken into account: the *anastolē*, the 'limpid eyes', the tilt of the head and the lack of a beard.

The *anastolē* is usually interpreted as the hair being parted over the brow and raised in a mane-like way. The phrase 'limpid eyes' is more problematic, as the sources are not specific whether the phrase denotes a physical aspect of the eyes, or the eyes' gaze and the emotions it conveys. Judging by the most common Alexander types in sculpture, it is commonly agreed that at least in art the notion referred to the upward turn of the large eyes, so that his gaze might express his famous *pothos* ('longing'). Dimitris Plantzos interestingly connects this melting gaze with the *aretē* ('virtue') of philosophical thought:

> With particular reference to eyes and vision, in peripatetic and related sources the belief that 'liquid' eyes are a sign of the brave and upright in character is repeated as a matter of course. In many such texts Alexander is mentioned as an example. However, there is more in these remarks than traditional physiognomics. The nature and function of the eye, as explained at length by Aristotle, formed the basis of an influential, albeit idiosyncratic, physiology which affected the views later expressed by the physiognomists.[13]

Apart from these traits, which can serve to idealize, the physical description of Alexander presented by the texts is hardly compatible with the most widespread types of portraiture. One major work has long been believed to convey a realistic likeness: the life-size *Azara Herm* (Figure 30.1), discovered in 1779 by a Spanish ambassador to the Papal States, amateur archaeologist and art collector, José Nicolás de Azara y Perera. In 1803, de Azara presented the herm, inscribed in antiquity with the legend 'Alexander, son of Philip, Macedonian', to the then First Consul of the French Republic, Napoleon Bonaparte, who bequeathed the sculpture to the Louvre, where it remains.

The herm is a Roman copy. It accorded with the general taste of the portrait galleries prominent men kept in their wealthy villas, like the

---

[13] Plantzos 1999: 69.

30.1 The *Azara Herm*. Paris, Louvre, Ma 436.

collection of Hellenistic kings from the Villa dei Papiri in Herculaneum, and it was actually discovered in a similar context: in the Villa dei Pisoni in Tivoli (ancient Tibur). The sculpture is executed in relatively poor-quality stone, which has suffered from erosion and chips, and this condition adds to a general expression of tiredness or sadness. Nonetheless, and even if it underwent minor reworking while in

Azara's possession, the herm is popularly believed to be a faithful copy of the portrait of Alexander made in life by Lysippus, and has been deemed to be realistic. This belief is partly due to the unique inscription.

The predominant model, however, was the idealized image, and the smooth face of a young godling was the one that was to be reproduced on coins, engraved gems, in sculpture, then in those portraits of later rulers who wished to emphasize their symbolic descent from Alexander, and eventually in the ideal male heads from the Hellenistic period, found both in the Greek kingdoms and in Italy, especially, in the latter case, in an Etruscan context.

Alexander: Lifetime Portraiture

Sculpture was *the* genre of art for the Greeks. Even though it was held to be a variety of *technē* ('craft'), like any other artisanal process, it was nonetheless believed to constitute the crown of human creative skills and to be the most perfect way of rendering reality. Therefore portraiture too, or what passed for portraiture in Greece (the Greeks did not develop the concept of a 'portrait' in the sense of a 'likeness' of a living person prior to the Hellenistic period), was executed in the first place in the medium of sculpture. It was the sculptors that dictated the rules of artistic representation, for example by establishing canons of beauty, as expressed in terms of the proportions and the harmony of the human body. Alexander's court sculptor, Lysippus, who was counted among the greatest artists not only of his own age, but of antiquity as a whole, was one of these codifiers. He proposed a new canon of proportions, associated with the 'late classicism' of the fourth century BCE. However, Alexander's sculpted portraiture does not start with Lysippus.

Around 338 BCE Alexander's father, Philip of Macedon, commissioned two works of art to commemorate his victory over the Greek states at Chaeronea, the victory that consolidated Macedon's hegemony in the Greek world. Both commemorations included the crown prince, whose cavalry manoeuvre was crucial to the outcome of the battle, but the goal was also dynastic: Alexander was designated by his father to become the next king, which in the complex system of Macedonian hereditary rule was an important gesture. Hence, Alexander was represented at his father's side in the group sculpted by Euphranor, showing the king and the prince as victors. The statue from the Munich Glyptothek, known as *Alexander Rondanini* (Figure 30.2), has long been considered to be a copy of this statue, not without reservation.

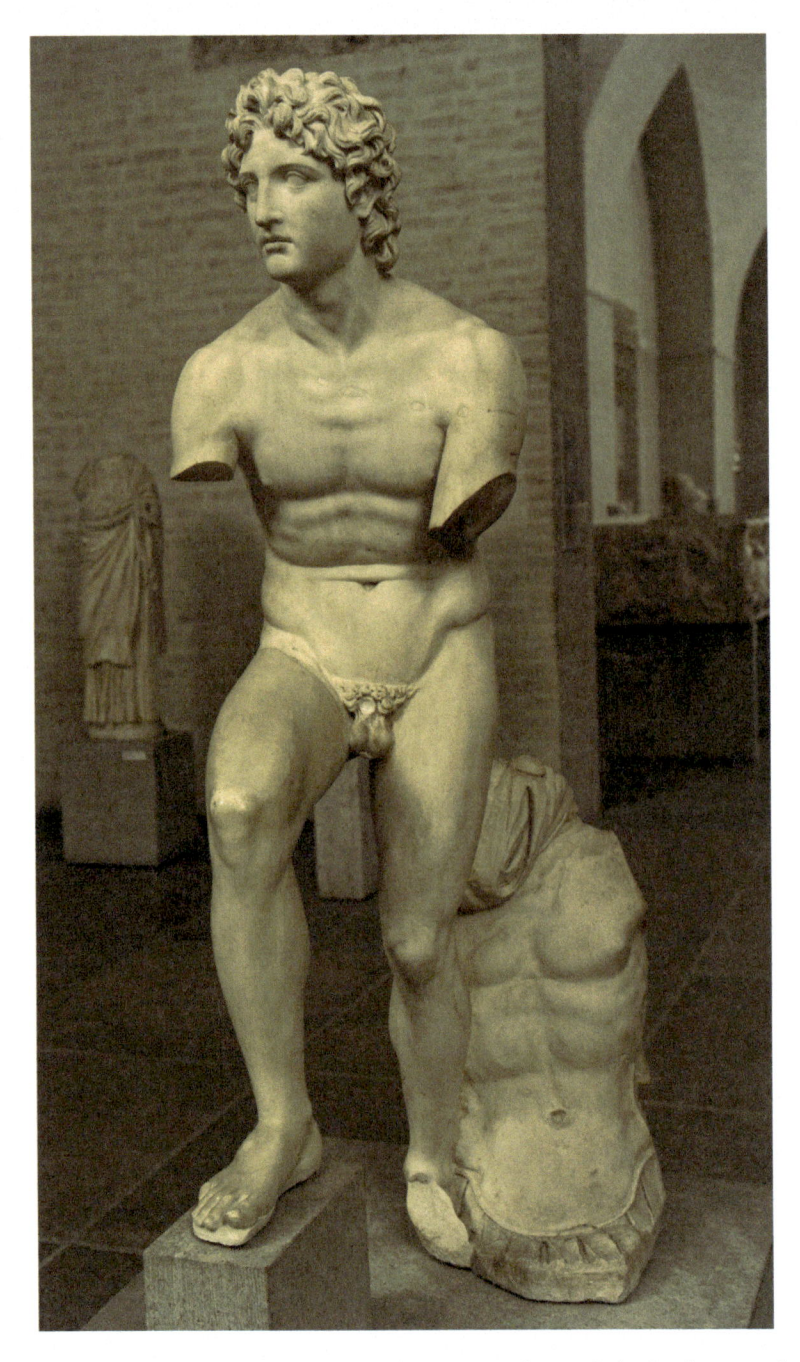

30.2 Euphranor. *The Alexander Rondanini*. Munich, Staatliche Antikensammlung, 9007172307.

The latter is based mainly on the idealistic approach to the subject, and its possible Hellenistic dating. Since only the incomplete statue of the young man is preserved, there is no certainty, either, that the sculpture was part of a group as Euphranor's was.[14]

A major work, however, especially from the point of view of royal propaganda aimed at the Greeks, was the royal family group commissioned for the Philippeum, that is, the ex voto for the Chaeronea victory, which was erected in the Altis at Olympia. Philip employed Leochares, one of the major names of his time, who would later cooperate with Lysippus in the execution of the sculptures. But what was significant about this commission was not the sculptor, but the medium and placement. The group was chryselephantine, which is to say that it used ivory for the visible body parts, gold for the decorations and wood or stone for the covered parts of the body, especially the torso.[15] This technique was usually reserved for images of the gods, and moreover, the statues of Philip and his family were to be placed in one of the most sacred sanctuaries of the Greek world. Alexander was again to be included in this almost deified group, together with his parents, Philip and Olympias, and paternal grandparents, Amyntas and Eurydice, which made an even clearer dynastic statement than the Euphranor commission.

Even though nothing is preserved from the Philippeum statues, apart from their bases, which show traces that may confirm their material, it is sometimes believed that a set of small ivory heads from Tomb II at Vergina are reduced versions of the Olympian portraits, and several life-size marble heads – the idealized youthful heads from Pella and the Athenian Acropolis, as well as the *Getty Alexander* – have been tentatively considered to be copies or reflections of them.[16] In the case of the two former sculptures, their find sites may corroborate the hypothesis, because the Macedonian capital and Athens are likely places for the images to be disseminated. Nonetheless, the question of the function of the Philippeum images remains unsolved: were they cult statues, as the material from which they were made might suggest, or not? Unknown too is their exact arrangement, since the only eyewitness

---

[14] See von den Hoff 1997 for discussion.
[15] For the chryselephantine medium of this group, see Barringer 2011; *pace* Schultz 2009. Cf. Lapatin 2001: 118 for the popular conviction that the technique was reserved for divine images only.
[16] Andronicos 1984: 115, 123–136. Note the debate between, for example, Kottaridi 1996: 100 and Worthington 2008b: 239.

to leave a surviving testimony is Pausanias, who travelled to Olympia in the second century CE. He gives the following description:

> The Metroum is within the Altis, and so is a round building called the Philippeum. On the roof of the Philippeum is a bronze poppy which binds the beams together. This building is on the left of the exit over against the Town Hall. It is made of burnt brick and is surrounded by columns. It was built by Philip after the fall of Greece at Chaeroneia. Here are set statues of Philip and Alexander, and with them is Amyntas, Philip's father. These works too are by Leochares, and are of ivory and gold, as are the statues of Olympias and Eurydice.
> Pausanias 5.20.9–5.20.10 (Jones and Ormerod trans.)

The arrangement, with either Philip or Alexander in the centre, could help to date the realization of the monument to either Philip's lifetime or to Alexander's reign, but this question must remain open for now.[17]

The textual evidence has both of the Chaeronea commemorations commissioned by Philip, which suggests that their general dynastic programme must have been laid out during his reign. However, if it was Alexander that brought the Olympian monument to completion after Philip's death only two years after Chaeronea, the meaning of the group could have changed, either with or without its arrangement changing too. Cult-like monuments of deceased ancestors were certainly considered less offensive to the gods than the same statues would have been if they represented persons still living. Even so, both Alexander and his mother remained alive after Philip's death, so the argument in favour of a heroic monument to the murdered father is only partly valid.[18]

During the decade of Alexander's rule and campaigns, Lysippus overshadowed all other sculptors and is duly called 'court artist' by Pliny and Plutarch.[19] This does not mean that other artists did not produce statues to honour the king and his deeds at this time. Lysippus was probably the preferred and official portraitist, but it is possible that others copied his two main types, with one of them predominating, to judge by the number of preserved copies. These two types were to be

---

[17] For the most up-to-date summary of the discussion on the arrangement of the statues, and detailed bibliography of the dispute, see Barringer 2011: 64–68, with notes.

[18] Schultz 2009: 129. [19] Pliny *Natural History* 7.57; Plutarch *Alexander* 2.2.

reproduced and disseminated in reduced scale and in materials other than bronze in all conquered lands; their role was to convey the king's image throughout his empire. The first type represents Alexander standing and holding a spear (Figure 30.3); the second represents Alexander on horseback (Figure 30.4). The former is known from numerous various-size reproductions, mostly in bronze, many of them small and of poor, simplified execution, as well as from detached heads and busts, including the *Azara Herm*. Copies of the latter are less abundant, but among them is one of supreme quality: the *Naples Alexander* from Herculaneum, a bronze dating most likely from the late Roman Republic. The equestrian Alexander originally formed a part of the so-called *turma Alexandri*, a monumental commemoration of the cavalry charge at Granicus, in which over thirty *hetairoi* perished. The monument, erected in the sanctuary of Zeus in Dion, that is, in the most important religious centre in Macedon, showed Alexander at the head of the charge, which contradicted the historical facts, but conveyed a very convenient image for the royal propaganda.

As far as life-size and monumental sculptures are concerned, what we possess are predominantly portrait heads, which tell us nothing about the way the rest of Alexander's body was represented. However, judging by the preserved reflections and by the codes of Greek statuary types in general, the standing Alexander was represented naked, while the one on horseback was equipped with a suitable panoply: armour and weapons. The body of the standing Alexander was arranged in contrapposto, with one hand raised in order to hold the spear; the head was slightly raised in an idealized rendition of his distinctive mannerism.

Among the preserved heads and busts, the *Azara Herm* is exceptional because of its inscription, but several other sculpted heads can be identified with confidence as copies of Lysippus' first type. They differ from the Louvre herm in their facial proportions in particular, but also in the degree of their idealization. While the Azara portrait exhibits elongated features (quite similar in proportions to a majority of the bronze statuettes), the other heads present a more rounded face, which also results in minor differences in the arrangement of the hair. In this respect the herm presents an image closer to the unflattering testimonies: the longish, slightly unkempt hair, the 'tired' look. The Schwarzenberg head from Munich, which is the second most important candidate for a faithful rendition of the Lysippus type, is more youthful in its general appearance, the features are smoother (which can only partly be attributed to the better quality of stone), and the hair is shorter and more harmoniously distributed around the face (Figure 30.5).

30.3 Bronze figurine after Lysippus, Paris, Louvre, Br 370.

30.4 Equestrian Alexander: bronze figurine. Naples, National Archaeological Museum, inv. 4996.

30.5 The *Schwarzenberg Alexander*. Munich, Staatliche Antikensammlungen, inv. GL 559.

Other marble heads identified with a high degree of certainty with the Lysippus type can be roughly divided into two groups as far as facial proportions are concerned. The *Dresden Alexander* bears a similarity to the Schwarzenberg Alexander, while the Erbach portrait appears to be the closest to the *Azara Herm*, even if it is more idealized; the *Pergamon Alexander* is mid-way between the two, as far as the proportions are concerned. The identified copies of the statue in whole body – reduced bronze figurines and paintings from Pompeii – prefer the oblong face. It would seem, therefore, that such differences are related to the artists' or workshops preferences, although it ought to be noted that the rounded face is more likely to appear on idealized portraits, which is not surprising if we look at the canons of proportions and statues of ideal male bodies from the late classical age.

Sculpted portraits were predominant, but Alexander was obviously represented in other media too, and one must bear in mind that, first and foremost, paintings were much more widespread in Greece than the state of their preservation may suggest, and moreover, that figural paintings, as well as mosaics, abounded in Macedonia, especially in funereal contexts, but also in wealthy houses and palaces.

According to our sources, the court painter was the famous Apelles, while Pyrgoteles, believed to be one of the greatest engravers of all time, supposedly executed portrait gems for Alexander.[20] However, nothing survives of their original work, which is known mainly from supposed reflections of it in other media dating from the Hellenistic and Roman periods. As for descriptions of the lost works, they are rare and not very detailed in content. The most comprehensive account is found in Pliny's remarks on monumental, allegorical paintings: he mentions one of Alexander in the company of the Dioscuri and Nike and another of Alexander as peacemaker, riding a triumphal chariot, accompanied by the personification of War with her hands tied.[21] No copy or reflection of these works survives to this day, even though they were displayed in the Forum Augusti in Rome, but one Pompeian fresco has been tentatively identified as a copy of a painting commissioned for the temple of Artemis in Ephesus: this is the image from the House of the Vettii, which shows Alexander seated on a throne, holding a thunderbolt in his left hand and a spear in his right.[22] This allegorical representation, with both divine and royal attributes, is believed to reflect the work of Apelles, owing to the famous

---

[20] Apuleius *Florida* 7; cf. Stewart 2003: 31, 34 for other testimonies.
[21] Pliny *Natural History* 35.36.   [22] Mingazzini 1961; *pace* Stewart 2003 : 39.

anecdotal quarrel between the painter and Lysippus over the use of such attributes in the portraiture of Alexander.[23]

This quarrel, as passed down in anecdote, concerned the acceptability of the use of divine attributes in representations of royal figures. According to the sources, it was Apelles that portrayed Alexander with the thunderbolt and Lysippus that objected to such a transgression. He argued that mortals, even those of elevated status, should not be portrayed with divine attributes, since this would be an act of hubris. However, it may be reasoned that Alexander's descent from Zeus, proclaimed at Siwah in 332 BCE, gave legitimacy to the use of this attribute, which is attested in minor representations of Alexander's image, such as the Neisos gem and the Porus medallions, apart from the posthumous Pompeii fresco. We will return to issue of attributes later.

A painting relatively well known for its content, and in all probability contemporary with Alexander, is that of the wedding of Alexander and Roxane by the painter Aetion, which is described in detail by Lucian.[24]

> The scene is a very beautiful chamber, and in it there is a bridal couch with Roxana, a very lovely maiden, sitting upon it, her eyes cast down in modesty, for Alexander is standing there. There are smiling Cupids: one is standing behind her removing the veil from her head and showing Roxana to her husband; another like a true servant is taking the sandal off her foot, already preparing her for bed; a third Cupid has hold of Alexander's cloak and is pulling him with all his might towards Roxana. The king himself is holding out a garland to the maiden and their best man and helper, Hephaestion, is there with a blazing torch in his hand, leaning on a very handsome youth – I think he is Hymenaeus (his name is not inscribed). On the other side of the picture are more Cupids playing among Alexander's armour; two of them are carrying his spear, pretending to be labourers burdened under a beam; two others are dragging a third, their king no doubt, on the shield, holding it by the handgrips; another has gone inside the corslet, which is lying breast-up on the ground – he seems to be lying in ambush to frighten the others when they drag the shield past him.
>
> Lucian *Herodotus or Aetion* 5 (Kilburn trans.)

---

[23] Plutarch *On Isis and Osiris* 24.
[24] It is commonly assumed that Aetion's floruit coincided with Alexander's reign.

However, there is no evidence to support the hypothesis of Pyrgoteles' authorship. Nor is there any to support the popular conjecture that sees Alexander on two coins related to the Indian expedition, the so-called Porus medallions with their standing figure and elephant-rider.[31] Equally doubtful is the attribution to Pyrgoteles of the Neisos gem, and so too the identification of the subject of this intaglio, a naked, wreathed male figure, with a thunderbolt in his right hand, an *aegis* on his shoulder, and an eagle at his feet.[32] However, despite the doubts, it can be assumed that the types presented on these coins and the gem do reflect Alexander's iconography.

The representations of Alexander made in his own lifetime can be divided into two main categories: those without attributes and those with them; the former are close to what we would now label as a 'portrait', whereas the latter are allegorical images, the aim of which was to convey a message about the ruler, rather than his likeness as such. Our knowledge of the sculptural types for Alexander, of the types for him in other arts, and of the quarrel between Lysippus and Apelles, even if anecdotal, points to an important difference in treatment of the royal figure between these media, with the preference of sculpture on the one hand for 'realism' and the preference of painting and glyptics on the other for allegories. The attributes given to Alexander in art during his own lifetime, however, are predominantly of a military sort, such as a spear or armour. A much richer repertoire of attributes will appear in the posthumous representations of the king, and these will allow for direct associations with the divine.

THE GOD ALEXANDER, THE LEGENDARY ALEXANDER: HELLENISTIC AND ROMAN IMAGERY

Alexander's death changed the rules of the portraiture game. The conqueror-king became the divine ancestor of the Hellenistic dynasties: it was for this reason that his imagery flourished in the centuries following his death, especially under the most successful Successors and their descendants, that is, the Ptolemies and the Seleucids. Even if it remains doubtful whether Alexander was deified in his lifetime, the Alexander embraced by Hellenistic kingdoms was a certainly the god Alexander first and foremost. For Hellenistic sculptors it was clear,

---

[31] Dahmen 2007: 6–9, with further literature.
[32] In favour of such attribution is Pollitt 1986: 23; Stewart 1997: 208 dates it, however, to the first half of the third century BCE.

therefore, that Alexander must be endowed with attributes pointing at his apotheosis, and syncretized or at least associated with numerous gods or heroes – Zeus, Dionysus, Pan, Apollo, Helios, Heracles, to name only the recurrent ones.

The process of divinization is most clearly visible in coin iconography. Even if we assume that Alexander's coins bear his own image in Heracles' guise, the ambiguity inherent in divine associations remains. However, in *c.* 297 BCE, one of the Successors, Lysimachus of Thrace, began minting coins exhibiting an image of Alexander with an obvious indicator of divinity, namely the ram's horns of Zeus-Ammon, god of the Siwah oracle,[33] and an obvious indicator of royalty, namely the fillet diadem (Figure 30.7). This issue marks a major shift in Alexander's iconography, which had hitherto been almost entirely devoid of attributes. The art of the Successors and their descendants – in the media of coinage, sculpture, mosaics and paintings – would add novel iconographic elements in the following centuries, such as the aegis, the *chlamys* (a short cloak), horns (ram's horns for Zeus-Ammon; goat's horns for Pan on a bronze figurine from Pella; and possibly bull's horns for Dionysus on a coin of Seleucus),[34] the *corona radiata* ('radiate crown'),

30.7 Alexander with ram's horns. Tetradrachm of Lysimachus. Paris, Louvre, FG 128.

---

[33] See Fulińska 2014 for detailed discussion of this attribute and its associations with a range of divinities.
[34] The dispute in this last case is summarized at Hadley 1974: 10–12.

the elephant scalp, etc. At times these attributes served the local propaganda of the Hellenistic kings, the *imitatio Alexandri* ('imitation of Alexander') performed by many of them, and so it is in that context that the meaning of these iconographic details should be sought rather than in the development of Alexander's legend per se. Alexander's traits, especially the symbolic ones, would also be appropriated by the kings, and even by the queens, by virtue of their association with a wide range of deities, including the divine founders of their dynasties.

Complex scenes are rare among the surviving Hellenistic images. A major exception is the Sarcophagus of Abdalonymus, which is decorated with the scenes Alexander's battles against the Persians (Figure 30.8). The figure of the youthful rider with highly idealized features on one of the long sides, reminiscent of the Alexandrian mints, and wearing a lion-scalp helmet, is almost unanimously considered to be a portrait of Alexander, Abdalonymus' benefactor. The similarities in composition with the Pompeii Mosaic, especially in the treatment of Alexander himself, suggest the hypothesis that the Philoxenus painting was a common source of these two depictions.[35] In the sarcophagus

30.8 Sarcophagus of Abdalonymus. Istanbul, Archaeological Museum.

[35] The best analysis of the sarcophagus, its dating and circumstances of execution, remains that of von Graeve 1970.

relief, nonetheless, the realism of the mosaic, and apparently that of the original, is replaced by a heroized figure, appropriate both for the funereal context and for the for date at which it was made, shortly after Alexander's death. The identification of the other prominent rider figure, in the lion-hunt relief on the opposite side of the sarcophagus, is controversial: devoid of any attributes, it is deemed to represent either the king himself (in whose iconography such scenes are noted), or his closest companion, Hephaestion, who was the one to actually make Abdalonymus king of Sidon, which would provide a context for him being accorded a place of honour here. The mixture of a historical theme with a subtle heroization places the sarcophagus on the cusp between the images of Alexander's lifetime and the posthumous ones.

Another important monument that showed Alexander in action was the Craterus *ex voto* ('dedication'), sculpted by Lysippus and Leochares and placed in the sanctuary at Delphi, only the platform of which now survives.[36] However, the arrangement of this group, which commemorated the episode in which Craterus saved the king's life during a lion hunt, may be attested in two major works of art that we do have: a mosaic from Pella (Figure 30.9) and an analogous relief from Messene, in the Louvre (Figure 30.10). Both show two men in Macedonian costume (*chlamys*-cloak and *kausia*, the broad-brimmed hat) fighting a lion, with the major distinction that on the mosaic both men are on foot, while the relief depicts one of them on horseback.

Surprisingly, the medium which testifies most copiously to the popularity of narrative, mostly legendary or half-legendary episodes from Alexander's life is that of Roman coins and other numismatic artefacts.[37] First and foremost, in 218–249 CE the *koinon Makedonōn* (the league of cities of the province of Macedonia) issued a series of coins in connection with games in honour of Alexander, the obverses of which replaced the usual portrait of the emperor with the image of the diademed Alexander, borrowed from Hellenistic tradition.[38] Complex scenes relating to Alexander were placed on the reverses; they either illustrate episodes from the *Alexander Romance* (Olympias with the siring serpent; the taming of Bucephalas), or reflect contemporary monuments to Alexander, constituting a unique, even if not very detailed, source of information for his late iconography. Similar imagery is featured on

---

[36] Plutarch *Alexander* 40.5; Pliny *Natural History* 34.63–34.64 (who mentions only Lysippus).
[37] One should, however, note that many works of art, sculptures and paintings featuring Alexander were transported to Rome after the conquest of Macedonia in the mid-second century BCE, and doubtless copied there: see Cohen 1997: 59.
[38] Dahmen 2007: 33. The coins were replicated by the city of Beroea.

30.9 Lion Hunt mosaic, Pella, Archaeological Museum.

30.10 Lion Hunt relief, Messene. Paris, Louvre, Ma 858.

a very particular issue made in late antiquity (fourth–fifth century CE), a series of jetons called *contorniati* ('contorniates') owing to their unusual articulated rim. Here, again, we find the scene of Olympias and the serpent (Figure 30.11), as well as Alexander fighting the barbarians on horseback.[39]

[39] Dahmen 2007: 37.

30.11 Contorniate with Olympias and the serpent. London, British Museum, R.4803.

The admiration of the emperors Caracalla and Heliogabalus for Alexander probably explains the existence of the most luxurious of the Roman items to carry Alexander's iconography: the hoards of gold medallions found in Tarsus and Aboukir, in 1863 and 1902 respectively. They show some iconographic similarities with the *koinon* coins, but amplify their imagery, possibly to suit the aims of Caracalla in his admiration and imitation of Alexander. In addition to the horseback Alexander and an unusual frontal portrait of the king (Figure 30.12), the medallions feature imagined portraits of Alexander's parents: a unique portrait of Philip II wearing a diadem, and two images of Olympias, namely a profile view, and the queen riding a taurocamp ('sea-bull'). Other scenes depicted include Alexander hunting and a winged Victory presenting the king with armour, probably in evocation both of *tropaion* ('trophy') imagery and of the divine gift of armour to Achilles, who was the mythical ancestor of the Epirote dynasty, and therefore of Alexander himself via his mother. In all three cases of the Roman numismatic evidence, the portraits of the Macedonian conqueror are generally consistent with the Hellenistic models as far as attributes are concerned, and do not deviate from the characteristics attributed to Alexander by the literary sources.

The only non-numismatic object featuring a scene which can be linked to the *Alexander Romance* is the unique fourth-century CE mosaic from Baalbek, showing episodes of Alexander's conception and childhood, with the figures named. Its content is rich: it shows both of

30.12 Gold medallion with frontal portrait of Alexander. Berlin, Münzkabinett, Staatliche Museen zu Berlin, 18200016 (1907/230).

Alexander's parents, the toddler Alexander in the care of a nymph, and probably the young prince with his teacher, Aristotle.[40]

Attributes and Their Meaning

Attributes are the most significant means by which portraits of prominent persons construct meaning. They usually carry both a literal and a symbolic or metaphorical meaning. In the case of ancient royal portraiture, these attributes fall into three main categories: the divine ones, the strictly royal ones and other objects with a significant iconographic role.

The imagery of Alexander's own lifetime, especially in the medium of sculpture, is very economical with additional iconographic elements. The only important attribute is the spear, which should not be mistaken for a simple piece of military equipment. In the context of the Macedonian concept of *gē doriktētos*, 'spear-won land', this attribute was a powerful symbol of earthly power and rule. The representation of the king as an idealized young man leaning on a spear conveyed the image of a heroized ruler, able to subjugate the whole world and become its

[40] See Ross 1963.

legitimate master, as in the anecdote, noted by Diodorus, of Alexander landing in Asia and throwing the spear into the land in order to claim dominion over it.[41] The spear in the hand of the personification of Macedonia on the allegorical fresco from Boscoreale is similarly the symbol of territorial power over Asia.[42]

In paintings and glyptics the figure of Alexander was more likely to be adorned with mere accessories as opposed to attributes as such, since representations of episodes, realistic or allegorical, required scenery, as can be seen in Lucian's description of the painting of the wedding with Roxane, and also in the details of surviving scenes such as the Pompeii Mosaic or the Vergina frieze. Warrior accessories would be present in sculptural groups related to battles or hunts, both those made in Alexander's lifetime, such as the Chaeronea monument and those made posthumously, such as Craterus' dedication. One of the Porus medallions shows a warrior, identified as Alexander, in armour and a Phrygian helmet, which attests that Alexander was represented with warrior accessories during his own lifetime.[43]

It is disputable whether any other iconographic elements that can be labelled either as mere accessory or as attribute were present in Alexander's imagery before the Hellenistic period, apart from garments and arms in the horseback representations. Among the accessories, a certain importance ought to be ascribed to the elements of Macedonian costume, that is, the *kausia*-hat and the *chlamys*-cloak, since they would play a considerable role in the Hellenistic reception of Alexander's imagery. Apart from the aforementioned Pella mosaic, a well-preserved bronze figurine from the British Museum shows Alexander in the *chlamys*-cloak, but without the headdress (Figure 30.13). The nakedness with which Lysippus chose to depict his standing Alexander should be considered equivalent to an attribute, since ideal nudity was the privilege of prominent figures in the Greek world: gods, heroes, winners of athletic games. Noteworthily, the application of single attribute or accessory, such as a cloak slung over the shoulder, or a weapon, while the body generally remains unclad, does not exclude the symbolism of nudity, and so the hunt imagery (the Vergina frieze apart) also falls into this category.[44]

---

[41] Diodorus 17.17.2.
[42] Smith 1994: 107, with further literature; cf. also Palagia 2014: 212–214.
[43] For discussion of the headdress, see Goukowsky 1981: 4; Stewart 1993: 203; Smith 2000: 16; Holt 2003: 118–119; Dahmen 2007: 6, 45 and 109–112; *pace* Olbrycht 2011b: 13–14.
[44] For discussion of the traditional notion of the concept of 'heroic nudity' and its problems, see Hölscher 1973; Himmelmann 1990; and Hallett 2005: 26–30.

30.13 Bronze statuette of Alexander. London, British Museum 1868,0520.65.

If we are to believe the anecdote about Apelles and Lysippus, and link in the Pompeian Alexander fresco, the only other actual attribute to have appeared during Alexander's own lifetime would have been the thunderbolt, but it is present on only one contemporary artefact, and that too a controversial one, one of the Porus coins, while even the Neisos gem is dated to the years after Alexander's death. Alexander *Ceraunophoros* ('Thunderbolt-bearer') is, however, attested soon afterwards, e.g., on a gold stater of Ptolemy of *c.* 300 BCE (this shows the deified Alexander with the *aegis*, the thunderbolt and cornucopia, driving a chariot drawn by four elephants),[45] and then later in Pausanias' description of a statue at Olympia:

> I have enumerated the images of Zeus within the Altis with the greatest accuracy. For the offering near the great temple, though supposed to be a likeness of Zeus, is really Alexander, the son of Philip. It was set up by a Corinthian, not one of the old Corinthians, but one of those settlers whom the Emperor planted in the city.
> Pausanias 5.25.1 (Jones and Ormerod trans.)

The Roman statue could have been modelled upon Hellenistic imagery, and the representation as such may echo Callisthenes' lost writings on Alexander; Callisthenes was the main propagator of the king's divine descent.[46]

Other attributes popularly given to Alexander in Hellenistic art refer to Zeus or Ammon. The aforementioned monetary issue of Lysimachus, representing the deified king with ram's horns in an image that was to become iconic, was not the first to do so; this tradition started with Ptolemy in the last decade of the fourth century BCE, before or after his proclamation as the king of Egypt, and it was followed by several others.[47] Ptolemy's types introduced one more attribute that was to be frequently repeated subsequently in Alexander's Hellenistic imagery (including statuary attested by reduced copies), namely the *aegis*, again an attribute related primarily to Zeus, even if it was presented by the father of the gods to his daughter Athena (a goddess who appeared on gold coinage during Alexander's lifetime): this is found in the 'Alexander Aegiochus (*Aegis*-bearing)' statue-type, which represented Alexander in his role as founder of Alexandria (Figure 30.14).

---

[45] Cf. the description of the grand procession of Ptolemy Philadelphus at Athenaeus 197d–203b.
[46] Stewart 1993: 10.   [47] For the list see Fulińska 2014: 123–124.

30.14 Alexander Aegiochus. Bronze statuette. London, British Museum, 1922,0711.1.

The most important royal attribute associated with Alexander in the art of the Hellenistic period onwards is the diadem in the form of a white cloth fillet, placed on the head, and knotted at the neck. It is disputed whether this was used by the king himself.[48] Two main points of origin for this item of insignia are proposed in the scholarship: the Persian fillet, which was placed around the royal tiara;[49] and the Dionysiac *mitra*, a ribbon present mostly in late fifth- and fourth-century iconography of Dionysus, placed on the brow, below the hairline, like the fillet given to athletic victors. The situation is additionally complicated by mentions of the *kausia diadēmatophoros* ('diadem-bearing *kausia*-hat'), which suggests that the traditional Macedonian hat was bound with some kind of ribbon. It is unclear whether this custom related to royalty.[50] The main flaw with the current academic discussion is the assumption that there can have been only one source for the diadem. It is possible that even if Alexander borrowed the *use* of such an item of insignia from the Persians, its ultimate *form*, as we know it from Hellenistic royal imagery, combined the three traditions. An intermediate stance of this sort is supported by the iconographic sources: on early Ptolemaic coins Alexander wears the Dionysiac *mitra* instead of the typical diadem, but the *mitra* is supplanted by the diadem after the appearance of Lysimachus' Alexander coinage.

Even though the Hellenistic dynasties associated the diadem with their own founders, it was not the most common attribute they gave to Alexander. It virtually disappears from his imagery during the first half of the third century BCE, only to reappear in imperial Rome. Rather, Alexander was represented with attributes of a divine significance, as befitted his posthumous status. Thus the headdresses he is given include the radiate crown, the lion scalp and the elephant scalp, relating to Apollo-Helios, Heracles and Dionysus respectively, in addition to the attributes described above. It seems that the diadem's brief appearance at the beginning of the Hellenistic age primarily served to legitimate his Successors in their role as kings. Like Alexander's spear, it remained a symbol of earthly power.

---

[48] The arguments are summarized by Fredricksmeyer 1997.
[49] Xenophon *Cyropaedia* 8.3.13; Polyaenus *Strategemata* 7.11.2.
[50] Duris of Samos *FGrH* / *BNJ* 76 fr. 14; Ephippus of Olynthus *FGrH* / *BNJ* 126 fr. 5. Discussion at Janssen 2007.

Conclusion

Our actual knowledge of Alexander's image in ancient art is limited to what has survived to date, and to the more or less cryptic descriptions of lost artworks provided by ancient authors that lived long after Alexander and at best quote his contemporaries or describe monuments preserved into their own times. Passing remarks scattered across various texts allow us to imagine that Alexander's iconography was much more complex than is indicated in what survives. For instance, a description of the king's hearse mentions an image of Alexander driving a chariot, and holding the Persian royal sceptre.[51] And uncertainties remain even about image types for which we have a physical record. Thus, we can guess from the wealth of preserved reduced figurines that the Alexandrian cult statue of Alexander in the role of the founder of the city represented him wearing the *aegis*, but whether it was a standing statue or an equestrian one remains the subject of dispute.[52]

Given the relative scarcity of incontestable imagery, we should not neglect the 'presence' of Alexander in the various Hellenistic and Roman 'imitations': just as Alexander was posthumously syncretized with his divine ancestors or cousins, the kings and emperors incorporated his figure into their own syncretization with divinities, with the result that he is present in their portraiture in the same way as the gods are present in his own. Moreover, Alexander's presence should be assumed in the generalized model of youthful beauty as found in the representations of gods and heroes, especially Heracles, Dionysus and Apollo-Helios, in Etruscan ideal heads produced for funerary purposes, in the Colossus of Rhodes made by Chares of Lindos and its reflections on Rhodian coins, in cameos and other luxurious objects from late antiquity, etc. The presence of Alexander in ancient art is not limited to the artefacts that can be labelled as his own portraits; his image permeated the art of the period, which continued to be fascinated by his life and legend.

Guide to Further Reading

Indispensable for the topic of Alexander's portraiture are the classic compilations: de Ujfalvÿ 1902; Schreiber 1903; Bernouilli 1905; and Gebauer 1938/39. Discussions of the particular attributions are provided by Bieber 1964; Hölscher 1971 and 2009; Stewart 1993; and Palagia 2022.

---

[51] Diodorus 18.4.5   [52] Thus Moreno 1987: 29–30 vs Ridgway 2001: 117.

Stewart provides a good starting point for the Hellenistic reinterpretations of Alexander's image; these are also discussed by Trofimova 2012, while the standard volumes on Hellenistic art and portraiture (Pollitt 1986; Smith 1988 and three volumes of Ridgway 1998–2002) provide insights into the art-historical context of these representations. The political and ideological contexts of the exploitation of Alexander's figure are discussed by Hazzard 2000 and Hölscher 2018. As for Alexander's representation in specific works of art, the Pompeii 'Alexander mosaic' is analysed in detail by Cohen 1997 and the 'Alexander sarcophagus' by Schefold 1968. For the most exhaustive discussion of numismatic issues, see Dahmen 2007; Holt 2003 deals with the Indian campaign coinage, while Palagia 2002 and Seyer 2007 deal with the imagery of the royal hunt. For Alexander's royal and/or divine insignia and attributes, and their Hellenistic afterlife, see Hammond 1989a (general); Ritter 1965 and Dahmen 2012 (the diadem); Janssen 2007 (the *kausia*); Fulińska 2014 (the ram's horns); Fulińska 2012 (oriental elements). For the Macedonian archaeological context, Andronicos 1984 remains the core publication; important papers can be found in the exhibition catalogues: Hansen et al. 2009; Kottaridi and Walker 2011 and Descamps-Lequime and Charatzopoulou 2011. The reception of Alexander's image in later art is discussed in, for example, Briant 2012 and Fulińska 2018, and the numerous papers included in Hadjinicolaou 1997.

Alexander's Timeline 356–321 BC

356	A. is born (6 Hecatombaeon = July 20) to Philip II and the Epirote princess Olympias.
353	(*c.*) Birth of A.'s full sister Cleopatra.
346	The 9-year-old A. is admired at Philip's court by Aeschines and Demosthenes.
343	Aristotle takes charge of A.'s education at Mieza (until. *c.* 340); supposed taming of Bucephalas.
340	A. left as regent as Philip campaigns in Thrace and at Byzantium; he puts down a rebellion by the Maedi; he founds Alexandropolis; he receives a Persian embassy.
338	Battle of Chaeronea; A., in charge of the left wing, destroys the Theban Sacred Band. A. leads the Macedonian embassy to Athens. Philip founds the League of Corinth.
337	Philip marries Cleopatra, niece of Attalus; after an argument at the wedding, A. flees to Epirus (escorting his mother home) and then on to Illyria; A. is restored to Macedon through the intercession of Demaratus of Corinth.
336	The Pixodarus affair; A. misguidedly competes for the hand of Ada, daughter of Pixodarus, satrap of Caria, against his half-brother Arrhidaeus; Philip exiles the Companions that have advised A. in this, including Ptolemy, Harpalus and Nearchus.
	Philip initiates an expedition against the Persian empire in Asia Minor under Attalus, Parmenion and Amyntas.
	Assassination of Philip by Pausanias of Orestis at the wedding of his daughter Cleopatra to her uncle Alexander of Epirus, Olympias' brother.
	A. secures the throne of Macedon.
	A. purges enemies and threats, Heromenes, Arrhabaeus, Attalus and Amyntas, son of Perdiccas III.

A. succeeds Philip as *archon* of Thessaly and *hegemon* of the League of Corinth.

335 A. mounts expeditions against Thracians, Triballians, Getae and Illyrians.

Thebes rebels against Macedonian rule and is extirpated.

334 A. resumes Philip's Persian expedition, leading it in person, and leaving Antipater as viceroy of Macedon; he starts out from Amphipolis with 40,000 men and crosses the Hellespont into Asia Minor (crossing from Sestos to Abydus, within the bridgehead established by Parmenion).

A. visits Troy; he sacrifices at the tombs of Achilles and Ajax. Battle of the Granicus: A. defeats a coalition of satraps and Greek mercenaries under Memnon of Rhodes.

A. dismisses most of his allied fleet.

Sardis is surrendered to A. by Mithrenes; Miletus and Halicarnassus are taken by siege.

A. reinstates Ada, sister of Pixodarus (aunt of the above Ada), as ruler of Caria and claims the land as his own inheritance by becoming her adopted son.

333 A. spends the winter in Lycia and Pamphylia; he sends his newly married troops back to Macedon for the duration to spend time with their wives.

At Phaselis, Alexander of Lyncestis, hipparch of the Thessalian cavalry, is detected in a conspiracy with the Persian King Darius III to murder A.; he is arrested and kept in chains.

A. solves (cuts?) the Gordian Knot at Gordium; he is rejoined here by the newly married Macedonians, who return with reinforcements.

A. falls ill after bathing in the river Cydnus near Tarsus in Cilicia.

Darius enters Cilicia to challenge A; he is defeated in the Battle of Issus; A. captures Darius' tent, family and treasures; Darius offers peace terms.

Damascus is captured by Parmenion.

332 Byblos and Sidon surrender to A., with A. installing Abdalonymus (he of the Alexander sarcophagus) as ruler of the latter.

The seven-month siege of Tyre, during which A. constructs a causeway from the mainland.

Darius offers peace terms again.

The two-month siege of Gaza.

A.'s visit to Jerusalem (?).

Alexander's Timeline 356–321 BC

A. enters Egypt without resistance

A. is crowned pharaoh in Memphis (?).

331 A. marches to the Siwah Oasis and is reputedly hailed as the son of Zeus/Ammon.

A. founds, or initiates the creation of, Alexandria (priority of this and Siwah unclear).

A. returns to Asia, crosses the Tigris; Darius offers peace terms yet again; A. defeats him at the Battle of Gaugamela.

Babylon is surrendered to A. by Mazaeus, and Susa by Abulites, who are both confirmed as satraps.

A. defeats the Uxians and circumvents the Persian/Susian Gates, strongly defended by Ariobarzanes, to reach Persepolis and its palace.

330 A. campaigns against the Mardians.

A. (partially) burns the Persepolis palace.

A. sends his Greek allies home from Ecbatana.

The fleeing Darius is killed by Bessus at Choara near the Caspian Gates; A. finds his corpse on the road.

Supposed visit of Amazon Queen Thalestris to A. in Hyrcania.

A. begins to adopt Persian dress.

There are mass defections to A. from the Persian army.

The conspiracy of Dimnus and Demetrius is exposed at Phrada; Philotas and Parmenion are executed, and so too Alexander of Lyncestis.

329 A. founds Alexandria in Arachosia (Kandahar) and Alexandria-in-the Caucasus (near Charikar).

A. passes over the Hindu Kush.

A. massacres the Branchidae in Sogdiana. Bessus is arrested by a group of Sogdian barons and left bound for A. to collect; he executes him.

A. founds Alexandria Eschate, near Khodjend.

Spitamenes revolts and massacres a Macedonian division at Maracanda (Samarkand).

328 A. campaigns against Spitamenes.

A. rejects a Scythian king's offer of his daughter as a bride.

A. captures the Rock of Sogdiana.

A. murders Clitus at Maracanda.

Spitamenes is murdered by his own allies, the Massagetae, and his head is sent to A.

327 Chorienes surrenders his Rock (Koh-i-Nor) to A. at Gazaba.

A. marries the Sogdian Roxane, daughter of Oxyartes.

A. attempts to introduce *proskynesis* at a drinking party in Bactria.

The conspiracy of Hermolaus and the Pages.

The arrest and execution of Callisthenes.
A. re-crosses the Hindu Kush to enter India.

326 Siege of Massaga, culminating in A.'s brief encounter with its ruler, Cleophis.

A. captures the Rock of Aornus (Pir-sar).

A. crosses the Indus and enters the kingdom of Taxiles, with whom he makes an alliance against Abisares and Porus.

The Battle of the Hydaspes (Jhelum) against King Porus and his elephants; A. defeats Porus and then comes to terms with him, confirming him as a client king; he founds Bucephala (in commemoration of the death of Bucephalas) and Nicaea on either side of the river. An alliance is made with Abisares also.

A. begins the construction of a fleet.

A. reaches the Hyphasis (Beas); the army mutinies and refuses to press on to the Ganges; A. sets up altars to the twelve gods on the far bank of the river, marking the eastern limit of the Persian empire and of his campaign.

A. returns to the Hydaspes, and progresses down it towards the Indus, with a fleet of 2,000 vessels and the army divided between the two banks, under Hephaestion and Craterus.

325 A. attacks the city of the Mallians; he is seriously wounded by an arrow.

A. dispatches Craterus through Drangiana to Carmania with part of army.

A. reaches the Indus Delta and the Indian Ocean.

A. dispatches the fleet under Nearchus from the port of Patala (Hyderabad?) to sail up the Persian Gulf, while himself leading the army in coordination with it through the hardships of the Gedrosian Desert.

The supposed Bacchic revel in Carmania.

A. rendezvouses with Craterus.

The defection of Harpalus.

A. punishes the rebellious satraps, in part, possibly, for their failure to supply the army in Gedrosia.

324 A. restores Cyrus' tomb after it has been plundered.

A. returns to Persepolis, then to Susa.

A. presides over mass marriages between (90+) Companions and Persian noblewomen at Susa; A. himself marries Stateira, daughter of Darius, and Parysatis, daughter of Artaxerxes III Ochus; he legalizes the common-law unions of 10,000 of the soldiery.

A. brings 30,000 Persians into the army as Epigoni.

A. sails with Nearchus to the mouth of the Tigris, and thence to Opis.

The army mutinies at Opis (Baghdad); A. demobs and dispatches 11,500 veterans, to return to Macedon with Craterus, who is to replace Antipater as viceroy of Macedon.

The Exiles Decree (designed to ensure homes for A.'s returning Greek mercenaries?) is proclaimed at the Olympic Games.

A.'s request to the Greek states for deification.

A. holds a sporting and artistic festival at Ecbatana; Hephaestion dies here; A. plans an extravagant mausoleum for him in Babylon.

323 A. campaigns against the Cossaeans.

A. returns to Babylon, where he receives ambassadors, possibly including ambassadors from Carthage and Rome.

A. dies of an unidentifiable disease (11 June), possibly malaria or typhoid.

The army entrusts the succession to A.'s brother Arrhidaeus, renamed Philip III, and to his unborn son, Alexander IV to be, both incompetent kings under the regency of Perdiccas.

321 Ptolemy appropriates A.'s funeral cortege, burying him initially at Memphis, subsequently in Alexandria.

References

Adams, W. L. 1986. 'Macedonian kingship and the right of petition' *Ancient Macedonia* 4, 43–52.
Adams, W. L. 1996. 'In the wake of Alexander the Great: the impact of conquest in the Aegean World' *Ancient World* 27, 29–37.
Adams, W. L. 2003. 'The episode of Philotas: an insight' in Heckel and Tritle 2003, 113–126.
Adams, W. L. 2005. *Alexander the Great: Legacy of a Conqueror*. New York.
Adams, W. L. 2007a. 'Alexander the Great: fact' in D. Buisseret ed. *The Oxford Companion to World Exploration*. Oxford. 32–34.
Adams, W. L. 2007b. 'The games of Alexander' in Heckel et al. 2007, 124–138.
Adler, W., and P. Tuffin 2002. *The Chronography of George Synkellos: A Byzantine Chronicle of Universal History from the Creation*. Oxford.
Aerts, F. C. W. 2010. *Alexander Magnus Arabicus: A Survey of the Alexander Tradition through Seven Centuries: From Pseudo-Callisthenes to Sūrī*. Paris.
Ager, S. 2017. 'Symbol and ceremony: royal weddings in the Hellenistic age' in A. Erskine, L. Llewellyn-Jones and S. Wallace eds. *The Hellenistic Courts*. Swansea. 165–188.
Agut-Labordère, D. 2021. 'Gods in the gray zone: a political history of Egyptian temples from Artaxerxes III to the end of the Argeadai (342–ca. 305 BCE)' in S. Honigman, C. Nihan and O. Lipschits eds. *Times of Transition Judea in the Early Hellenistic Period*. University Park, PA. 177–186.
Agut-Labordère, D. 2024. 'Alexander, "Prince of the Two Deserts": the geopolitical significance of the trip to Siwa' in A. Wojciechowska and K. Nawotka eds. *The Ancient Near Eastern Legacy and Alexander vs. Alexander's Legacy to the World*. Wiesbaden.
Akamatis, I. M. 2011. 'Pella' in Lane Fox 2011a, 393–408.
Albaladejo Vivero, M. 2005. *La India en la literatura griega: un estudio etnográfico*. Alcalá de Henares.
Almagor, E. 2023. 'Alexander the Great: historical or historiographic failure?' in M. Mendoza and B. Antela-Bernárdez eds. *Historiographical Alexander: Alexander the Great and the Historians in XIXth and XXth Centuries*. Coimbra.
Alonso Troncoso, V. 2007. 'Alexander, Cleitus and Lanice: upbringing and maintenance' in Heckel et al. 2007, 109–123.
Alonso Troncoso, V. 2013. 'The Diadochi and the zoology of kingship' in Alonso Troncoso and Anson 2013, 254–270.
Alonso Troncoso, V., and M. Álvarez Rico. 2017. 'Alexander's tents and camp life' in S. Müller, T. Howe, H. Bowden and R. Rollinger eds. *The History of the Argeads: New Perspectives*. Wiesbaden. 113–124.

References

Alonso Troncoso, V., and E. M. Anson eds. 2013. *After Alexander: The Time of the Diadochoi*. Oxford.

Alvar, J. 2000. 'Alejandro, explorador y hombre de ciencia' in J. M. Blázquez and J. Alvar eds. *Alejandro Magno: Hombre y mito*. Madrid. 83–98.

Amitay, O. 2006. 'The Story of Gviha Ben-Psisa and Alexander the Great' *Journal for the Study of the Pseudepigrapha* 16, 61–74.

Amitay, O. 2010 'The use and abuse of the argumentum e silentio: the case of Alexander in Jerusalem' in M. Mor, F. V. Reiterer and W. Winkler eds. *Samaritans– Past and Present; Current Studies*. Berlin and New York. 59–72.

Anderson, A. R. 1930. 'Bucephalas and his legend' *American Journal of Philology* 51, 1–21.

Anderson, A. R. 1932. *Alexander's Gate, Gog and Magog and the Inclosed Nations*. Cambridge, MA.

Andréadès, A. M. 1929. 'Les finances de guerre d'Alexandre le Grand' *Annales d'histoire économique et sociale* 1, 321–334.

Andronicos, M. 1984. *Vergina: The Royal Tombs and the Ancient City*. Athens.

Angiò, F. 2021. 'Ἀτενὰ Προναία nell' epigramma 31 Austin-Bastiannini di Posidippo?' *Zeitschrift für Papyrologie und Epigraphik* 220, 50–53.

Anson, E. M. 1985a. 'Macedonia's alleged constitutionalism' *Classical Journal* 80, 303–316.

Anson, E. M. 1985b. 'The hypaspists: Macedonia's professional citizen-soldiers' *Historia* 34, 246–248.

Anson, E. M. 1988. 'Antigonus, the Satrap of Phrygia' *Historia* 37, 471–477.

Anson, E. M. 1990. 'Neoptolemus and Armenia' *Ancient History Bulletin* 4, 125–128.

Anson, E. M. 1996. 'The "Ephemerides" of Alexander the Great' *Historia* 45, 501–504.

Anson, E. M. 2003. 'Alexander at Siwah' *Ancient World* 34, 117–130.

Anson, E. M. 2008. 'Philip II and the transformation of Macedonia' in Howe and Reames 2008, 17–30.

Anson, E. M. 2009. 'Philip II and the creation of the Macedonian pezhetairoi' in Wheatley and Hannah 2009, 88–98.

Anson, E. M. 2010. 'The introduction of the *sarissa* in Macedonian warfare' *Ancient Society* 40, 51–68.

Anson, E. M. 2013. *Alexander the Great: Themes and Issues*. London.

Anson, E. M. 2014. *Alexander's Heirs: The Age of the Successors*. London.

Anson, E. M. 2020a. *Philip II the Father of Alexander the Great: Themes and Issues*. London.

Anson, E. M. 2020b. 'The father of the army: Alexander and the Epigoni' in F. Pownall and E. Anson eds. *Affective Relations and Personal Bonds in Hellenistic Antiquity*. Oxford. 227–241.

Anson, E. M. 2021a. 'Alexander the Great: a life lived as legend' in Walsh and Baynham 2021, 14–32.

Anson, E. M. 2021b. 'Alexander's foundation of Alexandria' *International Journal of Military History and Historiography* 20, 1–23.

Anson, E. M. 2022. 'Philip and Alexander and the nature of their personal kingship' in Pownall et al. 2022. 17–31.

Antela-Bernárdez, B. 2005. *Alexandre Magno e Atenas*. Santiago de Compostela.

Antela-Bernárdez, B. 2007a. 'Vencidas, violadas, vendidas: mujeres griegas y violencia sexual en asedios romanos' *Klio* 90, 307–322.

Antela-Bernárdez, B. 2007b. 'Hegemonía y Panhelenismoconceptos políticos en tiempos de Filipo y Alejandro' *Dialogues d'histoire ancienne* 33, 69–89.

Antela-Bernárdez, B. 2010. 'El Alejandro homoerótico: homosexualidad en la corte Macedonia' *Klio* 92, 331–343.
Antela-Bernárdez, B. 2011a. 'El día después de Queronea: la Liga de Corinto y el imperio macedonio sobre Grecia' in J. M. Cortés Copete, E. Muñiz Grijalvo and E. Gordillo Hervás eds. *Grecia ante los imperios*. Seville. 187–196.
Antela-Bernárdez, B. 2011b. 'Simply the best. Alexander's last words, and the Macedonian kingship' *Eirene* 47, 118–126.
Antela-Bernárdez, B. 2012. 'Philip and Pausanias: a deadly love in Macedonian politics' *Classical Quarterly* 62, 859–861.
Antela-Bernárdez, B. 2016a. '*Like gods among men*: the use of religion and mythical issues during Alexander's campaign' in K. Ulanowski ed. *The Religious Aspects of War in Ancient Near East, Greece, and Rome*. Leiden. 235–255.
Antela-Bernárdez, B. 2016b. '*Poleis, Choras* and spaces, from civic to royal: spaces in the cities over Macedonian rule from Alexander the Great to Seleucus I' *Pyrenae* 47, 27–38.
Antela-Bernárdez, B. 2018. *Hellenismus: Ensayos de historiografía*. Zaragoza.
Antela-Bernárdez, B. 2019. 'Enfermedad, curación y poder: los Eácidas taumaturgos' in C. Sierra Martín and B. Antela Rodríguez eds. *Historia y Medicina en la Antigüedad*. Zaragoza. 63–74.
Antela-Bernárdez, B. 2022. 'The hungry years: Athenian grain supply and the impact of Alexander's conquest over Greece' in B. Antela-Bernárdez and M. Mendoza eds. *The Impact of Alexander's Conquest*. Alcalá de Henares. 65–74.
Antela-Bernárdez, B., and C. Sierra Martin 2018. 'Alexander and medicine' *Karanos* 1 (*Alexander's Gaze: Studies in Honor of A. B. Bosworth*) 35–54.
Aperghis, G. G. 2004. *The Seleukid Royal Economy: The Finances and Financial Administration of the Seleukid Empire*. Cambridge.
Archibald, Z. H. 2002. 'Space, hierarchy, and community in Archaic and Classical Macedonia, Thessaly, and Thrace' in R. Brock and S. Hodkinson eds. *Alternatives to Athens: Varieties of Political Organization and Community in Ancient Greece*. Oxford. 212–233.
Arnaud, P. 1983. 'L'affaire Metius Pompusianus ou le crime de cartographie' *Mélanges de l'École française de Rome – Antiquité* 95, 677–699.
Arthur-Montagne, J. 2014. 'Persuasion, emotion, and the letters of the *Alexander Romance*' *Ancient Narrative* 11, 159–189.
Arthur-Montagne, J. 2016. Parodies of paideia: Prose fiction and high learning in the Roman Empire. Diss., Stanford.
Arthur-Montagne, J. 2020. Review of Stoneman, Nawotka and Wojciechowska 2018, *Classical Review* 70.1, 70–72.
Asirvatham, S. 2005. 'Classicism and "romanitas" in Plutarch's *De Alexandri fortuna aut virtute*' *American Journal of Philology* 126, 107–125.
Asirvatham, S. 2010. 'His son's father? Philip II in the Second Sophistic' in Carney and Ogden 2010, 193–204.
Asirvatham, S. 2012. 'Alexander the philosopher in the Greco-Roman, Persian and Arabic traditions' in Stoneman et al. 2012, 311–326.
Asirvatham, S. 2017. 'Historiography' in D. Richter and W. Johnson eds. *The Oxford Handbook to the Second Sophistic*. Oxford. 477–492.
Asirvatham, S. 2018. 'Plutarch's Alexander' in Moore 2018, 355–376.

References

Asirvatham, S. 2021. 'Alexander's wet-nurse Lanice and her sons' in D'Agostini et al. 2021, 37–50.

Aston, E. M., and J. Kerr 2018. 'Battlefield and racetrack: the role of horses in Thessalian society' *Historia* 67, 2–35.

Atkinson, J. E. 1980. *A Commentary on Q. Curtius Rufus' Historiae Alexandri Magni. Books 3 and 4.* Amsterdam.

Atkinson, J. E. 1994. *A Commentary on Q. Curtius Rufus' Historiae Alexandri Magni. Books 5 to 7,2.* Amsterdam.

Atkinson, J. E. 1998–2000. *Curzio Rufo: Storie di Alessandro Magno.* 2 vols. Turin.

Atkinson, J. E. 2009. *Curtius Rufus: Histories of Alexander the Great, Book 10.* (Includes trans. by J. C. Yardley.) Oxford.

Atkinson, J. E., E. Truter and E. Truter 2009. 'Alexander's last days: malaria and mind games' *Acta Classica* 52, 23–46.

Auberger, J. 2005. *Historiens d'Alexandre. Textes traduits et annotés.* Paris.

Aufrère, S. H. 1999. 'Quelques aspects du dernier Nectanébo et les échos de la magie égyptienne dans "le roman d'Alexandre"' in A. Moreau and J.-C. Turpin eds. *La Magie.* 4 vols. Montpellier. i, 95–118.

Ausfeld, A. 1894. *Zur Kritik des griechischen Alexanderromans. Untersuchungen über die unechten Teile der ältesten Überlieferung.* Karlsruhe.

Ausfeld, A. 1907. *Der griechischen Alexanderroman.* Leipzig.

Ausfeld, A. 1909. *Die Sage vom grossen König Alexander.* Lörrach.

Austin, C., and G. Bastianini eds. 2002. *Posidippi Pellaei quae supersunt omnia.* Milan.

Bäbler, B., and H. G. Nesselrath 2016. *Philostrats Apollonios und seine Welt.* Berlin.

Bacon, R. 2013 [originally 1271]. *Compendium studii philosophiae.* J. S. Brewer ed. [originally 1859]. Turnhout.

Bader, F. 1998. 'Héraclès et le cheval' in C. Bonnet, C. Jourdan-Annequin and V. Pirenne-Delforge eds. *Le Bestiaire d'Héraclès: IIIe rencontre Héracléenne.* Kernos Suppl. 7. Liège. 151–172.

Badian, E. 1958a. 'Alexander the Great and the unity of mankind' *Historia* 7, 425–44. Reprinted in Badian 2012, 1–19.

Badian, E. 1958b. 'Alexander the Great and the creation of an empire' *History Today* 8.6, 369–76 and 8.7, 495–502.

Badian, E. 1958c. 'The eunuch Bagoas: a study in method' *Classical Quarterly* 8, 144–157. Reprinted in Badian 2012, 20–35.

Badian, E. 1960. 'The death of Parmenio' *Transactions of the American Philological Association* 91, 324–338.

Badian, E. 1961. 'Harpalus' *Journal of Hellenic Studies* 81, 16–43.

Badian, E. 1962. 'Alexander the Great and the loneliness of power' *Australasian Universities Modern Languages Association* [no serial no.] 80–91. Reprinted in Badian 2012, 96–105.

Badian, E. 1963. 'The death of Philip II' *Phoenix* 17, 244–250. Reprinted in Badian 2012, 106–112.

Badian, E. 1965a. 'The administration of the empire' *Greece and Rome* 12, 166–182.

Badian, E. 1965b. 'The date of Clitarchus' *Proceedings of the African Classical Association* 8, 5–11.

Badian, E. 1966. 'Alexander the Great and the Greeks of Asia' in E. Badian ed. *Ancient Society and Institutions: Studies Presented to Victor Ehrenberg on His 75th Birthday.* Oxford. 37–69. Reprinted in Badian 2012, 124–152.

Badian, E. 1974. 'The *Alexander Romance*' *New York Review of Books*. 19 September.
Badian, E. 1975. 'Nearchus the Cretan' *Yale Classical Studies* 24, 147–170. Reprinted in Badian 2012, 193–210.
Badian, E. 1977. 'The battle of the Granicus: a new look' *Ancient Macedonia* 2, 27–71.
Badian, E. 1982. 'Greeks and Macedonians' in B. Barr-Sharrar and E. N. Borza eds. *Macedonia and Greece in Classical and Early Hellenistic Times*. Studies in Art History 10. Washington, DC. 33–51.
Badian, E. 1985. 'Alexander in Iran' in I. Gershevitch ed. *The Cambridge History of Iran* II. Cambridge. 420–501.
Badian, E. 1994. 'Agis III: revisions and reflections' in I. Worthington ed. *Ventures into Greek History*. Oxford. 258–292.
Badian, E. 1996. 'Alexander the Great between two thrones and heaven' in A. Small ed. *Subject and Ruler*. Journal of Roman Archaeology Supp. 17. Ann Arbor. 11–26. Reprinted in Badian 2012, 365–385.
Badian, E. 1998. 'The King's Indians' *Antiquitas* 46, 205–224. Reprinted in Badian 2012, 386–401.
Badian, E. 2000. 'Conspiracies' in A. B. Bosworth and E. J. Baynam eds. *Alexander the Great in Fact and Fiction*. Oxford. 50–95.
Badian, E. 2007. 'Once more the death of Philip II' in *Ancient Macedonia* 7, 389–406. Reprinted in Badian 2012, 496–511.
Badian, E. 2012. *Collected Papers on Alexander the Great*. London.
Bagnall, R. 1979. 'The date of the foundation of Alexandria' *American Journal of Ancient History* 4, 46–49.
Baharal, D. 1994. 'Caracalla and Alexander the Great: a reappraisal' *Studies in Latin Literature and Roman History* 7, 524–567.
Balcer, J. M. 1978. 'Alexander's burning of Persepolis' *Iranica Antiqua* 13, 120–33.
Barbantani, S. 2014. 'Mother of snakes and kings: Apollonius Rhodius' *Foundation of Alexandria*' *Histos* 8, 209–245.
Barbantani, S. 2016. 'Alexander's presence (and absence) in Hellenistic poetry' in C. Bearzot and F. Landucci Gattinoni eds. *Alexander's Legacy*. Rome. 1–24.
Barbantani, S. 2017. '"His σῆμα are both continents": Alexander the Great in Hellenistic poetry' *Studi Ellenistici* 31, 51–128.
Bardon, H. 1961–1965. *Quinte-Curce: Histoires*. 2 vols. Paris.
Baron, C. 2013. *Timaeus of Tauromenium and Hellenistic Historiography*. Cambridge.
Barringer, J. M. 2011. 'The legacy of the Phidian Zeus at Olympia' in J. McWilliam, S. Puttock and T. Stevenson eds. *The Statue of Zeus at Olympia: New Approaches*. Cambridge. 61–77.
Basham, A. L. 1951. *History and Doctrines of the Ajivikas: A Vanished Indian Religion*. London.
Baynham, E. J. 1995a. 'An introduction to the *Metz Epitome*: its traditions and value' *Antichthon* 29, 60–77.
Baynham, E. J. 1995b. 'Who put the "romance" in the *Alexander Romance*?' *Ancient History Bulletin* 9, 1–13.
Baynham, E. J. 1998a. *Alexander the Great: The Unique History of Quintus Curtius*. Ann Arbor.
Baynham, E. J. 1998b. 'The treatment of Olympias in the *Liber de morte Alexandri Magni*: a Rhodian retirement' in W. Will ed. *Alexander der Grosse: Eine Weltroberung und ihr Hintergrund*. Bonn. 103–116.

Baynham, E. J. 1998c. 'Why didn't Alexander marry before leaving Macedonia? Observations on factional politics at Alexander's court in 336–334 B.C.' *Rheinisches Museum* 141, 141–152.

Baynham, E. J. 2001. 'Alexander and the Amazons' *Classical Quarterly* 51, 115–126.

Baynham, E. J. 2003. 'The ancient evidence for Alexander the Great' in Roisman 2003a, 3–29.

Baynham, E. J. 2007. 'Quintus Curtius Rufus on "the Good King": the Dioxippus episode in Book 9. 7. 16–26' in Marincola 2007, 427–433.

Baynham, E. J. 2009. 'Barbarians I: Quintus Curtius' and other Roman historians' reception of Alexander' in Feldherr 2009a, 288–300.

Baynham, E. J. 2012. '"The abominable quibble": Alexander's massacre of Indian mercenaries at Massaga' in P. G. Dwyer and L. Ryan eds. *Theatres of Violence*. New York and Oxford. 27–37.

Baynham, E. J. 2015. 'Cleomenes of Naucratis, villain or victim?' in T. Howe, E. E. Garvin and G. Wrightson eds. *Greece, Macedon and Persia*. Oxford. 127–134.

Baynham, E. J. 2022. 'Bosworth on Alexander and the Iranians revisited: Alexander's marriages to Persian brides at Susa: a study of Arrian, *Anabasis* 7.4.4–8' in Pownall et al. 2022, 151–170.

Baynham, E. J. and T. J. Ryan 2018. 'The "unmanly ruler": Bagoas, Alexander's eunuch lover, Mary Renault's *The Persian Boy* and Alexander reception' in Moore 2018, 615–639.

Bearzot, C. 2017. 'Alexander's *Ephemerides* (117)' *BNJ*.

Bearzot, C., and F. Landucci Gattinoni eds. 2016. *Alexander's Legacy*. Rome.

Beaujeu, J. 1955. *La Religion romaine à l'apogée de l'empire: I. La politique religieuse des Antonins*. Paris. 96–192.

Beck, M. ed. 2014. *A Companion to Plutarch*. Oxford/Malden, MA.

Becker, M. 2013. *Eunapios aus Sardes: Biographien über Philosophen und Sophisten*. Stuttgart.

Beckwith, C. 2015. *Greek Buddha*. Princeton.

Behrwald, R. 2016. 'Der Orient bei Curtius Rufus zwischen Thema und Motiv' in H. Wulfram 2016a, 263–300.

Beloch, K. J. 1912–1927. *Griechische Geschichte*. 2nd ed. 4 vols. Berlin.

Berg, B. 1973. 'An early source of the *Alexander Romance*' *Greek, Roman and Byzantine Studies* 14, 381–387.

Bernoulli, J. J. 1905. *Die erhaltenen Darstellungen Alexanders des Grossen*. Munich.

Berve, H. 1926. *Das Alexanderreich auf prosopographischer Grundlage*. 2 vols. Munich.

Bessios, M., I. Z. Tzifopoulos and A. Kotsonas eds. 2012. *Μεθώνη Πιερίας 1: Επιγραφές, χαράγματα και εμπορικά σύμβολα στη γεωμετρική και αρχαϊκή κεραμική από το 'Υπόγειο'*. Thessaloniki.

Best, J. G. P. 1969. *Thracian Peltasts and Their Influence on Greek Warfare*. Groningen.

Bieber, M. 1964. *Alexander the Great in Greek and Roman Art*. Chicago.

Bielman Sánchez, A. ed. 2019. *Power Couples in Antiquity: Transversal Perspectives*. London.

Bigwood, J. M. 1993. 'Aristotle and the elephant again' *American Journal of Philology* 114, 537–555.

Billows, R. A. 1995. *Kings and Colonists: Aspects of Macedonian Imperialism*. Leiden.

Billows, R. A. 1997. *Antigonos the One-Eyed and the Creation of the Hellenistic State*. Berkeley.

Billows, R. A. 2018. *Before and After Alexander: The Legend and Legacy of Alexander the Great*. New York and London.

Binder, C., H. Börm and A. Luther eds. 2016. *Diwan: Untersuchungen zu Geschichte und Kultur des Nahen Ostens und des östlichen Mittelmeerraumes in Altertum*. Duisburg.

Bingen, J. 2007. *Hellenistic Egypt: Monarchy, Society, Economy, Culture*. Berkeley and Los Angeles.

Blaineau, A. 2015. *Le Cheval de guerre en Grèce ancienne*. Rennes.

Blaze, E. 1837. *La Vie militaire sous l'empire ou mœurs de la garnison de bivouac et de la caserne*. Paris.

Bloedow, E. F. 2004. 'Egypt in Alexander's scheme of things' *Quaderni di cultura classica* 77, 75–99.

Bloedow, E. F., and H. M. Loube 1997. 'Alexander the Great "under fire" at Persepolis' *Klio* 79, 341–353.

Blue, L. and E. Khalil eds. 2010. *Lake Mareotis: Reconstructing the Past. Proceedings of the International Conference on the Archaeology of the Mareotic Region held at Alexandria University, Egypt, 5–6 April, 2008*. Oxford.

Blümel, W., and R. Merkelbach eds. 2014. *Die Inschriften von Priene*. Inschriften griechischer Städte aus Kleinasien 69. 2 vols. Bonn.

Boardman, J. 1990. 'I. Herakles and the horses of Diomedes (Labour VIII)' *LIMC* V.1, 67–71.

Boardman, J. 2019. *Alexander the Great: From His Death to the Present Day*. Princeton.

Bodhi, B. 1989. *The Discourse on the Fruits of Recluseship: The Sāmaññaphala Sutta and Its Commentaries*. Kandy.

Bodson, L. 1991. 'Alexander the Great and the scientific exploration of the oriental part of his empire: an overview of the background, trends and results' *Ancient Society* 22, 127–138.

Boeckh, A., et al. eds. 1828–1877. *Corpus inscriptionum Graecarum*. 4 vols. Berlin.

Bohm, C. 1989. *Imitatio Alexandri im Hellenismus*. Munich.

Böhme, M. 2009. 'Das Perserbild in den Fragmenten der Alexanderhistoriker' in M. Rathmann ed. *Studien zur antiken Geschichtsschreibung*. Bonn. 161–186.

Borza, E. N. 1967. 'Editor's preface: an introduction to Alexander studies' in U. Wilcken *Alexander the Great* [republication of Wilcken 1932]. New York. vii–xxviii.

Borza, E. N. 1972. 'Fire from heaven: Alexander at Persepolis' *Classical Philology* 67, 233–245.

Borza, E. N. 1982. 'The natural resources of early Macedonia' in W. L. Adams and E. N. Borza eds. *Philip II, Alexander the Great and the Macedonian Heritage*. Lanham, MD. 1–20.

Borza, E. N. 1983. 'The symposium at Alexander's court' *Ancient Macedonia* 3, 45–55.

Borza, E. N. 1987. 'The royal Macedonian tombs and the paraphernalia of Alexander the Great' *Phoenix* 41, 105–121.

Borza, E. N. 1990. *In the Shadow of Olympus: The Emergence of Macedon*. Princeton. 2nd ed. 1992.

Borza, E. N. 1995. 'An introduction to Alexander studies' in Roisman 2003a, 1–7.

Borza, E. N. 1999. *Before Alexander: Constructing Early Macedonia*. Claremont, CA.

Bosch-Puche, F. 2008. 'L' "autel" du temple d'Alexandre le Grand à Bahariya' retrouvé' *Bulletin de l'Institut français d'archéologie orientale* 108, 29–44.

Bosch-Puche, F. 2012. 'Alejandro Magno y los cultos a animals sagados en Egipto' *Aula Orientalis* 30, 243–276.

Bosch-Puche, F. 2013. 'The Egyptian royal titulary of Alexander the Great I: Horus, two ladies, golden Horus, and throne names' *Journal of Egyptian Archaeology* 99, 131–154.
Bosch-Puche, F. 2014. 'The Egyptian royal titulary of Alexander the Great II: personal name, empty cartouches, final remarks, and appendix' *Journal of Egyptian Archaeology* 100, 89–109.
Bosch-Puche, F., and J. Moje. 2015. 'Alexander the Great's name in contemporary Demotic sources' *The Journal of Egyptian Archaeology* 101, 340–348.
Boschung, D. 1993. *Die Bildnisse des Augustus*. Berlin.
Bosman, P. ed. 2014. *Alexander in Africa*. Pretoria.
Bossuet, J. 1681. *Discours sur l'histoire universelle*. Paris.
Bosworth, A. B. 1971a. 'Philip II and Upper Macedonia' *Classical Quarterly* 21, 93–105.
Bosworth, A. B. 1971b. 'The death of Alexander the Great: rumour and propaganda' *Classical Quarterly* 21, 112–136.
Bosworth, A. B. 1974. 'The government of Syria under Alexander the Great' *Classical Quarterly* 24, 46–64.
Bosworth, A. B. 1976a. 'Arrian and the Alexander Vulgate' in E. Badian, D. Van Berchem and B. Grange eds. *Alexandre le Grand: Image et réalité*. Entretiens Hardt vol. 22. Vandœuvres-Genève. 1–46.
Bosworth, A. B. 1976b. 'Errors in Arrian' *Classical Quarterly* 26, 117–139.
Bosworth, A. B. 1977. 'Alexander and Ammon' in K. H. Kinzl ed. *Greece and the Eastern Mediterranean in Ancient History and Prehistory*. Oxford. 52–64.
Bosworth, A. B. 1980a. 'Alexander and the Iranians' *Journal of Hellenic Studies* 100, 1–21.
Bosworth, A. B. 1980b. *A Historical Commentary on Arrian's History of Alexander*. I. Oxford.
Bosworth, A. B. 1981. 'A missing year in the history of Alexander the Great' *Journal of Hellenic Studies* 101, 17–39.
Bosworth, A. B. 1983. 'The Indian satrapies under Alexander the Great' *Antichthon* 17, 37–46.
Bosworth, A. B. 1986. 'Alexander the Great and the decline of Macedon' *Journal of Hellenic Studies* 106, 1–12.
Bosworth, A. B. 1988a. *Conquest and Empire: The Reign of Alexander the Great*. Cambridge.
Bosworth, A. B. 1988b. *From Arrian to Alexander: Studies in Historical Interpretation*. Oxford.
Bosworth, A. B. 1995. *A Historical Commentary on Arrian's History of Alexander*. II. Oxford.
Bosworth, A. B. 1996a. 'Alexander, Euripides, and Dionysos' in R. W. Wallace and E. M. Harris eds. *Transitions to Empire*. Oxford. 140–166.
Bosworth, A. B. 1996b. *Alexander and the East: The Tragedy of Triumph*. Oxford.
Bosworth, A. B. 1997. 'In search of Cleitarchus: review-discussion of Luisa Prandi: "Fortuna e realtà dell'opera di Clitarco"' *Histos* 1, 211–224.
Bosworth, A. B. 1998. 'Calanus and the Brahman opposition' in W. Will ed. *Alexander der Grosse. Eine Welteroberung und ihr Hintergrund*. Bonn. 173–203.
Bosworth, A. B. 2000. 'Ptolemy and the will of Alexander' in Bosworth and Baynham 2000, 207–241.
Bosworth, A. B. 2003. 'Plus ça change ... Ancient Historians and their sources' *Classical Antiquity* 22, 167–197.

Bosworth, A. B. 2004. '"Mountain or molehill": Cornelius Tacitus and Quintus Curtius' *Classical Quarterly* 54, 551–567.
Bosworth, A. B. 2006. 'Alexander the Great and the creation of the Hellenistic age' in G. R. Bugh ed. *The Cambridge Companion to the Hellenistic World*. Cambridge. 9–27.
Bosworth, A. B. 2007. 'Arrian, Alexander and the pursuit of glory' in Marincola 2007, 447–453.
Bosworth, A. B. 2009. 'Johann Gustav Droysen, Alexander the Great and the creation of the Hellenistic age' in Wheatley and Hannah 2009, 1–27.
Bosworth, A. B. 2012. 'Foreword' in Droysen 2012, xv–xxi.
Bosworth, A. B. 2019. 'The impossible dream: W. W. Tarn's *Alexander* in retrospect' *Karanos* 2, 77–95. Reprinted from *Ancient Society Resources for Teachers* 13.3 (1983), 131–150.
Bosworth, A. B., and E. J. Baynham eds. 2000. *Alexander the Great in Fact and Fiction*. Oxford.
Bowden, H. 2004. 'Xenophon and the scientific study of religion' in C. Tuplin ed. *Xenophon and His World: Papers from a Conference Held in Liverpool in July 1999*. Stuttgart. 229–246.
Bowden, H. 2013. 'On kissing and making up: court protocol and historiography in Alexander the Great's "experiment with *proskynesis*"' *Bulletin of the Institute of Classical Studies* 56, 55–77.
Bowden, H. 2014a. 'Alexander in Egypt: considering the Egyptian evidence' in Bosman 2014, 38–55.
Bowden, H. 2014b. 'Recent travels in Alexanderland' *Journal of Hellenic Studies* 134, 136–148.
Bowden, H. 2014c. *Alexander the Great: A Very Short Introduction*. Oxford.
Bowden, H. 2016. 'The eagle has landed: divination in the Alexander Historians' in Howe et al. 2017, 149–168.
Bowden, H. 2017. 'The Argeads and Greek sanctuaries' in S. Müller, T. Howe, H. Bowden and R. Rollinger eds. *The History of the Argeads: New Perspectives*. Wiesbaden. 163–182.
Bowie, E. 2002. 'Plutarch and literary activity in Achaea: A.D. 107–117' in Stadter and Van der Stockt 2002, 41–56.
Bowman, A., C. Crowther and K. Savvopoulos 2016. 'The "Corpus of Ptolemaic Inscriptions from Egypt" project: unpublished texts' *Zeitschrift für Papyrologie und Epigraphik* 200, 100–108.
Braccesi, L. 2014. 'Imitazioni di e da Curzio Rufo' in Mahé-Simon and Trinquier 2014a, 109–118.
Braun, M. 1938. *History and Romance in Graeco-Oriental Literature*. Oxford.
Bretzl, H. 1903. *Botanische Forschungen des Alexanderzuges*. Leipzig.
Briant, P. 1979. 'Des Achéménides aux rois hellénistiques: continuités et ruptures' in *Annales della Scuola Normale Superiore di Pisa* 9, 1375–1414. Reprinted at P. Briant *Rois, Tributs, Paisans*. Paris, 1982. 291–330.
Briant, P. 1996. *Histoire de l'empire perse de Cyrus à Alexandre*. Paris. Trans. as *From Cyrus to Alexander: A History of the Persian Empire*. Winona Lake, IN, 2002.
Briant, P. 2003. *Darius dans l'ombre d'Alexandre*. Paris. Trans. as *Darius in the Shadow of Alexander*. Cambridge, MA, 2015.

Briant, P. 2009a. 'The empire of Darius III in perspective' in Heckel and Tritle 2009, 141–170.
Briant, P. 2009b. 'Alexander and the Persian Empire, between "decline" and "renovation"' in Heckel and Tritle 2009, 171–188.
Briant, P. 2010. *Alexander the Great and His Empire*. Princeton.
Briant, P. 2012. *Alexandre des lumières: Fragments d'histoire européenne*. Paris. Trans. as *The First European: Alexander in the Age of Empire*. Cambridge, MA, 2017.
Briant, P. 2018. 'Alexandre à Troie: images, mythe et realia' in K. Nawotka, R. Rollinger, J. Wiesehöfer and A. Wojciechowska eds. *The Historiography of Alexander the Great*. Wiesbaden. 9–20.
Briant, P. 2020. Review of (*inter alia*) Djurslev 2020, *Topoi Orient-Occident* 23, 103–120.
Briscoe, J. 1976. Review of Lane Fox 1973, Schachermeyr 1973 etc., *Classical Review* 2, 232–235.
Brommer, F. 1986. *Heracles: The Twelve Labours of the Hero in Ancient Art and Literature*. New Rochelle, NY. Trans. of *Herakles: Die zwölf Taten des Helden in antiker Kunst und Literatur*. 2nd ed. Cologne, 1979.
Brosius, M. 1996. *Women in Ancient Persia* (559–331 B.C.). Oxford.
Brosius, M. 2003a. 'Alexander and the Persians' in Roisman 2003a, 169–193.
Brosius, M. 2003b. 'Why Persia became the enemy of Macedon' in W. Henkelman and A. Kuhrt eds. *A Persian Perspective: Essays in Memory of Heleen Sancisi-Weerdenburg*. Achaemenid History XII. Leiden. 227–37.
Brosius, M. 2007. 'New out of old? Court and court ceremonies in Achaemenid Persia' in A. J. S. Spawforth ed. *The Court and Court Society in Ancient Monarchies*. Cambridge. 17–57.
Brosius, M. 2021. *A History of Ancient Persia: The Achaemenid Empire*. Oxford.
Brown, T. S. 1949. *Onesicritus*. Berkeley.
Brown, T. S. 1950. 'Clitarchus' *American Journal of Philology* 71, 134–155.
Brown, T. S. 1951. Review of Schachermeyr 1949, *American Journal of Philology* 1, 74–77.
Brown, T. S. 1967. 'Alexander's book order' *Historia* 16, 359–368.
Bruhn, K. C. 2010. *Ammoniaca I. 'Kein Tempel der Pracht': Architektur und Geschichte des Tempels aus der Zeit des Amasis auf Agurmi, Oase Siwa*. Wiesbaden.
Brunt, P. A. 1963. 'Alexander's Macedonian cavalry' *Journal of Hellenic Studies* 83, 27–46.
Brunt, P. A, trans. 1976–1983. *Arrian*. 2 vols. Cambridge, MA.
Brunt, P. A. 1977. 'From Epictetus to Arrian' *Athenaeum* n.s. 55, 19–48.
Bucciantini, V. 2015a. 'Geographical description and historical narrative in the tradition on Alexander's expedition' in S. Bianchetti, H.-J. Gehrke and M. R. Cataudella eds. *Brill's Companion to Ancient Geography: The Inhabited World in Greek and Roman Tradition*. Leiden. 98–109.
Bucciantini, V. 2015b. *Studio su Nearco di Creta*. Alessandria.
Buckley-Gorman, R. 2016. 'If I were not Alexander ... ': An Examination of the Political Philosophy of Plutarch's Alexander-Caesar. Diss., Victoria University of Wellington.
Burliga, B. 2013. *Arrian's Anabasis: An Intellectual and Cultural Story*. Gdańsk.
Burn, A. R. 1951. Review of Schachermeyr 1949, *Classical Review* 1, 100–102.
Burstein, S. M. 1989. '*SEG* 33.802 and the *Alexander Romance*' *Zeitschrift für Papyrologie und Epigraphik* 77, 275–276.
Burstein, S. M. 1991. 'Pharaoh Alexander: a scholarly myth' *Ancient Society* 22, 139–145.

Burstein, S. M. 1999. 'Cleitarchus in Jerusalem: a note on the Book of Judith' in F. B. Titchener and R. F. Moorton eds. *The Eye Expanded: Life and the Arts in Greco-Roman Antiquity*. Berkeley. 105–112.

Burstein, S. M. 2007. 'The gardener became king or did he? The case of Abdalonymus of Sidon' in Heckel et al. 2007, 139–149.

Burstein, S. M. 2008. 'Alexander's organization of Egypt: a note on the career of Cleomenes of Naucratis' in Howe and Reames 2008, 183–194.

Buszard, B. 2008. 'Caesar's ambition: a combined reading of Plutarch's *Alexander-Caesar* and *Pyrrhus-Marius*' *Transactions of the American Philological Association* 138, 185–215.

Butler, M. 2008. *Of Swords and Strigils: Social Change in Ancient Macedon*. Stanford.

Butz, R., J. Hirschbiegel and D. Willoweit eds. 2004. *Hof und Theorie: Annaherungen an Ein Historisches Phänomen*. Vienna and Cologne.

Cagnat, R., P. Jouguet, G. Lafaye and J. Toutain eds. 1906–27. *Inscriptiones Graecae ad res Romanas pertinentes*. 3 vols. Paris.

Cagnazzi, S. 2015. *Carete di Mitilene: Testimonianze e frammenti*. Tivoli.

Cahill, N. 1985. 'The treasury at Persepolis: gift-giving at the city of the Persians' *American Journal of Archaeology* 89, 373–389.

Callu, J.-P. 2010. *Julius Valère. Roman d'Alexandre*. Turnhout.

Cammarota, M. R. 1998. *La Fortuna o la Virtu di Alessandro Magno: Seconda orazione*. Naples.

Caneva, S. 2013. 'Il coro del re. Capo e comprimari nella storiografia e nell'epos fra IV e III secolo a. C.' *Quaderni di storia* 77, 177–206.

Caneva, S. G. 2016. *From Alexander to the Theoi Adelphoi: Foundation and Legitimation of a Dynasty*. Studia Hellenistica 56. Leuven.

Carey, C. 2007. 'Epideictic oratory' in I. Worthington ed. *A Companion to Greek Rhetoric*. Oxford. 236–252.

Carlsen, J. 2014. 'Greek history in a Roman context: Arrian's *Anabasis of Alexander*' in J. M. Madsen and R. Rees eds. *Roman Rule in Greek and Latin Writing*. Leiden. 210–223.

Carney, E. D. 1980. 'Alexander the Lyncestian': the disloyal opposition' *Greek, Roman and Byzantine Studies* 21, 22–33. Reprinted in Carney 2015: 127–139 (with afterword).

Carney, E. D. 1981. 'The death of Clitus' *Greek, Roman, and Byzantine Studies* 22, 149–160. Reprinted in Carney 2015, 141–154 (with an afterword).

Carney, E. D. 1987. 'Olympias' *Ancient Society* 18, 35–62.

Carney, E. D. 1988. 'The sisters of Alexander the Great: royal relicts' *Historia* 37, 285–404.

Carney, E. D. 1992. 'The politics of polygamy' *Historia* 41, 169–189. Reprinted in Carney 2015, 167–190 (with afterword).

Carney, E. D. 1993a. 'Olympias and the image of the virago' *Phoenix* 47, 29–55.

Carney, E. D. 1993b. 'Foreign influence and the changing role of royal Macedonian women' *Ancient Macedonia* 5. 1, 3–23.

Carney, E. D. 1995. 'Women and *basileia*: legitimacy and female political action in Macedonia' *Classical Journal* 90, 367–391.

Carney, E. D. 1996. 'Alexander and the Persian Women' *American Journal of Philology* 117, 563–583.

Carney, E. D. 2000. *Women and Monarchy in Macedonia*. Norman, OK.

Carney, E. D. 2001. 'The trouble with Philip Arrhidaeus' *Ancient History Bulletin* 15, 63–89.
Carney, E. D. 2002. 'Hunting and the Macedonian elite' in D. Ogden ed. *The Hellenistic World: New Perspectives*. London. 59–80.
Carney, E. D. 2003a. 'Elite education and high culture in Macedonia' in Heckel and Tritle 2003, 47–64. Reprinted in Carney 2015, 191–206 (with afterword).
Carney, E. D. 2003b. 'Women in Alexander's court' in Roisman 2003a, 227–252.
Carney, E. D. 2006. *Olympias, Mother of Alexander the Great*. London.
Carney, E. D. 2007. 'The Philippeum, women and the formation of a dynastic image' in Heckel et al. 2007, 27–70. Reprinted in Carney 2015, 61–90 (with afterword).
Carney, E. D. 2015. *King and Court in Ancient Macedonia: Rivalry, Treason and Conspiracy*. Swansea.
Carney, E. D. 2017. 'Argead marriage policy' in S. Müller, T. Howe, H. Bowden and R. Rollinger eds. *The History of the Argeads – New Perspectives*. Wiesbaden. 139–150.
Carney, E. D, 2019. *Eurydice and the Birth of Macedonian Power*. Oxford.
Carney, E. D. 2021. 'Transitional royal women: Kleopatra, sister of Alexander the Great, Adea Eurydike, and Phila' in Carney and Müller 2021, 321–332.
Carney, E. D., and D. Ogden eds. 2010. *Philip and Alexander: Father and Son, Lives and Afterlives*. New York.
Carney, E. D., and S. Müller eds. 2021. *The Routledge Companion to Women and Monarchy in the Ancient Mediterranean World*. Abingdon and New York.
Carradice, I. 1987. 'The "regal coinage" of the Persian. Empire' in I. Carradice ed. *Coinage and Administration in the Athenian and Persian Empires*. London. 73–95.
Carter, M.L. 1992. 'Dionysiac festivals and Gandharan imagery' in R. Gyselen ed. *Banquets d'Orient*. Res Orientales 4. Bures-sur-Yvette. 51–9.
Carter, M. L. 2015. *Arts of the Hellenized East: Precious Metalwork and Gems of the PreIslamic Era*. London.
Cary, G. 1956. *The Medieval Alexander*. Cambridge.
Casey, C. 1956. *Les Vœux du paon*. Diss., Columbia University.
Cawkwell, G. L. 1978. *Philip of Macedon*. London.
Černý, J. 1962. 'Egyptian oracles' in R. Parker ed. *A Saite Oracle Papyrus from Thebes in the Brooklyn Museum*. Providence, RI. 35–48.
Chairman of the Joint Chiefs of Staff. 2006. *Joint Operations, Joint Publication 3–0, 17 September 2006*. Washington, DC. Revised version, October 2018.
Chandezon, C. 2010. 'Bucéphale et Alexandre: histoire, imaginaire et images de rois et chevaux' in A. Gadeisen, E. Furet and N. Boulbes eds. *Histoire d'équides.: Des textes, des images et des os*. Lattes. 17–96.
Chandezon, C. 2014. 'Chevaux et remonte dans le cavalerie d'Alexandre' in A. Gardeisen and C. Chandezon eds. *Équidés et bovidés de la Méditeranée antique: Rites et combats; jeux et savoirs*. Lattes. 157–171.
Charles, M. B. 2012. 'The Persian ΚΑΡΔΑΚΕΣ' *Journal of Hellenic Studies* 132, 7–21.
Chateaubriand, R. de 1815. *Précis de la vie de Bonaparte*. Paris.
Chateaubriand, R. de 1849. *Mémoires d'outre-tombe*. 2 vols. Paris.
Christesen, P., and S. C. Murray. 2010. 'Macedonian Religion' in Roisman and Worthington 2010, 428–445.
Chrysanthou, C. S. 2020. 'Plutarch and the "malicious" historian' *Illinois Classical Studies* 45, 49–79

Chrysostomou, A., and P. Chrysostomou. 2012. 'The "gold-wearing" Archaic Macedonians from the western cemetery of Archontiko, Pella' in M. Tiverios, P. Nigdelis and P. Adam-Velini eds. *Threpteria: Studies in Ancient Macedonia*. Thessaloniki. 491–516, 623–625.

Chrysostomou, P., and A. Chrysostomou. 2012. 'The Lady of Archontiko' in N. C. Stampolidis and M. Giannopoulou eds. *'Princesses' of the Mediterranean in the Dawn of History*. Athens. 366–387.

Chugg, A. M. 2004. *The Lost Tomb of Alexander the Great*. London.

Chugg, A. M. 2015. *Concerning Alexander the Great: A Reconstruction of Cleitarchus*. Hunstville, AL.

Classen, C. 1959. 'The Libyan god Ammon in Greece before 331 B.C.' *Historia* 8, 349–355.

Clausewitz, C. von 1812. 'Die wichtigsten Grundsätze des Kriegführens zur Ergänzung meines Unterricht bei Sr. Königlichen Hoheit dem Konprinzen'. Printed as appendix to Clausewitz 1832.

Clausewitz, C. von 1832. *Vom Kriege*. 3 vols. Berlin. Trans. as *On War*. Princeton, 1976.

Clay, J. S., I. Malkin and Y. Z. Tzifopulos eds. 2017. *Panhellenes at Methone: Graphe in Late Geometric and Protoarchaic Methone, Macedonia (ca. 700 BCE)*. Berlin.

Cloché, P. 1916. 'Les naopes de Delphes et la politique hellénique de 356 à 327 av. J.-C.' *Bulletin de correspondance hellénique* 40, 78–142.

Cohen, A. 1995. 'Alexander and Achilles – Macedonians and "Mycenaeans"' in J. B. Carter and S. P. Morris eds. *The Ages of Homer: A Tribute to Emily Townsend-Vermeule*. Austin. 483–505.

Cohen, A. 1997. *The Alexander Mosaic: Stories of Victory and Defeat*. Cambridge.

Cohen, G. M. 1995. *The Hellenistic Settlements in Europe, the Islands and Asia Minor*. Berkeley.

Cohen, G. M. 2006. *The Hellenistic Settlements in Syria, The Red Sea Basin and North Africa*. Berkeley.

Cohen, G. M. 2013. *The Hellenistic Settlements in the East from Armenia and Mesopotamia to Bactria and India*. Berkeley.

Colburn, H. P. 2015. 'Memories of the Second Persian Period in Egypt' in J. M. Silverman and C. Waerzeggers eds. *Political Memory in and after the Persian Empire*. Atlanta. 165–202.

Colin, F. 1998. 'Les fondateurs du sanctuaire d'Amon à Siwa (Désert Libyque). Autour d'un bronze de donation inédit' in W. Clarysse, A. Schoors and H. Willems eds. *Egyptian Religion: The Last Thousand Years*, II: *Studies Dedicated to the Memory of J. Quaegebeur*. Leuven. 329–355.

Collins, A. W. 2001. 'The office of chiliarch under Alexander and the Successors' *Phoenix* 55, 259–283.

Collins, A. W. 2009. 'The divinity of Alexander in Egypt' in Wheatley and Hannah 2009, 179–206.

Collins, A. W. 2012a. 'Alexander the Great and the office of *edeatros*' *Historia* 61, 414–420.

Collins, A. W. 2012b. 'Callisthenes on Olympias and Alexander's divine birth' *Ancient History Bulletin* 26, 1–14.

Collins, A. W. 2012c. 'The royal costume and insignia of Alexander the Great' *American Journal of Philology* 133, 371–402.

Collins, A. W. 2013. 'Alexander the Great and the kingship of Babylonia' *Ancient History Bulletin* 27, 130–148.

Collins, A. W. 2014a. 'Alexander's visit to Siwah: a new analysis' *Phoenix* 68, 62–67.

Collins, A. W. 2014b. 'The divinity of the pharaoh in Greek sources' *Classical Quarterly* 64, 841–844.

Collins, A. W. 2017. 'The Persian royal tent and ceremonial of Alexander the Great' *Classical Quarterly* 67, 71–76.
Connolly, P. 2000. 'Experiments with the *sarissa* – the Macedonian pike and cavalry lance – a functional view' *Journal of Roman Military Equipment Studies* 11, 103–112.
Cook, B. L. 2001. 'Plutarch's use of λέγεται: narrative design and source in *Alexander*' *Greek, Roman and Byzantine Studies* 42, 329–360.
Coppola, A. 2015. 'Virgilio, Licofrone e la tradizione su Alessandro Magno' *Museum Helveticum* 72, 21–33.
Coşkun, A., and A. McAuley eds. 2016. *Seleukid Royal Women: Creation, Representation and Distortion of Hellenistic Queenship in the Seleukid Empire.* Historia Einzelschriften 240. Stuttgart.
Culasso Gastaldi, E. 1984. *Sul trattato con Alessandro. Polis, monarchia macedone e memoria demostenica.* Padua.
Curtius, E. 1867. *Griechische Geschichte*. 3 vols. Berlin. Trans. as *The History of Greece*. 5 vols. London, 1873.
D'Agostini, M. 2021. 'Alexander the Great and his sisters: blood in the Hellenistic palace' in D'Agostini et al. 2021. 19–36.
D'Agostini, M., E. M. Anson and F. Pownall eds. 2021. *Affective Relations and Personal Bonds in Hellenistic Antiquity: Studies in Honor of Elizabeth D. Carney.* Oxford.
Dahmen, K. 2007. *The Legend of Alexander the Great on Greek and Roman Coins.* Abingdon.
Dahmen, K. 2012. 'Alexander und das Diadem – die archäologische und numismatische Perspektive' in A. Lichtenberger, K. Martin, H.-H. Nieswandt and D. Salzmann eds. *Das Diadem der Hellenistischen Herrscher: Übernahme, Transformation oder Neuschöpfung eines Herrschaftszeichens? Kolloquium vom 30.-31. Januar 2009 in Münster.* Bonn. 281–292.
Dahmen, K. 2018. 'The first generation of Alexander's influence: diversity of empire' in S. Glenn, F. Duyrat and A. Meadows eds. *Alexander the Great: A Linked Open World*. Scripta Antiqua 116. Bordeaux. 153–167.
Dandamaev, M. A., and V. G. Lukonin 1989. *The Culture and Social Institutions of Ancient Iran.* Cambridge.
D'Angelo, A. 1998. *La Fortuna o la Virtu di Alessandro Magno: Prima Orazione*. Naples.
Dani, A. H. 1986. *The Historic City of Taxila.* Tokyo.
David, W. 2018. *Das goldene Antlitz des unbekannten Makedonenkönigs: Makedonen und Kelten am Ohrid-See – ein Zusammenprall der Kulturen?* Manching.
Davidson, J. N. 2001. 'Bonkers about boys' *London Review of Books* 23.21, 7–10.
Debord, P. 1999. *L'Asie Mineure au IVe siècle (412–323 A.C.)*. Bordeaux.
De Callataÿ, F. 1982. 'La date des premiers tétradrachmes de poids Attique émis par Alexandre le Grand' *Revue Belge de numismatique* 128, 5–25.
De Callataÿ, F. 2011. 'Quantifying monetary production in Greco-Roman times: a general frame' in F. de Callataÿ ed. *Quantifying Monetary Supplies in Greco-Roman Times*. Bari. 7–29.
De Callataÿ, F. 2012. 'The fabulous wealth of the Hellenistic kings: coinage and Weltmachtpolitik' in V. Penna ed. *Words and Coins: From Ancient Greece to Byzantium.* Ghent. 91–101.
De Callataÿ, F. 2016. 'Monnaies, guerres et mercenaires en Grèce ancienne: un bilan actualisé' in J. Baechler and G.-H. Soutou eds. *Guerre, économie et fiscalité.* Paris. 41–54.

Dell, H. J. 1963. The Illyrian frontier to 229 B.C. Diss., University of Wisconsin.

Del Socorro, N. 2012. 'Social status as reflected through metal objects found in archaic burials from Macedonia' *Haemus* 1, 57–69.

Demandt, A. 2009. *Alexander der Grosse: Leben und Legende*. Munich.

Depuydt, L. 1995. 'Murder in Memphis: the story of Cambyses's mortal wounding of the Apis Bull (*ca.* 523 B.C.E.)' *Journal of Near Eastern Studies* 54, 119–126.

Depuydt, L. 1997. 'The time of death of Alexander the Great: 11 June 323 B.C. (-322), *ca.* 4:00–5:00 PM' *Die Welt des Orients* 28, 117–135.

De Rachewiltz, I., trans. 2015. *The Secret History of the Mongols*. Madison, WI.

Descamps-Lequime, S., and K. Charatzopoulou eds. 2011. *Au Royaume d'Alexandre le Grand: La Macédoine antique*. Exhibition catalogue. Paris.

Desideri, P. 2017. 'Plutarch's *Lives*' in D. S. Richter and W. A. Johnson eds. *The Oxford Handbook to the Second Sophistic*. Oxford and New York. 312–326.

Despini, A. 2009. 'Gold funerary masks' *Antike Kunst* 52, 20–65.

Despini, A. 2016. *Σίνδος I, II, III*. 1980–82. 3 vols. Athens.

De Temmerman, K. ed. 2020. *The Oxford Handbook of Ancient Biography*. Oxford.

De Temmerman, K., and E. van Emde Boas 2017. 'Character and characterization in ancient Greek literature: an introduction' in K. De Temmerman and E. van Emde Boas eds. *Characterization in Ancient Greek Literature*. Leiden. 1–26.

Deuchler, F. 1996. 'Heldenkult im Mittelalter: Alexander der Grosse' in M. Bridges and J. Ch. Bürgel eds. *The Problematics of Power*. Bern. 15–27.

De Ujfalvÿ, C. 1902. *Le Type physique d'Alexandre le Grand d'après les auteurs anciens et les documents iconographiques*. Paris.

Develin, R. 1981. 'The Murder of Philip II' *Antichthon* 15, 86–99.

Devine, A. M. 1975a. 'Grand tactics at Gaugamela' *Phoenix*, 374–385.

Devine, A. M. 1975b. 'The Battle of Gaugamela: a tactical and source-critical study' *Ancient World* 13, 87–115.

Devine, A. M. 1985a. 'The strategies of Alexander the Great and Darius III in the Issus Campaign (333 B.C.)' *The Ancient World* 12, 25–38.

Devine, A. M. 1985b. 'Grand tactics at the Battle of Issus' *Ancient World* 12, 39–59.

Devine, A. M. 1986. 'Demythologizing the Battle of the Granicus' *Phoenix* 40, 265–278.

Devine, A. M. 1988. 'A pawn sacrifice at the Battle of the Granicus: the origins of a favourite strategem of Alexander the Great' *Ancient World* 19, 3–20.

DeWitt, N. J. 1942. 'Caesar and the Alexander legend' *Classical World* 36, 51–53.

Dillon, J. 2002. 'The social role of the philosopher in the second century C.E.: some remarks' in Stadter and Van der Stockt 2002, 29–40.

Di Serio, C. 2020. 'Signs and premonitions for Alexander's reign' *Acta Antiqua Academiae Scientiarum Hungaricae* 60, 229–240.

Dittenberger, W. 1915–1924. *Sylloge inscriptionum Graecarum*. 3rd ed. 4 vols. Leipzig.

Djurslev, C. T. 2017. '*Alexander Romance*' *Encyclopedia of Ancient History* https://doi.org/10.1002/9781444338386.wbeah30507.

Djurslev, C. T. 2018. 'Revisiting Alexander's gates against "Gog and Magog": observations on the testimonies before the *Alexander Romance* tradition' in Stoneman et al. 2018, 201–214.

Djurslev, C. T. 2020. *Alexander the Great in the Early Christian Tradition*. London.

Djurslev, C. T. 2021a. 'Four beasts and a baby: the "baleful birth" omen of Alexander's death in its Hellenistic context' *Mnemosyne* 74, 29–55.

Djurslev. C. T. 2021b. 'Heracles, Macedon and Alexander the Great' in D. Ogden ed. *The Oxford Handbook of Heracles*. New York. 432–446.
Djurslev, C. T. 2022. 'Educating Alexander: high culture in the Argead court through ancient texts' in Pownall et al. 2022, 225–253.
Djurslev, C. T., and D. Ogden 2018. 'Alexander, *agathoi daimones*, Argives and Armenians' *Karanos* 1, 11–21.
Dmitriev, S. 2004. 'Alexander's Exiles Decree' *Klio* 86, 348–381.
Dodge, T. 1890. *Alexander: A History of the Origin and Growth of the Art of War from the Earliest Times to the Battle of Ipsus, 301 BC, with a Detailed Account of the Campaigns of the Great Macedonian*. Boston.
Dods, M. trans. 1871. *Augustine: City of God*. 2 vols. Edinburgh.
Domínguez Monedero, A. 2022. 'La Grecia que dejó atrás Alejandro' in B. Antela-Bernárdez and M. Mendoza eds. *The Impact of Alexander's Conquest*. Alcalá de Henares. 37–64.
Dönitz, S. 2011. 'Alexander the Great in Medieval Hebrew tradition' in Z. D. Zuwiyya ed. *A Companion to Alexander Literature in the Middle Ages*. Leiden. 21–39.
Doufikar-Aerts, F. 2010. *Alexander Magnus Arabicus: A Survey of the Alexander Tradition through Seven Centuries, from Pseudo-Callisthenes to Ṣūrī*. Mediaevalia Groningana n.s. 13. Paris, Leuven, and Walpole, MA.
Dowden, K., trans. 1989. 'Pseudo-Callisthenes, *The Alexander Romance*' in B. P. Reardon ed. *Collected Ancient Greek Novels*. Berkeley. 650–735.
Dreyer, B. 2009. '"Jeder hat Alexander-Bild, das er verdient": the changing perceptions of Alexander in ancient historiography' in Wheatley and Hannah 2009, 56–71.
Droysen, J. G. 1833. *Geschichte Alexanders des Grossen*. Berlin. Reprinted Darmstadt, 1998.
Droysen, J. G. 1836–43. *Geschichte des Hellenismus*. 2 vols. Hamburg. [i. *Geschichte Nachfolger Alexanders*; ii. *Geschichte der Epigonen*.]
Droysen, J. G. 1877–1878. *Geschichte des Hellenismus*. 2nd ed. 3 vols. Gotha. [This edition incorporates a revised version of *Geschichte Alexanders des Grossen* as a new first volume.]
Droysen, J. G. 2012. *History of Alexander the Great*. F. Kimmich trans. Philadelphia. [Trans. of Droysen 1877–8 vol. I.]
Duff, T. 1999. *Plutarch's Lives: Exploring Virtue and Vice*. Oxford.
Dunand, F. 1969. 'Les representations de l'Agathodémon: à propos de quelques bas-reliefs du Musée d'Alexandrie' *Bulletin de l'Institut français d'archéologie orientale* 67, 9–48.
Dunand, F. 1981. 'Agathodaimon' *LIMC* i.1, 277–282.
Dunn, C., and E. D. Carney eds. 2018. *Royal Women and Dynastic Loyalty*. London.
Dunn, C., and P. Wheatley 2012. 'Craterus and the dedication date of the Delphi Lion Monument' *Ancient History Bulletin* 26, 39–48.
Edmonds, R., III ed. 2011. *The Orphic Gold Tablets and Greek Religion: Further Along the Path*. Cambridge.
Edmunds, L. 1971. 'The religiosity of Alexander' *Greek, Roman and Byzantine Studies* 12, 363–391.
Edward, W. A. 1928. *The Suasoriae of Seneca the Elder*. Cambridge.
Edwards, C. 2003. 'Incorporating the alien' in C. Edwards and G. Woolf eds. *Rome the Cosmopolis*. Cambridge. 44–70.
Eggermont, P. H. L. 1975. *Alexander's Campaigns in the Sind and Baluchistan and the Siege of the Brahmin Town of Harmatelia*. Leuven.

Ehrenberg, V. 1938. *Alexander and the Greeks*. Oxford. 52–61.
Elias, N. 1969. *Die höfische Gesellschaft*. Neuwied. Trans. as *The Court Society*. Oxford, 1983.
Ellis, J. R. 1969. 'Population-transplants under Philip II' *Makedonika* 9, 9–16.
Ellis, J. R. 1971. 'Amyntas Perdikka, Philip II and Alexander the Great: a study in conspiracy' *Journal of Hellenic Studies* 91, 15–24.
Ellis, J. R. 1976. *Philip II and Macedonian Imperialism*. London.
Ellis, J. R. 1981. 'The assassination of Philip II' in H. J. Dell ed. *Ancient Macedonian Studies in Honor of Charles F. Edson*. Thessaloniki. 99–137.
Empereur, J.-Y. 2018. 'New data concerning the foundation of Alexandria' in Zerefos and Voardinoyannis 2018, 3–12.
Engels, D. W. 1978. *Alexander the Great and the Logistics of the Macedonian Army*. Berkeley.
Errington, R. M. 1969. 'Bias in Ptolemy's *History of Alexander*' *Classical Quarterly* 19, 233–242.
Errington, R. M. 1970. 'From Babylon to Triparadeisos, 323–320 B.C.' *Journal of Hellenic Studies* 90, 49–77.
Errington, R. M. 1990. *A History of Macedonia*. C. Errington, trans. Berkeley.
Erskine, A. 1989. 'The πεζέταιροι of Philip II and Alexander III' *Historia*: 38, 385–394.
Erskine, A. 2002. 'Life after death: Alexandria and the body of Alexander the Great' *Greece and Rome* 49, 163–179.
Erskine, A., and L. Llewellyn-Jones eds. 2011. *Creating a Hellenistic World*. Swansea.
Fakhry, A. 1973. *The Oases of Egypt I: Siwa Oasis*. Cairo.
Faraguna, M. 2003. 'Alexander and the Greeks' in Roisman 2003a, 99–130.
Faraguna, M. 2011. 'Lykourgan Athens?' in V. Azoulay and P. Ismard eds. *Clisthène et Lycurgue d'Athènes: Autour du politique dans la cité classique*. Paris. 67–86.
Faraguna, M. 2020. 'Alexander the Great and Asia Minor' in K. Trampedach and A. Meeus eds. *The Legitimation of Conquest: Monarchical Representation and the Art of Government in the Empire of Alexander the Great*. Stuttgart. 243–261.
Faraone, C. A., and S. Torallas Tovar eds. 2022. *Greek and Egyptian Magical Formularies* I. Berkeley.
Faure, P. 1982. *La Vie quotidienne des armées d'Alexandre*. Paris.
Faust, S. 2018. 'Alexander's hearse and the Alexander Sarcophagus: power politics and commemoration in a changing world' in C. M. Draycott, R. Raja, K. Welch and W. T. Wooton eds. *Visual Histories of the Classical World: Essays in Honour of R. R. R. Smith*. Turnhout, 87–96.
Fears, J. R. 1974. 'The Stoic view of the career and character of Alexander the Great' *Philologus* 118.1, 113–130.
Fears, J. R. 1975. 'Pausanias, the assassin of Philip II' *Athenaeum* 53, 111–135.
Feis, O. 1918–1919. 'Die Geburt Alexanders des Grossen (Die Wandlung einer Geburtsgeschichte)' *Sudhoffs Archiv für Geschichte der Medizin und der Naturwissenschaften* 11, 260–277.
Feldherr, A. ed. 2009a. *The Cambridge Companion to the Roman Historians*. Cambridge.
Feldherr, A. 2009b. 'Introduction' in Feldherr 2009a, 1–8.
Ferguson, W. S. 1932. Review of Wilcken 1931, *American Historical Review* 37, 528–529.
Ferrando, S. 1998. 'La nascita di Alessandro Magno: una nuova ipotesi di datazione' *Maia* 50, 257–266.

Ferrario, M. 2020. 'Cherchez la femme: power and female agency in Bactria at the dawn of the Hellenistic age' *Karanos* 3, 85–101.

Finn, J. 2014. 'Alexander's return of the tyrannicide statues to Athens' *Historia* 63, 385–403.

Finn, J. 2022. *Contested Pasts: A Determinist History of Alexander the Great in the Roman Empire*. Ann Arbor.

Fisher, N. R. E. 2001. *Aeschines: Against Timarchos*. Clarendon Ancient History Series. Oxford.

Flintoff, E. 1980. 'Pyrrho and India' *Phronesis* 25, 88–108.

Flower, M. 2000. 'Alexander the Great and panhellenism' in Bosworth and Baynham 2000, 96–135

Fol, V. 2009. 'The anthropodaimons with gold masks from the upper stream of Tonzos' *Thracia* 18, 35–42.

Franks, H. M. 2012. *Hunters, Heroes, Kings*. Princeton.

Fraser, P. M. 1972. *Ptolemaic Alexandria*. 3 vols. Oxford.

Fraser, P. M. 1994. 'The world of Theophrastus' in S. Hornblower ed. *Greek Historiography*. Oxford. 167–191.

Fraser, P. M. 1996. *Cities of Alexander the Great*. Oxford.

Frederick II of Prussia. 1741. *L'Antimachiavel, ou Examen du Prince de Machiavel avec des notes historiques et politiques*. London.

Frederick II of Prussia. 1787. *Réflexions sur le caractère et les talens militaires de Charles XII*. Paris.

Fredricksmeyer, E. 1997. 'The origins of Alexander's royal insignia' *Transactions of the American Philological Association* 12, 97–109.

Fredricksmeyer, E. 2000. 'Alexander and the kingship of Asia' in Bosworth and Baynham 2000, 136–166.

Fredricksmeyer, E. 2003. 'Alexander's religion and divinity' in Roisman 2003a, 253–278.

French, V., and P. Dixon. 1986a. 'The Pixodaros affair: another view' *Ancient World* 13, 73–86.

French, V., and P. Dixon 1986b. 'The source traditions for the Pixodaros affair' *Ancient World* 14, 25–40.

Fulińska A. 2012. 'Oriental imagery and Alexander's legend in art: reconnaissance' in Stoneman et al. 2012, 383–404.

Fulińska A. 2014. 'Son of Ammon: ram horns of Alexander reconsidered' in Grieb et al. 2014, 119–144.

Fulińska A. 2018. 'Alexander and Napoleon' in Moore 2018, 545–575.

Fuller, J. F. C. 1936. *Memoirs of an Unconventional Soldier*. London.

Fuller, J. F. C. 1958. *The Generalship of Alexander the Great*. London.

Gabriel, R. A. 2010. *Philip II of Macedonia: Greater than Alexander*. Washington.

Gaca, K. L. 2015. 'Ancient warfare and the ravaging martial rape of girls and women: evidence from Homeric epic and Greek drama' in M. Masterson, N. S. Rabinowitz and J. Robson eds. *Sex in Antiquity: Exploring Gender and Sexuality in the Ancient World*. New York, 278–297.

Gadaleta, A. P. 2008. 'La vita di Nearco di Creta' *Annali della Facoltà di Lettere e Filosofia dell'Università di Bari* 51, 63–94.

Gaebel, R. E. 2002. *Cavalry Operations in the Ancient Greek World*. Norman.

Galbois, E. 2018. *Images du pouvoir de l'image: Les 'médaillons-portraits' miniatures des Lagides*. Bordeaux.

Galli, D. 2016. 'L'uso delle sententiae per delineare la psicologia dei personaggi nelle *Historiae* di Curzio Rufo' in Wulfram 2016a, 159–170.

Gallo, P. 2006. 'Ounamon, roi de l'oasis libyenne d'Ighespep (El-Bahreïn) sous la XXXe dynastie' *Bulletin de la Société française d'égyptologie* 166, 11–30.

Gamble, N., and E. F. Bloedow. 2017. 'A medical-historical examination of the death of Alexander the Great' *Journal of Ancient History and Archaeology*, 4, 18–29.

Gantz, T. 1993. *Early Greek Myth: A Guide to Literary and Artistic Sources*. Baltimore.

Garfield, J. L. 1990. 'Epoché and Śunyatā: skepticism east and west' *Philosophy East and West* 40, 285–308.

Garstad, B. 2016. 'Alexander's return to Greece in the *Alexander Romance*' *Greek, Roman and Byzantine Studies* 56, 679–695.

Garstad, B. 2018a. 'Alexander's circuit of the Mediterranean in the *Alexander Romance*' in Stoneman et al. 2018, 129–158.

Garstad, B. 2018b. 'Alexander the Great, the disguised dinner guest' *Symbolae Osloenses* 92, 171–197.

Gaullier-Bougassas, C. 2014. *La Fascination pour Alexandre le Grand dans les littératures euopéennes (X^e-XVIe siècle)*. 4 vols. Turnhout.

Gebauer, M. 1938/39. 'Alexanderbildnis und Alexandertypus' *Mitteilungen des Deutschen archäologischen Instituts: Athenische Abteilung* 63.64, 1–105.

Gehrke, J.-H. 2015. 'The revolution of Alexander the Great' in S. Bianchetti, H.-J. Gehrke and M. R. Cataudella eds. *Brill's Companion to Ancient Geography: The Inhabited World in Greek and Roman Tradition*, Leiden. 78–97.

Geus, K. 2003. 'Space and geography' in A. Erskine ed. *A Companion to the Hellenistic World*. Oxford. 232–245.

Gibson, C. 2004. 'Learning Greek history in the ancient classroom: the evidence of the treatises on *Progymnasmata*' *Classical Philology* 99.2, 103–129.

Gilhaus, L. 2017. *Fragmente der Historiker: Die Alexanderhistoriker (FGrHist 117–153): Übersetzt, eingeleitet und kommentiert*. Stuttgart.

Gilley, D. L. 2009. Damn with Faint Praise: A Historical Commentary on Plutarch's On the Fortune or Virtue of Alexander the Great. Diss., University of Missouri.

Gilley, D. L. and I. Worthington 2010. 'Alexander the Great, Macedonia and Asia' in Roisman and Worthington 2010, 186–207.

Gillies, J. 1789. *A View of the Reign of Frederick I of Prussia, with a Parallel Between that Prince and Philip II of Macedon*. London.

Gimatzidis, S. 2010. *The City of Sindos: A Settlement of the Late Bronze Age to the Classical Period on the Thermaikos Gulf in Macedonia*. Rahden.

Giommoni, F. 2019. 'Epigrams on the Persian Wars: an example of poetic propaganda' in M. Kanellou, I. Petrovic and C. Carey eds. *Greek Epigram from the Hellenistic to the Early Byzantine Era*. Oxford. 272–287.

Gitti A. 1953. 'L'età di Clitarco' *Rendiconti dell'Accademia dei Lincei* 8, 38–51.

Giustiniani, V. 1961. 'Sulle tradizioni latine delle Vite di Plutarco nel quattrocento' *Rinascimento* 1, 3–63.

Gleason, M. 1995. *Making Men*. Princeton, NJ.

Goddio, F., and D. Fabre eds. 2008. *Egypt's Sunken Treasures*. 2nd ed. Munich.

Gómez Espelosín, F. J. 2010. 'La imaginación geográfica en la expedición de Alejandro' in F. M. Simón ed. *Viajeros, peregrinos y aventureros en el mundo antiguo*. Barcelona. 49–63.

Gómez Espelosín, F. J. 2014 'Alejandro y los confines' in A. Pérez Jiménez ed. *Realidad, fantasía, interpretación, funciones y pervivencia del mito griego: Estudios en honor del Profesor Carlos García Gual*. Zaragoza. 329–342.
Gómez Espelosín, F. J. 2017 'Alejandro y el océano' in G. Santana Henríquez and L. M. Pino Campos eds. *Παιδεία καὶ ζήτησις: Homenaje a Marcos Martínez*. Madrid. 371–379.
Gómez Espelosín, F. J. 2023. *Las geografías de Alejandro*. Alcalá de Henares.
Goukowsky, P. 1976. *Diodore de Sicile: Bibliothèque historique, Livre XVII*. Paris.
Goukowsky, P. 1981. *Essai sur les origines du mythe d'Alexandre (336–270 av. J.-C.)* II: *Alexandre et Dionysos*. Nancy.
Goukowsky, P. 2022. *Arrien: Anabase d'Alexandre: Introduction générale, Livres I & II*, Paris.
Gounaropolou, L. and M. Hatzopoulos 1998. *Επιγραφές Κάτω Μακεδονίας: μεταξύ του Βερμίου όρους και του Αξιού ποταμού: τεύχος Α΄: Επιγραφές Βέροιας = Inscriptiones Macedoniae inferioris: Inter Bermium montem at Axium flumen repertae: Fasciculus primus: Inscriptiones Beroeae*. Athens.
Graninger, D. 2010. 'Macedonia and Thessaly' in Roisman and Worthington 2010, 306–325.
Green, P. 1974. *Alexander of Macedon, 356–323 B.C.: A Historical Biography*. London. [Revised ed. of his *Alexander the Great*. London, 1970.]
Green, P. 1978. 'Caesar and Alexander: aemulatio, imitatio, comparatio' *American Journal of Ancient History*, 3.1, 1–26.
Green, P. 1990. *Alexander to Actium: The Historical Evolution of the Hellenistic Age*. Berkeley.
Green, P. 2016. 'Bucephalas the hero' in D. A. Powers, J. G. Hawke and J. Langford eds. *Hetairideia: Studies in Honor of W. Lindsay Adams on the Occasion of His Retirement*. Chicago. 29–41.
Greenwalt, W. S. 1985. 'The introduction of Caranus into the Argead king list' *Greek, Roman and Byzantine Studies* 26, 43–9.
Greenwalt, W. S. 1986. 'Herodotus and the foundation of Argead Macedonia' *Ancient World* 4, 117–122
Greenwalt, W. S. 1989. 'Polygamy and succession in Argead Macedonia' *Arethusa* 22, 19–45.
Greenwalt, W. S. 1992. 'The iconographical significance of Amyntas III's mounted hunter stater' *Ancient Macedonia* 5, 95–104.
Greenwalt, W. S. 1994. 'A solar Dionysus and Argead legitimacy' *Ancient World* 25, 3–8.
Greenwalt, W. S. 1997. 'Thracian influence on the ideology of Argead kingship' in *Actes 2ᵉ Symposium international des études thraciennes* I. Komotini. 121–133.
Greenwalt, W. S. 1999. 'Why Pella?' *Historia* 48, 158–183.
Greenwalt, W. S. 2002. 'A Macedonian counterpart to the Thracian rider: Alexander and Bucephalas' in A. Fol. ed. *Thrace and the Aegean: Proceedings of the Eighth International Congress of Thracology* I. Sofia. 281–291.
Greenwalt, W. S. 2006. 'The development of a middle class in Macedonia' *Ancient Macedonia* 7, 179–188.
Greenwalt, W. S. 2010a. 'Argead dunasteia during the reigns of Philip and Alexander III: Aristotle reconsidered' in Carney and Ogden 2010, 151–163.
Greenwalt, W. S. 2010b. 'Macedonia, Illyria and Epirus' in Roisman and Worthington 2010, 279–305.

Greenwalt, W. S. 2011. 'Royal charisma and the evolution of Macedonia during the reigns of Philip and Alexander' *Ancient World* 42, 148–156.
Greenwalt, W. S. 2015. 'Thracian and Macedonian kingship' in J. Valeva, E. Nankov and D. Graninger eds. *A Companion to Ancient Thrace*. Malden, MA. 337–349.
Greenwalt, W. S. 2017a. 'Alexander II of Macedon' in Howe et al. 2017, 80–91.
Greenwalt, W. S. 2017b. 'Infantry and evolution of Argead Macedonia' in T. J. Howe, E. E. Garvin and G. Wrightson eds. *Greece, Macedon and Persia: Studies in Social, Political, and Military History in Honor of Waldemar Heckel*. Oxford. 41–46.
Greenwalt, W. S. 2019. 'The assassination of Archelaus and the significance of the Macedonian royal hunt' *Karanos* 2, 11–17.
Greenwalt, W. S. 2021a. 'Hermolaus, the royal Argead hunt and royal Prerogative' in *Ancient Macedonia* 8, 513–518.
Greenwalt, W. S. 2021b. 'Callisthenes the prig' in D'Agostini et al. 2021, 187–194.
Grell, C. 2014. 'Alexandre le Grand ou le rêve des prices: lectures de Quinte-Curce et de Plutarque au xviie siècle' in Mahé-Simon and Trinquier 2014a, 265–304.
Grenfell, P. B. et al. eds. 1898-. *The Oxyrhynchus Papyri*. London.
Grethlein, J. 2010. 'Beyond intentional history' in L. Foxhall, H. Gehrke and N. Luraghi eds. *Intentional History: Spinning Time in Ancient Greece*. Stuttgart. 325–341.
Grieb, V., K. Nawotka and A. Wojciechowska eds. 2014. *Alexander the Great and Egypt: History, Art, Tradition*. Wiesbaden.
Griffith, G. T. 1963. 'A note on the hipparchies of Alexander' *Journal of Hellenic Studies* 83, 68–74.
Griffith, G. T. 1964. 'Alexander the Great and an experiment in government' *Proceedings of the Cambridge Philological Society* 10, 23–39.
Griffith, G. T. 1977. 'Alexander's generalship at Gaugamela' *Journal of Hellenic Studies* 67, 77–89.
Griffith, G. T. 1981. 'Peltasts and the origins of the Macedonian phalanx' in H. J. Dell and E. N. Borza eds. *Ancient Macedonian Studies in Honor of Charles F. Edson*. Thessaloniki. 161–167.
Groag, E., A. Stein, L. Petersen, K. Wachtel, M. Heil, M. Horster, A. Krieckhaus, A. Strobach, W. Eck and J. Heinrichs eds. 1933–2015. *Prosopographia imperii Romani: Saec I. II. III.* 2nd ed. Berlin.
Grote, G. 1853. *History of Greece*. XI. London.
Grote, G. 1857. *History of Greece*. XII. London.
Gruen, E. S. 1998. 'Rome and the myth of Alexander' in T. W. Hillard, R. A. Kearsley, C. E. V. Nixon and A. M. Nobbs eds. *Ancient History in a Modern University*. Grand Rapids, MI. 178–191.
Guermeur, I. 2005. *Les Cultes d'Amon hors de Thèbes: Recherches de géographie religieuse*. Turnhout.
Habib, I., and V. Jha 2004. *Mauryan India (A People's History of India* vol. 5). New Delhi.
Habicht, C. 1997. *Athens from Alexander to Anthony*. London.
Habicht, C. 2017. *Divine Honors for Mortal Men in Greek Cities: The Early Cases*. Ann Arbor.
Hadjinicolaou, N., ed. 1997. *Alexander the Great in European Art*. Thessaloniki.
Hadley, R. A. 1974. 'Seleucus, Dionysus, or Alexander?' *Numismatic Chronicle* 14, 9–13.
Hägg, T. 2012. *The Art of Biography in Antiquity*. Cambridge.
Hägg, T. 2014. 'Historical fiction in the Graeco-Roman world: Cyrus, Alexander, Apollonius' in P. A. Agapitos and L. B. Mortensen eds. *Medieval Narratives between History and Fiction*. Copenhagen.

Haight, E. H. 1955. *The Life of Alexander of Macedon*. New York (trans. of Kroll's edition of *alpha*).
Halfmann, H. 1986. *Itinera principum: Geschichte und Typologie der Kaiserreisen im römischen Reich*. Stuttgart.
Hallett, C. H. 2005. *The Roman Nude: Heroic Portrait Statuary 200 BC–AD 300*. Oxford.
Hamilton, J. R. 1965. 'Alexander's early life' *Greece and Rome* 12, 116–125.
Hamilton, J. R. 1969. *Plutarch: Alexander: A Commentary*. Oxford.
Hamilton, J. R. 1973. *Alexander the Great*. London.
Hamilton, J. R. 1977. 'Cleitarchus and Diodorus 17' in K. H. Kinzl ed. *Greece and the East Mediterranean in History and Prehistory: Studies presented to Fritz Schachermeyr on the Occasion of his 80th Birthday*. Berlin. 126–146.
Hammond, N. G. L. 1972. *A History of Macedonia* I. Oxford.
Hammond, N. G. L. 1978. 'A note on "pursuit" in Arrian' *Classical Quarterly* 28, 136–140.
Hammond, N. G. L. 1980a. *Alexander the Great, King, Commander, and Statesman*. Park Ridge, NJ.
Hammond, N. G. L. 1980b. 'The Battle of the Granicus River' *Journal of Hellenic Studies* 100, 73–88.
Hammond, N. G. L. 1980c. 'Training in the use of a *sarissa* and its effect in battle, 359–333 BC' *Antichthon* 14, 53–63.
Hammond, N. G. L. 1983. *Three Historians of Alexander the Great: The So-Called Vulgate Authors, Diodorus, Justin and Curtius*. Cambridge.
Hammond, N. G. L. 1989a. 'Arms and the king: the insignia of Alexander the Great' *Phoenix* 43, 217–224.
Hammond, N. G. L. 1989b. 'The battle between Philip and Bardylis' *Antichthon* 23, 1–9.
Hammond, N. G. L. 1989c. *The Macedonian State: Origins, Institutions, and History*. Oxford.
Hammond, N. G. L. 1990. 'Royal Pages, personal pages, and boys trained in the Macedonian manner during the period of the Temenid Monarchy' *Historia* 39, 261–290.
Hammond, N. G. L. 1992a. 'Alexander's cavalry charge at the Battle of Issus in 333 B.C.' *Historia* 41, 395–406.
Hammond, N. G. L. 1992b. 'The archaeological and literary evidence for the burning of the Persepolis palace' *Classical Quarterly* 42, 358–364.
Hammond, N. G. L. 1992c. 'The regnal years of Philip and Alexander' *Greek, Roman and Byzantine Studies* 33, 355–373.
Hammond, N. G. L. 1993. *Sources for Alexander the Great: An Analysis of Plutarch's 'Life' and Arrian's Anabasis Alexandrou*. Cambridge.
Hammond, N. G. L. 1994. *Philip of Macedon*. Baltimore.
Hammond, N. G. L. 1996a. 'Alexander and Armenia' *Phoenix* 50, 130–137.
Hammond, N. G. L. 1996b. 'Alexander's non-European troops and Ptolemy I's use of such troops' *The Bulletin of the American Society of Papyrologists* 33, 99–109.
Hammond, N. G. L. 1996c. 'Some passages in Polyaenus' *Stratagems* concerning Alexander' *Greek, Roman and Byzantine Studies* 37, 23–53.
Hammond, N. G. L. 1997a. 'What may Philip have learnt as a hostage at Thebes?' *Greek, Roman and Byzantine Studies* 38, 355–372.
Hammond, N. G. L. 1997b. *The Genius of Alexander the Great*. London.

Hammond, N. G. L. 1998. 'Cavalry recruited in Macedonia down to 322 B.C.' *Historia* 47, 404–425.
Hammond, N. G. L. 2000. 'The Ethne in Epirus and Upper Macedonia' *The Annual of the British School at Athens* 95, 345–352.
Hammond, N. G. L., and G. T. Griffith 1979. *A History of Macedonia*. II. Oxford.
Hammond, N. G. L., and F. W. Walbank 1988. *A History of Macedonia* III. Oxford.
Hansen, S., A. Wieczorek and M. Tellenbach eds. 2009. *Alexander der Grosse und die Öffnung der Welt: Asiens Kulturen im Wandel. Exhibition catalogue*. Mannheim.
Hanson, V. D. 1999. *The Other Greeks: The Family Farm and the Agrarian Roots of Western Civilization*. Berkeley.
Harders, A.-C. 2014. 'Königinnen ohne König: zur Rolle und Bedeutung der Witwen Alexanders im Zeitalter der Diadochen' in H. Hauben and A. Meeus eds. *The Age of the Successors and the Creation of the Hellenistic Kingdoms (323–276 B.C.)*. Leuven. 345–378.
Harding, P. 1985. *From the End of the Peloponnesian War to the Battle of Ipsus: Translated Documents of Greece and Rome*. Cambridge.
Hatzilambrou, R. 2019. 'A lesson of self-control to Alexander in an Ashmolean ostracon' *Chronique d'Égypte* 94, 116–121.
Hatzopoulos, M. B. 1982. 'A reconsideration of the Pixodarus affair' in E. N. Borza and B. Barr-Shararr eds. *Macedonia and Greece in Late Classical and Early Hellenistic Times*. Washington, DC. 59–66.
Hatzopoulos, M. B. 1996. *Macedonian Institutions Under the Kings*. 2 vols. Meletemata 22. Athens.
Hatzopoulos, M. B. 1997. 'Alexandre in Perse: la revanche et l'empire' *Zeitschrift für Papyrologie und Epigraphik* 116, 41–52.
Hatzopoulos, M. B. 2001. 'Macedonian palaces: where king and city meet' in I. Nielsen ed. *The Royal Palace Institution in the First Millennium BC*. Aarhus, 189–200.
Hatzopoulos, M. B. 2005. 'The reliability of Diodorus' account of Philip II's assassination' in C. Bearzot and F. Landucci Gattinoni eds. *Diodoro e l'altra Grecia: Macedonia, occidente e ellenismo nella Bibiloteca storica*. Milan. 43–65.
Hatzopoulos, M. B. 2008. 'The burial of the dead (at Vergina) or the unending controversy on the identity of the occupants of Tomb II' *Tekmeria* 9, 91–118.
Hatzopoulos, M. B. 2011. 'Macedonia and Macedonians' in Lane Fox 2011a, 43–9.
Hatzopoulos, M. B. 2015. 'L'organization de la guerre macédonienne: Philippe II et Alexandre' in P. Contamines, J. Jouanna and M. Zinc eds. *Colloque la Grèce et la guerre*. Paris. 105–120.
Hatzopoulos, M. B. 2020. *Ancient Macedonia*. Berlin.
Hatzopoulos, M. B., and L. D. Loukopoulou eds. 1980. *Philip of Macedon*. Athens.
Hatzopoulos, M. B., and P. Paschidis. 2004. 'Makedonia' in M. H. Hansen and T. H. Nielsen eds. *An Inventory of Archaic and Classical Poleis*. Oxford. 794–809.
Hau, L. I. 2021 'The fragments of Polybius compared with those of the "tragic" historians Duris and Phylarchus' *Histos* 15, 238–282.
Hausner, S. L. 2007. *Wandering with Sadhus: Ascetics in the Hindu Himalayas*. Bloomington.
Haverkost, A. 2023. Death and politics: effects of kingship on Classical Macedonian tombstones. Diss., The University of Nebraska-Omaha.
Hazzard, R. A. 1992. 'Did Ptolemy I get his surname from the Rhodians in 304?' *Zeitschrift für Papyrologie und Epigraphik* 93, 52–56.

Hazzard, R. A. 2000. *Imagination of a Monarchy: Studies in Ptolemaic Propaganda*. Toronto.
Heckel, W. 1977. 'The conspiracy against Philotas' *Phoenix* 31, 9–21.
Heckel, W. 1979. 'Philip II, Kleopatra and Karanos' *Rivista di Filologia e di Istruzione Classica* 107, 385–393.
Heckel, W. 1980. 'Alexander at the Persian Gates' *Athenaeum* 58, 168–174.
Heckel, W. 1981a. 'Philip and Olympias (337/6 BC)' in G. S. Shrimpton and D. J. McCargar eds. *Classical Contributions: Studies in Honour of Malcolm F. McGregor*. Locust Valley. 51–57.
Heckel, W. 1981b. 'Polyxena, the mother of Alexander the Great' *Chiron* 11, 79–96.
Heckel, W. 1986. '"Somatophylakia": a Macedonian "cursus honorum"' *Phoenix* 40, 279–294.
Heckel, W. 1988. *The Last Days and Testament of Alexander the Great: A Prosopographical Study*. Stuttgart.
Heckel, W. 1992. *The Marshals of Alexander's Empire*. London.
Heckel, W. 2003a. 'Alexander and the "limits of the civilised world"' in Heckel and Tritle 2003, 147–174.
Heckel, W. 2003b. 'King and "Companions": observations on the nature of power in the reign of Alexander' in Roisman 2003a, 195–225.
Heckel, W. 2006. *Who's Who in the Age of Alexander the Great: Prosopography of Alexander's Empire*. Chichester.
Heckel, W. 2007. 'The earliest evidence for the plot to poison Alexander' in Heckel et al. 2007, 265–275.
Heckel, W. 2008. *The Conquests of Alexander the Great*. Cambridge.
Heckel, W. 2012. 'The royal hypaspists in battle: Macedonian *hamippoi*' *Ancient History Bulletin* 26, 15–20.
Heckel, W. 2016. *Alexander's Marshals: A Study of the Makedonian Aristocracy and the Politics of Military Leadership*. 2nd ed. of Heckel 1992. London.
Heckel, W. 2017a. 'Dareios III's military reforms before Gaugamela and the Alexander Mosaic: a note' *Ancient History Bulletin* 31, 65–69.
Heckel, W. 2017b. 'Geography and politics in Argead Makedonia' in S. Müller, T. Howe, H. Bowden and R. Rollinger eds. *The History of the Argeads: New Perspectives*. Wiesbaden. 67–78.
Heckel, W. 2018. 'Ptolemy: a man of his own making' in Howe 2018c, 1–19.
Heckel, W. 2020a. 'Creating Alexander: the "official" history of Kallisthenes of Olynthos' in R. A. Faber ed. *Celebrity, Fame, and Infamy in the Hellenistic World*. Toronto. 199–216.
Heckel, W. 2020b. *In the Path of Conquest: Resistance to Alexander the Great*. Oxford.
Heckel, W. 2021. *Who's Who in the Age of Alexander and his Successors: From Chaironeia to Ipsos (338–301 BC)*. Barnsley. 2nd ed. of Heckel 2006.
Heckel, W., J. Heinrichs, S. Müller and F. Pownall eds. 2020. *Lexicon of Argead Macedonia*. Berlin.
Heckel, W., T. Howe and S. Müller 2017. '"The giver of the bride, the bridegroom, and the bride": a study of the murder of Philip II and its aftermath' in Howe et al. 2017. 92–124.
Heckel, W., and L. A. Tritle eds. 2003. *Crossroads of History: The Age of Alexander*. Claremont, CA.
Heckel, W., and L. A. Tritle eds. 2009. *Alexander the Great: A New History*. Chichester.

Heckel, W., L. A. Tritle and P. Wheatley eds. 2007. *Alexander's Empire: Formulation to Decay*. Claremont, CA.
Heckel, W., C. Willekes and G. Wrightson. 2010. 'Scythed chariots at Gaugamela: a case study' in Carney and Ogden 2010, 103–109.
Heckel, W., and J. Yardley. 2004. *Alexander the Great – Historical Sources in Translation*. Malden, MA.
Heinrichs, J. 1987. '"Asiens König": die Inschriften des Kyrosgrabs und das achaimenidische Reichsverständnis' in W. Will and J. Heinrichs eds. *Zu Alexander d. Gr.: Festschrift für G. Wirth*. I. Amsterdam. 487–540.
Heinrichs, J. 2020a. 'Achaimenids' in W. Heckel et al. 2020, 32–7.
Heinrichs, J. 2020b. 'Alexander I' in W. Heckel et al. 2020, 55–60.
Heinrichs, J. 2020c. 'Panhellenism' in W. Heckel et al. 2020, 376–377.
Heinrichs, J. 2020d. 'Kyros II, as a reference' in W. Heckel et al. 2020, 307–309.
Heinrichs, J., and S. Müller. 2008. 'Ein persisches Statussymbol auf Münzen Alexanders I. von Makedonien' *Zeitschrift für Papyrologie und Epigraphik* 167, 283–309.
Heisserer, A. J. 1980. *Alexander the Great and the Greeks: The Epigraphical Evidence*, Norman.
Hekster, O. 2005. 'Propagating power: Hercules as an example for second-century emperors' in L. Rawlings and H. Bowden eds. *Herakles and Hercules: Exploring a Graeco-Roman Divinity*. Swansea. 205–222.
Helmreich, F. 1927. *Die Reden bei Curtius*. Paderborn.
Higgins, W. E. 1980. 'Aspects of Alexander's imperial administration: some modern methods and views reviewed' *Athenaeum* 58, 129–152.
Himmelmann, N. 1990. *Die ideale Nacktheit in der griechischen Kunst*. JDAI Ergänzungshefte 26. Berlin.
Hinge, G., and J. A. Krasilnikoff eds. 2009. *Alexandria, a Cultural and Religious Melting Pot*. Aarhus.
Hoffmann, W. 1907. *Das literarische Porträt von Alexanders des Grossen im griechischen und römischen Altertum*. Leipzig.
Högemann, P. 1985. *Alexander der Grosse und Arabien*. Munich.
Hölbl, G. 2001. *A History of the Ptolemaic Empire*. London and New York.
Hölscher, T. 1971. *Ideal und Wirklichkeit in den Bildnissen Alexanders des Grossen*. Heidelberg.
Hölscher, T. 1973. *Griechische Historienbilder des 5. und 4. Jahrhunderts v. Chr*. Würzburg.
Hölscher, T. 2009. *Herrschaft und Lebensalter: Alexander der Grosse: politisches Image und anthropologisches Modell*. Basel.
Hölscher, T. 2018. *Visual Power in Ancient Greece and Rome: Between Art and Social Reality*. Oakland, CA.
Holt, F. L. 1982. 'The Hyphasis mutiny: a source study' *Ancient World* 5, 33–59.
Holt, F. L. 1988. *Alexander the Great and Bactria: The Formation of a Greek Frontier in Central Asia*. Leiden.
Holt, F. L. 2003. *Alexander the Great and the Mystery of the Elephant Medallions*. Berkeley.
Holt, F. L. 2005. *Into the Land of Bones: Alexander the Great in Afghanistan*. Berkeley.
Holt, F. L. 2016. *The Treasures of Alexander the Great: How One Man's Wealth Shaped the World*. Oxford.
Holton, J. 2018. 'The reception of Alexander in the Ptolemaic dynasty' in Moore 2018, 96–118.
Hornblower, S. 1982. *Mausolus*. Oxford.
Howe, T. 2008a. 'Alexander in India: Ptolemy as Near Eastern historiographer' in Howe and Reames 2008, 215–233.

REFERENCES

Howe, T. 2008b. *Pastoral Politics: Animals, Agriculture and Society in Ancient Greece.* Claremont.
Howe, T. 2013. 'The Diadochi, invented tradition and Alexander's expedition to Siwa' in Alonso Troncoso and Anson 2013, 57–70.
Howe, T. 2014. 'Founding Alexandria: Alexander the Great and the politics of memory' in Bosman 2014, 72–91.
Howe, T. 2015a. 'Cleopatra-Eurydice, Olympias, and a "weak" Alexander' in Wheatley and Baynham 2015, 133–146.
Howe, T. 2015b. 'Introducing Ptolemy: Alexander and the Persian Gates' in W. Heckel, S. Müller and G. Wrightson eds. *The Many Faces of War in the Ancient World.* Newcastle upon Tyne. 166–195.
Howe, T. 2017. 'Plain tales from the hills: Illyrian influences on Argead military development' in S. Müller, T. Howe, H. Bowden and R. Rollinger eds. *The History of the Argeads: New Perspectives.* Wiesbaden. 99–111.
Howe, T. 2018a. 'Kings don't lie: truthtelling, historiography and Ptolemy I Soter' in Howe 2018c. 155–184.
Howe, T. 2018b. 'Ptolemy (138)' *BNJ.*
Howe, T. 2018c. ed. *Ptolemy I Soter: A Self-Made Man.* Oxford and Philadelphia.
Howe, T. 2021. 'The "pursuit" of kings: *imitatio Alexandri* in Arrian's Darius and Bessos "chase scenes"' in Walsh and Baynham 2021, 54–70.
Howe, T., and S. Müller 2012. 'Mission accomplished: Alexander at the Hyphasis' *Ancient History Bulletin* 26, 21–38.
Howe, T., S. Müller and R. Stoneman eds. 2017. *Ancient Historiography on War and Empire.* Oxford.
Howe, T., and J. Reames eds. 2008. *Macedonian Legacies.* Claremont.
Howgego, C. 2005. 'Coinage and identity in the Roman provinces' in C. Howgego, V. Heuchert and A. Burnett eds. *Coinage and Identity in the Roman Provinces.* Oxford. 1–17.
Hughes, G. R. and R. Jasnow. 1997. *Oriental Institute Hawara Papyri: Demotic and Greek Texts from an Egyptian Family Archive in the Fayum (Fourth to Third Century B.C.).* Chicago.
Humm M. 2006. 'Rome face à la menace d'Alexandre le Grand' in E. Caire and S. Pittia eds. *Guerre et diplomatie romaines (IVe-IIIe siècles av. J. C.).* Aix-en-Provence. 176–196.
Huß, W. 2001. *Ägypten in der hellenistischer Zeit, 332–30 v. Chr.* Munich.
Hussein, H. H. 2019. 'Mapping an ancient Egyptian highway of North Sinai: the ways of Horus' in J. K. Hoffmeier ed. *Excavations in North Sinai: Tell el-Borg* II. University Park, PA. 348–354.
Ignatiadou, D. 2012. 'The Sindos priestess' in N. C. Stampolidis and M. Giannopoulou eds. *'Princesses' of the Mediterranean in the Dawn of History.* Athens. 389–411.
Immerwahr, H. 1966. *Form and Thought in Herodotus.* Cleveland, OH.
Inscriptiones Graecae 1873–. Berlin.
Jacob, C. 1991. 'Alexandre et la maitrise de l'espace' *Quaderni storici* 34, 5–40.
Jacob, C. 2008. *Geografía y etnografía en la Grecia antigua.* Barcelona. Trans. of *Géographie et ethnographie en Grèce ancienne.* Paris, 1990.
Jacobs, B. 1994. *Die Satrapienverwaltung im Perserreich zur Zeit Darius' III.* Wiesbaden.
Jacobs, B. 2006. 'Achaemenid Satrapies' in *Encyclopaedia Iranica.* https://iranicaonline.org/articles/achaemenid-satrapies
Jacobs, B. 2020. 'Satrap, satrapies' in W. Heckel et al. 2020, 462–466.

Jacobs, B. 2021. 'The residences' in B. Jacobs and R. Rollinger eds. *A Companion to the Achaemenid Persian Empire*. II. Oxford. 1005–1034.

Jacobs, B., W. F. M. Henkelman and M. W. Stolper eds. 2017. *Die Verwaltung im Achaimenidenreich: Imperiale Muster und Strukturen*. Wiesbaden.

Jacobs, S. 2018. *Plutarch's Pragmatic Biographies: Lessons for Statesmen and Generals in the Parallel Lives*. Leiden and Boston.

Jacoby, F. 1921. 'Kleitarchos (2)' *RE* xi.1, 622–654.

Jacoby, F. et al. 1923– eds. *Die Fragmente der griechischen Historiker*. Multiple volumes and parts. Berlin and Leiden.

Jaeger, W. 1948. *Aristotle: Fundamentals of the History of his Development*. 2nd ed. Oxford.

Jäger, O. 1866. *Geschichte der Griechen*. Gütersloh.

James, D. 2023. '*Translatio Fortunae*: Curtius Rufus' Alexander, Livy's Hannibal, and intertextuality' *Classical Philology* 18, 210–231.

Jamzadeh, P. 2012. *Alexander Histories and Iranian Reflections*. Boston and Leiden.

Janni, P. 2000. 'Los límites del mundo entre el mito y la realidad' in G. Cruz Andreotti and A. Pérez Jiménez eds. *Los límites de la tierra: El espacio geográfico en las culturas mediterráneas*. Madrid. 23–40.

Jansari, S. 2023. *Chandragupta Maurya: The Creation of a National Hero in India*. London.

Janssen, E. 2007. *Die Kausia: Symbolik und Funktion der makedonischen Kleidung*. Göttingen.

Johnson, C. G. 2000. 'Ptolemy I's epiclesis Soter: origin and definition' *Ancient History Bulletin* 14, 102–106.

Johnston, A. 1989. 'The coinage of Smyrna' *Journal of Roman Archaeology* 2, 319–325.

Jones, W. H. S., and H. A. Ormerod trans. 1918–35. *Pausanias: Description of Greece*. Loeb Classical Library. 5 vols. Cambridge, MA.

Jouanno, C. 2002. *Naissance et metamorphoses du Roman d'Alexandre: Domaine grec*. Paris.

Jouanno, C. 2013. 'Alexander's friends in the Alexander Romance' *Scripta Classica Israelica* 32, 67–77.

Jouanno, C. 2016. 'Alexandre à Jérusalem: variations byzantines sur un thème hérité de Flavius Josèphe' *Anabases* 23, 75–95.

Jouanno, C. 2018a. 'Byzantine views on Alexander the Great' in Moore 2018, 449–476.

Jouanno, C. 2018b. 'The Alexander historians in Byzantium' in K. Nawotka, R. Rollinger, J. Wiesehöfer and A. Wojciechowska eds. *The Historiography of Alexander the Great*. Wiesbaden. 187–210.

Jouanno, C. 2020. 'The *Alexander Romance*' in K. De Temmerman ed. *The Oxford Handbook of Ancient Biography*. Oxford. 209–220.

Juhel, P. 2009. 'The regulation helmet of the phalanx and the introduction of the concept of uniform in the Macedonian army at the end of the reign of Alexander the Great' *Klio* 91, 342–355.

Julien, P. 1914. *Zur Verwaltung der Satrapien unter Alexander dem Großen*. Diss., Leipzig.

Kahil, L., et al. eds. 1981–1999. *Lexicon iconographicum mythologiae classicae*. 9 vols. in 18 pts. Zurich and Munich.

Kalitzi, M. 2016. *Figured Tombstones from Macedonia, Fifth–First Century BC*. Oxford.

Kapetanopoulos, E. 1996. 'Philip II's assassination and funeral' *Ancient World* 27, 81–87.

Karamitrou-Mentesidi, G. 2008a. Αιανή: Αρχαιολογικοί χώροι και Μουσείο (αρχαιολογικός οδηγός). Kozani.

Karamitrou-Mentesidi, G. 2008b. Η Αιανή και η συμβολή της στη διαμόρφωση της νέας ιστορικής φυσιογνωμίας της Άνω Μακεδονίας. Thessaloniki.

Karamitrou-Mentesidi, G. 2011. 'Aiani-: historical and geographical context' in Lane Fox 2011a, 93–112.
Karathanasis, K. 2019. 'A game of timber monopoly: Atheno–Macedonian relations on the eve of the Peloponnesian War' *Hesperia* 88, 707–726.
Karla, G. 2012. 'Folk narrative techniques in the *Alexander Romance*' *Mnemosyne* 65, 636–655.
Karunanithy, D. 2013. *The Macedonian War Machine: Neglected Aspects of the Armies of Philip, Alexander, and the Successors, 359–281 BC*. Barnsley.
Kasseri, A. 2015. Archaic Trade in the Northern Aegean: The Case of Methone in Pieria, Greece. Diss., Oxford. https://ora.ox.ac.uk/objects/uuid:48f2cf91-f266-4d32-9521-680da39f0acd.
Keith, A. B. 1909. 'Pythagoras and the doctrine of transmigration' *Journal of the Royal Asiatic Society*, [no serial no.] 569–606.
Kennedy, G. A. 1994. *A New History of Classical Rhetoric*. Princeton.
Kent, R. G. 1950. *Old Persian: Grammar – Texts – Lexicon*. New Haven.
Kern, O. 1938. 'Der Glaube Alexanders des Grossen' in his *Die Religion der Griechen*. 3 vols. Berlin. III, 38–57.
Kholod, M. M. 2010. 'The garrisons of Alexander the Great in the Greek cities of Asia Minor' *Eos* 97, 249–258.
Kholod, M. M. 2013. 'On the financial relations of Alexander the Great and the Greek cities in Asia Minor: the case of *syntaxis*' in A. Mehl, A. Makhlayuk and O. Gabelko eds. *Ruthenia Classica Aetatis Novae*. Stuttgart. 83–92.
Kholod, M. M. 2016. 'The cults of Alexander the Great in the Greek cities of Asia Minor' *Klio* 98, 495–525.
Kholod, M. M. 2017. 'The financial administration of Asia Minor under Alexander the Great: an interpretation of two passages from Arrian's Anabasis' in Howe et al. 2017, 136–148.
Kholod, M. M. 2018. 'The Macedonian expeditionary corps in Asia Minor (336–335 BC)' *Klio* 100, 407–446.
Kholod, M. M. 2021. 'The administration of Syria under Alexander the Great' *Klio* 103, 505–537.
Kienast, D. 1969. 'Augustus und Alexander' *Gymnasium* 76, 430–456.
Kienast, D. 1973. *Philipp II. von Makedonien und das Reich der Achaimeniden*. Abhandlungen der Marburger Gelehrten Gesellschaft 6. Marburg.
Kiilerich, B. 2017. 'The head posture of Alexander the Great' *Acta ad Archaeologiam et Artium Historiam Pertinentia* 29.15 (n.s.), 1–23.
Kilburn, K., trans., 1959. *Lucian* VI. Loeb Classical Library. Cambridge, MA.
King, C. J. 2010. 'Macedonian kingship and other political institutions' in Roisman and Worthington 2010, 371–391.
King, C. J. 2018. *Ancient Macedonia*. London.
Kirkland, N. B. 2019. 'The character of tradition in Plutarch's *On the Malice of Herodotus*' *American Journal of Philology* 140, 477–511.
Klęczar, A. 2014. 'Bones of the prophet and birds in the city: stories of the foundation of Alexandria in ancient and medieval Jewish sources' in G. Volker, K. Nawotka and A. Wojciechowska eds. *Alexander the Great and Egypt: History, Art, Tradition*. Philippika 74. Wiesbaden, 391–400,
Klęczar, A. 2019. *Ha-Makdoni: Images of Alexander the Great in Ancient and Medieval Jewish Literature*. Kraków.

Klinkott, H. 2000. *Die Satrapienregister der Alexander- und Diadochenzeit*. Stuttgart.
Klinkott, H. 2005. *Der Satrap: Ein achaimenidischer Amtsträger und seine Handlungsspielräume*. Frankfurt am Main.
Klose, D. A. O. 1987. *Die Münzprägung von Smyrna in der römischen Kaiserzeit*. Berlin.
Koch, H. 2000. *Hundert Jahre Curtius-Forschung (1899–1999): Eine Arbeitsbibliographie*. St Katharinen.
Koch, H. 2017. Review of Wulfram 2016a, *Gymnasium* 124, 67–69.
Konstan, D. 1998. 'The *Alexander Romance*: the cunning of an open text' *Lexis* 16, 123–138.
Konstantakos, I. 2015. 'Death in Babylon: Alexander and the fatal portent (*Alexander Romance* III.30)' *Eikasmos* 26, 253–274.
Kornemann, E. 1935. *Die Alexandergeschichte des Königs Ptolemaios I. von Aegypten*. Leipzig.
Kosmin, P. 2013. 'Apologetic ethnography: Megasthenes and the Seleucid elephant' in E. Almagor and J. Skinner eds. *Ancient Ethnography: New Approaches*. London. 97–116.
Kosmin, P. 2014. *The Land of the Elephant Kings: Space, Territory and Ideology in the Seleucid Empire*. Cambridge, MA.
Kottaridi, A. 1996. 'Art monumental et art miniature' in S. Drougou, C. Saatsoglou-Paliadeli, P. Faklaris, A. Kottaridou and E.-B. Tsigarida eds. *Vergina, le Grand Tumulus: Guide archéologique*. Thessaloniki.
Kottaridi, A. 2011. 'The palace of Aegae' in Lane Fox 2011a, 297–333.
Kottaridi, A. 2012. 'The Lady of Aigai – Tomb AZVII' and 'The Lady of Aigai' in N. C. Stampolidis and M. Giannopoulou eds. *'Princesses' of the Mediterranean in the Dawn of History*. Athens. 70–81 and 412–433.
Kottaridi, A. 2013. *Aigai: The Royal Metropolis of the Macedonians*. Athens.
Kottaridi, A. 2017. 'Παλιές προκαταλήψεις και νέα ευρήματα: "Μακεδόνες ἢ Βοττιαῖοι"' in M. Giannapoulou and C. Kallini eds. *Ηχάδιν* I. *Τιμητικός τόμος για τη Στέλλα Δρούγου*. Thessaloniki. 612–639.
Kottaridi, A., and S. Walker eds. 2011. 'Heracles to Alexander the Great: treasures from the royal capital of Macedon' in *a Hellenic Kingdom in the Age of Democracy*. Oxford.
Koulakiotis, E. 2006. *Genese und Metamorphosen des Alexandermythos im Spiegel der griechischen nichthistoriographischen Überlieferung bis zum 3. Jh. n. Chr*. Konstanz.
Kouremenos, A. 2022. '"The city of Hadrian and not of Theseus": a cultural history of Hadrian's Arch' in A. Kouremenos ed. *The Province of Achaea in the Second Century CE: The Past Present*. Abingdon. 345–374.
Kraeling, C. H. 1938. *Gerasa, City of the Decapolis*. New Haven.
Kraft, K. 1971. *Der 'rationale' Alexander*. Kallmünz.
Kremydi, S. 2011. 'Coinage and finance' in Lane Fox 2011a. 159–178.
Kremydi-Sicilianou, S. 2005. 'Belonging to Rome, remaining Greek: coinage and identity in Roman Macedonia' in C. Howgego, V. Heuchert and A. Burnett eds. *Coinage and Identity in the Roman Provinces*. Oxford. 95–106 (with pl. 7.1–7.3).
Kristeller, P. et al. 1960–. *Catalogus translationum et commentariorum: Medieval and Renaissance Latin Translations, Commentaries, Annotated Lists, and Guides*. Washington, D.C.
Kroll, J. H. 1977. 'An archive of the Athenian cavalry' *Hesperia* 46, 83–140.
Kroll, W. 1919. 'Kallisthenes' *RE* X.2. cols. 1707–1026.
Kroll, W. 1926. *Historia Alexandri Magni*. Berlin.
Kubica, O. 2016. 'Greek literature and cultural life of the Euphrates: the Greeks and Buddhism' *Eos* 102, 143–147.
Kuhlmann, K. P. 1988. *Das Ammoneion: Archäologie, Geschichte und Kultpraxis des Orakels von Siwa*. Mainz.

Kuhlmann, K. P. 2013. 'The realm of the "Two Deserts": Siwa Oasis between east and west' in F. Förster and H. Riemer eds. *Desert Road Archaeology*. Cologne. 133–166.

Kuhlmann, K. P., and W. M. Brashear 1988. *Das Ammoneion: Archeologie, Geschichte und Kulturpraxis des Orakels von Siwa*. Mainz.

Kühnen, A. 2005. *Die* Imitatio Alexandri *in der römischen Politik (1. Jh. v. Chr.–3. Jh. n. Chr.)*. Münster.

Kuhrt, A. 2007. *The Persian Empire: A Corpus of Sources from the Achaemenid Period*. London.

Kumaniecki, C. F. 1929. *De Satyro Peripatetico*. Krakow.

Kunst, C. 2021. *Basilissa – Die Königin im Hellenismus*. 2 vols. Rahden in Westfalen.

Kunze, M. 2000 *Alexander der Grosse, König der Welt: Eine neuentdeckte Bronzestatue*. Berlin.

Kunze, M. 2007. *Meisterwerke antiker Bronzen und Metallarbeiten aus der Sammlung Borowski I: Griechische und römische Bronzen*. Ruhpolding and Mainz.

Kuzminski, A. 2008. *Pyrrhonism: How the Greeks Reinvented Buddhism*. Plymouth.

Kyriakou, A. 2014. 'Exceptional burials at the sanctuary of Eukleia at Aegae (Vergina): the gold oak wreath' *Annual of the British School at Athens* 109, 251–285.

Ladynin, I. A. 2012. 'К вопросу о характере полномочий и формальном статусе Клеомена из Навкратиса' *Проблемы истории, филологии, культуры* 4.38, 89–100.

Ladynin, I. A. 2016. 'Defense and offense in the Egyptian royal titles of Alexander the Great' in K. Ulanowski ed. *The Religious Aspects of War in the Ancient Near East, Greece and Rome*. Leiden. 256–271.

Landucci Gattinoni, F. 1994. 'I mercenari nella politica ateniese dell'età di Alessandro: parte I' *Ancient Society* 25, 33–61.

Landucci Gattinoni, F. 1995. 'I mercenari nella politica ateniese dell'età di Alessandro: parte II: Il ritorno in patria dei mercenari' *Ancient Society* 26, 59–91.

Landucci Gattinoni, F. 1997. *Duride di Samo*. Roma.

Landucci Gattinoni, F. 2009. 'Cassander's wife and heirs' in Wheatley and Hannah 2009, 261–275.

Landucci, Gattinoni, F. 2018. 'Alexander, the crown prince' *Anabasis: Studia Classica et Orientalia* 9, 9–20.

Landucci Gattinoni, F., and L. Prandi 2013. 'P.Oxy LXXI 4808: contenuto e problemi' *Rivista di Filologia e Istruzione Classica* 141, 79–97.

Lane Fox, R. 1973. *Alexander the Great*. London.

Lane Fox, R. 2007. 'Alexander the Great: "last of the Achaemenids?"' in C. Tuplin ed. *Persian Responses: Political and Cultural Interaction with(in) the Achaemenid Empire*. Oxford. 267–311.

Lane Fox, R., ed. 2011a. *Brill's Companion to Ancient Macedon: Studies in the Archaeology and History of Macedon, 650 BC–300 AD*. Leiden.

Lane Fox, R. 2011b. 'Philip of Macedon: accession, ambitions, and self-preservation' in Lane Fox 2011a, 335–366.

Lane Fox, R. 2011c. 'Philip's and Alexander's Macedon' in Lane Fox 2011a, 367–392.

Lane Fox, R. 2011d. 'The 360s' in Lane Fox 2011a, 257–269.

Lane Fox, R. 2016. 'Alexander and Babylon: a substitute king' in K. Nawotka and A. Wojciechowska eds. 2016. *Alexander the Great and the East: History, Art, Tradition*. Wiesbaden. 103–116.

Lapatin, K. 2001. *Chryselephantine Statuary in the Ancient Mediterranean World*. Oxford.

Larsen, J. A. O. 1932. Review of Wilcken 1931, *Classical Philology* 27, 97–99.
Larson, J. 2016. *Understanding Greek Religion: A Cognitive Approach.* London.
Lasslett, L. 2020. The Making of Philip's Macedonia: The Archaeology of the Macedonian Kingdom from the Persian Wars to the Fall of Perdiccas III (c. 510-359 BC). 2 vols. Diss., Oxford.
Lateiner, D. 1989. *The Historical Method of Herodotus.* Toronto.
Law B. C. 1954. *Historical Geography of Ancient India.* Paris.
Lazaridis, N. 2012. 'Crossing the Egyptian Desert: epigraphic work at Kharga Oasis' *MAARAV, A Journal for the Study of the Northwest Semitic Languages and Literatures* 19, 117–129.
Lazaridis, N. 2015. 'Amun-Ra, Lord of the Sky: a deity for travellers of the Western Desert' *British Museum Studies in Ancient Egypt and Sudan* 22, 43–60.
Leclant, J. and G. Clerc. 1981. 'Ammon' *Lexicon iconographicum mythologiae classicae* i.1, 666–89 and i.2, 534–554.
Lee, H. D. P. 1948. 'Place-names and the date of Aristotle's biological works' *Classical Quarterly* 42, 61–7.
Lehmann-Haupt, C. F. 1921. 'Satrap' *RE* II.2 82–188.
Lendon, J. E. 2005. *Soldiers and Ghosts: A History of Battle in Classical Antiquity.* New Haven.
Lenfant, D. 2009. *Les Histoires perses de Dinon et d'Héraclide.* Paris.
Lenfant, D. 2011. *Les Perses vus par les Grecs.* Paris.
Lenfant, D. 2013. 'The study of intermediate authors and its role in the interpretation of historical fragments' *Ancient Society* 43, 289–305.
Leon, D. 2019. 'Arrian's Scythian *logos*' *Mnemosyne* 72.4, 550–560.
Leon, D. 2021. *Arrian the Historian: Writing the Greek Past in the Roman Empire.* Austin.
Leprohon, R. J. 2013. *The Great Name: Ancient Egyptian Royal Titulary.* Atlanta.
Le Rider, G. 1997. 'Cléomène de Naucratis' *Bulletin de correspondance hellénique* 121, 71–93.
Le Rider, G. 2007. *Alexander the Great: Coinage, Finances, and Policy.* Philadelphia.
Lerner, J. D. 2018. 'Alexander's settlement of the Upper satrapies in policy and practice' *Anabasis* 9, 110–128.
Lerouge-Cohen, C. 2014. 'Alexandre, Rome et les Parthes dans les *Histoires d'Alexandre* de Quinte-Curce' in Mahé-Simon and Trinquier 2014a, 199–210.
Leroy, P. 2022. 'Historiography and tactics: some thoughts about the dating of Arrian's *Anabasis*' in Rollinger and Degen 2022, 161–188.
Leuze, O. 1935. *Die Satrapieneinteilung in Syrien und im Zweistromlande von 520–320.* Halle.
Leventopoulo-Giouri, E. 1971. 'The sanctuary of Zeus-Ammon at Aphytis' *Athens Annals of Archaeology* 4, 356–367.
Lianou, M. 2010. 'The role of the Argeadai in the legitimation of the Ptolemaic dynasty: rhetoric and practice' in Carney and Ogden 2010, 123–133 and 280–284.
Lichtenberger, A. 2011. *Severus Pius Augustus: Studien zur sakralen Repräsentation und Rezeption der Herrschaft des Septimius Severus und seiner Familie (193–211 n. Chr.).* Leiden.
Lichtenberger, A., and R. Raja 2020. 'Roman city coins of Gerasa: contextualizing currency and circulation from the Hellenistic to the late Roman Period' in A. Lichtenberger and R. Raja eds. *Hellenistic and Roman Gerasa: The Archaeology and History of a Decapolis City.* Belgium. 369–381.
Liddell-Hart, B. H. 1926. *Scipio Africanus: Greater than Napoleon.* London.

Liddell-Hart, B. H. 1927. *Great Captains Unveiled.* London.
Liddell-Hart, B. H. 1941. *The Strategy of Indirect Approach.* London.
Liotsakis, V. 2019a. *Alexander the Great in Arrian's Anabasis: A Literary Portrait.* Berlin.
Liotsakis, V. 2019b. 'Why Arrian wrote the *Indike*: narrative suspense as a defense of Alexander' *Rivista di filologia e di istruzione classica* 147, 96–128.
Llewellyn-Jones, L. 2012. 'The Great kings of the fourth century and the Greek memory of the Persian past' in J. Marincola, L. Llewellyn-Jones and C. Maciver eds. *Greek Notions of the Past in the Archaic and Classical Eras: History without Historians.* Edinburgh. 317–348.
Llewellyn-Jones, L. 2013. *King and Court in Ancient Persia 559–331 BCE.* Edinburgh.
Lloyd, A. B. 2011. 'From satrapy to Hellenistic kingdom: the case of Egypt' in Erskine and Llewellyn-Jones 2011, 83–105.
Loar, M. 2021. 'Hercules, Caesar, and the Roman Emperors' in D. Ogden ed. *The Oxford Handbook of Heracles.* Oxford. 507–521.
Loar, M., C. MacDonald and D. Padilla Peralta eds. 2018. *Rome, Empire of Plunder: The Dynamics of Cultural Appropriation.* Cambridge.
Long, A. A. 2002. *Epictetus: A Stoic and Socratic Guide to Life.* Oxford.
Lonsdale, D. 2007. *Alexander the Great: Lessons in Strategy.* London.
Lorberbaum, Y. 2011. *Disempowered King: Monarchy in Classical Jewish Literature.* London.
Lord, C. 1978. 'Politics and philosophy in Aristotle's *Politics*' *Hermes* 106, 336–357.
Loukopoulou, L. D. 2011. 'Macedonia in Thrace' in Lane Fox 2011a, 467–476.
Low, P. 2018. 'Panhellenism without imperialism? Athens and the Greeks before and after Chaeronea' *Historia* 67, 454–471.
Luccioni, J. 1961. *Démosthène et le panhellénisme.* Paris.
Łukaszewicz, A. 2012. 'Second thoughts on the beginnings of Alexandria' *Institut des Cultures Méditerranéennes et Orientales de l'Academie Polonaise des Sciences, Études et Travaux* 25, 206–211.
Lunt, D. 2014. 'The thrill of victory and the avoidance of defeat: Alexander as a sponsor of athletic contests' *Ancient History Bulletin* 28, 119–134.
Luvaas, J. 1966. *Frederick the Great on the Art of War.* New York.
MacDowell, D. M. 2009. *Demosthenes the Orator.* Oxford.
Macherei, A. 2016. 'Die Medizin in Curtius' Tarsos-und-Mallerstadt-Episode' in Wulfram 2016a, 219–238.
Machiavelli, N. 1531. *I discorsi sopra la prima deca di Tito Livio.* Rome. Reprinted London, 1584.
Machiavelli, N. 1532. *Il principe.* Venice. Reprinted (A. Borgianni, ed.) Florence, 2006.
Machiavelli, N. 1546. *Libro dell'arte della guerra.* Venice. Reprinted, Milan, 1875.
McInerney, J. 2007. 'Arrian and the Greek *Alexander Romance*' *Classical World* 100, 424–430.
McKechnie, P. 2009. 'Omens of the death of Alexander the Great' in P. Wheatley and R. Hannah eds. *Alexander and His Successors: Essays from the Antipodes.* Claremont, CA. 206–226.
McKenzie, J. 2007. *The Architecture of Alexandria and Egypt, 300 BC–AD 700.* New Haven.
McQueen, E. I. 1995. *Diodorus Siculus: The Reign of Philip II: The Greek and Macedonian Narrative from Book XVI: A Companion.* Bristol.
McRoberts, S. 2018. 'Caesar's "Virgilian" katabasis at Troy' in Lucan *Bellum Civile* 9.950–99' *Ramus* 47, 58–77.

Macurdy, G. H. 1932. *Hellenistic Queens: A Study of Woman-Power in Macedonia, Seleucid Syria, and Ptolemaic Egypt*. Baltimore and London.

McVey, A. 2019. Reading Character in Suetonius' *De vita Caesarum*. Diss., University of Illinois.

Madreiter, I. 2012. 'Stereotypisierung – Idealisierung – Indifferenz' in *Formen der Auseinandersetzung mit dem Achaimeniden-Reich in der griechischen Persika-Literatur*. Wiesbaden.

Magee, P., C. Petrie, G. Knox, R. Knox, F. Khan and K. Thomas 2005. 'The Achaemenid empire in South Asia and recent excavations in Akra in northwest Pakistan' *American Journal of Archaeology* 109, 711–741.

Magnetto, A. 1994. 'L'intervento di Filippo II nel Peloponneso e l'iscrizione *Syll.³* 665' in S. Alessandrì ed. *Ἱστορίη. Studi offerti dagli allievi in onore di G. Nenci in occasione del suo settantesimo compleanno*. Galatina. 283–308.

Mahé-Simon, M. 2014. 'Quinte-Curce et ses sources: le case de Parménion' in Mahé-Simon and Trinquier 2014a, 91–108.

Mahé-Simon, M. and J. Trinquier eds. 2014a. *L'Histoire d'Alexandre selon Quinte-Curce*. Paris.

Mahé-Simon, M. and J. Trinquier 2014b. 'Avant-Propos' in Mahé-Simon and Trinquier 2014a, 7–27.

Mairs, R. 2014. *The Hellenistic Far East: Archaeology, Language and Culture in Greek Central Asia*. Berkeley.

Majumdar, B. K. 1960. *The Military System in Ancient India*. Calcutta.

Mann, C. 2020. 'Alexander and athletics *or* how (not) to use a traditional field of monarchic legitimation' in K. Trampedach and A. Meeus eds. *The Legitimation of Conquest: Monarchical Representation and the Art of Government in the Empire of Alexander the Great*. Stuttgart. 61–75.

Manning, S. 2020. *Armed Force in the Teispid-Achaemenid Empire: Past Approaches, Future Prospects*. Stuttgart.

Manteghi, H. 2018. *Alexander the Great in the Persian: Tradition, History, Myth and Legend in Medieval Iran*. London.

Manti, P. 1992. 'The *sarissa* of the Macedonian infantry' *Ancient Word* 33, 32–42.

Manti, P. 1994. 'The Macedonian *sarissa*, again' *Ancient World* 25, 77–91.

Mari, M. 2002. *Al di là dell'Olimpo: Macedoni e grandi santuari della Grecia dell'età arcaica al primo ellenismo*. Athens.

Mari, M. 2011a. 'Archaic and early Classical Macedonia' in Lane Fox 2011a, 79–92.

Mari, M. 2011b. 'Traditional cults and beliefs' in Lane Fox 2011a, 453–465.

Marincola, J. 1997. *Authority and Tradition in Ancient Historiography*. Cambridge.

Marincola, J., ed. 2007. *A Companion to Greek and Roman Historiography*. London.

Marincola, J. 2009. 'Ancient audiences and expectations' in Feldherr 2009a, 11–23.

Markle, M. M. 1977. 'The Macedonian *sarissa*, spear, and related armor' *American Journal of Archaeology* 81, 483–497.

Markle, M. M. 1978. 'Use of the *sarissa* by Philip and Alexander of Macedon' *American Journal of Archaeology* 82, 483–497.

Marsden, E. W. 1964. *The Campaign of Gaugamela*. Liverpool.

Martin, D. J. 1998. 'Did Pompey engage in *imitatio Alexandri*?' in *Studies in Latin Literature and Roman History* 9 (C. Deroux ed.), 23–51.

Massar, N. 2004. 'Le rôle des richesses dans les relations entre le souverain, la "maison du roi" et les savants de cour: un état des lieux' in A. S. Chankowski and F. Duyrat eds.

Le Roi et l'économie: Autonomies locales et structures royales dans l'économie de l'empire Séleucide. TOPOI 6. Paris. 189–211.

Mathéus, P. 2022. 'From Epictetus to Arrian and beyond: how Stoicism influenced the *Anabasis*' in Rollinger and Degen 2022, 131–143.

Matijašić, I. 2018. *Shaping the Canons of Ancient Greek Historiography: Imitation, Classicism, and Literary Criticism.* Beiträge zur Altertumskunde 359. Berlin-Boston.

Mattingly, H. et al. eds. 1923–94. *Roman Imperial Coinage.* 10 vols. London.

Maurice of Nassau 1616. *The Taktiks of Aelian,* Or The *Art of Embattling an Army in the Grecian Manner.* J. Bingham, trans. London.

Mayor, A. 2014. *The Amazons: Lives and Legends of Warrior Women across the Ancient World.* New Jersey.

Meadows, A. 2001. 'Money, freedom, and empire in the Hellenistic world' in A. Meadows and K. Shipton eds. *Money and Its Uses in the Ancient Greek World.* Oxford. 53–63.

Meadows, A. 2014. 'The spread of coins in the Hellenistic world' in P. Bernholz and R. Vaubel eds. *Explaining Monetary and Financial Innovation: A Historical Analysis.* New York. 169–194.

Meadows, A. 2018. 'What is an Alexander? PELLA and the classification or interpretation of coinage in the name of Alexander the Great' in S. Glenn, F. Duyrat and A. Meadows eds. *Alexander the Great: A Linked Open World.* Scripta Antiqua 116. Bordeaux. 55–74.

Meeus, A. 2008. 'The power struggle of the Diadochoi in Babylon, 323 B.C.' *Ancient Society* 38, 39–82.

Meeus, A. 2009a. 'Alexander's image in the age of the Successors' in Heckel and Tritle 2009, 235–250.

Meeus, A. 2009b. 'Kleopatra and the Diadochoi' in P. van Nuffelen ed. *Faces of Hellenism.* Leuven. 63–92.

Menu, B. 1999. 'Alexandre le Grand ḥqꜣ n Kmt' *Bulletin de l'Institute français d'archéologie orientale* 99, 353–356.

Merkelbach, R., and J. Trumpf. 1977. *Die Quellen des griechischen Alexanderromans.* Munich.

Meyer, E. 1919. *Caesars Monarchie und das Principat des Pompeius.* Stuttgart.

Meyer, M. 1989. *Alexander Complex: The Dreams That Drive the Great Businessmen.* New York.

Michel, D. 1967. *Alexander als Vorbild für Pompeius, Caesar und Marcus Antonius.* Brussels.

Millar, F. 1995. *The Roman Near East.* Cambridge, MA.

Millett, P. 2010. 'The political economy of Macedonia' in Roisman and Worthington 2010, 472–504.

Milns, R. D. 1967. 'Philip II and the Hypaspists' *Historia* 16, 509–512.

Milns, R. D. 1971. 'The Hypaspists of Alexander III: some problems' *Historia* 20, 186–195.

Milns, R. D. 1987. 'Army pay and the military budget of Alexander the Great' in W. Will and J. Heinrichs eds. *Zu Alexander dem Grossen: Festschrift G. Wirth zum 60. Geburtstag am 9.12.86.* Amsterdam. 233–256.

Milns, R. D. 1992. Review of Bosworth 1988a, *Ancient Society Resources for Teachers* 22.2, 98–103.

Miltner F. 1952. 'Der Okeanos in der persischen Weltreichidee' *Saeculum* 3, 522–555.
Mingazzini, P. 1961. 'Una copia dell'Alexandros Keraunophoros di Apelle' *Jahrbuch der Berliner Museen* 3, 6–17.
Mitchell, L. G. 1998. *Greeks Bearing Gifts: The Public Use of Private Relationships in the Greek World, 435–323 BC.* Cambridge.
Mitchell, L. G. 2012. 'The women of ruling families in Archaic and Classical Greece' *CQ* 62.1, 1–21.
Mittag, P. F. 2015. 'Alföldi and the contorniates' in J. H. Richardson and F. Santangelo eds. *Andreas Alföldi in the Twenty First Century.* Stuttgart. 259–269.
Moje, J. 2014. 'Die privaten demotischen Quellen zur Zeit Alexanders des Großen. Ihre Entwicklung am Beginn einer neuen Epoche der ägyptischen Geschichte im 4. Jh. v. Chr' in Grieb et al. 2014, 241–272.
Molina Marín, A. I. 2011. *Geographica: Ciencia del espacio y tradición narrativa de Homero a Cosmas Indicopleustes, Antigüedad y Cristianismo.* Monografías de la Antigüedad Tardía XXVII. Murcia.
Molina Marín, A. I. 2017. 'Under the shadow of Eratosthenes: Strabo and the Alexander historians' in D. Dueck ed. *The Routledge Companion to Strabo.* New York. 294–305.
Molina Marín, A. I. 2018. *Alejandro Magno (1916–2015): un siglo de estudios sobre Macedonia antigua.* Zaragoza.
Molina Marín, A. I. 2022. 'Alexander the reader: Herodotus and the Royal House of Macedonia' in B. Antela-Bernárdez and M. Mendoza eds. *The Impact of Alexander's Conquest.* Alcalá de Henares. 161–175.
Moloney, E. P. 2015. 'Neither Agamemnon nor Thersites, Achilles nor Margites: the Heraclid kings of ancient Macedon' *Antichthon* 49, 50–721.
Monaco Caterine, M. A. 2017. 'Alexander-imitators in the age of Trajan: Plutarch's Demetrius and Pyrrhus' *Classical Journal* 112, 406–430.
Monfasani, J. 2016. 'Diodorus Siculus' in Kristeller et al., vol. xi, 61–153.
Montaigne., M.de 1875. *Essais de Michel de Montaigne: Texte original de 1580, avec les variantes des éditions de 1582 & 1587.* Bordeaux.
Montecuccoli, R. 1973. *Aforismi dell'arte bellica* (E. Faccioli ed.). Milan.
Montecuccoli, R. 1988. *Trattato della guerra* = R. Luraghi ed. *Opere di Raimondo Montecuccoli* I. Rome.
Montesquieu, C.-L., de Secondat, Baron de 1748. *De l'Esprit des lois.* Geneva.
Montgomery, H. 1965. *Gedanke und Tat.* Lund.
Monti, G. 2016. 'Le lettere di Alessandro: storia degli studi' *Histos* 10, 17–33.
Mookerji, R. K. 1966. *Chandragupta Maurya and His Times.* Delhi.
Moore. K. ed. 2018. *Brill's Companion to the Reception of Alexander the Great.* Leiden.
Moore, P. 1995. Quintus Curtius Rufus' *Historiae Alexandri Magni*: A Study in Rhetorical Historiography Diss.,Oxford.
Moreno, P. 1987. 'Vita e opera di Lisippo' in J. Chamay and J.-L. Maier eds. *Lysippe et son influence.* Genève.
Moreno Hernandez, J. J. 2004. 'La caballería Macedonia: teoría y práctica' *Gladius* 24, 109–122.
Morgan, J. 2017. 'At home with royalty: re-viewing the Hellenistic palace' in Erskine and Llewellyn-Jones 2011, 31–68.
Mørkholm, O. 1991. *Early Hellenistic Coinage from the Accession of Alexander to the Peace of Apamea (336–186 AD).* Cambridge.

Morris, E. F. 2010. 'The pharaoh and pharaonic office' in A. B. Lloyd ed. *A Companion to Ancient Egypt*. Malden, MA. 201–217.
Mortensen, K. 2007. 'Homosexuality at the Macedonian court and the death of Philip II' *Ancient Macedonia* vii, 371–387.
Mossman, J. 1988. 'Tragedy and epic in Plutarch's *Alexander*' *Journal of Hellenic Studies* 108, 83–93.
Mossman, J. 1992. 'Plutarch, Pyrrhus, and Alexander' in P. Stadter ed. *Plutarch and the Historical Tradition*. London. 90–108.
Muccioli, F. 2013. *Gli epiteti ufficiali dei re ellenistici*. Stuttgart.
Muckensturm-Poulle, C. 1998. *Les Gymnosophistes dans la littérature grecque de l'époque impériale*. Diss., Université de Paris X, Nanterre.
Müller, K. 1841–70. *Fragmenta historicorum graecorum*. 5 vols. Paris.
Müller, K. 1846. *Arrianus; fragmenta scriptorum de rebus Alexandri Magni; Pseudo-Callisthenes* Paris.
Müller, K., and H. Schönfeld 1954. *Geschicte Alexanders des Grossen*. Munich.
Müller, S. 2009. 'Mehr als König Alexander has du getrunken' in R. Bernasconi and C. Hoffstadt eds. *An den Grenzen der Sucht / On the Edge of Addiction / Aux confins de la dépendance*. Aspekte der Medizinphilosophie 8. Bochum. 205–222.
Müller, S. 2010. 'In the shadow of his father: Alexander, Hermolaus and the legend of Philip' in Carney and Ogden 2010, 25–32.
Müller, S. 2011. '*Oikos*, Prestige und wirtschftliche Handlungsräume von Argeadinnen und hellenistischen Königinnen' in J. E. Fries and U. Rambuscheck eds. *Von wirtschaftlicher Macht und militärischer Stärke*. Münster and New York. 95–114.
Müller, S. 2012a. 'Onesikritos und das Achaimenidenreich' *Anabasis* 2, 45–66.
Müller, S. 2012b. 'Stories of the Persian bride: Alexander and Roxane' in Stoneman et al. 2012. 295–309.
Müller, S. 2013. 'Das symbolische Kapital von Argeadinnen und Frauen der Diadochen' in C. Kunst ed. *Matronage Handlungsstrategien und soziale Netzwerke antikern Herrsherfrauen im Altertum in diachroner Perspektive*. Rahden. 31–42.
Müller, S. 2014. *Alexander, Makedonien, und Persien*. Berlin.
Müller, S. 2015. 'A history of misunderstandings? Macedonian politics and Persian prototypes in Greek *polis*-centered perspective' in R. Rollinger and E. van Dongen eds. *Mesopotamia in the Ancient World: Impact, Continuities, Parallels*. Münster. 459–480.
Müller, S. 2016a. 'Alexander, Dareios und Hephaistion: Fallhöhen bei Curtius Rufus' in Wulfram 2016a, 13–48.
Müller, S. 2016b. *Die Argeaden: Geschichte Makedoniens bis zum Zeitalter Alexanders des Großen*. Paderborn.
Müller, S. 2016c. 'Kambyses II, Alexander und Siwa: die ökonomisch-geopolitische Dimension' in Binder, Börm and Luther 2016, 223–246.
Müller, S. 2016d. 'Make it big: the "new decadence" of the Macedonians under Philip II and Alexander the Great in Greco-Roman narratives' in T. Howe and S. Müller eds. *Folly and Violence in the Court of Alexander the Great and His Successors: Greco-Roman Perspectives*. Bochum. 35–45.
Müller, S. 2016e. 'Poseidippos, Ptolemy, and Alexander' in K. Nawotka and A. Wojciechowska eds. *Alexander and the East: History, Art, Tradition*. Wiesbaden. 179–192.
Müller, S. 2017a. *Perdikkas II – Retter Makedoniens*. Berlin.

Müller, S. 2017b. 'Chares of Mytilene (125)' *BNJ*.
Müller, S. 2018. 'The miracles of water and oil in the historiography on Alexander' in K. Nawotka, R. Rollinger, J. Wiesehöfer and A. Wojciechowska eds. *The Historiography of Alexander the Great*. Wiesbaden. 131–147.
Müller, S. 2019. *Alexander der Große: Eroberung – Politik – Rezeption*. Stuttgart.
Müller, S. 2020a. 'Argead Macedonia and the Aegean Sea' *Ricerche ellenistiche* 1, 9–20.
Müller, S. 2020b. 'Legitimization' in Heckel et al. 2020, 311–313.
Müller, S. 2020c. '*Proskynesis*' in Heckel et al. 2020, 441–443.
Müller, S. 2020d. 'Ptolemy, son of Lagos' in Heckel et al. 2020, 448–453.
Müller, S. 2021a. 'Alexander at Naqsh-e Rostam? Persia and the Macedonians' in Walsh and Baynham 2021, 107–128.
Müller, S. 2021b. 'Argead women' in Carney and Müller 2021, 294–306.
Müller, S. 2021c. 'Barsine Antigone and the Macedonian War' in D'Agostini et al. 2021, 81–96.
Müller, S. 2021d. 'On a dynastic mission: Olympias and Kleopatra, agents of their house' in K. Droß-Krüpe and S. Fink eds. *Perception and (Self)Presentation of Powerful Women in the Ancient World*. Melammu Workshops and Monographs 4. Vienna. 223–240.
Müller, S. 2021e. 'Perspectives in Europe in the Middle Ages and in the modern era' in B. Jacobs and R. Rollinger eds. *A Companion to the Achaemenid Persian Empire* II. Oxford. 1479–1494.
Müller, S., T. Howe, H. Bowden and R. Rollinger eds. 2017. *The History of the Argeads: New Perspectives*. Wiesbaden.
Murison, C. L. 1972. 'Darius III and the Battle of Issus' *Historia* 21, 399–423.
Murray, O. ed. 1990. *Sympotica: a Symposium on the Symposion*. Oxford.
Nabel, J. 2018. 'Alexander between Rome and Persia: politics, ideology, and history' in Moore 2018, 197–232.
Nagel, D. B. 1996. 'The cultural context of Alexander's speech at Opis' *Transactions of the American Philological Association* 126, 151–172.
Naiden, F. S. 2007. 'The invention of the officer corps' *Journal of the Historical Society* 1, 35–60.
Naiden, F. S. 2008. Review of Lonsdale 2007, *Journal of Military History* 4, 1275–1276.
Naiden, F. S. 2019a. *Soldier, Priest, and God: A Life of Alexander the Great*. Oxford.
Naiden, F. S. 2019b. 'The war aims of Alexander the Great' in F. S. Naiden and D. Raisbeck eds. *Reflections on Macedonian and Roman Grand Strategy*. Bogotá 41–59.
Napoleon I. 1858–69. *Correspondance de Napoléon Ier*. Paris.
Narain, A. K. 1965. 'Alexander and India' *Greece and Rome* 12, 155–165.
Narain, A. K. 2003. *The Indo-Greeks: Revisited and Supplemented*. Delhi.
Naveh, J., and S. Shaked eds. 2012. *Aramaic Documents from Ancient Bactria (Fourth Century B.C.E.) From the Khalili Collections*. London.
Nawotka, K. 2003. 'Freedom of Greek cities in Asia Minor in the Age of Alexander the Great' *Klio* 85, 15–41.
Nawotka, K. 2004. *Aleksander Wielki*. Wrocław.
Nawotka, K. 2012. 'Persia, Alexander the Great and the Kingdom of Asia' *Klio* 94, 348–356.
Nawotka, K. 2017. *The Alexander-Romance by Pseudo-Callisthenes: A Historical Commentary*. Leiden.

Nehru, J. 2004. *The Discovery of India*. Gurgaon (1st ed. 1946).
Neudecker, R. 2015. 'Collecting culture: statues and fragments in Roman gardens' in M. Wellington Gahtan and D. Pegazzano eds. *Museum Archetypes and Collecting in the Ancient World*. Leiden. 129–136.
Nicolai, R. 2007. 'The place of History in the ancient world' in Marincola 2007, 13–26.
Nicolet, C. 1991. *Space, Geography and Politics in the Early Roman Empire*. Ann Arbor.
Nikolitsis, N. T. 1974. *The Battle of the Granicus*. Stockholm.
Nilakanta Sastri, K. A. 1957. *A Comprehensive History of India II: Mauryas and Satavahanas*. Bombay.
Nousek, D. L. 2008. 'Turning points in Roman History: the case of Caesar's elephant. denarius' *Phoenix* 62.3/4, 290–307.
Nylander, C. 1997. 'Darius III – the coward king: point and counterpoint' in J. Carlsen et al. eds. *Alexander the Great: Reality and Myth*. 2nd ed. Rome. 145–159.
O'Brien, J. M. 1992. *Alexander the Great, the Invisible Enemy – A Biography*. London.
Ogden, D. 1996. 'Homosexuality and warfare in Ancient Greece' in A. B. Lloyd ed. *Battle in Antiquity*. London. 107–68. Reprinted in M. Bronski ed. *Lesbian, Gay, Bisexual and Transgender History: Critical Readings*. 4 vols. London. II, 38–86.
Ogden, D. 1999. *Polygamy, Prostitutes and Death: The Hellenistic Dynasties*. London.
Ogden, D. 2007a. 'A war of witches at the court of Philip II?' *Ancient Macedonia* VII, 425–437.
Ogden, D. 2007b. 'Two studies in the reception and representation of Alexander's sexuality' in Heckel et al. 2007, 75–108.
Ogden, D. 2008. *Perseus*. London.
Ogden, D. 2009a. 'Alexander, Scipio and Octavian: serpent siring in Macedon and Rome' *Syllecta Classica* 20, 31–52.
Ogden, D. 2009b. 'Alexander's sex life' in Heckel and Tritle 2009, 203–217.
Ogden, D. 2009c. 'Alexander's snake sire' in Wheatley and Hannah 2009, 136–178.
Ogden, D. 2011a. *Alexander the Great: Myth, Genesis and Sexuality*. Exeter.
Ogden, D. 2011b. 'The royal families of Argead Macedon' in B. Rawson ed. *A Companion to Families in the Greek and Roman Worlds*. Oxford. 92–107.
Ogden, D. 2012. 'Sekandar, Dragon-Slayer' in Stoneman et al. 2012, 277–294.
Ogden, D. 2013a. *Drakōn: Dragon Myth and Serpent Cult in the Greek and Roman Worlds*. Oxford.
Ogden, D. 2013b. 'The Alexandrian foundation myth: Alexander, Ptolemy, the *agathoi daimones* and the *argolaoi*' in Alonso Troncoso and Anson 2013, 241–252.
Ogden, D. 2013c. 'The birth myths of Ptolemy Soter' in S. L. Ager and R. A. Faber eds. *Belonging and Isolation in the Hellenistic World*. Toronto. 184–198.
Ogden, D. 2014a. 'Alexander, Agathos Daimon and Ptolemy: the Alexandrian foundation myth in dialogue' in N. Mac Sweeney ed. *Foundation Myths in Ancient Societies: Dialogues and Discourses*. Philadelphia. 129–150.
Ogden, D. 2014b. 'Alexander and Africa (332–331 BC and beyond): the facts, the traditions and the problems' in Bosman 2014, 1–37.
Ogden, D. 2015. 'Nectanebo's seduction of Olympias and the benign anguiform deities of the ancient Greek world' in Wheatley and Baynham 2015, 117–132.
Ogden, D. 2016. 'The legend of Seleucus: his signet ring and his diadem' in C. Bearzot and F. Landucci-Gattinoni eds. *Alexander's Legacy: Atti del Convegno Università*

Cattolica del Sacro Cuore. Centro Ricerche e Documentazione sull'Antichità Classica Monografie 39. Rome. 141–156.

Ogden, D. 2017a. Review of Carney 2015, *Journal of Hellenic Studies* 137, 251–252.

Ogden, D. 2017b. *The Legend of Seleucus: Kingship, Narrative and Mythmaking in the Ancient World*. Cambridge.

Ogden, D. 2018. 'Legends of Seleucus' death, from omens to revenge' in T. Howe and F. Pownall eds. *Ancient Macedonians in the Greek and Roman Sources: From History to Historiography*. Swansea. 201–214.

Ogden, D. 2019. 'The waters of Daphne *or* The *drakōn* source again' *Les Études classiques* 87 (special edition: M.-C. Beaulieu and P. Bonnechere eds. *L'Eau dans la religion grecque: paysages, usages, mythologie*), 41–63.

Ogden, D. 2020. 'Warfare and the legend of Seleucus' in K. Ruffing, K. Droß-Krüpe, S. Fink and R. Rollinger eds. *Societies at War*. Melammu Symposia 10. Vienna. 177–197.

Ogden, D. 2021a. 'Labour VIII: the Mares of Diomede' in D. Ogden ed. *The Oxford Handbook of Heracles*. New York. 113–123.

Ogden, D. 2021b. 'The theft of Bucephalas' in D'Agostini et al. 2021, 143–161.

Ogden, D. 2022a. 'The serpent sire of Alexander the Great: a palinode' in Pownall et al. 2022. 211–232.

Ogden, D. 2022b. 'Seleucus and the typology of Heracles' in E. Anagnostou-Laoutides and S. Pfeiffer eds. *Culture and Ideology under the Seleukids: Unframing a Dynasty*. Berlin. 77–96.

Ogden, D. 2023. *Polygamy, Prostitutes and Death: The Hellenistic Dynasties*. 2nd ed. Swansea.

Olajos, J. 1981. 'Le monument du triomphe de Trajan en Parthie quelques renseignements inobservés (Jean d'Ephèse, *Anthologie grecque* XVI 72)' *Acta Antiqua Academiae Scientiarum Hungaricae* 29, 379–383.

Olbrycht, M. J. 2004. *Aleksander Wielki i świat irański* (*Alexander the Great and the Iranian World*). Rzeszów.

Olbrycht, M. J. 2008. 'Curtius Rufus, the Macedonian mutiny at Opis and Alexander's Iranian policy in 324 BC' in J. Pigon ed. *The Children of Herodotus: Greek and Roman Historiography and Related Genres*. Newcastle. 231–252.

Olbrycht, M. J. 2010. 'Macedonia and Persia' in Roisman and Worthington 2010, 342–369.

Olbrycht, M. J. 2011a. 'First Iranian units in the army of Alexander the Great' *Anabasis* 2, 67–84.

Olbrycht, M. J. 2011b. 'On coin portraits of Alexander the Great and his Iranian regalia: some remarks occasioned by the book by F. Smith, *L'immagine di Alessandro il Grande sulle monete del regno (336–323)*' *Notae Numismaticae/Zapiski Numizmatyczne* 6, 13–27.

Olbrycht, M. J. 2014. '"An admirer of Persian ways": Alexander the Great's reforms in Parthia-Hyrcania and the Iranian heritage' in T. Daryaee, A. Mousavi and K. Rezakhani eds. *Excavating an Empire: Achaemenid Persia in Longue Durée*. Costa Mesa, CA. 37–62.

Olbrycht, M. J. 2015. 'The Epigonoi – the Iranian phalanx of Alexander the Great' in W. Heckel, S. Müller and G. Wrightson eds. *The Many Faces of War in the Ancient World*. Newcastle. 196–212.

Olbrycht, M. J. 2016. 'Alexander the Great at Susa (324 B.C.)' in C. Bearzot and F. Landucci eds. *Alexander's Legacy: Atti del Convegno Università Cattolica del Sacro Cuore Milano*. Rome. 61–72.
Oliver, P. 1986, 'Numismatique et iconographie: le cavalier macédonien' *Suppléments au Bulletin de Correspondance Hellénique* 14, 67–76.
Olivier, J., F. Duyrat, C. Carrier and M. Blet-Lemarquand. 2018. 'Minted silver in the empire of Alexander: old bullion and new' in S. Glenn, F. Duyrat and A. Meadows eds. *Alexander the Great: A Linked Open World*. Scripta Antiqua 116. Bordeaux. 127–146.
O'Neil, J. L. 1999. 'Olympias: "The Macedonians will never let themselves be ruled by a woman"' *Prudentia* 31, 1–14.
Osing, J. 1984. 'Siwa' in W. Helck and W. Westendorf eds. *Lexikon der Ägyptologie* V. Wiesbaden. Cols. 965–968.
O'Sullivan, L. 2015. 'Callisthenes and Alexander the invincible god' in Wheatley and Baynham 2015, 35–52.
O'Sullivan, L. 2016. 'Augustus and Alexander the Great at Athens' *Phoenix* 70, 339–360.
O'Sullivan, L. 2019. 'Court intrigue and the death of Callisthenes' *Greek, Roman and Byzantine Studies* 54, 596–620.
O'Sullivan, L. 2020. 'Reinventing *proskynesis*: Callisthenes and the peripatetic school' *Historia* 69, 260–282.
Pabst, S. 2009. 'Bevölkerungsbewegungen auf der Balkanhalbinsel am Beginn der Früheisenzeit und die Frage der Ethnogenese der Makedonen' *Jahrbuch des Deutschen Archäologischen Instituts* 124, 1–74.
Palagia, O. 2000. 'Hephaestion's pyre and the Royal Hunt of Alexander' in Bosworth and Baynham 2000, 167–206.
Palagia, O. 2010. 'Philip's Eurydice in the Philippeum at Olympia' in Carney and Ogden 2010, 33–42.
Palagia, O. 2014. 'The frescoes from the villa of P. Fannius Synistor in Boscoreale as reflections of Macedonian funerary paintings of the early Hellenistic period' in H. Hauben and A. Meeus eds. *The Age of the Successors and the Creation of the Hellenistic Kingdoms (323–276 B.C.)*. Leuven. 207–231.
Palagia, O. 2018. 'Alexander the Great, the royal throne and the funerary thrones of Macedonia' *Karanos* 1, 23–34.
Palagia, O. 2022. 'The image of Alexander in ancient art' in Stoneman 2022a, 42–64.
Panichi, S. 2018. 'Alexander and Cappadocia' *Anabasis* 9, 62–79.
Papadoulou, M. 2017. 'Shaping space and territory: Alexander's *chlamys* and the foundation myth of Alexandria' in M. Oller, J. Pàmias and C. Varias eds. *Tierra, territorio y población en la Grecia antigua* II. Mering. 209–224.
Parker, R. A. 1962. *A Saite Oracle Papyrus from Thebes in the Brooklyn Museum*. Providence, RI.
Parker, V. 2009. 'Source-critical reflections on Cleitarchus' work' in Wheatley and Hannah 2009, 28–55.
Parsons, P. J. 1979. 'The burial of Philip II' *American Journal of Ancient History* 4, 97–101.
Paschalis, M. 2007. 'The Greek and Latin *Alexander Romance*: comparative readings' in M. Paschalis et al. eds. *The Greek and Roman Novel: Parallel Readings*. Groningen. 70–102.
Paschidis, P. 2006. 'The interpenetration of civic elites and court elite in Macedonia' in A.-M. Guimier-Sorbets, M. B. Hatzopoulos and Y. Morizot eds. *Rois, cités,*

nécropoles: Institutions, rites et monuments en Macédoine. Meletemata 45. Athens. 251–268.

Paspalas, S. A. 2000. 'On Persian-type furniture in Macedonia: the recognition and transmission of forms' *American Journal of Archaeology* 104, 531–560.

Patsavos, C. C. 1973. *The Unification of the Greeks under Macedonian Hegemony*. Athens.

Pauly, A., G. Wissowa, and W. Kroll eds. 1893– *Realencyclopädie der klassischen Altertumswissenschaft*. Multiple volumes and parts. Munich.

Pausch, D. 2016. 'Alexander in der Toga? Techniken der Aktualisierung bei Curtius Rufus zwischen *delectare* und *prodesse*' in Wulfram 2016a. 73–98.

Pearson, L. 1960. *Lost Histories of Alexander the Great*. New York.

Pédech P. 1980. 'L´expédition d´Alexandre et la science grecque' in K. Babouskos ed. *Μέγας Αλέξανδρος: 2300 Χρόνια από τον θάνατο του*. Thessaloniki. 135–156.

Pédech, P. 1984. *Historiens compagnons d'Alexandre*. Paris.

Pedersen, B. 2015. 'Callisthenes and the creation of a Homeric hero' *Classica et Mediaevalia* 66, 103–127.

Pelling, C. 2002a. *Plutarch and History: Eighteen Studies*. Swansea.

Pelling, C. 2002b. 'Plutarch's *Caesar*: a *Caesar* for the Caesars?' in Stadter and Van der Stockt 2002, 213–226.

Pelling, C. 2009. 'Biography' in B. Graziosi, P. Vasunia and G. Boys-Stones eds. *The Oxford Handbook of Hellenic Studies*. Oxford. 608–616.

Peltonen, J. 2018. 'Church Fathers and the reception of Alexander the Great' in Moore 2018, 477–502.

Peltonen, J. 2019. *Alexander the Great in the Roman Empire, 150 BC to AD 600*. London.

Penella, R. J. 2019. 'Declamation and extempore speech as hallmarks of Philostratus's Second Sophistic' *Eranos* 110, 89–106.

Pepys, S. 1893. *The Diary of Samuel Pepys M.A., F. R. S.* H. B. Wheatley ed. London.

Perlman, S. 1957. 'Isocrates' *Philippus* – a reinterpretation' *Historia* 6, 306–317.

Perlman, S. 1967. 'Isocrates' advice on Philip's attitude towards barbarians' *Historia* 16, 338–43.

Perlman, S. 1969. 'Isocrates' *Philippus* and Panhellenism' *Historia* 18, 370–374.

Perlman, S. 1976. 'Panhellenism, the *polis* and imperialism' *Historia* 25, 1–30.

Perrin, B. trans. 1919. *Plutarch: Lives* VII. Loeb Classical Library. Cambridge, MA.

Pfieffer, S. 2014. 'Alexander der Große in Ägypten: Überlegungen zur Frage seiner pharaonischen Legitimation' in Grieb et al. 2014, 89–106.

Pfister, F. 1961. 'Das Alexander-Archiv und die hellenistisch-römische Wissenschaft' *Historia* 10, 30–67.

Pfister, F. 1976. *Kleine Schriften zum* Alexanderroman. Meisenheim am Glan.

Plantzos, D. 1999. 'Alexander's gaze: peripatetic concepts of vision and their influence on Hellenistic royal portraiture' *Archaiognosia* 10, 65–86.

Poddighe, E. 2012. 'Alexander and the Greeks: the Corinthian League' in I. Worthington ed. *Alexander the Great: A Reader*. New York. 129–151.

Pollitt, J. J. 1978. 'The impact of Greek art on Rome' *Transactions of the American Philological Association* 108, 155–171.

Pollitt, J. J. 1986. *Art in the Hellenistic Age*. Cambridge.

Porod, R. 1987. Der Literat Curtius: Tradition und Neugestaltung: Zur Frage der Eigenständigkeit des Schriftstellers Curtius. Diss., Graz.

Porod, R. 2016. 'Rhetorische Spezifika bei Curtius Rufus' in Wulfram 2016a, 99–126.
Power, T. 2013. 'Suetonius and the date of Curtius Rufus' *Hermes* 141, 117–120.
Pownall, F. 2010. 'The symposia of Philip II and Alexander III of Macedon: the view from Greece' in Carney and Ogden 2010, 55–68.
Pownall, F. 2013. 'Aristoboulos (139)' *BNJ*.
Pownall, F. 2014. 'Callisthenes in Africa: the historian's role at Siwah and in the *proskynesis* controversy' in Bosman 2014, 56–71.
Pownall, F. 2018. 'Was Kallisthenes the tutor of Alexander's Royal Pages?' in T. Howe and F. Pownall eds. *Ancient Macedonians in the Greek and Roman Sources: From History to Historiography*. Swansea. 59–76.
Pownall, F. 2020a. 'Alexander historiographers' in Heckel et al. 2020, 50–55.
Pownall, F. 2020b. 'Kallisthenes of Olynthos' in Heckel et al. 2020, 287–291.
Pownall, F. 2021. 'Ptolemaic propaganda in Alexander's visit to Ammon' in Walsh and Baynham 2021, 33–53.
Pownall, F. 2022a. 'Arrian's propinquity to Ptolemy and Aristobulus: a reassessment' in Rollinger and Degen 2022, 243–262.
Pownall, F. 2022b. 'Introduction' in Pownall et al. 2022, 1–14.
Pownall, F., S. Asirvatham and S. Müller eds. 2022. *The Courts of Philip II and Alexander the Great: Monarchy and Power in Ancient Macedonia*. Berlin.
Prakash, B. 1964. *Political and Social Movements in the Ancient Panjab*. Delhi.
Prandi, L. 1985. *Callistene: Uno storico tra Aristotele e i re macedoni* Milan.
Prandi, L. 1996. *Fortuna e realtà dell'opera di Clitarco*. Historia Einzelschriften 104. Stuttgart.
Prandi, L. 2012a. 'Anonymous on Alexander (148)' *BNJ*.
Prandi, L. 2012b. 'New evidence for the dating of Cleitarchus (*P.Oxy* LXXXI.4808)?' *Histos* 6 15–26.
Prandi, L. 2013. *Diodoro Siculo: Biblioteca storica, Libro XVII: Commento storico*. Milan.
Prandi, L. 2015. 'Alessandro il Grande in Giustino' in C. Bearzot and F. Landucci eds. *Studi sull'Epitome di Giustino*. II. Milan. 3–15.
Prandi, L. 2016. 'Kleitarchos of Alexandria (137)' *BNJ*.
Prandi, L. 2018. 'A monograph on Alexander the Great within a Universal History: Diodoros, Book XVII' in L. I. Hau, A. Meeus and B. Sheridan eds. *Diodoros of Sicily: Historiographical Theory and Practice in the* Bibliotheke. Leuven. 175–185.
Preisendanz, K. and A. Henrichs eds. 1973–4. *Papyri Graecae Magicae: Die griechischen Zauberpapyri*. 2nd ed. 2 vols. Stuttgart.
Price, M. J. 1991. *The Coinage in the Name of Alexander the Great and Philip Arrhidaeus*. 2 vols. Zurich and London.
Psoma, S. 2011 'The Kingdom of Macedonia and the Chalcidic League' in Lane Fox 2011a, 113–135.
Raabe, R. 1896. *Ἱστορία Ἀλεξάνδρου*. Leipzig.
Rahe, P. 2022. 'Anatomy of an error: Machiavelli's supposed commitment to a "citizen" militia' in S. Chauduri and P. Chakravarty eds. *Machiavelli Then and Now: History, Politics, Literature*. Cambridge. 31–53.
Rankin, D. 1987. *Celts and the Classical World*. London.
Rapin, C. 2014. 'Du Caucase au Tanaïs : les sources de Quinte Curce à propos de la route d'Alexandre le Grand en 330–329 av. J.-C.' in M. Mahé-Simon and J. Trinquier 2014a, 141–186.

Rashidzad, B. 2009. *I Am Timour, World Conqueror: Autobiography of a 14th Century Central Asian Ruler.* Indianapolis.

Raun, C. 1868. *De Clitarcho Diodori, Iustini, Curtii auctore.* Diss., Bonn.

Ravazzolo, C. 2012. *Liber de morte Alexandri Magni.* Alessandria.

Reames, J. 2008. 'Crisis and opportunity: the Philotas affair – again' in Howe and Reames 2008, 165–181.

Reames, J. 2010. 'The cult of Hephaistion' in P. Cartledge and F. Greenland eds. *Responses to Oliver Stone's Alexander: Film, History, and Cultural Studies.* Madison, WI. 184–217.

Reames-Zimmermann, J. 1999. 'An atypical affair? Alexander the Great, Hephaistion Amyntoros and the nature of their relationship' *Ancient History Bulletin* 13, 81–96.

Rhodes, P. J., and R. Osborne 2003. *Greek Historical Inscriptions, 404–323 BC.* Oxford. Revised ed., 2007.

Rice, E. 1983. *The Grand Procession of Ptolemy Philadelphus.* Oxford.

Richardson, L. 2000. *A Catalog of Identifiable Figure Painters of Ancient Pompeii, Herculaneum and Stabiae.* Baltimore.

Ridgway, B. S. 2001. *Sculpture I: The Styles of ca. 331–200 B.C.* Madison, WI.

Ritter, H.-W. 1965. *Diadem und Königsherrschaft: Untersuchungen zu Zeremonien und Rechtsgrundlagen des Herrschaftsantritts bei den Persen, bei Alexander dem Großen und im Hellenismus.* Munich.

Robert, C., 1921. *Die griechische Heldensage* ii. Berlin; = L. Preller, C. Robert and O. Kern 1894–1926. *Griechische Mythologie.* 4th ed. II.2. Berlin.

Robinson, C. A. 1953–1963. *The History of Alexander the Great.* 2 vols. Providence.

Robinson, C. A. 1932. Review of Wilcken 1931, *American Journal of Philology* 53, 383–385.

Robinson, D. and A. Wilson eds. 2010. *Alexandria and the North-Western Delta.* Oxford.

Rohan, H. de 1640. 'Traité de la guerre' in *Le Parfaict capitaine, autrement L'Abrégé des guerres de Gaule des Commentaires de César, avec quelques remarques sur icelles, suivy d'un recueil de l'ordre des guerres des anciens, ensemble d'un traité particulier de la guerre par Henry, duc de Rohan.* Paris. Translated as *The Compleat Captain.* Cambridge, 1694.

Roisman, J. 1984. 'Ptolemy and his rivals in his *History of Alexander*' *Classical Quarterly* 34, 373–385.

Roisman, J. ed. 2003a. *Brill's Companion to Alexander the Great.* Leiden.

Roisman, J. 2003b. 'Honor in Alexander's campaign' in Roisman 2003a, 279–321.

Roisman, J. 2012a. *Alexander's Veterans and the Early Wars of the Successors.* Austin.

Roisman, J. 2012b. 'Royal power, law and justice' *Ancient History Bulletin* 26, 131–148.

Roisman, J. and I. Worthington eds. 2010. *A Companion to Ancient Macedonia.* Chichester.

Rollinger, R. 2013. *Alexander und die grossen Ströme: Die Flussüberquerungen im Lichte altorientalischer Pioniertechniken.* Wiesbaden.

Rollinger, R. 2014. 'Das teispidisch-achaimenidische Großreich' in M. Gehler and R. Rollinger eds. *Imperien und Reiche in der Weltgeschichte* I. Wiesbaden. 149–192.

Rollinger, R., and J. Degen eds. 2022. *The World of Alexander in Perspective: Contextualizing Arrian.* Wiesbaden.

Romm, J. 1989. 'Aristotle's elephant and the myth of Alexander's scientific patronage' *American Journal of Philology* 10, 566–575.

Romm, J. 1992. *The Edges of the Earth in Ancient Thought.* Princeton.

Rop, J. 2019. *Greek Military Service in the Ancient Near East, 401–330 BCE.* Cambridge.

Rosellini, M. 2004. *Julius Valerius: Res gestae Alexandri Macedonis.* Munich.
Rostovzeff, M. 1941. *Social and Economic History of the Hellenistic World.* 3 vols. Oxford.
Rubinsohn, R. 1977. 'The Philotas affair? A reconsideration' Ancient Macedonia 2, 409–420.
Ruzicka, S. 1988. 'War in the Aegean, 333–331 B.C.: a reconsideration' *Phoenix* 42, 131–151.
Ruzicka, S. 1992. *Politics of a Persian Dynasty: The Hecatomnids in the Fourth Century B.C.* Norman, OK.
Ruzicka, S. 2010. 'The "Pixodarus affair" reconsidered again' in Carney and Ogden 2010, 3–12.
Ryder, T. T. B. 1965. *Koiné Eirene: General Peace and Local Independence in Ancient Greece.* London.
Rzepka, J. 2016. 'Kallisthenes (124)' *BNJ.*
Saatsoglou-Paliadeli, C. 2001. 'The palace of Vergina-Aegae and its surroundings' in I. Nielsen ed. *The Royal Palace Institution in the First Millennium BC.* Aarhus. 201–214.
Sales, J. de C., 2005. 'Prodígios e presságios como marcas de sobrenaturalidade de um herói predestinado: o caso de Alexandre Magno' *Cadmo* 15, 71–104.
Samuel, A. E. 1986. 'The earliest elements in the *Alexander Romance*' *Historia* 35, 427–437.
Samuel, A. E. 1988. 'Philip and Alexander as kings: Macedonian monarchy and Merovingian parallels' *American Historical Review* 93, 1270–1286.
Sancisi-Weerdenburg, H. 1993. 'Alexander and Persepolis' in J. Carlsen B. Due, O. S. Due and B. Poulsen eds. *Alexander the Great: Reality and Myth.* Analecta Romana Instituti Danici, Supplementum 21. Rome. 177–188.
Sanders, D. H. 1996. *Nemrud Dagi: The Hierothesion of Antiochus I of Commagene.* 2 vols. Winona Lake.
Sansone, D. 1980. 'Plutarch, Alexander and the discovery of naphtha' *Greek, Roman and Byzantine Studies* 21, 63–74.
Saripanidi, V. 2017. 'Constructing continuities with a "heroic" past: death, feasting and political ideology in the Archaic Macedonian kingdom' in A. Tsingarida and I. S. Lemos eds. *Constructing Social Identities in Early Iron Age and Archaic Greece.* Brussels. 73–170.
Saripanidi, V. 2019. 'Macedonian necropoleis in the Archaic period: shifting practices and emerging identities' in H. Frielinghaus, J. Stroszeck and P. Valavanis eds. *Griechische Nekropolen, Neue Forschungen und Funde.* Beiträge zur archäologie Griechenlands 5. Möhnesee. 175–196.
Sawada, N. 2010. 'Social customs and institutions' in Roisman and Worthington 2010, 392–408.
Schachermeyr, F. 1944. *Indogermanen und Orient.* Stuttgart.
Schachermeyr, F. 1949. *Alexander der Grosse: Ingenium und Macht.* Graz.
Schachermeyr, F. 1970. *Alexander in Babylon und die Reichsordnung nach seinem Tode.* Vienna.
Schachermeyr, F. 1973. *Alexander der Grosse: Das Problem seiner Persönlichkeit und seines Wirkens.* Vienna.
Schäfer, D. 2011. *Makedonische Pharaonen und hieroglyphische Stelen: Historische Untersuchungen zur Satrapenstele und verwandten Denkmalern.* Leuven.

Schäfer, D. 2014. 'Pharao Alexander "der Große" in Ägypten – eine Bewertung' in Grieb et al. 2014, 153–168.
Schlude, J. 2020. *Rome, Parthia, and the Politics of Peace: The Origins of War in the Ancient Middle East.* Abingdon.
Schmidt, E. F. 1939. *The Treasury of Persepolis and Other Discoveries in the Homeland of the Achaemenians.* Chicago.
Schmitz, T. 2014. 'Plutarch and the Second Sophistic' in Beck 2014, 32–42.
Schneeweiss, G. 2007. Review of Duff 1999, *Gnomon* 79, 591–597.
Schorn, S. 2013. 'Überlegungen zu P.Oxy. LXXI 4808' *Rivista di filologia e istruzione classica* 141, 105–122.
Schreiber, T. 1903. *Studien über das Bildnis Alexanders des Grossen: Ein Beitrag zur alexandrinischen Kunstgeschichte mit einem Anhang über die Anfänge des Alexanderkultes.* Leipzig.
Schultz, P. 2007. 'Leochares' Argead portraits in the Philippeion' in P. Schultz and R. von den Hoff eds. *Early Hellenistic Portraiture: Image, Style, Contexts.* Cambridge. 205–233.
Schulz, P. 2009. 'Divine images and royal ideology in the Philippeion at Olympia' in J. Jensen, G. Hinge, B. Wickkiser and P. Schultz eds. *Aspects of Ancient Greek Cult: Context, Ritual, Iconography.* Aarhus. 125–193.
Schulze, C. 2016. 'Der Arzt bei Curtius Rufus: medizinische und literarische Funktionen' in Wulfram 2016a, 209–218.
Schunk, H. 2019. *Arrians* Indiké: *Eine Untersuchung der Darstellungstechnik.* Wiesbaden.
Schütze, A. 2017. 'Local administration in Persian-period Egypt according to Aramaic and Demotic sources' in B. Jacobs, W. Henkelman and M. Stolper eds. *Die Verwaltung im Achämenidenreich Imperiale Muster und Strukturen.* Wiesbaden. 489–516.
Schwartz, E. 1901. 'Curtius (31)' *RE* IV.2, 1871–1891.
Schwenk, C. J. 1985. *Athens in the Age of Alexander: The Dated Laws and Decrees of the Lykourgan Era, 338–322 BC.* Chicago Ridge.
Seager, R. 1981. 'The freedom of the Greeks of Asia: from Alexander to Antiochus' *Classical Quarterly* 31, 106–112.
Seager, R., and C. Tuplin 1980. 'The freedom of the Greeks of Asia: on the origins of a concept and the creation of a slogan' *Journal of Hellenic Studies* 100, 141–154.
Sealey, R. 1993. *Demosthenes and his Time: A Study in Defeat.* Oxford.
Sears, M. 2019. *Understanding Greek Warfare.* New York.
Sears, M., and C. Willekes. 2016. 'Alexander's cavalry charge at Chaeronea, 338 BCE' *The Journal of Military History* 80, 1017–1035.
Seibert, J. 1985. *Die Eroberung des Perserreiches durch Alexander den Großen auf kartographischer Grundlage.* Wiesbaden.
Sekunda, N. V. 2001. 'The *sarissa*' *Acta Universitatis Lodziensis: Folia archaeologica* 23, 13–41.
Sekunda, N. V. 2010. 'The Macedonian army' in Roisman and Worthington 2010, 446–471.
Sekunda, N. V. 2014a. 'The chronology of the Iphicratean peltast reform' in N. V. Sekunda and B. Burliga eds. *Iphicrates, Peltasts and Lechaeum.* Gdansk. 126–144.
Sekunda, N. V. 2014b. 'The importance of the oracle at Didyma' in Grieb et al. 2014, 107–117.
Selden, D. 2010. 'Text networks' *Ancient Narrative* 8, 1–23.

Seyer, M. 2007. *Der Herrscher als Jäger: Untersuchungen zur königlichen Jagd in persischen und makedonischen Reich vom 6–4. Jahrhundert v. Chr. sowie unter den Diadochen Alexanders des Großen*. Vienna.

Shayegan, M. R. 2007. 'Prosopographical notes: the Iranian nobility during and after the Macedonian conquest' *Bulletin of the Asia Institute* 21, 97–126.

Sherwin-White, A. N. 1966. *The Letters of Pliny*. Oxford.

Siemoneit, G. 2016. 'Lob und Datierung: Johannes Freinsheims Überblick über den Stand der Curtius-Forschung im Jahr 1639' in Wulfram 2016a, 369–388.

Singh, U. 2009. *A History of Ancient and Medieval India*. London and Delhi.

Sircar, D. C. 1945. 'Puranic list of Peoples' *Indian Historical Quarterly* 21, 297–318.

Sirinelli, J. 1993. *Les Enfants d'Alexandre: La littérature et la pensée grecques (331 av. J.-C. – 519 ap. J.-C.)*. Paris.

Sisti, F., and A. Zambrini. 2001–2004. *Arriano: Anabasi di Alessandro*. 2 vols. Rome.

Skinner, M. B. 2010. 'Alexander and ancient Greek sexuality: some theoretical considerations' in F. Greenland and P. Cartledge eds. *Responses to Oliver Stone's Alexander: Film, History and Culture Studies*. Madison, WI. 119–134.

Smith, F. 2000. *L'immagine di Alessandro il Grande sulle monete del regno (336–323 A.C.)*. Milan.

Smith, R. R. R. 1988. *Hellenistic Royal Portraits*. Oxford.

Smith, R. R. R. 1993. 'Kings and philosophers' in A. Bulloch, E. S. Gruen and A. A. Long eds. *Images and Ideologies: Self-Definition in the Hellenistic World*. Berkeley. 202–212.

Smith, R. R. R. 1994. 'Spear-won land at Boscoreale: on the royal paintings of a Roman villa' *Journal of Roman Archaeology* 7, 100–128.

Smith, R. R. R. 1996. 'Typology and diversity in the portraits of Augustus' *Journal of Roman Archaeology* 9, 30–47.

Sohlberg, D. 1972. 'Zu Kleitarch' *Historia* 21, 758–759.

Spann, P. O. 1999. 'Alexander at the Beas: fox in a lion's skin' in F. B. Titchener and R. F. Moorton eds. *The Eye Expanded: Life and the Arts in Greco-Roman Antiquity*. Berkeley. 62–74.

Spawforth, A. J. S. ed. 2007a. *The Court and Court Society in Ancient Monarchies*. Cambridge.

Spawforth, A. J. S. 2007b. 'The court of Alexander the Great between Europe and Asia' in Spawforth 2007a, 82–120.

Spence, I. 1993. *The Cavalry of Classical Greece: A Social and Military History*. Oxford.

Spencer, D. 2002. *The Roman Alexander: Reading a Cultural Myth*. Exeter.

Sprawski, S. 2010. 'The early Temenid kings to Alexander I' in Roisman and Worthington 2010, 127–144.

Squillace, G. 2004. Βασιλεῖς ἢ τύραννοι: *Filippo II e Alessandro Magno tra opposizione e consenso*. Soveria Mannelli.

Squillace, G. 2010. 'Consensus strategies under Philip and Alexander: the revenge theme' in Carney and Ogden 2010, 69–80.

Squillace, G. 2018. 'Alexander after Alexander: Macedonian propaganda and historical memory in Ptolemy and Aristobulus' writings' in Moore 2018, 119–139.

Squillace, G. 2022. *Filippo II di Macedonia*. Rome.

Stadter, P. A. 1975. 'Arrianus, Flavius' in Kristeller et al. 1960, III, 1–20.

Stadter, P. A. 1980. *Arrian of Nicomedia*. Chapel Hill, NC.

Stadter, P. A. 2002. 'Introduction: setting Plutarch in his context' in Stadter and Van der Stockt 2002, 1–26.
Stadter, P. A. 2007. 'Biography and history' in Marincola 2007, 528–540.
Stadter, P. A. 2010. 'Parallels in three dimensions' in N. Humble ed. *Plutarch's Lives: Parallelism and Purpose.* Swansea. 197–216.
Stadter, P. A. 2014. 'Plutarch and Rome' in Beck 2014, 13–31.
Stadter, P. A., and L. van der Stockt eds. 2002. *Sage and Emperor: Plutarch, Greek Intellectuals and Roman Power in the Time of Trajan.* Leuven.
Steenkamp, J.-B. 2020. *Time to Lead: Lessons for Today's Leaders from Bold Decisions That Changed History.* Austin, TX.
Stephens, S. S. 2003. *Seeing Double: Intercultural Politics in Ptolemaic Alexandria.* London.
Stewart, A. 1993. *Faces of Power: Alexander's Image and Hellenistic Politics.* Berkeley.
Stewart, A. 2003. 'Alexander in Greek and Roman Art' in Roisman 2003a, 31–66.
Stibbe, C. M. 2003. *Trebenishte: The Fortunes of an Unusual Excavation.* Studia Archaeologica, Roma 121. Rome.
Stöcker, C. 1976. 'Der Trug der Olympias: ein Beitrag zur Erzählkunst antiker Novellistik' *Würzburger Jahrbücher für die Altertumswissenschaft* 2, 85–98.
Stoneman, R. 1991. *The Greek* Alexander Romance. London.
Stoneman, R. 1994a. 'The *Alexander Romance*: from history to fiction' in J. R. Morgan and R. Stoneman eds. *Greek Fiction: The Greek Novel in Context.* London. 117–129.
Stoneman, R. 1994b. 'Who are the Brahmans?' *Classical Quarterly* 44, 500–510.
Stoneman, R. 1995. 'Naked Philosophers' *Journal of Hellenic Studies* 115, 99–114.
Stoneman, R. 1997. *Alexander the Great.* London.
Stoneman, R. 2004. *Alexander the Great.* 2nd ed. London.
Stoneman, R. 2007–. *Il romanzo di Alessandro.* 3 vols. Milan.
Stoneman, R. 2008. *Alexander the Great: A Life in Legend.* New Haven.
Stoneman, R. 2009. 'The author of the *Alexander Romance*' in M. Paschalis, S. Panayotakis and G. Schmeling eds. *Readers and Writers in the Ancient Novel.* Groningen. 142–154.
Stoneman, R. 2012. *The Book of Alexander the Great: A Life of the Conqueror.* London.
Stoneman, R. 2015. *Xerxes: A Persian Life.* New Haven.
Stoneman, R. 2016. 'The origins of Quintus Curtius' concept of Fortuna' in Wulfram 2016a, 301–322.
Stoneman, R. 2018a. '*Alexander Romance*' in Oxford Research Encyclopedias (ORE). https://doi.org/10.1093/acrefore/9780199381135.013.8245.
Stoneman, R. 2018b. 'Introduction: on using literature for history' in Stoneman et al. 2018, vii–xv.
Stoneman, R. 2019. *The Greek Experience of India: From Alexander to the Indo-Greeks.* Princeton.
Stoneman, R. 2021a. 'Alexander and Dionysus' in F. Doroszewski and D. Karłowicz eds. *Dionysus and Politics: Constructing Authority in the Graeco-Roman World.* London. 46–59.
Stoneman, R. 2021b. *Megasthenes'* Indica: *A New Translation of the Fragments.* Abingdon.
Stoneman, R. ed. 2022a. *A History of Alexander the Great in World Culture.* Cambridge.
Stoneman, R. 2022b. 'Arrian's *Indica* in its second-century context' in Rollinger and Degen 2022, 95–110.
Stoneman, R. 2022c. 'Introduction' in Stoneman 2022a, 1–13.

Stoneman, R., K. Erickson and I. Netton eds. 2012. *The* Alexander Romance *in Persia and the East*. Groningen.
Stoneman, R., K. Nawotka and A. Wojciechowska eds. 2018. *The* Alexander Romance: *History and Literature*. Groningen.
Strauss, B. S. 2003. 'Alexander: the military campaign' in J. Roisman ed. *Brill's Companion to Alexander the Great*. Leiden. 133–158.
Strootman, R. 2012. 'Alexander's Thessalian cavalry' *Talanta* 42, 51–67.
Strootman, R. 2014. *Courts and Elites in the Hellenistic Empires: The Near East after the Achaemenids, c. 330 to 30 BCE*. Edinburgh.
Strootman, R. 2021. 'Women and dynasty at the Hellenistic imperial courts' in Carney and Müller 2021, 333–345.
Supplementum epigraphicum Graecum 1923–. Leiden.
Swain, S. 1989. 'Plutarch: chance, providence and history' *American Journal of Philology* 110, 272–302.
Swire, O. 1951. *Skye: The Island and Its Legends*. London.
Tarn, W. W. 1919. *The Treasure of the Isle of Mist*. London.
Tarn, W. W. 1927. 'Alexander: the conquest of Persia' *Cambridge Ancient History* VI, 352–386.
Tarn, W. W. 1933. 'Alexander the Great and the unity of mankind' *Proceedings of the British Academy* 19, 1–46.
Tarn, W. W. 1948. *Alexander the Great*. 2 vols. Cambridge.
Tarn, W. W. 1951. *The Greeks in Bactria and India*. 2nd ed. Cambridge.
Taylor, L. R. 1931. *The Divinity of the Roman Emperor*. Middletown, CT.
Taylor, M. 2015. 'Ozymandias the dreamer: *Watchmen* and Alexander the Great' in G. Kovacs and C. W. Marshall eds. *Son of Classics and Comics*. Oxford. 201–214.
Thapar, R. 2002. *Early India: From the Origins to AD 1300*. London.
Theodossiev, N. 1998. 'The dead with golden faces: Dasaretian, Pelagonian, Mygdonian and Boeotian funeral masks' *Oxford Journal of Archaeology* 17, 345–367.
Theodossiev, N. 2000. 'The dead with golden faces II: other evidence and connections' *Oxford Journal of Archaeology* 19, 175–210.
Thomas, C. 2008. 'Centering the periphery' in Howe and Reames 2008, 1–16.
Thomas, C. 2010. 'The physical kingdom' in Roisman and Worthington 2010, 65–80.
Thomas, C. G. 1968. 'Alexander the Great and the unity of mankind' *Classical Journal* 63, 258–260.
Thomas, C. G. 1974. 'Alexander's garrisons: a clue to his administrative plans?' *Antichthon* 8, 11–20.
Thomas, K. R. 1995. 'A psychoanalytic study of Alexander the Great' *Psychoanalysis Review* 82, 859–901.
Thomas, P. H. 1966. *Epitoma rerum gestarum Alexandri Magni*. Leipzig.
Thompson, D. J. 2022. 'Alexander and Alexandria in life and legend' in Stoneman 2022a, 14–41.
Thonemann, P. 2012. 'Alexander, Priene and Naulochon' in P. Martzavou and N. Papazarkadas eds. *Epigraphical Approaches to the Post-classical Polis: Fourth Century BC to Second Century AD*. Oxford. 23–36.
Thurn, N. 2016. 'Imitation als Indikator für Lesegewohnheiten: Curtius Rufus und Juan Ginés de Supúlvedas *De rebus Hispanorum gestis ad Novum Orbem Mexicumque*' in Wulfram 2016a, 411–420.

Tiverios, M. A. 1998. 'The ancient settlement in the Anchialos-Sindos double trapeza: seven years (1990–1996) of archaeological research' in B. D'Agostino and M. Bats eds. *L'Eubea e la presenza euboica in Calcidica e in Occidente*. Naples. 243–253.
Todd, R. A. 1964. 'W. W. Tarn and the Alexander ideal' *The Historian* 27, 48–55.
Tomlinson, R. A. 1970. 'Ancient Macedonian symposia' *Ancient Macedonia* 1, 308–315.
Tonnet, H. 1988. *Recherches sur Arrien: Sa personnalité et ses écrits atticistes*. Amsterdam.
Touratsoglou, I. 2008. 'Tarsos, Aboukir, etc.: before and after, once again' *American Journal of Numismatics* 20, 479–492.
Touratsoglou, I. 2010. *A Contribution to the Economic History of the Kingdom of Ancient Macedonia (6th–3rd Century BC)*. Athens.
Trinquier, J. 2014. 'Alexandre au miroir des rois indiens: le développement du livre VIII des *Histoires d'Alexandre* consacré aux souverains de l'Inde' in Mahé-Simon and Trinquier 2014, 211–264.
Tritle, L. A. 2003. 'Alexander and the killing of Cleitus the Black' in Heckel and Tritle 2003, 127–146.
Trnka-Amrhein, Y. 2018. 'The fantastic four: Alexander, Sesonchosis, Ninus and Semiramis' in Stoneman et al. 2018, 23–48.
Trnka-Amrhein, Y. 2020. 'Interpreting Sesonchosis as a biographical novel' *Classical Philology* 115, 70–94.
Trofimova, A. A. 2012. *Imitatio Alexandri in Hellenistic Art: Portraits of Alexander the Great and Mythological Images*. Rome.
Trumpf, J. 2006. '*Pap. Berl.* 21266: ein Beleg für die historische Quelle des griechischen Alexanderromans?' *Zeitschrift für Papyrologie und Epigraphik* 155, 85–90.
Tsigarida, E. B. 2011. 'The sanctuary of Zeus Ammon at Kallithea (Chalcidice)' *Kernos* 24, 165–181.
Tsigarida, E. B., and D. Ignatiadou 2000. *The Gold of Macedon: Exhibition Guide*. Thessaloniki.
Tsitsiridis, S. 2013. *Beiträge zu den Fragmenten des Klearchos von Soloi*. Untersuchungen zur antiken Literatur und Geschichte 107. Berlin.
Tzifopoulos, Y. 2010. *'Paradise' Earned: The Bacchic-Orphic Gold Lamellae of Crete*. Washington, DC.
Tzifopoulos, Y., M. Bessios and A. Kotsonas 2017. 'Panhellenes at Methone, Pieria (*ca.* 700 BCE): new inscriptions, graffiti, dipinti and (trade)marks' in C. Morgan and X. Charalambidou eds. *Interpreting the Seventh Century BC: Tradition and Innovation*. Athens. 364–374.
Van Creveld, M. 1982. *Fighting Power: German and US Army Performance, 1939–45*. Westport, CT.
Van Creveld, M. 1991. *The Transformation of War*. New York.
Van Creveld, M. 2007. 'It will continue to spread and it will conquer' in A. Karp, R. Karp and T. Terriff eds. *Global Insurgency and the Future of Armed Conflict*. London. 58–69.
Van der Spek, R. J. 2003. 'Darius III, Alexander the Great and Babylonian scholarship' in W. Henkelman and A. Kuhrt eds. *A Persian Perspective: Essays in Memory of Heleen Sancisi-Weerdenberg*. Achaemenid History XIII. Leiden. 289–346.
Van der Spek, R. J. 2006. 'How to measure prosperity? The case of Hellenistic Babylonia' in R. Descat ed. *Approches de l'économie hellénistique*. Paris. 287–310.
Van Hoof, L. 2010. *Plutarch's Practical Ethics: The Social Dynamics of Philosophy*. Oxford.

Van Oppen de Ruiter, B. F. 2020. 'Amastris: the first Hellenistic queen' *Historia* 69, 17–37.
Van Thiel, H. 1974. *Leben und Taten Alexanders von Makedonien: Der griechische Alexanderroman nach der Handschrift L*. Darmstadt.
Van Wees, H. 2004. *Greek Warfare: Myths and Realities*. London.
Vasilev, M. I. 2011. 'Thucydides II. 99 and the early expansion of the Argeadae' *Eirene* 47, 93–105.
Vasilev, M. I. 2012. 'Herodotus VIII 137–139 and the foundation of Argead Macedonia' *Ziva Antika* 62, 37–47.
Vasilev, M. I. 2015. *The Policy of Darius and Xerxes towards Thrace and Macedonia*. Leiden and Boston.
Vasilev, M. I. 2016. 'The date of Herodotus' visit to Macedonia' *Ancient West and East* 15, 31–51.
Verdejo Manchado, J., and B. Antela-Bernárdez 2021. '*IG* II^2 1623, 276–285: Athens versus pirates: between recovery, need and patriotism' *Klio* 103, 42–58.
Visscher, M. S. 2020. *Beyond Alexandria: Literature and Empire in the Seleucid World*. Oxford.
Vogelsang, W. J. 1990. 'The Achaemenids and India' in H. Kuhrt and A. Kuhrt eds. *Achaemenid History* 4. Leiden. 93–110.
Völcker-Janssen, W. 1993. *Kunst und Gesellschaft an den Höfen Alexanders d. Gr. und seiner Nachfolger*. Munich.
Von den Hoff, R. 1997. 'Der Alexander Rondanini: Mythischer Heros oder heroischer Herrscher?' *Münchner Jahrbuch der Bildenden Kunst* 48, 7–28.
Von Graeve, V. 1970. *Der Alexandersarkophag und seine Werkstatt*. Berlin.
Von Reden, S., and R. Strootman 2022. 'Imperial *metropoleis* and foundation myths: Ptolemaic and Seleucid capitals compared' in C. Fischer-Bovet and S. von Reden eds. *Comparing the Ptolemaic and Seleucid Empires*. Cambridge. 17–47.
Waley, A. 1952. *The Real Tripitaka*. London.
Wallace, S. 2018a. 'Communication and legitimation: knowledge of Alexander's Asian campaign in the Greek world' in K. Trampedach and A. Meeus eds. *The Legitimation of Conquest*. Stuttgart. 123–144
Wallace, S. 2018b. '*Metalexandron*: receptions of Alexander in the Hellenistic and Roman Worlds' in Moore 2018, 162–196..
Wallace, S. 2020. 'Communication and legitimation: knowledge of Alexander's Asian campaign in the Greek world' in K. Trampedach and A. Meeus eds. *The Legitimation of Conquest*. Stuttgart. 123–144.
Wallach, L. 1947. 'Yosippon and the *Alexander Romance*' *The Jewish Quarterly Review* 37, 407–422.
Walsh, J. 2012. 'Antipater and early Hellenistic literature' *Ancient History Bulletin* 26, 149–62.
Walsh, J., and E. J. Baynham eds. 2021. *Alexander the Great and Propaganda*. London.
Walton, F. R., ed. and trans. 1957. *Diodorus Siculus* XI: *Books xxi–xxxii*. Loeb Classical Library Cambridge, MA.
Wardman, A. E. 1955. 'Plutarch and Alexander' *Classical Quarterly* 5, 96–107.
Warren, J. 2018. 'Avoid nation building in Afghanistan: an absent insight from Alexander' in Moore 2018. 739–753.
Waterfield, R. trans. 2008. *Plutarch: Greek Lives*. Oxford.

Waterfield, R. 2011. *Dividing the Spoils: The War for Alexander the Great's Empire*. Oxford.
Weber, G. 2009. 'The court of Alexander as a social system' in Heckel and Tritle 2009, 83–98.
Weippert. O. 1972. Alexander-*Imitatio* und Römische Politik in Republikanischer Zeit. Diss., Augsburg.
Welch, K., and H. Mitchell 2013. 'Revisiting the Roman Alexander' *Antichthon* 47, 80–100.
Welles, C. B. 1951. Review of Schachermeyr 1949, *American Journal of Archaeology* 55, 433–436.
Welles, C. B. 1962. 'The discovery of Sarapis and the foundation of Alexandria' *Historia* 11, 271–298.
Welles, C. B., trans. 1963. *Diodorus Siculus* VIII. Loeb Classical Library. Cambridge, MA.
Wheatley, P., and E. J. Baynham eds. 2015. *East and West in the World Empire of Alexander*. Oxford.
Wheatley, P., and C. Dunn. 2020. *Demetrius the Besieger*. Oxford.
Wheatley, P., and C. Dunn 2021. 'Coinage as propaganda: Alexander and his Successors' in Walsh and Baynham 2021, 162–198.
Wheatley, P., and R. Hannah eds. 2009. *Alexander and his Successors: Essays from the Antipodes*. Claremont.
Wheatley, P., and W. Heckel 2011. 'Commentary' in *Justin: Epitome of the Philippic History of Pompeius Trogus* II: *Books 13–15: The Successors to Alexander the Great*. Oxford. 43–309.
Wheeler, E. 2012. 'The general's métier: the lists of "Great Captains" and criteria for selection' in C. Wolff ed. *Le Métier de soldat dans le monde romain: Actes du cinquième congrès de Lyon, 23–25 septembre 2010*. Collection du Centre d'études romaines et gallo-romaines 42. Paris. 417–449.
Whitby, M. 2011. 'Onesikritos (134)' *BNJ*.
Whitby, M. 2012. 'Nearchos (133)' *BNJ*.
Whitmarsh, T. 2002. 'Alexander's hellenism and Plutarch's textualism' *Classical Quarterly* 52, 174–192.
Whitmarsh, T. 2004. Review of Stadter and van der Stockt 2002, *Bryn Mawr Classical Review* 04.32.
Whitmarsh, T. 2005. *The Second Sophistic*. Oxford.
Whitmarsh, T. 2018. *Dirty Love: The Genealogy of the Ancient Greek Novel*. Oxford.
Wieland, C. M. 1796. 'Der *Panegyrikos* des Isokrates: Anmerkungen' *Attisches Museum* 1.1, 71–110.
Wiemer, H.-U. 2011. 'Held, Gott oder Tyrann? Alexander der Grosse im frühen Hellenismus' *Hermes* 139, 179–204.
Wiesehöfer, J. 1993. *Das antike Persien von 550 v. Chr. bis 650 n. Chr*. Zurich.
Wiesehöfer, J. 2001. *Ancient Persia: From 550 BC to 650 AD*. London. Trans. of Wiesehöfer 1993.
Wiesehöfer, J. 2011. 'The "accursed" and the "adventurer": Alexander the Great in Iranian tradition' in Z. D. Zuwiyya ed. *A Companion to Alexander Literature in the Middle Ages*. Leiden. 113–132.
Wiesehöfer, J. 2021. 'The Achaemenid empire: realm of tyranny or founder of human rights?' in B. Jacobs and R. Rollinger eds. *A Companion to the Achaemenid Persian Empire* II. Oxford. 1649–1669.
Wilcken, U. 1931. *Alexander der Grosse*. Leipzig. Trans. as *Alexander the Great*. London, 1932.

Willekes, C. 2015. 'Equine aspects of Alexander the Great's Macedonian cavalry' in T. Howe, E. E. Garvin and G. Wrightson eds. *Greece, Macedon and Persia: Studies in Social, Political and Military History in Honour of Waldemar Heckel*. Oxford. 47–58.

Williams, D. 2009. *Masterpieces of Classical Art*. Austin.

Williams, M. F. 2016. 'Patrokles (712)' *BNJ*.

Winiarczyk, M. 2007. 'Das Werk *Die Erziehung Alexanders* des Onesikritos von Astypalaia (*FGrHist* 134 F 1–39)' *Eos* 94, 197–250.

Winiarczyk, M. 2011. *Die hellenistischen Utopien*. Berlin.

Wirth, G. 1976. 'Alexander und Rom' in O. Reverdin ed. *Alexandre le Grand: Image et réalité*. Genève. 181–210.

Wirth, G. 1988. 'Nearch, Alexander und die Diadochen' *Tyche* 3, 241–259.

Wirth, G. 1993a. *Der Brand von Persepolis: Folgerungen zur Geschichte Alexanders des Großen*. Amsterdam.

Wirth, G. 1993b. *Der Weg in die Vergessenheit: Zum Schicksal des antiken Alexanderbildes*. Vienna.

Wirth, G. 2020. 'Philip II' in Heckel et al. 2020, 415–420.

Wiseman, T. P. 1998. 'The publication of *De bello Gallico*' in K. Welch and A. Powell eds. *Julius Caesar as Artful Reporter: The War Commentaries as Political Instruments*. London. 1–9.

Wojciechowska, A., and K. Nawotka 2014. 'Alexander in Egypt: chronology' in Grieb et al. 2014, 49–54.

Wolohojian, A. M. trans. 1969. *The Romance of Alexander the Great by Pseudo-Callisthenes: Translated from the Armenian Version*. New York.

Woodcock, G. 1966. *The Greeks in India*. London.

Worthington, I. 1999. 'How "great" was Alexander?' *Ancient History Bulletin* 13, 39–55.

Worthington, I. 2003. 'Alexander, Philip and the Macedonian background' in Roisman 2003a, 69–98.

Worthington, I. 2004. *Alexander the Great: Man and God*. London.

Worthington, I. ed. 2007–. *Brill's New Jacoby*. Leiden. (Online resource.)

Worthington, I. 2008a. '*IG* II² 236 and Philip's Common Peace of 337' in L. G Mitchell and L. Rubinstein eds. *Greek History and Epigraphy: Essays in Honour of P. J. Rhodes*. Swansea. 213–223.

Worthington, I. 2008b. *Philip II of Macedonia*. New Haven, CT.

Worthington, I. 2010. 'Worldwide empire versus glorious enterprise: Diodorus and Justin and Alexander the Great' in Carney and Ogden 2010. 165–174.

Worthington, I. 2014. *By the Spear: Philip II, Alexander the Great and the Rise and Fall of the Macedonian Empire*. Oxford and New York.

Worthington, I. 2015. 'From east to west: Alexander and the Exiles Decree' in Wheatley and Baynham 2015, 93–108.

Worthington, I. 2016a. 'Ptolemy I as Soter: the silence of epigraphy and the case for Egypt' *Zeitschrift für Papyrologie und Epigraphik* 198, 128–130.

Worthington, I. 2016b. *Ptolemy I, King and Pharaoh of Egypt*. Oxford.

Wrightson, G. 2010. 'The nature of command in the Macedonian *sarissa* phalanx' *Ancient History Bulletin* 24, 73–94.

Wrightson, G. 2019. *Combined Arms Warfare in Ancient Greece: From Homer to Alexander the Great and His Successors*. New York.

Wulfram, H. ed. 2016a. *Der römische Alexanderhistoriker Curtius Rufus*. Vienna.

Wulfram, H. 2016b. 'Einleitung' in Wulfram 2016a, 7–12.

Wüst, F. R. 1953. 'Die Rede Alexanders des Grossen in Opis, Arrian VII, 9–10' *Historia* 2, 177–188.
Xydopoulos, I. K. 2012a. 'Anthemus and Hippias: the policy of Amyntas I' *Illinois Classical Studies* 37, 21–37.
Xydopoulos, I. K. 2012b. 'Upper Macedonia' in M. Tiverios, P. Nigdelis and P. Adam-Veleni eds. *Threpteria: Studies on Ancient Macedonia*. Thessaloniki. 520–539.
Xydopoulos, I. K. 2017. 'Macedonians in Bottiaia: "warriors" and identities in Late Iron Age and Archaic Macedonia' in I. K. Xydopoulos, K. Vlassopoulos and E. Tounta eds. *Violence and Community: Law, Space and Identity in the Ancient Eastern Mediterranean World*. London.
Yakoubovitch, I. 2014. 'Echos, diptyques et effets de bouclage: la construction du portrait d'Alexandre chez Quinte-Curce' in Mahé-Simon and Trinquier 2014a, 125–138.
Yardley, J.C., and W. Heckel 1984. *Quintus Curtius Rufus: The History of Alexander*. Harmondsworth.
Yardley, J. C., and W. Heckel eds and trans. 1997. *Justin: Epitome of the Philippic History of Pompeius Trogus* I: *Books 11–12: Alexander the Great*. Oxford.
Yates, D. 2019. *States of Memory: The Polis, Panhellenism, and the Persian War*. Oxford.
Zahrnt, M. 1984. 'Die Entwicklung des makedonishen Reiches bis zu den Perserkriegen' *Chiron* 14, 325–368.
Zahrnt, M. 1996. 'Alexanders Übergang über den Hellespont' *Chiron* 26, 129–147.
Zahrnt, M. 2016. 'Von Siwa bis Babylon: Alexanders Weg vom Gottessohn zum Gott' in Binder, Börm and Luther 2016, 303–323.
Zambrini, A. 2007. 'The historians of Alexander the Great' in Marincola 2007, 210–220.
Zambrini, A. 2013. 'Néarque, un ami fidèle à Alexandre jusqu'à la fin?' *Geographia Antiqua* 22, 35–41.
Zecchini, G. 1989. *La cultura storica di Ateneo*. Milan.
Zerefos, C. S., and M. V. Voardinoyannis eds. 2018. *Hellenistic Alexandria: Celebrating 24 Centuries*. Oxford.
Ziegler, K. ed. 1968. *Plutarch: Vitae parallelae* II.2. Leipzig.
Ziegler, R. 2014. 'Alexander der Große als Städtegründer: Fiktion und Realität' in U. Peter ed. *Stephanos nomismatikos: Edith Schönert-Geiss zum 65*. Berlin. 679–698.
Zumpt, C. G. Q. 1849. *Curtii Rufi De gestis Alexandri Magni*, Edinburgh.
Zuwiyya, D. ed. 2011. *A Companion to Alexander Literature in the Middle Ages*. Leiden.

INDEX

Abdalonymus of Sidon, 11, 328, 403, 506, 519
Abisares, 115, 290, 521
Abulites, 303, 310, 313
Acesines, 72, 74, 115–116, 118, 298
Achilles, 32, 37, 69, 75, 167, 327, 362, 449, 509, 519
Ada, 301, 309, 371, 519
Adea Eurydice, 219–220
administration, 290–316
Aeacides, 219
Aegae, 49–50, 140, 149, 153, 166, 168, 172, 180, 186, 193–194, 196, 213, 227, 425, 495, 502–503
aemulatio (Alexandri), 440, 444, 447, 449–450
Aeschines, 33, 460, 518
Aetion, 501
Agalasseis, 118
Agathos Daimon, 427
Agis III of Sparta, 61, 108, 371
Agrianes, 247, 252
Ai Khanum, 126
Aiane, 163, 194
Alexander Aegiochus, 513
Alexander Ceraunophoros, 513
Alexander I, 39, 97, 152, 154–155, 169, 176, 182, 200, 212, 244
Alexander II, 157, 159, 175, 182
Alexander IV, 142, 219, 224
Alexander of Epirus, 49, 159, 215, 217, 518
Alexander of Lyncestis, 49–52, 201
Alexander Romance, 68, 87, 133, 241, 426, 434, 452–474, 476, 480, 482–483, 486–488, 507, 509
Alexanderland, 9–10

Alexandria, 69, 74, 82, 86–90, 92, 94–96, 140–143, 237, 239, 281, 315, 318, 357, 367, 383, 393–394, 396–399, 403, 406, 426–428, 434–437, 443, 449, 453, 459, 462–463, 465, 480–481, 488, 503, 513, 516, 520, 522
Alexandria Eschate, 322
Alexandropolis, 12, 32, 38, 69, 518
Amastris, 106, 223–224
Amazons, 68, 373–374, 395–396, 398, 462
Amminapes, 304, 310
Ammon, 30, 78, 82, 89–91, 93–95, 104, 117, 140, 151, 233, 237–239, 241–242, 319, 359, 373, 386, 403, 433–434, 445, 459–460, 465, 484, 505, 513, 520
Ammonius, 349
Amphictyony, 160, 229
Amphipolis, 161, 182, 199, 226, 281, 287, 519
Amyntas I, 39, 97, 152–154
Amyntas III, 32, 157, 159, 170, 175, 177, 244, 495–496
Amyntas, satrap of Bactria, 305
Amyntas, son of Perdiccas III, 48, 51, 200, 518
anastolē, 490–491
Andromachus, 302
Androsthenes of Thasos, 327
Anthela, 229
Antigonus I Monophthalmus, 142, 300–301, 415, 461
Antioch, 434, 436–437
Antiochus III, 433, 446
Antiochus IV, 477
Antipater, 33, 38, 40, 50, 52, 55, 62, 129, 136, 140, 157, 163, 183, 200–201, 214,

218–220, 224, 279, 291, 359, 371, 429, 433, 462, 519, 522
Aornus, 114, 118, 382, 521
Apama, 106, 223–224
Apamea, 434
Apelles, 65, 69, 232, 447, 500–501, 504, 513
Aphytis, 91
Apis bull, 84–85
Apollo, 432–433, 505, 516
Apollophanes, 305, 313
Arachosia, 109, 125–126, 292, 296, 298, 304–305, 311, 520
Arcesilaus, 303, 313
Archelaus, 151, 156, 159, 169, 173, 177, 182, 199, 212, 237
Archon, 303
Archontiko, 193–194, 196
Areia, 292, 296, 304, 310, 312
argyraspides, 182
Arimmas, 302
Ariobarzanes, 520
Aristander of Telmessus, 227
Aristobulus, 72–73, 334, 358–360, 367, 369, 379–380, 385–391, 403, 406, 413
Aristotle, 32–33, 48, 50, 65, 70, 111, 207, 320–322, 325–326, 359–360, 408, 411–412, 462, 484, 491, 518
Armenia, 292, 295, 299, 302, 310, 456, 460
army, 151 and *passim*
Arnobius of Sicca, 484
Arrhabaeus, 50, 151, 156–157, 199–200, 518
Arrhidaeus, escort of Alexander's body, 140–141, 425
Arrian, 347–347 and *passim*
Arsaces, 304, 310, 312
Arsames, 304, 310
art, 517
Artabazus, 305, 307, 311
Artaxerxes III Ochus, 84, 95, 98, 106, 222–223, 522
Arthur, King, 259
Asander, 301, 308
Asclepiodorus, 302, 308
Asclepius, 30, 38
Assos, 325

Astaspes, 303, 313
Atheas, 39
Athens, Athenians, 29, 33, 39–40, 42, 55–56, 58–63, 67, 70, 97, 100, 103, 149, 151, 155–156, 161–162, 169, 193, 198, 202, 214–215, 218, 230–232, 240, 243–244, 273, 279, 398, 413, 449, 459, 495
Atropates, 303, 310, 314
Attalus, 43–45, 50, 98, 217, 359, 518
Audata, 157–158, 215
Autophradates, 304, 310
Axios, 147, 149, 152, 155, 162
Azara herm, 491, 493, 497, 500

Babylon, Babylonia, 9, 32, 63, 69, 73, 76, 78, 95, 101, 104, 106, 129–131, 134–135, 138–141, 219, 223–224, 227, 233–235, 256, 258, 266, 273, 279, 281, 283–284, 295, 297, 300, 302, 307–308, 310, 313, 324, 356–358, 382, 396, 398, 412, 425, 429, 434, 462, 478, 520, 522
Bactria, 101, 104–105, 113, 196, 200, 203, 205, 208, 223, 296, 305, 307, 311, 376, 382, 521
Badian, 3, 5–8, 10, 211
Baeton, 319
Bagoas, 10, 36, 372–374
Bahariya, 30, 104, 233, 239
Balacrus, 302, 308, 314
Bardylis, 157, 244
Barsine, 135, 221, 223–224
Bebrycia, 459
Bellerophon, 35
bematists, 319, 321
Bermion, 147, 149
Bernadotte, 265
Beroea, 194, 445, 507
Berve, 3–4
Bessus, 75, 101, 104–105, 107, 185, 339, 381, 385–386, 460, 520
birth, birth myth, 30
Bisaltia, 154, 198
Bossuet, 264
Bosworth, 8
Bottiaea, 149, 152, 194, 199
Brahmans, 114, 120, 123, 125, 418
Brasidas, 156, 162

Brunt, 8
Bubares, 97, 154, 182, 198
Bucephala, 33, 69, 74, 521
Bucephalas, 33–35, 273, 326, 356, 372, 436, 458, 461, 488, 518, 521
Buddha, 124
Byblos, 519
Byzantium, 98

Caesar, Julius, 142, 256, 258–259, 261, 264–265, 272, 319, 355, 361, 368, 402, 450
Calanus, 122–125, 128–129, 342–344, 358, 413, 418
Calas, 300–301
Callisthenes of Olynthus, 32, 65, 69, 82, 90–91, 105, 174, 180, 185, 206–207, 211, 240, 326, 334, 359, 367, 385, 387–388, 403, 406–411, 416, 456, 513, 521 see also *Alexander Romance*
Callixeina, 36
Cambyses, 84, 91–92, 94, 238
Candace, 428, 461
Candragupta, 115, 125
Cappadocia, 22, 34, 292, 294, 299, 302, 309, 443
Caracalla, 143, 445, 447, 509
Caranus, Argead founder, 168, 177
Caranus, son of Philip, 45, 53
Caria, Carians, 47, 103, 198, 217, 221, 294, 301, 309, 371, 373, 406, 518–519
Carmania, 36, 237, 295, 303, 310, 313, 358–359, 414, 521
Carthage, 88, 136, 522
Caspian, 323
Cassander, 129, 132–133, 219–220, 224, 387, 462, 502
Cassandreia, 387
cavalry, 102, 104, 118–119, 136, 139, 141, 156, 159–160, 165, 172, 183–184, 199, 216, 243–248, 250–252, 254–255, 261–262, 264, 276, 350, 381, 493, 497, 519
Chaeronea, 39–40, 42, 45, 53, 55–57, 61, 67, 160, 183, 199, 216, 245, 248, 255, 349–350, 410, 493, 495–496, 511, 518
Chaldaeans, 131, 228
Chares of Mytilene, 99, 180, 202, 207, 359, 367, 406, 411–413, 416, 420

Charlemagne, 259
Charles XII of Sweden, 264
Chateaubriand, 266–267
Choaspes, 114
Chorasmia, 324
Chorienes, 521
Christianity, 2, 9, 257, 471–485, 487
Cilicia, 103, 136, 251, 282, 291, 295, 302, 307–308, 443, 519
Clausewitz, 256–257, 267–268, 270
Clement of Alexandria, 484
Cleomenes of Naucratis, 94, 302, 314
Cleopatra, daughter of Philip, 49, 140, 214–216, 218–219, 518
Cleopatra, niece of Attalus, 45, 47, 50, 53, 217, 458, 518
Cleophis, 374
Clitarchus, 11, 21, 89–90, 359, 367, 369, 376, 384, 392–406, 428
Clitus the Black, 30–31, 105, 158, 184–185, 205–206, 211, 258, 300, 305, 357, 377, 383–384, 387, 410–411, 468, 521
Clitus the White, 211
Coenus, 303, 313, 323
Coeranus, 291
coinage, 170, 273–289, 442–446, 509
Companions, 78, 165–166, 171–173, 175, 179–191, 198–202, 205, 243, 246, 248–249, 381, 522
conspiracies, 212
Constantine, 485
Córdoba, 261
Cossaeans, 296, 358, 522
Court, 179–225
Craterus, 46, 115, 117–118, 132, 136–137, 139, 151, 183, 187, 205, 208, 211, 219, 223–224, 262, 357, 359, 362, 382, 507, 511, 521
Crestonia, 154
Curtius, 364–378 and *passim*
Cydnus, 460, 519
Cynnane, 157, 215, 220
Cyrene, 88–89, 92–93, 104, 218, 238–239, 318, 393
Cyrus, 339, 522

Damascus, 519
Dandamis, 121–122, 124, 342–343, 358

Daphne, 435
Darius I, 339, 481
Darius III, 48, 62, 84–85, 92, 94–95, 98, 100–106, 184, 201–202, 221, 223, 251–253, 255, 258, 260, 269, 278, 299, 310, 339–340, 371–373, 381, 403, 409, 434, 459–460, 462, 468, 490, 502, 519, 522
Davidson, 8, 10–11
death, 129–135, 138–143
Delos, 281
Delphi, 149, 188, 218, 228–229, 240, 281, 319, 357, 458–459, 507
Demades, 60, 460
Demaratus of Corinth, 518
Demarchus, 301
Demetrius Poliorcetes, 425
Demosthenes, 33, 55, 59, 103, 186, 460, 518
Derdas of Elimeia, 151, 158
Derriopus, 151–152
Didyma, 231, 433
Dimnus, 105, 203, 205, 520
Diodorus, 20, 48–50, 52, 403
Diogenes, 65, 320, 341, 352, 357, 419
Diognetus, 319
Diomede, 35
Dion, 149, 172, 186, 194, 198, 227, 281, 408, 497
Dionysius of Messene, 130
Dionysus, 36, 91, 114, 119, 168, 235, 237, 324, 362, 505, 515–516
Dodona, 281
Doloaspis, 94, 314
Drangiana, 292, 296, 298, 304, 310, 521
Dresden Alexander, 500
Droysen, 2, 4–5, 9, 56, 65, 211
Drypetis, 221–223
Duris of Samos, 402
Dysoron, 153, 155

Ecbatana, 38, 106, 204, 276, 409, 520–522
edeatros, 186
education, 30–33
Egypt, Egyptians, 72, 76–77, 82–96, 102, 104, 135–137, 140–142, 149, 227–228, 233–235, 238–239, 241–242, 258, 265–266, 269, 272, 281, 295, 300, 302, 308, 314, 353, 356, 380, 382–384, 386, 390, 393, 403, 415, 425–426, 443, 457, 459, 462, 465, 467, 481, 486, 502, 513, 520
Elagabalus, 445
elephants, 112, 232, 239, 325–326, 504, 506, 515
Elimeia, 151, 156, 158–159, 163, 194, 199
emperors, Roman, 438–451
Eordaea, 151–152, 157, 199
Epaminondas, 160, 261, 267
Ephemerides, 131, 227, 360, 406, 415, 419–420
Ephesus, 230–232, 281, 500
Ephorus, 321, 399
Epictetus, 345
Epigoni, 2, 77–80, 209–211, 522
Eratosthenes, 318–319, 359–360, 394, 399
Erbach Alexander, 500
Eudoxus, 321
Eugnostus, 314
Eumenes of Cardia, 131, 223, 406, 419
Euphorion, 433
Euphranor, 493, 495
Euphrates, 103, 135, 287, 429, 433, 462
Euripides, 172, 177
Eurydice, mother of Philip, 214–216, 495–496
Eusebius, 476, 478–479, 485
Exiles Decree, 62

Ferdinand of Aragon, 261
finance, 273–289
Frederick the Great, 264–265
Fuller, 269–270

Gandhara, 113, 116, 297, 298, 305
Ganges, 70, 114, 116–117, 321, 323, 358, 521
Gaugamela, 75–76, 101, 104, 106, 151, 156, 160, 201, 246, 248, 252, 266, 269, 299, 307, 309–311, 336, 338, 356–357, 409, 502, 520
Gaza, 31, 83, 415, 519
Gedrosia, 109, 125, 292, 296, 298, 304–305, 312–313, 345, 521
Genghis Khan, 70
geography, 317–329
Getty Alexander, 495

Godolphin, 263, 267
Gog and Magog, 453, 481–482
Gordian Knot, 389, 483, 519
Granicus, 61, 102, 156, 160, 206, 230–231, 246, 249, 252, 280, 357, 371, 408, 448, 497, 519
Gryneum, 63
Gustavus Adolphus, 265
Gygaea, 97, 154, 198
Gymnosophists, 121–125, 341, 393, 396, 461, 487
gynnis, 33, 38

Haliacmon, 147, 149–150
Halicarnassus, 103, 371, 519
hamippoi, 183, 246–247, 250
Hannibal, 265, 448
Harmatelia, 120, 123, 427, 436–437
Harpalus, 47, 60, 63, 328, 371, 396, 518, 522
Heckel, 3–4
Hector, 259
Hegel, 2
Heliodorus, 127
Hellespont, 98, 102, 162, 228, 244–245, 410, 519
Hephaestion, 37, 74, 113–114, 118, 121, 129, 134, 136, 180, 222–223, 328, 357–358, 362, 371–373, 375, 382, 411, 490, 501, 507, 521
Heracles, hero, 35, 90–91, 117–118, 149, 167, 171, 235–238, 240, 258, 267, 285, 352, 362, 402, 409, 430, 433, 441, 459, 481, 503, 505, 515–516. *See also* Pillars of Hercules
Heracles, son of Alexander, 135, 221, 224
Herculaneum, 492, 497
Hermias of Atarneus, 32, 320
Hermippus, 359
Hermolaus, 105, 174, 185, 187, 206–208, 211, 263, 375, 521
Herodotus, 167
Heromenes, 50, 200, 518
hetairoi. *See* Companions
Hindu Kush, 113, 322, 377, 520
Hippocrates, 327
Hitler, 6, 256, 259, 269–270, 272
Holcias, 132–133, 462

House of the Faun, 502
Hydaspes, 33, 73–74, 115, 118, 125, 246, 298, 369, 390, 406, 414, 521–521
Hyderabad, 121
hypaspists, 182–184, 188, 246, 249–250, 252–254
Hyphasis, 70–71, 73–74, 77–78, 105, 113, 116–117, 209, 228, 323, 521
Hyrcania, 184, 202, 296, 298, 304, 307, 310, 312, 314, 394, 396, 400, 520

Iasus, 64
Illyria, Illyrians, 43, 47, 149, 152, 155–159, 161, 163, 175, 183, 199, 215, 217, 244, 518
imitatio Alexandri, 349, 360–361, 375, 438–441, 443, 446–447, 450–451, 506
India, 77, 91, 105, 111–128, 258, 290, 460, 504, 521–521
India I (satrapy), 297, 298
India II (satrapy), 297, 298
India III (satrapy), 297–298
Indo-Greeks, 126–128
Indus, 70, 72–74, 105, 109, 111, 113–114, 116–118, 120, 125, 128, 228, 231–232, 237, 271, 297, 298, 305–306, 321, 323, 326, 414, 521–521
Iolaus (Iollas), son of Antipater, 132–133, 462
Iolaus, father of Antipater (?), 183
Iphicrates, 214
Ipsus, 4, 387, 390
Isocrates, 57, 67
Issus, 32, 34, 85, 103–104, 156, 160, 201, 221, 246, 251, 253–254, 269, 299, 310, 357, 371, 375, 396, 412, 444, 450, 502, 519
Isthmia, 228–229

Jacoby, 4, 21
Jaddus, 474
Jalalabad, 114
Jaxartes, 74, 228, 321
Jeremiah, 480
Jerome, 478
Jerusalem, 259, 327, 474, 476, 478, 480, 519
Jesus, 3, 5, 9, 258, 481
John Moschus, 480

Josephus, 474, 476, 480, 483, 486
Judaism, 2, 9, 259, 471–487
Judas Maccabee, 271
Julian, 257–259, 264, 267
Julius Valerius, 455, 457
Justin, 20–21, 49

kardakes, 251
Karnak, 233
Kazia, 483
Khyber Pass, 113
kingship, 165–178

Lactantius, 480
Lagus, 429
Lampsacus, 284
Lane Fox, 7
Lanice, 30–31, 41, 214
Laodice, mother of Seleucus, 432–433
Laodicea, 434
Last plans, 136–138
League of Corinth, 43, 53, 55–59, 61–64, 66–67, 98, 160, 229, 247, 290, 518
Leochares, 495–496
Leonnatus, 152, 211, 381
Libya, 117, 136, 314, 323, 459
Liddell-Hart, 269
Louis XIV, 263
Luther, 2
Luxor, 82, 233
Lycaonia, 294, 299
Lycia, 292, 294, 298, 301, 307, 519
Lycurgus, 55
Lydia, 294, 301, 308
Lyncestis, Lyncus, 50–51, 151–152, 156–158, 199–200, 519–520
Lysimachus, 30–31, 106, 187, 208, 224, 239, 356, 399, 419, 433, 505, 513, 515
Lysippus, 65, 69, 408, 446, 448–449, 490, 493, 495–497, 500–501, 504, 507, 511, 513

Maccabees, 477–478, 482, 485
Macedon, Macedonia, 147–164
Machatas, 158
Machiavelli, 257, 259–262, 264, 266–267
Maedi, 518
Mallians, 119–120, 358, 384, 411, 521

Manasseh, 474
Mandanis, 121
Mao, 270, 272
Maracanda, 184–185, 205, 377, 520
Marcus Aurelius, 258
Mardians, 296, 298, 520
Mardonius, 154
Marduk, 102, 234
Marlborough, 263
Mazaces, 84, 104, 233
Mazaeus, 302, 308, 310, 520
Medates, 376
Media, 223, 296, 303, 307, 310–311, 314, 460
Megabazus, 152–154
Megasthenes, 122, 125–126
Meleager, 136, 138–139
Memnon, 102–103, 221, 519
Memphis, 83–87, 90–95, 140–142, 233–234, 238, 314, 383, 386, 426, 459, 462, 520, 522
Menander (satrap), 301
Mendelsohn, 2
Menon, 302, 304, 311
Mentor, 221, 223
Meroe, 461
Mesopotamia, 103–104, 295, 298, 303, 313, 328, 414, 465
Methone, 149, 193, 458
Metropolitan, 11
Metz Epitome, 370, 464
Midrash, 483
Mieza, 32, 65, 321, 518
Miletus, 63, 284, 519
Mithrenes, 300, 302, 310, 519
Molossia, 217–219
Montaigne, 257, 261, 267
Montecuccoli, 261–263
Montesquieu, 263, 265, 270
Montgomery, 267
Mossalamus, 483
Musicanus, 120, 419
Mygdonia, 152, 154
Mytilene, 325

Nabarzanes, 374
Napoleon, 256–257, 259, 264–269, 491

Nearchus, 111, 118–119, 122, 126, 223–224, 301, 307, 345, 367, 406, 413–417, 419–420, 522
Nebuchadnezzar, 481
Nectanebo II, 92, 238, 426, 429, 457–459, 465, 468
Neisos gem, 504, 513
Nemrud Dağ, 430
Nicanor, 305
Nicesipolis, 160, 215
Nicias, 308

O'Brien, 8
Octavian (Augustus), 143, 448–449
Odrysians, 161–163
Ohrid, 150, 157, 194
Olympia, 29, 53, 188, 216, 228–229, 495–496, 513
Olympias, 30–31, 35–36, 41–43, 46–47, 49–51, 53, 132–133, 159, 180, 213–220, 224–225, 237, 241, 360, 362, 372, 375–376, 433, 445, 457–458, 462, 464, 478, 495–496, 507, 509, 518
Olynthus, 22, 60, 65, 131, 160, 214, 243, 406, 408, 515
omens, 131
Onesicritus, 99, 120, 122–123, 320, 352, 359, 367, 401, 403, 406, 413, 415–419
Opis, 77–79, 105, 163, 185, 192, 209, 211, 328, 371, 522
Oreitae, 296
Orestis, 48–50, 149, 151, 158, 199, 518
Origen, 476, 479
Orontes, 300
Oropius, 303, 313
Orosius, 485
Orsodates, 358
Orxines, 303, 313, 372, 388
Oxathres, 313
Oxicanus, 120
Oxyartes, 223, 305, 312, 314, 358, 521
Oxyathres, 184, 202
Oxydates, 303, 310
Oxydracae, 119, 123, 411

Paeonia, 151–153, 155, 157, 198, 246
Pamphylia, 292, 294, 298, 301, 307, 359, 519

panhellenism, 57
Pantaleon of Pydna, 94, 314
Paphlagonia, 292, 294, 299
paradeisoi, 328
Paraetacene, 313
Paraetonium, 88–89, 435, 459
Parapamisadae, 296, 298, 305, 311–312, 314
Parmenion, 43, 47, 51, 58, 63, 98, 102, 151, 157, 200, 203, 205, 255, 276, 287, 375, 385, 417, 518–520
Parnassus, 322
Parthia, 296, 298, 304, 307, 310, 312, 314, 443, 445
Parysatis, 105, 222–223, 522
Pasargadae, 104, 276, 413
Patala, 121, 521
Patrocles, 326, 400
Patroclus, 37
Pausanias (Companion), 308
Pausanias of Orestis, 51–52, 58, 158, 175, 518
Pegasus, 35
Peithagoras, 129
Peithon, 306
Pelignas, 180
Pella, 22, 39, 94, 98, 106, 150, 157, 172, 180, 186–187, 193–194, 198, 213, 282, 284, 431, 495, 505, 507, 511
Pelusium, 83, 88, 92, 94, 314
Perdiccas I, 149, 167, 177
Perdiccas II, 151, 156, 159, 162, 167, 169, 177, 199, 243, 327
Perdiccas III, 155, 162, 183
Perdiccas, regent, 46, 51, 106, 120, 132, 135–142, 151–153, 156, 166, 168, 198, 211, 220, 222–223, 244, 382, 384, 425–426, 522
Perinthus, 98
Peritas, 69
Perrhaebia, 151, 159
Persepolis, 75, 100–101, 104, 108–109, 202–203, 229, 276, 279, 339, 359, 362, 373–374, 396, 398, 409, 520–522
Perseus, hero, 90, 238, 409
Persia, Persians, 32, 36, 38–39, 47–48, 57–58, 61–64, 67–68, 71–76, 78–79, 84–85, 95, 97–110, 113, 121, 129,

135, 141, 152–154, 158, 161, 164, 171, 174–175, 180–188, 190, 192–193, 195–199, 202–203, 205–206, 208–212, 217, 221–225, 227–228, 231, 233–236, 238–239, 241, 248, 250–252, 254–255, 258, 260, 266, 269, 272–274, 276–277, 279–280, 288, 290–291, 298–300, 307–308, 310–314, 318, 323–324, 328–329, 335, 337–340, 357, 365, 367, 371–377, 381, 388, 393, 395–396, 398, 409–410, 413, 431–432, 434, 449, 457–458, 460, 467, 472, 479, 487, 502, 515–516, 518–521

Persis, 295, 300, 303, 310, 313, 357
Petisis, 94, 314
Peucelaotis, 114
Peucestas, 94, 119, 303, 313–314
pezhetairoi, 78, 182–183, 188, 202, 245–246, 248, 250, 252–254
phalanx, 40, 78–79, 151, 158, 245, 247–248, 252, 254, 279
pharaoh, 76, 141, 242, 256, 269, 457, 461, 465
Pharasmenes, 324
Pharos, 88
Phila, wife of Philip, 158
Philinna, 46, 160
Philip II, 35, 39–40, 45, 48–51, 53, 55–58, 60, 67–68, 78, 97–99, 102, 137, 147, 149–151, 155–163, 169, 175, 182–183, 195, 198–200, 215, 217, 229, 243–245, 264, 335, 356, 372, 380, 410, 419, 429, 434, 458, 478, 493, 496, 503, 518–519
Philip III Arrhidaeus, 48, 135–136, 138–139, 157, 160, 217, 219, 518, 522
Philip, satrap of Bactria, 305
Philip, satrap of India I and II, 306
Philip, son of Machatas (satrap of India I and II), 305–306
Philippeum, 53–54, 216, 495–496
Philippi, 22, 161–162, 276–277
Philippopolis, 38, 163
Philotas, 43, 47, 102, 151, 173, 183, 200–201, 203–205, 211, 216, 258, 262, 302, 308, 357, 365–366, 375, 381, 385, 387, 402, 520

Philoxenus (satrap), 291, 301
Philoxenus of Eretria, 34, 502, 506
Phoenicia, 136, 291–292, 295, 443
Phrasaortes, 303, 310, 313
Phrataphernes, 304, 307, 310, 314
Phrygia, 98, 294, 299–301, 307, 313
Pieria, 147, 149–150, 159, 194, 199
Pillars of Hercules, 321, 323
Pixodarus, 42, 45–48, 54, 309, 380, 415, 518–519
Plutarch, 29, 348–363 and *passim*
Polemon, 314
polygamy, 42–43, 53, 158, 215, 224
Polyperchon, 151, 219, 224
Polytimetus river, 384, 389
Pompeii, 500–502, 511
Pompey, 258
Porus, 33, 70, 114–116, 125, 232, 271, 290, 369, 438, 460–461, 468, 488, 504, 511, 513, 521
Posidippus, 106
pothos, 86, 113, 320, 342, 482, 491
Potidaea, 183, 387
Priene, 63, 281
Proexes, 305, 310, 312
proposography, 3
proskynesis, 105, 107, 174, 185, 206–208, 235, 242, 357, 410, 521
Ptolemy I Soter, 47, 72–73, 87, 89, 132, 140, 223, 239, 309, 326, 334, 367, 369, 379–388, 390, 396–400, 406, 425–437, 456, 462, 513, 518, 522
Ptolemy II Philadelphus, 239, 383, 397, 400
Ptolemy III Philometor, 397
Ptolemy IV Philopator, 142, 400
Ptolemy of Alorus, 160, 175
Ptolemy X, 142
Punjab, 112, 118
Pydna, 149, 194
Pyrgoteles, 65, 69, 500, 503–504
Pyrrho, 65, 125

Quellenforschung, 6, 10–11
Questions of King Milinda, 124–125, 127

regency, 39
religion, 226–242
Richelieu, 263
Rohan, 262
Rome, 438–451
Rondanini Alexander, 493
Roxane, 39, 105–106, 135–136, 214, 217, 219, 222–224, 314, 376, 460, 462, 501, 511, 521
Royal Pages, 159, 171, 174, 183–184, 209, 375, 385, 521

Sabictas, 302, 309–310
Sacred Band, 40, 42
Samaritans, 474, 478
Sangala, 116
Sarapis (Serapis), 130–131, 420, 434, 459, 465
Sardis, 231, 284, 308, 357, 519
Sargon of Akkad, 324
sarissa, 158, 163, 244–245, 247–248, 250, 254
Satibarzanes, 304, 310, 312
satrapies, 316
satraps, satrapies, 316
Satyrus, 43, 45
Schachermeyr, 4–6
Schwarzenberg Alexander, 500
science, 317–329
Scylla, 130
Scythia, Scythians, 39, 74, 152, 228, 254, 269, 339, 520
Second Sophistic, 350, 360
Seleucia-in-Pieria, 434
Seleucia-on-the-Tigris, 435, 437
Seleucus I Nicator, 106, 125, 223–224, 326, 328, 400, 425–437, 505
Semiramis, 461
Septimius Severus, 143, 439, 446
Sesonchosis, 461–462, 465, 467
sexuality, 35–38
Sibyrtius, 303–305, 313
Sidon, 519
Sind, 112
Sindos, 193–194
Sirras, 156–157
Sisygambis, 221, 373, 375–377
Sitalces, 162

Siwah, 30, 82, 86–87, 89–94, 96, 135, 140, 236–242, 357, 386, 403, 409, 427, 434, 501, 505, 520
Socrates, 172
Sogdiana, 105, 296, 305, 307, 311, 382, 520
Solomon, 481
somatophylakes, 183–184
Sopeithes, 116, 118, 127
Sostratus, 208
Sparta, 56, 58, 61, 98, 108, 231, 410, 459–460
Spitamenes, 105, 111, 223, 336, 384, 389, 520
Stalin, 269
Stamenes, 302, 313
Stasanor, 304, 312
Stateira I, 221
Stateira II, 105, 221–223, 522
Stillman, 11
Stranga, 460
strategy, 67–81
Strymon, 38, 149, 152, 154–155, 161
succession, 53, 136
Successors to Alexander, 425–437, 478, 480, 504–505, 515
Susa, 77, 79, 95, 104–107, 109, 113, 184, 201, 209, 222–223, 235, 276, 280, 284, 356, 358, 371, 376, 412, 414, 416–417, 520, 522
Susiana, 295, 303, 310, 313
symposium, 185, 187
Syria, 136, 141, 291–292, 295, 298–299, 302, 415, 443, 445

Talmud, 471, 474, 476, 482–484, 486
Tanais, 321
Tapuria, Tapurians, 292, 296, 298, 304, 310
Tarn, 4–5, 7, 76
Tatian, 484
Taxila, 111, 114–115, 121, 123, 125
Taxiles, 401, 521
Tertullian, 481
Thais, 373–374, 396, 398–399
Thalestris, 373–374, 396, 520
Thebes, Thebans, 40, 42, 56, 60–61, 63, 91, 131, 160, 238, 244, 261, 277–278, 335, 350, 356, 371, 404, 459, 478, 519

584

Themiscyra, 374
Theophrastus, 327
Theopompus, 399
Thermodon, 374
Thessalonice, 160, 215, 220
Thessaloniki, 7
Thessalus, 47
Thessaly, Thessalians, 34, 36, 46, 60, 154, 159–160, 163, 200, 215, 229, 245, 247, 250, 252–253, 255, 458, 519
Thoas, 305
Thrace, Thracians, 35, 38–39, 69, 97, 102, 136, 149, 152–154, 161–163, 167, 169, 183, 195, 198, 200, 278, 433, 458, 505, 518
Timagenes, 367, 398
Timocleia, 278
Tito, 269
Tlepolemus, 303, 313
Trajan, 258, 348–349, 352, 360, 363, 439, 443–444, 446, 449
Triballians, 163, 371, 519
Triparadisus, 297
Troy, 75, 137, 228, 281, 410, 449, 459, 519
Turenne, 265
Tymphaea, 151, 199

Tyre, 100, 459, 519
Tyriespes, 305, 311–312

Uxians, 295, 520

Van Creveld, 257, 270–272
Vergina. *See* Aegae
Villa dei Papiri, 492
Villa dei Pisoni, 492
Vulgate, 21, 359

warfare, 243–255, 272
Wilcken, 4
women (in Alexander's court), 213–225

Xerxes, 58, 76, 97, 101–102, 104, 108, 113, 154–155, 202, 229, 395
Xuan Zang, 123

Yosippon, 486

Zeus, 30, 55, 77–78, 89–91, 93–94, 117, 159, 231–232, 236–237, 240, 258, 266, 285, 319, 410, 429, 431, 433–434, 445, 449, 462, 497, 501, 503, 505, 513, 520
zoology, 326

CAMBRIDGE COMPANIONS TO THE ANCIENT WORLD

Other Titles in the Series

The Cambridge Companion to the Age of Justinian
Edited by Michael Maas

The Cambridge Companion to Ancient Greek Law
Edited by Michael Gagarin and David Cohen

The Cambridge Companion to the Age of Augustus
Edited by Karl Galinsky

The Cambridge Companion to the Hellenistic World
Edited by Glenn R. Bugh

The Cambridge Companion to the Age of Pericles
Edited by Loren J. Samons II

The Cambridge Companion to Archaic Greece
Edited by H. A. Shapiro

The Cambridge Companion to Ancient Greek Political Thought
Edited by Stephen Salkever

The Cambridge Companion to the Age of Constantine, Second Edition
Edited by Noel Lenski

The Cambridge Companion to the Roman Economy
Edited by Walter Scheidel

The Cambridge Companion to the Ancient Rome
Edited by Paul Erdkamp

The Cambridge Companion to the Roman Republic, Second Edition
Edited by Harriet I. Flower

The Cambridge Companion to the Age of Attila
Edited by Michael Maas

The Cambridge Companion to Roman Law
Edited by David Johnston

The Cambridge Companion to the Age of Nero
Edited by Shadi Bartsch, Kirk Freudenburg, and Cedric Littlewood

The Cambridge Companion to Ancient Athens
Edited by Jenifer Neils and Dylan Rogers

The Cambridge Companion to Constantinople
Edited by Sarah Bassett

The Cambridge Companion to the Ancient Greek Economy
Edited by Sitta von Reden

Printed by Printforce, United Kingdom